The World Encyclopedia of
MODEL SOLDIERS

Stadden. *Part of the 'Waterloo' chess set, made by Stadden and painted by a team of artists, issued in 1975 (N. Saunders Metal Products).*

The World Encyclopedia of
MODEL SOLDIERS

John G. Garratt

THE OVERLOOK PRESS
WOODSTOCK   NEW YORK

Other books by the same author

Landscape Drawing in Pen and Ink
Model Soldiers: A Collector's Guide
Model Soldiers for the Connoisseur
Bramber and Steyning: An Illustrated History
Collecting Model Soldiers

Dedicated to
collectors of model soldiers
throughout the world

First published in the United States in 1981
by The Overlook Press, Lewis Hollow Road
Woodstock, New York 12498

Published in Great Britain 1981 by
Frederick Muller Limited, London

Library of Congress Cataloging in Publication Data

Garratt, John Geoffrey
  The world encyclopedia of model soldiers.
  1. Military miniatures — Dictionaries.
  I. Title
  NK8475.M5G38   745.592'82'0321   80-84376

  ISBN 0-87951-129-X

Printed in Singapore

Title-page: *Detail from a diorama by* **H. Cawood** *(National
Army Museum)*.
Opposite: *A few examples from a vast range of card and paper
sheets and cut-outs (Author)*.

CONTENTS

ACKNOWLEDGEMENTS

The author is only too conscious that without the altruistic cooperation of a large number of collectors this work would never have been written. This assistance has been spread over twenty years of research, and many acknowledgements have been given in preceding publications. Many of the makers and manufacturers mentioned in the present volume were not only eager to supply information,but models as well, and to them the author is grateful. It must be said, however, that in some instances this was not forthcoming, and the author was unable to obtain either information or photographs. Curators and directors of museums and other institutions, both civil and regimental, also collaborated most willingly, even to the extent of indicating other sources of reference.

The author wishes to express his thanks for specific information to the following, who have given of their time and knowledge in the fields in which they specialize: J.M. Allendesalazar, Madrid (information on Spanish models); G.R. Allison, Otago (New Zealand and Australian makers); G. Alschner, Munich (modern flats); E. Basseterre, Olwas, Argentina (Argentinian makers and manufacturers); L. Bozzetti, Bologna (Italian models); D. Brett, Morristown, Va. (aluminium); W.Y. Carman, Sutton (early English solids and hollow-casts); Lloyd Corning, Arlington, Va. (contemporary United States makers); Jock Coutts, London (English makers); C.A. Cutileiro, Lisbon (Portuguese makers); Rev. Sir Dickon Durand Bart; S. Southall (Wooten); Mrs. F. Farquharson, Coventry (Marx; loan of books on early U.S. models); Walter Fischer, Cassel (German societies); C. Frazer, Amsterdam (paper sheets); F.G. Frisella, San Carlos, Cal. (American plastics); D. Frost, Edmonton (modern solids); R. Gennari, Rome (Italian and other models); G. de Giorgis, Turin (manufacturers in Italy, Poland and Russia); Dr. Estelle Goldstein, Paris (contemporary French makers); P. Greenhill, Wimbledon (Courtenay); G.M. Haley, Halifax (hollow-casts); Mr. J. Hanington, Wimbledon (hollow-casts and solids); D.F. Hawkins, Oystermouth (Elastolin); M.V. Hitrovo, Ambler, Pa. (early United States solids and hollow-casts); Mrs. F. Howard, Hockley (concerning her father, F. Wolavka); O. Høyer, Glostrup (Danish and Swedish makers); M. Juplin, Cramlington (plastics); G. Kearton, Stockton-on-Tees (plastics); J.S. Kuster, San Diego (Marx sets); M.A. Longoni, Milan (Italian makers); E. Morazzoni, Turin (paper sheets); H.R.W. Morrison, Ottawa (Canadian manufacturers); B. & J. Newman, Elnora, N.Y. (paper sheets, cardboard models); M. O'Brien, London, Ontario (Canadian and United States models); J. Opie, London (plastics); H. Pestana, Waterville, Me. (American models); D. Pielin, Wheeling, Ill. (early American manufactures); R. Polaine, London (Elastolin); N. Polk, Jersey City, N.J. (gift of Spanish models); Major E. Roche-Kelly, London (French manufacturers); M. Roubicek, Jerusalem (Czechoslovakian and Israeli models); the late J. Sandars, Gosport (armoured fighting vehicles); Justin G. Schiller, New York (paper sheets); A. Speyer, Weisbaden (German semi-solids); the late D.C. Stokes, Harpenden (dioramas); P. Van Tuycom, Brussels (Belgian makers); G. Vergnano, Pinerola (contemporary Italian makers and paper sheets); F. Weinberg, Cape Town (S.A.E.); E. Wiseman, Sydney (Wooten); M. Wohl, New Orleans (American makers); D. Wollheim, U.S.A. (Argentinian manufacturers).

Without wishing to be invidious, the author must give his most special thanks to a number of individuals who took upon themselves the task of self-appointed researchers. Henry F. Anton, of Meriden, Conn., not only searched every highway and byway, large shop and junkstore, for models which he sent in profusion to the author (models, which, incidentally, the author would never have otherwise seen or even heard of) but also elucidated points of piracy and pseudonimity which proved invaluable, and all this whilst often in grave ill-health. Professor A. Balil, of Valladolid, was equally enthusiastic in researching Spanish and Portuguese paper sheets. Valentine Bean of Brookline, Mass., not only proved an inspiration at times when the sheer enormity of the author's task appeared too great for him to carry, but produced and circulated at his own expense a questionnaire to societies in the United States of America. Peter MacCallum, of Watson's Bay, Sydney, was as active as Mr. Anton in chasing references to the model makers of Australia. Don and Honey Ray, English-born though working in Canada, told him much of the early history of modelling in England and of later productions in Canada and the United States. To all these keen collectors the author can only say "thank you".

Thanks are also due to Andrew Dransfield, a fifteen-year old neighbour who painted a number of the author's models, to Bill Duinker, also of Farnham, who undertook a similar task most beautifully; and to Martin Rice, of Downing Street Studios, who photographed the majority of the models in the author's collection and spared neither time or energy in attempting to achieve what was required of him. Finally, a special word of thanks to Tom Hartman, who painstakingly and most thoroughly checked the whole of the text, made valuable comments and criticisms, and saved the author from making numerous blunders in dates of battles and the like.

PREFACE

A number of books have already been written on that fascinating little object, the 'Model Soldier', or, as the Americans prefer to call it, the 'Military Miniature'. Indeed, some might say that saturation point has been reached. Most of the publications, however, deal with certain specific aspects of the subject, such as pre-Second World War 'toys', the making of models in various modern compounds or the conversion of polystyrene kits. This book is the first, to the author's knowledge, to attempt to gather together as many facts as possible regarding the model soldier as a collector's item. The idea has lain dormant in the author's mind during the twenty years since he himself began collecting, and, whilst he is aware that he has written a certain amount on the subject, and that others have done the same, he feels that there is still room for a comprehensive volume dealing with the many types of figures, whether in lead or plastic, in wood or in cardboard, in polystyrene or in paper sheets, in 5mm or in 120mm, as a single unit or in a diorama, that have been issued in many countries and in many eras. Every aspect, therefore, whether important or seemingly trifling, has been dealt with: every maker, however shortlived or remote geographically, every painter who has assisted in the promotion of the hobby, every person employed on the construction of a diorama, whether their role be primary or secondary, of whom the author has knowledge, has been included.

It must be made quite clear that this book is primarily for the collector rather than for the spare-time maker, and whilst one cannot fail to acknowledge that today there is a growing tendency for a model to be purchased for the purposes of the recreation of something entirely different, at the same time twenty years' of correspondence with collectors all over the world has amply proved that there are many more enthusiasts who are content to leave a model as it is, and are at the same time intensely interested in the works of makers in countries other than their own. The processes of production grow yearly more and more technical, especially with the advent of such materials as resin and fibreglass, and the author is only too aware of his ignorance as to chemical matters. He therefore leaves the technical side of production to those specialists who have already written about them.

He realizes also the growing interest in armoured fighting vehicles featuring so prominently in journals and in society exhibitions, but their connection with the model soldier as a collector's item is remote, and, as an ancillary to the mainstream, the makers of the actual original models or kits have been mentioned, as it were, in passing: there is in any case a volume of literature on the subject, enough to satisfy any enthusiast. Similarly, he has regarded the wargame as an entity in itself, already written about by many far more competent authorities than himself, and has confined his remarks to the makers of the actual models as distinct from their application.

His most difficult decision was what to do about the hundreds (possibly thousands) of quasi-collectors who make an occasional model for their own pleasure, or those who, calling themselves 'military modellers', endeavour by much ingenuity, and even at times genius, to alter existing models or convert polystyrene kits in order to create something entirely different from the original conception of the maker. It is these final efforts which feature so largely in magazines and exhibitions, and whilst acknowledging that they have expanded the conception of the model soldier, and produced something of which they may well and justifiably be proud, they are in a sense working in a backwater, in as much as, after photography or exhibition, the conception returns to the home of the conceiver, there to be seen by a limited number of friends. It became apparent early in the writing of this book that it would be possible to include only those who passed a rigid test. The following guide-lines were therefore adopted: (a) the modeller had to be of such quality that he worked to commission or (b) was employed regularly as a painter or convertor by one or more specialist firms or (c) that he was represented in a museum or other institution, where his work was on permanent display. The mere winning of a prize at a competition, or the inclusion of his work in a magazine was not considered sufficient justification for selection, just as, if one exhibited an occasional painting at a local exhibition, one would hardly expect to be included in an Encyclopaedia of World Art. Similarly, only those collectors who have contributed to the history of the model, either by their altruistic impartation of knowledge to others or by their bequests to posterity, can expect to find a place in these pages. Without their presence, however, this book would never have been written.

JOHN G. GARRATT

Farnham, Surrey

GENERAL INTRODUCTION

The collecting of tiny replicas of a military character is of comparatively recent origin. The interest was certainly latent before the Second World War in a comparatively minor form, but by 1959, when the author's first book on the subject was published, it was increasing. It would, however, have been a bold prophet indeed who could have foreseen that a gentle hobby indulged in mainly by professional men would have developed into the all-absorbing passion that it is today. At one time the 'model soldier', as it is now almost universally called, was a toy, produced in thousands for the juvenile market. The manufacturers were not working for posterity, merely for a profitable living, and it must not be forgotten that these toy soldiers are no better for being called 'models' in modern nomenclature. They are still comparatively simply designed objects with a utilitarian purpose (e.g. Britains, Mignot); and the fact that a few manufacturers with vision (e.g. Lucotte, Authenticast) made better models does not invalidate this contention. The normal manufacturer could never have foreseen that his sometimes clumsy approximation of a human figure, selling for a few pence, would eventually achieve the status of a collector's object at the same number of shillings or even pounds. In fact, a curious aspect is that this same figure is at times sold at a higher price than many a much finer 'model'.

Economic factors of production after the Second World War broke the hegemony of the toy soldier, causing the manufacturers to turn to an alien plastic material, and it was this that was responsible in part for the evolution of the maker of better-class models (e.g. Stadden, Imrie, Greenwood) rather than the 'manufacturer'. These makers worked either singly or with a small staff, and their initial output was limited in quantity. It is their work that has brought the model soldier to its present interest and stature, and above all there is the master-maker who lavishes a lifetime of experience and craftsmanship on his art, which may well be performed only to commission.

The beginnings of the model soldier go far back into antiquity. The Egyptian, Cretan and Roman specimens so far unearthed are in the main of a votive nature, although there is ample evidence that some at least were intended as playthings. Even in these early times it is possible to observe the basis of the future development of the two most important types of production: the solid, or three-dimensional, and the flat, silhouette-like model. Both these types disappeared, as did most other things of social value, during the days of the barbarians, to reappear in the early Middle Ages in France and Germany in flat tin, in the Eastern European countries in round clay or earthenware, and, universally, as jointed jousting puppets, sometimes of simply carved wood, sometimes of elaborate craftsmanship in metal.

Apart from the occasional wooden models made for royal personages, and silver tactical ones commissioned by French royal fathers in the seventeenth and eighteenth centuries, little in the way of commercial military models appeared until the time of the French Revolution, when the firm of Lucotte produced a series of designs in solid of such quality that they are still paramount in the history of the toy soldier. Here indeed was a toy that could well be called a model, and which anticipated present-day figures by its sensible design and its separately cast riders and equipment. Other French makers, working in the middle of the nineteenth century left little mark, but the amalgamation of three of them (Cuperly, Blondel and Gerbeau), taking over Lucotte, and themselves being taken over later by Mignot (still flourishing) provided a link between the two centuries.

In Germany the semi-solid figure must have been in existence in quantity in the early days of the nineteenth century, but it was the firm of Georg Heyde, commencing fifty or sixty years' later, that established the all-pervading era of the German solid. Here again, as with Lucotte, was a better than average model, also with some separate equipment. Their most successful rival, Haffner, made better models, some of which are today being reproduced for a German museum. The characteristics of all these models were a torso of solid lead with plug-in heads and detachable riders, the smaller ones kept in place on the horse by a tiny peg fitted to the seat of the figure. Heyde continued to churn out vast quantities of toys until the advent of the Second World War, since when Germany has made few commercial solids.

A further development in the making of round models for children occurred in 1893, when William Britain introduced his 'hollow-cast' specimens. Economics dictated a cheaper production, made possible by a process which involved the construction of a shell of light metal alloy enclosing a vacuum (as in a hollow Easter egg). Once established, the firm never looked back, and up to its cessation of metal models in about 1965 it must have provided more boys with more fun than any other manufacturer, besides being first in the field to have a truly worldwide influence. The establishment of the size of 54mm (except in their cheaper ranges) broke the German practice of producing models of anything between 40 and 90mm size, thus forming a basis for a serious collection of units of uniform size. Later, when more serious models were made by craftsmen, this was the generally accepted scale, (within a few millimetres either way) and it is only in comparatively recent years that it has become almost obsolete. Competition was fierce, and from 1900 to 1965 many other firms, large and small, competed with Britains in the hollow-cast style, and such was its influence that some of the later Heyde and Mignot specimens were made in this manner. Apart from these isolated examples, however, and a few in the United States, the hollow-cast still remained a specially English contribution.

The 'flat', mainly in the form of either religious tokens on fairings, was in existence in Germany and France in the 13th century and isolated examples occur in Germany of those of a military and civil nature from about 1680 to 1730, but no commercial production on a grand scale occurred until the advent of Johannes Hilpert (c.1775), coinciding with the resurgence of the national Germanic spirit after the wars of Frederick the Great. Now, for the first time, thousands of models in tin were available for the reconstruction of battles. The models were in various sizes from 50 to 90mm, with special portrait pieces made to commission. The German foundries were soon in full swing, until the firm of Heinrichsen dominated the scene. He later reduced the size to 28mm, which lasted well into the present century, when the slightly larger one of 30mm was generally considered as allowing for greater detail of engraving. Heinrichsen was as prolific as Heyde, outstripping all his rivals (principally Allgeyer) by the variety and

Under Two Flags. *The Iron Duke, by* **T. Richards,** *commissioned from Phoenix, 54mm. Painted by Andrew Dransfield (Author).*

size of his sets. These 'flats', as they soon came to be called, were easy to manufacture, granted the engraving was adequate, and were painted or partially painted by home labour. Germany has remained faithful to the concept, although in execution the present-day specimens are far superior, but other countries who began their production early had disappointing results.

In between these two main streams, the solid and the flat, occurred the bastard 'semi-solid' and 'semi-flat', confined mainly to the Germanic countries in the 1850 to 1890 period, which have happily vanished except for a few isolated instances such as Cutileiro in Portugal and Wollner in Austria.

The commercial solid and the hollow-cast were replaced by a new and cheaper material – plastic – which had its heyday between about 1950 and 1970. A few firms (e.g. Herald, Starlux, Marx) determined to achieve a high standard, but seldom did their rivals produce anything better than a throw-away. Similar in material was the French *carton-moulé* of the end of the nineteenth century, and the German composition group led by Elastolin and Lineol.

In the 1930s came the first groping towards a better model, one which would be superior in all aspects to the toy. This development, taking place simultaneously in most countries, was responsible for the 'model' soldier rather than the toy. The pioneers (e.g. Carman, Courtenay, Ping, Baldet, Greenwood, Eriksson) designed separate entities rather than complete units: each model was the result of long hours of research, careful anatomical sculpture, meticulous casting in solid metal and skilful painting. A finished model consisted of a torso to which the arms, legs, head and equipment were soldered. A few of these makers are still alive, whilst they have been joined by a whole host of others from practically every country. It must not be forgotten that their efforts were made at the time when hollow-casts and then plastics were being turned out in their thousands, and it took immense courage to place their special models in front of a buying public. The passing of the hollow-cast, and the sheer exhaustion and staleness of the plastic, together with the use of more malleable material and increasing skill in

Anderson. *The models are either conversions of Historex kits or original designs in polystyrene. (R. Anderson)*.

moulding and casting methods coincided with a desire on the part of the collector to acquire a fine model, even at a much higher price. The further development of the model in broken-down or unassembled form in its turn created a new public, that of the collector who wished to 'animate' the models himself. It was then that the present-day school of makers came into their own, and indeed some of them, although maintaining a high standard, could be classed as commercial concerns, so many models emerged from their workshops. On the other hand, a number of mastermakers refused to enter this particular kind of competition, and continued to execute masterpieces to commission only.

A similar movement occurred in Germany about the same time, when erudite collectors questioned the suitability of the existing flats for the historic study that was their passion. As a result of their efforts the quality of the flat improved, the services of designers such as Madlener and engravers such as Frank resulting in the superb series that are available today, and led the way to a veritable explosion of private or semi-private designers, engravers and distributors that still remains a feature of the Germany of the present period.

Many other materials have at times been used, such as carved wood, clay, plaster and paper sheets, but none has achieved the popularity of metal. The most amazing development which has split the model soldier world apart, however, is that of the polystyrene kit, the chief, (though not the first), exponent being Historex S.A. The collector may now indulge his passion by assembling his own model. Cost does not matter, as the price of a kit is equivalent to that of a metal model, but the fun is there, and, furthermore, by clever manipulation and the amalgamation of many disparate pieces from many disparate kits, startling and novel results may be achieved. Such has been its influence that many have formed the basis of an extension, that in which part of a kit forms the foundation of a model developed further by the use of almost every imaginable medium.

Another branch of the main stream is the fast-growing 'wargame', in which, although models have of necessity to be used, there is now little of the element of collecting as such, as the models are acquired simply as a means to an end. Allied to this is the invasion of the armoured fighting vehicle, a logical development of the model aeroplane.

The solid Germanic and French toy soldiers were the stock import into most European countries right up to the beginning of the Second World War, even though the British hollow-cast outstripped them in popularity. At the same time Denmark, Sweden, Italy, Spain and the United States began their own manufacture, in some cases even during the last decade of the nineteenth century, and by 1950 each could show not only a native manufacture but some-times a more worthy individual product. Today, whilst many commercial firms have died away, or the original designs are still being reproduced, there is a large and growing group of fine craftsmen making excellent models to offset the plastic toy and the kit, and nowhere more so than in Great Britain and the United States of America. In the latter, indeed, many designers and sculptors work free-lance, offering the results of their labours to a number of different producers (just as do the engravers of German flats). In Scandinavia, Italy and Spain commercial manufacturers have made their mark, and their better craftsmen are among the finest in the world.

The flat, developed to such a high degree in Germany, met with success at first in other countries, and even as early as the end of the eighteenth century such countries as France, Portugal, Spain, Italy and even Finland had their own native makers. The Strasbourg venture, after a long period of popularity, fell before the onslaught of the paper sheet, and flats were not to emerge again in France until 1935. Italy soon fell by the wayside, whilst Spain struggled on for a few years, but Swedish firms developed the idea much later in the nineteenth century. A few flats may have been made in America in the early days of the same century, but the sole effort of Great Britain in 1935 was doomed to failure.

Paper sheets of uniformed troops, mostly in serried ranks, were first printed in France, Germany and Italy in the eighteenth century. Originally intended to be coloured by hand, the rise of coloured lithography ensured speedier and cheaper production, and soon they were flooding from the presses of many of the European countries and, in the early days of the present century, in the United States of America. The interest has not died, and sheets of varying quality are still being produced in Germany, France, Poland, Italy, Spain and Russia. Some are still intended for children, others for collectors.

With the rise of the maker rather than the manufacturer, the number of collectors in all parts of the world has grown rapidly, and the enterprise of societies in staging exhibitions and competitions, together with an increase in the number of books devoted to military subjects in all languages (some erudite, some merely enthusiastic) and on all allied branches of militaria, together with the growing awareness of institutional authorities and even of owners of stately homes, is sufficient to ensure that the interest in the model soldier is not likely to decline in the foreseeable future.

A NOTE ON SYMBOLS AND OTHER MATTERS

1 DATES

Where possible the dates of the actual working life of the person portrayed in each entry has been given. If this is not known absolutely accurately, a 'c' has been used to indicate 'circa' (or 'about'); 'fl.' ('flourished'); a - means that as far as the author is aware work is still proceeding; (?) that the date is uncertain. Where no date is given the sense of the entry should indicate either that the author has been unable to establish a working life or that the subject of the entry is contemporary (e.g. a maker of polystyrene armoured fighting vehicle kits).

2 SOURCES

It would be impossible to list the thousands of references that the author has acquired over the last twenty years. However, specific information that was to be found in a published work, or which was conveyed to him by one or two collectors only, has been acknowledged at the end (or sometimes in the text) of the entry. Thus, [Anton] means that the information was supplied by a collector; (Ortmann) that the information came from a published work.

3 ENTRIES

The brevity of some entries is not entirely the fault of the author. It occasionally denotes that no àmount of correspondence elicited a response.

4 TIME-FACTOR

It must be emphasized that the time that elapses between the completion of any work and its eventual publication is quite considerable, and that therefore the author felt compelled to limit his investigations to the end of 1979, since when a number of new makers have emerged.

5 SCOPE

The book is not intended as a directory, and the actual addresses of present-day makers and manufacturers are therefore omitted.

A

'Aarau (Alt)'. An affectionate name given to the early Swiss makers of flats (e.g. Martin Beck, Gottschalk and Wehrli) from either the town or the area. In 1969 *Figurina Helvetica* began to reissue some of the originals.

Abadal, Joan, Barcelona (1854?-60?). A prolific publisher of paper sheets.

Abadie, Austria (1914-18). A cigarette factory which issued sheets depicting 6-8 figures or groups for cutting out.

Abbey, Norman, Chesterfield, Derbyshire. A maker of commissioned dioramas and a professional painter, especially noted for his work in both fields for *Military Modelling*. He is especially happy when creating groups of models by his friend Sanderson, as, for instance, in his 1975 'Isandhlwana'.

ABC Manufacturing Co. *See* Battalions in Miniature.

Abel & Fry, London (c.1910-14). Hollow-cast, 50mm, poor quality. A small collection of 45mm models were made with bases which could be inserted into trays. This information was given by Richards to Wade, who passed it to the author.

About Face (Larry N. Byrd) Van Nuys, California (1975). Solids, 54mm, of 'Bad Men': Billy the Kid (a masterpiece of criminal vacuity, taken from a famous photograph), Jesse James, etc. Also a free-lance designer.

Abraham, Nils. *See* Santessonska.

Acedo (Domage et Cie), Paris (c.1965). Plastic, 6.5cm. Their range included Alpini, American, English, French, Belgian and Russian infantry; colour-sergeants; Horse Guards; St Cyr cadets; sailors; firemen; Westerners; Gauchos, and wild and domestic animals.

Ace Model, Pasadena, California (c.1942). Balsawood kits, including a US jeep towing an anti-tank gun. [*Newman*]

Ace Toy Mold Company. *See* Kast A Toy.

Ackermann, R., Wissembourg. *See* Imprimerie de Wissembourg.

Acland, Tony. *See* Asgard; Citadel Minatures Ltd.

Acorn Figures. *See* Robinson, C.; Sanderson, C.

Action Pack. *See* Timpo.

Acuña, F., Cali, Colombia. A professional painter of models and maker of wooden figures to commission. In 1975 he informed the author that he intended issuing his own range of solid models.

Adams Action Model, Hawthorne, California (?1960-). Polystyrene kits of armaments, with figures to scale.

Adams, D., Australia. Landscape designer for the dioramas at the Australian War Memorial at Canberra.

Advance Guard (Miniatures) Ltd (Miss F. Adams) Motherwell (1979-). Marketer of 15mm Napoleonic and fantasy figures, sculptured by Tom Park.

ADVERTISING. Since the Second World War model soldiers have proved popular with commercial firms as a means of advertising. Suitable displays in the foyers of cinemas have attracted the attention of patrons going to see such films as *The Black Knight of Tolworth, War and Peace, Richard III, Zulu* and *Waterloo*. One insurance firm staged a show in its window in 1960 of part of the author's collection of medieval period models, with the slogan: 'In those days a shield was your defence – today *we* shield you'; and a campaign for National Defence Bonds was emphasized by a small diorama showing ancient Britons drawn up on the cliffs of Dover as Roman galleys approached. The advent of the interest in armoured fighting vehicles was shown in displays for *D-Day* and *Stalingrad*, while the recent attention paid by makers to the Crimean War was used to effect in one display for *The Charge of the Light Brigade*. Single large models of guardsmen and Yeomen of the Guard are common in such places as Piccadilly Circus. Napoleonic models are often used in glossy magazines and colour supplements by tobacco firms and distillers of spirits, and in one instance wargamers were shown in animated argument. There appears to be wide scope for such advertisement, and it can only do good to the hobby as a whole, especially when even a banking house, the First National Bank of Boston, commissioned students of the Theodore B. Pitman Studios of Cambridge, Mass., to make models of famous events in American history.

Agencia Portuguesa de Revistas, Portugal. Producers of paper sheets.

A.H.I., Japan (c.1960). Plastic piracies of 30mm models by S.A.E.

AHM, USA, (1975). Plastic kits of armoured fighting vehicles.

Ahnert, Klaus, Halle a.d. Saale. Maker of flats of Aztecs

1 **Airfix** *polystyrene kits assembled by J.B. Ratsey.*

and Teutonic knights, engraved by Hartmann. (*Katalogue der Formen, 1976*)

Ahrens, Karl M. *See* H.A.M. Miniatures Ltd.

Aiglon, Paris (c.1962–67). Polystyrene kits in 70mm in solid pieces similar in idea to those of Segom. Of good quality, they succumbed to the popularity of Historex.

Ailor, France (post-1945). Producers of paper sheets of Napoleonic troops, printed in colour on glossy paper.

Airfix, London (c.1962–). Plastic, 20, 54mm; polystyrene, 54mm, 12cm. The first product was a series of polystyrene kits, akin to statuettes, obviously inspired by those of Aurora and Selcol, but very much simpler, smaller and cheaper, including such models as a Guardsman, a Joan of Arc (an atrocious model), a Yeoman of the Guard, a Napoleon, and a Black Prince (probably the best, but with far too large a shield). They proved immensely popular, but remained without addition until 1974, when they were joined by a Queen Elizabeth I and an Anne Boleyn, and in 1978 by a Queen Victoria. About 1964 they went to the other extreme in size, and began their now world-famous sets of 20mm alkathene models. Although wargame models in metal had been current for some years and Britains had issued a lone example in Alkathene, Airfix were the first to make a large series of sets of 48 figures, attached to the sprues, and packaged in single boxes at a remarkably cheap price. Each set consisted of several combat positions, so that for a modest price a number of boxes could be purchased, thus yielding complete armies. The disadvantages were the tiny projections under the hooves of the horses, which were intended to fit into microscopic holes in an irregular-shaped base, and a wavering of spears, lances and swords. They were designed originally by John Niblett, who retired from the firm about 1970. They more than held their own until the sudden upsurge about 1969–70 of the makers of wargame models in metal. To go with these tiny figures

were cannon, and, starting in 1970, scale polystyrene kits of forts, both Roman and French Foreign Legion, and a medieval castle. In 1971 they began to issue 54mm polystyrene kits, both foot and mounted, which were immediately welcomed by converters as a cheaper complement to those of Historex. These have come under some severe criticism by some purists (especially in uniform detail and the anatomy of George Washington's horse), but they have survived, and their sales are still astronomical. Unfortunately, the management of Airfix declined to disclose the names of their designers. It is known, however, that Ronald Cameron has designed for their 'Multipose' and 'Collector' series. The 20mm models have been pirated in many parts of the world, and in 1975 those in 12cm, which, surprisingly, had not hitherto appeared in the United States of America, appeared under the name of S.S. Kresge & Co., labelled 'Made in Hong Kong'. Airfix also make small-scale armoured fighting vehicles with their own crews.

In 1975 the firm started 'Battlefront' — complete dioramas, comprising moulded terrain, vehicles and figures, for D-Day, Alamein, Stalingrad and Guadalcanal; and 'Assault' sets of a similar nature (gun emplacements, pontoon bridges, coastal defences, each with vehicles, guns, figures and accessories, and including a set for Waterloo). Whereas the 54mm figures were in kit form and entitled 'Collectors' Series', the 'Military Series' in the same size issued in 1975 were in solid plastic. Early in 1976 they expanded the 54mm range by the introduction of polystyrene figures in kit form on sprues entitled 'Multipose', and two years later revived an old form of model-making, that of the 'home-cast'. The firm issues a house magazine and an annual publication for modellers and converters.

Airmodel, Germany. Armoured fighting vehicle kits in polystyrene.

Alaiss, Raoul, Argentina (1952–60). Manufacturer of a

range of 36 types of Argentine Cadets and Second World War Americans, copied from Britains and Timpo. [*Basseterre*]

Alarçon, José M. *See* Soldat.

Albatross, Czechoslovakia (1975). Publishers of a cardboard village and castle. (*Newman*)

Alberken, England. *See* Miniature Figurines.

Albrecht, A., Garmisch-Partenkirchen (c.1940-). Publisher of 30mm flats, specializing in the Middle Ages, and including townsfolk and market-scenes, together with a siege of a town in 1476. Engraved by Block and Mohr, and designed by Lecke, many of his models were used by Denny Stokes in his dioramas.

Albrecht, Dr Fritz. *See* Ara-Kunst.

Alcocer, Lucio. *See* Saez-Alcocer.

Aldrich, Tony, Chelmsford (1979-). 30mm solids, starting with Second World War Germans.

Alexander, William, Michigan (c.1970-). Maker of Alexander Scale Models, railroad accessories. Has worked for the Smithsonian Institution and has a steady outlet for commissioned 54mm models.

Alexandre, A. *See* Palx.

Alexandre, E. *See* Jacklex.

Alkathene. *See* Plastics.

'All The Queen's Men' series. *See* DEK.

Allen, H.R., Westerham (1969). Maker of a metal copy of the National Maritime Museum cork assault craft at the time of Wolfe. This copy is at Quebec House, Westerham.

Allen, Peter. *See* Maritime Models.

Allen, T., London (fl.1953-71). Professional painter employed by Willetts.

2   *Typical solid and semi-solid figures. 30mm, probably by* **Allgeyer,** *c.1867 (Courtesy Tunbridge Wells Museum).*

Allgeyer, Fürth, (before 1800-1896). A famous firm of manufacturers of flats, semi-solids and solids. (Flats, 5-7cm, later 30mm. Semi-solids, from 1860. Solids, 40mm.) Mark: ALLGEYER. Created by Johann Christian, (c.1790-1820) succeeded by Johann Friedreich (1821-76) and Konrad (1843-96). The founder began work as a maker of children's clocks in tin. His son, J.F., was the first to sign the family name on the footstands of the models, and both he and Konrad were originally employed as engravers by Heinrichsen. In many ways their products rivalled those of Heinrichsen, and on occasion were superior in technique. An outstanding achievement was a set of 25 tournament figures in 5.7cm. Their output must have been colossal, and they are still to be found in fairly large quantities. Their semi-solids were shown at the Great Exhibition in 1851, where they were stated to be in 'solid pewter'. They are noted by D'Allemagne as having won a medal at the Paris

Exposition of 1867. The solid models were a logical extension. As with most German firms of the period, their boxes were elegant and with elaborately decorated lids and labels.

Allison, R., Burnham, New Zealand (1973-). Maker of 54mm solids to commission.

All-Nu Products, (Frank Krupp) USA (1940-42). Manufacturers of a small range of hollow-casts, the best-known being a machine-gunner and a drum-majorette band. [*Pielin*] Krupp was formerly employed by Barclay. (*R. O'Brien*)

Allsop, D.J. *See* Frei Korps.

Almark, London (1970-). Manufacturer of plastics, 20mm: solids, 54mm. A comparatively limited range of modern troops for the wargamer, designed by Stadden and known in the United States as 'WD' series. In 1974 metal kits in 54mm of British guardsmen, 1815, at the halt, advancing, kneeling, with an officer, were issued, together with Germans of the Second World War. Optional plastic bases were obtainable. This group was marketed in the United States as the 'Sentinel' series. The firm is more notable for its printed publications.

Almeida, A.J., Lisbon (1926-). Publishers of paper sheets.

Almeida Filhos Ltda (Gaspar Luiz de Almeida), Lisbon (fl.1967-before 1974). Solids, 54mm, and later plastics. An advertisement in a Portuguese trade magazine claims that the firm was founded about 1870, but Portuguese collectors are unable to verify this statement, nor is detailed information about the models themselves available.

Almirall, José, Barcelona (1962-). Solids, 54, 90mm. His output is comparable with that of a large commercial venture, but the models themselves are of good quality and eminently collectable. They are issued painted, and on plastic bases, with a printed descriptive label. A vast range is available, together with an invaluable collection of spare heads and equipment. A notable achievement is a set of historical models of the Spanish monarchy. He also designs the 'Canadian Collectors' series of Canadian historical figures for R. Payen of Iberville. Export to a number of countries has been effected, and one Dutch collector must have everything that he has issued. The artillery series is important, covering many periods, and the horses are magnificently sturdy. Initially, his cavalry horses were poor, but he has improved them over the years. His models, all in all, are among the best known to emanate from Spain. Not content with the 54mm size, in 1975 he started a series of 130 solids in 90mm, in one-piece castings, of the American Revolution, the Napoleonic wars, Germany and Russia in 1910, France, 1914, Great Britain, France, Italy, Denmark and India, 1970. He also employed Casadevall to make for him an EKO series in 54mm, issued painted or in kits.

Almond, Richard J., London (1977-). Designer for Sea Gull (Real Models) of solid 120-140mm models in kit form, starting with Julius Caesar and a hoplite. He also designs for Barton Miniatures.

Alou, France (19th century). Publishers of paper sheets.

Alpha Accessories, Herne Bay (1974-). Wargame terrains of vacuum-formed plastic, consisting of sheets of bricks, doors, windows, etc., in 54mm scale.

Alter, Johann Adam, Nuremberg (d.1788). A caster of flats, including possibly those of Hilpert.

3   *Selection of* **Alymer** *models (Author).*

Altona, Hamburg (19th Century). A few flats are known bearing this name. [*Kollbrunner*]

Aluminium. A somewhat intractable material occasionally used for making models. An exceptional example is the 31-inch 'The Bruce at Bannockburn', by the late C.d'O. Pilkington Jackson. Generally speaking the material precludes the use of sharply cut detail, and was used as a cheap substitute for the hollow-cast, being certainly more durable. It is easily recognized by its metallic *timbre* when knocked. Beton Toys experimented with it around 1940, and in France Berne produced standard-size models, while about 1930 Mignot attempted a cheaper variety of their lead models, christening them 'Mignalu'. Between 1947 and 1953 Wend-Al of Blandford imported models designed by Quiralu-Quirinal. Models by Petrich of Hanover and by Krolyn (under the pseudonym Rode Orm) of Denmark are also known.

Aluminium Paste Resin. *See* Composite Models.

Alymer (Angel Comes Plasençia), Burjasot, Valencia (c.1928-). His first products were a long series of 20mm models entitled 'Miniploms'; in fact, he claims priority in this size. They covered a wide range of historical costume from the earliest times to the present day. Normally they were issued in sets of three (occasionally four) models, each in the same pose (based on a few stiff prototypes and some merely painted in different colours to denote different troops), one of the figures being either an officer or a standard bearer. They are still available on occasion in America or England at an exorbitant price. Much more attractive are the pairs of ancient warriors, the single horsemen, the chariots and the war elephants. Also available, although not listed in their admirable coloured catalogue, are nuns and priests, a wedding group, children, builders, street vendors and musicians. In 1972 they started to issue models in 33mm. Again in three or four pieces, they showed a great improvement in design, although the horses were much coarser in execution and the medieval warriors were in anachronistic armour. The range of chariots was extended, and birds and animals appeared for the first time. Their most important contribution was, at the beginning in 1973, of models in 54mm, designed by Casadevall. A long range of ancient peoples, including such little-represented races as the Canaanites, the Semites, the Hittites, the Iberians, the Celtiberians, the Mycenaeans and the early Chinese, of the most attractive and exciting appearance, is followed by a more normal collection of Second World War and more recent times, including portraits of modern war leaders. A smaller range of cavalry includes Saracens, Attila, El Cid, the medieval Moorish King Zeit, knights, Napoleonics, Bengal Lancers, Nigerian Presidential guards, Ethiopian Guards, Royal Canadian North-West Mounted Police and combatants of the Six-Day War. The horses are stoutly built, the riders cast separately and soldered on. Up to 1976 they were obtainable only in painted state. This painting is probably the best of its kind for what must be a fairly mass-produced effort. The smaller models are attractively boxed in clear stiff plastic, with a label attached to a black base, as are the 54mm infantrymen, but the cavalry have bases of light polished wood and flimsy cellophane-like covers. If the price were more reasonable they might become among the most sought-after of Continental models. Unfortunately, the firm does not fulfil orders from collectors abroad.

Amades, J. Collector of a vast number of Catalan sheets of printed soldiers deposited by him at the Barcelona Museum.

Amati (Franco and Primo Marletti), Turin (1975-). Makers of 54 and 22mm solids, some being designed and sculpted by Boggio. Their initial output was an attractive mixture, including a Roman legionary, an archer, a crossbowman, a member of Rogers' Rangers, a Mohican Indian, a Kuban Cossack, Austrians and French troops (1792-8) and delightful naval officers of the eighteenth century. A variety of weapons were cast separately. The smaller models were all naval, for the manning of the rigging and the handling of the carronades of model ships. The brothers hope to expand greatly over the years.

Amelia, Etruria. The site of a find of 40mm semi-solid lead figurines dating from the 5th century BC.

American Alloy (Louis Picco), North Bergen, New Jersey (1940-41). Manufacturers of hollow-casts. R.O'Brien says that he had this information verbatim from Picco (formerly of Barclay) who told him that the models were sculpted by Olive Kooken (also formerly employed by Barclay and 'Tommy Toy') but was vague as to the extent of their production and character, except that they were influenced by Barclay. The firm would appear to have been revived after the Second World War as Toy Creations. A mysterious firm whose products appear to be known rather than by hearsay.

'American Classics' series. *See* Heritage Miniatures.

'American Heritage' series. *See* Sutty, M.

American International Miniatures Ltd, Oxford, Connecticut (1979-). 'Toy' soldiers in solid, specializing in the armies of America.

'American Liberty' chess set. *See* Goodbrand, James.

American Metal Figures (William H. Long), Bay City, Michigan (c.1949-60). 54mm solids, brittle, and on very heavy stands. One knows of sets of 12 Spaniards of 1520, and 14 Romans. The moulds were purchased in 1976 by R. Eccles, of Burlington, Iowa, who is recasting the figures. [*Pielin*]

'American Revolution' chess set. Designed by C.C. Stadden and produced by N. Saunders in 1976. The models range from 3-6½ inches, are of sculptured pewter and hand-coloured. They are in a limited edition. A

4   **American Soldier Co.** *Early United States hollow-casts (M.V. Hitrovo).*

splendid array, a curiosity being that the queens are Generals Sir William Howe and Horatio Gates. (For other sets of the same subject *see* Carlton; Hinton; Imrie-Risley.)

American Soldier Co., (Parker Bros) Salem/Glendale, New York (c.1890-1918) Hollow-cast 54mm derivatives of Britains' oval-base models. They are known to have exhibited toy soldiers at the Columbian Exposition, Chicago, in 1893. These may have been of cardboard, as in the previous year they issued 'The Battle Game', consisting of a box containing 'one large army gorgeously arrayed', with a toy pistol. (*McClintock*). Also in cardboard came sheets of forts and military camp scenes. During the First World War they issued a pamphlet entitled 'Good Reasons for *not* Buying Military Games', in which the pages were blank!

Amesbury, Lieutenant Dennis. Assisted in the diorama of Waterloo at the Canadian Forces Base at Chilliwack.

Amis du Musée-Wellington à Waterloo, Les. *See* Franklin Mint.

Ammann, Hans. *See* Ara-Kunst.

Ammon, Nuremberg (1770-1921). Flats 30mm, 7-9cm; semi-solids 20mm. Johann Wolfgang Ammon became Master in 1794. He was succeeded by Christoph (1812-72) and Christian (1845-1921). Marks: C. AMMON IN NURNBERG : C. AMMON ; C.A. (cursive). The firm had a prolific output in the traditional style, especially notable being tournaments and English Lancers, and they were early in the field of making flats representing the newly invented railway. They began making 20mm semi-solids about 1860. They employed Ludwig Frank as an engraver before 1890. The moulds were purchased by Rieche.

AMT Corporation, USA (1973). Makers of a 6-inch plastic model of 'Mr Spok'.

Anatomy Of Glory, The. *See* Sykes J.

Anderson, Raymond, Manhattan Beach, California (1970-76). He began as a skilled convertor of Historex kits, while at the same time working polystyrene independently for his 54 and 75mm models. While thus engaged, he assumed the name of 'Western Dioramas'. Having mastered his technique until he no longer used any pre-prepared kits, he concentrated on the building of his own dioramas, and designed one or two models for

Valiant, but in 1976 he decided to transfer his energies and abilities to fine art.

Anderson, T., Newton Abbey, N. Ireland (1975-). Maker of commissioned models in large size in plasticine over wire and wood and painted in enamels.

Anderson, W. Wallace, Melbourne, Australia (b.1888). One of the sculptors of the dioramas at the Australian War Memorial, Canberra.

Andra, Martin, Germany (1975-). Engraver of flats.

'Andy' (M. Longhurst, G. Brown, J. Booth), London (1978-). Makers of diorama accessories in hard plaster, marketed by Trevis.

Andy Gard Toy Company, New York. Poor quality plastics of American infantry, the Civil War and Westerners.

Angel Square. *See* Cross W.F.

Angenot, General, Aix-en-Provence (b.1893). After the First World War he began carving exquisite equestrian models of the statuette-size variety, and is today one of the leading exponents of his craft. As a breeder of horses, he knows their action intimately (see his *Celebration du Cheval*, privately printed, Limoges, 1967) and visualizes horse and rider as a complete entity, sacrificing unnecessary detail. By using basswood he is able to achieve a balance which would be impossible in any other material. The riders are clothed with natural materials, and the weapons, reins, horsehair, etc. made from leather, metal and the like. He works only to commission, and is so self-critical that many of the models are destroyed.

Anholm R.F., Copenhagen (1956-). A most capable maker of 54mm solid models, who has done much for the popularity of the hobby in Denmark. His most notable achievement is the creation of a collection of 64 models covering Denmark's war with Sweden, made for the Danish Society, the moulds being destroyed after casting has taken place.

ANIMATION. The bringing to 'life' of an inanimate object. When models were made of softish metal with a high pure lead content, and cast in one piece, legs and arms could be altered by gentle pulling or twisting, thus altering the appearance of the stance of the figure. When the practice evolved of casting the models in a spread-eagle position, legs and arms could still be adjusted to the required posture. The larger firms employed special artists or 'animators' to do this. To a large extent the collector began to replace the professional animator when many makers supplied their models in kit form, in some cases with alternative arms, legs, heads, and weapons, so that the purchaser could assemble the figure to suit his own predilection.

Annad, Dalmondo Revergali di, Naples. Fine solid models seen on sale in Capri by a correspondent in 1976. Enquiries produced no results.

Anrefer, Madrid. Publishers of paper sheets of US army and the Wild West.

ANRI, Italy. Contemporary makers of fine chess sets in softwood, stained or gilded. Two sets, one medieval, the other of Americans and Indians, were sold at Christie's in London in March, 1980.

Ansell, Brian. *See* Asgard; Citadel Miniatures Ltd; Conquest.

Anteojito Magazine, Argentina (1975). Issued plastic 54mm and stamped metal 80mm flats of regional costume of all countries. [*Basseterre*]

ANTIQUITY. The ancestors of the model soldier as we know it were the products first of religions and cults. At the same time a certain number were undoubtedly made for play. Most of the evidence comes from grave-tombs. Obviously, the dead would have been a warrior of distinction in his time on earth and would therefore be honoured by a squadron of miniature followers to accompany him on his journey to the other world (and not always by small figures, as evinced by the mass of life-size warriors discovered in 1975 in a grave-mound in China). Prince Emsah (or Mesheta) took with him a group of war-like followers (now in Cairo Museum) when he died about 2000 BC, and was entombed at Assiut, Upper Egypt. The same votive process was current throughout the ancient world, whichever god was worshipped. Thus crude bronze and lead figures dating from the 5th-6th centuries BC have been found at Frögg and Rosegg in Carinthia, Olbia on the Black Sea, Hierapolis in Syria (one wearing a conical Greek hat), Amelia in Etruria, and in Cyprus (a Roman 60mm, now in the Cyprus Museum). Flat Trojans and Greek equestrians have been unearthed, together with clay and terracotta figurines, which are likely to have been playthings, as examples have mostly been found in the graves of children, notably at Sestieri in Greece (5th century BC). In this category also comes a warship (Greek, 7th century BC) containing five warriors with shields (British Museum); an Athenian war chariot (Kunsthistorisches-museum, Vienna) and a complete group of 400 cavalry found at Wasit, South Iraq, in 1942. The Shardanus left much evidence of their presence, while specimens of Roman occupation in the form of miniature figurines are in many museums. One at the British Museum is conceded by the authorities to be in all probability a toy.

Anton, Javine Cuadrados. *See* Jecsan.

Antonini, F. *See* FIGIR.

Aøhnas. *See* Athina.

Aoshima Plastic Colour Model, Japan (1976–). Manufacturers of sets of Japanese medieval warriors in polystyrene on sprues. Some are concerned with the 'Legend of the Forty-Seven Ronin'.

Apelcraft, Leicester (1972). Large and terrible plastic wall plaques.

Apex Spielwaren, Germany (1977). Solids, 54mm. Napoleonic, some mounted.

AQUA-MANILE. While this cannot be in any sense regarded as a model-soldier *per se*, being a utilitarian medieval household object, it is important as indicating the style of figure that was produced in wood or metal purely as a model. Its purpose, that of an ewer, afforded great opportunity for the display of contemporary armour. Important examples are to be seen in the Bargello (Florence), the National Museum, Copenhagen, and in the British Museum.

Aquila. *See* Marca Aquila.

Ara, Mexico City (fl.1950-68). A toy shop which produced 54mm composition models of Mexican, Spanish, French and Austrian uniforms of the beginning of the 20th century.

Ara-Kunst (Dr Fritz Albrecht), Bayer-Wald (1972–). Solids, 54mm, in several pieces. Periods covered: 1425-90; 1618-48; 1700; 1740-86; 1900-14, with Adam and Eve and Ancient Greece. Also makers of facsimile coins, seals, tokens, and amulets. The firm began by taking over the models produced by Hans Ammann of Usingen, adding recent designs by Claus S. Kowallik and produced by Gunther Koch. The set of medieval figures based on contemporary illustrations is delightful.

Arbogast, Strasbourg (1795-1800). Publisher of paper sheets which are now extremely rare.

Arcade, USA (c.1945). Manufacturers of cast-iron artillery.

Archer, L., London. Designer of medieval 56mm models for Tradition, sculpted by Stadden.

Archibald, Stephen, England. Commissioned designer and converter, especially for *Military Modelling*.

Archive Miniatures (Nevile Stocken) San Francisco (1974-). 15 and 25mm solid models of Huns and Napoleonics.

5　**Argentina.** *Solids by EG-Toys, except military figure by Viruta (Author).*

ARGENTINA. Of all the countries of South America, Argentina is the only one which apparently takes any significant interest in the model soldier. Determined enquiries from consulates and trade officials of the other countries met with courtesy but nothing more tangible. As with so many other countries, imports were made from Britain, Germany and France, with the result that piracy was rampant. The first well-known maker may have been Yelmo, starting in 1927 and working consistently through to 1960. (This statement is queried by the *Boletin del Club del Soldado de Plomo*, No. 1, Buenos Aires, 1971, giving his working dates as 1957-61.) From 1930 to 1950 there was a small number of anonymous manufacturers of solids and semi-solids (30, 45, 54, 70 and 90mm) with a few hollow-cast and papier-mâché models. These mainly featured Argentinian troops and gauchos. Carlos Sommer (1947-66) was a German expatriate who made a large number of semi-solids in 35mm of good quality of the usual miscellaneous types. Viruta (1947-52), 54mm solids, again influenced by Mignot, had a large range of Argentinians (1800-1914), gauchos, Chinese, Conquistadores, native farmers, chuck wagons and pampas vehicles, and a special series of better quality of historic Argentinian heroes. Austrandia, Alais, Reyco, Astesiano, Terry (hollow-cast), Grafil (semi-solid and hollow-cast), Mambru (hollow-cast), Birmania (40 and 54mm), Falucho and Grammar (hollow-cast), all in business between 1949 and 1956, had one factor in common - they either blatantly pirated Britains and Timpo, or made independent models in the same style. The firm of EG-Toys (1955 onwards) was an exception, and while their products were mainly rural communities and were some-what crude in finish, they had a freshness and originality of approach. Tanks and artillery were made by Grafil, Talin, and Minimarquet in the middle 1950s. Plastics, nearly all of Westerners, are made by Oklahoma and Wells Fargo, while El Huinca have a wider range, with detachable riders, although still copying Timpo, and include vehicles and artillery. Paper sheets have occasionally appeared. Chedel (formerly Austrandia) later turned to the production of better models, and Girardo and Balagner work to commission. Although collectors are few, a society keeps them in touch with each other. [*Basseterre and Wollheim*, in part]

Argosy. *See* Carman, W.Y.; Riviere, R. Briton.

Arias, Perez, Barcelona. Wargame solids in 30mm designed by Casadevall.

Aries, Madrid (fl.1960s). Manufacturers of 54mm plastics.

Arii, Italy. Polystyrene armoured fighting vehicle kits.

Aristo-Monogram Merité. *See* Monogram Models.

Arjoplast, Belgium (c.1968–). Manufacturers of hard plastic 54mm models. One remarkable set consists of bandsmen wearing bowler hats with feathers: there is probably some local connection here. [*Kearton*]

Armbrite Industries. *See* Scruby, J.

Armée, Belgium (c.1935). Manufacturers of composition Elastolin-type 7cm models. [*Polaine*]

Armitage, London (pre-1939). Manufacturers of poor quality 54mm hollow-casts.

Arm-Model (José Cacharach), Gerona (1975–). Maker of 30mm wargame models of the German army; publisher of paper sheets in colour of Spanish, French, Austrian and Prussian troops of the Napoleonic War, designed by J.Pla. Dalmaū.

Armont, Pierre (calling himself 'Petrocochino'), Paris (1928–c.1960). A collector of flats who, with designers Hamel and Rousselot and artists Métayer and Rousselot, was responsible for the production of 30mm flats for Mignot. In this he was assisted by Pierre Simon. He also privately employed Frank and Maier as personal engravers.

Armour Accessories, Paris. An offshoot of Historex, providing polystyrene accessories of scale model equipment, such as trenching tools, water flasks, etc, issued on the sprue in packets.

ARMOURED FIGHTING VEHICLES. This heading includes not only the obvious, but also all the impedimenta that goes with the warfare of the two World Wars. There were, of course, specimens made during the war of 1914–18, in the form of mechanized lead or tinplate tanks, but these were comparatively few. With the advent of the plastic kit, however, every conceivable vehicle of every nation began to be made, and the pages of journals and magazines became studded with descriptions, scale plans, criticisms, and suggestions for their conversion. Indeed, a whole literature has grown up, and the enthusiast will turn to these specialist publications for the information he requires. We ourselves, while acknowledging their popularity and obvious legitimacy in the world of model soldiers, regard them as ancillaries, and do not have the technical knowledge to give them the treatment they deserve. They are indeed in a class of their own, and those who are interested in them do not of necessity include model figures in their perimeter, except where they are either issued specifically with the kits, or made or converted by the collector. Listings of the principal makers (mostly, it should

6 **Armoured Fighting Vehicles.** *A typical diorama: Russia 1942, the Germans pushing towards Moscow. Tamiya KVKW IV with 54mm figures from various kits (Richard Frizzell).*

be noted, the Japanese) are given in alphabetical order, but these may well be far from complete as it early proved an impossible task to keep abreast of the wave of production, and dozens more may well have appeared by the time this book is published. One infuriating aspect is that a number of dealers advertise kits without giving any identification, and it is a bore to try to obtain an answer from those whose sole interest is to sell them. Another frustrating feature is that the makers have so completely ignored the normal nomenclature of sizes of models that it takes a mathematician to glean the exact size of any model that is advertised. The most important contributions as regards figures as a separate entity are by Airfix, Tamiya (often badly proportioned), Monogram, Fujimi, Ital-Lobby, Preiser, Roco and Almark, with smaller contributions by Heroics (6mm), Miniature Figurines and Old Guard (all the latter in metal). Societies proliferate, and there must be as large a following for the offensive armour of the two World Wars as there is for the wargame. Many and protean are the changes effected on the kits, and more and more dioramas or mini-dioramas are appearing as enthusiasts exhibit their skill in picture making.

Arms Pack (K.S. Bradley) Northfield, Birmingham (1976–). Manufacturer of polystyrene scale armour parts.

Armstrong, Peter, Kendal, Westmorland (1976–). Maker of 54mm solids to commission. He is particularly attracted to the Peninsular War.

Armtec (Don Winar), Enfield, Connecticut (1973–). Maker of polystyrene armoured fighting vehicles and artillery. In 1974 he made a set of Italian tank officers, 54mm, in metal.

Arnold, Germany (c.1945). Maker of a clockwork model of a US army jeep with figures. [*Wade*]

Arnold, Arnold, USA (1966). Publishers of *A Book of Toy Soldiers*, consisting of 409 punch-out cardboard figures of English and Napoleonic troops in 40mm.

Arpax, Japan. Manufacturers of plastic 54mm models, probably piracies.

Arquette, Cliff, Idaho. A comedian by profession, up to 1959 he had made over 40 carved wooden 12-inch models of Civil War figures each taking about six weeks to carve, paint and dress in real cloth and leather. They form the foundation for his own museum at Gettysburg. Replicas in 54mm in metal were cast by Thomas Industries.

Arrington, USA (1964). A short-lived range of 54mm and 20mm models, the larger ones of Custer's war, the smaller of ancient Greeks and Romans. The name of the actual sculptor or designer is not known.

Artcraft, USA (1964). Printers of cardboard figure books, one in particular dealing with the adventures of Daniel Boone.

Arte & Commercie, Milan. Chromolithographed paper sheets.

Arte Grafica (A. de Giacomo), Italy. Publisher of paper sheets.

Arthur, H.J., London (fl.c.1956-70). Carved wood figures, large and attenuated, with more than a hint of caricature about them. Although the carving and painting were striking, they were never in the top rank. Those to be seen at Hummel's and 'Tradition' are of the American Revolution, the American Civil War, the British Army from 1650, Highland clansmen, the French Army from 1745 the Indian Army, Germans (1870-1914), Bersaglieri, Evzones, Russians (1808-14), Colonials, and British naval units. The same tradition is continued by his son. (*See* Karthage Figures)

Arthur, K. *See* Karthage Figures.

Artia, Prague (1973-). Maker of a cardboard castle.

ARTILLERY. Engines and mechanical weapons of war are only of interest to the author as part of the general overall conception of the model soldier, and he is certain that an authoritative book will some day be written (if it has not been already) dealing with models of cannon, guns, howitzers, mortars and the like. Such models have always formed a part of many a maker's or manufacturer's list, and it would be a difficult task to enumerate them. It would also take an expert in artillery to deal with the actual items. However, as specimens appear regularly in groups and dioramas, some token description at least is called for. Field guns of all periods were, and are, made to go with flat figures, in many cases incorporated on the same footstand. When exceptionally well-painted they become three-dimensional, especially when used in quantity, as in many of the large Continental dioramas. In the days of semi-flats and semi-solids the wheeled artillery was often made in the round, but still pulled by flat or semi-flat horses. By the time of Mignot, Heyde and Britains they had lost the hybrid horse and were drawn by fully-rounded animals, and it can be said that they have formed the basis for succeeding generations of craftsmen. (In the United States many models were made in cast iron and wood between 1840 and 1880.) Britains showed great technical accuracy in their artillery, and their many specimens, some now very rare, are eagerly sought after. Of present-day craftsmen, Alcocer and Almirall have a long list to their credit, while those made by Hinchliffe are masterpieces in their own right, especially admirable being the horses to go with them (as are the later efforts in this class by Almirall). Imrie has produced several smaller pieces, but his Revolutionary War artillery team ranks high in esteem, as does his anti-tank gun, while the howitzers, anti-tank guns and Renaissance cannon of Superior are of very fine quality. Cavalier's Gardner gun is so detailed that it requires an expert to assemble.

Most of the wargame figure-makers supply the most exquisite tiny models, which well repay the time taken in assembling and painting them, and the scale is usually very accurate. Historex has produced some impressive artillery teams; in their particular case so involved is the process of assembly that this is sometimes carried out by a team rather than by an individual. Of the other kits produced in polystyrene, (mainly in Japan and Italy) there is seemingly no end, and again they increase in complexity - a far cry, indeed, from the Victorian schoolboy's spring-loaded cannon! During the last decade the popularity of ancient siege weapons has increased, and there are now a number of working models of ballistas, catapults, onegas and the like, together with siege towers, in lead, plastic or polystyrene. But for the really enthusiastic collector of the unusual, what could be more highly recommended than the 'pneumatic cannon' issued by Schiercke?

Artillery and Wheelcraft, Harlow (1976-). Makers of scale-model wheels in wood and metal, of an 18-pounder garrison gun with accessories, and of wooden plinths for models.

Art Miniature (Jean-Pierre Lobel) Noisy-le-Grand, France (1979-). Models in 54mm metal, in kit form, of French troops between 1734 and 1870.

Arturo, Barcelona and Paris. An artist of great ability, whose speciality is the painting of Labayen models for the shop run by Segom. [*Bièville*]. A certain amount of confusion has been caused by some collectors classifying him as a maker and not simply as a painter of existing models.

Aschberg. *See* Tenngjuteriet Mars.

Asgard Miniatures (Brian Ansell) Nottingham (1971-). Maker of fantasy 25mm models in metal, some designed by Tony Acland.

Asheton-Bayard, Westfield, New Jersey (1970-?). An American journal mentioned that someone by this name had in 1970 commissioned a model of Bayard, the famous late medieval knight, from J. Lane Casey.

Ashworth, George, Watford (1965-). A maker of commissioned models in barbola.

Assasition, Spain. Publishers of paper sheets, designed by Father Carlos Garcia Iturri, finely printed on cardboard. [*Frazer*]

'Assault' series. *See* Airfix.

Assegai Miniatures (K. Nolan), Linmeyer, Transvaal (1975-). Only two models were issued, both in 54mm metal, the first, a Zulu, as a kit, the second, a British officer, 1879, as a one-piece casting.

Assiut, Upper Egypt. The site of Prince Emshah's bodyguard of infantry dating from c.2000 BC (now in Cairo Museum).

Association of Tinsmiths and Tinfigure Manufacturers. A group of German manufacturers of flats who in the 1850s formed themselves into a type of co-operative, possibly in order to save costs by sharing their labour-force. The members were: Bunau, Schundler and Loblich of Leipzig, Scheller of Kassel, Vaterlein of Freiburg, Schepp of Breslau and Leschorn of Randten.

Aster, Madrid (fl.1965-70?). Manufacturer of 54mm plastic foot models.

Astesiano, Argentina (1952-57). Manufacturers of 54mm solids based on Britains' designs. [*Basseterre*]

Astra, Italy. Maker of a 6-barrel rocket gun. [*Opie*]

Astro Model, Genoa. Agents for the models of Grifo and

Rocchiero.

Astro-Pharos, England (pre-1939). Manufacturers of tanks and guns in metal. [*Wade*]

Asturias, Mexico. In 1978 Wade had a model of a parachutist, the parachute itself of cloth with wire strings.

'At The Front'. *See* Lincoln Logs.

Athina OE, Athens (1968-). Manufacturers of 56mm plastic models of Evzones, ancient (with chariots) and modern Greeks (with printed linen standards) and police. A number of the models have movable arms, and some of the ancient Greeks' helmets are removable. Mark: MADE IN GREECE/A⊕HNAS/ in circle or surrounding the representation of an armed warrior.

Atlantic, Rome (1972-). Manufacturers of unpainted 20, 56mm plastics. The very curious range includes sets of Mao, Hitler, Stalin and Mussolini and their troops, a rickshaw kit with bearer and passenger, and a sampan kit. The smaller models (especially fine being a set of Egyptians) are as popular in Italy as those of Airfix are in Britain.

Atwell, Hicks, USA. Creator and painter of dioramas for the series 'They Nobly Dared'.

Attwood, Stephen. *See* Parade Miniatures.

Auburn Rubber Corp. (Auburn, Indiana/Deming, New Mexico (1936-c.1960). Manufacturers of very crude 60mm hard rubber figures, desiged by Edward McCandish, and issued painted in violent light or mid-brown. Tanks and artillery were included in their range. They must be unique in advertising the name of the designer, Martin Ullman, on some of their boxes. Known also as Aub-Rub'r. (*O'Brien*)

AUCTION SALES. The earliest auction of models that we are able to trace was in 1892, as reported in the *Gazette Anecdotique*, at the Hotel Drouet, Paris, where there was '*une vente de soldats de plomb. . . un grénadier de la Garde Imperiale fut alors coté trente-cinq francs or, un sapeur, quarante-deux francs*' (*Vaultier*). The occasional box or small collection has appeared regularly through the years, generally catalogued as 'toys', and fetching negligible prices (as at Lancing, Sussex, in 1960, when a collection of Authenticast barely exceeded the modest reserve). However, in 1953 the firm of Wallis and Wallis, of Lewes, in Sussex, began a series of sales devoted entirely to militaria, where a large number of lots were specifically but badly catalogued, and a collection of Silbermann paper sheets aroused great interest when shown at Sothebys in 1968. In 1969 Phillips of London began their now famous sales devoted entirely to model soldiers, and employed experts to catalogue the lots. The Brocke Collection of Heinrichsen flats was sold at Sotheby Belgravia in March, 1974, making a high price, and other collections, such as the Boersch and the Schmidt, both of paper sheets, were sold on the Continent in recent years. In the period from 1969 onwards the most surprising prices were paid for the 'toys of yesteryear' (Britains, Heydes, Elastolin). Apart from public auctions, many societies have for years held their own auctions, generally annually. These, of course, are restricted to the property of members only.

Audy, Mario don, USA. Modeller for Authenticast.

'Aufsitzen'. A form of flat in which a rider is cast separately from his horse, only one leg being shown.

Augé, Les Editions Jean, Paris (up to 1950). Paper sheets, in covers, 8 figures to each, each one different, and of fine quality. Napoleonics and French First World War

featured.

Auger, Paris. (1939-45). Maker of 60mm solids, although better known as a painter of fine quality. Also made figures in tin-plate of 18th-century French troops, 54mm, with apparently only one cavalryman— a Napoleonic cuirassier, the rider detachable. Carman says that he was partly financed by Peter Young.

Aurend, Germany (1975-). Designer of flats.

Aurora Plastics Corp, W. Hempstead, Long Island (1955-). Polystyrene kits of United States infantrymen and Marines; excellent historic armour and poor 40mm crews for armoured fighting vehicles.

'Austerlitz' series. *See* McNeil, Gordon.

Austincraft, USA (c.1935). Manufacturers of balsawood kits of armaments.

7   **Australia and New Zealand.** *At back: Dinah Penman (wood); second row: Allison, Sykes, Wooten, Sykes; third row: Turton; front row: Sykes wargame figures (Author).*

AUSTRALIA. The youngest Continent to show an interest in model soldiers. This is understandable, owing to its geographical position. In pre- and post-Second World War days the only models were Britains' and Stadden's imports, several large collections of which are still in existence. In 1963-4 Peter Wooten failed, even with a good native-produced model, to interest Australian collectors, and in England his agent, the Rev Sir Dickon Durand, had no success with English dealers. Today, however, the hobby is flourishing, models from all countries are collected, and there are several societies. Among the members are a number of private makers. Communications within the Continent itself are still difficult, as vast areas have to be covered for meetings, and the postal service from the rest of the world is appalling. It is hardly surprising that the arrival of models is an event, as there are as yet few dealers. Wargaming by younger members is popular. Apart from the efforts of Wooten, interest has centred on the works of John Sykes. In 1966 a series by him entitled Australian Military Miniatures was designed for and marketed by the Australian Society. They were also known as Milartex. Sykes still sells his models at his shop 'The Anatomy of Glory' in Sydney. A new line in

8   **Authenticast.** *Early models designed by Eriksson (Hanington).*

36mm solids was started in 1977 by Derek Brown. The most impressive group of models to be seen in public is the collection of dioramas at the Australian War Memorial at Canberra. The models are from 3 to 30 inches, and made by a team of over a dozen artists who have been working on them for years. In quality they are quite equal to anything to be seen elsewhere. [part *MacCallam*]

Australian Military Miniatures. *See* Sykes, John.

Austrandia (Fernando Chedel), Argentina (1949–1954). Manufacturer of 54mm solids, pirated from Britains and others. In 1964 he changed to the making of fine models, to commission only, under the trademark Roche. [*Basseterre*]

AUSTRIA. Owing to the confused political history of the country it would be difficult to separate its model-soldier activities from those of Germany. However, it is safe to say that the traditional flat has always been eagerly collected, and Ludwig Gärtner (b.1900) and Hofrat Dr Werner, who publicly staged a huge display during the First World War, together with Colonel Willy Teuber-Wickersdorff, set the tone for later collectors. Gärtner showed a diorama of the Battle of Hochstadt (1703) in 1940, which led to a meeting with Roger de Riedmatten, with whom he immediately began to co-operate, but, with the Second World War intervening, they were unable to work together until 1954, their reunion resulting in several large dioramas, including ones of Zenta and Wagram. In 1959 an exhibition in Vienna showed a Battle of Sacile (1809) now at the Military Academy, in which the two collectors were joined by Dr Erich Kröner-Grimm. A new version of Zenta by Gärtner and Riedmatten was shown in 1960, followed a year later by a Gärtner/Kröner-Grimm 'Prince Eugen's Crossing'. An incredible Siege of Vienna (Heeresmuseum) was made by all three collaborators, assisted by Frau Gärtner. Gärtner and Kröner-Grimm were now joined by Dr Erich Diener in the construction of the 'Battle near Prague, 1620' (5,000 flats), whilst Gärtner and Kröner-Grimm did a 'Leipzig'. Reference to the supplement under 'Places' will reveal the interest in dioramas taken by the museums. Solids have never been very popular in Austria, apart from the naive and nostalgic Wollner 38 and 55mm solids and semi-solids, reflecting as they do the vanished days of the Emperor Franz Josef. Founded in 1868, models were made by the firm up to 1914, but they can still be obtained at Kober's in Vienna. They hold the same place in Austria as Britains do in England and Mignot does in France. One lone figure hardly known outside his native country, Herbert Hahn (d.1957), for a few years manu-

factured small plaster models and lay-outs, but towering head and shoulders over all his contemporaries in every country is the amazing Helmut Krauhs (b.1913). In adopting the larger statuette type of figure, he has been able to give full rein to his majestic art of welding wood, plaster, cloth and metal into an incredible whole, and museums eagerly seek for his military and non-military creations. One man, Franz Wolavka, has since 1914 been building his own private museum, his models, in a material of his own devising, dealing exclusively with the misery of the trench warfare of the First World War. The Austrian Collectors' Society, which has a resounding name, usually abbreviated to '1683', began about 1940 and its journal was, until the end of 1975, enthusiastically edited by Dr Kröner-Grimm.

Authenticast. *See* Comet.

Authenticast Reproductions Company, New York (fl.1965). A balsawood and metal range of medieval siege engines and war machines.

Authentic Miniatures, Glasgow (1979–   ). Producers of 75 and 80mm solids in kit form designed by Tom Park.

AUTOMATA. A popular form of mechanical entertainment (and sometimes of instruction) of considerable variety. An actual army in silver was made by Jacob Wolrab in 1672, for Louis de France, Duc de Viennois, the eldest son of Louis XIV, which was activated by mechanical devices designed by Hans and Gottfried Hautsch, goldsmiths, silversmiths and compass-makers. In the same year John Wells patented a 'certain Engine. . . to performe by artificiall horses the usuall exercises of a complete horseman generally taught in academys' (*Bevan*). Gröber illustrates a solid lead coach with postilions, 9cm high, made in Nuremberg about 1780, which was worked by clockwork, and in D'Allemagne there are a number of plates of mechanical soldiers, some being set in motion by the action of a musical box. *La Nature* (1896) features two cavalrymen worked by a spinning top. Fortresses with movable figures, and complete battles, often with hundreds of troops, set in motion by a crankshaft, were popular in Germany in the late 19th century and Maximilian I of

9   **Automata.** *Clock in the form of a ship by Hans Schlott, 2ft 6in x 4ft. The figures surrounding the Emperor Rudolph II revolve when the clock strikes. c.1580 (British Museum).*

Bavaria ordered a representation of the capture of the Fort of Scharutz by the French, comprising 300 such figures. Another, of the Battle of Leipzig, with 800 models, is also known (*Fritch & Bachmann*). Less costly toys of wood and papiermâché, made at Erzegebirge in the 18th-19th centuries were set in motion by a contrivance similar to a roundabout, with horses, mounted Turks, and sentries riding and marching endlessly. In this category the examination of a catalogue of a toy-maker of Biberach published about 1836 throws a penetrating light on the immense variety of the wooden models for sale. They are in all shapes and sizes, some being highly finished products that would obviously be very expensive, others of a more humble nature. A large number are single mounted figures on rockers, showing great animation, rearing horses being provided with a support. Other models on footstands are fitted with various types of springs, in some instances again of a pair of combatants as one unit on the same stand. Wheels instead of rockers or coiled springs are frequently used, and occasionally wheels and springs are combined. Units of six to twelve men are also made on one wheeled stand. Free-standing infantry are common, and some must have been quite small, judging from the size of the boxes into which they fit. A large number of illustrations depict not only trellis tongs for both infantry and cavalry, but single figures or pairs of figures on a box from the side of which a handle projects. Obviously these performed some military action, such as a sentry emerging from and retreating into his box, or drummers performing. The armies of Germany predominate, but there are also Scottish troops and portrait models of Napoleon. One large model of an infantrymen of the Old Guard must have been expensive, as the very tall plinth (doubtless enclosing clockwork) appears to have ormolu or brass acanthus feet. Forts, castles, town houses, farm activities and hunting groups abound, many of these also being of a mechanical nature. A very popular type of automation was the 'home-bank' in many forms, such as a rifleman shooting a dime into a slot in a tree (America), a Highlander placing a coin in his mouth, etc, of which Britains also made a few examples. At Dorking in Surrey there is a model of a rider from the Viennese Riding Academy (said to be a favourite gift from Napoleon to children of soldiers in his Old Guard) which is set in motion by a lead fulcrum. Single figures in more or less standard size are not common, but Britains produced a set of 'Soldiers to shoot' (c.1895) and an archer with a target, 7cm (c.1930), examples of which may be seen at their offices. An amusing example of the use of models in lithographed sheet tin, $3\frac{1}{2}$ inches high, is a 'West Point Parade', advertised in the catalogue of a large store in 1930: 'The cadets march in never-ending parade.' Berdou has produced one or two models with a spring as a footstand, and, in quite a different category, the author has a Don Quixote (made in New York) so arranged that the brave knight trembles when touched. An American firm has recently issued a mortar-gun team complete with a clicking mechanism to produce the sound of fire, and this has even been done with cardboard models (*Alberini*). A clock is an obvious vehicle for mechanical ingenuity, as shown by the 'Edward VII' Chinese specimen (London Museum) and that of Rudolf II (British Museum), while specimens in public places may be noted in numerous medieval towns, where quarter-jacks appear or a joust takes place. The modern example in the childrens' television programme 'Trumpton' should not be despised, and it is a great joy to stand in the square in Coventry when Godiva and Peeping Tom emerge, or watch the elegant hourly masquerade of the rococo pair at Fortnum and Mason in Piccadilly. (*See also* Evolutions.)

Autopiano, USA (c.1918). Makers of a metal 8-inch model of a US infantryman of the First World War, possibly a recruiting figure. [*Pestana*]

Avondoglio, Carlos D. *See* Mambru.

Azco (Cards) Ltd, Birmingham. (post–1945-1955). Unlikely named manufacturers of 54mm hollow-casts.

B

Baarlen, Frau von, Amstelreen, Holland (1968–   ). Maker of polystyrene armoured fighting vehicle kits.

Bacciarini, Barcelona (c.1830–31). Engraver for Ortelli. (*Allendesalazar*)

Backman, Roland, Germany. Designer of flats for Sivhed.

Badajoz. A diorama, composed of over 350 different models, 52mm solid, with pins in the feet, was said to have been on show at the Crystal Palace near London before the fire of 1939. In 1974 we saw two of the models, which may well have been by Greenwood.

Bader, Strasbourg (c.1800). Publisher of paper sheets of the French armies of the Napoleonic era, together with portraits of Bonaparte and his marshals.

Baker, C.W. *See* Reka Ltd.

Balaguer, José, Argentina. Maker of 54mm solids to commission. [*Basseterre*]

Baldet, Marcel, Paris (1898–1972). He began making solid 54mm models in 1940. A basic torso was used, animated to the required action, the costume built up by sheet lead or brass, and the equipment added. He made a very wide range, with many commissions for private collections, and institutions, with a preference for French history (e.g. at Anderson House, Washington, and the Musée Militaire at Montreal). As a man he was a revered figure in France, and contributed much to the appreciation of the model soldier not so much by his technical excellence as by his erudite yet readable writings.

Ballada, Michael, Paris (c.1940–68). A maker of 54mm solid models, he worked originally under his own name, then formed a company with his son called 'Le Gaulois France'. Later he worked to commission only. The models are of fine quality, with the emphasis on the First Empire, military musicians and artillery regiments. (See *Le Retour des Cendres de Napoleon I* at Compiègne and two splendid cavalry pieces made in 1946 illustrated by Cowan in his *Militaria* Catalogue Vol. 10.) After his death and up to 1970 his models were marketed by his widow.

Balsawood. A very light, tough-grained wood used by makers mainly for their prototypes, although from time to time it appears as the material for a complete model. Weapons are also made from it to accompany models in other material, e.g. Isopon.

Banbury, B. *See* Jupiter Models.

Band, Percy, Canada. On his death in 1962 his collection, (mainly Britains and Heinrichsens) was bought by the Metropolitan Toronto Museum and is housed at Black Creek Pioneer Village.

Bandai, Japan. Polystyrene armoured fighting vehicle kits.

Bandsmen Figures. At a Phillips' sale, 29 June, 1976, a set of 13 Bandsmen of the Fijian Regiment was catalogued thus.

Banks, R. *See* Regimental Enterprises.

Banner-Model, Copenhagen (1948–1970). Manufacturers of commercial 47–49mm solids.

Bantock, J.R. Granville and **Dr Alastair,** England. The foremost advocates of flats in England. They are indefatigable in their enthusiasm, and have always been liberal with their talent for instructing collectors in the art of casting. Their knowledge of current European makers has been only one of the many contributions they have made to the *Bulletin* of the British Model Soldier Society. Without their valuable assistance many collectors would have remained in virtual ignorance of the fascination of the flat model.

Baptiste, E. *See* Hubert, André.

Baranella, Italy. Manufacturer of 54mm plastic models.

'Barbarian' series. *See* Valiant Miniatures.

Barber, John. *See* Jackboot.

Barbola. A type of malleable paste akin to sealing-wax, originally intended for young ladies in the 1930s to make into artificial flowers, it has on occasion been used for conversion (as by Don and Honey Ray), and even formed the basis of complete and original models, as by J.F. Morrison of Glasgow, who, in 1950, made a set of six models, each one foot high, now in the Museum of the Royal Army Service Corps at Aldershot. The only other recorded maker is George Ashworth.

Barclay (Leon Donzé) New York/Union Town, New Jersey (c.1924–1965). Manufacturers of 54 and 60mm hollowcasts. The American equivalent of Heyde in their scope, which included over 200 vehicles and guns. The majority of the models were of American troops of the First World War. Changes were effected from time to time: for example, in the earliest models no eyes were indicated, or, if so, by the merest dot (later changed to the shape of a recumbent comma), a tin helmet was glued on after the painting had been done, the tunics were khaki, the puttees orange, and the footstand green. Some of

10   Barclay. *Late examples (Author).*

the few mounted troops (including a bugler and a cavalryman with a sword or a revolver) had movable arms. In about 1940 the helmet was riveted, and the puttees changed to leggings. The helmet was then cast on to the figure, and the name of the manufacturer or the series number,700, marked on the base. Red Cross personnel, civilians and scouts were given the numbers 900, 600 and 800 respectively. After the Second World War new moulds were made, and again in 1955 the models were redesigned with a round base to each foot, while the last phase reverted to the 'no eyes' and eliminated the numbers. Even so, they were supplied with a curved or half-moon eyebrow, except in the very latest version. The round base (or 'pod feet', as they are generally called) produced an incredibly naive figure. A charming, non-military, series of winter sports (c.1940) was later pirated in plastic. Two of their sculptors are known: Frank Krupp and Olive Kooken [*R. O'Brien, Pielin et alia*, in part]. Castings from four original Barclay moulds were issued by Eccles in 1978. Some of their models were pirated in Japan, the name of that country being rubber-stamped on the underside of the footstand. (*R. O'Brien*)

Bard, Robert, New York. A collector and dealer, and the author (1957) of the first modern book on model soldiers.

Barecki, Roger, Grand Rapids, Michigan. Maker of commissioned 54mm solids, and represented at Grand Rapids Public Museum.

Barefoot Soldier, The. *See* The Barefoot Soldier.

Barnes, Dr J. Lovell. *See* Carman, W.Y.; The Sentry Box.

'Barrack Bawds' series. *See* Old Guard.

Barracks Square, Liverpool, 1974. Marketers of Hinton chess sets.

Barreira, Barcelona. A dealer featuring several well-known Spanish makers, and also issuing (1978) a range in 45mm of 'toy' soldiers.

Barrett & Sons. *See* Taylor & Barrett.

Barrientos, Luis, Madrid. Maker of magnificent 54mm commissioned solids, especially of cavalry.

Bartel, Hanover. A collector of flats who assisted in the construction of a Waterloo diorama at Hanover, 1957.

Barthel, Strasbourg (c.1800). One of the earliest publishers of paper sheets.

Bartle, W., Great Britain (1915). Manufacturer of plaster 20-inch trenches with barbed wire. (*Model Soldier*, October, 1978)

Barton, A. & C. (Toys) Ltd, New Addington, Croydon (1963). Plastic 40mm model of a mother and her children.

Barton Miniatures (J. Barton) London, (1978-). Producer of 90mm solids sculpted by Richard J. Almond.

Baschieri, A., Bologna (1973-). Maker of magnificent

54mm commissioned solid models of a variety of subjects.

Baselsoder, J.A., Nuremberg (1870-1939). Maker of 30mm flats, semi-solids; 54mm solids.

Bassett-Lowke, Northampton. A long-established firm specializing in scale-model railways. In 1979 they announced 1/10th scale kits of cannon in metal and timber.

Baston, Prescott, USA (1976-). Maker of '76' models for Hudson Pewter and his own Sebastian Miniatures. [*Trautmann*]

Baston, P.W. The author has a polychrome equestrian model in plaster, 3 inches high on a thick stand, inscribed PAUL REVERE on the front of the stand and COPR: 1950: P.W. BASTON on the rear.

Bata, Prague (c.1935). Manufacturers of probably the most grotesque military toys ever made. These consisted of plastic flats in 6cm, plastic solids 5cm (gold-plated knights), 12cm and 20cm. [*Roubicek*]

Battaglia, Ernesto, Venice (1970-). Large composite figures of wood and cloth, the whole rather archaic and doll-like in appearance, but most colourful.

Battalions in Miniature (Darrell Combs), Woodbridge, Virginia (1974). A shortlived venture of four somewhat crude 54mm solids of the American Civil War, together with battlefield equipment.

Battle Building Soldiers (Lyon Ltd), Glasgow (c.1916). Stiff card cut-outs, colour printed, with wooden struts, and scenic accessories. (*Model Soldier*, October, 1978)

'Battle for Freedom' (1947). A series of dioramas made by Stokes, Greenwood and Ball in 20mm: Badajoz; Waterloo; the Alma; the Somme; the Battle of Britain; the Blitz; Bir Hacheim; the Rhine Crossing. They travelled extensively throughout Great Britain, but their whereabouts are now unknown to the author.

'Battlefront' series *See* Airfix.

'Battle Game, The'. *See* American Soldier Co.

11   Barrientos. *Spanish artillery, c.1730. 1/30th scale.*

'Battle of Agincourt' chess sets. *See* Chessmen; Minimodels.

'Battle of Bunker Hill'. Diorama made by the Military Collectors of New England for the Sun Life Assurance Company of Canada and given by that firm (1975) to the Bunker Hill Museum. Size 12 x 8 feet, using 5,400 models in 9mm, created by S. Holmes, H. Lion and V. Bean.

'Battle of Pavia' chess set. *See* Chessmen; Willie.

'Battle of the Pyramids' chess set. *See* Chessmen; Willie.

'Battle of Waterloo' chess sets. *See* Chessmen; Lamming; Stadden Studios Ltd.

'Battle of Waterloo' set. *See* Timpo.

Baumgarten, R., Alfeld, West Germany. Flats, 30mm. Specializes in the publication of a small range of the 1790-1815 period, including a drinking party, Prussian cuirassiers with women, and Austrian and Jager artillery.

Baumgartner, Fritz. *See* Tim-Mee Figures.

Bayer, Emil, Mengersgerenth-Hammern, Austria (c.1965-?). Manufacturer of plaster composition Indians and trappers for juveniles.

Beaumont, London (fl.1895). A virtually unknown manufacturer of 54mm hollow-casts in as much as hardly a model survives.

Beaumont, Ernest, New York (fl.1938) Assisted in the making of the dioramas at the Museum of the City of New York.

Beck, Franz, Kassel. Publisher of 20 and 30mm flats. Some of the smaller variety were designed by Fritsch and engraved by Redlin. A long series of the Siegfried sagas, designed by Madlener, engraved by Frank, Emmerling and Lecke; also Prussians, 1760 and 1920. Mark: FB.

Beck, Hans and **Brandstetter, Horst.** *See* Big Spielwarenfabrik.

Beck, Martin, Aarau, (fl.1800-05). Beginning as a journeyman to W. Gottschalk, he later began his own manufacture of large-size flats.

Becker, Henry, USA (fl.1960). A maker of Civil War cannon, for which Murray provided the crews.

Becker, H.K., Frankfurt, Constructed a number of war machines for the Royal United Service Institution collection of dioramas.

Becker, Horst, Nuremberg. Designer of flats for Hafer and Kebbel.

Becker, Kurt, Kassel. Publisher of 30mm flats. Responsible for a diorama of Rossbach with 20mm flats for Kulmbach, 1975.

Beckman, Alan C. *See* Parade Square.

Beek, R. van, Holland. With A. Beerhorst constructed an RAF Base with plastic models for the Leiden Army Museum in 1975.

Beerhorst, A., Holland. Reconstructed a parade of Spanish troops for the Leiden Army Museum. (*See also* Beek, R. van.)

Beersman & Delhovennes, Holland (19th century). Publishers of paper sheets.

Beersman & Jacobs, Holland (19th century). Probably a later amalgamation of the foregoing firm.

Beeswax. A smooth substance, which, when hardened, forms like barbola. Used on occasion for large models, especially in the United States.

Beffara et Cie, *See* Starlux.

Beffoid, France (1970-). Manufacturer of models in hard plastic. [*Kearton*]

Beiser, C.W. *See* Eureka American Soldiers.

Belaubre, Jean, Colombes, France. Publisher of 20mm flats of the 15th-18th centuries. First mentioned in 1974 in the BMSS *Bulletin.*

BELGIUM. The Belgian Society was one of the earliest to be formed, but the making of models never appears to have been very popular. Those of Emmanuel Steinback (MIM) are universally known; there have been a few makers of composition figures such as Fabrique Belge, and certain establishments produced paper sheets, but the only modern makers of originals that we have been able to trace are Léon Hames and Le Sellier. On the other hand, there are many collectors of great taste, and a number who have produced an occasional unique model for their own pleasure. Historex is in great demand, and there are many converters. The Society does not hold competitions but collectors are known to get together to pool their resources for cultural exhibitions.

Bell, Rev J., Camberley, Surrey (1975). Maker of a series of minidioramas of the history and present-day activities of Chaplains to the Forces, composed of converted models. Housed at R.A.Ch.D. Museum, Bagshot Park.

Bellahoj, Copenhagen (1890-1920). Publisher of lithographed sheets of soldiers for cutting out.

Bellerophon, New York (1974). Publishers of a series of books of cardboard cut-out figures such as *Paper Soldiers of the American Revolution,* consisting of 80 figures each of American and British troops in separate volumes. They also published (1975) separate models of Henry VIII and his wives and Queen Elizabeth I.

Bell-Knight, C.A., Bath. Creator of the Bell-Knight Collection of British Bygones at Bath, which includes many conversions for dioramas, and a collection of separate models.

'Bellona'. *See* Deltorama.

Belmont-Maitland, Roy, London. The first dealer to recognize the high quality of the work of Courtenay and of Stadden. Through his efforts both were placed on a high pinnacle at a time when there were few specialist makers. He began as a dealer in Shepherd Market, moving later to Dover Street, where he assumed the same of Norman Newton Ltd. Later, when in Piccadilly, he established the International Society of Military Collectors, naming his business 'Tradition' after the title of the journal. In 1976 the business moved to Mayfair. He himself designed many of the Stadden German range. (*See also* 'Tradition'.)

Beltramino, Alejandro. *See* Birmania.

Benassi, Major Julian, England (1975-). First began as a designer of 78mm Italians (1813 and First World War) and Spanish Napoleonics for Hinchliffe. He followed these (1976) with a Sumerian warrior and a nude Nubian Amazon, both very clumsy in anatomy, for Warrior, and a Scottish clansman for Caledonian. Any originality of period or in pose is negated by a lack of anatomical knowledge and an almost complete lack of taste.

Benbros (London) Ltd, London (1951-c.1967). Manufacturers of reasonably good 6.5cm hollow-casts, mainly of standard types: the British Army, the Wild West and Robin Hood. Later they made a range of plastics, mainly copies of Herald or Lone Star.

Bendix Radio Premium, USA (1944). Publishers of 8 varieties of 5½-inch-high cut-out coloured photographs of Second World War troops. (*Newman*)

Benecke, Else, Trieb uber Lichtenfels. Publisher of flats, listed as an exhibitor at Kulmbach in 1973.

Benkert, Dr A.J. *See* Monarch.

Benorden (David) Miniatures, Lincoln, Nebraska. He was noted in 1972 in the BMSS *Bulletin* as producing 75mm solids of the French and Indian War. No amount of correspondence to the given address produced an answer, but one United States collector has actually seen a single example, of which he gave a lukewarm opinion.

Benoy, Brigadier J.F., England (pre-1950). Maker of 30mm solids.

Benson, London (c.1950). Maker of hollow-casts, 54mm.

A firm so elusive that only a few are known, including a Wild West bandit, similar in appearance to Timpo, and a drover. (*Wade*)

Berdin, Paris (c.1930). Maker of metal artillery. [*Nicollier*]

Berdou, Roger, Paris/Aiguebelle (1907–1976). Connoisseur maker of 54mm solids. A legendary figure in France and among collectors of taste in other countries. As he worked strictly to commission, few examples are to be seen outside the collections of those who employed his skill, and he himself said that if one visited his studio he would have been unable to show one anything other than the model on which he was currently working. In his early days (1945) he began making models in series, but found this irksome. Thereafter no model was ever duplicated. Each torso was built up in the French manner by soldering, with the addition of separate articles of clothing and equipment. Although his horses were assembled from seven different basic pieces, no one is exactly alike, as he kept an elaborate chart of the position of each one as completed. And what horses they are! Careful examination will reveal that every strand of hair is a separate piece of the thinnest possible metal, and not for him an overall colour of hair and tail. His scrupulous accuracy, his marvellous though restrained painting, his sheer integrity of craftsmanship, and the dignity of everything that he undertook are sufficient to ensure his pre-eminence among the makers of all times. His great passion was for mounted troops of the Napoleonic Army, but after heavy persuasion he did on one occasion undertake a task alien to his nature when Lyle Thoburn commissioned United States Cavalry from him, and he also provided horses for Imrie riders. Only he could design a graceful metal wave or a spring as a base and get away with it. Many an established model maker would find it rewarding to study a collection of some fifty Berdou models, as the author has been fortunate enough to do, and observe horse anatomy and painting that makes the work of many a currently lauded professional model-maker and painter appear cheap and tawdry. The hallmark of his work was dignity, and one cannot visualize him ever having been willing to lend his art to the creation of a model in violent or sadistic action. He rejected modern trends in this direction, and his *corpus* of work shines the more brilliantly for it. Unfortunately, no more will be made, as his eyesight deteriorated to such an extent that he was compelled to give up work in 1976. (For a fuller assessment of Berdou, see the present author's *Model Soldiers for the Connoisseur.*)

Bergen Toy and Novelty Co. Inc. *See* Beton Toys.

Berger-Levrault & Fils, Strasbourg (c.1875). Publishers of paper sheets.

Berglund, George, Sweden (d.1972). A noted collector who collaborated with Dahlback in the construction of the dioramas at Leksand.

Bergmann, Strasbourg (c.1770–1904). The most important of the makers of Strasbourg flats, originally in the prevalent very large size (mainly 6.5cm). Many can be seen at the Musée de Strasbourg. One of the earliest efforts was a 12cm copy of Hilpert's 'Frederick the Great'. Founded by Antoine-Joseph (d.1830), his successor was Charles Théodore (1830–58), then Charles (1858–1904) and, finally, Eugène Marchand. A prolific industry, concentrating mainly on the armies of Louis XV and Frederick the Great, with excursions into the

12 **Bergmann.** *Flats 12.5cm from Strasbourg, 1830–45 (Musée Alsacien, Strasbourg).*

more exotic realms of Croatia.

Berking, Erik, Hanover (fl.1965). Designer of 30mm flats.

Berliner-Miniatur-Plastiken, (Walter Merten), Berlin, (c.1940–). Manufacturer of solids (20–40mm) of Indians, cowboys, gauchos (in all 94 on foot, 24 mounted, riders detachable), railway staff, civilians and wild animals (all probably no longer obtainable). In plastic composition in the same size, a remarkable collection of troops of the Middle Ages, the action of some excellent, of others execrable, those of the mounted troops appalling. On the other hand the archers are excellent, even though one or two are shooting off the wrong foot. Some of the knights have detachable cloaks, and there are scaling ladders, pavisses and mantlets. A brilliantly coloured set of Landschnechts on foot and mounted, the riders again detachable, were among the first of this period to be obtainable, the weapons being interchangeable, and variety on basic figures given by changes of headwear. The design of the horses again is poor. Further sets include Westerners, Bedouins, German and United States Second World War, Centaurs, a riding school, a bathing party, medieval ladies going hawking, and delightful civilians and children of the same period. Pirated (very badly) by a number of makers, especially Fairylite (20mm) and Reamsa (60mm).

Berliner Zinnfiguren Werner Scholtz (Werner and Anna Scholtz), Berlin (1904–). Publisher of flats of all sizes. One of the most vital figures in the *zinnfiguren* industry. Having been apprenticed to Roskopf, in 1934 he produced his first flat, which was engraved by Sixtus Maier. His first essay into the larger figure (7.5cm) was issued in the same year. He soon began to make his mark, conducting courses for painting models, and acquired various nicknames. His first catalogue was issued with painting instructions. He planned many of his productions on the colossal scale of a Heinrichsen, in some cases as many as 400 figures going to make up a set. Probably the most famous is the 'Retreat from Moscow', comprising three separate entities: the Retreat, the Crossing of the Beresina, and the Burning of the Standards. Every aspect of the Retreat is covered, and the many 'kombination' figures give ample scope for colossal presentations. Moreover, it is perhaps the starkest presentation of military folly and suffering ever portrayed. Similar in scope is his series depicting the troops of Frederick the Great (including the 'Choral of Leuthen'), an achievement which earned him yet another sobriquet: 'Friederichianer'. Large sets are obtainable of magnificent medieval knights and foot-soldiers of the Maximilian period, and, more recently, English bowmen in several stances. Slightly later in period is a long series of Landschnechts, and there are further sets of Greeks, Romans, Sumerians, Egyptians, Huns and prehistoric animals. Not content with military matters, he enriched the civilian range with church-goers, sedan chairs, Greek athletes and bathers, desert folk, town and country types from the 17th to the 20th centuries, including a street photographer with clients, and a complete series of costumes from the earliest times to the mid-1920s. Many of the designs were by himself or his wife, but others have been done by Madlener and M. Block, while for engraving he employed the services of Lecke, Maier, his son, Hans Gunther Scholtz, and Sollner. In 1970 he began a series of 12cm or *vituren* figures, including magnificent Landschnechts, bowmen, dancing peasants, rococo huntsmen and ladies, Napoleon, Madame Récamier, an antiquarian studying books, Prince Eugen, Maria Theresa, street musicians, and vases of flowers. These were engraved mainly by Lecke and Sollner. Perhaps the most attractive of his ventures is a rococo garden (30mm), every conceivable kind of clipped hedges and bushes, flowerbeds, fountains, statues and gardeners being available. In 1974 he took over the moulds of Sandow's Boer War series. Scholtz, who died in 1977, was the essence of courtesy, willing at all times to collaborate with a collector or an author. The business continues with his widow and son in charge.

Berlin Scale. An arbitrary size of 40mm used by mid-19th-century makers of flats in the Berlin area. It was superseded by the Nuremberg scale of 28mm.

Bern, Gerald, Toronto (fl.1969). Producer of cardboard press-out colour-printed models of Canadian forts: Halifax Citadel, Fort Louisbourg, Fort Chambly, Fort York, Fort George, Fort Garry.

Berne, Maurice, Paris (fl.1935). Manufacturer of toys in metal, aluminium and papiermâché, of no great quality, 54 and 60mm. Modern and Napoleonic French troops (with portrait models of Napoleon and Joffre) German, Scottish, Russian, American and Italian combatants, Westerners (foot and mounted), Romans, Middle Ages (including Joan of Arc), fixed and removable cavalry, firemen, railway staff, circuses, hunts, polar exploration, domestic and wild animals. Accessories were in papiermâché. More famous, perhaps, as a producer of 'Rivollet' armaments in aluminium.

Berton, Joseph, St Charles, Illinois. A free-lance designer of 54mm solids (including a Lawrence of Arabia for Valiant) and a skilled professional painter.

Berwick's Toy Co Ltd, Liverpool (pre-1939). A manufacturer with a small output of 54mm hollow-casts.

Besold, Nuremberg. (1800-93). Producers of 30mm flats. Carl Ludwig Friedrich Albert Besold (1800-57) was apprenticed to Schweigger; Johann Andreas (1835-93) succeeded him. Friedrich Besold, moving to Fürth, sold the business in 1877 to Fortner and Haffner, who in turn sold it to Schildnecht in about 1890. The earlier flats were of fine quality, especially five mounted knights with movable arms in the Nuremberg Museum. Marks: B; BESOLD/NURNBERG.

Bestermaier, G.H., Nuremberg (1798-?). A toy-dealer, one of whose catalogues (1809) contained a mass of flats and animals in papiermâché.

Best Toy Company, Manhattan, Kansas (c.1920-30). Manufacturers of toys, the only items we have heard of being a six-piece set of farm machinery and a few cars.

Betal Products, London (c.1955). Manufacturers of 54mm hollow-casts of whom nothing is known apart from the fact that Opie has a box of cowboys marked thus.

Beton Toys (Bergen Toy & Novelty Co. Inc.,) Carlstadt, New Jersey (fl.c.1938-c.1960). Manufacturers of models in aluminium and later in plastic (60mm), some figures being mounted. During 1955-60 they were in unpainted polystyrene. The bases of the earlier models were oval, later rectangular. The feet of the plastic models were plugged into holes in the base, with the mark BERGEN TOY & NOV CO INC in a circle around USA on the left; on the right C in circle. Other marks: BETON/CARLSTADT N.J./USA; BETON/MADE IN USA; and, post-1945, ⬚.

Betts, George H. and **Harling, Donald,** Kingston, Ontario (1973-). For Kingston's 300th Anniversary (1973) they were commissioned to make a series of 54mm solid models of Count Frontenac and Indians and priests. Copies are stocked by Payen of Iberville. Those which we have seen are somewhat doll-like in their anatomy. They are also making a series of the Canadian army of the late 19th century.

BG of GB (Brian Gildea), Gosport (1979-). Manufacturers of 'toy' soldiers in Britains' style.

BIBLIOGRAPHY. (For the actual titles of the books mentioned in this section the reader should refer to the Bibliographical Supplement at the end of the book.) The first factual reference to model soldiers that has been found is that contained in the diary of Dr Heroard (1600-1628), quoted extensively by Crump (1929), in which are described in detail the models used as playthings by the French royal family. A long gap ensues until George Augustus Sala reported on the products displayed at the Great Exhibitions of London and Paris in 1851 and 1867 respectively, but as far as he was concerned the articles he described were simply one aspect of the toy trade. Forgeais (1858) wrote about the tin industry, this time from an archaeological viewpoint, followed after a long interval by Forrer (1905), who wrote with the collector of flats in mind, an example that was elaborated on by Hampe (1924) in the first serious attempt at a history of the Germanic flat, but dealing almost exclusively with the products of Nuremberg and Fürth. Claretie (1894 and again in 1920) and d'Allemagne (1903) looked more seriously at models as collectable objects, even though incorporating their remarks in works on toys in general, as did Mrs Neville Jackson (1928), von Bohn, Gordon Holme and Grober (all in 1932). The awakening interest of the 1920s to '40s was evident in a number of journals, prominent among them being *The Illustrated London News* and *L'Illustration*, while distinguished French and German makers and collectors were at the same time issuing small, limited editions of erudite works confined solely to the products of their own countries. Paper sheets were written about by Percout (1912), Martin (*Les Petits Soldats de Strasbourg*, 1950) and Amades, whose monumental book on Catalan sheets appeared in 1946. However, the first attempt at a review of solid toys and models was not made until 1957, when Bard's book appeared. Sketchy though it was, it did at least establish the importance of the solid, although of necessity it was circumscribed in its choice of American and French examples. At any rate, it inspired the present author to investigate the history of the model soldier in all periods and in all its aspects in a much fuller manner (1959). It was followed quickly by Baldet (1961), Harris (1962) and Featherstone (1964), each of whom touched on aspects not hitherto approached. Peter Blum's tiny gem (1964) not only crystallized the art, but brought to the fore the photographic genius of Philip Stearns, which was later shown again in the slim volume by Alberini (1972). The author's *Model Soldiers for the Connoisseur* (1973) for the first time brought together the skill of the maker and the enthusiasm of the collector as allied to one another. His third book (1975) took a more popular view, and attempted to bring up to date his previous publications.

Serious works on specialized subjects within the main framework include Richards on hollow-casts in general and Britains in particular (1969), Ortmann (1972) and Pleticha (1976) on flats, and Polaine (1979) on Elastolin; while works dealing with specific countries include Gripenberg (1973) on Sweden, and Allendesalazar (1978) on Spain.

The last decade has produced a whole flood of works, mostly short, some mere flimsy sketches, concerned mainly with the art of conversion, both of plastic and of polystyrene kits. They do no more than elaborate on magazines devoted more to modelling than to collecting. Works of greater value in this field, aimed at the collector interested in creating his own models, while at the same time skimming lightly over the philosophy and history of the model, have been written by Stearns (mainly for casting in metal) and Cassin-Scott (fibre resin and other materials).

'Kriegsspiel' had been written about since the 1840s, and the 'wargame' since 1872, but it really came into its own between 1965 and 1975, when a veritable flood of publications emerged, headed in bulk by the works of Featherstone, although probably the most attractive were Young's *Charge!* and Grant's *The War Game*. The study of armoured fighting vehicles is a separate one, and a perusal of publishers' lists will show the vast literature there is on this subject.

Bickerton, Graham, England. Professional painter employed by the Dover branch of Historex.

Biebel, F, Berlin. An early 20th-century collector who made flats for his own amusement and for exhibition. He began in 1924 by employing Frank and Maier and later Thiel and Bolling as engravers. Sets to his credit include Wallenstein, Kronstadt, Frederick II and General Wrede. He also made solids from separate moulds and fully-round vehicles. He exercised a great influence on German collecting circles.

Biener, Heinz, Leipzig. Maker of flats. (*Katalog der Formen, 1976*)

Biéville, P. *See* SEGOM.

Big Bang, USA (1950). Manufacturers of tin-plate artillery.

Big Spielwarenfabrik (Hans Beck and Horst Brandstetter), Nuremberg (1971-). Makers of a series of polystyrene movable models, 5 inches high, entitled 'Busy Bodies' in England. They are nursery figures, with movable arms and separate equipment: knights, cowboys, Indians, nurses, hospital staff and road workers.

Bihari, Robert, Roselle, Illinois. Free-lance artist, who has designed for Valiant.

Billiken Magazine, Argentina (1940). Publisher of paper sheets of Argentinian uniform 1807-1820 and modern troops. [*Basseterre*]

Bilsland, Dale A. *See* Vulcan Miniatures

Bing Gebr, Germany. Manufacturers of long-standing of mechanized tin-plate military vehicles. About 1960 they produced a number of the early Elastolin-type models in 60mm, one being of a Grenadier Guardsman with a wooden sentry box. [*Wade*]

Bircher, H., Sulgen, Switzerland (before 1920). Maker of flats of Swiss troops.

Bird, Pat. *See* Series 77.

Birkman, Nuremberg. Exhibited a metal coach in 1867.

Birmania (Alejandro Beltramino), Argentina (1955-60, 1975-). Maker of 40mm solids, 54mm hollow-casts, with heavy emphasis and often blatant piracy of Britains and Timpo. [*Basseterre*]

Bischoff, Joseph, Nuremberg (19th-20th centuries). Flats and (?) semi-solids.

Bisgood, D., Cheltenham (1975-). Maker of 30cm and upward foot and mounted models of the British army, using synthetic air-drying clay over a metal and wood armature, with all equipment in natural materials. He works only to commission (e.g. Queen's Own Hussars Museum, Warwick).

Biswell, Alan. *See* Greenwood and Ball (Pearce).

Bittard, Jacques, Paris (fl.1950). One of the specialist French makers of 54mm solids, with a wide range of subjects, all his work being commissioned. Especially interested in the 1900-1914 period, but not restricting himself to this by any means (for instance, his 'Hundred Swiss' at Coppet Castle on Lake Geneva). Impeccable in detail, rich in texture of painting, with plumes and feathers of incredible beauty. Still working, but only for a limited clientele.

Bittner, Heinz, Hof a.d. Saale, E. Germany (fl.1965). Producer of flats of Egyptians (engraved by Frank) Hussites (engraved by Braune, Neumeister and Frank), the Middle Ages and the Renaissance (engraved by Mohr).

Bivouac Military Miniatures (David Brown), Kansas City, Missouri (1977-). Maker of 90mm solids of disparate subjects, including Sherman, an American slave, a Roman retiarius, an American cowboy, a Cheyenne warrior, a Robin Hood, a Cyrano de Bergerac, a Maid Marian, and 'Tarlock, King of Hell's Demons'. Most of the sculpting is done by James Payette.

Blackman, Rear-Admiral C.M., Southampton. Converter of commercial models with additional hand-made equipment. He made 18 for the Regimental Museum of the Duke of Wellington's Regiment (33rd Foot) at Halifax, and 35 for the Royal Marine Museum, Eastney Barracks, Southampton.

Black Watch, The (J.P. Janssen), Van Nuys, California (1978-). A firm promoting the making of models in two series: 1. Signature Series, 90-150mm, medieval to 1900, designed or sculpted by Terry Worster, J. Payette, D. Kennedy, M. Tapavica, D. Burgess, E. Lelièpvre, S. Paine, D. Hawley. 2. Ordnance Miniatures, 90mm ordnance designed by D. Hawley. All are in kit form.

Blair-Smith, Crewe (1975-). Maker of a 54mm solid Persian cavalryman, dismounted, in kit form.

Blanc-de-Meudon. The French equivalent (in particular the original pre-war Starlux) to the composition material used in the early Elastolin-style models. [*Hawkins*]

Blenheim Military Models (Frank and Janet Scroby) London/Pontycymmer, Bridgend, S. Wales (1973-). The Scrobys began making Britains-type models in solid, with movable arms, selling them in Portobello Road. These were not an immediate success, but they soon began making models for Shamus Wade under the name Nostalgia, a project which has kept them occupied up to the time of writing. In 1976 they recommenced the Blenheim models, issuing drum horses and Chelsea Pensioners. Together with the figures one would expect to find, they include such items as bands and bandstands, a campfire set of the 1870 to 1900 period, and transport wagons. A foot figure set consists of six soldiers, a cavalry one of three, both sets being boxed. In 1977 they made a Jubilee set of Her Majesty the Queen, the Duke of Edinburgh, the Archbishop of Canterbury, pages and gentlemen-at-arms. Special commissions have included a large collection of thirty-nine different regiments of the American Army of the War of Independence (for Princeton Battlefield Preservation Society, N.J.), a Colour-party for West Point, and Fort Henry Guards. A break with the Blenheim figure are the 'Derek Knight Originals', commissioned by the Scrobys from Knight in 1978. These are not 'toy' soldiers, but finely designed 54mm solids, in kit form and available in the unpainted state only.

Block, Martin, Germany. Designer of flats for Lecke, Sivhed, Ochel and others.

Blocquel, Lille (19th century). Publisher of paper sheets.

Blondel et Fils, Paris (fl.1838-51). Solids. Mentioned in the *Almanach Bottin* from 1838 to 1851, linked with a separate establishment of Blondel only, together with yet another, Cuperly-Blondel, as all producing '*montres, ménages, soldats*' etc. *See also* Mignot.

Blue Box/Red Box, Hong Kong. Plastic, 30/54mm. The first are piracies of models by Marx. The 54mm range, made in hard, metallic, plated plastic, and entitled 'Famous Historical Characters', comprises such an assortment as Robin Hood, Julius Caesar, Richard I, Henry VIII, Geronimo (with full eagle head-dress) and Lord Nelson, a ridiculous figure. No attempt at portraiture is achieved, although the card to which each model is attached states 'Masterpieces by well-known top-notch artists'! Probably flagrant piracies of other plastics unknown to us.

Blum, Eugen, Zurich (d.1965). A collector of high sensitivity, who busied himself with the editing of many sets of flats of outstanding quality. The most impressive is that for the Battle of Morat (1476) between the Swiss and the Burgundians. 140 postures were made, and a useful leaflet issued with the set giving instructions for the painting of the banners and a diagram and description of the tactics employed by the crossbowmen. To these were added similar designs made for Otto Gottstein, so that a most comprehensive collection emerged. Numerous dioramas have been made of this set, one of which is illustrated in some detail in Martin, *Le Monde Merveilleux.* He also issued sets of mamelukes, and Gottstein's moulds of ancient British chieftains and the sovereigns of Great Britain. An enthusiastic personality, whose loss is keenly felt in collecting circles. However, his moulds were purchased by Neckel in 1972 for reissue.

Blum, Peter, New York. Collector and author of a delightful pocket-book on models. Now the owner of The Soldier Shop and an enterprising salesman of native and imported models.

Blumentritt, Germany (1975). Designer of flats.

BMC, London (before 1918). Commercial manufacturer of hollow-casts, 60mm, fixed or movable arms. Their range included First World War, Wild West, Zulus, the Rifle Brigade, a mounted Cossack, firemen, ships, tents, and a Scout brigade. Shamus Wade, who has probably seen more hollow-casts than any other collector, considers them to be one of the best of Britains' rivals.

BMS, London (fl.1965). Plastic, 54mm. Arabs, Foreign Legion, Westerners.

'Bobs, A Boer War Game', London (1900). A board game, with flat metal stamped-out military figures.

Boehm, M.F., Strasbourg (1850). Lithographer of paper sheets, mainly for Maison Froereisen.

Boecker (or Broker), August, Berlin (c.1850-76). Engraver of flats of the Thirty Years' War, the Siege of Magdeburg, the Crimean War, and of Serbians. The moulds were sold to Fraas, Meyerheine and possibly Heinrichsen. (*Scholtz.*)

Boerse, Ch., Strasbourg (fl.1835). Publisher of paper sheets.

Boersch, Martin, Strasbourg (fl.1805-15). Born in 1790 and dying in 1861, he was an artist who, when still a boy, began to draw and paint his own paper soldiers. According to Paul Martin, Boersch married the niece of Benjamin Zix. His collection passed to his son and then to the Kolb family. After being exhibited in 1913, the collection disappeared, to reappear at auction in Antwerp in 1971. The sale catalogue shows the incredible artistry of the figures, which comprised 4,360 sheets, depicting French troops from 1794 to 1811. A good selection is now at the Musée d'Histoire Militaire, St Sulpice le Verdon.

Boettcher, Dr, Berlin (c.1930). One of the earliest converters of flats.

Bofors Models (B.A.C. Forder and M. Jackman) Gorleston-on-Sea, Norfolk (1978-). Producers of 90mm models, with a United States trooper on a rearing horse.

Boga (Ediziona), Bilbao, Spain (c.1935). Publishers of paper sheets.

Boggio, G., Turin (1973-). An architect by profession, he is also a maker of commissioned models in 54 and 110mm. He specializes in the troops of the Kingdom of Sardinia (1730-60), especially King Carlo Emanuele III. Of splendid quality and impeccable painting. Has also designed for Amati.

Bohl, Klaus-Peter, Frankfurt (1979-). Publisher of flats.

Bohler, L., Berlin (1881-?). Manufacturer of flats. A shadowy figure of whom practically nothing is known. (*Scholtz*)

Boitard, Martin. He was directed by Napoleon in 1804 to construct a diorama of Lodi, 50 x 67 inches. The models were semi-flat, the infantry being 15mm and the cavalry 25mm, mounted on pins. Cardboard and other materials were used for gun carriages, and shell-torn buildings were incorporated. It is now at the Musée de l'Armée.

Boland, N.T. *See* Sovereign Figures.

Boldetti. *See* Lebrun & Boldetti.

Bolling, Werner, Berlin (fl.1960). Designer and engraver of flats for Frauendorf and Emmerling. His own in-

Above: **Berdou**. *An unusual solid showing the wave-like support he occasionally used (Lyle Corburn)* 2 Right: **Acuña**. *Skinner's Horse. Carved balsawood painted in acrylics (Acuña).* Below: **Berdou**. *Napoleonic cavalry, including the Emperor himself. (E.L. Puffer).*

4 Composition. *British and Zulus; models by Howard Willetts approx 7in. high, arranged by Kurt Stackhouse. (Eugene and Wilma Custer).*
5 Right: Allgeyer. *Armoured train with original box (Gennari).*

6 Left: Coronet. *A fine facsimile of the Reynolds' portrait of Sir Banastre Tarleton. The decorative quality was such that the author decided to give it a finish equivalent porcelain (Author).* **7 Below: Conversion.** *The 21st Lancers at Omdurman made by Joseph Berton from various Historex kits (Shepherd Paine).*

frequent productions were designed by Frank and engraved by Sambeth, and were of the 1870 and First World War periods.

Bolling, Werner, jr., Hellendorf. Publisher of 30mm flats, mainly of the periods of 1792-97 and 1913-14. Owner of some of Thiel's moulds.

Bollman, J., Bremen (fl.1866). Maker of flats.

Bombled, Germany. Designer for the Mignot series of flats; engraver for Ochel.

BONE CHINA. *See* Ceramics.

Bonham, R. *See* Fife & Drum.

Bonness, August (1890-1944). A German publisher and collector, who was the prime mover in the foundation of the Kulmbach collection of dioramas.

Boode, C.G., Holland. One of the Dutch enthusiasts, he added to the Koekkoek paper cut-out dioramas at Leiden Army Museum, 1964.

Booden, G.Q., Rotterdam. A private maker of 54mm solids who exhibited at the first exhibition held by the Dutch Society in 1956.

Bookwalter, Thomas and **Glanzer, Stanley.** *See* Bugle & Guidon.

Booth, James, London (1978-). Sculptor for 'Andy' diorama accessories.

Bordas, Jorge. His collection of flats by Lleonart is at the Barcelona Municipal Museum.

Borie, Commandant. *See* Figur.

Bormioli, Amanzio, Milan (1972-). Commissioned maker of 54mm solids of fine quality, mainly of the Piedmontese army.

Bornemann, Strasbourg (1850). Publisher of paper sheets.

Börnig, Bernhard, Hanover/Brunswick (fl.1930). Maker of 30mm flats. In 1913 he constructed, with the aid of Hermann Meyer, a diorama of Leipzig. His workshop is preserved intact at the Stadtisches Museum, Brunswick. (*Ortmann*)

Borst, Victor, Strasbourg (1840-58). A prolific producer of flats, although apparently his signature appears on only one model, that of a gun-carriage.

Bos, J., Holland. Assisted in the improvement of a diorama by Ipey at Leiden Army Museum in 1967.

Bosch, Antoni, Barcelona (1823-75). Producer of paper sheets, whose business was acquired by Joan Millat.

Boston Evening Post, Boston (c.1920). Publishers of sheets of cardboard figures, 12-15 in number, 6 inches high, stencilled, with fold-back stands.

Boston Sunday Post Supplements, Boston (c.1900). Publishers of cardboard cut-outs, 6 inches high, with foot-stands.

Boucquin, Paris (late 19th century). Publishers of paper sheets lithographed by Garsave.

Boughton, Stephen, Tunbridge Wells (1976-). *Military Modelling*, July, 1976, advertised him as issuing a 'New Series' of 54mm solids. These have not yet appeared.

Bouquet, H., Paris (c.1915-55). Maker of sheet-tin models, in sets of six, 54mm, enamelled on both sides, and mounted on wooden blocks; also of paper sheets entitled 'Pro Patria', printed on both sides, and dealing with medical services. It is possible that the same firm was concerned in Support Breveté (*q.v.*).

Boutet, Reginald, Granada Hills, California (1966-). A free-lance sculptor of immense ability, and certainly one of the best that the United States has produced. He is most famous for the range of Second World War leaders that he made for Cameo. He has also made a Vietnamese

soldier for Valiant. He works well within his limitations, and, unlike so many of his contemporaries, produces relatively few models. Before working for Cameo, he had made models of American troops in Vietnam.

Boverat, R., Paris/Mareil/Marly/Yvelines (d.1968). Producer of 30mm flats, designed and engraved by Pepin, of the French Revolution and later. The business is still carried on by his widow.

Bowles, William Leslie, Canberra (1885-1954). Head sculptor for the Australian War Memorial, Canberra.

Boyle, K. *See* Castile Miniatures.

Bozzetti, Leonardo, Bologna (1970-). Designer for Dulcop Italiana, Italobby, Italiaeri, etc.

Braat, K., Holland. Constructor of a diorama, using Elastolin Landschnechts, 1975; added to an existing 'Siege of a Medieval Castle', 1967; both for Leiden Army Museum.

Bracey, D.C. *See* Lancer Collectors Toys.

Bradley, K.S. *See* Arms Pack.

Bradley, Milton, Springfield, Massachusetts, (c.1860-1925). An early American manufacturer of toys, jigsaw puzzles, etc., and a long range of single chromolithographed cardboard figures for children to shoot at.

Brady, Richard F. *See* Kenneth Speciality Company.

Bragaglia, G., Bologna (1974). Maker of 54mm solid commissioned models, of excellent quality, in the Continental style.

Braidwood, Scotland (1971-). Manufacturer of 54mm plastic Indians, US Cavalry Indians, and cowboys. [*Kearton*]

Braithwaite, John. *See* Greenwood and Ball (Pearce).

Bramwell, Colin. *See* Sea Gull Model.

Branchline Figures. *See* Dawson, Malcolm; New Hope Design.

Brand, Leipzig (fl.1960s). Flats. Mark: B.

Brandani, Massimo, Rome (1970-). Maker of fine 54mm models to commission.

Brandstetter, Horst and **Beck, Hans.** *See* Big Spielwarenfabrik.

Brandt, Gerhard, Paris (fl.1950s). Collaborator with Keller in a series of flats of French infantry, 1786, and representatives of the Cantons at the occupation of Basle, 1792, distinguished by the mark GB.

Braun, Strasbourg (1850). Publisher of paper sheets.

Braun & Schreider, Munich (19th century). Publishers of paper sheets of civil and military subjects, under the name '*Müncherier Bilderbogen*'.

Braune, Helmut, Meissen (b.1928). A fairly prolific designer, engraver and producer of flats. He has a varied range (with some '*kombination*' figures) including Napoleonics (with horse artillery, gun caissons, and a forge), Royal Horse Artillery in action, uniforms of the period 1870-73 (including Cossacks), South Americans, African tribes, Egyptians, Romans, North American Indians, Custer's last stand, United States troops 1850-1900 and the Thirty Years' War. He also makes delightful non-military figures, such as a 17th-century dentist, a 15th-century boar hunt, Leonardo da Vinci, Riemenschneider working on an altar piece, and a set of four models featuring the painter Goya.

Brépols (P.J. Établissements), Turnhout, Belgium (before 1806-1916). A prolific publisher of paper sheets, mainly of Belgian and French troops. Later named P.J. Brépols and Diercky. The woodcuts were extremely crude with a curious number of left-handed combatants. The text was in Dutch and French.

Bresica, N. Hollywood, California (1973–). The firm began well with 24mm wargame models, and 54mm solids designed by the American Ray Lamb, including a fine Napoleon standing by his chair (after the painting by David), a Blackbeard and a Geronimo. No further models can be traced.

Bretegnier, Pierre, Chaussy d'Ivry, Paris (c.1965–72). Flats, 30mm. He made a parade of 1870 (engraved by Pepin), Napoleonic artillery, cyclists of 1916–18, paratroops of 1950, and Leonardo da Vinci displaying his portrait of Francis I. The moulds are now in the possession of Ochel.

Brethiot Family. *See* Mokarex.

Bret' Hist. Another name for reissues of the original Mokarex hard plastic models.

Breuel, Hamburg (1975–). Moulds in 33mm for home-casting.

Brevett. *See* Figur Brevett.

Breyer Moulding Company, Chicago, Illinois (1979–). Makers of plastic horses in various sizes, excellent for military modellers.

Bridges, E.N., Canberra, Australia (1924). Made a number of the models for the dioramas at the Australian War Memorial, Canberra.

Bridle Models, Croydon. Dealers, who at the same time offer painting and converting services.

Brieger, Ulrich, Kottbus, E. Germany (fl.1968). 50mm flats, especially of a barricade of 1848.

Brigader-Statuette (Carl Andersen), Copenhagen (1946–). Commercial manufacturer of 45mm solids. These are in the Heyde tradition, but of good design and finish. There is a wide variety of posture, the horses are well modelled and the painting, in the Britains' style, is fresh and sparkling.

Brigadier. *See* Comet.

Bright, D.P. *See* Leviathan Models.

5. 1956. BRITAINS LTD ENGLAND.

French office:

1. 1910. Wm. BRITAIN JRN. COPYRIGHT-DÉPOSÉ MADE IN FRANCE. (date of first issue of basic figure and date of introduction to France).

2. BRITAINS LTD COPYRIGHT PROPRIETORS.

3. 1939. As above, with DÉPOSÉ added.

Britains is the most famous name in English model soldiers, and the earliest. William Britain senior had been in business for a number of years, making mechanical toys, money-boxes, and the like, when in 1893 he issued something entirely new, a light-weight 'hollow-cast' model which he himself designed with his son Alfred as producer and overseer, and sold at a much cheaper price than the heavy, solid German and French imports. After a few years of struggle, the firm became firmly established, and indisputably held the premier place in England, if not in the world, until, under the Statutory Regulation of 1967 (q.v.), amid mounting economic difficulties and owing to the system of 'home-painting' they employed, they were forced to turn to the growing medium of plastic. The first hollow-cast model they produced heralded a vast range of models unique in that they were all in a uniform size of 54mm to the height of an un-capped soldier's head, so that purchasers could be assured that every set of models they acquired would be of the same size. Furthermore, by their avowed plan of reproducing every unit of the British Army, they were assured of success. At the same time, the firm featured foreign armies, especially when war broke out in other countries, when models already in existence would be hurriedly adapted, or new models speedily made and issued before the war was over. By the end of the hollow-cast era, they had issued several thousand sets, mainly in boxes of five cavalry or eight infantry, usually with an officer; troopers were normally all in the same posture, with an officer on a

13 **Britains.** *Hollow-cast 54mm. Royal Horse Artillery 14-pounder gun and team. (Photo: P. Greenhill; collection Hanington).*

Britain, William, Ltd, London (1893–). Hollow-cast, mainly 54mm, but also 45, 47, 70, 83mm, and 'Lilliput', 19-21mm; 1966, hollow-casts ended; 1954, Herald Miniatures incorporated; 1957, 'Lilliput' battle-dress troops in Alkathene, reduced in size from the Herald models, Britains' name on base (soon discontinued); 1958, farm animals in Alkathene; 1965, 'Eyes Right' series of Alkathene copies of early hollow-casts; 1971, 'Deetail', Alkathene with metal base and equipment; 1973, 'New Metal,' alloy revival of old style. Marks:

1. 1900-12. COPYRIGHT Wm. BRITAIN or Wm BRITAIN JRN (date) and sometimes MADE IN ENGLAND.

2. 1913. BRITAINS LTD. COPYRIGHT. PROPRIETORS.

3. 1937. MADE IN ENGLAND BRITAINS LTD COPYRIGHT PROPRIETORS.

4. 1946. COPYRIGHT BRITAINS LTD MADE IN ENGLAND.

rearing horse, and the infantry all in similar stance. Large boxes *à la* Heyde were built up, and bands added. The boxes themselves were distinguished by their uniformity, only the label being altered as required. Not all the numbers in their catalogue denoted new models; many were constantly remodelled, or those already issued were re-painted as uniforms and weapons changed, or anatomical inaccuracies were corrected. Horses also underwent dramatic changes, some of the original ones (the 'rocking horse', the 'one-eared' horse and the 'twisted leg' horse) being extremely clumsy. Experiments were constantly being made with movable arms, affixed either by a bolted shaft which ran straight through the side of the shoulder, or by a circular fitting on the end of the arm sliding over a projecting knob on the torso. (With wear, the arms tended to swing too freely.) Metals of various kinds were also used for swords. Bases also varied, the earliest being oval or circular. Others were square or oblong. Of the horses, only those rearing were fitted with a footstand. Cheaper models ('B' range) were made with fixed arms in 45mm between 1897 and 1907, to be succeeded by a greatly inferior range made exclusively for Woolworths (W range) ending, without any loss, at the beginning of the Second World War. Others were the 'A' series of cheap second-quality 54mm models, 'B' bulk line of selected figures for sale singly and 'C' series, also of second grade, for retailing singly. The 'H' series were 70mm, the 'HH' 83mm, while 'M' and 'P' and a later 'Crown' range were used from time to time. Britains were also well to the fore with their cannon, and, as they were developed, with contemporary missiles. Their catalogue showed a long list of armoured transport and ambulance vehicles.

Experiments were made with special slotted cards ('Parade Soldiers') and automata ('Soldiers to Shoot'). There were also trial figures which were never produced, and special displays on turntables identified by a small piece of metal on the base, or chipped out of the base [Wade]. An example is an exceptional 'Exploding Trench'. The first known specimen was discovered by G.M. Haley, an English dealer (Old Toy Soldier Newsletter, August, 1978). It is, he says, 13 x 4 x 2½ inches, made of green card and nailed to a heavy wood frame. This encloses a platform pivoted on two nails at either end of the trench. A spring attached to one of these is held in place by a swinging brass trigger with a cap hammer to strike the screwed-on plate for the cap. The trigger in turn is held in place by a flagstaff with a flag. When a hit is registered by the wooden shell of a 4.7-inch naval gun the trench immediately explodes. Under the trench is a blue-stamped Patent Number and date 1915. It is surmised that it was either made as a prototype for consideration by the firm and rejected, or withdrawn very hastily if issued.

Britains' excursions into the past were few, consisting of a Waterloo gun set, a tournament (two poorly conceived Henry VIII-period tilting knights, a good Marshal, elegant squires and colourful trumpeters), a standing Henry VIII in full armour, and a truly magnificent set of 'Agincourt' knights (see R. Selwyn-Smith). For some years after the issue of this set examples were being beautifully and heraldically correctly painted, and with some slight improvements, by Freddie Ping for Hamley's and for private collectors. Special selections were made up from time to time, for export only, such as representative and variant unlisted models, boxed exclusively for F.A.O. Schwartz in the United States under the title 'Historical Soldier Collections'.

After the First World War, when military objects were frowned upon for some years, Britains turned their attention to more placid subjects: farm animals and implements, together with miniature gardens, and civilians such as a parson, a village idiot, aged inhabitants (clothed in the style of the 1900s), station staff, trapeze artists, roundabouts, and country cottages in wood, decoratively painted. The famous Salvation Army set was born, and achieved a face- (and skirt) lift nearer our own time. Specially commissioned models were made for Madame Tussaud's (Henry VIII, Elizabeth I, the Duke of Windsor, Robin Hood, Red Riding Hood, Cinderella, and a bust of the lady herself):

14   **Britains.** *A selection of their 54mm hollow-cast models, some with moveable arms. (J. Hanington).*

for J. Lyons a Victory Parade, and for Cadbury's Cocoa a set of 'Teddy Tail' characters (a sow, a frog, a duck, a robin, a fox, etc. varying in size from 1 to 2½ inches, stamped COPYRIGHT CADBURY'S BRITAINS' PROPRIETORS). Wade calls these 'the rarest of all Britains' figures'.

The full story of Britains' models is told by L.W. Richards in his *Old British Lead Soldiers* (added to by McKenzie). To the present author, not being a Britains, or even a British Regimental, enthusiast, and in any case entering the collecting field late in the hollow-cast era, the fascination that surrounds this pioneer firm in many quarters has been a perennial mystery. As models, they are no better (and at times worse) than some of their competitors and Continental rivals. One supposes that an inherited collection, well preserved, and in the original boxes, may spark off a latent enthusiasm to collect more and more examples. Britains' models are, of course, ideal for those collectors whose bent is for serried rows of marching, firing, kneeling or running models, all exactly the same, or for massed parades with bands and mounted officers. Certainly the founding of the British Model Soldier Society might have been delayed indefinitely but for them, and they were in their day the only models suitable for conversion. Another factor is the search for the elusive variation, of which there are so many: early version, second version, later version; all these phrases appear regularly in dealers' and auctioneers' catalogues, and some incredible prices are asked for them. Nor have they relinquished their title as the most collected commercial figures in the world. It will be interesting to see whether, after their return in 1973 to a new type of metal substitute, in which only three models have so far appeared, these will in future years be collected with the same enthusiasm as the old ones. Their entry into the field of plastic models began with their purchase of Herald, (broken into in 1965 by a comparatively short-lived venture entitled Eyes Right) and they are now so inextricably bound together that whether the models appear in their catalogues as 'Britains' or as 'Herald' means nothing, as they are designed by the same artist. They are described in this book under 'Herald'. A new range of plastic with metal bases under the title 'Deetail' was introduced in 1971, of which the best are those depicting modern troops. The medieval range is flamboyant, and all the horses suffer from a strange rigid bar extending (one supposes for support) from the footstand to the belly of the horse. Naturally piracy of all Britains' models has always been rife, and Herald and Deetail are unashamedly offered in various parts of the world under different 'maker's' names, while the hollow-casts are being cast in solid form by enthusiasts in Great Britain, Canada and the United States. (It is to be hoped that they are marked as recasts.) Their memory is being perpetuated by a sudden renaissance, started in 1974 by Nostalgia, and now being copied by an increasing number of small firms or individuals, whereby the ideal as expressed by Britains' range is being made in solid.

'Britannia Brand'. See Johillco.

Britannia Ltd (John Sandy), San Francisco (1978-). Manufacturers of 54mm Britains-type models in solid.

British Bulldog (M. Drewson and P. Jones) Swansea (1975-). Manufacturers of Britains-type solids.

Britya, London (c.1900). Manufacturers of poor quality guardsmen and an army camp of the Boer War period. Sold in boxes, the name probably being chosen as a challenge to Britains. [Hannington; Haley]

Brocke, Germany. A collector of Heinrichsen flats. One half of the collection was presented to the museum at Nuremberg, the other dispersed at a sale at Sothebys, Belgravia in 1974.

Brockley Forges Ltd. See Ku-Zu Models.

Broker. See Boecker, A.

Broman, C.R. See H.R. Products Ltd.

Brookes, S., Hastings, Sussex. In 1963 he made a series of solid 54mm (swords removable from scabbards) for a diorama of Minden at Woolwich Arsenal.

Brooks, Henry H., USA. Assisted in the creation of the diorama of Bunker Hill at the First National Bank, Boston.

BROTTEIG. See Edible Models.

Brown, Colonel, London. Designer of one of the dioramas at Woolwich Arsenal.

Brown, David. See Bivouac Military Miniatures.

Brown, Giles S. See Dorset Soldiers.

Brown, Graham, London (1978-). Sculptor for 'Andy' diorama accessories.

Brown, Michael, Broadbottom, Cheshire. Maker of numerous models of Roman forts and Norman castles, with converted models, commissioned by the Bowes/Durham School series for touring education purposes. He also created a life-size Roman centurion for the Centurion Public House, Melander Castle Road, Gamesley, Glossop.

Browning, George, Australia (1918-). Official war artist in New Guinea and Borneo in 1943-46; also employed on the Australian War Memorial dioramas at Canberra.

Bruck, Carl Gottfried Daniel, Freiburg (1834-66). Apprenticed as a maker of flats to Pilz, he began on his own account in 1834, leaving the business in 1866 to G. Vaterlein.

Brückner, C. Herman, USA (fl.c.1872-1912). Brückner emigrated to the United States just after the end of the Civil War, establishing himself as a clothing manufacturer. In about 1872 he began work on a remarkable wood-carved 'Continental Palace', 41 inches high, with 50 individual figurines, some civilians, others troops, both on foot and mounted, continuously adding to it up to his death. It came as an heirloom to Hank Spermon, a plumber with the New York Port Authority, and was auctioned at Christie's, New York, being bought for $5,000 by Malcolm Forbes (American Collector, April, 1979)

Brugnera Editorial, Barcelona (?-1945). Publisher of paper sheets.

Brüller, Hans, Göttingen (1979-). Designer and publisher of flats.

Brumm, Hans Siegfried, Berlin (1979-). Publisher of flats.

Brundick Miniatures (Mel Brundick), USA (1974-). The only model we have seen is a Nazi in 54mm solid.

Brunoe, Søren. See Rollo.

Brutsch, Jean, Paris (fl.1950). Collaborator with Keller in a series of flats of the Third Swiss Grenadier Guards. Mark: KB.

Bruzzone, Gianetto, Genoa (1975-). Large composition models, dressed in natural materials. [Frost]

Bryant & May, London (1978-). Siege engines in wood in the form of constructional kits.

Buccaneer. See Squadron Shop.

Buckingham. Boxed 54mm hollow-casts under this name appeared in Macy's Department Stores in the United States between 1950 and 1960, probably imported from Britains and Johillco. [Anton]

Buckingham Pewter. See Stadden, Chas C., Studio.

Buckley, Paul A., USA. Constructor of dioramas, including a number at the US Army Military Historical Research Collection, Carlisle Barracks, Pennsylvania, and the Newburgh Museum, Vails Gate, New York State.

Bueno, José Maria, Malaga. His collection of paper sheets is at the Museo del Ejercito, Malaga.

Buffalo Indestructible Malleable Iron and Steel Toy Works, New York (1880-90). The catalogue of a large American store illustrates a gun-team in iron.

Buffey, David. See Greenwood and Ball (Pearce).

Bugle & Guidon (Thomas Bookwalter and Stanley Glanzer) Cincinnati, Ohio (1968-). They began work with 30mm solids of Plains Indians and fighting US cavalry, the horses being quite astonishingly bad. In 1973 they turned to 54mm size, with models for Little Big Horn, a Hun, a Chasseur Alpin and a Mountain Man of 1830. Little improvement was apparent, although it is certain that Chernak did at least one figure for them, and a later Southern Cavalry Commander is excellent. In 1974 they became a subsidiary of a typical octopoid American firm called Custom Cast. In 1975 they joined other makers with 45mm fantasy figures.

Built-Rite. See Warren Paper Products.

Buliker, A., Berlin (fl.1890. Publisher of flats of the Thirty Years' War, engraved by H. Wildt, including several figures on one stand. (Ortmann)

Bull, London (fl.1877). An enigma. An article on toys, written by G.C. Bartley, and published in British Manufacturing Industries in 1877, is the only reference that can be found. He is classed as a 'pewterer' and said to have 'in his possession a number of gun-metal moulds in one piece', which he had 'produced over the last seventy years'. They were of Wellington, Napoleon and other celebrated characters of the early part of the 19th century. No size is given, but as they are mentioned in the section of the book dealing with toys, it must be assumed that they would be manageable, and not commemorative pieces for the mantleshelf. Whether the

15   **Animals in War.** *Camel, elephant and oxen by Buntzen; Six-Day War Camel trooper by B. Gordon; German South-West Africa camel by Cavalier; artillery horses by Almirall; Landschnecht donkey by R. Young for New Hope (Author).*

moulds were for flats or solids is not stated. It is not clear whether he himself cast from them: if this were the case he would be the first English producer of either flats or solids.

Buma, J.C.H., Arnhem. A collector who exhibited his models at the first Dutch exhibition in 1956.

Bunau, Rudolf von, Leipzig (c.1850). A producer of flats and one of the seven manufacturers comprising the 'Association of Tinsmiths and Tinfigure Manufacturers' (*q.v.*). He was joined later by Schündler in the production of semi-flats.

Buntzen, John, Copenhagen (1976-). A collector who also works to commission, or collaborates with colleagues who require elephants, which he makes superbly in 10 pieces. In 1976 he added draught-oxen and camels, to which he gives a covering of flock.

Bunzel, Ruthard. *See* Herbu.

Burckhardt, C. *See* Imprimerie de Wissembourg.

Burgess, Donald, Claymount, Delaware. For years one of the leading American professional painters of solid models; in 1978 he began designing models for The Black Watch.

Burke, Bernard, USA. Professional painter employed by Cowan and others.

Burkhalter, France (fl.1950). Professional painter of flats, mainly for exhibition purposes.

Burmann, Israel, Stockholm (fl.1770-80). A tinsmith whose only claim to inclusion is that he had as his apprentice Erik Lodin. (*Gripenberg*)

Burns, Ned J., New York (fl.1938). A creator of dioramas at the Museum of the City of New York.

Burns, Stephen, Massachusetts. Painter of figures for the series of dioramas 'They Nobly Dared'.

Burton, Michael. *See* Mike's Models.

Busch, A. Hanover (fl.1850). A little-known maker of flats.

Bussler Miniatures (Dr K.G. Bussler), Wollaston, Massachusetts (before 1948-). One of the earliest makers of specialized solid models in the United States. He began as a collector, until, after early efforts at making his own models, he was commissioned by the United States Marine Corps to make models of their entire history, showing major changes of uniform (Smithsonian Institution). After this he decided to work commercially. Several hundred models ensued, cast in separate pieces and then assembled, the mounted riders being detachable, and all in various postures. Notable were the West Point Colour Guard, 1953, and the United States Colour Guard, both designed by Captain Leo Meyer. An outstanding achievement was a Civil War artillery piece available in two styles, either with the horses attached to individual stands, or to interlocking stands forming a deeply-rutted road. By inventing the 'Busslerama', (groups of related figures on the same stand, and designed for the purpose) he anticipated what has since become quite commonplace with makers. About 1968 he transferred most of his attention to the making of 25mm wargame models. With his later 54mm efforts he has been linked by a number of critics with the numerous plagiarists of other makers such as Stadden and Cameo that seems to be the curse of the United States.

Busy Bodies. *See* Big Spielwarenfabrik.

Butcher, Neil. *See* Miniature Figurines.

Buwe, Celle, Germany (fl.1830). Engraver of flats for Heine and J.G. Richter. Mark: Buwe fecit. (*Kollbrunner*)

Buxton, R.A. *See* Valhalla Wargames Ltd.

Byrd, Larry N. *See* About Face.

C

'Cabalt'. *See* Rose Miniatures.

Caberfeidh Miniatures (Graham Hilditch), Forres, Scotland (1979-). Manufacturers of Britains-style models, in solid, with detailed painting. The boxed sets, each of six figures, are all of Scottish regiments and designed by Hilditch himself.

Cacharach, José. *See* Arm-Model.

Cadbury, William., London (c.1935). A cocoa firm who gave Britains' humanized animals away in their packets.

Cade, Ronald G., Pomona, Kansas. A free-lance designer, whose models occur in the ranges of Old Guard and Valiant. (*See also* Lotus.)

Café Storme, Mouscron, Belgium (1965-9). A coffee-exporting firm of rare intelligence, who included one of their models in each tin of their product. These models were made of a type of brittle but tough, hollow plastic, un-painted, with convertable limbs. Upwards of 350 models of Belgian history were made. Produced for them by Historex, some of the designs were by Lelièpvre. Normally they were 54mm, but on occasion the horses were sadly out of scale. Their greatest interest is the range of period, and the inclusion of non-military models. They are still available, but only if purchased in bulk. They also issued a house magazine, showing how the figures could be converted and how dioramas could be made with them.

Caiffa, M.C. A mystery. In 1973 Søren Brunoe was given a plastic model from which he made a number of metal castings, one of which he gave to the author. It is of an English actress, Lady Martin (née Helena Saville Faucit, 1817-1898) who played many Shakespearean roles, and bears the inscription 'Madame Martin. M.C. Caiffa.' In appearance it is akin to the Café Storme models. It remains so far unidentified.

Calder Craft. *See* Hinchliffe, F. and R.

Caldwell, Chuck, Oak Ridge, Tennessee. Sculptor of 6-inch-high models in a material called 'Sculpy', equivalent to a type of modelling clay. In 1975 he did a series of 100mm bronzes of Westerners for the Franklin Mint and in 1977 two Civil War bronzes of the same size in a limited edition for Militaria.

Caledonian Castings Ltd (A. McCalum), Glasgow (1977-). Producers of 75mm metal kits of Scottish clansmen by Benassi and medieval 90mm models by Carruthers. In 1979 they produced a 90mm model of Robert the Bruce by Peter Rogerson.

Calex International. *See* Supercast.

Camarado, Portugal (?-1970). A newspaper for young people, publishing sheets of Portuguese uniforms up to 1970.

Cameo (Max Eastman, later Sydney P. Chivers) USA (1968-). A firm which has issued a very limited number of 54mm solids of an almost uniformly high quality, the earliest and best being by Reginal Boutet. They include MacArthur, Churchill, von Richthofen, Rommel, Eisenhower, Mussolini, Hitler, Goering, a German World War II Luftwaffe Pilot, and a Japanese pilot. A Robert E. Lee was designed for them in 1974 by Lionel Forrest. Further (1976) models included Georges Guynemer (French fighter ace, d.1917) and Eddie Rickenbacker. In the following year the American Ray Lamb began an 'Empire series' in 80mm. In 1975 they produced models of Laurel and Hardy which are sadly out of touch with the rest of their productions. In 1970 arrangements were made with Greenwood and Ball for the production of their models in England.

Cameron, Ronald, London (1960-). Maker of 110 and 120mm metal models in kit form, or assembled for 'Tradition'. He has also designed in 54mm for Britains, for Airfix ('Multipose' and 'Collectors' series) crew members for vehicles and aircraft kits, and also works in ceramics. [*Dilley*]

Camp, Robert, USA. A free-lance designer of 54mm solid models for various makers.

Campaign (Peter Johnstone) Hatfield, Herts (1970-). Maker of 54mm solids based on the traditional Britains' style. His troops of the British Empire, 1870-1935, are entirely original except for the hands, and designed and cast by himself.

Campaign Miniatures (Ben Michel), USA. A professional painter employed by Cowan. The Barefoot Soldier catalogue of August, 1973, announced that not only would he be probably working for Valiant in the future, but that he would himself be starting a series of models entitled 'Campaign Miniatures'. To date nothing is known of this venture.

Campaigns, Los Angeles (1976-). T. Richards of England sculpted a 75mm officer of the Zieten Hussars for them.

16 **Canada**. *The four rear figures are by Lipton's Red Rose (plastic); second row by Betts and Harling (Frontenac); the two standing hollow-casts by unknown makers; the solid wounded man by London Toys (Author).*

Campbell, A.M. *See* Sea Gull Models.

Campbell, J. *See* Squadron Shop.

Campos Bros, Lisbon. Manufacturers of poor quality semi-solids from German moulds.

CANADA. Until the beginning of the Second World War the only models to be seen in Canada were Britains' importations. During the war these became virtually impossible to obtain and their place was taken by crude semi-flats in khaki service dress, varying in size between 4 and 6cm. Imports from Japan were easier to obtain. These were of a plaster composition, with walking horses, of very poor quality, but complete with bell-tents and cannon. Made in Canada, but similar in size and style, were some crude plaster-type models, representing the four major armies that appeared in the Second World War, together with Reliable Toys (plastic) and London Toys (solid) [*Morrison*]. All these efforts were distinguished only by their crudity, as were a series of 60mm hollow celluloid-type models of Mounties and Canadian sailors and infantry. Cheaper types still were models in cardboard mounted on wood blocks, and lithographed tin cut-outs, 3 inches high. Antiquarian booksellers discovered that Canadians stationed in or passing through England were astonished at the variety of books that could be found, and bought freely. It may well be that a view of a Courtenay or a Greenwood inspired a latent collector or two. Whatever the reason, it is significant that after the war Canadians set about collecting in earnest. Dioramas and single models were commissioned from Baldet by museums, and Sam Jackson, who worked under the name of 'Jane Jackson', began a series of unusual models. Even so, it was Britains who, until a few years ago, still filled the demand for models and it is only re-

cently that societies have been formed, dealers become established, and native makers made their appearance. Prominent among them are McNeill, with his varied - size 'Austerlitz' solids, Robinson-Sager with a fine set of paper sheets in a limited edition in book-form, and, in 1974, new series by Stevenson, Coronet Miniatures and Scimitar Miniatures. Collectors are also being commissioned to make models, as in the case of Betts and Harling. Don and Honey Ray have had a great influence on the Canadian scene with their long experience, their craftsmanship in carved wood and their remarkable and ever-growing 'Fields of Glory'. One of the most ambitious projects is that of the Canadian Historical Miniature Society's construction in Vancouver of a titanic Waterloo, which (1979) was still uncompleted. It incorporates models by Stadden, Gammage and Cooke, with artillery by Hinchliffe. Canada is such a vast and sparsely-populated country that travel is a problem, and, while societies do exist, there are also numerous tiny groups of collectors in various Provinces who meet together from time to time in their own homes. Wargames also flourish.

'Canadian Collectors'. *See* Almirall, José.

Candlegrease. Strange as it may seem, this material appears to have been used by one maker at least, Lucie Delarue-Mardrus, who specializes in civilians, but occasionally makes a military model. (*Nicollier*)

Candy, Germany (1970-). Models in plastic composition. The name is in Gothic type; although purchasable in Spain, they are probably of German origin.

Cannon Miniatures, Southport (1976-). 20mm houses, churches, bridges, castles.

Cantelli, Georges, Rome (1968-). Maker of large wooden models with cloth and metal accessories.

Cantey, Emory, USA. Professional painter for Cowan.

Capell, J. *See* La Guerra.

Carbago. *See* Carman, W.Y.

Carbonel, Saintonge, France. A range of 65mm plaster models of Provençal civilians, delightful in expression and colour. Discovered in a small Surrey village in 1979.

CARDBOARD. Models in cardboard fall into three categories: 1. Issued as a separate entity; 2. Issued in book-form; 3. Buildings. These models should not be confused with those issued originally in paper sheets, for subsequent mounting on card (*See* Paper Sheets). The most obvious is the third section; as early as the 1880s Gothic castles were published in profusion in Germany. The Germans still remain the chief sponsors of 'scissor art', as their productions may be called. Indeed, such models as those of Cologne Cathedral or Neuschwanstein Castle tax the ingenuity of many an adult when faced with the incredible array of pieces to be cut or folded. Houses of all kinds have always been popular, especially those with which a complete town or even a village square can be created (ideal for dioramas) or a country farm, complete with wind or water mill. These are, of course, more familiar to model railway enthusiasts. So far as the model soldier collector is concerned their place is rapidly being taken over by polystyrene mouldings (*See* Wargame terrains). Prominent among the makers of the models just mentioned are Schreiber, Scholz, Teubner, Geru-verlag, and Uhlmann, all of Germany; Pellerin (with hundreds of examples), Editions Volumetrics and Ingenia, of France; Monte Enterprises, with famous United States buildings; KS Models, of Holland (farms and windmills); Terence Wise, of England (domestic buildings); Sea Gull of England (York Minster); Zeuner of Germany (countryside and farms), and Honrath (pre-pressed-out trees). Forts have been made by Bern of Toronto, and in 1973-4 Chapman in England issued a short series of military buildings. The next category, that of individual figures, has been with us for many years. They were normally 5 to 6 inches high, colour-printed, pre-cut and mounted on the stoutest of cardboard, their ultimate fate being their massacre by spring-loaded cannon, which were usually issued with them. In 1892 one firm in the United States issued them in boxes of 90, together with tin stands. It would be an impossible task to attempt to identify their producers, but it is known that such firms as Samuel Lowe (c.1942), the *Boston Sunday Post* Supplements (c.1900) and the *Boston Evening Post* (c.1920), all of the United States, and Ward Lock & Co. and Raphael Tuck of London, issued many such. Indeed the latter went further and issued stout embossed figures. Another aspect is the figure issued in series, not necessarily to be fired at, such as a notable set of 10-inch-tall, colour-printed figures meant for cutting-out and folding back issued by Kellogg's Cornflakes. Lastly there are the many complete books, mainly of a juvenile nature, but some more mature, whose pages contain any number of coloured or plain figures, each pre-cut for pressing out. Such books have been issued by many publishers, Vasco Americana of Bilbao currently issuing a long series, while many American publishers are or have been active in this field, such as Singleton (1949) - Revolutionary War, War of 1812 and the Civil War (3 inches); Saalfield; Jay Line (1943) - airplane hanger and figures; Bergen Toy Company (c.1944) - invasion barge; Arnold's *Book of*

17 **Card Cut-outs.** *'The History and Adventures of Little Henry', London 1810. One of a set of four hand-coloured aquatint plates, with a printed booklet. One of the earliest cut-out stand-up sheets published in England.* (Author).

Toy Soldiers, with 409 English and French soldiers of the Napoleonic period; Hasselfield; Artcraft (1964) - Daniel Boone; Woodburn (c.1943) -aeroplanes; The Golden Press (1959-68) - the Round Table, Ben Hur and the Alamo. A final aspect was a series of thin cardboard cards depicting French cavalry and British squares at Waterloo, uncoloured, for cutting out, and produced by René North in 30mm size, for dioramas. One of the earliest publishers were J. & B. Fuller of London (1810-20) with a single quasi-military offering, and they may well be considered as exceptional.

Cardigan Model Soldier Studios, Gwbert on the sea, Cardigan (1972-). Professional painting service offered.

Carl, Theodore, Strasbourg (1880-1904). Publisher of paper sheets.

Carlson, Ernst, Wiesbaden. Appears in the Kulmbach list as a producer of flats.

Carlton, Anne, Studio (Anne Finestein), Hull (c.1970-). Maker of chess sets, including Romans, the king 10cm, and the American Revolution (in reconstituted marble).

Carman, W.Y., London/Sutton, Surrey. One of the first makers of specialist solid 54mm models, author, curator, and authority on military uniform. As early as 1920 he had tried casting his own models, but it was not until 1937 that, having received assistance from Courtenay and Ping in the mechanics of the art, he began a commercial venture with 45mm Waterloo troops, and a year later with Magna Carta characters, Henry VIII, Elizabeth I, medieval warriors and civilians. In his representations of the British Army he collaborated with H.R. Robinson and was the first to make models of this type. In addition he made a series of 30mm Marines. The 54mm models were continued after the Second World War as Carbago, representing a triumvirate of Carman, Lovell Barnes and Otto Gottstein, who taught him the art of casting flats. When financial difficulties obliged the firm to close confusion reigned, and eventually some of the models were re-issued under the name Argosy. At that time Briton Riviere (*q.v.*) became associated with the figures and produced some new models. Purchase tax difficulties made further complications, and Riviere took control, manufacturing military models under the name of Matchlock and civilians in hard plaster as Faber. Carman was one of the founders of the British Model Soldier Society, and one of those who welcomed Otto Gottstein to England. He has always encouraged collectors and given freely of his expert knowledge. His own preference in collecting is the school of makers existing before the Second World War.

Carroccio. *See* Casa Editrice.

Carreras, V.M. *See* Miniaturas Militares.

Carrigg, Edward J., Massachusetts. Creator of dioramas and painter of figures for the series 'They Nobly Dared'.

Carrington, John. *See* Reynard; 'Tradition'.

Carroccio Cartoccino, Monza, Italy (c.1920-30). Publishers of very fine paper sheets.

Carruthers, Colin, Scotland (1977-). Designer for Caledonian Castings.

CARTON-COMPRIMÉ. *See* Composition.

Carvalho, Este Vao de, Lisbon (19th century). Publisher of paper sheets.

Casadevall, Ramon, Madrid. Designer of solids for Spanish firms, including Alymer and Soldat.

Casa Editrice (Carroccio), Milan (c.1914-20). Publishers of paper sheets of First World War figures.

Casanellas, Baldomero. *See* La Guerra.

Casey, J. Lane. *See* Asheton-Bayard.

Casey, Michael, Dublin (c.1967). Made 8 models in lead for Cork Museum, 6 inches high, $\frac{1}{8}$ inch thick, engraved and moulded on one side only.

Casa Pardo, Buenos Aires, Argentina (c.1970-?). 60mm solids of Argentinian infantry and cavalry, 1799-1840.

Caspari, Artur, Hof a.d. Saale. A dealer in flats, who is in possession of a number of moulds, especially the 'Gothick' set by Lorenz (*see* Garratt, *Model Soldiers: a Collector's Guide, plate II*). The equestrian model is described in his catalogue as 'Knight George, weaponded'. Also makes a good onega.

Cassin-Scott, Jack, London (c.1956-). Maker of commissioned models in various media. The plasticine masters are built up on wire armatures, the moulds made in plaster and rubber, and the whole model (normally 45cm) is assembled from the component parts. The materials used include metal and latex composition. He includes a number of non-military figures in his collections, which may be seen in numerous institutions. During the 1960s a retail firm in Berkeley Street marketed his models, naming them 'Regimental' (the name of the firm). His methods of working are described in his own publication.

Castalluchi, L. & F. *See* Chambers Mfg Co.

Castano, David. *See* Columbia Miniatures.

Castel Sant' Angelo, Rome. A notable exhibition of dioramas arranged by Mauke was exhibited here in 1937.

Castiglioni, Turin (late 18th century). One of the earliest known Italian makers of flats.

Castiglione, E. de, & Co. *See* Fabbrica Nationale d'Immagini.

Castile Miniatures (K. Boyle, T. Davidson, J. Douglas, B. McKenzie, J. Rae), Carluke, Lanarkshire (1978-). 25mm medieval solids of good quality.

CASTING. The name given to a model produced from a mould. This may be in the form of a complete torso, with arms, legs and accoutrements as an integral part, or with these soldered to the torso. In all cases no paint has been applied, although many are sold already undercoated.

CAST IRON. An intractable and seemingly highly unsuitable material for the making of model soldiers. However, catalogues of American stores issued between 1880 and 1900 illustrate numerous examples of artillery teams, some on wheels, including a set of soldiers 2 inches high. Unfortunately, these wholesale stores did not disclose the names of the makers, although it is known that some artillery came from Buffalo Iron Toy Works. The only maker with any pretentions to accuracy was the Grey Iron Casting Co (*q.v.*) whose products appear to have achieved the popularity accorded to the hollow-casts of Britains.

Castlemaster. *See* Sinclair Toys Ltd.

'Castle Of The Commander-in-Chief, The: A New Game for Artillery', Germany, (c.1840). A collection of 14 coloured, lithographed paper-sided blocks for the construction of a castle, and a paper and wood cannon, to be seen at Sudbury Hall, Sudbury, Derbyshire.

Castresana, Julio Garcia. *See* Marte.

CATALOY PASTE. A polyester filler paste composed of talcum powder, resin and slate powder. *See* Composite Models.

Catel, P.F., Berlin. A dealer in toys, whose catalogue of 1790 lists a vast array of models in all materials and styles.

Caton, Alan, London (1974-). Employed originally by 'Tradition' as a converter and painter of Stadden's models, he started making his own models in 1974, starting with single-piece castings in 90mm of the American Revolution and 1812 Bavarians. The following year appeared a series of cavalry in the same size, each an individual piece, skilfully designed and finished, with detachable riders, originally issued painted only at £125 each, but later available as castings. In the same year he produced a series of 54mm models of Indian Colonial Forces, South African soldiers and Zulu warriors, a fine Punjab Frontier Force cavalryman (1900), a Lieutenant Chard, together with a surgeon at Rorke's Drift (with buckets), a Plains Indian, etc. In 1976 a series of models appeared depicting the Retreat from Moscow, each of which has a dogged, wind-swept appearance which just fails to convince, and a group of the Greenjackets. He also produced a set of a wedding party of 1900, complete with photographer, tripod camera, military bridegroom, a page boy, a dog, and the bride and her father. A set of 'Danjou's Last Stand' and a 'Retreat from Corunna' (in some of which he was assisted by David Scheinemann) and a continuing series in 80mm, entitled 'The British Army', were also made for 'Tradition'. In 1977 he joined in the DEK venture with 80mm 'All The Queen's Men'.

Cattle, G.B., Hull (1975-). Maker of 100mm solids, starting with Continental Line Infantry and a Greek Hoplite, of which the anatomy was woeful. He began designing for New Hope in 1977, and making small buildings to complement GHQ armour.

Cavalier (Allan Silk and Edward Lober) Brooklyn, New York (1970-). Prolific producers of 54mm solids of a more varied interest. Silk himself designed a number (e.g. a Colonial South-West African German Schutztruppe on a camel and Second World War Germans), while Lober was responsible for motorcycle units and kits. Other designs were commissioned from Stackhouse, Chernak, McGerr, Fabre, Rubin (Napoleonics), Goddin (1977) and Saunders (a German soldier with his girl friend). Plains Indians and US Cavalry officers, together with North African Desert Rats and a fine von Rundstedt, were of varied quality, but a French Foreign Legionnaire was a disaster. New models are constantly being issued, and the firm, from its sheer output, must be regarded as a major one. In 1976 they purchased the Vallance moulds, as well as the masters of a four-figure group on one stand in the form of a vignette of the French Revolution by Major Robert Rowe and his son, Sergeant Robert, which had been made in 1972 for The Barefoot Soldier, but never issued.

Cavendish Miniatures Ltd (Michael Martin), London (1958-70). A small firm of producers of 54mm plastics which were certainly the only rivals to Herald for quality. One of the most delightful sets ever made in any medium was the seven-piece 'Henry VIII and his wives', and another outstanding one was of four military types of 1748. Both sets were designed by Stadden. Other models included a Gentleman Warder of the Guard, a Beefeater and a policeman. The only criticism that might be offered is that the paint flaked easily from the 1748 set. The firm should certainly have received more encouragement, and their small output should be cherished.

Cawkwell, Lance W., Hull (1976-). Maker of card models for Wild West scenes entitled 'Period Setting'.

Cawood, H.H., London (fl.1935). A maker of models in plaster, clay, wood and metal for dioramas at the Imperial War Museum. They comprise: an officer's dugout; a front-line trench, 1916; an officer and runner; King George V and the Prince of Wales inspecting a 12-inch howitzer; a 13-pounder and a mounted gun team of four; machine gunners during the Great Offensive of 1918; and a camouflaged tree with an Observation officer, an orderly, and a telephonist. The scale is 1 inch to 1 foot.

CGB (Cuperly, Blondel and Gerbeau). *See* Mignot.

C.C., Milan, Italy (fl.1935). Publishers of poor plastic composition figures.

C & C, USA (1973). Makers of 20mm wargame models.

Cedarwood Accessories, Welwyn Garden City (1975-). Makers of 20mm trees and hedges.

Cenni, Quinto, Turin (fl.c.1895-1910). A prominent designer for Italian publishers of paper sheets.

Centrum, Warsaw (fl.1970). Manufacturers of plastic flats, 50cm, unpainted, of modern infantry and artillery. [*Pestana*]

CERAMICS. Any object made in an earthy substance capable of being hardened by fire. The commonest form is clay, easily obtainable in most countries, and by its

18 **Ceramics.** *Statuettes in bone china by the Royal Doulton Company to commemorate the American War of Independence. (Royal Doulton Company).*

very nature inviting moulding by the hands or on a machine. It was the natural material for the production of drinking vessels and platters and the obvious choice for any peasant population. It was obvious, also, that toys would be made of this medium, and there are many examples in terra-cotta of a military nature to be found all over Europe, especially in Rome and Greece and the adjacent islands, and Iran. Specimens of this folk art are illustrated in a number of books (e.g. Fraser; Hercik). Owing to the fragility of the material many thousands of models must have vanished, and it is perhaps surprising that in recent years there has been a revival of the material in model soldier circles. In Belgium Léon Hames uses a type of modelling clay which, when painted resembles porcelain; in the United States Caldwell, Tunison and Forrest make 6- to 10-inch models, Caldwell in 'Sculpy', Tunison in 'Duron', while in England Sowden uses it occasionally for his 12-inch models. He also goes a stage further, and produces stoneware on occasions. It will be noted that all the models described are fairly large, and perhaps the more normal use of the material is for preliminary studies for scaling down.

The highest form of the art is exhibited in the porcelain varieties. It is not proposed to discuss in detail the military models made in this material. Many factories in Europe (e.g. Meissen, Dresden, Copenhagen) have produced many outstanding examples, but their object would not be to cater for the enthusiastic collector of model soldiers, but as a normal vehicle of the potter's art, and in the past there does not appear to have been a regular pattern of production of military figures in series. Their place belongs in the general history of porcelain. However, in recent years one or two individuals and firms have used it with effect. Foremost of these is the team of Rousselot and Lelièpvre with a steadily mounting series of models of the Napoleonic period, in which metal is added for weapons. Porcelain models of earlier periods, both foot and mounted, are made by Lelièpvre and his partner for Van Gerdinge (illustrated in Nicollier) and currently the latest range is featured in The Soldier Shop catalogues. Those privileged to have seen the magnificent creations in polychrome bone china by Michael Sutty will have been astonished by the incredible versatility of execution and complete command of material in his 12-inch to 24-inch medieval battle scenes and personalities. Their price places them beyond the scope of the average collector, as do the Wellington and Napoleon made by the Royal Worcester factory. These, the largest the factory has made, form 'The Military Commanders' series, and were made by Bernard Winskill in respectively 1969 and 1974. They are $16\frac{1}{2}$ x $14\frac{1}{2}$ inches. The same firm's 'Historical Figures' series by Frederick Gertner (8-10 inches) began in 1960 and contains eight models, mainly of Kings and Queens of England. Their 'Papal Figures' series, by Neal French (of which the first two were by Gertner) comprises five figures. The 'Military Figure' series (again by Gertner) includes an Officer of the 17th Dragoon Guards, c.1814. Untitled, but known all over the world, are the sculptures by Doris Lindner. The most famous, produced in 1947, is her equestrian H.M. Queen Elizabeth as H.R.H. Princess Elizabeth on Tommy. This was issued in a strictly limited edition. It was followed by an Officer of the Life Guards, an Officer of the Royal Horse Guards (both in 1961) and a Constable of the Royal Canadian Mounted Police, 1966. Thomas Morrison, of Edmonds, Washington, D.C., has also specialized in editions limited to 100 copies of ethnic types of Alaska, North American Indians and European costume. Like Sowden, he uses many media, including stone, wood, metal and aluminium paste. Events such as the American War of Independence offer an ideal opportunity, in this instance seized upon by Aldo Falchi for Dave Grossman Designs of the United States. The models are limited to editions of 200, 600 or 800 and comprise Betsy Rose, Francis Scott Key, the Spirit of '76 (3 models on one stand) and the Signing of the Declaration of Independence (12 models grouped together). The sizes vary from 8 to 15 inches. Similar also in concept is the thirteen figures on foot, with a mounted George Washington, completed in 1977.

Ceregumil Food Company, Spain, Producers of pre-cut paper tanks.

CFE, England (1913). A retail firm selling Britains' C.I.V. waggon, and boxing them with this imprint. [*Wade*]

Chad Valley, London (c.1925). A famous manufacturer of games, dolls and toys, they produce a series of printed-paper-over-plywood foot soldiers, 5 inch high (the horses 6 inches) including Seaforth and Gordon Highlanders, Grenadier Guards, King's Royal Rifle Corps and the Buffs, in a box which converted into a fort with a drawbridge. Probably issued contemporaneously in Germany. An example is in the Museum of Childhood, Menai Bridge.

Chambers Mfg Co. (L. & F. Castalluchi) West Hoboken, New York (fl.1925-27). Manufacturers of 45mm hollow-casts strongly influenced by Barclay. The Castalluchis were formerly employed by Barclay. (*R. O'Brien*).

Chambers, Ron. *See* Cromwell Pewterers.

Chang, Wah, Carmel, California (1971-). In 1976 he issued a series of four equestrian models of Westerners in two editions: one in bronze, the other in pewter, 959 and 1450 sets respectively under the title 'The Official Western Sculpture Collection', and available only by subscription. The brochure describing them gives no size, the indications are that they are about 90mm. They are obviously influenced by the work of Frederick Remington.

Chanter, G. England (1975). A converter of models to be seen at Tiverton Museum.

'Chapayev's. Soldiers' series. *See* U.S.S.R.

Chapman, Charles E. Massachusetts. He and his son assisted in the painting of the models and the creation of the dioramas for 'They Nobly Dared'.

Chapman, Ken. *See* Military Buildings.

Charbens & Co. Ltd, London (c.1920-68). Founded by Reid Brothers (one of whom was formerly an employee of Britains). Manufacturers of lesser quality 45-54mm hollow-casts of British troops, Yeomen of the Guard, Westerners, medieval period, American GIs. Some of the riders were detachable. Later they turned to plastic, but only to more or less reproduce their existing moulds.

CHARIOTS. This ancient form of fighting vehicle has always been popular for portrayal. In flat form they can be really magnificent if skilfully painted (e.g. a series of seven by Mignot, eight by Ochel, and others by Heinrichsen, Rössner, Nechel and Gottstein). Heyde made a few in metal for his Roman triumphs and his 'Siege of Troy', and Alymer made some lovely little ones in 20mm. The Egyptian one by Gammage is a masterpiece; not quite so good is the stouter Roman one by Series 77. Several wargame makers include them in their lists (e.g. Silvercross, Miniature Figurines and Hinchliffe). Hahn made several in plaster, while Multi-color issued one in plastic to stand on a tiny box-like bookcase. Cherilea produced a British one with an unattractive and clumsy Boadicea. Marx had several, including those for the film *Ben Hur*; Timpo, Britains and Elastolin made slightly better ones. The best in kit form was by Revell.

Charles, A., Walsall (1975-). Maker of 54mm solids. His first published models were period caricatures for Phoenix. In 1977 he designed 54mm semi-flats, moulded on one side only, with three figures on one footstand, for Mainly Military and in the same year began making solids of Nazis and refugees, medieval troops engaged in looting, and 80mm models of females at war (clothed, for a change.) All these were for Greenwood and Ball; in 1978 for the same firm he began a fine series of knights and footmen at Crécy, issued in kit form.

Chassel, Georges, Nancy/Paris (fl.1650). The Kings of France never did things by halves and in 1650 Chassel was instructed to design an army in silver to supplement one by Nicolas Roger that belonged by descent to Louis XIV. This second silver army was actually made by the goldsmith Merlin at a cost of 5,000 écus. It comprised '*tout le cavalerie, infanterie et les machines de guerre*', and was contained in a number of specially made boxes. (*Crump*)

Chauve, Barcelona. Publisher of paper sheets, re-issues in 1974 of four sheets of Spanish infantry of 1910. He is also a leading dealer and encourager of Spanish craftsmen.

Chedel, Fernando. *See* Austrandia.

Chein, J., USA (c.1950). A tin-plate clockwork toy of a marching US sergeant.

Cherband, Paris (c.1900). Hampe does him the honour of mentioning him as a maker of a few ranges in 'ronde-bosse'.

Cherilea Products, Blackpool (1948-). Hollow-casts, 54mm and slightly smaller: plastics 40, 54, 70mm. In 1950 they incorporated Fylde Mfg Co. A fairly prolific manufacturer of models for the juvenile trade, although some were of a more collectable quality. The range included the British Army, Westerners, Crusaders, and a British chariot. About 1960 some of their boxes were named 'Monarch'. Three of their models require special mention: The Black Prince, Marlborough, and a charging mounted knight. The same horse was used for the first two, but the third was quite different, as it had interchangeable weapons and a removable (though over-large) great helm. All three riders were removable from their mounts. It is possible that these three models were designed by Wilfred Cherrington, whom Greenhill quite recently discovered was also associated with Richard Courtenay. The plastic models were mainly adaptations from those in hollow-cast, apart from the ballet set poorly copied from Herald. Although the firm was purchased in 1973 by Sharna Ware, a very small range of the plastics are still available under the name of Ellem Action Models. A medieval chess set in black and white plastic with a king 2¼ inches high was marketed in 1972 under the name Crespak Ltd.

Chernak, Andrew, Springfield, Pennsylvania (1972–). A free-lance designer and sculptor of 54mm solids for firms and to commission. His first commercial contract was with Old Guard, beginning with a Samurai, followed by work for Cavalier, Bugle & Guidon, Walthers, (so far unpublished), Squadron/Rubin and others. In 1974 he joined forces with Rubin as Grenadier, with the production of 25mm models, and in a year is stated to have made 250 different figures. The Franklin Mint 'American People' pewter figures are also by him (105mm). Some of his models, such as his Czar Nicholas II, reach a high standard of excellence.

Cherrington, Wilfred, Birmingham/Blackpool (d.1962). Maker of moulds for Courtenay and later for Cherilea. [*Greenhill*].

CHESSMEN. Although not strictly to be classed as model soldiers, they lend themselves particularly well to the modelling of military subjects, and have a fascination of their own. One of the most famous is the set found at Uig on the Island of Lewis in 1831. From the archaic style and carving they have popularly been thought to be of 10th-century Scandinavian workmanship, but Hammond states that several authorities now consider them to be no earlier than 1650 and the stock-in-trade of a Nordic merchant. Apparently there are 78 pieces in the British Museum and 67 in the National Museum of Scotland. Furthermore, records exist of Icelandic chessmen in walrus ivory of the 17th century

which are practically identical. Reproductions are made by the British Museum and several commercial firms. A famous single figure, known as 'Charlemagne King' (Bibliothèque Nationale, Paris) depicting an Eastern potentate mounted on an elephant with an encircling row of cavalry, is possibly not a chessman at all. Its date is fixed very roughly between the 8th and 10th centuries (*Mackett-Beeson*). A fine 12th-century king of English work is to be seen at the Salisbury and South Wiltshire Museum, while several 13th-century knights have been found in different places in Sweden. Many Cantonese and Indian sets, while giving the principal characters the rôles of mandarin or rajah, make free use of the war-elephant as the rook. Usually the military aspect is portrayed in the pawns, especially in the 'John Company' sets. A magnificent set, formerly owned by the architect Sir Albert Richardson (Garratt, '*Model Soldiers: a Collector's Guide*', Plate 71) is of French 18th century origin and depicts the combatants at Agincourt, while a similar set (*Hammond*, plate VIII(2)) in coloured ivory, is of the Battle of Tolbiac between Clovis and Alaric. A 17th-century Dutch set is anachronistic as the pawns are in 12th-century armour, with cloaks and large shields, while the rooks are contemporary cavaliers. A mid-18th-century French set comprised opposing British and French forces, the French in their normal uniforms, the British having feathered Indians as pawns, and mounted ones as knights. It would have been made to commemorate the war in Canada, although the French should strictly have also had Indians on their side (*Mackett-Beeson*, fig. 14). French sets depicting Revolutionary troops were popular, and another set, this time German, shows the armies of the Catholics and the Huguenots at the Battle of Jarnac. Early in the 19th-century sets portraying Crusaders and Saracens were in great demand, while a magnificent set, probably made in 1848 by Juvina, was carved in wood for the Emperor Franz Joseph. Each figure is a masterpiece, representing the large bronze figures surrounding the tomb of Maximilian. The Punic Wars and the Napoleonic Wars are well represented, and Hammond illustrates one commemorating the Italo-Abyssinian War (plate XLVII). Nor must the sets of Hilpert be forgotten, even though they are of a non-military nature. Such is the popularity of the vehicle that many modern makers are doing outstanding sets. Surén (Willie) has produced a 'Battle of Pavia' and a 'Battle of the Pyramids', Hinton several, including one of the American Revolution (the subject also of one by

19　**Chessmen.** *Busts by Lamming to commemorate the Battle of Waterloo. Issued solid and unpainted (Author).*

Imrie/Risley). Ping made a number of specially-commissioned sets, all of medieval subjects, Stadden a 50mm plastic 'Battle of Agincourt' for Minimodels, which is most colourful (albeit some of the heraldry is suspect), a magnificent 'Waterloo', a fine 'American Revolution', and, most recent, a 'Tower of London'. Dickinson's Egyptian gods and goddesses break new ground, and others (e.g. Mokarex, Morrison, Fouillé and Classic Games Company) have made their own different contributions, while the International Silver Company (a firm established in 1808) celebrated the American Bicentennial with a set in pewter by Robert Sullivan in 500 numbered sets [*Anton*]. Lamming has done a set composed entirely of busts of the participants at Waterloo. The earliest modern commercial set of quality that we have been able to trace was one of Normans by Waddingtons (plastic, c.1966). Anonymous sets abound: Napoleonics from Italy, Joan of Arc in several sizes and varied quality, Frederick the Great, the Reformation, and a poor caricature set of current political leaders. Even an 'erotic' set was advertised in *Men Only*. One would imagine that in this case there would be no checking either mate if it were used.

Chevrillon, Dr. Converter of 12 SEGOM models at the Museum des Hussars, Tarbes.

Chialu, Italy (1960-). Plastic composition models, 4 inches high, of pre-war Elastolin type, of the Swiss Guard, the Italian Army, Scots Guards, United States First World War troops, and Boers. Of poor quality, they are easily broken.

Chiappa, Ernesto, Turin (c.1965-). A maker of models in various sizes including 54mm, but mainly in 30-35cm. The torso is of papiermâché on a wire armature, the head, legs and arms carved from wood. Actual cloth, leather and metal complete the models, which are extremely elegant. His speciality is the old Piedmontese Army and Italian naval uniforms 1775-1918. He is represented at the Risorgimento and Pietro Milo Museums, and does much commissioned work.

CHINA. *See* Ceramics.

CHINA, REPUBLIC OF. Plaster models, such as those of the Imperial Guard with halberd at the time of the Boxer Rebellion (made about 1930), different sets of mounted polychrome figures of an Emperor and his staff and of peasant figures (imported into England from 1960) appear to be the only solid figures known. Paper sheets issued after the accession of Chairman Mao were used for propaganda purposes.

Chiswell, L.E. London (fl.1937-60). Maker of a few solid models, including an equestrian Queen Elizabeth II (8cm) and painter of many of the flats for the R.U.S.I. dioramas and others by Stokes.

'Chivalry Figures'. *See* Matheson Models.

Chivers, Sidney P. *See* Cameo.

Chodnicki, L., U.S.A. (c.1935). One of the forerunners of the modern school of American makers of models in solid.

Chota Sahib (Sydney Horton) Brighton (1977-). Maker of 90mm solid kit-form models, starting with an officer of the Indian army. The first mounted model was issued in 1978.

Christ, Dr Heinrich, Bonn (fl.c.1930-65). Noted for dioramas at Kulmbach of flats of the German army of 1875 and 1913 (with vehicles and guns in the round), and for the section of the Battle of Gravelotte which centred round the village of St Privat (at Gravelotte Museum).

Christensen, Jack, Panorama City, California. Painter of models (not his own) at the History Room, University of Wyoming.

Christie, Lewis David. *See* Ideal Toy Company.

Christopher's Model Outfitters (C.P.D. Parsons-Gorham) Cranleigh, Surrey (1975-). Makers of dioramas and scenic backgrounds (e.g. at West Point).

Chromoplastic, Italy (1976-). Rubber-like plastic, the bases so marked [*Anton*].

Chuckles, London (1914-23). A few issues of this children's comic contained cut-out models of a village and a school.

Churchill, Rt Hon. Sir Winston. Wrote about model soldiers with great feeling in *My Early Life*. Commissioned the D-Day diorama formerly at the R.U.S.I., and the model at Arromanches.

CIGARETTE CARDS. These would normally be classed under illustrated reference material, or even militaria, but on a few occasions they have proved to be collectable as model soldiers. About 1914 Major Drapkin & Co. of London produced a set of 25 cut-out folding-back figures, size 60 x 80mm, entitled 'Soldiers and their Uniforms'; in 1932 Stephen Mitchell & Son of Glasgow issued a set of 30 cards, size 67 x 36mm, of army uniforms and vehicles, punched to stand up. About 1931 Greys Cigarettes put out a large collection of flats of the Napoleonic War. W.Y. Carman discovered a broken one in a street in Belgium and, after much research, established that the complete set was made by Ochel, engraved by Frank, and imported by the proprietors of Greys. A second set followed, this time of the Crimean War, but much inferior in quality. Both Carman and Patrick Murray possess large numbers [*Carman; Murray*]. Just before and during the Second World War the German Government issued very thin metal colour-printed pre-cut cards, with a metal flange at the foot.

CINEMA AND TELEVISION. Several films made during the latter days of the Second World War (e.g. *Till We Meet Again*) used models in their context, and much use has subsequently been made of static massed troops in backgrounds together with model aircraft and tanks. Makers of models, both commercial and specialist, have, in reverse, benefited from films, for example Timpo (*Ivanhoe, Quentin Durward*), Ping (*Richard III*), Marx (*Ben Hur* and Walt Disney's animal cartoons), Reynolds (*Treasure Island*) and Sanderson (*Zulu*). Television has been active in this direction, with Sacul making *Andy Pandy*, Timpo *Hopalong Cassidy*, Trojan *Roy Rogers*, while Britains' latest offering is *Black Beauty*. Every now and then one finds a programme devoted to some aspect of the model soldier (the interviewer usually in a state of amused tolerance) and one hears some extravagant pronouncements, one, from a dealer, on *Pebble Mill at One* (1975) that Ray Lamb's *Saburai* cost £100 painted; one undoubtedly skiller converter was classed as a 'model maker extraordinary'. Members of the British Model Soldier Society have shown how to make and convert figures, while the wargame has featured from time to time. The author, strange as it may seem, never saw a once-popular series entitled *Callan*, but every other intelligent collector appears to know that in it the wargame forms an integral part. One well-known dealer tells the author that he has done much commissioned work in artillery, vehicles, ships and planes, often entailing weeks of work, that appear for a fleeting instance which he may see quite by chance, he himself remaining in ignorance of the programme in which it will appear. (For instance, the Roman soldiers in BBC2 *Scrolls from the Son of a Star*, 12 February, 1976.)

Citadel Miniatures (Brian Ansell) Newark, Notts (1978-). Makers of 25mm fantasy figures, designed by Ansell, Humphrey Ledbetter, Alan and Michael Perry and Tony Acland (who also designs for Asgard). Each model is individually packed and bears the name of the designer.

Ciuffo, John, London (1970-). Plasticine models, 54mm, moulded entirely in self-coloured plasticine, thus eliminating all but the minimum of painting. These are sold in twos or threes, enclosed in glass cases, a very necessary precaution against handling. He has made several dioramas for the Forbes Museum in Tangier.

C.K., Hong Kong. Flagrant piracies of plastics.

Clairet, F., Paris (c.1964-68). Makers of 55mm plastics, apparently taken over by Starlux. [*Opie*]

Clark, USA. Models purporting to have been made by someone of this name were advertised in 1964 as the property of a collector coming up for disposal. Probably apocryphal. [*Pielin*]

Clark, John, Massachusetts. Painter of figures for the dioramas 'They Nobly Dared'.

Clarke, A.J. *See* RA Cannons.

Clarke, Frederick, Sheffield (1920-58). During the First World War he was employed as an orderly at a German prisoner-of-war camp in England and became intrigued by the activities of the prisoners carving wooden figures. He himself started sculpting figures from blobs of solder, the limbs and weapons being of ordinary household pins set in the solder. The result was a most remarkable collection, each figure 18mm high, painted in gloss colours, all of incredible accuracy and with impeccable horse anatomy. The collection comprised the Trooping of the Colour, the American Civil War, the Indian wars in America, and Napoleonic guns and supply teams. His name is included as being the only known maker to have worked in such a manner and with such remarkable results. [*Furness*]

Clarke, H.G. & Co, London (fl.1870-80). Publishers of folders 4½ x 6 inches, entitled 'Penney Packets' (*sic*), marked '1d. PLAIN, 2d. COLOURED', unfolding to large illustrated sheets of buildings and people, including Windsor Castle, a model farm and a working windmill. (*Newman*)

Clasen, Harald, Torgelow, E. Germany. Producer of flats. (*Katalog der Formen, 1976*)

Classic Games Company Inc., New York (c.1963-). Makers of chess sets of Ancient Rome, the American Revolution, the Napoleonic army and others of more traditional style. Of fine quality polystyrene, and beautifully sculpted, the 'Kings' are 4⅞ inches in the most expensive sets, 4⅛ inches in the cheaper ones. Each of the principal pieces is an actual portrait model. The sets are limited, and issued in white or grey polystyrene, or bronzed or silvered, or fully painted with a high porcelain-like glaze. [*Anton*]

Classic Miniatures (E. Deal), Yanceyville, North Carolina (1975-). A maker of 42mm solids of First World War American troops. By 1977 he had issued some 250 different types. The heads are larger than usual, and the figures rough in finish (possibly because he is a black-smith by trade) and the painting extremely crude. He himself says, 'Figures are 100% lead so as to eliminate brittleness. Rifles are of babbit, which, although brittle, is essential to stiffen such a small part. Shop coat is heat-resistant aluminium which preserves from oxidation and takes acrylic water paints with the minimum of curdling. The limitations of hand-pouring may have slightly blurred [the detail] and we do not recommend them to the highly fussy collector.' It is nice to know of a maker who is modest in his claims.

Clemence, Paris (mid-18th century). At Compiègne may be seen the '*magnifique ensemble de figures en bois sculpté*' representing military types of the 18th century carved by Clemence for Louis XV and the Dauphin.

Clendennin, P. Dana, London (fl.1930-50). One of the earliest of the English collectors to foresee the possibilities of the 'specialist' model and whose enthusiasm and military knowledge proved of great service in the early days of the British Model Soldier Society. He also assisted in the creation of the R.U.S.I. dioramas.

Clidinst, Robert, Indianapolis (1973-). Maker of 54mm solids, nine of which, all of the Second World War, have been produced by Monarch. At times he has also made models of cars, military vehicles and aircraft for Monogram, Strombecker, Tootsie Toy, and his own 'Clidinst Models'.

Clifford Toys, Hong Kong (1977-). Piracies of Cherilea. 'Swappet'-type 45mm plastic imported into England and sold in boxes.

Cloninger, Margaret. *See* Tommy Toy.

CLOTHES-PEGS. It is a never-ending source of surprise to collectors to come across the ingenious use of unlikely materials and objects. R. Hibbert (England) makes his models for exhibition purposes; Craig Herron of Baltimore goes one better, clothing his 65mm models in most materials, and offering them for sale. Perhaps the best are the creations of R. Kostelnik.

'Cloudesley Collection', London (1978-). The name given to a series which began with a 90mm Shakespeare, and to which nothing further has so far been added. The promoter is David Hawkesworth, but the name of the designer could not be discovered.

Clydecast Products, Glasgow (1978-). Makers of 30mm solids, starting with the Zulu Wars.

C.M., Italy. Publishers of paper sheets of the First World War.

C.M.V., Hong Kong (1974-). Manufacturers of plastics, all piracies of Herald.

Cockade Miniatures (Martin L. Kaufmann), Brookline, Massachusetts (1960-67). Maker of 54mm solids, including a set of NATO troops (based on one torso, with variations in uniform only); fine Landsknechts, a 'Desert Rat', a Mexican cavalryman c.1845, and a Luftwaffe officer with his dog. An unusual achievement was an Aztec litter-bearer party, in kit form. Taken over in 1976 by Excalibur.

Código Alimentoso. *See* Spain.

Cody Models (David Oddy and George Cowburn) Manchester, (1979-). Makers of 54mm solid 'Collector's Models', sculpted by John Howard and Ian Fenton.

Cofalu, Labrède, France (1973-). Plastic, 54mm, of modern troops, Far West, medievals. Poor quality and obviously derivative.

Coignet, Captain. A Napoleonic veteran, famous for his

Cahiers, which mention his 200 wooden soldiers used for evolutions, which accompanied him on his campaigns.

Coisel. An eccentric Parisian dealer who flourished in the 1920s.

Colección Mexico, Mexico City (c.1936-?). A manufacturer of 54mm solids of Aztec-Jaguar warriors, with portrait figures of Montezuma, Cortez and Columbus.

COLLECTORS AND COLLECTING. The collecting of model soldiers is a comparatively recent phenomenon. It would be wrong to assume that because tiny figurines of a military nature have been made for many centuries they would *ipso facto* be preserved for posterity. Indeed, their fragility made them extremely vulnerable to the ravages of time and the barbarism of youth, and although it is evident that special flats were carefully put aside by certain individuals in Europe at the turn of the present century, to be bequeathed later to museums with imaginative curators (e.g. Zurich, Strasbourg), it would seem fairly safe to assume that the collecting of model soldiers as distinct from playing with them hardly began until just after the First World War. This led to the formation of societies with enthusiastic members, many of whom advocated a quality of craftsmanship superior to the toy. The importance of these groups cannot be sufficiently emphasized, for it is due to their influence that we have today such a rich diversity of makers of fine models. Discussion among members led to the interchange of information and ideas and ideals with members of societies in other parts of the world, leading to mutual visits; the inauguration of exhibitions and competitions did much to promote the interest of the general public. Not only were the finest models collected, but the humbler toy was conserved as being of historic interest, albeit that in some cases the impetus came from sentiment or nostalgia. The meaning of the word 'collect' is deceptively simple: 'to assemble or bring together'. The easiest method is to go and buy the complete stock of whatever is available at any given time, as when an American bought every single Courtenay on display at Hummel's. Whether there is any real pleasure in such buccaneering feats is debatable, and in any case our American would soon discover that he had failed to acquire the withdrawn or the variant models. He would then, if he were a true collector, begin the search for the missing models. Another simple method of acquisition is inheritance, and many collectors have had large accumulations handed down to them. These may be preserved intact, or sorted out and the dross discarded, or the bulk added to in later years.

Anyone who, twenty years ago, purchased the models of Vertunni has a collection valuable in three senses — a distinguished maker, scarcity, and price, and those observant enough to recognize the intrinsic worth of Courtenay have done even better. One has only to attend an auction sale of average (and sometimes rare) hollow-casts, Elastolins, Heydes, and the like, to realize not only the collectability in terms of variety of these 'toys' but the gaps that need to be filled by the collector who formerly neglected them and now has to pay an incredible price. But he must ask himself first of all, 'Do I like this model or this type of figure sufficiently for it to give me pleasure, irrespective of what happens to it in the end?' In his book *Model Soldiers for the Connoisseur* the author described the collections made by a number of enthusiasts in different parts of the world. The

20 **Vertunni.** *Solids and hollow-casts slightly larger than standard size. (Greenhill).*

chapter headings are indicative of the varied interests of collectors: Flats, *l'Idée Fixe*, Means to an End, New Worlds to Conquer, Miscellany. The following is a summary.

Flats. The virtue of the flat does not immediately disclose itself, and it tends to be appreciated more by connoisseurs of history than by the general collector. In Germany it is almost a natural habit, but in other countries it is still relatively small, although there are growing signs of greater interest. One of the reasons for its slowness of appreciation is the difficulty of obtaining models, which, perforce, have to be ordered 'blind' as few catalogues are illustrated, allied to the sometimes poor business methods of Continental dealers or agents and the savage levy of customs duties and VAT. These difficulties surmounted, however, the collecting of flats is very rewarding, and a number of collectors make an annual pilgrimage to Kulmbach in order to inspect the latest productions. The advantage of these little models is the relatively small space that they occupy, and the cost, if castings only are purchased, is still most reasonable. Owing to the almost uniform size, it is possible to acquire models of the same period of history or even of the same battle, by a number of different editors, and to add to them regularly as fresh designs are issued. Flats from the 1870s to the beginning of the First World War can be found, but eighteenth century specimens are difficult to acquire. The variety is so great that the possibilities are endless, and the joy of acquisition unbounded.

L'Idée Fixe: There are many collections containing either a predominant subject or maker, as evinced by one collector who has 285 Courtenays, and another who is the possessor of 175 Berdous (with no more, alas, now to come), or a third whose collection consists of Household troops of all nations. The 'single maker' collector is obviously so attracted to his chosen master that he is indifferent to the actual period that the model represents: the Courtenay collection, nominally concentrating on the Middle Ages, also contains his Assyrians and his George V and Queen Mary, and perhaps it is coincidental that Berdou concentrates on one period only. Collecting the works of a single maker can be rewarding (for example Courtenay's transition from his early models made with Doran to his later productions, and Stadden's tentative beginnings which were either completely withdrawn, or amended, or redesigned). Collecting an era is exciting: so many portrayals of the same theme lead to a great understanding of the uniforms and decorations of the period, and one learns to seek out the less well-known maker for the model not already featured by the specialists. Allied to this is the acquisition of the models produced by the great manufacturers such as Mignot, Heyde and Britains, where the various sizes, the withdrawals, the variations, the altered models, the special issues, the different and successive methods of providing equipment, and the new methods of production lend an added zest to the search; and what is more rewarding than the discovery of a hitherto unknown figure? Above all, the specialist gains a deeper insight into regimental history, uniforms and fashion, and is on occasion able to offer information of value to a maker, or, indeed, supply his own designs for translation into more permanent form.

Means to an End: In this group the collector, while appreciating to the full the pleasure that most model soldiers provide, does not allow them to exist in a vacuum. Possibly he has a diorama or a whole series of dioramas in view; he therefore carefully chooses the models necessary for his purpose. Or perhaps he wishes on his death to donate his collection to a particular institution, and accordingly collects with the aim of homogeneity always before him. Or, again, it may be that he wishes, by means of his models, to illustrate certain events in history. Another aspect is the creation of a complete unit with all its military impedimenta, in which case manuscript records may be kept as in real life, and barracks, store-houses and the like built to scale. The well-known collector Henry Harris assembled his models with the sole purpose of displaying them for Army recruitment, and used the buildings he made for the background as storage and transport units. It is in this type of collection that makers of all types will figure, so long as they conform to the collector's requirements.

New Worlds to Conquer: A few collectors are endowed with such material wealth that they are able to collect in quantity what would be beyond the capacity of the majority to even think of acquiring. To them it is essential to have the best, and they have the means to indulge their passion. So it is that one can occasionally see together an assembly of Courtenay, des Fontaine, Berdou, Lelièpvre, Angenot, Krauhs, and the commissioned models of the known and the unknown masters, together with conversions specially made for the collector by the most skilled modellers. It is especially for these collectors that the master maker can exercise his skill in complete freedom, unrestricted by questions of commercialism, and for whom the professional painter is specially hired to do his finest work.

Miscellany: It is probable that the majority of collectors come under this heading. It implies a catholic urge, perhaps not very critical, to acquire models of all types and of all periods. This means that all materials are welcomed, so that a typical collection might include the solids and hollow-casts of the commercial manufacturers (Britains, Timpo, Johillco, Heyde, Mignot, Lincoln Logs, Wollner), plastics (Herald, Starlux, Crescent, Elastolin, Mokarex, Reamsa), plastic kits (Revell, Airfix, Segom, Historex), wargame models (Miniature Figurines, Hinchliffe, Garrison, Airfix,

21 **Courtenay**. *Some typical examples of his work. (Greenhill).*

Laing), solids (Ping, Stadden, Scruby, Monarch, Rose, Labayen, Brunoe, Cavalier), flats (Ochel, Neckel, Scholtz, Hinsch, Rössner, Mignot), semi-flats and semi-solids, plaster composition (Willetts, Patmore, Elastolin), large models (Sentry Box, Cameron, Superior), small models (Surèn, Stadden), caricatures, souvenirs, and so on, with perhaps some paper sheets and a highly prized commissioned model or two. These collections form the core of the model soldier world, and guarantee its survival. The specialist at times can become too precious, and the master model sometimes palls by its very excellence, but the honest-to-goodness model, costing little, may often delight the collector either by its inspiration or its sheer ineptitude. In the early days of collecting, the variety was limited. Many collectors built up assemblies of Britains regiment by regiment, complete with artillery, and horse and mechanical transport. The models themselves were restricted to a few set actions, either marching, running, firing or at attention, the cavalry being somewhat more lively in their movement. Mignot's models were almost entirely static, but those of Heyde were more flexible. The makers who catered for their more selective clients followed the same tradition, and the 'Review Order' model, at attention, or at least in non-violent action, was universally accepted as the classic convention. In those days the collector was content with the single figure as an entity in itself (the 'cabinet figure'). Only Courtenay came outside this range. However, with the passing of the hollow-cast, the appearance of the plastic, and new methods of casting (and, perhaps, a new philosophy) models began to exhibit more violent action, and the collector was obliged in many instances to group several together to bring out the best in each. The Napoleonic era has now reached saturation point, to be succeeded by what some impartial observers might consider to be the most repugnant and uncouth of all periods, that of the Third Reich. It is here that the two clashes of interest occur – the 'parade' soldier and the man of action. In representing the first, all the skill of generations of craftsmen and the humbler efforts of the manufacturers have allied to produce a resplendent figure to be painted as a spruce example of martial costume. In the second, it is an anomaly to create a man of action unless the collector is willing to house an unkempt, delapidated, travel-stained miniature figure, with a growth of stubble, torn trousers, mud-caked boots and puttees, or even, as Moore's Portuguese allies did in the Peninsular War, wearing the uniform of a dead enemy. If a maker is intent on realism his figure

8 Left: **Composite.** *Detail of model 45cm high of the drum horse Crusader by Douglas Bisgood (Bisgood). 9 Above:* **Cassin-Scott.** *Napoleon in contemplation (Cassin-Scott). 10 Below:* **Continental Models.** *Bandsmen (40mm solid) and bandstand are German; the spectators (semi-solid) from makers including Wollner, Schweizer and (probably) Mignot. (Gennari).*

11 Above: **Chiappa.** *A group of composite models (Chiappa). 12* Right: **Diorama** *(Mini) 'Love among the Ruins'. A setting for the delightful female by Rollo and her escort by Ping. The archway was intended for a tropical fish tank; the column is a modern German flat; the pond, rocks and masonry from Britains' garden series and their plastic rough-stone walls. (Author).*

13 Left: **Diorama** *(Mini) The Coronation of Richard II. Front row: Bishop by Stadden fr plastic chess set; Richard II by Frontier; pa and trumpeters from Britains' medieval set repainted; throne by Britains. Painted and composed by the author (Author). 14* Below: **Des Fontaines.** *Jousting scene, one of the la from this great maker (Nathan Polk).*

must reflect that fact that his clothing will be stained, torn, and filthy, that he will probably have lost his footwear and that his feet will be swathed in dirty linen; as for medieval footmen, what a motley collection of brigands or scarecrows they must have been. Therefore, it behoves the maker to think very hard, and, if planning to make a series of models in which much bloodshed is obvious, the painter or collector must join him in this, and represent his models as shabby, uncouth, dirty and dull, and subdue his colours accordingly, so that a gallant but filthy collection of fighting men emerge. Perhaps the answer is that there is room for both, but not under the same roof. One, the static, could remain in the cabinet, the other, the violent, be made into a diorama. The collector has in recent years undoubtedly been assisted by the emergence of the specialist dealer, who has a lifetime of experience behind him. Some of them display a professional acumen in stocking imports from other countries, but others, alas, seem remarkably reluctant to deal in any but the established lines. Makers seem only too eager to cooperate with the more enterprising model shops, who certainly do all within their power, by assembling and painting samples, to bring their models to the notice of the public.

Collectors are to be found in all walks of life and have proliferated during the past few years. Whatever their social status, they fall roughly into two distinct categories. The first is the fanatic. For him his whole way of life (and that of his family, if he has one, and is lucky enought to keep it) revolves round the model soldier. In the end he may well become a bore. The other is the more balanced individual who still believes that collecting should be a pleasurable part-time occupation, to be indulged in without detriment to human or other cultural relations. Both contribute much to the hobby. The first, unfortunately, has on rare occasions broken the bounds of convention and cast covetous eyes (and hands) on his neighbour's goods. It may well be that the second group has most to give to the hobby by the encouragement of younger or newly-interested collectors and by their willingness to share acquired knowledge. This group also brings a critical conservatism to the hobby as a whole, acknowledging excellence where it is due, and rightly condemning the much-lauded trumperies that sometimes masquerade as masterpieces. It is good to see the manner in which the collector has influenced museums and institutions during the past few decades. The number now displaying permanent or semi-permanent collections, single pieces, or dioramas has grown rapidly, as is shown in the supplement on *Places*. Not only does today's curator take an interest in forgotten basement collections but actively encourages local groups to produce models for special occasions. The genuine collector is altruistic, and it is through his beneficence that we can today share his pleasure. There are, for example, the gifts of Armand Gritton, J. Laurent and A. Ternisien to Compiègne; the Ake Dahlback collection at Leksand; the Hickmott collection at Trinity College, Hartford, Connecticut; the Lilly collection at Heritage Plantation, Sandwich, Massachusetts; the Lewis collection at Springfield Armory; the Rieder collection of dioramas at the Musée de l'Armeé, Paris; the Bibault de l'Isle paper sheets at the Carnavalet Museum, and those of P. Vila at Barcelona. Others, such as the Nelli, Testi, Spandauw

and Ruddle collections are also open to the public. Above all, it is the sensitivity of the knowledgeable collector that influences the style and artistic merit of the maker, and in turn communicates it to the uninitiated.

Three aspects of collecting have never been touched upon by previous authors. Two of them come from collectors with widely varying interest. The first (from Cornelius Frazer) is that of the elderly person who, in his retirement, looks around for an interest. The model soldier may well fulfil this desire, either in the beginning of a collection, or perhaps in the painting of models for other collectors. A parallel can be found in the psychological and therapeutic value experienced by those who have take to oil or watercolour painting late in life. The assembling of Airfix and similar uncomplicated kits and their subsequent painting is also now recommended by hospital boards in cases where a patient does not have to lie flat on his back and is likely to be confined to bed or to the ward for some time.

The second is a strong plea from Hank Anton for low-priced models for young people. Obviously the master-pieces and the more expensive commercial products are out of their range, leaving them with the alternative of plastic or wargame models, either of which they may not like. Nothing has yet taken the place of Britains' hollow-casts, which could always be afforded by the young. It had been hoped that the appearance of the Britains-style solid model, started by Nostalgia and now made by many other firms, would have fulfilled this need, but they are far too expensive for a youngster, and dear enough in all conscience for the older collector. Perhaps if they were issued unpainted in bulk they might be a viable proposition.

The third idea, which may be peculiar to the author, is one of a series of figures commemorating all aspects of the Christian Church. Under the possible title 'Soldiers of Christ' there are untold opportunities for an imaginative designer: surely St Peter was as important as Napoleon, St Paul as Genghis Khan, St Louis of France as Richard I, St Francis as the Emperor Barbarossa? Spain has always produced its 'Corpus Christi' processions, and day schools and junior Church groups would greatly benefit by sets of figures of the clergy in their distinctive clothing (deacons, curates, deans, bishops,

22 **Britains' Revivals.** *Solids. These look back to the colourful hey day of the 'toy' soldier (Author).*

archbishops) and by Palm Sunday and Rogation Day processions. It might be done if two firms could amalgamate, one providing master models for collectors, the other making mass-produced commercial figures at a much cheaper price and possibly in a variant material. Vincent Pfab has already given a lead with his series of Biblical figures (which may well remain unknown to the majority of collectors), and Don and Honey Ray scored an outstanding success when they exhibited in Canada their wood-carved Biblical tableaux.

In violent contrast is the ever-increasing wave of 20-25mm models of witches and warlocks and even more ghastly creations of fevered imaginations culled from American pulp magazines. However, these may be dismissed as being sought for by only a certain section of the model soldier world that is interested solely in the more grisly side of the imagination. The craze spread after about 1970 into the making by master craftsman of small groups or single figures in 54mm and upwards, in which exquisite workmanship has been used on the creation of sadistic or erotic themes which look out of place in any normal collection of models.

Collector Enterprises (Michael Russo and Ronald von Klein) Rockaway, New Jersey (1974-). Makers of 60mm solid models, designed by Russo, sculpted by Klein. To date a curious mixture has emerged: a Marine and a recruit, Satan and a woman.

'Collector' series. *See* Airfix; K. Mart; Sykes, J.

Collett, A.C. *See* Springwood Models.

Collins, J.A. & W.A. *See* Jac Models.

Collins, J.K., Christchurch, New Zealand (1970-). Maker of 54mm solids to commission. He is represented at the Rocks Historical Gallery, Sydney (Regular Army, Territorials of 1912, Boer War, Zulu War, Sudan Campaign); and at Russell, Bay of Islands, New Zealand.

Colominas, J.M. His collection of paper sheets is at the Barcelona Museum.

Colonial Craftsmen Pewter Workshop (K. Ewer), Cape May, New Jersey (1970-). A maker mainly of miniature pewter reproductions of dolls' house furniture and American Colonial bygones. He has, however, also made a range of 25, 30 and 56mm military models in pewter, chiefly of the American Revolution. These are no longer available. In 30mm he produces American Revolution flats from, he says, 'old moulds', which may originally have been made for home-casting.

Colorgraphics Sculpture-ettes, USA (1943). Publishers of thin cardboard three-dimensional models, mainly of domestic subjects, but including a marine and an infantryman. (*Newman*)

Coltrero, Argentina (c.1976-). Manufacturers of plastic models. One set they have copied is Herald's 7th Cavalry (dismounted), which have been re-styled in the colours of Union and Confederate troops. [*Kearton*].

Columbia Miniatures (David Castano), Ruxford, Pennsylvania (1977-). Advertised in *Vedette*: 'Wooden figures of the Colonial period, 1745-1783. Hand-carved and painted in the Old World tradition'.

Columbo, Christopher, Bethesda, Maryland (1976-). Designer for Valiant.

Comansi, Spain (1976-). Manufacturers of 60mm plastics of US cavalry, modern Spanish Army and Second World War Americans, probably piracies. [*Kearton*]

Combs, Darrell. *See* Battalions in Miniature.

Com-E-Tec (Robert Kramer and A. Schwartz) USA (1972-). A confusing amalgam of K-S Historical Prints and K/S Pewter Miniatures. A number of kit-form pewter 54mm models of the American Revolution and the Civil War, with artillery, were designed by Cooke and Greer. A set depicting Laudonnière (the French Huguenot discoverer of Florida) and the Indians he met passed to The Barefoot Soldier in 1973. In 1975 Cooke began a further American Revolution series in 85mm.

Comet Metal Products Inc., New York (1919-). Founded by Abraham Slonim, joined in 1932 by his son Joseph, and in 1936 by another son, Samuel. Having originally made aircraft and ship recognition models for the Navy Department (which are now very rare), they were persuaded in about 1940 by the Swede Curt Wennberg to begin making model soldiers, which were marketed under the name Brigadier. They began with troops of 1776 in what became known as the 'knees-bend' style, with thick oval stands and a rectangular projection at either end. In 1944 Wennberg introduced the firm to Holger Eriksson and persuaded them to commission this Swedish master to design 54 and 40mm solids for them. In order to create a market in England and perhaps on the Continent of Europe, a firm called Galterra Eireaan was set up at Spiddal, Co. Galway, Eire, with Henning Renfeld as manager [*Wade*], and it was there that the new Eriksson range, entitled Authenticast, were made (a few were marked L.N., a sculptor who has not been identified.) To these were added semi-flats of pastoral subjects designed by Frank Rogers, Arturo Levi and Mario don Audy. A few models labelled H R with a date and technical details on the underside of the base (in the possesion of Shamus Wade) may be prototypes given out for painting. The factory failed after a few years and the moulds (a number of which had never been used) were returned to Comet, the remainder going to Malleable Mouldings, who adapted them for issue in a type of plastic. Since 1957 Comet has only made semi-solid railroad figures.

Comisa Miniaturas, Spain (1974-). Models in 150mm, either in metal or in composition (*Cowan's Militaria Catalogue Number 2*).

'Command Group'. *See* Phoenix Model Developments.

Command Post (George van Tubergen), USA (1968-). Van Tubergen began making 54mm and smaller solids of United States naval types for Waterloo Galleries, but set up his own business under the above name in 1971.

Commerzbank, Hamburg (1977-). Publishers of large flats in the 18th-century style. (*Klio*)

Compagnie Colonial, Chocolates y Café, Madrid. Publishers of ready-cut scrapbook figures.

COMPOSITE MODELS. The maker of model soldiers is nothing if not versatile, and while undoubtedly the prime medium is metal, there has always been a number of artists who have used materials of many kinds, expressing themselves in a manner which it would be impossible to achieve otherwise. Many of the results could be called 'mannequins' by virtue of the fact that they exceed the normal size and usage, and undoubtedly the majority are made to commission for the benefit of museums or military establishments. The mixture of wood, cloth and leather is a very popular one, while plaster or the equivalent, also finished with cloth and metal, has appealed to a number of makers. The march of chemistry has led to the exploration of the possibilities of many *media* unthought of ten years' ago, and the

23 **Composite.** *Rare 18th-century models of Austrian make using real skin and cloth (Gennari).*

artist is no longer content to use traditional materials but to explore the whole gamut of synthetic resin, fibreglass and cataloy paste. It would be wrong to assume that every aspect has been covered in this review, and there must undoubtedly be many makers privately pursuing their own experiments, and occasionally exhibiting their models at a society gathering. It would be impossible to track them all down, and the best that can be done is to record those who work to commission or are represented in institutions, or have an international reputation. The use of plaster by itself will be discussed under the heading **Composition**, but it has, of course, been used in conjunction with other materials (e.g. at Leningrad, where there are units of the Russian Imperial Guard made of plaster with brass and steel equipment [*C. Robinson*], and even commercially, as in the case of a collection of British and French troops, 300mm high, at the Imperial War Museum. These are clothed in actual cloth uniforms and were sold in Paris in aid of charities during the First World War (*Carman*). This is a fairly isolated case, but in the early 1950s the firm The Sentry Box made a large number of plaster models which they subsequently metallized or 'cupronized' to ensure durability. These were later completely redesigned and turned out in metal kits. Plaster and wood, the latter for horses, are used by Major Alan Coppin and his son (formerly assisted by Patrick Synge-Hutchinson, and now called Midleton Models) and their efforts may be seen at the National Army Museum and the National Maritime Museum. Perhaps the most brilliant exponent of mixed materials is Helmut Krauhs. He clothes a skeleton of wire with cotton upon which he builds up all the clothes, weapons and accoutrements in cloth and metal. His models are to be found in many museums, especially in his native Austria. In France, Rousselot and Lelièpvre are the chief exponents, while Marcel Riffet clothes his 7in lead models with cloth uniforms. In Italy many models of a similar type are made by Pranzetti, Chiappa, Battaglia and Cantelli. Charles d'O. Pilkington Jackson (died 1973, at the age of 87) was long famous as the creator of a magnificent set of carved wood models depicting Scottish uniforms, but in later years he turned to other materials, including polyester resin, non-ferrous metal, aluminium, and gold and platinum leaf. Furthermore, he mounted some of the models on movable turn-tables. Many of his very large (up to 3 foot) models are housed in Calgary and New York. H.H. Cawood (fl.c.1935) combined plaster, wood and metal for his work at the Imperial War Museum, and E.W. Saunders, while making many models in traditional lead and size, has also had success with 6- to 9-inch models in plastic wood, with heads of plaster, and natural materials as clothing, Peter Wilcox employs every type of material for his 54mm creations of ancient times. Based on a lead torso, he uses filling plaster, thick art paper, lead, nylon and Bristol board. J.D. Shakespeare combines cataloy paste resin, barbola, lead and wood in his 13-inch creations, while Alan Kemp's 60mm models are of metal or wood, with faces of hardened plasticine, clothed with treated paper, reduced polythene, and other materials. John Darnell and Pierre Turner both use fibreglass, while Arthur Woolford, although strictly speaking a private maker, has by his female models in the same material greatly influenced the production of certain professionals. Jack Cassin-Scott, whose large models are to be seen in numerous museums, makes his figures in sections, subsequently joined together. He begins with plasticine strengthened with aluminium wire, and the moulds are of plaster or rubber. The finished product emerges in either metal or latex composition. Dreyer of Copenhagen makes 16cm models of varied composition, mainly in the form of caricatures, but with a few military specimens. Wolavka has his own museum which he has been building since the end of 1914, the models, based on a wood torso, being impregnated by a hard wax of his own invention, which, when still pliable, is moulded to the required effect. All metal parts are of actual metal. The latest ventures (1975) of which we have heard are by R. Reeves for Warrior of 14-inch models in synthetic resin with metal, cloth and leather and 90mm essays in aluminium resin by Kilmore (1976). Finally, there are two sculptors, each of whose models are entirely in the one medium they have chosen as being most appropriate. T.B. Sowden makes starkly realistic figures either in fibreglass or metal or stoneware: and Thomas Morrison uses either clay, wood, metal, porcelain or aluminium paste according to the need.

COMPOSITION. Plaster, papiermâché, and other non-metallic materials have been used for making model soldiers from the earliest days. Perhaps the first recorded example is that of Elias Ridinger, who, at Ulm at the end of the 17th century, made whole squadrons of models in papiermâché (*Von Boehn*). It would be a difficult material to preserve, and the next we hear of it is in a Bestermaier catalogue of 1815. Sonneburg was the centre of a complete industry in papiermâché and compressed sawdust (but in France in the 19th century, under the name of *carton-comprimé*, it was developed by a Monsieur Eckel (*d'Allemagne*)). These would be large models, and it is evident by their survival that they proved popular, being much cheaper to manufacture than if lead had been used. (Fleischman exhibited a large model at the Great Exhibition.) That the material is still occasionally used is shown by the models of Kurt Schwartz of the United States.

Plaster itself, an improbable material, also has a long history. A complete set of 75 figures was made for Napoleon III between 1855 and 1865, only to be destroyed by the Commune. A fine example is a set of the Emperor Franz Joseph and his staff, made about 1856, to which additions in metal were made, and a similar set of Napoleon III and his marshals (thirteen models) was exhibited in Paris in 1922. In more recent years it has been extensively used by Herbert Hahn (40-50mm), R. Fowler (10-18cm), Albert Selley (a short-lived venture), Clive Patmore and Howard Willetts, in a long and distinguished series. The Sentry Box went further and metallized their models for strength. In commercial use it has been the prerogative of the German and Italian manufacturers, mainly in very clumsy figures (e.g. Bayer, Chialu, Figur, Brevett, Hopf, NB, Roder and Rupp). Allied to this material is the peculiarly German mixture of sawdust, casein, kaolin, dextrin, bone-glue and water. The greatest exponent of this medium is the firm of O. & M. Hausser, under the famous trade mark Elastolin. Basically moulded on wire armatures, these large models poured into England and the United States in vast numbers, and are still collected. Other firms such as Leyla and Lineol followed suit, at times producing much better figures. (After the bombing of their plant Elastolin turned to another material and the quality improved beyond all recognition.) The models made by Italian competitors are almost always extremely poor. The original Starlux models were in *blanc-de-Meudon*.

Confalonieri, O. & Co., Milan (c.1965-). Plastic models 8cm, of Bersaglieri, Ascari, Scottish troops, Koreans, Italians, American Civil War, the Middle Ages, Romans, Westerners, portrait models of Garibaldi, Pecos Bill, Belle Starr, Colonel Crockett. Mounted figures 11cm.

Conise, Barcelona, Spain (c.1973-). A firm making solids in sizes varying from 54 to 160mm.

CONJOINT TIN. A form of sheet tin in which a rounded form is obtained by pressing the tin into curves and clipping with a metal flange. Originating in Germany about 1840, it became one of the cheapest forms of toymaking, and was marketed in the 'Penny Bazaars'. Strangely enough it anticipated the principle upon which William Britain based his hollow-casts. It was used for many other objects, such as wagons, carriages and horses (especially in USA), and the author remembers them as a boy. Many of them incorporated clockwork mechanism. Its modern equivalent is the large polythene children's pull-along toy found in Woolworth's. Military examples in various sizes turn up from time to time, but the only identifiable maker that we can discover was drawn to our attention by Wade. In 1974 he had a box of four horizontal sections with scenic backgrounds, containing 60mm British Hussars and Infantry of the Line. They were marketed by M. Laas of Paris, the label on the box bearing the initials F.V. (possibly Vasquez, mentioned by name in an early Mignot catalogue). The date is about 1915. M.D. Griffith, in his *Toy Soldiers of the World*, an article published in 1898, describes the process in the following words: 'For stamped soldiers, an artist and expert in martial affairs carves out of metal the model to be represented. He carves the two sides separately. Then follows the stamping. An enormous roll of tin hangs from a steel windlass, and, by means of an automatic steel knife, is cut into sheets as easily and rapidly as if it were paper. At the next table the sheets of tin are placed over the matrices, and, by means of a rammer, pressed into every cavity. When removed, they are exact facsimiles of the matrices. In this way hundreds are struck in an hour. Perfect in every detail, even the hair on the horses is accurately reproduced. The two halves are then soldered together by means of metal flanges, and every superfluous bit of metal is trimmed away, so that the outline of the figure is clear and well defined.' When completed, the model passed through a vat of coloured spirit-varnish. The spirit, on evaporation through heat, left a brilliant film of colour, with the shining metal showing through on the curves, or, alternatively, the whole could be sprayed with paint. Many thousands must have been sold in the famous Lowther Arcade in England, while in the United States conjoint tin was used from as early as 1840 for the production of carriages and other wheeled transport. Examples of its use in the military sphere occur in the illustrated pages of the large American stores from 1880 until 1914. The Germans were particularly prolific in its use, mainly for army vehicles and artillery (e.g. Märklin, Tipp, Lineol and Hausser).

Conley, Frank, Tipton, California (c.1954-68). Maker of 40-50mm solid models. He was originally associated with Scruby as Historical Miniature Figures. Conley made a number of the models, and did the painting of most of them.

Connett, Percy, London. As a collector of insight, he was probably the first to commission models in England, giving designs of ancient races to Courtenay, who sculpted and cast them for him, and, on Connett's death, added them to his own range. The designs were of Cleopatra as a priestess, an Egyptian soldier, a Nubian, a Nubian woman (Hitrovo says that Connett said that she was 'not quite a lady') and Mesopotamian and Assyrian cavalrymen. [*Ping*]

'Connoisseur Figures'. *See* S.K. Models.

'Connoisseur Range'. *See* Spencer-Smith Miniatures.

Connolly, William. *See* Waterloo Galleries.

Conquest (Skytrex Ltd) Leicester (1977-). Manufacturers of solid 25mm models of the Han Dynasty designed by Brian Ansell.

Conrad, Charles, France (1976-). A 90mm flat, engraved on one side only, of a Belgian Lancer, 1831, was commissioned from him by the Belgian Society.

Conrad, Pierre, France. A professional painter, mainly of Historex figures for the Dover branch of that firm and for The Soldier Shop.

Construcciónes Pepi. *See* Roma (Editorial).

CONVERSION. The practice of altering a model, either wholly or in part, from its original state. One of the earliest examples we have come across is the conversion of flats in the Leipzig Exhibition of 1930, but it was a stock-in-trade of many collectors in England before the Second World War. The models most commonly altered were Britains, and many and varied were the transformations, not always very successful. With the passing of the hollow-cast and the ever-increasing appearance on the market of the models of skilled

24 **Conversion** *by Norman Abbey using a number of Historex Napoleonic kits to create a scene from U.S. history (N. Abbey).*

makers, often in kit form, the necessity no longer existed, but the arrival of the polystyrene kit, notably by Historex, opened up entirely new vistas. No longer was the collector content with the figure made up as per the printed instructions — it had to be altered, no matter how slightly, so as to be different. Indeed, a single kit did not suffice, but a whole arsenal of parts was built up from diversified units, so that any single model when completed might well consist of the separate elements of a dozen designs. The results were in many cases quite remarkable, displaying incredible ingenuity. At times, when allied to expert painting and display, it was quite impossible to tell whether the model was an original, and the practice of omitting this vital piece of information when it was photographed and commented upon in a journal or a magazine set the historian a difficult problem. It also created trouble for the collector, who might well consider the model an original worthy of purchase. Finally, it had an effect on the younger school of collectors, who at times were inclined to be scathing of the works of the professional sculptor in metal, into which some had put the experience of a lifetime, and it also blinded them to the fact that many models made before they were born were worthy of admiration if not collection. In fact, one might be justified in classifying these converters (or 'modellers' as they prefer to be called) in a separate category from their fellow collectors, especially when one sees exhibitions at such divergent shows as those of the Model Engineering Society and the International Plastics Society, while illustrations frequently occur in journals quite remote from that of the model soldier.

In the days of the hollow-cast, solder or plastic wood were the most commonly used materials for the repositioning of a leg or an arm. Today, however, such substances as Isopon, Greenstuff, Plastic Padding and the like have rendered the early crude methods obsolete, and impact adhesives have largely solved the problem of binding parts together. As far as polystyrene models are concerned, the material itself has been turned to good account, the sprue from the parts being used in a liquefied form as an adhesive or as a moulding compound. The fact that the material is sensitive to heat has led to the expedient of moulding *in situ*, while the advent of the pyrogravure is as important to the worker in plastic as the soldering iron to the metallist. To attempt

to explain how a conversion is made would be pointless, as there are innumerable ways of setting about any specific task, and in any case military journals and society bulletins publish *ad nauseam* the step-by-step efforts of the creator, usually written by himself, and several books have been written expressly on the subject. Unless the reader is prepared to attempt the same transformation nothing could be more boring, but usually among the welter of technical and chemical phrases a few points stand out clearly: the would-be converter must be prepared to provide himself with a separate room in which to work; he should be capable of cleaning up afterwards, as conversion appears to be an extremely messy business; and he must supply himself with a whole battery of aids (admirably listed by Dilley) and have the mind of a magpie; the most unlikely screw, piece of string, button, circular paint-lid, or hairpin may become the vital part necessary for a model. The alert mind which spots an alternative posture or gesture is usually content with making a minor alteration without disturbing the concept as a whole, and there are many examples where this has been done in a regular series for display in a civic or regimental museum. Of late years, however, there have appeared a number of enthusiasts in many parts of the world to whom the basic figure is used merely as a torso on which to experiment, so it might be that a Plains Indian becomes a Nazi stormtrooper and a Luftwaffe pilot a Plains Indian. It is even done with Airfix 20mm wargame figures. The ultimate is reached when a complete diorama consists solely of conversions. The fact remains that such kits as Historex and Airfix have released a hitherto latent talent, and caused dealers to employ special converters, and schools of painting have emerged which have had their influence on the whole philosophy of the model soldier, whether for good or ill only remains for the future to assess.

Cook, John M., Massachusetts. One of the painters employed for the dioramas 'They Nobly Dared'.

Cooke, Norman and **Lisl.** *See* Lance Historical Miniatures.

Copada, Mexico (fl.1968). Makers of 54mm plastics.

Copestick, James H., Lancashire. Maker of Ludendorf Bridge model at the National Infantry Center, Fort Benning, Georgia, USA.

Copitzky, M., Villingen, W. Germany. Publisher of flats.

Copley, David, London (1973-   ). A commissioned convertor. (*Stearns*)

Coppin, Major Alan and **David.** *See* Midleton Models.

Coppinger, John, London. Assisted in the dioramas at Wilton House.

Copy-Cat (Brian Gildea), Gosport, Hants (1979-   ). Producer of 'toy' soldiers in Britains-style.

Cora, Mexico (c.1965). Manufacturers of 54mm hollow-casts, similar to those of Britains.

Corgi, England (1974-   ). Manufacturers of polystyrene AFVs, with drivers; metal tanks in 1975. (*See also* Mettoy Co. Ltd.)

Cork. Wolfe's victory at Quebec was celebrated by a small but interesting group of cork models. Soldiers and sailors made of painted cork embarking in wooden transports two or three feet long are to be seen at the Castle Museum, York, the National Army Museum and the National Maritime Museum. At Quebec House, Westerham, there is a variation made in the present century by H.R. Allen, where although copied from the original at the National Maritime Museum, the figures and weapons are in metal.

'Coronation' set. *See* Farish; Nicholson; Rose Miniatures.

Coronet Miniatures (John Gauthier and Peter Twist) Toronto, Ontario (1974–   ). A combine which began with a North-West Mounted policeman, a winged Polish Hussar, an equestrian Thomas Beauchamp, 12th Earl of Warwick, a Sir John de Plessis with his squire, and a Banastre Tarleton (after the original oil painting by Sir Joshua Reynolds). These were followed by a Yeoman of the Guard, a Fort Henry Guard, and a crossbowman with mantlet. All are attractive and well sculpted by Twist from Gauthier's designs, the Tarleton being outstanding.

Cortum, George, Hamburg (b.1915). Designer of flats. Mark: c. He first began in 1948, the models being mainly engraved by Frank. The most important are sets of Romans on the march and the Battle of Issus.

Cosson, Paris. Painter of flats for the Mignot range.

Courtenay, Richard, Slough (1928-65). Richard Courtenay was one of the first in England to try to create a new form of model, intended for collectors. He served his apprenticeship, as it were, in a partnership of a commercial character with E. Doran, producing 45mm medieval models which were of little moment from the artistic aspect, the armour being left unpainted. At the same time, he innovated the 'two on a stand' type of figure. Neglected for many years by collectors, they are important for a study of Courtenay, as they display the germs of later characteristics. Like Beethoven, as seen in his sketch books, he was not an instant genius; indeed, some of the earliest and smaller models were badly conceived and executed; and his notebooks and drawings (in the ownership of his son, but a photocopy in Greenhill's possession) show the slow and careful stages by which he arrived at his final conclusion. The original Doran models are seen to emerge, by alteration, into the later Courtenay. His main range consisted of medieval warriors, mainly of the fourteenth and fifteenth centuries, and comprised some three hundred variations. The early ones had some peculiar characteristics, especially when one looks at the horses, many of which might almost be regarded as ponies, when comparison is made with the great, rearing destriers which show so much animation. His painting was exceptional, and his heraldry impeccable. In this he was greatly helped by Ping, with whom he soon became friends, the latter doing much of the research into rolls of arms and contemporary accounts. Each model bore the name of the person on the upper part of the footstand. Although riders were cast separately and then soldered to the saddle, the reins and horse trappings were moulded in one; very occasionally he used a movable lance-arm. Not only did the obvious personalities appear, but also little-known ones culled from Froissart and Monstrelet. Armour and arms were varied, as were faces, some being bald-headed, and one at least had a patch over one eye. Up to the beginning of the Second World War the models were hollow-cast, but at the suggestion of Ping they were then issued solid. Again owing to Ping's influence, the range greatly expanded, and it was decided that some sort of identification should be used. This led to the grouping of figures in several series, and a basic formula of twenty-two foot and thirteen horses emerged, upon which the changes were rung. After the

25   **Courtenay.** *Solids, 50mm. (Trinity College, Hartford).*

'fifties he redesigned the majority of his models in nearer 54mm size, and completed a set of twenty different figures made up from about two dozen new moulds, all of which he prefixed 'Z'. Another series was named after his wife Vida, and a few specimens were unnumbered, including a Scottish axeman, a tournament horse, a Richard I, a Henry V horse, and a series of foot soldiers. Among the rarities is a group of crossbowmen made specifically for Ping, and a Sir Walter de Manny bearing the legend 'Made by Courtenay'. Although the mature Courtenay displays all the beauty that a collector could wish for (and seen in bulk they are magnificent), he was not perhaps so happy in periods other than the medieval (although the very rare First Foot Guards; 1660 are still as good as anything made since) and his Raleigh, Nell Gwynne (two versions), Charles II (two sizes), George V and Queen Mary are unremarkable. More attractive are his series of 'Ladies of the Garter', and a superb Nefertiti. Percy Connett got him to make him a number of models of ancient races, including Nubians, and Babylonians, and on Connett's death Courtenay incorporated them into his own range. Added to these were three $4\frac{1}{2}$ inch models (the Black Prince, Edward III and Henry VIII) which he seldom cast (but were later revived by Ping), and a set of racehorses with jockeys specially for the Aga Khan. Greenhill has recently discovered that Wilfred Cherrington was his pattern maker, so much of the credit must go to him for the translation of the Courtenay designs. When Courtenay died his son, in collaboration with Webb of Hummel's, who had nurtured Courtenay's products for years, commissioned Ping to take charge of the moulds and continue to make castings. These were so successful that permission was granted to give Ping a free hand in rearranging the positions and the weapons, place new riders on different horses, and generally create an entirely new range, known as 'Courtenay/Ping'. Nobody could have been a better choice, and such was Ping's affinity to his friend that, although his methods of painting were different, the essential Courtenay, with the impeccable armour and heraldry, was preserved, and given new life. Many other makers have delved into the medieval period since Courtenay, but one has the feeling that they regard any model they make as a vehicle for their own display of erudition, often false, and usually the result is a stiff, heavy, lifeless puppet. However, one of Courtenay's most fervent admirers, the collector Peter Greenhill, is in the process of producing an exciting new series, not copying Courtenay, but in memory of him. Furthermore Greenhill is now the owner of the original Courtenay moulds. And so the Courtenay tradition will march on, and shed its refulgent light over the German Paratroopers and the Japanese suicide squads and the other thugs who today crowd the makers' lists.

Courtenay, William, London (c.1935–1950). A maker of 54mm hollow-casts of little significance.

Coutts, J. & C. *See* 'Under Two Flags'.

Couturier, Pierre, Paris (fl.1669). Responsible for the painting of the paper cut-out figures for the Duc de Viennois.

Covington, Edward G., Hurst, Texas (1972–). A maker, for Cowan, of an as yet small range of 54mm metal models, each limited to 50 copies. William the Conqueror, a Cuero Dragoon, and Sir Geoffrey de Trumpington are all in kit form. The last assembles well, and has an unusual and attractive base of grass and flowers, these and the arms on the shield and neck protectors being in relief.

Cow, P.B., & Co. Ltd, London (1949). Half-a-dozen British Second World War battle-dress troops, 54mm, plastic, were issued for a short period as a sideline only.

Cowan, P.J. *See* Mark-Time Figures.

Cowan, R. *See* Militaria.

Cowburn, George. *See* Cody Models.

Cox, T., USA (c.1965). Maker of 30 and 54mm solids. At one time he was associated with Scruby in the production of the smaller size models, especially of a mule train.

'Crab'. The trademark of E. Fontanini. It has been placed here as the only guide to identification.

Crafts For The Collector, Lamorna, Cornwall. Makers of facsimile cannon, 1790–1825, in metal and wood.

Crancroft Engineering Ltd, Warnham, Surrey (1978–). Makers of acrylic show-cases.

Craus, Philip, USA. A professional painter employed by Cowan.

'Crécy' chess set. *See* Warrior.

Crécy series. *See* Charles, A.; Greenwood and Ball (Pearce).

Crepax, Guido, Milan (1965–). Designer of a set of paper sheets of the Battle of Pavia, colour printed for Linus of Milan.

Crescent Toy Co. Ltd, Tottenham, London/Cwmcarn, Wales. (1922–?). Manufacturers of passable hollow-cast and plastic models, 54 and 60mm, although they were badly painted. The range consisted mainly of British Regiments, the Italo-Abyssinian War, troops in khaki, trotting Guards, Westerners, and poor medievals. One remarkable figure, albeit clumsy, was based on the contemporary drawing by John Rouse of the pole-axe combat between Richard Beauchamp, Earl of Warwick, and Sigismondo Malatesta. The medievals in plastics were better than those in hollow-cast, although the shields were far too large. Those in 40mm were very poor, the body and legs of the horses hollowed out for economy. They also made an excellent metal catapult, as well as tanks in 1975. They may have purchased some of Reka's moulds, as a number of the early models show marked similarity and certainly they reissued some of Fry's [*Wade*]. They actually began making military models in 1930; detachable riders and movable arms were introduced in 1948, plastics in 1956, and second-grade plastics, 40mm, in 1958.

Crespak Ltd, Gwent (1975). Medieval plastic chess set promoted by Cherilea.

Crider, Doris, USA. Employed by Cowan as a professional painter.

CRITICISM AND CRITICS. With the increase in recent years of journals and magazines devoted to the model soldier and its ancillaries much more detailed analysis of models old and new has been noticeable. Ten years ago the collector in many cases searched for his own models, or was influenced by any of a number of makers, and to a large extent made up his own mind. But criticism is nothing new: at the Great Exhibition an anonymous critic said of the German models, 'They bend almost with their own weight, and the colouring matter upon them stains a moist finger . . . they are certainly no better than are often made at school or at home.' In 1867 George Augustus Sala questioned 'the fierce martial display of Bavaria, Hesse and Wurtemberg'. This moral aspect was taken up in France, with a criticism of Heinrichsen 'in whose boxes there are printed slips describing battles in which the Prussians were always either victorious, or painted in the most favourable light'. Every collector is obviously a critic, or he would never become a collector, but it would seem that every model issued is now subjected to a more intensive scrutiny than was evident in the past. One reason for this is the flood of models from new makers, another the current interest in militaria in general.

Cromwell Pewterers (Ron Chambers), Cromwell, Connecticut (1970–). Manufacturer of semi-flats, 30-60mm, of American First World War infantry and cavalry, said to be from 'old moulds', probably from those of defunct home-casting outfits.

Cross, D. *See* DEK Military Models.

Cross, W.F., London (1969-72). Maker of a set of six *Samurai* (solid, 54mm, and rather poorly cast, but historically accurate) and a Japanese puppeteer of better quality. They were marketed by one or two smaller dealers in London, one of whom called himself 'Angel Square' (now 'Angel Armoury'). No mark was placed on the models, and they have consequently been given the name of 'Angel Square' by one or two American collectors who purchased them in London.

Crowe, Raymond. *See* Monarch.

Crowfoot, Timothy, USA. Designer for Bugle & Guidon and Deauville/Brigade.

Crown, London. Manufacturers of polystyrene AFV kits.

Crown Personalities (Ivor Pollock) Stockport, Cheshire (1970–). 60mm solids, which are more elliptical than round. The series, each figure of which is separately boxed, on individual stands and given a dull metal finish, consists of Henry VIII, the Black Prince, Shakespeare, John Bull and Queen Elizabeth I. They are all designed by Pollock and are somewhat clumsy in appearance.

'Crown' series. *See* Britain, William, Ltd.

Croxford, Jenny, London (1978–). Designer of a four-sheet cut-out English village with figures.

C.S. & D., Denver, Colorado (1976–). Wargame, solids, 25mm.

Culpitt, P.J. and **Musgrave, G.** *See* Gem-Models.

Cushing, Peter, London. A collector who used his models as a vehicle for his profession – that of an actor. He built his own theatre, and thought out his entrances and exits with the aid of his models, many of which were made specially for him by Ping. Others he himself made from papiermâché. His collection was sold at auction in 1970.

Custer, Eugene B., Jamaica, New York (1945-). One of the first of the self-taught school of American specialist-makers. During the course of some ten years he turned out a number of models of the American Revolution and the Civil War, together with a cannon and gun team of that period. The painting was done by his wife, Wilma. The newly-arriving imports from England proved too much competition for Custer, however, and he refrained from any further marketing. But their interest did not cease, and he continued to advise and design for such contemporaries as Greer, Murray and Imrie. They were, and still are, altruistic in their help to many a collector and author.

Custom Cast Inc., USA. Dealers in and makers of 25mm Confederates and fantastics. Purchased Bugle & Guidon in 1974.

Cutileiro, A.J.C. *See* Diorama Miniaturas Militares.

CZECHOSLOVAKIA. Production began at about the beginning of the 19th century with commercially produced, crudely painted wooden figures, both foot and mounted, the height of the equestrians roughly 20cm, the foot 15cm. Much later there appeared both flats and semi-flats of cavalry and infantry, 60 and 50mm respectively, together with paper sheets of all units of the army in parade order, the sizes varying from 65 to 80mm. Towards the end of the century a firm in Prague specialized in figures carved in wood and dressed in cloth, with leather and metal accoutrements, weapons and musical instruments, these being detachable. These figures were approximately 6 inches high, of Czechs and Germans, the former being sold singly or as a complete band, the latter having only a bugler and a drummer. For some reason Senegalese sharp-shooters were also fairly common. During the first Republic (1918–39) the old moulds continued in use, together with more up-to-date ones of infantry and cavalry of the Republican troops (some with gas masks) and artillery in flats, in many positions. To these can be added semi-flat mounted knights and the ubiquitous Westerners, all in 50-60mm size. In the late 20's, however, these began to be superseded by troops in papiermâché (9cm) in many poses, together with German, French, British, Chinese and Japanese troops. The Czechs included airmen carrying propellors, and ski troops. The cavalry were of two types, the riders moulded to the horse or detachable, all horses at the walk, and of Czech, German, French and British units, the French Republican Guards with glittering breastplates and the Czechs with gas masks. The infantry included Senegalese, British and French airmen, United States sailors, a British admiral, Czech telegraph troops (one atop a pole), doctors and nurses, and smaller-size Highlanders and pre-1914 Frenchmen. Allied to the papiermâché productions there were also reinforced plaster representations of the same troops with the addition of Grenadier Guards and Ethiopians, and somewhat smaller West Point Cadets. They were very badly made, and few have survived; they died a natural death, as did a few attempts in conjoint tin. During the middle 30's the firm of Bata made some quite exceptionally crude 6cm flats in a type of synthetic rubber, the subjects being, fantastically, Negro troops with a mounted officer. These were followed by solid rubber 12cm horrors, consisting of Czech infantry and huge (20cm) cavalry. These, again, did not last long, nor did 5cm lead, gold-plated knights. Various military sheets, however, some with both sides printed, were of good quality. Under the German régime the whole tenor changed, all the moulds disappearing, and being replaced by new ones portraying only Germans and Czechs. The reinforced plaster, the lead, and the rubber disappeared completely, together with the paper sheets. In 1942 new papiermâché Westerners appeared, but towards the end of the same year all production ceased. After the war a fresh start was made with a set of ill-cast solid Czech infantry, 9cm high. These in their turn disappeared in 1946, when new sets of foot and mounted troops appeared from moulds which must have been secreted years before. Crippling trade restrictions caused a revival of the paper sheet industry, but, since the political change, production of all forms of model soldiers appears to have stopped completely. [*Roubiecek*]

CZZPP, Warsaw (fl.1970). Producers of 40mm plastic semi-solids of modern infantry, cavalry and artillery all unpainted. [*Pestana*]

D

Dahlback, Ake, Leksand, Sweden. His own collection of flats, in the form of beautiful dioramas, is to be seen at Leksand. He was responsible for the bulk of the figure painting.

D.A.L., California. Advertised in *Soldier,* October 1968, as makers of 54mm solids, but no further information is forthcoming.

Dalmau, Joaquin, Gerona (1977-). Publisher of paper sheets.

Dalmaū, J. Pla. *See* Arm-Model.

Dancaster, Samuel and **Dr Augustus,** Jersey, Channel Islands (before 1900-1914). Although strictly makers for their own amusement, their 28mm woodcarvings, especially with slings made separately, and in vast quantities, are so unusual that they deserve a mention. Shamus Wade had a large collection of them in 1970.

Daneri, A. *See* Life Model.

Dangschat, Dr P., Germany. Designer of flats.

Daniel, René. *See* MDM.

Daniel, Lee N. *See* Steadfast.

Danolin, Denmark (c.1940-). Manufacturers of Elastolin composition-type models.

Dansk Aubeijde, Denmark. Paper sheets of Danish troops.

Danske Billeder. *See* Jacobsen, (Alfred) Forlag.

Darnell, John, London (1972-). Maker of commissioned 54mm models in fibreglass, carving directly from the composition.

Davenport, William, Quincey, Massachusetts. Maker of commissioned 50-60mm models in composition and cloth.

David, Peter, Montreal (1968-). A private maker of models that are so unusual that they must be included. He casts semi-flats, 45mm, in which the front is completely sculptured, the back completely flat. Great animation and character is expressed.

Davidson, T. *See* Castile Miniatures.

Davies & Co., London (1903). Manufacturers of a few inferior hollow-casts. Remembered only for their prosecution by Britains for piracy.

Davies-Sparke, E. *See* Wend-Al.

Davis, Gordon, USA. Professional painter employed by Cowan.

Davis, John. *See* Drumbeat.

'Davy Crockett' series. *See* Lone Star Diecasting Tools Ltd.

Dawson, Malcolm, England (1970-). Known for some time as a modeller who made balsawood figures with the addition of other materials. In 1973 he joined the English branch of Old Guard as a designer of 54mm solids of the Thirty Years' War, and the following year began a series of station staff and travellers of the 1917-20 era in 20mm, entitled Branchline Figures, in which he was assisted by Roslyn Young. His more recent work includes a medieval member of the Codrington family, work for New Hope and for The Franklin Mint (q.v.).

Deal, E. *See* Classic Miniatures.

Dean (Publishers), London. In 1945 they issued a 'Victory Cut-Out Book' with pre-pressed models of the Allied troops.

Dean, Robert M., Clovelly, N. Devon. Professional painter of Historex kits.

Deauville Models (John Stonesypher) Decatur, Illinois (1974-). A retail shop, advertising a painting service. To this was added a small series of 54mm solids. In *Vedette,* 1974, Stonesypher advertised 150 models in kit form as being available. Whether these were actually ever issued is in doubt, Stonesypher making no response to numerous applications for them or at least for a list of them. However, a group of three Napoleonic figures in off-duty poses were eventually obtained. These proved interesting but not remarkable. In 1975 the name was changed to Deauville/Brigade, with Tom Crowfoot as designer. In the same year Deauville models were advertised under the blanket name New Hope Design, in England, and it appears that a two-way process was emerging, whereby some American models were being exported to England and some English models finding their way from New Hope to Stonesypher. One instance is a set depicting Blücher being unhorsed at Ligny, consisting of five men and two horses, designed in England, the men by John Patterson, the horses by William Taylor. A British nurse of the South African War period, looking remarkably like Nurse Cavell, designed by Roger Saunders, is a beautiful figure.

DB Figurines (Derek Brown), Sydney, Australia (1977-). Began sculpting and casting about 1971, after his own collection had been stolen. In 1977 he issued World Wars I and II airmen, including personalities, in 36mm solids. He is contemplating the issue of

54mm models.

Debler, Schwäbish-Gmünd. Maker of stamped and cut tin models in 30mm of flora and fauna. (*Ortmann*, unfortunately giving no date)

De Bono, Joseph, London (1976-). Maker of 35mm pewter models for Willie of ancient Japanese warriors.

Decker, Colmar (1850). Producer of paper sheets.

Deckherr, Th. Fred., Montbéliard, France (1830). Publisher of paper sheets of the Imperial family.

Decofigur. *See* Reamsa.

Deconinck, Jean, Belgium. One of the leading figures in Belgian collecting circles, exerting a great influence on the fostering of solids.

Decorator Speciality Co. Inc., Allston, Massachusetts (1974). Manufacturers of diorama display cases on birchwood bases.

'Deetail' series. *See* Britains Ltd.

De Gissey, Henri, Paris (fl.1670). On 27 September, 1670, he was paid '*6,000 milles francs [sic] en payment de partie des petites figures des soldats composant une armée de XX escadrons de cavalerie et X bataillons infanterie de carte que Sa Majesté à commandé.*' This was followed on 11 February, 1671, by '*pour parfait remboursement de 26,963 livres 14 sous, à quoi monté de dépense de la petite armée de carte . . 963 livres 14 sous*'. This paper army may have been either hand-drawn or engraved, and then brilliantly coloured and heightened with gold, mounted on thin card, and fixed to small footstands.

De Gruyter, Holland. Manufacturer of crude 54mm plastics.

De Jong, J., Utrecht. A private maker of solids who participated in the first Dutch International Exhibition in 1956.

De Jong's Cacao, Holland (1890–1915). Manufacturers of coloured and pressed-out paper figures in relief, issued in packets of cocoa.

DEK Military Models (A. Caton and D. Cross) Leicester (1977-). Makers of 80mm solids in kit-form entitled 'All the Queen's Men'. In 1978 they were joined by Esmond Jago and David Kayson, and in the same year the first mounted model was produced. They now have a remarkably large range, of which a kettle-drummer of the Royal Scots Greys (c.1892) is outstanding.

Delacroix, Paris (fl.1830-51). Carried on a business at 15 rue Grenetat. First mentioned in *Le Bazar Parisien*, as makers of 'soldiers of all kinds', and again in the *Almanach Bottin*. In all probability the models were of lead or some kind of composition.

Delarue-Mardrus, Lucien, Paris. Mentioned (without date) by Nicollier as making models in candle-grease.

Delez, F.J. *See* Empire Military Miniatures.

Delhalt, C. & C.W., Nancy, France (19th century). Producers of paper sheets.

Delmas, A. Converter of 20 Aiglon models for the *Musée International des Hussars* at Tarbes.

Deltorama, Bury, Sussex, (c.1963-72). Manufacturers of war buildings and entrenchments in unbreakable rubber composition for use with 20 and 30mm troops under the name 'Bellona'. They were designed by W. Holmes (d.1970), whose last work was done in 1968. Later taken over by Micromold the range also included scale drawings and vehicles.

'De Luxe Soldier Review'. *See* McLoughlin Brothers.

Dembour. Only a collector who has devoted himself exclusively to the study of paper sheets could attempt to sort out the ramifications of French family businesses, especially those of the mid-19th century. Such a one, which we admit we have been unable to clarify, has the following permutations: Dembour et Gangel; Gangel, Gangel et Didion; Gangel frères et Didion; Didion et Gangel. Places of publication were Metz and Paris.

Demong, Ernst Carl, Hanover (1830-7). Maker and engraver of flats who also employed Schaper. Marks: C.E. DEMONG in HANNOVER; C. SHAPER FEC.

Denecke, Christian August Wolrath, Brunswick (1804–42). Manufacturer of flats, 30mm and 8-9cm. Succeeded by his son Wolrath who sold the business in 1870 to L. Link, who left it to his two sons. One of these died about 1890, the other, Albert, an engraver, in 1916. Moulds were then purchased by Rieche of Hanover. Another branch, belonging to Denecke's widow, was sold in 1820 to Carl Wegmann. Wollrath started with the then traditional large models of Brunswick and Napoleonic troops, especially those of the Egyptian expedition. Later he turned to the smaller size. (See *Catalogue of the Leipzig Exhibition, 1930*, diorama 18.) Wegmann, in turn, left his business to his son Theodor (1825-95) which was then purchased by B. Bornig. Wegmann used many of the original Denecke moulds, erasing the mark WD and substituting CW.

Denis, L. *See* D.F.H.

DENMARK. The earliest production of flats began about 1760, and a few other examples occur which are dated 1791. The most famous example is that of an equestrian portrait model of King Frederick VII, wearing his aluminium helmet. This is by H. Høy, is 12cm high, dates from about 1848-50, and is signed in Gothic script. The Teknisk Museum, Copenhagen, a few years' ago made a limited number of about 20 castings for collectors. Traditional flats of 30mm size were made by S.E. Gallaus (first exhibited at Amsterdam in 1956), which were designed by Rössner. Commercial solids were started about 1948 by Banner-Model of Copenhagen. These were of excellent quality, size about 47-49mm, but the most popular and best-known are those of Brigader-Statuette (Carl Andersen), 45mm in the Heyde style, but far superior in workmanship and painting, and with good horses. They are still being produced. In 1946 the firm of G. Krohn-Rasmussen of Copenhagen incorporated the aluminium models of a former firm whose trade mark was Rode-Orm. In a curious 75mm size, among the products were Vikings, knights and Robin Hood, an Ivanhoe set, Danish Royal Guards, and the ubiquitous Westerners. Plastics were made by Kai Reisler, but much of the interest has been transferred to the ever-increasing monopoly of the Historex polystyrene range. Of specialist models, *Chakoten*, the Danish Society, started production of the War of 1864, both in 30mm flats and 54mm solids, the latter reaching a total of some sixty-odd models by R.F. Anholm and I.H. Johansen. The models of Søren Brunoe (Rollo) are of the highest quality. Official artist to the Danish navy, he began model-making as a pastime, but soon found that his figures were in demand. He has concentrated on the history of his own country, especially in the 17th-19th centuries, but with excursions into other countries and periods. Working in the traditional Continental style, everything he turns out displays grace and elegance, and he is particularly successful with female models and small dioramas, upon which he is at the moment concentrating, especially those depicting naval actions. His 'Homage to Watteau' group places him head and shoulders above all other contemporary makers in any country. The models of Ole Høyer (cast by J. Hansen) are very fine. John Buntzen is also occasionally seen on the market, making some outstanding elephants to go with Stadden and Rose Colonial troops. Three authors joined in the production of a delightful little book *Tinge-linge-later tinsoldater* (1966) dealing with the hobby in Denmark.

Deppe, Horst, Germany. Designer of flats.

De Rham, Casimir, Zurich. Nicollier illustrates a field gun of 1760, with team, in flat, and states 'castings and painting by Casimir de Rham, engineer'.

Des Fontaines, Josianne, Boulogne-sur-Seine (1955–1977). Perhaps the most immediately breath-taking of all makers. Each model, 54mm, solid, was built up on a torso by means of sheet lead and soldering, the equipment being added. Her range was all-embracing, from Carthaginian war-elephants to North American Indian chiefs. The earlier models were slightly wooden facially and rather dumpy, but this was later brilliantly overcome. Her models received great acclamation wherever they were exhibited. She worked solely to commission, but even so only the richest of collectors could hope to own one of her models. Unlike the majority of the French masters, who are traditional in their reticence, des Fontaines expressed extreme animation at times, and perhaps this is illustrated most clearly in the above-mentioned elephant group owned by Nathan Polk (See Garratt, *Collecting Model Soldiers*, p.34). The excellence of her work has been expressed in several other publications (notably in Garratt, *Model Soldiers for the Connoisseur*). The above review would appear to be too short for the pre-eminence of this master, but she herself has proved inaccessible, at least by post, although Nathan Polk describes her as being most charming and friendly. Since 1977 she has been unable to work owing to a persistent eye infection, and the collector must sadly reconcile himself to the loss of an adornment to the hobby.

Des Granges, H. *See* Quiralu.

DESIGNER. One who is responsible for the conception of a model, and who produces working drawings for the use of the sculptor or master maker. Alternatively, his function may be limited to research into, and drawings of, a particular uniform, the sculptor himself then working out the way in which he wishes to proceed. A number of makers see the project through from start to finish (e.g. Eriksson, Berdou, des Fontaines Schreiber, Surèn, Ping, Greenwood, Sanderson, Imrie-Risley, Stadden, Lelièpvre, Gammage, the early Selwyn-Smith, Niblett when working in metal, Labayen, Høyer, Brunoe, Parisini) and of course the majority of makers who work solely to commission. In large firms, however, and even in smaller ones, particularly in the United States, there appears the dual partnership of designer-maker and producer, or the triumvirate of designer, sculptor and distributor, and in many instances the designer is seldom mentioned. Who, for example, designed the many thousands of models that go under the name of Britains, Heyde, Elastolin, Crescent, Timpo and the like? It was not through Malleable Mouldings themselves that we discovered that the designers of these

models were Niblett, Harris and Nicholson; nor until recently did we know that C.R. Broman's models were mainly designed by Tom Sibbitt, and the identity of the designer/sculptor of the first Deauville Models and the earlier Airfix models in 54mm still remains undiscovered, in the first instance by indifference, in the second by point blank refusal by the distributors to acknowledge their respective debts. On the credit side is the obvious eagerness of many of the Americans to acknowledge that such and such a model made for, say, The Barefoot Soldier, is by Greer, that Beverly Gordon has worked for Waterloo Galleries, that Monarch use the services of Greer, McGeer, Olmstead, Fabre and Benkert, that Cavalier have or have had Stackhouse,

26 **Des Fontaines.** *Sitting Bull. Solid, 54mm. (M. O'Brien).*

Chernak and others in their employ, and that Old Guard, besides still marketing the models of the founder, Murray, have recently branched out with designs by Chernak, Dawson and Stadden. Many designers, however, remain for ever anonymous, as some makers of solids are jealous lest their craftsman may be stolen from them. Free-lance designers are not a prerogative of the United States, however, as the careers of Stadden, Niblett and Erik show; and Hinton and Surén are known to have designed for firms other than their own. In fact, the whole matter is so complicated that one has no recourse but to call a model Cavalier, Stadden or Hinchliffe.

In the case of flats the base of the figure normally bears the initials or trade name of designer, engraver and marketer or 'editor' (e.g. the names of the designers Block, Backman or Willie Ericson, the engravers Lecke, Frank or Knoll, are in evidence on the models 'edited' by Sivhed), and a pretty exhaustive list is published regularly in many Continental journals.

Despeñaperros, Spain. Bronze equestrian warriors 7-8cm, 5th century BC, were found here.

Deutsche Zinnfiguren-Werkstatte, Berlin, Berlin (after 1918–?). Producer of HS-Zinnfiguren depicting the German Army. Only seven small sets were issued. (*Scholtz*)

Dew, James. *See* Pride of Europe.

D.F.H., Paris (fl.1950–65). A combination of L. Denis, Pierre Fouré and G. Hourtoule, who together made a few individual flats (e.g. a medieval litter by Denis) and sets of 1800-06 and 1808-11 French troops, horse and foot, privately, for members of the French Society. Marks: DF;DFH.

Dia-D-Hora, Spain (1970–). Manufacturers of 54mm plastics of the Moorish Guard of General Franco; mounted Barcelona police; German Infantry; a Russian mine-detector dog; Second World War troops, and sandbag wall sections in polystyrene.

Diaz-Del-Rio, Chile. A contemporary maker of commissioned models. [*Duinker*]

Dickey, R., USA. A professional painter employed by Cowan.

Dickinson, Neville. *See* Miniature Figurines.

Didion. *See* Dembour.

Diedrich, Ludwig, Brussels (c.1965). Editor of 33mm flats of Belgian carabiniers, 1813-15, designed by Oehlschlagel, engraved by S. Maier.

Diedrich-Jacques, H.J.G., Amsterdam. A collector who has been the inspiration of the Dutch Society. He occasionally makes a 54mm solid for his friends.

Dier, E.A., Berlin. Designer of flats for Scholtz.

Diercky. *See* Brépols.

Dietelbach, Berlin (c.1860). Maker of flats.

Dietrich, Walter, Germany. Designer for Eichhorn of flats of the Thirty Years' War.

Dietz, Eugen, Nuremberg. Specifically mentioned in *Dawk*, 1975, as a maker of plastic models. Communication failed to elicit a reply.

Diez, Leopold, St Polten, Austria. Maker of three-dimensional siege weapons, Guns, Wagons, etc, of the medieval period in 30mm (*Kulmbach Almanac, 1977*)

Diezemann, Germany. Home-casting moulds in semi-solid. [*Fischer*]

Dihm, Dr. Leipzig (fl.c.1950). A collector and occasional maker of flats.

Dill, J. England (c.1937). The only works that can be ascribed to him are a series of 54mm hollow-cast 'Buck Rogers' characters.

Dillon, Rear-Admiral C.J., Canada. Supervisor of the 'D-Day' diorama at the Canadian War Museum, Ottawa.

Dilly, USA (c.1965). Featured in a Polk exhibition as being on a par with Berdou, but further investigation reveals that Polk himself can remember nothing about him.

Dinglinger, Johann Melchior. *See* 'Grand Mogul's Birthday Party'.

Dinky (Meccano) Ltd, Liverpool (1933–). Originally called Modelled Miniatures. Concerned mainly with tiny mechanical (as distinct from mechanized) vehicles, and beloved of children of all ages. The incidental 20mm

models sometimes had the distinction of being designed by Stadden. In 1975 they began the production of metal German Second World War guns with plastic shells, a two-man crew in 60mm and a tank-destroyer.

Dior, Germany (pre-1939). Plaster composition, similar to pre-1939 Elastolin models.

DIORAMA. A representation by the use of models of a particular scene or event, traditionally in boxed form, but more recently of a much freer nature. The necessities are a given number of suitably sized models and a simulated terrain. The urge to create a diorama stems on occasion from the reading of a description of an historic encounter, from the desire to re-create a painting in three-dimensional form, from the wish to commemorate a happening, or from the direct commission by a group, an association, or a museum, for permanent display. With all forms of diorama presentation, proportion is the main ingredient. The actual moment it is wished to portray is the equivalent of a frozen moment, and must speak for itself without a long description being necessary. The artist must therefore familiarize himself with all the happenings before and after, for errors cannot be corrected once the box is sealed. Due prominence must be given to the participants, so that they become the centre of attraction. A training in stage-craft is a distinct advantage in this respect, and a knowledge of great plays and operas with their figure-groupings a great help. Problems of light and shade, distance, foreground, background and action are all present, especially if the grouping is an original conception, and not a copy of an existing picture. Flats appear to be ideal for many dioramas; indeed, the original conception of the modern maker was for their use in pictorial tableaux, hence the long series issued by many of them, to which are often allied the works of other makers extending the original idea, together with the *komposition* figure and the advantages that accrue from its use. With flats, of course, many more separate models may be, and often have to be, used than with larger figures, and in large, massed formations it is usually only necessary to vary the action of the foreground combatants. It is also possible, by the skilful use of accessories, and the subtle employment of atmosphere and proportion, to use a mere half-dozen flats to achieve the end in view. There are many versions of the very large diorama, employing thousands of flats and extending over vast areas, on the Continent of Europe in particular. These are normally the work of dedicated teams of experts, using pooled sets of models, some doing alterations if necessary, others the painting, and others the landscape or other natural features, with a general co-ordinator in charge. Examples are the famous series by Kröner-Grimm and his colleagues in Austria, and the somewhat smaller collection supervised by Gottstein formerly in the Royal United Service Institution Museum. The smaller, more intimate, groups employing a few models are to be seen in many club exhibitions, and it is with them that the work of a single individual is usually associated. One remembers vividly an exhibition of the works of Denny Stokes, in which one diorama, consisting solely of Courtenay's model of Nefertiti placed amid a simple setting of stylized Egyptian columns constructed from the embossed paper found inside the lid of a chocolate box was by far the most striking. The smaller-sized models, such

27 Diorama. *Made of Duron with some wood in weapons and equipment by Displayer Inc, N.Y.C. (Marine Corps Museum, Quantico, Va).*

as those of Surén, or the even tinier wargaming ones, are ideal for dioramic purposes, and have indeed been used to good effect; it appears likely that they may supercede the use of flats, at least in non-Germanic countries. Problems occur, however, when larger sizes are visualized. Large numbers of large models need space, and a corresponding increase in the size of the landscape detail such as trees and buildings; the prized model which looks so handsome in the cabinet may appear lifeless when placed in a setting with a mass of similar figures. The ideal number of models of a 50-60mm size is probably about a dozen, which number enables them to be housed in a box of reasonable size. Each model then tends to complement the other in a satisfactory manner. This tendency is reflected in the growing practice of placing a mere half a dozen figures or less within a scenic setting on a single base and dispensing entirely with a protective cover. In this way the problems of the sky and background are eliminated, and the viewer is enabled to see the representation from all sides. Now the maker can indulge his fancy by the creation of a series of tableaux illustrating successive incidents, and the interest is centred more on the actual models used. Another practice that has emerged of recent years is the placing of a related group of tiny figures on a single base with little or no scenery, the simulated ground being 'bled-off' into an irregular shape. Here again there is great scope for ingenuity. Yet another method, worthy of close attention, is that used by Valentine Bean. Well-versed in stage techniques, he creates impressions rather than factual representations, by using flats painted to suit the mood of the event and grouping them in tiers on contours of naked wood. Whichever method is used, and whatever the means employed to achieve the end, taste and proportion are essential to the final outcome, and it may appear to some that the overlarge

bees-wax models used in some of the dioramas exhibited in American museums fail by being both too large and too factual. With a large diorama it is necessary to employ some scheme whereby the contours of the ground will be sustained, and it is usual to use either chicken wire coated with a paste-like material or with papiermâché, or graded wooden slabs treated with a covering. Upon this may be sprinkled or dredged any of the innumerable simulated grass and earth materials used by model railway enthusiasts, together with Plaster of Paris or Polyfilla or similar material for ruts and excrescences. Matt oil paint will have to be used, and such oddments as sisal and manufactured moss for greenery. Hedges and trees (those designed by Herald are superb) are easily bought, as are stone walls, gates, etc. Scenes of carnage will inevitably include broken artillery wheels, odd rifles and other weapons, and natural objects such as pebbles and stone chippings, dry twigs and the like will readily be thought of. (Teague, *Discovering Modelling for Wargamers*, contains many hints.) Broken revetments, rutted roads, scorched and ruined buildings are all available, as are domestic articles such as tables, chairs, mugs, and plates. Indeed, Phoenix Enterprises have produced a polystyrene pressed-out interior, occupying three sides of an oblong, which the purchaser may paint and then arrange his figures and accessories (also supplied by the firm) as a conversation piece. This, again, eliminates the necessity of the painting of a sky or other drop cloth, the part of a diorama which inevitably proves the ability of the artist to tackle something other than a uniform. The makers of wargame figures have gone one better, and have issued complete sets of diorama equipment, particularly for the Second World War (e.g. Micromold), and Hinchliffe not only produce battle lay-outs but the models to scale.

We are indebted to Marcel Baldet for much valuable

information on early dioramas. One of the earliest appears to be that of the Battle of Dettingen, the models used being cast in continuous strips, the infantry 6mm, the cavalry 11-12mm. It was made by a 'former Guards officer' after a survey made by Le Seigne, 'the General of Engineers and later engineer in charge of constructions for the King'. It is in the Musée de l'Armée in Paris, as is another, much more impressive, diorama of the Battle of Lodi, executed in 1804 by Martin Boitard, on Napoleon's orders. It is 50 x 67 inches, incorporates wonderfully realistic shell-torn buildings and has a remarkable atmosphere of suspense. The models are not quite half-round, 15mm for the infantry, 25mm for the cavalry, and each is stuck into the ground by a single pin. Extreme ingenuity is apparent in the making of the accessories, with paper being used for saddle-cloths, belts, etc, and cardboard for gun-carriages and wagons. Unfortunately, many of the figures are now in very frail condition. At the same Museum can be seen a remarkable model of the 'Bridges of Paris', the perspective owing much to the *vues optiques* of the period. The figures, carved in wood, are by Thirot, who made the model in 1817. Another fine diorama of the 'Arrival of the Duke of Orléans at the Town Hall in Paris, 1830' by Pierre-Louis Foulley is peopled with 20mm figures, which, though individually clumsy, are remarkably impressive as a whole. This is at the Musée Carnavalet. Another early diorama is at Lucerne Glacier Garden. In 1798 a young man named Niederost watched from the heights of Illgau the bloody Battle of the Muothatal Valley. It made such an impression on him that he spent two years making a model of it, using semi-flat one-inch-tall figures. In 1927 Alfred Ternisien donated his princely collection of flats and solids to the Museum at Compiègne, where they have been arranged in dioramic style. The most impressive display is that of the Battle of Waterloo, which took the maker, Laurent, eighteen years to complete. Another, of a Review of the French Army in 1901, by Alfred Silhol, took thirty-two years. Solid figures, by Baldet and Durand-Grimaldi, occur in a diorama of the return of the ashes of Napoleon I to France. There are other fine dioramas in most of the French museums, not least being those executed under the partnership of Lelièpvre and Métayer.

In Germany it is an essential part of model-collecting and the line is not drawn at flats or 54mm solids. The main place of pilgrimage is the Castle of Plassenburg, at Kulmbach in Bavaria, where the massive display of dioramas is constantly being added to. Switzerland also has its centres of attraction, notably at Coppet Castle, while in Italy there are numerous examples, some involving the use of paper-sheet figures. A small diorama at Bethnal Green Museum using semi-solids, and with a documentary history dating it accurately to 1834, is German in origin, and the first English products that we can trace are the pair of panoramas constructed by Captain Siborne to illustrate various aspects of the Battle of Waterloo. The first, an overall view, uses thousands of pin-size models, but the second, that of a single period of the battle, has recognizable models, even with removable breast-plates. In the 1930s Milliken showed the way at Croydon with a series of incidents, mainly of a non-military nature, but the towering figure in early English diorama-making was

28 **Diorama.** *Troops on foremost river bank by Métayer; the others and setting by Lelièpvre. 54mm solids. (Lelièpvre).*

undoubtedly Denny Stokes, collaborating with Gottstein and others in the production, with flats, of perfect scenes illustrating English history that were at one time a magnet for all collectors (*See* Royal United Service Institution). When flats became unobtainable he enlisted the services of Greenwood and Ball, using 20mm solids. This collaboration led to other work, including a 'Battle for Freedom' series shown in 1947, and 'Proclaim Freedom', depicting Jewish history. Stokes, although semi-retired, was still working until his death, and there are many examples of his craft in English museums.

Since the end of the Second World War the diorama has spread rapidly, and there is hardly a regimental or civic museum that does not possess at least one example. Some are quite small, others very large, and employ all kinds of visual aids and effects (e.g. at Yeovilton). Many are the work of museum staffs, but on occasion the aid of a local collecting group is sought. Even stately homes are finding that dioramas swell their takings (e.g. Wilton House, Woburn Abbey), and there has arisen a whole school of professional commissioned dioramists (e.g. Kemplay, Valhalla). In the United States the emphasis on the whole was originally on over-size models (e.g. the Marine Corps Museum, Quantico), the figures in bees-wax or Duron, but there are many in smaller sizes, even 20mm (e.g. Crécy at West Point). Perhaps the most remarkable solo effort was that of the Pfabs in creating the Kennesaw Battlerama, at Kennesaw, Georgia, using a colossal number of 54mm solids of their own making. The work of a club is shown in the creations by members of the Military Collectors of New England of fourteen dioramas of the War of Independence entitled 'They Nobly Dared' in 1975 for the American Mutual Insurance Company, and later for the Fine Arts Museum at Boston, while at Sandwich Plantation the Cookes have placed the vast Lilly collection in appropriate settings and added many models of their own. In Vancouver the Rays have used a huge inherited collection of hollow-casts, have purchased thousands of plastics and have made many of their own, together with all the accessories, to create a whole series of tableaux, military and civil, as a permanent exhibition entitled 'Fields of Glory'. As a family effort this is comparable to that of the Pfabs. The most remarkable example we have come across is the 'D-Day Landing on the Normandy Coast' at the Canadian War Museum, Ottawa. Here the scheme incorporates a full-size model of a German soldier looking through the slit of a simulated concrete pill-box. As the catalogue says, 'You brush him aside and gaze on the activity three hundred yards away.' Added to this, not only are there natural battle sounds in evidence, but also the smell of oil and cordite. The models are 20mm wargame conversions, with plastic-kit landing barges, tanks, planes and the like. But perhaps the most impressive of all dioramas using solids are to be seen at the Australian War Memorial at Canberra — a whole series of three-to-six-inch-high models — and it is refreshing to know that the art flourishes on the other side of the world. It took years to complete, and a group of twenty-odd sculptors and dioramists were employed. This is perhaps not remarkable in itself, but is unique in that each has a distinguished career in the arts in general.

Diorama Construction Sets. *See* Verlinden, F.

Diorama Miniaturas Militares (A.J.C. Cutileiro), Lisbon (1843-). Manufacturers of a long range of semi-flats, still being cast from the original moulds. They are obtainable only from the Centro de Coleccionadores at Lisbon.

Diplo, Milan. Publishers of paper sheets of modern troops and Wild West figures.

Disney Productions, New York. Manufacturers of 54mm plastic figures derived from films.

Displayers Inc., New York. Makers of dioramas for museums.

Distributive Products Inc. *See* Grey Iron Casting Co.

Ditta Landi. *See* Landi.

Dixon's Miniatures (T.A. Dixon) Longwood, Huddersfield (1976-). Dixon worked for some years for a firm of model-makers before branching out on his own. A small range of 54mm solids in kit-form includes a Portuguese Irregular and a French Infantryman in fatigue dress (1796-1815) which had a badly-fitting head shaft. In 1977 he began 25mm wargame figures, starting with Mongols.

D.J.'s Miniatures (D.J. Porter), Arrada, Connecticut (1978-). Manufacturer of 'toy' soldiers with a difference. Designed by Greer, they feature American troops in Europe, 1914-1918, under the title 'Over There', and include groups lining up for food, complete with tables, utensils, and the like, being administered to by ladies of the Salvation Army.

Dobson & Crowther, Llangollen, N. Wales (1977). Publishers of a pre-pressed cardboard model of Caernarvon Castle.

Domage et Cie. *See* Acedo.

DOMES AND DUST COVERS. In recent years an increasing number of models have proved too large to fit into a normal case. Protection has therefore to be effected by the provision of either a dome or an oblong glass case. These in the past have proved both expensive and dangerous but their place has now been taken

by clear, strong, transparent plastic or perspex (e.g. Doyle, Historex, Titan, Drumbeat). Similarly, small dioramas can be housed in the same material (e.g. Decorator Speciality Co.).

Donath, Rudolf, Simbach-Inn, W. Germany. The most important agent for the distribution of flats by outstanding makers. Excellent as a businessman and equally courteous.

Donsco Inc., (1974). *See* Grey Iron Casting Co.

Donzé, Leon. *See* Barclay.

Doran, E., London (1928-35). Maker of 45-50mm hollow-casts. His was merely a reflected glory, by virtue of the fact that he began in partnership with Richard Courtenay. With him he produced a number of medieval models, sometimes in pairs, with the simple mark 'Patented'. Many of these formed the nucleus of Courtenay's later models.

Dorfler, Hans, Fürth (c.1890-1945). One of a number of German makers of 40mm semi-solids, and 70mm solids, similar to Heyde, who had a regular export business to England. These were mainly of European armies, the riders detachable. He, however, made better quality 6cm models of Frederick the Great and German pre-war mounted troops.

Dorset Box. *See* Segal, P.

Dorset Soldiers (Giles S. Brown), Shaftesbury, Dorset (1975-). Adaptations of original Britains, with some original designs, all solid. A range of additional heads and arms for old hollow-casts is available. In 1978 he began a 'Women at War' series, and added wargame models in 25mm.

Douchkine, Vladimir, Paris. '*Peintre de figurines plats*' (*Origine du Musée de la Figurine Historique, Compiègne,* c.1950). He assisted in the painting of the R.U.S.I. diorama flats, and his specimens may be seen in many collections. Amazingly he was still collaborating with Denny Stokes in 1975.

DOUGH. *See* Edible Models.

Douglas, J. *See* Castile Miniatures.

Douglas Miniatures (J.D. Johnston), Leicester, (1969-). He began making 54mm solids some years before 1969, but ill-health prevented any activity for some years. When he recommenced he added 20mm models and restored the defunct Skybird wargame figures. His models include a clansman, a Royal Fusilier (1689), a Mahdi warrior, an Aztec, a Russian Guard Grenadier, a British Pikeman (1540), 19th-century troops, First and Second World Wars and, in 20mm, the Marlborough, Cromwellian and Napoleonic eras. In 1974 he changed the title from Douglas Miniatures to M.J. Mode, and began redesigning existing models and adding new ones. In 1977 he started making traditional 'toy' soldiers designed by A. Rose. (*See also* On Parade.)

Downes, W.H., USA. Author of *The Tin Army of the Potomac. See* Wargames.

Doyle, Ronald, Newquay, Cornwall (1974). Manufacturer of plastic domes.

Dragon Miniatures (John Holt) Glasgow (1978-). Maker of 25mm science fiction models.

Dragon Tooth (Tom Loback), USA (1977-). Maker of 'fantasy' models in roughly 25mm. An incredibly tasteless collection of evil beings, Indian animal-headed gods, unicorns, hippogryphs, etc., clumsily produced and reeking with flash. A large dragon, in six pieces, is quite frightening.

'**Dragoon Models**'. *See* Jarvis, D.

Drapkin, Major, & Co., London. *See* Cigarette Cards.

Dressler, Dresden (fl.c.1870). Flats. Specimens may be seen at the Staatliches Museum fur Volkunst at Dresden. (*Ortmann*)

Drewson, M. and **Jones, P.** *See* British Bulldog.

Dreyer, Carl, Copenhagen. Maker of composite 16cm caricatures, mainly of non-military subjects.

Droste, Dr F. von, Marbach/Neckar (1915-). Maker and editor of a large and continuing series of the Thirty Years' War in flats, designed by Madlener and engraved by S. Maier II and Lecke, and a series of Austrian Dragoons in bivouac during the Seven Years' War.

DRPA, Germany (c.1935) Tin-plate artillery and vehicles.

Drumbeat (John Davis), Cheltenham/Painswick (1975-). Manufacturer of plastic covers. In 1977 he began the exclusive marketing of 'toy' soldiers designed by Walter and Witts in boxed sets entitled 'Militia Models'. In 1979 the makers withdrew from his sponsorship and set up on their own as 'Militia Models Worldwide'.

Du Bois, J.E. Hanover (1830-c.1890). One of the most intelligent and able makers of 3-7cm flats. Beginning as engraver to Wegmann, he had his own business by 1830. This was continued by his son Ernst Conrad. The moulds (seldom signed) are in the Vaterlandisches Museum. A stickler for accuracy, he catered for the emergent interest of the collector. Most famous for his Hanoverian army (displayed at Celle in 1956), troops of 1816, a portrait model of General Hugh Halkett, the surrender of Cambronne at Waterloo, a medieval knight with movable arm and visor, Napoleonic troops and mamelukes, and Romans on horse and on foot one set of which was sold at auction in London in 1969. Evidence of the emergence of the German solid is shown in the elder DuBois' group of 30cm models, comprising ten figures, dating from 1839, made for the King of Hanover, and a pair of the King's German Legion (both exhibited at Celle in 1956). There is some doubt as to a collection of 140 figures made for Frederick William III. Baldet discovered two specimens in the Phillipot Collection. He found them to be of Britannia metal, screwed to an iron base. Previously assigned to DuBois, Baldet considered them to be by Söhlke. Mark: Vgl. duBois

Ducal Models (Jack and Thelma Duke) Eastleigh, Hants (1975-). Britains-style revivals in solid, made under the patronage of 'Under Two Flags'. Originally entitled 'Dukeson Models'.

Ducker, P.B. *See* Toydell.

Duesing, Gustav, Hamburg. Publisher of flats.

Duffy, Thomas E., Mahopac, New York. About 1965 he issued a pamphlet illustrating a series of eleven 54mm solids, consisting of the Court of Frederick the Great, complete with chairs and a harpsichord. No amount of correspondence brought any reply, and we know nothing further of them.

Duke, Jack and **Thelma**. *See* Ducal Models

Dukeson Models. *See* Ducal models.

Dulcop Italiana, Italy. Manufacturer of 54mm plastics, designed by Leonardo Bozzetti.

Dullap Models, Italy. Manufacturers of 54mm plastics.

Dumesnil, Paris (c.1965-). Maker of commissioned 54mm models. These are facially distinguished, with real fur on hats and packs. All are of French military subjects. He also makes models of French peasant costume. [*Goldstein*]

Dunbee Combex Marx Group. *See* Marx Miniatures.

Dunekate, L. Germany. One of the painters employed on the R.U.S.I. dioramas.

Dunham, White & Co. Ltd, London (fl.1929). Manufacturers of 54mm hollow-casts. A short-lived firm with a limited range of a mounted Guards Officer and Standard Bearer and a few Highlanders on foot.

Durand, Rev. Sir Dickon, Bart. *See* Wooten, Peter.

Durand-Grimaldi, Paris. Assisted Ballada in the creation of several dioramas including the 'Return of the Ashes of Napoleon I' at Compiègne.

Durham, Keith. *See* New Hope Design.

Duro, Germany (c.1925-1946). Manufacturers of poor quality composition models.

Durolin, Brno, Czechoslovakia (c.1925-1936). Manufacturers of Elastolin-type models, but smaller and cruder. Taken over by Elastolin in 1936.

Durso, Germany (fl.1935). Manufacturers of poor quality composition models.

Dusch, Strasbourg (c.1872-80). Publisher of paper sheets.

Dusing, Gustav, Hamburg (1977-). Publisher of flats of the 20th century. (*Klio*)

Duvinage and Harinkonck, Paris. The Paris Exposition of 1867 contained a Roman baggage wagon drawn by oxen with attendant soldiers, all carved in wood and signed.

E

Eagle Miniatures (Paul Shingle), Barry, Glamorgan (1976-). Maker of 54mm solids in kit form. He began with a French First World War pilot, an Indian officer of the Gurkha Rifles (1880), a French Foreign Legionnaire, a United States Marine (1928) and a sadistic Hun. These were followed by a set of 7 models to commemorate the 'Last Stand at Gandamack', Genghis Khan and Florence Nightingale with patients. The following year saw the appearance of models in 90mm.

Eagle Wall Plastics Ltd, Dorking, Surrey (fl.1959). Manufacturers of Dan Dare characters in 54mm plastics; no mark.

Eastman, Max. See Cameo.

Eberhardt, Eritz, Delmenhorst, W. Germany (1979-). Publisher of flats.

Eberhardt, Klaus, Elmenhorst, W. Germany (1977-). Publisher of flats of ancient times and 19th-20th century. (Klio)

E.B.V.-Product, Hamburg. Flats of Napoleonic troops exhibited at the Nuremberg Trade Fair, 1975.

Eccles Brothers Molding, Burlington, Iowa. Purchasers of old home-cast moulds, from which they re-cast, and of American metal figures. In 1978 they reissued four of the original Barclay figures.

Echeverria, Jorge Hernandez, Barcelona (1965-70). A gifted maker of 54mm solids to commission.

Eckel, M. D'Allemagne states that in 1845 a certain Monsieur Eckel proposed to establish an industry whereby all toys hitherto made of lead or of tin could be made of carton-comprimé, the weapons only being made of metal. These had success for a number of years, and d'Allemagne illustrates a diorama using these figures made at the time of the Crimean War.

EDIBLE MODELS. Strange as it may seem, such did and do exist. (1) Brotteig, made of gum-tragacanth, sugar and meal, hardened in moulds and then painted, were popular in Swabia from the 17th to the 19th century. Usually about 4 to 6cm in height, when painted they assumed a sheen not unlike porcelain. Peter III certainly possessed a number, and a few may be seen at Kulmbach.

(2) Dough. This was used by an enthusiast to the extent of two thousand figures, suitably painted, decorating an organ at the Altdorf Museum, to celebrate the Battle of Waterloo. Very naive (See illustration 113 in Nicollier.)

(3) Gingerbread. Gingerbread moulds were a commonplace on the Continent, and many outstanding military examples exist.

(4) Sugar. The Great Exhibition of 1851 produced nothing but marvels, including an assortment of 'toys made of sugar' by Froeglen.

Ediciónes Recontables. See Toray.

Editions Nouveau Brunier, Paris (c.1935). Publisher of paper sheets, including one of 17 pieces depicting St Louis dispensing justice, and one of the coronation of Napoleon. (Newman)

Editions Volumetrics, Paris (1930-49). Publishers of $9\frac{1}{2}$ x $12\frac{1}{2}$ inch cardboard buildings.

Editorial Roma. See Roma (Editorial).

Edizioni Europa, Italy (c.1950-). Paper sheets, printed on both sides, and pre-cut, for the connoisseur.

Edman, Ab. Jan, Vagnhärad, Sweden (1958-). Distributors of Prins August series of moulds for home-casting, the originals being from designs by Eriksson, in 40mm size and easily the best of their kind. In 1979 a 25mm range designed by Christopher Tubb was added. The Company is now run by Lars Edman, son of the founder.

Edmonds, Yvonne. See Sentry Box, The.

Educoll UNICEF (1977). Issued four cut-out sheets on stiff card of models of African villages.

Eggiman, F., Aarau (1800-30). Engraver of flats for Gottschalk. Mark: E. EGGIMAN; FE.

EG-Toys (Ezio Guggiari) Argentina, (1955-). Manufacturer of 54-60mm hollow-casts, mainly of peasants of the Argentine. Riders are detachable. The trademark occasionally appears on the seat. In 1960 they turned over to the making of plastic models. [Basseterre]

Ehrlich, Robert, Leipzig (1849-?). Producer of flats.

Eichhorn, Johannes, Grossenheim-Naundorf. Producer of flats of the Thirty Years' War, designed by Walter Dietrich, and himself a designer and engraver.

Eichhorn, Klaus, Erfurt, E. Germany. Maker of flats. (Katalog der Formen, 1976)

Eichinger, Austria. Painter of dioramic backgrounds, as at Schloss Pottenbrunn.

Eidai, Japan. Manufacturers of polystyrene tank kits and figures in plastic. In 1974 they issued a diorama setting for the Second World War complete with a stronghold, gun emplacements, vehicles and look-out figures.

Eikon Verlag & Druck Asta Gobel, Grafath/Amper. Listed as an exhibitor of flats at the Kulmbach exhibition of 1973.

Einco Battle Packs, Hong Kong (1976–). Atrocious 25mm polystyrene piracies.

EIRE. The first mention of model soldiers being produced in the Republic of Eire was the ill-fated venture of Comet in establishing a factory at Spiddal, Co. Galway in 1947–48 under the auspices of the Irish Government for the production of Eriksson's Authenticast models and for semi-flats. A long lull followed, when the collectors had to rely on imports. Around the 1970s, however, the enthusiasm of Henry Harris and Shamus Wade led to the formation of a society which, in turn, produced a number of private makers and the opening of several model shops. The museums even began to take notice (e.g. Haulbowline Naval HQ, Cork Public Museum, the Curragh). Collectors now have contacts with all parts of the world and their varied tastes are indicated by their collections.

EKO, Valladolid, Spain. Manufacturers of polystyrene AFVs and other vehicles. Known previously as pirates of Airfix 20mm figures. In 1977 they began making 54mm metal kits.

EKO series. *See* Almirall.

Elastolin Fabrikaten (Otto & Max Hausser) Ludwigsberg/Neustadt bei Coburg (1904–). A firm pre-eminent in the making of large composition models for the toy trade, and later for polystyrene models of a different style and quality. The combination of glue, sawdust and linseed oil, when fused and compressed together, was discovered about 1850, and was used mainly for the manufacture of large dolls. It was improved upon and first used for smaller objects by Pfeiffer of Vienna in 1898. The Hausser brothers, formerly trading under the name of Muller & Freyer, toy manufacturers and wholesalemen in dolls, absorbed the Pfeiffer firm in 1904 (*Polaine*). The first models to appear were 10 to 14cm animals, military types in 7cm being issued in 1912. The peculiar substance of which the figures were made necessitated the use of wire armatures, and the result was a plaster-like oil-painted model, with plugged-in heads and a minimum of detail, standing on very thick bases. (Hawkins says that the very early models were first carved in wood, and then transposed into composition.) The figures from 1912 to the early 1920s often sported moustaches. At the same time the firm issued tin-plate vehicles, the later ones with rubber wheels. These were added to by the purchase in 1925 of the firm of Tipple Topple, which was one of Pfeiffer's subsidiaries. Otto Hausser died in 1956, his sons Kurt and Rolfe, who both joined the firm in 1930, being the present owners.

Owing to war demands, production of composition figures ceased in 1943, when the plant was switched to making wooden objects, but making of figures recommenced in 1946.

Before the advent of the Third Reich Hausser made a number of personality figures, including Frederick the Great, Ziethen, Seydlitz (mounted), Hindenburg and Washington. With the advent of the Hitler régime concentration began on the portrayal of German troops, to the virtual exclusion of other nations. In fact, it can safely be said that practically every aspect of the German war-machine was portrayed. In 1936, probably

29 **Elastolin.** *Typical examples in various sizes. (Author).*

at the instigation of the Nazi hierarchy, special portrait models of the Axis leaders were made in many poses and uniforms, some having movable arms and a few with faces of porcelain. In 1938 'goose-stepping' troops were first introduced, together with riflemen firing explosive caps and electric rat-tat-tat machine guns (*Polaine*). The models that were not of German troops were made by repainting existing figures. Anomalies inevitably occurred: British Lifeguardsmen appeared on white horses and British infantry wore brown boots, while an 'English Goldstream Guard' is an amusing entry in their 1972 catalogue. Wild West scenes were also popular, including as they did covered wagons, buffaloes and scenic equipment, totem poles, teepees and camp-fires, and up to 1939 combatants of the First World War, with pigeon lofts, pontoon bridges and field emplacements. The horses (the riders removable) were naïve in the extreme, in some cases being mounted on wooden stands with wheels, even for horse-drawn vehicles and artillery. However, all their models more than held their own with other products, and were lavishly exported to England for many years, although the material was subject to deterioration by damp and easily chipped. After 1945 only non-military sets, such as Westerners, were allowed by the Allied Forces of Occupation, apart from a small set of the Swiss army, but Hawkins states that most ranges continued in their catalogues until 1968, and that he was able to purchase the old models direct from the factory in 1976. A few of the historical sets (e.g. the American War of Independence) were revived in 1978.

In the early 1940s Rolf Hausser carried out experiments in many forms of plastic, resulting in a completely new range of polystyrene models in 70 and 40mm of a most delightfully crisp and colourful character. These consisted of Romans, Vikings, Huns, Turks, medieval troops and Landsknechts, some of the riders being detachable from the saddles. These were accompanied by siege-engines, scaling-towers and cannon. Incredibly 'Gothick' castles, originally made in composition, were re-introduced in vacuum-formed plastic. Gone, happily, were the wheeled horses, the new ones being lively and full of movement. Outstanding were two sets of Nativity figures. In the early 1960s a short-lived range of malleable plastics was made, which Hawkins says are now extremely rare. Later (1974) the 'Swoppit' principle invented by Britains was adopted for entirely new designs of Westerners and knights, while Indians appeared on metal bases, as in Britains' 'Deetail' range. (Both these types are shown in the 1975 catalogue). Marks: ELASTOLIN; ELASTOLIN/GERMANY; ELASTOLIN (Cursive) /GERMANY, all within oval depressions. The firm has suffered much from Hong Kong piracies.

'El Cid' set. *See* Reamsa.

Elgström, Ossian, Sweden. Designer of a set of Lapps and reindeer for the firm of Tenngjuteriet Mars.

El Huinca, Argentina (1975–   ). Manufacturers of poor-quality 54mm plastic models, riders separate, in many ranges. [*Basseterre*]

'Elite Figures'. *See* Fabre, C.

Elite Figures (Geoffrey Phillipson), Oadby, Leicester (1973–5). Essentially a painting and diorama-making enterprise, Phillipson occasionally made an original 54mm model to commission. A 75mm range of originals

was contemplated by him in 1975, but nothing materialized.

Elite-Men, USA. An advertisement in *Soldier World*, 1974, carried an advertisement that Civil War generals in 54mm solids were being issued under this name. A few only were ever marketed.

Elite Toys, USA (c.1968). Monstrous 11-inch rubber-like playthings for the very juvenile market.

Ellem Action Models. *See* Cherilea.

Ellfeldt, Hans Gunter, Stuttgart (1912-14). Producer of 30mm flats.

'Ellison, George'. *See* New Hope.

Elzeverina y Libreria Co Imprenta, Barcelona (pre-1900). Publishers of paper sheets.

Embleton, G., England (1975–   ). Designer of a range of double-figures for Series 77, announced in 1975, and issued two years later.

Emerson, Arthur T. Jr. *See* Waterloo Galleries.

EMI. *See* S.A.E.

E.M.I. Ltd, London (c.1950–   ). Manufacturers of 54mm hollow-casts of the British Army in battledress, lettering on base very similar to that of Britains. [*Wade*]

Emmanueli, Italy. A professional painter of flats.

Emmanueli, Paris (fl.1961). Maker of commercial solids.

Emmerling, Joachim, Weimar (d.c.1970). A designer and engraver of flats, including a set for the Revolution of 1848-1849. Engraver for Bolling, Neumeister, Ochel, Ortmann, Otte and Pahle, and also collaborator with Staal. An expert painter. Mark: EW.

Empire Military Miniatures (F.J. Delez), Sheffield (1973-8). Although two 54mm solids, in kit-form, or assembled, were announced in 1973 they did not appear until two years later. As one was of General Gordon and the other a staff officer with sand-veil and goggles, it would appear that a 'Gordon Relief' series was contemplated. This was not, however, proceeded with, and other models of different types were then issued. Of these Dennis Johnson designed four, and transferred them in 1979 to his newly formed 'Mitrecap' range.

'Empire of the Petal Throne' series. *See* Old Guard.

Eneret, N.C.W., Copenhagen (20th century). Publishers of paper sheets of Danish troops, 1914-40.

Engels, A.G.F., Verden, W. Germany (1766-1841). Maker of flats in small quantities as a side-line. He made a copy (engraved on one side only) of the mounted knight in 7cm by Lorenz shown in plate 2 of Garratt, *Model Soldiers: a Collector's Guide*. Mark: A.G.F.E. His son, G.F.C. (1825-1914) carried on the business, signing his models G.F.E.

Ensign Miniatures. *See* Rowe, R.O.

'Entertainers, The', series. *See* Superior Models Inc.

Erdmann, Hesse, Germany, Designer of flats.

Ericson, Willie, Sweden. Designer of flats for Sivhed.

Erik, George, Wimbledon/Madrid/Tunbridge Wells (1963–   ). A designer of models of all kinds. The first we heard of was a 6-inch Robin Hood, made specially for sale in Nottingham only. About 1968 he went to Madrid to begin remodelling the original Reamsa figures. He was particularly successful with the humans in the El Cid set (which was spoiled by the adherence, probably at the insistence of the firm, to the original anachronistic horses), and portraits of bull fighters. A set of Spanish and French 1810 models was marred by production difficulties. In 1974 he opened a militaria shop in Tunbridge Wells, continuing his commerical designing

30 **Eriksson**. *30 and 45mm models (Author).*

for such firms as Subbuteo (non-military).

Eriksson, Holger, Karlstad (c.1946–   ). Maker of solids in 30, 40, 50, 54, 80 and 90mm sizes. He began carving 90mm equestrians in wood, but, turning to metal, soon started to interest the intelligent collector. He became a household word by his designs for Authenticast, at that time the only commercially produced models of superior quality. This led to his designing 30mm troops for the Swedish African Engineers, of which the castings were disgracefully inadequate. Although he issues a catalogue listing some 200 models in 30mm, 25 in 40mm, and 100 in 54mm (with additions, in 1977, of 85-90mm), he does not seek publicity and prefers to work to commission. For all this, in 1972 he produced a series of designs in 40mm of 18th-century Swedish troops, combatants in the Second World War, Westerners and sportsmen as home-castings for Ab.Jan Edman. He is revered on the Continent, where he has had an immense influence. His models are of the traditional style, sculpted as an entity, and, apart from Lelièpvre and Berdou, no one can design a better horse. His painting is simple but eloquent, and dignity is inherent in all his work. He makes no concessions to the latest trends of popular taste, and his models speak for themselves. The larger size models were begun in 1977.

Ernst, Jean, Brussels. Professional painter of solids.

Errington, Norman. *See* Greenwood and Ball (Pearce).

E.S.C.I. Modellistica, Italy (1974–   ). Manufacturers of polystyrene AFV kits and terrains. In 1975 William Hearne began designing figures for them, which may be the ones in plastic in 35mm of World War II advertised in 1977.

Eschleman, Samuel, USA. Designer for Grey Iron Casting Co.

Españocraft, Spain. Carved wood models, 2 feet high, polychromed, with gilt bases and a simulated antiquity, of the Napoleonic period. Seen once only at Hamleys in 1972.

Española de Juguetes-Garanta. *See* Monta-Plex.

Essayer, Nuremberg (fl.1851). Exhibited an open landau in lead at the Great Exhibition of 1851. It was 4 feet 6 inches in length and contained figures of Queen Victoria and the Prince Consort.

Estivill Cabot, Ignasi, Spain (1840-60). Publishers of paper sheets.

Établissements Brépols. *See* Brépols.

Etchells, Arthur, Philadelphia. A professional painter of solids.

Euller, Ch. *See* Imprimerie de Wissembourg.

Eulner, Halle (fl.1930). Maker of 30mm flats. At Leipzig in 1930 he exhibited a fine medieval town, trench-war-

fare in 1918, German army units of the 19th century, an Egyptian temple, and cars and vehicles in the round.

Euramerica, Madrid (1970–   ). Producers of paper sheets, especially of Wild West subjects.

Eureka American Soldiers (C.W. Beiser), New York (fl.1898–   ). 54mm solids, displayed on a cardboard tray with metal fixtures.

EVA (Ediciones Vasco Americana), Bilbao, Spain. Publishers of paper sheets of military subjects, together with buildings.

Evans, D., Canberra. Painter for the backdrops of the Australian War Memorial dioramas.

Evans, D. Runcorn, Cheshire (1974). At the age of 16 he made models in plastone for a diorama of the Battle of Alexandria for a history of the King's Regiment (8th of foot), exhibited at Liverpool Museum. A model he kindly sent to us arrived in fragments, and we wonder whether plastone is to be seriously considered as a vehicle for expression.

Everready Casting, USA (c.1930). A firm making home-casting moulds of three soldiers and three boy scouts.

EVOLUTIONS. The use of models to simulate drill exercises, or for the study of tactics, must be of some antiquity, but the first mention we can trace is of the 'little lead soldiers', 7cm high, which Heroard states that Louis XIII, when Dauphin, himself made in lead in 1610. They were pegged so as to fit into a board. Another Dauphin, Louis de France, Duc de Viennois (born 1661) son of Louis XIV, had a magnificent army of silver models, made by Jacob Wolrab, supervised by the great Colbert himself. They had automatic devices provided by Hans and Gottfried Hautsch, goldsmiths, silversmiths and compass-makers, and were from designs made by Vauban. 'They went through their usual manoeuvres very ably; they marched to left and right, doubled their ranks, lowered their weapons, struck fire, shot them off and retreated. Then the pike-men tried to knock the cavalry out of the saddles, but these were quite prepared to defend themselves by firing their pistols' [*Crump*]. In 1672 John Wells took out a patent for a very curious instructional toy: 'A certaine Engine which will be of very greate use and benefitt to the publique in teaching to performe by artificiall horses the usuall exercizes of a complete horseman, generally taught in academys: the running at the ring, throwing of the lannce, shooting of the pistoll, and takeing upp of the head, and that att such easy and cheappe rates as may encourage many to learne the same who are otherwise, by the greatnesse of the expense, prevented from acquireing the said exercizes.' In the 18th century quite a number of pamphlets accompanying picture blocks were issued by the well-known military publisher J. Millan, and these enjoyed a long period of popularity. Others of German origin are in the Castle Museum, York and the Queen's Own Hussars Museum, Warwick. A Mr West made similar items about 1797. Examples are in the Tower of London and the National Army Museum. Francis Edwards Ltd had a set in 1975, but without instructions. In 1973 Shamus Wade owned 'Military Drill Models. For Illustrating the Drill of a Squad, Company, Battalion, or Brigade, adapted to the plates of the Field Exercise and Evolutions of Infantry as revised in 1870. By Captain Gamble, Royal Marine Light Infantry. Harrison & Sons, Military Publishers, 59 Pall Mall, London.' This consisted of 59 wooden shapes in black and white, representing 11 different officers and NCOs and four different bodies of men, in a wooden box 4¾ x 7½ x 1¼ inches. At the Antiquarian Booksellers' Exhibition in 1972 an exhibitor had a three-tiered wooden box made about 1870, containing a large number of 40mm semi-solids obviously of German origin, the top shelf consisting of a mechanical device whereby the cavalry performed evolutions. During the European wars of the 19th century some ingenious devices were used. In Germany wooden horsemen were placed on springs; others on castors (Colmar Museum); specially large models were placed on planchettes; in 1832 Captain Augustus Wathen favourably impressed the War Office with his device of miniature rocking horses moved by springs; similar movements were performed with figures by Lieut-General Rozniecki in Poland. Trellis tongs were also much in use in England and in Europe in the 1860s–90s, and in America between 1880 and 1900, and are illustrated in the journals of the period. One is on view at the National Army Museum. Captain Rivière's 'Military Figures on a Mechanical Base for the practice of Company Drill' sounds very similar to the German models. A most unusual collection is that made for the King of Rome under Napoleon's direction by J.B. Claude Odiot, goldsmith, presented to the little King in 1812. These could be mounted by pins on a machine which moved the models in drill formation. They are fully described and illustrated in Harris, *Model Soldiers*. Those with a literary bent will remember the *Carnets de Capitain Coignet*, who demonstrated tactical theories by means of 200 wooden soldiers. (*See also* Automata.)

Ewart, Lieutenant-Colonel, Stockholm. Creator of 10 dioramas, using 25-30mm flats, at the Arme Museum, Stockholm.

Ewer, K. *See* Colonial Craftsmen Pewter Workshop.

Ewers, Raymond, Australia (1917–). Employed on the Australian War Memorial dioramas.

Ewing, Houston, Texas. In 1975 he commissioned Søren Brunoe to make six models of the American Revolution.

Excalibur Miniatures, Arlington, Massachusetts (1976–) Re-issuing Cockade miniatures. [*Pielin*]

Excelsior-Immagini (E. Grixoni), Rome. Publishers of paper sheets printed in colour, including a magnificent one of the Papal Court and the Papal Guard.

EXHIBITIONS. No collector wishes to hide the light of his collection under a bushel. Short of inviting the public to visit him, he perforce places his models on view, so that many who would never otherwise see them may have the benefit of assessing their quality or interest. Not only is the individual collector thus involved but, in joining with others of a kindred nature, the hobby is en-

riched and the sight of hundreds of models at a time, while indigestible to some, is instrumental in the making of new collectors. The aspiring maker of original models, the painting enthusiast, the 'modeller' of plastic kits, the converter of metal models, the wargame participant, are all able to display their frequently excellent productions. So many exhibitions are staged so often in so many places by so many societies that the healthiness of the hobby is self-evident. To the purist there might seem to be a danger that with such a welter of talent saturation point must at some time be reached, especially as model soldiers (mainly conversions) are now included in alien exhibitions. An important aspect of the exhibition is the interest shown by city and town councils in the recording of a special event, such as the Battle of Hastings or the Battle of Tewkesbury. On occasions this leads to the permanent acquisition of a diorama for posterity to view. In the earlier days of the hobby an exhibition was a rarity. Probably the most important one ever staged was that held at Leipzig in 1930 under the auspices of 'Klio'. This consisted of an immense number of dioramas, all of flats, by the finest makers of the time and incorporating Heinrichsens. It set alight a latent desire for the finer models. Similar in concept was an exhibition arranged by Mauke at Castel Sant' Angelo in Rome in 1937. In England E.K. Milliken, with far-seeing vision, staged a show of his own creative dioramas, this time using solids, in the 1930s. The creation of the former exhibition of dioramas at the R.U.S.I. Museum, overseen by Denny Stokes, led to separate temporary exhibitions of his own dioramas, using both flats and solids, which attracted much attention. The most important temporary assembly staged by the British Model Soldier Society was held at the R.U.S.I. to commemorate the Battle of Waterloo, which brought together models by the finest makers of the day (many specially made for the occasion) and attracted a great number of overseas enthusiasts. The latest and finest display of models is the annual series staged by the *Club Italiano* at the Sforza Castle, where master makers are invited to contribute. The ones held from 1974 onwards produced some magnificent pieces, mainly from Italy and Denmark. (English makers, though approached, sent no models.) Permanent exhibitions are listed in the Supplement.

Exin Lines Bros SA, Barcelona. In 1972 they issued a polystyrene castle ('Exincastillos'), or what they called a castle, together with a rabble of incredibly bad 25mm models of all periods pirated from Elastolin and others, including a ghost!

'Exploding Trench, The'. *See* Britain, William, Ltd.

'Eyes Right' series. *See* Britain, William, Ltd.

F

FA, Germany. Named by Hampe as an engraver of flats using the initials FA. Even Kollbrunner cannot trace his place of origin or the date at which he worked.

Fabbrica Italiana Giocattoli Infrangibili Roma. *See* FIGIR.

Fabbrica Nationale d'Immagini (E. de Castiglione & Co.) Milan (c.1895-1917). Publishers of paper sheets.

Fabbrica Nationale d'Immagini. *See* Macchi Elizeo.

Faber. *See* Carman; Riviere.

Fabergé, Carl, Russia (1846-1920). His workmen made a number of military models, usually about 12cm, in semi-precious stones, enamelled and jewelled. A full review of his work is found in Kenneth Snowman's *The Art of Carl Fabergé*.

Fabre, Christian L., Upper Derby, Pennsylvania (c. 1965-). Originally a collector who occasionally made a 6 inch model for his personal pleasure, he later became a designer of models of the German Army of the First World War, Napoleonic cuirassiers and the modern French Army which, in 1971, he entitled 'Elite Figures'. He has designed for Cavalier and Monarch.

Fabrication Belge, Brussels (c.1965). Manufacturer of 60mm plaster composition figures of poor quality, in the early Elastolin style.

Fabrique des Feuilles, Nancy (c.1815). Publishers of paper sheets.

Fairbanks, Douglas, Jr, USA. A famous actor whose collection (mainly of Britains, with some Courtenays and other makers) made astounding prices at Phillips' Auction Rooms in 1977.

Fairylite, Hong Kong (fl.1965). Blatant and crude piracies in 40mm polystyrene of Berliner and others.

FAKES. *See* Piracy.

Falcao, Ricardo. *See* Lito Lusitania.

Falchi, Alda. *See* Grossman, Dave, Designs Inc.

'Falcon' series. *See* Greenwood and Ball (Pearce).

Faller, W., Germany. Manufacturers of polystyrene AFV kits.

Falucho, Argentina (fl.1950-65). Maker of a small series of 54mm solid models for use with vehicles and wheeled equipment.

'Famous Fighters' series. *See* Timpo.

'Famous Historical Characters'. *See* Blue Box/Red Box.

Fantasyland, Hong Kong (1975-). Crude metal 20mm Second World War models sold in packets of 24 for use with AFVs. [*Anton*]

Farish, Graham, Ltd, London (fl.1950-53). A commercial firm which had many interests, model soldiers being in the nature of a sideline. For the Coronation of Queen Elizabeth II they commissioned the then hardly-known Russell Gammage and Lieut-Colonel Nicholson to make a series of models which received immediate acclamation. At the same time they commissioned other models, including hussars, Frederick, Duke of York, a high-lander, an officer of the Horse Guards (1821), Bonnie Prince Charlie, and military fashions of the 1830s from Nicholson, and a King John from Niblett, which, how-ever, according to Gammage, was never issued.

Farmer, Stephen. *See* Old Campaign Figures.

Farnham, George, Loughborough. Instigator of, and painter for, the model of the Battle of Bosworth at Ambion Farm.

Fasoli, C. and Ohlmann, 'Strasbourg (1840-50). Publishers of paper sheets.

Fechner, Werner, Schwäbish-Hall. Publisher of flats, mentioned as having exhibited at Kulmbach in 1973.

Federal Sales Co., USA (1942). Publishers of candy and chewing gum cards, pre-cut, pressed-out figures, $2\frac{3}{4}$ x $4\frac{1}{2}$ inches, of a tank officer, of Marines advancing through gas, using hand grenades, and a machine-gunner attacking a tank under fire. (*Newman*)

Feldwick, Martin, London (1977-). Designer for Sea Gull and Starcast.

Feltham, J.C., Canberra. A constructor of models for army exercises, and responsible for the diorama 'A Village in Vietnam' at the Australian War Memorial.

Felton, Donald G. *See* Tru-Craft.

Fenerin, William, USA. A professional painter employed by Cowan.

Fenton, Ian. *See* Cody Models.

Ferguson, Michael. *See* Soldiers Unlimited.

Ferguson, Neil, London. A professional painting service advertised in 1973.

Fermor, A. *See* Frontier.

Ferner, Andreas, Nuremberg (c.1880-1937). Apprenticed to Stadtler, and later an engraver of flats for Scheller, Heinrichsen and Schirmer, and of semi-solids for Spenküch.

Fessard, Paris (fl.1844-51). The *Almanach Bottin* states that during these years Fessard made '*jouets d'un*

31   **Fabre.** *Solid 6 inches.*
An early example.

nouveau genre: bivouacs, combats, figures imitant le natural avec yeux en émail mobiles'. We have no way of telling the size of these models, or the material used.

FF, Belgium (c.1945). Manufacturers of old Elastolin-like models, the only ones seen being of US troops. [*Anton*]

FGT. *See* Taylor & Barrett.

FHQ, Rochester, New York (1979–). Reproductions of Britains' models in solid.

Fibreglass. Literally glass in fibre form, sold in rolls in either woven mat or chopped strand form. (*See* Composite Models.)

FIBREGLASS. Literally glass in fibre form, sold in rolls in either woven mat or chopped strand form. (*See* Composite Models.)

FIBREGLASS RESIN. Polyester resin, used to bond fibreglass, the two materials when bound together often referred to as resin-fibreglass: (*See* Composite Models.)

Fiedler, Harry, Berlin (1979–). Publisher of flats.

'Fields of Glory'. *See* Ray, Don and Honey.

Fife & Drum Miniatures (John Gross), Havertown, Pennsylvania (1977–). Metal 'toy' soldiers sculpted by R. Bonham, starting with Apache scouts. These were withdrawn as unacceptable, and replaced by others made by Greer.

'Fighting Men of The British Empire' series. *See* Franklin Mint.

FIGIR (Fabbrica Italiana Giocattoli Infrangibili Roma (Francesco Antonini) Rome (1927–). Manufacturer of naive 55mm solids of the Italian army, the French 18th century and Napoleonic periods, Romans, Uhlans, Bavarians, Bengal Lancers, and other types, comprising a vast range. Although poor in quality, they enjoy immense popularity in Italy, equalling that of Britains in England. More recently they moulded the same range in 55mm plastic, with the addition of the American Civil War and Westerners. In 1974 they negotiated with Pranzetti for him to use his designs for wooden models to be turned into metal. There is no evidence that this ever transpired.

Figur (Le Soldat de Plomb Historique) (Commandant H.

Borie), Ablon, Seine et Oise (fl.1950-65). A maker of 30mm semi-solids and flats. In 1956 his catalogue listed several ranges, obtainable in five different ways:
1. Box of 5 infantry (officer, colours 3 infantry).
2. Box of 10 infantry (officer, colours, musician, 7 infantry).
3. Box of 5 cavalry.
4. Box of 20 infantry (mounted officer, colours, 6 musicians and sappers, 12 infantry).
5. Box of 10 cavalry (officer, standard bearer, trumpeter, 7 troopers).

For collectors, certain figures were mounted on socles, and beautifully painted, usually consisting of two to four figures, including a 'personality range'. The models have always been difficult to obtain outside France, except in the United States. The small range of flats that he produced were designed by Rousselot and engraved by Pepin.

Figur Brevett, Italy (1969–). Manufacturer of clumsy 60mm plaster composition models of the Vatican Guards. These break easily and the paint chips.

Figurines Historiques. *See* Mokarex.

Figurines Karlis (Carlos Maria Naon) Buenos Aires (fl.1950-70). Maker of commissioned 54mm solids of the 18th-19th century. A collector of rare intelligence, liberal in imparting his knowledge.

Fillge, G.G. and E.C. *See* Juersch Boghandel.

Finestein, Anne. *See* Carlton, Anne, Studio.

FINLAND. The remotest country in Europe, Finland seems to have seldom taken any interest in the model soldier. The fact that its physical geography consists mainly of innumerable lakes interspersed with vast forests, and that it has only occasionally been involved (albeit with tragic consequences) in actual warfare, may account for its lack of interest. Gripenberg has been unable to trace more than one maker of flats, Eric Lodin, who, surprisingly, flourished about 1782 to 1801. Apprenticed between 1777 and 1782 to a Swedish tinsmith who never made a model soldier, he settled in Finland in 1786, and carried on a unique manufacture of naive pre-Hilpertian-style troops, a number of which are to be seen at the Borga Museum and in Finland's National Museum. No one else seems to have followed his lead, and the sole modern representative we have been able to trace is Lohmann. No society exists, but today there are a number of collectors of all types of models.

Fischbach, G. and Kieffer, F. *See* Kieffer, F.

Fischer, Herbert, Munich. Producer of flats, including a set of 150 of the French Revolution (including sailors), a balloon ascent, and war elephants, with figures to be placed in the howdahs.

Fischer, Johann Ernst, Halle (c.1800). Maker and engraver of flats. A set of Olympian figures formerly ascribed to Fleegel are now thought to be by him. (*Kollbrunner*)

Fischer Thermoplastics (Kai Reisler) Norway-Denmark (1958–). Manufacturer of poor quality 54mm plastics, heavily influenced by Timpo, of battledress troops, Arabs (some mounted), firemen, and some farm and wild animals derived from Herald.

Fischtner, L., Reuthingen (fl.1950-60). Maker of 30mm flat trees suitable for dioramas.

Flacke, Dieter, Schönebeck a.d. Elbe, E. Germany. Maker of flats. (*Katalog der Formen, 1976*)

FLASH. The extraneous material left on a figure after casting. This occurs particularly on mould joins, on thin weapons, under legs and arms, between the head of a horse and its bridle, etc. The model issued by the scrupulous maker (e.g. Rowe, Gammage, Stadden) is presented to the public with these excrescences removed, but many a model, especially in kit form, bears witness to hasty production and lack of checking. The worst case we have ever seen was on a set of Strombecker figures, where the flash assumed the proportions of a shoulder pack. Especially bad are some wargame models. Normans by Hinton had the lance and the pennon of the mounted knights joined to the body, and the studs projecting from the feet were intolerable. Any model showing such flash should be returned to the maker for cleaning up or replacement. Small quantities may be removed by paring down with a sharp blade, but with hard metal a small file may be necessary. Flats on the whole normally require a smaller amount of attention. Plastic figures are not so easy to trim, as the material tends to rough up, but polystyrene carves quite easily.

Flasshaar, Alphonse, Berlin (1965–). A reviver of the medieval jointed wood and metal tilting knights, with removable riders, in 50cm. These are most attractive, being based on specimens in Continental museums.

FLATS. The English description of a thin, silhouette-like model, barely a millimetre in thickness, known in Germany as *zinnfigur* and in France as *plat d'étain*. It is as different in its philosophy from the solid as chalk is from cheese. The principle of its manufacture is basically the same: two separately engraved moulds clamped together and tin alloy poured through. When drainage has occurred a resultant figure emerges; but whereas the round model can be viewed from all sides, the flat can be seen only from the front and the rear; it is the engraving and painting that brings it to life. There is a wide gap between the two styles that is not bridged by the hybrid semi-flat, and the *zinnfigur* has remained the predominant German contribution to the art from its inception to the present day, even though challenged from time to time by Germanic makers of solids and semi-solids; other countries, although in some cases commencing with flats, or taking to them later, have produced but a tithe of the millions that have been issued over the centuries. Discounting the archaic specimens which were made in ancient times, the first concerted attempts at the making of tiny, flat objects in tin occurred early in the Middle Ages, and these were mainly of a religious nature. The 'Pilgrims' tokens' found in England and France are typical. The medieval mind was a mixture of many things, but undoubtedly religion played the greatest part in the lives of the people, whether poor or rich, and a pilgrimage to some shrine or other for the absolution of sin was considered essential if one was to receive the eternal blessing of the Almighty. The poor, in purchasing a 'token', not only claimed protection, the object being in the nature of a passport, but were able, on their return, to prove that they had actually taken the long road to Compostella or the longer one to Jerusalem, or even the reasonable one to Winchester or Canterbury. Some spent their whole lives doing nothing else, and although there may have been many who obtained their tokens by tricks, undoubtedly for every one of these there were thousands who died in distant lands, their ragged hats decorated

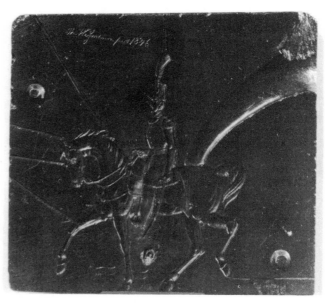

32   **Flats.** *Original mould by Weyman made in 1846 (Musée Alsacien, Strasbourg).*

by the tiny tokens of the saints whom they invoked. The rich, many without the grace of God and at best merely land-seekers, wore them also, either on their jewelled caps or suspended round their necks. In a materialistic age such as ours it is difficult to project one's mind into the past when a mystery was a mystery, but perhaps of all living writers Zoë Oldenbourg, in her *The Heirs of the Kingdom*, best conjured up these pilgrims when writing the story of the Crusade of Peter the Hermit. It is not too great a jump from the token to the toy, the isolated examples furnished with footstands (one of St Denis) that are in the museums in Paris, forming the prototype of later development. A long lull ensued, and it is not until about 1730 that there is evidence of a fairly substantial industry in being in Germany, where naïve examples of a military nature were being manufactured. Nor was it confined to Germany alone, for we know that the same techniques were being employed in Portugal and Denmark. Gradual improvement in anatomy evolved, until about 1775, when Johann Gottfried Hilpert (b.1732) displayed a technical and artistic ability that brought a new dimension to a crude folk-art. Above all, he organized his business to produce vast quantities of models, and thus anticipated modern methods of production. The popularity of the figures grew and rivals soon appeared, especially in Strasbourg. Within a short period of time the cult had spread far and wide, and these models (mainly 6 to 16cm) became almost a national industry. Before long other countries had their own makers (e.g. Castiglione in Italy, 1780: Lodin in Finland, 1786: Ortelli in Spain, 1828). The process was comparatively easy, engravers plentiful, material inexhaustible. The result was that in the 18th century one finds a large, engraved, silhouette-type model, not particularly correct as to anatomy as yet (the riders tending to be too large for their steeds) or to uniform, but pulsating with life. Indeed, the charm of the flats of this period is their naïvety and total disregard for convention. Apart from special commissions, they were made for children, and the children must have loved them. Colour was brushed on in patches in the most arbitrary way (although some were heightened with gold) and one cannot conceive that the makers had any thought for posterity. The designs were based mainly on the printed engravings of the period, and reproduced more or less faithfully the curiously shaped horses and the flashing sabres of the engravers. Above all they reflected the spirit of the times. Prominent among Hilpert's successors were Lorenz, Ammon, Wehrli, Gottschalk, Besold, Denecke, Wegmann, Weygang and du Bois. Many of these changed their style later, but Schweizer, the oldest existing firm, remained faithful to the 18th-century conception. With the coming of the industrial revolution, the process of making flats underwent drastic technical developments, and Ernst Heinrichsen (b.1806) went much further than Hilpert. Not only did he bring some order to the size of the models, establishing a uniform 28mm, but expanded the range of subjects to include countries never previously depicted. Hilpert and his rivals and successors had concentrated mainly on the Germanic States, with some more exotic figures from Hungary and Turkey, but now every country in Europe was represented, and by the end of their working lives Heinrichsen and his

33   **Flat.** *Roman flat of the 4th century. (British Museum).*

sons and their successors had recorded the military achievements of all countries. Their greatest rival, Allgeyer, also created a vast range of subjects, delving, like Heinrichsen, into the past on numerous occasions, and often exceeding him in skill, while at the same time not being averse to pirating his ideas. A whole host of other makers (many of whom had been plodding on since the late 18th century) became prominent by their individualism. Heinrichsen completely changed the conception of the flat. No longer was it a large, colourful and extravagant model. The smaller size of his productions precluded any engraving other than the essential, and generally speaking the models are utilitarian. That is not to say that they are without charm, but it is a charm of a much lesser degree. For one thing the anatomy is better, and the riders are proportioned properly. The old stiffness of the parade troops disappeared, and in their place came figures in all positions, sometimes a number of combatants being portrayed on one stand. Vast numbers of models went to each set, so

that it was possible to build up complete armies with their armaments, or complete engagements, all the models being on the same scale. Painting was crude, as befitted mass-produced models, and done mainly by home-labour, on a part-time basis, as in 1898, at Fürth, where one hundred and fifty school-children between the ages of six and thirteen were employed (*Fritch and Bachmann*). The models were sold by weight, $\frac{1}{8}$, $\frac{1}{4}$, $\frac{1}{2}$ and 1lb, each box containing anything from 25 to 200 figures. For a special subject up to 200 figures were issued, together with trees and houses in weights of half a pound or one pound. Packaging consisted of oval or square chipwood boxes, lined with shavings. A curious metallic paint was used to depict armour, and occasionally gold was added. Scarlet was very much in evidence. Lances, spears and swords were subject to breakage; a rearing horse was extremely fragile where it joined its base. Heinrichsen and his followers made no pretensions—they simply produced as many models as they could, and sold them at a competitive price. But in the early part of the present century collectors began to ask for something better. While assiduously preserving these relics of the past, they demanded a type of model which would exhibit both accuracy, artistic conception and a tour-de-force of engraving. That this ideal was soon achieved was amply demonstrated by an exhibition in 1930, when vast numbers of dioramas displayed the 'new look' in flats. Under the skilful guidance of such designers as Madlener and Gottstein, and the genius of the engravers Frank and Maier, an entirely new school of engravers and manufacturers arose, giving new life to a traditional industry and joy to collectors. A new size of 30mm enabled the most skilful engraving to be performed, and the figures achieved a hitherto unheard-of fluidity. Furthermore, new constitutions of chemistry ensured that the metal itself was harder, and consequently less damage to the figures occurred. Every figure could now in its own right be regarded as a 'vitrinen' or 'cabinet' model. The market was now provided by the collectors and the curators of museums, although some of the firms, notably Neckel and Ochel, still produced painted models for cheaper sale. This painting, as with the 19th-century figures, was merely adequate, and a modern collector will purchase his figures uncoloured or ask for them to be painted by professionals.

The industry of present-day makers is prodigious. The impetus stems from the collector, and is fostered by society journals and exhibitions, the chief of which is the annual event held at Kulmbach. Scholtz conceived his subjects in vast sets, and a characteristic is the '*kombination*' figure invented by Schirmer. The triple role of designer, engraver and distributor makes it difficult to give credit to any one individual. Ideally one should speak of a 'Madlener-Lecke-Donath' flat and, indeed, many of the footstands do bear the initials of all of the participants. Many present-day enthusiasts issue a very limited edition, specially produced for a certain purpose, and it often happens that one set of producers will issue fresh figures to add to an existing set by another set of makers. Gone is the mass production, and many of the sets and single figures are produced in the studios of students of history rather than by the full-time professional. One of the best methods of assessing the tremendous growth in recent times is to compare the number of makers given in Hampe (1924) and in Ortmann exactly fifty years later. The range covered is enormous—every conceivable era, every campaign, every battle, every skirmish, every uniform, appears to be available, and the variety of posture is never-ending. Yet with every list and in every issue of a Germanic society journal there appear new items to whet the appetite. Nor does the military aspect entirely predominate. From the earliest times the makers took note of the world around them, and, indeed, nothing could exceed the grace and fascination of the mid-18th century explorations into realms human and vegetable. zoological and piscatorial, anthropological and social; and, with the coming of industry and the opening up of communications, the 19th century produced its carriages and its railways, its country and town fairs and its pleasure gardens. Saints and sinners, kings and queens, marriages, photographers, mythical gods and goddesses, scenes from Biblical history, from the stage, opera, literature, and from fairy tales were all available, and provide one of the most interesting and rewarding aspects of this fascinating industry.

Earlier it was remarked that the modern flat may stand on its own as a display piece but in general the sets have been produced for a special purpose — for use in a diorama. In the early part of the present century the mass of Heinrichsen and Allgeyer models were used in this way in the creation of huge battle-pieces, and the tradition lingered on with those created for the R.U.S.I. and the more recent ones made by Kröner-Grimm and his associates. Recently, however, due possibly to our present restriction of space, collectors are assembling much smaller numbers of figures, and creating tableaux rather than dioramas. One collector, Valentine Bean, goes further, and arranges small groups on stepped levels, devoid of scenery, thus creating atmosphere rather than realism.

In France, the Strasbourg makers survived for many years, displaying the rococo period at its most interesting. The industry was killed more or less by the rise of the paper sheet and the importation of Germanic solids, and it was not until about 1928 that any lasting interest was taken in them, when the firm of Mignot assembled an enthusiastic team of artists and engravers, headed by Armont, and made a notable series. A few private designers exist, but on the whole the solid model as exemplified by the master makers is more popular. In Italy the art, getting off to an early start, seems to have faded early, while in Portugal and in Finland, again both early starters, nothing much developed. Denmark had a short spell in which it produced a few flats, notably by Høy, while in Sweden Mars and Santessonska held the field for many years (the most notable recent exponent is Sivhed). There may have been a few native American makers in the early 19th century, but the interest was not large enough for their survival. Similarly, in Great Britain, even the influence of Otto Gottstein was insufficient to create more than a passing interest when he and Carman got together to produce the first and only English-produced flats. Spain was much more enthusiastic at first, but dropped out of the field (with the exception of a few isolated cases) around 1870.

Looking back on this record of beginnings and endings in various countries, it is interesting to reflect on how

34   **Flats,** *the King and Queen by Gottstein, the remainder by Rössner (Author).*

popular the imported Germanic flat has now become. Although on the whole the solid is still the most popular style in most countries, there are small coteries of enthusiasts in many places. There are, however, still many difficulties in obtaining flats. In England, for example, a packet ordered from a Continental dealer bears not only Import Duty but VAT (formerly Purchase Tax) often up to a third of the value. Lists are usually printed in German, which forms an obstacle to those unaccustomed to the language. To obtain anything from France is almost impossible – what is generally regarded historically as a nation with impeccable manners contains a number of dealers who are so offhand that all letters pass unheeded. Despite these barriers, however, a few shops in England and the United States are beginning to build up small but representative stocks of specimens.

Accustomed as we are to the tremendous skill and accuracy of the modern flat it is hard to visualize the larger models of the 18th century (although Scholtz, Rössner and Walter have revived them) with all their rococo naïvety, or the graceful tiny confections of fairs and booths, of circuses and families promenading in the park, and indeed, Adam and Eve in Paradise [Scheizer]. Perhaps the modern flat is too perfect. As a footnote, it should be mentioned that in an American magazine *Call to Colors* (1973) there appeared a number of somewhat murky and unconvincing photographs of what purported to be moulds dating from 1635 to 1821, all said to emanate from the workshop of a certain von Wooster family, the initials of whose founder, F. von Wooster, are claimed to appear on the earliest one. Such a claim, if serious, deserves thorough investigation, as the earliest mould would antedate any known flats by a hundred years, and some serious rethinking on the history of the flat would have to be made. The author endeavoured several times to get in touch with the author of the article and with the magazine itself, with the logical request for the actual negatives for study, or proof in some other documentary form, as it seems entirely at variance with the fact that no Continental collector or writer, with all their acknowledge and acumen in research, had ever heard of or seen them. He is still awaiting a reply, so at the time of writing the authenticity of both F.v.W. and the moulds remains a large question mark.

FLATS, SEMI-. In the interval between the passing of the golden age of the flat (c.1880) and its modern revival, the texture of the model became much coarser and the bulk greater, so that instead of the engraving being in alignment with the surface, relief modelling took its place, although technically speaking it was still a two-dimensional figure. Less emphasis was placed on the engraving, and casting became much cruder, and the figure consequently became thicker from back to front. The later Söhlke and other makers such as Haffner and Haselbach (and, surprisingly, the much earlier Schweizer) produced quantities of these models. Many were cast during the First World War from home-casting moulds, and are still being perpetuated in Portugal and certain Eastern European countries. They are neither one thing nor the other, and have no qualities to recommend them. An unusual aspect is the attempt by some firms to create a semi-flat in plastic, especially in Czechoslovakia and Israel, and in modern times Lelièpvre and the collector Mathiot made an abortive start. The best is a curious half-round silhouette in lead, the rear being perfectly flat, by David of Canada, an amateur maker. Cutileiro of Portugal still turns out semi-flats from his moulds of 1845, but in the main those that emanate from Germany are of a stereotyped home-casting type.

Fleegel, J.F.C., Hildesheim/Wolfenbuttel (1771-1821). A maker and engraver of large flats. A set of the gods on Mount Olympus signed 'F', formerly ascribed to him, is now considered to be by Fischer (*Kollbrunner*). Unusual specimens are a set of fifty-five animals, birds and fishes, copied from illustrations in *Bilderbuch für Kinder* (1790-1818). Marks: FLEEGEL, HILDESHEIM; F; F.H. His son, F.C. Fleegel (1805-38) signed his models F.C.F. HILDESHEIM; FLEEGEL, HILDESHEIM. His grandson, J. Friedrich, worked in Wolfenbuttel between 1848 and 1886, engraving also for Denecke. Marks: F.F.; FLEEGEL WOLFENBUTTEL.

Fleetline, Gosport (1978-). Models of British naval officers in solid 54mm.

Fleischman, USA (c.1930). Maker of 54mm solids.

Fleischmann, A., Sonneberg, E. Germany (1851). At the Great Exhibition he exhibited a model in papiermâché.

'Flexitoys'. *See* Marx Miniatures.

Floor Games. See Wells, H.G.

Fohler, Frau Edith, Vienna (1966-). Private publisher of flats. A long series of the Siege of Vienna, the Napoleonic period, the Boer War, a French mountain battery (1830), and Sikh ('*kombination*') figures (1900), mainly engraved by Kovar.

'Folk Heroes' series. *See* On Parade.

Fontanini, E., Presepi Artistici, Florence (1955-). Plastic composition models, 54mm up to 10 inches, of Danes, Vikings, knights and the Three Musketeers, mounted with swivel screws on plastic bases. On the whole they are pretty crude, except for a series of rococo civilians, and sold in either gold or silver plate over black paint. The Italian armour specimens, however, are quite attractive. The large models are enlarged identically from the smaller ones. They are identifiable by the words ITALY DEPOSE with the design of a small crab. This trade-mark occurs under the footstand. They have been subjected to an enormous amount of piracy, especially in Hong Kong, an effort which would appear hardly to be worthwhile. They have also issued a Napoleonic period chess set, bronzed, using their 54mm upwards models.

Forbes, Malcolm, USA. A collector who houses his remarkable assembly of over 60,000 models at the Forbes Museum of Military Miniatures, Palais Mendoub, Tangier. These include cases devoted to Britains, Heyde, French manufacturers, flats and semi-flats, Spanish manufacturers and makers, and modern makers from many countries. Especially interesting is a diorama by Surèn, using 600 figures, of the 'Battle of the Three Kings', representing the Moorish victory over the Portuguese near the Qued el Magazen river in north-west Morocco on 4 August, 1578. Other dioramas are of the 'Road to the Somme' and 'Dien Bien Phu', with plasticine models by Ciuffo. A further diorama of Leuthen, using 40,000 flats, is under construction. He was also responsible for the creation of the Musée des Ballons at Château de Balleroy, France. Purchaser of the neo-classical 'Palace' made by C. Herman Brückner.

Ford, George, London (fl.1950-60). One of the designers and modellers employed by Britains.

Forder, B.A.C. *See* Bofors Models.

Fordham, David, London (1971-?). A maker of 85mm solids to commission. A consummate artist who had a fresh approach to model making, especially up to the Renaissance. Each model started as a hand-carved metal torso, to which all parts were made and attached individually. In 1974 it was stated that there was a possibility of his joining Stearns in a model-making venture, but nothing has since been heard of him.

Forgeries. *See* Piracy.

Forget, Robert C., USA. Assisted in the painting of the dioramas 'They Nobly Dared'.

Forrest, Lionel, Wrightsville Beach North Carolina (1963-). A free-lance artist for United States makers, including a Robert E. Lee for Cameo, and several in 90mm for Superior. He has also made a number of limited editions of 10-inch models in 'Duron' for The Soldier Shop.

Forsyth, Ella D., New York (fl.1938). Assisted in dioramas at the Museum of the City of New York.

Fortner, Andreas. *See* Haffner, J.

Fouillé, Georges, Châtillon-sous-Bagneux (b.1909). The official painter to the French navy, he has always been intensely interested in ships and ship models, and has peopled a number of these with lovely miniature crews and passengers, especially of the 17th-18th centuries. He studied model-making under Lelièpvre, starting his first tentative attempts with work on dioramas for the Musée de la Marine, Paris. In 1955 he began a series of splendid foot and mounted models of the French army, mainly of the Napoleonic period, and also some of the American Revolution. The details are soldered on, and the models painted with exquisite taste. They have a statuesque quality that places them in a class of their own. Outside his native country they may be seen at The Soldier Shop in New York.

Foulley. A French prisoner of war, 1805-15, who constructed a wooden model of Norman Cross prison.

Fouré, Pierre. *See* D.F.H.

Fowler, USA. 'A fantastic painter' (*Scale Modeller*, March, 1968). Unfortunately, no United States collector can offer any information.

Fowler, R, London (fl.1957). A minor maker of 10-18cm plaster composition models of Queen Elizabeth II (mounted), Pickwickian and Shakespearian characters.

Fraas, Johannes Carl, Breslau (1854-1912). One of the

earliest makers of German solids. He also made a few flats, some of civilians.

FRANCE. The most conservative of countries in the history of the model soldier, France has produced solids, plastics and flats, but little to fill the gap between the connoisseur model and the toy. It is probable she produces more private makers whose works appear only at exhibitions and of which the greater public must perforce be unaware than any other country. If her greatest asset is her splendid body of master makers, her greatest fault is her reticence. It is extremely difficult, at times even impossible, to open up avenues of approach among collectors, and no amount of correspondence with many of her great craftsmen elicits a reply. The result is that one can only comment on what one sees, or is told about by other, non-French, collectors who have visited the country. The earliest known models are 13th-14th century flats, clumsy, certainly, but recognizable. (*See* Flats.) Solid models of the time of Henri IV and of Louis XIII are well-documented, and many forgeries of these were made in the 19th century, and sold to 'connoisseurs' as originals (*Forgeais*). The most popular pastime among the children of the later nobility was mock warfare, especially when France was the master of Europe. Dr Heroard, physician and guardian of Louis XIII as Dauphin, describes how in 1604 the Prince had model soldiers made of pottery, and in 1608 his mother gave him three hundred silver models, the work of Nicolas Roger. He was not satisfied with these, however, and, like many a latter-day collector, turned his own hand to producing 7-inch-tall lead warriors, pegged for arranging in battalions, and cannons which 'fired without bursting'. Wood and cardboard models also figured in his collection. On his death they passed to Louis XIV, who augmented them with another silver army, this time made by the goldsmith Merlin. Even this was not sufficient, so he commissioned for his son, the Duc de Viennois, yet another army made by Wolrab, each figure 7cm tall, and fitted with automatic devices by the best German craftsmen, which performed evolutions. Finally, there was what must have been a magnificent collection of cardboard models by de Gissey and Pierre Couturier (*Crump*).

Large models in pottery were mentioned early in the 19th century by the author Goethe, who compared them with his native flats, and there are many paintings extant of scenes depicting children playing with what are obviously tall wooden models. We know that Captain Coignet carried a collection of these about with him during his service days, and during the mid-19th century there are many references to models, mainly of a large size, in plaster, papiermâché, carton-comprimé, conjoint tin and other materials. The art of making metal models from moulds must have been in existence in France well before the Revolution, but the only named maker of whom any trace exists is the famous Lucotte, whose models were stamped on the base with the Napoleonic emblem of a bee with the letters L and C on either side. These models were a revelation. Well-proportioned, 58-60mm, solid, with detachable riders, saddles and saddle-cloths, the reins were also made separately and soldered on. Authorities seem to agree that the Lucottes that one sees were made between 1850 and 1870; therefore it is impossible to know precisely when they created their particular style. Nor is it known

35 **Flats.** *Typical examples by modern Continental makers (Bantock).*

how long they existed as a firm in their own right. The firm of Mignot CBG claims that they took over the Lucotte business early in the 19th century, but it is possible that Lucotte flourished independently alongside the firms of Cuperly, Blondel and Gerbeau, who are known to have been producing models in the 1850s. Mignot themselves have confounded matters of dates of take-overs by confusing statements made in successive catalogues. In one they claim that they were founded under the name 'CBG' as early as 1828. Later they claim that they called themselves 'CBG' in 1902, and in yet another that 'Margat' and 'Vasquez' were now '*réunies*' with the firm. All that is known with certainty about the early origins of Mignot is that they made models for the Emperor Napoleon III about 1854. The fact remains that Mignot CBG, whatever its amalgamations, is accepted by all authorities as the oldest existing firm of makers of model soldiers. Like Britains, they have become a household word, not by any inherent quality that their models possess, but through sentiment. Designing of new models ceased after the First World War, but castings continue to be made from the old moulds, and the firm still forms the core of the French commercial model. A number of firms making composition and plastic models have been active from time to time, the most important being Starlux, in both media. Their models have an elegance about them hard to match elsewhere. The polystyrene kit commemorating Napoleon and his armies, made almost exclusively by Historex, and designed by Lelièpvre, made a shattering and worldwide impact, even if the idea itself, in a much simpler form, came originally from Segom.

A very large industry engaged in the production of flats began early in Strasbourg, and produced a style of its own. It died out, however, and was not replaced until the middle of the present century, when an inspired group of artists produced an exquisite range of flats for Mignot. The paper sheet, the cause of the demise of the early flat, also originated in Strasbourg, and throughout the 19th century printing presses were busy turning out the famous Épinal and Pellerin sheets, some printed in colours, which, when the figures had been coloured by hand, pasted onto strong cardboard, cut out with great care, and then mounted on little wooden blocks, gave immense pleasure to thousands of children. They are now collected with avidity by connoisseurs. The number and scope of the production needs a work of its own, so intricate are the ramifications of editions and printers.

France's greatest contribution to the model soldier world is the work produced by her legendary craftsmen, Baldet, Bittard, Ballada, Berdou, Métayer, Fouillé, des Fontaines, Lelièpvre, and Vanot, mainly in 54mm solid, but occasionally, as with Lelièpvre, in composite forms. Each has a style of his own, but they are all united in the same ideal: that of a torso to which are lovingly added all the necessary solderings to ensure that an absolutely authentic model, beautifully made, beautifully painted, full of grace, élan and artistry, emerges. Few are interested in marketing them, in the accepted sense, and work mainly to commission, either for collectors or for museums. Tastes and fashion pass them by, and they will have no truck with metal models in 'kit' form, nor will they farm out their models for painting by others. The wargame is hardly catered for, unless one considers the 25mm Segom and Starlux examples as such, which we do not think they are.

The French Society was founded in 1931 and is still flourishing, and France possesses the finest military artists in the world. Their knowledge of the Napoleonic period is overwhelming, as evinced by the publications of Rousselot and Lelièpvre. Museums have also taken a keen interest in military models, and there are many collections in Paris and other places of breathtaking proportions.

Frances Turton Figures (Byllee Turton), Tryphena, Great Barrier Island, New Zealand (1970-). A maker of 54mm models. To date she has made mainly New Zealand troops of 1845 to 1902. Each is limited to a numbered edition of 50 castings. They have a sound, if uninspired quality, the painted ones with strangely pale faces. As an example of the research that goes into any particular figure, we would like to quote her description of a Forest Ranger: 'This is the field dress of the Forest Ranger section of the Armed Constabulary. Originally there were two companies, No. 1 commanded by Major Jackson, and No. 2 by Carl Gustavus von Tempsky, the early military hero . . . These troops were issued with basic kit, e.g. ammunition, pouches and rifles, but very little uniform, so that they wore mostly civilian kit. One thing they all wore in common, however, was the 'Rapaki', or coloured blanket wrapped about them kiltwise. It was never meant to represent a kilt as such, but it is thought that it was merely a convenient way of carrying a sleeping blanket. They were issued with Bowie knives, an idea von Tempsky had picked up in America, but Major Jackson was very much opposed to it, and his men seldom wore them, and when they did for the sole purposes of hacking at undergrowth and digging themselves in.'

Francis, Field & Francis. *See* Philadelphia Tin Toy Manufactory.

Franco. *See* Soldat.

Frank, Ludwig, Nuremberg (1870–1957). Engraver of flats. Marks: FRANK; L. FRK. One of the outstanding engravers of all times. He began in 1885 as an apprentice, along with Stadtler, to Heinrichsen, then to Ammon, then to Scheller. He rejoined Stadtler in 1893 when the latter became independent. In 1899 he engraved some semi-flats. He returned to Heinrichsen from 1899 to 1924. He also worked for Spenküch, and did private work for Walter Lockwood, Armont, Wilke, Biebel, Hähnemann, and Hans Müller. Later he was in great demand by Hafer, Beck, Neckel and many others. He was outstanding for his unerring feeling for period and style, guaranteeing that each model was a gem. He had a profound influence on the whole of the later development of the German *zinnfigur* industry. His workbench and tools are preserved at Kulmbach.

Franke, Kurt, Reutlingen. Designer, painter and publisher of flats, mainly of the Napoleonic period and the French Revolution. Has engraved for Sivhed.

Franklin, Dwight, USA. Maker of 7-inch models in beeswax for American museums.

Franklin, Ian. *See* New Hope Design.

Franklin Mint, The, Franklin Center, Pennsylvania (1975-). Publishers of models in various series and various sizes, designed by different artists, and issued in limited editions. The first consisted of 10 models, each 70mm, in pewter, designed and sculpted by Andrew Chernak, illustrating the ten generations of American life from 1776 to 1976, comprising: the First Citizen, the Pathfinder, the Canal Boatman, the Prospector, the Homesteader, the Gibson Girl, the Immigrant, the Jazz Man, the G.I. and the Astronaut. This series was followed by bronzes of Westerners by Caldwell in the same size as those by Chernak, and American Revolution figures in pewter by Imrie/Risley. The first few of a miscellaneous collection of subjects in pewter in 75mm by Hinote have been issued, and it is intended that another series in 54mm by the same artist will total about one hundred. In 1978 they began a fine and complete set of English monarchs in 60mm pewter by Saunders, followed in 1979 by a series of 50 painted pewter models in 62mm by Malcolm Dawson of men in action at the Battle of Waterloo. In this they were sponsored by 'Les Amis du Musée-Wellington à Waterloo'. Their latest venture (1980) is 'The Fighting Men of the British Empire', a set of 50 painted 54mm solids by Malcolm Dawson, issued in an edition of 7,500 sets. (*See also* Nathan, Philip.)

Franz Josef, Emperor of Austria. In 1856 he commissioned sets of large plaster portrait models of himself and his staff, comprising Erzherzog Albrecht, Fürst Windisch-Graz, Count Jelacic, Count Coronini, Colonel Pefacsexics, Cronberg, Field-Marshal Radetzky, the Archduke Ferdinand and the Archduke Charles Louis. One set was owned by Marcel Baldet, another by Baron Huber. (*See* coloured plate in *The Saturday Book*, No. 20.)

Frauendorf, Johannes, Halle (1889–1972). He began producing flats in 1925, with designs for Ochel and Waibel, and engravings for the latter. He specialized in the Napoleonic period, the Franco-Prussian War and the First World War. Many were exhibited at Leipzig in 1930, and a number were used in the R.U.S.I. dioramas. Mark: JF.

Frazer, Cornelius, Amsterdam. A collector whose assembly of paper sheets from all over the world is open to inspection; his modest house is a magnet for overseas collectors. He has also done much to foster the art of collecting and many are in his debt.

Frederick William III of Prussia (1770-1840). He commissioned a set of 140 models of Prussian regiments from either DuBois or Söhlke. These were of Britannia metal screwed to an iron base, standing 25cm high. One set was formerly at the Hohenzollern Museum in Berlin (its whereabouts unknown since 1959), and Baldet traced two sets in the collection of Maître Philipot.

Frei Korps (John O'Loan), Belfast (1978-). Producer of 15mm solids of models of the Seven Years' War, designed and sculpted by D.J. Allsop.

Fremiet, Paris (fl.1854). Was commanded by Napoleon III to design 75 different units of the army of the Second Empire for the Prince Imperial. They were cast in lead by Mignot. After the death of the Prince the Empress Eugénie preserved the models for a long time, then gave some to collectors, the remainder passing to the Duke of Alba in 1910.

French, Neal, England (1963-). Maker of porcelain models for Royal Worcester. Trained by Gertner. Completed the 'Papal Figures' series.

Frenchal, France (c.1935). Aluminium, 54mm. A small range, including cavalry, Legionnaires, Arabs, bull-fighters and a Papal procession. A circular paper label pasted on the underside of the footstand reads: MADE IN FRANCE/FRENCHAL/UNBREAKABLE. Riders and foot in the exact positions of Quiralu indicate either an amalgamation or two-name ranges. [*Brett*]

Frentzel, Matthias, Meissen, E. Germany. Maker of flats. (*Katalog der Formen, 1976*)

Fritsch, Hans, Dresden. Designed for several well-known producers of flats, including 20mm Prussians of 1760 and 1920 engraved by Redlin and issued by Beck.

Fritz, Heinrich, Nuremberg. Mentioned as exhibiting flats at Kulmbach in 1973.

Fritz, Max, Kernnath, Stuttgart. Publisher of flats with a range covering 1400-1700, including the Thirty Years' War, Turkish Janissaries of 1800 and the French Revolution.

Froeglen, G., Ulm. A curiosity! At the Great Exhibition of 1851 he produced a large assortment of 'toys' made of sugar; one, a large group depicting an Arabian lion hunt, was considered to be worthy of 'a better material'.

Froemter, Hans, Hilpoltstein, W. Germany. Mentioned in *Dawk*, 1975, as a producer of models. We suspect that they are plastic, but have so far obtained no reply to letters.

Froereisen, Strasbourg (c.1845). Publisher of paper sheets, lithographed by M.F. Boehm.

Frog, USA. Manufacturer of polystyrene AFV kits.

Frögg, Carinthia, Austria. Lead horsemen of archaic design were discovered here in 1882.

Frontier (Anthony Fermor), Bletchley, Bucks (1969-). He began as a collector who turned his hand to the making of an occasional 54mm solid model. Soon he found that friends wanted them, and he not only began making more, but sought out collectors' interests (most makers do the reverse). The result is that he now has a long list of the most diverse periods that could be imagined, from an Etruscan warrior to the Second World War. He has made a series of English Kings and Queens, (including a seated Queen Victoria) which are a refreshing change, and a number of civilians, such as a lady in a sedan chair with bearers and a link boy. For the benefit of the Historex enthusiast he has made a Heavy Dragoon and a British Hussar (both of 1900) as riders for the numerous styles of polystyrene horses available. There is a certain uneasy pose in some of the models, over-long arms and crudity in the bend of an elbow, but the originality of the range more than compensates for these inaccuracies. In 1978 he arranged with C. Robinson to produce his models on a more commercial basis.

Fry, A., Ltd, London (1914-18). A short-lived manufacturer of hollow-casts of the principal contestants of the First World War, mostly charging infantry. Really nothing more than a piracy of Britains' models. Mark (some): A FRY LTD/LONDON, sometimes dated. Some moulds fell into the hands of Crescent. [*Wade*]

FT. See Metal Miniatura.

Fuhrmeister, Helmut, Kulmbach. Listed as exhibiting flats at Kulmbach in 1973.

Fujimimokei Co. Ltd, Japan. Usually known by the abbreviation Fujimo. Manufacturers of polystyrene AFV kits, together with tank traps, pill-boxes, tents, bricks and jerrycans for diorama sets; plastic figures of poor quality.

Fulgarex, Spain. Issues 40mm Elastolin style models, probably piracies.

Fuller, S. & J. *See History and Adventures of Little Henry, The.*

'Furio'. A clockwork tank, place and date of origin unknown, was catalogued under this name in a Phillips auction sale in June, 1975.

Fürst, Austria (d.c.1970). Diorama maker.

Fusilier, La Puenta, California. 'The Barefoot Soldier' advertised 54mm solid models under this name in 1973, but nothing further is known.

Fuste, J.A., Barcelona (fl.1950-60). Maker of 54mm solids.

F. v. W [?**o̸oster**]. *See* Flats; von Wooster

Fylde Manufacturing Co, Blackpool (post-1945-50). Manufacturer of poor Westerners (riders detachable), British Infantry (mainly Grenadier Guards). Absorbed by Cherilea c.1950.

G

Gabriel Industries Inc., Lancaster, Pennsylvania (1965-). Distributors of 56mm die-cast figures. The military models are subtitled 'Hubley Division', under the name Metallions. The packages carry the inscription 'Made in England by Lone Star'. We have seen (by courtesy of Anton) White Eagle, Black Hawk, Pat Garrett, Kit Carson, Bat Masterson. Some models are identical with those of Kresge, while undoubtedly a number are piracies.

Galio, Edizione, Italy. Publishers of paper sheets of troops up to the First World War.

Galipeau, Florence, Australia. Engaged on painting models for the D-Day diorama at the Australian War Museum, Canberra.

Gallaus, S.E., Copenhagen (d.1966). Producer of 30mm flats of Danish forces of early 1800, designed by Rössner. The moulds are owned by the Danish Society.

Galterra Eireaan. *See* Comet.

GAMA (G.A. Mangold) Fürth (fl.1935). Manufacturer of tin-plate vehicles.

GAMA (Manuel Ribes), Barcelona (fl.1959). Manufacturer of 54mm plastics.

Gamage's, London. A large store (no longer in existence), which promoted Britains' models.

Gamble, Captain, London (1870). Inventor of wooden blocks for military evolutions.

'Game of Fortification, The,' Germany (1840). An engraved sheet with a grid and four illustrations, with instructions in three languages, and 53 turned wood soldiers.

Gammage, Russell. *See* Rose Miniatures Ltd.

Gangel. *See* Dembour.

Ganier-Tauconville, H., Strasbourg (1860-1920). Producer of paper sheets of fine quality. He also collaborated with J. Schneider.

Garcia, Father Carlos C., Nuria, Spain. Designer of the drawings for paper sheets issued by Assasition.

Garfield, R.G. *See* Parade Square.

Garrick Miniatures. *See* Greenwood and Ball (Pearce).

'Garrison'. *See* Greenwood and Ball (Pearce).

Garsave. *See* Bouçquin.

Gärtner, Ludwig (d.c.1962) and **Frau,** Vienna. A team of diorama makers. (*See* Austria; Dioramas.)

Gastaldi, Dominique, Colombes, Paris, (fl.1950). Producer of flats of Napoleonic troops.

'Gaulois France, Le'. *See* Ballada, M.

Gauthier, John. *See* Coronet Miniatures.

Gavin, William, Massachusetts. Painter of figures and maker of dioramas for the series 'They Nobly Dared'.

Gay, USA (fl.1960). Maker of 54mm solids.

Geelhaar, Carl Gottfried, Meissen (before 1810, d.1865). A maker of delightful circuses, fairs and fêtes in flats in the German romantic tradition. Ortmann records that over 1000 moulds are known.

Gehle, H., Hamburg. He is credited with making war machines for the dioramas formerly at the R.U.S.I.

Gellert, Kassel (fl.1956). Producer of flats.

Gemeinhardt, Sgt W.P., USA. Dioramist for United States military museums.

Gem-Models (G. Musgrave and P.J. Culpitt), Croydon (1960-?). Makers of 60mm plastic models of fairytale figures and for cake decorations.

'Genesis' series. *See* Minot, B.

Gepner, Captain S., Warsaw. Formerly curator at the Army Museum in Warsaw, he designed a number of figures for the French Society and for Ochel, and in 1939 began production of his own flats with a model of Poniatowski. The author has seen 20mm flats (*kombination* figures). Correspondence with Poland now being virtually impossible, we cannot say whether he is still working.

Gerard, Raoul. He donated his large collection of flats to the Cantonal & University Library at Lausanne.

Gerbeau. *See* Mignot.

Gerhardt, J.H. and **J.G.,** Strasbourg/Landau (fl.1795-1810). Important and early publishers of paper sheets, and among the first to depict both sides of the figure.

GERMANY. The sprawling mass of states which finally merged into the Germany as it was before the end of the Second World War are important in giving to the model soldier world both the flat and the commercial solid. There is early evidence of the making of models in clay and wood; at Magdeburg a series of most curious continuous strips of lead figures dating from about AD 1250 was found in 1956, while the 12th century manuscript of the Abbess of Landsberg known as *Hortus Deliciarum* illustrates manipulated puppets of fighting foot soldiers. Equestrian tilting knights (see *Weisskünig*) were engraved by Burgkmaier at the time of Maximilian I, and elaborate models of this type, some in bronze, are preserved at Munich, Innsbruck and the Vienna State Museum. They were evidently made for princely patrons, as were the 'Little tilting horsemen which were moved by clockwork', given as gifts by Duke William of Bavaria; and a certain little Felix Platter was presented on his sixth birthday with a 'little wooden man which when pulled (could) fight'. Woodcarving was an inherent German accomplishment and it is no surprise to learn that in 1674 Matthias Schutz was commanded by the Prince Elector of Bavaria to repair 27 soldiers and drummers, and to replace their muskets. Furthermore, he had to carve six more original musketeers and six gun-carriages for the same patron. Goldsmiths and pewterers abounded, and give evidence of their art in the *Kunstschrank* ('casket of miniatures') given by Augsburg to Gustavus Adolphus in 1632. One incredible example of the work of the goldsmiths and silversmiths of the early 18th century is 'The Grand Mogul's Birthday Party', at the Staatliche Kunstsammlungen, Dresden. Included in this Oriental confection of gold, silver-gilt and enamels, besides elephants and camels bearing gifts, are 132 men of aesthetic quality and anatomical excellence unsurpassed by craftsmen of later centuries. Made by a team led by J.M. Dinglinger, it was given to the Elector Augustus.

The thickly forested areas of Germany were responsible for a vast home industry, particularly in the Sonneberg, Berchtesgaden and Frankfurt areas, producing countless thousands of crude carved or turned military toys, both foot and mounted, together with cannon, forts and emplacements, as illustrated by a number of toy catalogues of the early 19th century. Farm animals, trees and Mr and Mrs Noah and their flock existed until the early days of the present century, and one occasionally comes across a partial revival. The military interest was so strong that gum-tragacanth, sugar and meal were all pressed into service for 'Brotteig' figures, and compressed sawdust was extensively used in place of wood. Mid-19th-century industrialism, however, gradually killed off these amusing products, which were superseded by metal and pewter, more stable materials. Little groups of round figures, 32mm in height, with accessories of wood, were made in Nuremberg in the latter part of the 18th century [*Hampe*]. Intermittent attempts at half-round (or semi-solid) models were made from time to time quite early in the 19th century and can be dated with some accuracy by a passage in, of all things, *Travels in Brazil* (1824) by two Bavarian travellers, Spix and Martius. To the Coroados Indians the travellers gave as barter 'pins, narrow ribbons, leaden soldiers and horsemen. They tied the latter to strings which they suspended round their necks. . . . They felt the head, mouth and feet of the horses, and those of the leaden soldiers, and seemed desirous of convincing themselves whether they were animate or inanimate.' As these models obviously had a solidity about them they could hardly have been flats, and they must have been quite small for carrying with all the other baggage through the Brazilian jungles, which seems to preclude them from being the massive solids that are usually characteristic of German production. Indeed, German models of a semi-solid type were made for many years, and obviously in bulk, and were criticized in no uncertain fashion when shown at the Great Exhibition of 1851. Although in 1839 DuBois had made large solids for presentation purposes, the first firm to turn in a commercial way to the production of smaller mass-produced solids was probably Gebr. Haffner, some of whose models were of exceptional quality. Pirates soon followed, including Fraas, Schildknecht, Heinrich, Spenküch and Dorfler (models by the last still being cast up to 1945). The seal was set on the industry by the efforts of Georg Heyde of Dresden, who from about 1870, turned out the most astounding variety and quantity of solid models until the factory was destroyed during the Second World War. Not only did he embrace every conceivable size, variety and era, but his models showed a modernity in their action positions far ahead of his time. His 45-65mm products were clumsily conceived, but even so his output remained the largest in the world until the hollow-cast was invented, and every country in Europe, especially Britain, France only excepted, eagerly imported the elaborate sets, often extending to as many as 60 separate models, together with armaments, accessories and impedimenta. The fact that many of the uniform details were inaccurate meant little to the boys for whom they were intended, and it was only in the larger models (up to 90mm) that better workmanship and more research were apparent. Once Heyde, Haffner and Heinrich became established, there was little room for competitors, and although there were a few other makers who made smaller contributions, the Heyde style of solid models lasted until the beginning of the Second World War. It should be noted that the models have, in their native country, never been regarded as other than toys (except in the case of Haffner, some of whose better efforts are at this moment being re-issued for collectors), but in other parts of the world they have been avidly collected.

The other aspect of the model in metal, the flat, must surely be considered Germany's unique contribution. It is possible that the military idea developed from the Pilgrim token, as has already been suggested (*see* Flats). However, there seems to have been no continuity in the French effort, and the combination of tin mines in Nuremberg and the formation of the Guild of Pewterers in 1578, led to the setting up of commercial ventures for the production of religious trinkets. But a minor trade of this kind cannot exist when pressure of war needs metal, and for generation after generation internal wars racked the Germanic States. However, about 1730 there emerged tentative, clumsy and exploratory ventures here and there, leading by 1750 to a considerable advance in technique; by 1770 it is evident that an industry of small dimensions had been established in Frankfurt, and that the idea had found its way to other countries. Impetus was given by Johann Gottfried Hilpert, born in Coburg, whose father Andreas was already a tinsmith, though not necessarily of military inclinations. Learning his trade between 1746 and 1750, Johann moved to Nuremberg as an apprentice, and finally set up his own establishment, making models that are the epitome of his time. His masterly technique brought him numerous commissions for large equestrian models, and his work was pirated and plagiarized. His smaller models were issued with children in mind, and his success was so great that many rival factories were founded, and his ideas spread to Strasbourg, Fin-

15 Left: **Eriksson.** *Queen Christiana, a 54mm equestrian solid (Allendesalazar).* 16 Below left: **Fibreglass.** *French 3rd Hussars c.1808. A 9-in. model in fibreglass by Pierre Turner (Turner).* 17 **Flats.** *First row: by Maier, second and third rows by Hafer (Author).* 18 Below: **Flats.** *Top 'Christ before Pilate' – models by Retter, engraved by Frank, painted and staged by Valentine Bean (Bean).*

19 **Higgins.** *A delightful 60mm solid of Mr Pickwick. (Author)*

20 **Imrie/Risley.** *Private La Sarre Regiment 1755-60. A splendid 54mm solid painted by F. Acuña (Soldier Shop).*

21 **Lamb Saburai.** *A masterpiece of design, casting and painting, made of 26 separate pieces. 90mm (Courtesy Hinchliffe).*

22 **Gutierrez Comte.** *Spanish infantry, 1910. c.1965 (Allendesalazar).*

23 Left: **I.S.A.** *Typical Italian toy soldiers manufactured by I.S.A. (Testi). 24 Below:* **Lineol.** *Spanish infantry, 1900. Composition figures (Allendesalazar).*

36 **Germany.** *Plaster, plastic and composition examples by Hahn (first figure, top left),* JEAN *(3 large figures), anonymous (2), and the painted ones all by Merten (Author).*

land and Switzerland, and later to Italy and Spain. The idea of the flat was established, and in its various styles has remained to this day. The main history of its progress is described in the appropriate place, and it only remains to emphasize the importance of Heinrichsen in establishing a uniformity of scale, and to mention once more the profound effect that the collectors of the early part of the present century had in ensuring the continuation of what to many is the most delightful and skilful aspect of the making of the model soldier.

Germany's final contribution is again based on easily available materials, in this case a curious combination of sawdust, resin, glue and casein, forming a plaster-like substance built around an armature. The firm of O. & M. Hausser began about 1904 to make their crude, clumsy and easily-broken 60mm figures. They were marketed under the name 'Elastolin' and achieved immense popularity with German children, and were later widely exported to other countries. Inevitably other firms, such as Lineol and Leyla, began to manufacture in the same style, to be pirated in Italy and Belgium. Pre-war examples are today highly prized by collectors. After the Second World War the firm changed to other substances, and both they and Merten (founded about 1950) display a high technical skill, the latter being, however, far more conservative in their range.

Finally the paper-sheet, which established itself firmly in Germany, production, especially after the introduction of chromo-lithography, being enormous; but today it has been superseded by the complicated cut-out card model. Since the last war the collecting world in Germany, although still dominated by its love of the flat figure, has gradually become aware of the old solids and semi-solids, one or two makers (e.g. Ara-Kunst, Lacina)

making beautiful figures, while brusquely rejecting any representation of Hitlerian troops.

Gertheis, Dr Klaus, Trier (1975-). Private designer and engraver of flats, 20mm, having learned the craft from Trips. Among his productions he includes medieval miners, a war wagon (20cm), Napoleonics and a set to illustrate *Struwwelpeter*.

Gertner, Frederick, England (1917-). Maker of porcelain models for Royal Worcester: 'Historical Figures' series (8), 'Military Figures' series (7), and two of the 'Papal' series.

Geru-Verlag, Germany. Publishers of cardboard castles, towns and villages. [*Ortmann*]

Gestcha, Germany (pre-1945-). Manufacturers of mechanical tanks.

Geyser, Darmstadt. A producer of flats known only by his signature. [*Kollbrunner*]

GHQ (Micro Armor), Minneapolis (1968-). Manufacturers of metal AFVs and accessories. An agency was established in Britain in 1975 under the auspices of Old Guard, and 20 and 25mm wargame models, including French Line Grenadiers and artillery, and also 54mm models, all under the name 'Guardsman', were announced in that year. In 1976 25mm models were issued in kit form, and in 1977 buildings were designed for them by Cattle.

Giacomo, A. de. *See* Arte Grafica.

Giant Plastics Corporation, New York (1962-). Manufacturers of plastic 54mm unpainted figures, mainly piracies made in Hong Kong. 30mm plastic flats under their name are also known. [*Pestano*]

Gibbs, USA. A maker of 30mm plastic, unpainted figures of 'Custer's Last Stand'.

Gibson, F., England. Assisted in the construction of the dioramas 'Arroyo dos Molinos' and 'The Landing Zone at Arnhem' at the Border Regiment Museum, Carlisle.

Gilbert & Schiercke Miniatures, USA (fl.1960). Makers of a varied range of 54mm moulds for home-casting. (may be connected with Henry C. Schiercke.)

Gilbert, Charles Webb, Melbourne (1869-1925). One of the artists employed on the Australian War Memorial dioramas.

Gilbert Toy Co, New York (1965-). Manufacturers of plastic figures, 11 inch, 60 and 40mm, of television and movie characters, mainly made and painted in Hong Kong.

Gildea, Brian. *See* B.G. of G.B.; Copy-Cat.

Gilder, Peter, Southampton/Meltham, Yorks. About 1965 he became associated with Dickinson in the production of wargame models under the name Alberken. Later he was a designer for Hinchliffe, and in 1976 began his own Foremost models. A great advocate of the wargame, his painting of tiny models is superb, and he has boundless energy.

Gillet, R., Paris. Originator, with Lelièpvre, of the Historex polystyrene kits. A skilled engraver, he worked, again with Lelièpvre, on the series issued by Café Storme. He is also a professional painter of models.

Gilling, Harold, New York (fl.1938). Assisted in dioramas at the museum of the City of New York.

Gin, E. (b.1817) and **F.E.**, (b.1845) Naples. Professional painters of an outstanding collection of paper figures, cut out and mounted, at the San Martino Museum, Naples. (*Alberini*)

GINGERBREAD. *See* Edible Models.

Giore, Aristide, Milan (c.1895-1910). Publisher of paper sheets.

Girardo, Ernesto, Argentina (c.1927-61). Blatant copies of S.A.E. models, converted to local requirements. Solids, 54mm, Napoleonic and Franco-Prussian Wars, under the name Yelmo-Batalla. Since 1961 he has worked to commission only.

Gissey, Henri de, Paris (1669). Maker of a cardboard army for Louis XIV.

GKS, Austria (c.1760). Maker of a chess set comprising Austrian and Turkish troops, in silver and silver-gilt, some pieces bearing the above initials, sold at Christie's, London, on 18 June, 1979.

Glanzer, Stanley, USA. Designer of models for Bugle & Guidon.

Glaser, O., Leipzig (fl.1930). A private collector who specialized in the painting of flats, and made one of the earliest attempts at converting them.

Glassorama (S.P.Whitehead), Petersfield, Hants (fl.1973-4). In 1973 he advertised his new invention, the placing of microscopic figures, in suitable terrain, in brandy glasses. Nothing further was heard of him after 1974.

'Glory that was India' series. *See* Sutty, M.

'Glory to the Russian Weapon' series. *See* USSR.

Goddin, John, Milton Keynes (1975-). Son-in-law of Major Robert Rowe, he worked with the latter on one or two of the later Vallance models. His first solo effort was of a Reservation Indian in 1975 for Vallance, followed by an Indian scout (1977) for Cavalier.

Goebel, W. Germany (1974-). Makers of a series of 18cm hand-painted porcelain models of varied uniforms ranging from 1805 to 1809.

Goethe, Wolfgang von. In a story entitled *The New Paris*, written in 1770, but not published until 1811, he men-

tions models which were not 'flat . . . like ours . . . but man and horse were round and solid, and most finely wrought '(*Dichtung und Wahrheit*). Later the story states that they were shattered by cannon fire, which indicates that they were made of some kind of ceramic material. A partial translation, leaving out this important fact, caused authors and collectors to assume that Goethe had the French solid in mind when he wrote his story. However, Ortmann's true and full translation makes it clear that the models concerned were frangible.

Gold and Silver. An advertisement in a military journal in August, 1976, announced 9-carat gold and silver collectors' sets of 25mm wargame figures made in Guernsey. No further information was forthcoming in spite of numerous inquiries.

Goldberg, C.P., Kaltenkirchen, W. Germany (1977-). Publisher of flats of the Middle Ages and the 17th-18th centuries. (*Klio*)

Golden Press Inc, USA (1959-68). Press-out figures in cardbook form of Ben Hur, the Alamo, Knights of the Round Table, and the War between the States.

Gonzalez, D. Eulogio, Barcelona, Spain (1900-c.1945). Manufacturer of good quality 54mm solids and indifferent models in 45mm. It is difficult at times to distinguish them from those of Capell. (*Allendesalazar*)

Goodbrand, James, London (1973-4). Maker of an 'American Liberty' chess set, silver and silver-gilt, in a limited edition, hallmarked and signed with initials. The size of the pieces varie from 4 inches to 1 inches, with fitted wooden box. It was sold at Christie's, London, on June 8, 1979.

Gordine, Liège (19th century). Publisher of paper sheets.

37 **Gordon.** *Beverly Gordon with some of her models (Gordon).*

Gordon, Beverly A., Reseda, California (1970-). A freelance maker of 54mm solids. For Waterloo Galleries she made a small group commemorating the Six-Day War, which included a fine camel-trooper (the rider detachable). In 1972 she made models for Scale Specialities Miniatures, and in 1974 traded under the name of Gordon Miniatures Ltd Series. She has also designed for Polk's Merité (1975, six models), and for Waterloo Galleries in the same year a mounted Peking Marine and a Genghis Khan. For the Model Soldier Collectors of California she designed 77mm models of the American Revolution. She is represented at the Penman Collection, Lincoln Room, Metamore Court House, Illinois, and in museums in Los Angeles. One of the most gifted of American makers.

Gordon, Owen, Fairlawn, New Jersey. Designer of artillery for The Old Guard and Imrie/Risley, including a Renault tank for the latter.

'Gordon Relief' series. *See* Empire Military Miniatures.

Gosling, Alan, Liverpool. Designer of a First World War diorama at Merseyside Museum, Liverpool.

Gottschalk, J. Wilhelm, Nuremberg/Fürth (1768–1843). One of the earliest mass-producers of flats, notably of civilians. He began as a journeyman for Martin Beck, and was trained by R. Wehrli. His principal engraver was F. Eggimann (mark: name in full or FE). An outstanding example is a country market of 120 figures.

Gottstein, Otto, Leipzig/London/New York (d.1952). One of the outstanding personalities of his time, he exercised a profound influence on both the growth of the hobby and on the making of flats and dioramas. A collector of rare sensibility, he was one of the group which sought to raise the standard of the design of flats. A furrier by trade, he was a member of both the French and the German societies and had already produced flats before he was forced by anti-Semitic pressure to leave Germany in 1934, seeking a welcome in England, where he already had many friends. Two of these, E.K. Milliken and Charles Lockwood, were approached by him with a view to the formation of an English society. This led to a meeting of fifteen enthusiasts, and, with Gottstein's financial backing, the British Model Soldier Society was founded in 1935. At this auspicious meeting (Sir) Charles Foulkes presented each member with a damaged original Siborne model (*Carman*). Flats from Continental makers still being available, Gottstein persuaded a group of enthusiasts to use them in the construction of a series of dioramas illustrating great events in English history and by 1937 had assembled sufficient flats to set up a work-force, headed by Denny Stokes, for the construction of the actual diorama work. The flats were painted either on the Continent or in England and when they became unobtainable on the outbreak of war he turned to Greenwood and Ball for 20mm solids to use in the last two or three dioramas, although Carman says that Gottstein was never entirely happy with the transition from flats to solids.

Meanwhile he formed a partnership with Carman and Lovell Barnes and together they established a firm called Carbago. Medieval subjects and a fine set of forty-two English monarchs resulted. However, they were not appreciated at the time and the project was abandoned. He and Harry Levine sponsored a series of thirty-five dioramas of Jewish history, created by Greenwood and Ball and Stokes.(It is now in Jerusalem.)

Gottstein was the first to appreciate the talent of Roy Selwyn-Smith, assisting him financially in the production of a set of 'Knights of Agincourt', in 54mm solids. Designed by Madlener, they were for export to the United States only. A few models, however, occasionally turn up in England and Courtenay was so impressed by them that he managed to obtain one or two of the castings and painted them in his own style [*Greenhill*]. On the death of Gottstein in New York in distressing circumstances the moulds were sold to Britains, who re-issued them in hollow-cast. The moulds for the flats of the Swiss-Burgundian Wars passed to

Eugene Blum, the collector, who added a number to them, making a magnificent set of 204 figures. These in turn were purchased in 1974 by Curt Kollbrunner of Zollikon, who arranged with Neckel for their re-issue, together with a number of other sets which Gottstein had edited during his days in Germany. These comprised the following, the parentheses in each case indicating the number of figures in each: Ancient Britons (39); Ancient Egyptians (22); Assyrians and Babylonians (101); Babylonian slave market (8); Carthaginians (57); Charge of the Light Brigade (43); Charles the Bold (72); Charles the Great (30); Cortez (73); Death of Wolfe (15); Ethiopian Court (26); Falcon Hunt, Henry IV (13); Field of the Cloth of Gold (48); Battle of Hastings (78); Henry VIII and his Court (30); Hittites (47); Landschnechts (99); Last of the Valois (98); Libyans (8); Mamelukes (10); Napoleon and his Court (15); portraits of ancient leaders (14); inhabitants of Punt (6); Elizabeth I at Tilbury (44); Sumerians (22); Thirty Years' War (25); Zulus (16); war elephants (14) and prehistoric animals (23). Added to these was the set of English monarchs produced in England. Fortunately he died before his beloved dioramas at the R.U.S.I. were distributed to other museums. He would certainly have wept at the neglect of those now in the Glenbow Institution, where they appear, Ray says, to have been partially broken up and individual figures sold to collectors.

Gottstein, Aarau (c.1800). Flats of peasant costume, of which the moulds are at the Landesmuseum, Zurich.

Gould, L, New York (c.1910–1930). Maker of poor-quality 54mm hollow-casts of United States troops.

Gould, R., England (c.1968). Maker of 20mm solids of the British army.

Grace Toys, Hong Kong (1975–). Pirates in plastic of Herald 'Swoppets'. [*Kearton*]

Grack, Karl, Berlin (fl.1866). Publisher of paper sheets.

Graf, Bernd, Erfurt. Publisher of flats of the Californian Gold Rush, United States army (1880–1900) and two cannon of the Crécy period, all designed and engraved by himself. (*Katalog der Formen, 1976*)

Grafil (Francisco Grosso y Cia) Argentina (1950–55). Manufacturers of 54mm hollow-casts and semi-solids of good quality. [*Basseterre*]

Graham, A. *See* Silvercross.

Grammar, Argentina (c.1956). Manufacturer of hollow-casts similar to those of Britains. [*Basseterre*]

'Grand Mogul's Birthday Party; The' An exotic Oriental fantasy created by Johann Melchior Dinglinger, assisted by his two brothers and a team of goldsmiths, silversmiths, and enamellers for the Elector Augustus between 1701 and 1708, incorporating 132 men with elephants and camels, all of the most marvellous technical skill (*Staatliche Kunstsammlünger, Dresden*). Reproduced in colour in a Ferranti Computers calendar for 1979.

Grande Illusion, La. *See* Roma (Editorial).

Grant, USA. Mentioned in an article in the *Bulletin* of the British Model Soldier Society, December, 1965, as a maker of solids. No further information is available.

Grassi, Joseph, London (fl.1965). Maker of moulds for Willetts.

Grau, Barcelona (1821). Publisher of paper sheets.

Gravey, Fernande. A French actor who, as a private maker of flats, collaborated with the Mignot group.

38   **Great Britain.** *The Black Prince by Kirk; Joan of Arc by Hinton; Henry V by Jac; standing knight and Dutch hussar by Stadden; mounted knights, left by Jac, right by Harlech (Author).*

Grazia, Maria. *See* Quadri-Animata.

GREAT BRITAIN. The earliest account of model soldiers in Great Britain occurs in the Rolls at Alnwick Castle, home of the Percys of Northumberland, dating from 12 February, 1599, to 27 March, 1602, which contain accounts of money spent 'for trymnge of 4000 leaden soldiers', for quicksilver, verdigris and copper, moulds of brass to cast the 'Manykeys' (? mannequins), and wire to be drawn for the pikemen. It is also recorded that this army was used both at Alnwick and at Syon, the home of Thomas Hariot, the mathematician and scientist, by Henry Percy, ninth Earl of Northumberland. Both were members of an intimate circle which included Grenville and Raleigh. Hariot in particular made experiments with cannon shot, and it does not seem too far-fetched to suggest that some sort of tactical military game was played with this considerable lead army. It is possible that it was later either loaned or given to Henry, Prince of Wales (d.1612), for such an army is recorded in the inventory of the Armoury of St James's Palace (*Rukeyser*). The entries in the Rolls confirm stray references by dramatists of the period. A long gap now occurs until 1759, when the combined operations which culminated in the seizure by Wolfe of the Heights of Abraham were commemorated in cork models of barges full of troops. In the 1830s wooden soldiers attached to trellis tongs were used for the demonstration of evolutions, but the second model by Captain Siborne made to illustrate the Battle of Waterloo leaves the question unanswered as to whether the models were made in England or in Germany. In 1877 a 'Mr Bull' is credited with pewter models of military characters, but the imports of Germanic solids and semi-solids that saturated England at the time must have been suffi-

cient to stifle any native aspirations. Small firms may well have produced the odd model or two, but it was not until 1893 that William Britain produced his first 'hollow-cast'. After a few years of anxiety his models became so well established that the Continental hegemony was broken for ever. Hollow-casts were now the rage, and many firms, large and small, began making them. Some, like Britains, continued production up to 1964. The early makers were followed after the Second World War by a new wave, thus preserving the continuity of this unique form of presentation. Continental models continued to be imported up to 1939, but in constantly diminishing numbers, the most popular being the composition-type models of Elastolin.

The efforts of members of the British Model Soldier Society, founded in 1935, by such collectors as Milliken, Lockwood, Carman, Gottstein, Cass, Connett and Lord Greenway, led to the beginning of a new type of model—the historically accurate one. Aimed at the intelligent collector rather than the accumulator of commercially mass-produced toys (which, after all, was all that was then available), such artists as Courtenay, Carman, Ping and Greenwood began in a quiet, unobtrusive way to lay the foundations of a native school of craftsmanship that still continues to flourish. The end of the Second World War saw a new impetus in this direction, and brought to the fore the models of Gammage, Stadden, Hinton and Niblett, all of whom are still active. An even greater impetus can be traced to the demise of the hollow-cast in 1964, which culminated in the emergence of the present school of artists, represented by Minot, Marrion, Cameron, Sanderson, Braithwaite, Hinchliffe, Surèn, Bird (now in USA), Tassell, Rowe, the late Higgins and the like. In fact the momentum has increased to such an extent that each month a new maker emerges.

Over the years the size of models has changed. In Britains' hey-day the 54mm size was predominant, even though many of the makers of hollow-casts produced specimens varying between 45 and 60mm. The first makers of solids adhered pretty rigidly to the traditional size, as being ideal for their purpose, although Ping and Courtenay were always a shade smaller. Later makers (starting with Stadden) increased their size to a more robust 56-60mm, and it is now the exception to find models in the old size. In recent times even more makers are presenting their figures in anything from 70-90mm, some going as far as 180mm. Conversely, a keen interest has grown up in the smaller models, those in 30mm being beautifully made by Gammage, Stadden, Hinton and Surèn. About 1945 Groves and Benoy made a number of models in this size, fitting into slotted stands, which were used by the comparatively small number of wargames enthusiasts that existed in those days. However, they made no impact for years, until suddenly, about the beginning of 1970, a wave of enthusiasm for this pastime swept the country. Makers immediately began to cater for the demand, and soon tiny models in 20 to 25mm appeared. Prominent in this direction were Airfix (plastic) and Dickinson. Stadden, Gammage and Hinton had been making models in this size for some years. Others, such as Garrison, Hinchliffe and Lamming, followed, and some makers even reduced the size to a mere 5mm.

The short-lived venture into flats by Gottstein and Carman was never repeated, but the collecting of Continental specimens is gaining ground, and the standard of the collectors' painting and presentation is high. Paper sheets are almost entirely unknown, and, although one comes across the occasional Victorian or Edwardian cut-out or press-out, there seems little doubt that there was never a British industry. Plastics began to appear just after the Second World War, pioneered by Malleable Mouldings. Britains were again in the forefront, with their Herald Models, admirably designed by Roy Selwyn-Smith, and naturally other firms such as Cherilea, Charbens and Timpo followed suit, mainly transferring their old hollow-cast designs into the new material. A few are outstanding, such as the set of Henry VIII and his wives by a minor maker, Cavendish Miniatures, and the mounted model of a specimen of armour at the Tower of London issued at a prohibitive price by John Niblett. Large plaster models had a vogue in the 1960s (Willetts, Patmore, The Sentry Box). The advent of the Historex polystyrene kits brought forth a new type of enthusiast, one who, while not able to make his own models, was now able to use his ingenuity to create something original from the pieces provided.

Now that Germany produces few solid models, and Mignot are so stuffy with their business arrangements and so expensive, the only importations that are to be seen are from the United States, usually in kit form, and occasionally painted models from Brunoe in Denmark and Soldat and Alymer of Spain (again prohibitive in

39 **Great Britain.** *Back row: Armstrong, Carman, Courtenay (4); Centre: Crown (60mm), Deauville (Saunders), Dixon, Douglas (2); Front: Falcon (4) (Author).*

price), along with a sprinkling of Starlux Napoleonics (but not the medievals) and a solid block of Elastolins.

Dealers now proliferate, and several auction houses hold regular sales of models. Dozens of local societies exist, especially those devoted to the wargame, the armoured fighting vehicle and the conversion of polystyrene kits; exhibitions are unending. There is now a representative display of models and dioramas in many museums. There is still a hard core of collectors of hollow-casts and pre-war Elastolins, but with the upsurge of interest in ancient times, the average collector is becoming far less insular.

Britain has yet to produce a Berdou or a des Fontaines, but many fine models are produced by Stadden and Gammage and Surèn, of what one might with no disrespect call the older school, and more recently by Rowe, Dawson, Lamb, Sanderson (when at his best), Saunders and Richards. The competition is so great that the younger makers appear to find it necessary to go to extreme lengths to create something entirely new, at times abandoning the principles of anatomy and taste, especially in some of the larger models. In this they would appear to be attempting to compete with some of the products of the American market. More disturbing is the tendency of commercial painters to blatant theatricality. The wargame models vary immensely.

Great War Game, The. See Wargame Models.

GREECE. Archaic Greece may well have been the watershed of the model soldier, albeit mainly in the form of flat votive offerings, but no records exist of anything to bridge the intervening centuries. In our own time only one maker of plastics can be recorded – neither the Athenian Board of Trade nor the Embassy could do other than provide the author with a list of twenty-two firms making plastic toys, only two of whom bothered to reply to a circular letter, and these proved useless.

Green, J.K., London (fl.1870). Publisher of paper sheets for the juvenile theatre, including the Battle of the Alma (26 sheets), Balaclava and Inkerman (12 sheets) and the 'Life of a Soldier' (22 sheets), usually accompanied by a playbook.

Green, Kenneth, California (c.1947). One of the earliest of the modern school of American private makers.

Greene, Dr Albert. *See* Tommy Toy.

Greene, Ian, Dublin, Eire. Painter of 5-inch flats at Cork Museum.

Greenhill Medieval Miniatures (Peter Greenhill),

Wimbledon, London (1976–). A collector of impeccable taste and a skilful artist in many spheres, he began dealing in model soldiers as an adjunct to his Toy Guild shop. A profound admirer of Courtenay and Ping, he owns a photocopy of Courtenay's complete working data which was given to him by Courtenay's son. In 1976 he arranged with Christopher Lief, as pattern-maker, to produce a series of models of the 14th century, designed and personally painted by Greenhill himself. They are 50mm, with a hand that will grip, and there are alternative helms and visors and interchangable weapons. Each design is taken from the medieval *Armorial of Gelre* by Claus Heinen (1700 coats of arms) and Greenhill is endeavouring to portray faithfully the devices shown therein. They form a natural complement to the Courtenay models, and revert to the old practice of the designer refusing to allow his models to be painted commercially. Mark: GREENHILL/ENGLAND/ serial number and date. In 1978 he was entrusted with the original Courtenay moulds, from which he began casting the following year. He has also designed and produced three cut-out card sheets: Wimbledon windmill (1971), Wimbledon Centre Court and Jodrell Bank (both 1977).

Greenin, D.H., Fancy Repository, East Street, Brighton (1867). A box of Haffner's semi-solid 30mm models with the above label enables them to be dated. Now in the Luton Museum.

Greening, F.J., Dorking (1974-6) Maker of 10mm wargame models, Second World War and present-day troops, issued in packs of five.

Greenway, Lord. The first patron of the British Model Soldier Society. He commissioned Gammage and Ray to make models for him.

Greenwood, John A. and **Ball, Miss K.N.,** Wellington, Shropshire/Yorkshire/London/Yorkshire (1936–1966). Greenwood's earliest efforts were 40mm medieval types, and no more than competent. However, when he was joined in 1938 by Miss Ball he transferred his attention to the larger 54mm size, his female assistant doing the soldering and painting. Altogether they produced some 500 representations of the British Army, the Indian Army, Yeomanry regiments, the Air Force and the Navy. If one was inclined to cavil, it would be at the excessively large noses of all the figures, and certainly his later efforts at more animated models of a period in which he was ill at ease, that of the Second World War, were a sad ending to a brilliant career. Miss Ball retired

40 **Greenhill.** *Examples of models after the style of Courtenay. (Greenhill Miniatures).*

41 **Greenwood.** *Early examples of his 40mm models. (Hanington).*

from the business in 1961, when she became Mrs Nathaniel. Their most important work was done in the world of the 20-28mm figure, the idea emanating from the fertile brain of Gottstein, who needed his R.U.S.I. dioramas completed. Once started, orders for dioramas kept the pair busy for the rest of their careers, and these little gems paved the way for subsequent makers. Many museums in all parts of the world have their dioramas as treasured posessions. Greenwood was in ill health in 1966, and, although he lingered on until 1971, he passed all his moulds to an old friend W.F. Pearce, who purchased the name and the business.

Greenwood and Ball (W.F. Pearce), London/Thornaby-on-Tees (1966-). Pearce continued to produce Greenwood's 54mm models, though in diminishing numbers and with painting which showed a sad decline from the skill of Miss Ball. He soon began adding other makers, hitherto not well known: John Braithwaite ('Garrison' range of 25mm wargame figures, with one 54mm Roman legionary); Olive (R.J. Marrion, 1968-72); Barry Minot (1968-74); Lasset (John Tassell, formerly with Tradition and later a partner in Series 77, at intervals from 1972 to the time of writing); and Cliff Sanderson (1972-4). In 1975 Pearce relinquished the production side and retired into semi-obscurity, his place being taken by Braithwaite, who later in the same year began making the 'Falcon' series of 54mm combatants in pairs, beginning with Ancient Races. In 1976 he added Peter Hinton to the team, while in 1977 they were joined by Al Charles, who began with medieval plunderers and subsequently added an impressive series of models for the Battle of Crécy, Alan Biswell, with mythical figures, also in 54mm, and 90mm models of the Battle of Stamford Bridge, and Norman Errington, with beautifully sculptured combatants of the English Civil War, also in the larger size. In 1979 David Buffey began 125mm metal kits of warriors of the ancient world, under the title Garrick Miniatures. (*See also*: Old English: Pearce.)

Greer, William E., Apalachicola, Florida (1950-). A former collector who had great influence on the emergent American specialist makers. A profound knowledge of costume and period led him to design for Custer and Murray, and he had the ability to create and paint his own 54mm solids, many of which were commissioned. Early in the 1960s he began the discreet production and sale of many of these, including soldiers of the American Revolution, United States infantrymen

(1835-39), Confederates, units of the Charleston S.C. Militia, the Highland Company (1860), Plains cavalrymen dismounted, clansmen (1715/45), Danish Guard infantry (1777), Ole Rye (killed at Jutland, 1849), and a First World War pilot. In 1974 he joined R.G. Cade in a series entitled 'Lotus Miniatures', and in 1976 produced his own 'Greer Miniatures', cast in 'Cerrosafe', in limited editions, including some re-makes of earlier models. He has also worked free-lance for Monarch, Com-E-Tec and Fife and Drum, and in 1978 began making 'toy' soldiers for D.Js. He is permanently represented at the Old Barracks, Trenton by a series of dioramas incorporating over 200 figures of his own making.

Gregor, Heinrich Immanuel, Freiburg (1792-1846). A little-known maker of flats, specializing in markets and fairs. (*Ortmann*)

Greiner, Walter, Ahnatal. Appears in the Kulmbach list of 1973 as a producer of home-casting moulds, 45 to 70mm, semi-solids. (*Fischer*)

Grenadier. *See* Chernak; Squadron/Rubin.

Greyart. *See* Grey Iron Casting Co.

Greycraft. *See* Grey Iron Casting Co.

Grey Iron Casting Co., Mount Joy, Pennsylvania (1881-). Manufacturers of cast-iron 40mm and 70mm models, which, because of the material, are clumsy specimens. Cast iron was quite commonly used in the United States towards the end of the 19th century for toys, mainly horses and carts, wagons, home banks, miniature baby carriages and the like, and it was a long time before model soldiers were made by this firm, which underwent a bewildering succession of changes of ownership and amalgamations: 1903, National Novelty Corporation or 'Toy Trust'; 1906, Hardware and Woodenware Manufacturing Co.; Assets Realisation Co. (date not known): 1913, John Jenks, Philadelphia; c.1916, Riverside Foundry & John Wright Inc.; 1958, W.A. Coventry; 1974, Donsco Inc. They also had an agency under the name of Distributive Products Inc. Wrightsville Hardware Co. The first models, were made in about 1917 and were nickel-plated. They were later painted in khaki, and in 1938 were issued fully painted and entitled 'Uncle Sam's Defenders'. These were discontinued in 1942. Over a hundred sets of Westerners, United States troops (riders in two pieces, the man fixed to the horse by a long rivet), the Red Cross, pirates, the 'American Family' in several settings with scenic backgrounds to the boxes, together with silk-printed flags, tents, guns and trench sections, and a lone medieval knight, all in 70mm, were first produced in 1933, under such titles as Greycraft and 'Iron Men'. Animals were also made under the name Greyart. Designers of the figures included Wright, Eschleman, Musser and Schmidt. One special range, Greyklip, was designed to slip into a metal slot. Production ceased about 1942 but during their life they were as popular in the United States as were Britains in England. The latest owners have revived them. [*Zipple*]

Greyklip. *See* Grey Iron Casting Co.

'Greys'. *See* Cigarette Cards.

Grieve, David. *See* Sea Gull Models.

Griffin, Murray, Australia. One of the team that produced the diorama's at the Australian War Memorial, Canberra.

Griffin & Farran, London, (c.1885). Publishers of 'Home Pastimes or the Child's Own Toy Maker', consisting of 12 card sheets showing, in outline, a yacht, a railway engine, an omnibus, a windmill, etc., each 10 x 7 inches. (*Newman*)

Griffiths, Eric, England. Designer for the Royal Doulton Company.

Griffiths, H., Cardiff (d.1972). The maker of 8 clay models, 50mm high, for a diorama at the South Wales Borderers Museum in Brecon.

Grifo (Fabrizio Prudenziali and Jonny Tranquil) Genoa (1978-). Solids, made especially with the convenience of the converter in mind.

Grimes, A., Cardiff. Maker of a diorama of Rorke's Drift, using 20mm Airfix models, at the South Wales Borderers Museum in Brecon.

Grimoni, E., Rome. Publisher of paper sheets.

Grittner, Strasbourg (fl.1790-1800). Publisher of paper sheets.

Gritton, Armand., France. A collector liberal with his gifts, including those to the Museum at Compiègne.

Grixoni, E. *See* Excelsior-Immagini.

Grosch, Robert, Mannheim (fl.1950s). Maker of flats of German colonial history.

Gross, John. *See* Fife & Drum.

Grosse, Herbert, Karl Marx Stadt. Publisher of flats. (*Katalog der Formen, 1976*)

Grossman (Dave) Designs Inc., USA (1975-). Producers of commemorative porcelain designs by Alda Falchi, consisting of: Betsy Rose (10 inches, 800 copies); Francis Key Scott (8 inches, 800 copies); Spirit of '76 (3 figures on one stand, 15 inches, 600 copies); the Declaration of Independence (12 figures on one stand, 13 inches, 200 copies).

Grosso, Francisco, y Cia. *See* Grafil.

Grube, Harry, Indianapolis, Indiana. One of the first of the American collectors and private makers to foresee the emergence of a native school of American makers.

Grunewald, Rudolf, Wedemark-Elze. Publisher and designer of flats. He has a fairly large range, including many of the Seven Years' War (he has also engraved figures of the same period for Wagner); 1810-15 Russians and French; Prussians, 1756-63, 1870-1, 1914--19; Plains Indians; a peasant dance, 1630; witches and warlocks; Tzigane gypsies; minnesinger; Mozart before Maria Theresa; Wellington and Blücher at Waterloo. The gypsy set is somewhat sadistic.

Gryffyn Miniatures, Hull (1977-). Professional painting service.

Gryga, Robert, Grand Rapids, Michigan. Represented at the Grands Rapids Public Library by his paintings.

Grykiewicx, Joseph, Whitehall, Ohio. (1963-). Creator of 8-inch carved and painted pinewood models of police, both military and civil, of all times from the Egyptians onwards. The collection is permanently stationed at the United States Military Police School, Fort Gordon, Georgia, but exhibited elsewhere on occasions.

Guard House. *See* Hinton Hunt Figures Marketing Ltd.

'Guardsman'. *See* G.H.Q. (Micro Armor).

Guggenberger, Th. *See* Screiber.

Guggiari, Ezio. *See* EG-Toys.

Guilbert E.P., Paris (1965-). Manufacturer of 56mm plastics.

Guild of Model Soldier Manufacturers. Founded in 1966 'To protect the integrity and interest of manufacturers of high quality military miniatures'. The present members (and it is surprising that there are not more) are Almirall, Hinton, The Sentry Box and Surén.

Gum Tragacanth. *See* Edible Models.

Gunson, William, Seaton, Wellington, New Zealand (1973-). An industrious maker of solids in various sizes, some of which were purchased for publication by Matai Industries in 1974. K.F. Meates also has a collection of 30mm models dealing with New Zealand history, including ceremonies and campaigns, Trooping the Colour, the Band of the Black Watch, Australians, Punjabis, Fijians, Camel Corps, the Arab Legion, and a Royal Artillery 13-pounder gun and crew. He has also made Maoris, rugby footballers and race horses in their correct colours, and designed 90mm models for Scruby. The remoteness of New Zealand and the unwillingness of English importers to handle models outside those of the established makers makes it extremely unlikely that his fine models will ever become known to more than a tiny number of collectors.

Gunther, Joachim, Germany. Designer and engraver of flats. (*Katalog der Formen, 1976*)

Gutierrez Solana, José, Spain (1960-). Founded by José Gutierrez Compte (d.1969), and continued by his son in a more desultory fashion. 45mm solids of good quality. (*Allendesalazar*)

GZ (or ZG). *See* Zerwick Gebr.

H

Hacker, Robert, Mantel, W. Germany. Exhibited flats at Kulmbach, 1973.

Hafer, Ruediger, Kassel. Designer of flats. Son of Wolfgang Hafer.

Hafer, Wolfgang, Kassel/Staufenberg-Lanvehrhagen (b.1926). One of the most interesting and enterprising editors of flats. His figures are designed and engraved for him by Madlener, Lecke, Frank, Retter and Kroger. His great love is of ancient times, and we are indeed indebted to him for his superb portrayal of ancient Egypt, including a beautiful set of Pharaoh wild-fowling on the Nile, accompanied by attendants, papyrus plants and flying game, taken from contemporary Middle Kingdom wall paintings. In this period also is a set (with furniture) of Thutmosis sculpting the head of Nefertiti (from drawings by Fortunino Matania) and Nefertiti waiting on her husband Akhnaton (again from a wall-painting). Ancient Greece is represented by three figures from the Elgin Marbles; the Homeric set with 'the figure of eight' shields; Phryne posing for Praxiteles (again with furniture, and taken from a painting by H. Herget in the *National Geographic Magazine*) with *hetaerae* and flute players. Mythology follows, with Leda and her swan, the rape of Europa and Odysseus and the Sirens and a Minoan Bull-jumping set. There are also Assyrians and Macedonians, and a whole series from Biblical history, including Adam and Eve, the dance of Salome, Joseph and Potiphar's wife, Moses in the bullrushes, David and Bathsheba, Samson and Delilah, and the Golden Calf. Roman cavalry, Numidians and Hamilcar and Scipio follow, and lead to a delightful Moghul hawking set. Hafer's interpretation of the falconry party from *Les Très Riches Heures du Duc de Berri* (1250) is one of the loveliest of all sets of flats, while the hunting party of the 18th century French court, with dozens of figures, and completed by an extraordinary tree complete with birds of all kinds, and a hunting lodge or pavilion, is a masterpiece. It must not be imagined, however, that Hafer limits himself to ancient times. He also issues military models for the Seven Years' War, a boarhunt of 1739, Napoleonics, Bavarians of 1846-66, Uhlans of 1866 (including a panorama of Rozenville), the War of 1870-1, and, in 1971, British footguards. He has also made figures in 50mm of Roman garden herms, and an Inquisition set.

Haffner, Johann, Fürth/Nuremberg (1863-93). A vigorous manufacturer of flats, semi-flats, solids and semi-solids, 30, 40mm and up to 7cm. He won a medal for 'pewter toys' at the Paris Exposition of 1867. His production, mainly of French and Prussian troops, can be numbered in thousands, and his main export was to France and England. His greatest achievement was in the solids. While the infantry are typical of their period, but still superior to Heyde and the like, the mounted troops are outstanding, and akin to Lucotte in their elegance, exhibiting a feature shown only in the best makers, that of separately-cast reins, stirrup leathers, bugle cords, etc. In 1973, in fact, Bernhard Helmbrecht and Johann Reischl of Munich began making copies in 40 and 55mm by permission of the Bayerisches National museum, Munich, which holds many of the originals. Warships are also known, in semi-flat, for a 'Grand Review at Spithead' (eight battleships and jollyboats). His son Johann (1859-85) succeeded him, while his grandson Konrad (1885-92) appears to have joined Andreas Fortner (about 1880, and still existing in 1924) as United Toy Factories. Later still Albrecht Stadtler appears to have succeeded Haffner. Mark on box labels: J.H.N. [NUREMBERG] around a standing knight: 'FEINE ZINN-COMPOSITIONS FIGUREN: FIGURES EN COMPOSITION: SUPERFINE PEWTER FIGURES', (In one instance at least with the spelling 'Pewter').

Hahn, Herbert, Vienna (d.1957). A maker of plaster composition 40-50mm models, with a wire armature. He began before the Second World War to make models more or less as a hobby, but after the end of the war he turned out small numbers of figures and buildings from ancient times to the Middle Ages, including siege weapons, chariots, a Roman temple and houses; he also made a few models of the 17th century, including guns, horse litters and fortifications. Hardly known outside his own country.

Hähnemann, Kiel (fl.1930s). A collector who did much to improve the quality of flats by employing Ochel and Frank to engrave models for him.

Haines, George, London (1977-). Designer for Sea Gull.

Halberd Castings, London (1950-?). Manufacturers of 54mm hollow-casts of which a group of the Nigerian Regiment is apparently the only known specimen. [*Opie*]

42 **Haffner**. *Two subjects in solid lead, 1886 (Bayerisches Nationalmuseum).*

Hales, A.A., England. Retailers. *See* King White.

Haley, M. *See* Quality Model Soldiers.

Hall, Charles, Edinburgh (1977-). Producer of 54mm solids of Scottish troops commissioned from Niblett, together with another range of 'toy' soldiers of Scottish characters.

Hamblen's Authentic Miniatures (G.B. Hamblen & Son Inc.) Norwell, Massachusetts (1960-64). Manufacturer of 45mm solids, available plain or painted, including mounted troops and artillery, and all, except one, of the American Civil War. The exception was a fine figure of Decatur. Also concerned with the Charley Weaver (Cliff Arquette) Museum at Gettysburg. Mark: USA/ H. Taken over by UN Art Co.

Hamel, Paris. One of a group of enthusiasts who designed and painted the famous Mignot flats.

Hames, Léon, Lambermont, Belgium (1970-). A maker of fine equestrian models 16cm high in modelling clay, which, when painted, resembles porcelain. He was formerly a pupil of Lelièpvre.

Hamley's Toyshop, London. One of the first of the large English stores to encourage the sale of 'specialist' models. In the mid-1960s one could see there a selection of Greenwood and Ball, Niblett, Carman, Stadden and The Sentry Box, together with an occasional diorama. Every individually-boxed set of Britains' models was stocked, together with unpainted castings for the exclusive use of members of the British Model Soldier Society. From 1970 to 1977 the stock consisted of Britains/Herald plastics, together with Elastolin, but their 'specialist' range shrunk gradually to a token offering of the later Greenwood and Ball, Lasset and the occasional Alymer or the odd anonymous Continental model about which the staff knew nothing. In the latter part of 1977 they opened a department dealing exclusively in models well away from their main store, with a predominance of plastic kits and a still-restricted offering of metal models.

Hammant & Morgan Ltd. *See* H. & M.

H. & M. (Hammant & Morgan Ltd), Watford (1979-). Manufacturers of model trees and other accessories for dioramists.

H.A.M. Miniatures Ltd. Inc. (Karl M. Ahrens) Woodhaven, New York (1965-70). A comparatively short-lived maker of good solid 54mm models. These comprised British troops of 1800-1900, French 1806-15, Germans 1939-45. An unusual and sculptoresque figures is an ancient Greek from a classical original, another, in 60mm, the epitome of a swashbuckling Landschnecht.

Hammond, D., Australia. One of the team responsible for the dioramas at the Australian War Memorial, Canberra.

Hampe, T. Author of *Der Zinnsoldat* (1924), one of the first penetrating essays on the history of the flat figure, concentrating on the progress of the industries of Nuremberg and Fürth until about 1900, with vague references to solids. Never translated into English, and now extremely difficult to acquire.

Hampshire Figures (D.J. Noyce), Southampton (1972-3). A maker of an extremely small range of 20mm solids for the wargame, which were so badly cast that they were soon withdrawn.

Handscomb, John, Northampton (1973-). Designer of 20, 25mm guns and vehicles for Renown (part of Phoenix).

Hanks Brothers & Co., London (c.1900-14). Manufacturers of 56-70mm hollow-casts, many of which were more or less derivative of Britains, but slightly better in quality than the majority of their contemporaries. Mark: H. HANKS/COPYRIGHT, underneath oblong stands, or round the top of oval ones.

Hanley, Terry, Vancouver. The inspirer of a large diorama of Waterloo still under construction (1979) by the Canadian Historical Miniature Figure Society.

Hansen, J.W. *See* HH.

Hardie, J.W., Brisbane (1968-). Included, although strictly a collector, as unique in that, not content with the large Aurora and Airfix polystyrene kits as issued, he injects them with a material which can subsequently be sculptured into something entirely different.

Haring, Artur, Fürth (19th century). He appears to have owned some of Hilpert's moulds, later selling them to the Hamburg Museum.

Hariot, Thomas, London (1560-1622). Sharer with Henry Percy, ninth Earl of Northumberland, of an army of 4000 'leaden solders'. (*Rukeyser*)

Harle, William and **Dorothy**, Washington, D.C. A husband-and-wife team of collectors who, at the same time, made their own very competent 54mm solids, and exercised an influence on the nascent American movement during the latter part of the 1940s.

Harlech Models. *See* Trophy.

'Harlequinade'. *See* Willie.

Harling, Donald. *See* Betts, G.H.

Harms, Carl, Hamburg (fl.1960). A producer of a small number of flats.

Harnisch, G.F., Hanover (1824- at least 1850). Maker and engraver of flats. The founder (1824-40) signed his works H; G.H.; G.F.; HARNISCH IN HANOVER. He had two sons, J.L.H. and Adolf, both producers of flats.

Harper's Ferry Center, National Park Service, Harper's Ferry, West Virginia. Producers of museum exhibits, including those at the Custer Battlefield.

Harris, C., USA. Professional painter for Cowan.

Harris, Major H.E.D., Frimley Green/Portsmouth. An enthusiastic collector who until 1975 staged many exhibitions of his models for Army recruiting and educational purposes, and did much to establish the museum at The Curragh. He specialized in the British

Army from 1914 to the present day and converted large numbers of models to this period, at the same time making realistic buildings as backgrounds. He designed some of the Treforest Mouldings figures and was active in the formation of Malleable Mouldings. Author of several works on collecting, including *Model Soldiers* (1962). His own collection was sold at auction in 1976-7.

Hartmann Gebr., Hanover/Linden (1973-). Designers and manufacturers of flats.

Hasbro, USA (1966-). Manufacturers of polystyrene AFV kits.

Hasegawa, Japan (1973-). Manufacturers of polystyrene AFV kits.

Haselbach, F., Berlin (c.1848-?). Maker of flats. (*Scholtz*)

Haselbach, J.C., Berlin (c.1848-1900). A prolific producer of 40-50mm flats, some 5,000 moulds being recorded, including troops of Frederick the Great, cuirassiers, dragoons, grenadiers, hussars, the Thirty Years' War, Crusaders and sailors. They were packed in cardboard boxes bearing a large H in the middle. Several groups depicted more than one figure on the same stand. He employed the engraver Wildt between 1848 and 1855. Marks: H.; H.W.; FÜR H. WILDT; J.C. HASELBACH; H. WILD (*sic*). The moulds were purchased by Rieche. Scholtz queries the prevalent use of the initials 'J.C.', as, he says, there was another foundry in the same city owned in 1881 by F. Haselbach.

Haselup, Alan, Cranbrook, Kent. Professional painter for the Dover branch of Historex.

Hasenpflug, Wolfgang, Wachtersbach (1979-). Publisher of flats.

Haskell, Ted, Maryland (1955-?). Solid, 54mm models of an Indian and a trapper, both caricatures, advertised by Bard in 1955. [*Pielin*]

Hasselfield Bros, USA (1959-?). Publishers of cardboard cut-out books, including *G.I. Joe*, 1959.

Hathaway, John, San Pedro, California (1965-). Best known as a maker of plastic field guns for 30 and 40mm dioramas, but also produces a series of paper sheets in this size for the American War of Independence.

Hauck, Dr, Birkenheid (1975-). Maker of 30mm solids of Frederick the Great shown at Kulmbach, 1975. [*Fischer*]

Hauck, Hilde, Neustadt bei Coburg (1979-). Publisher of flats.

Hausser, O. & M. *See* Elastolin Fabrikaten.

Hautsch, Hans & Gottfried, Nuremberg (fl.1670-1700). Goldsmiths, silversmiths and compass-makes who supplied automatic devices for the animation of a silver army made for Louis XIV for the use of the Dauphin.

Havard, L. Strasbourg (1850). Publisher of paper sheets, each figure having interchangeable heads.

Hawk, USA. Manufacturers of polystyrene AFV kits.

Hawke, USA (1974-). Solids, 54 and 105mm, of a Second World War German and an American backwoodsman in hunting shirt. (Noted by Pielin, but source of information lost.)

Hawkesworth, David. *See* 'Cloudesley Collection'.

Hawley, David, USA (1978-). Maker of ordnance for The Black Watch.

Haynes, George. *See* Starcast Miniatures.

Hayward, R.W., England. Constructor of two dioramas for the Queen's Regiment (Queen's Surreys) HQ, Kingston-upon-Thames.

Hazelwood Miniatures (Wayne Morris and Paul Toms) Ratlby, Leicester (1974-). An initial offering of well-designed 54mm solids of ancient Egyptian warriors by Morris and Hittites by Toms appeared in 1974.

HC Model Craft, USA. Manufacturers of polystyrene AFV kits.

HCP, Sweden. Publishers of paper sheets, including a Wild West set.

Hearn, Michael. *See* W.M.H. Models.

Hearne, William, London/Blackborough/Exeter (1970-). His incredible conversions of kits, with special additions, first brought him into prominence, and as a private maker he enjoyed great fame by his portrayal of armoured motorcycles, all made entirely from original materials. Several of his conversions and his dioramas utilizing these machines are in private hands. In 1975 he turned professional, designing for the kits issued by E.S.C.I. Modellista, and a year later began the first of a series of 90mm models in kit-form entitled 'Real Models' for Sea Gull Model. In 1977 he issued 90mm metal kits under the title 'Hearne Originals', and the following year added others (some in 19 parts) in 130mm.

Hebden, W. *See* Wend-Al.

Heber, Stephen, Vienna (1820-?). A little-known producer of flats. Martin Ruckert was in his employ at one time as an apprentice engraver.

Hedrick, J.C., USA (1974-). Began as a professional painter for Cowan. In 1977 Cowan's catalogue *Militaria* announced a solid mounted Prussian Hussar, 8 inches high, made by Hedrick, at $1,000.

Heid, Albert, Roth/Nuremberg. Listed in *Dawk* (1975) as a maker of plastic models.

Heideloff, Alexander von (c.1840). Engraver for Heinrichsen.

Heidorn, C.A.F., Lübeck (1823-90). Maker of flats. Mark: A. HEIDORN. A number of his figures and the moulds are in the Lübecker Museum.

Heine, H. *See* Richter, A.C.

Heine, Jorg, Ellhöfen. Manufacturers of showcases. (*Kulmbach Almanac, 1977*)

Heinisch, Günther, Ocholt (1979-). Publisher of flats.

Heinrich, Johann Conrad and **Johann Georg,** Fürth (19th-20th century). Flats(?), semi-solids, solids. Within the last decade it has been established by Richards that

43   Heinrichsen. *Examples of flats, c.1885 (Author).*

many of the solids previously attributed to Heyde were made by Gebr. Heinrich. Their trademark was of a knight with a banner and shield on an armoured horse, with GH above the horse's head.

Heinrichs, K, Germany. Designer of flats for Hafer and Scholyz.

Heinrichsen, Nuremberg. The most prolific manufacturers of flats and semi-flats of their time, A succession of relations followed the founder Ernst (1806-88); Wilhelm (1834-1908); Ernst (1868-1938); and Johannes (1914-45). The widow of the latter is still alive, and, although officially not in business, a few favoured clients do occasionally obtain a model or two on request. Marks: E.H.; E.HEINRICHSEN FECIT; E.HEINRICHSEN GRAVIERT; W. HEINRICHSEN. The initials L.F. are also occasionally found, as Ludwig Frank was employed by the firm as an engraver in 1885 and again between 1899 and 1924. By the sheer magnitude of their production and the size and variety of the sets which they made the firm of Heinrichsen towers above all its contemporaries. The elder Heinrichsen exerted a profound influence on his own and successive generations and the fruits of his labours and those of his family may be seen in many Continental museums. Although in design and in execution the firm has been far outstripped by modern makers, its name will always be regarded with esteem by collectors as the most representative figure of its time. Indeed, it is only in recent years that Scholtz has tried to emulate the scale of Heinrichsen's production. As with Heyde's solids, the Heinrichsens made models in every conceivable position. If by present-day standards of criticism the figures appear naïve, they have to be judged against the artistic background of Germany at the time, which was at an extremely low ebb, and the anatomy of the horses is merely a reflection of the artistic conventions of the period. The painting was basic, and no concessions were made to facial expression, indeed, the area for engraving was far too small, and in any case the figures were mass-produced for children. They are the most fragile models ever produced, and it is indeed a miracle that so many have survived. Heinrichsen broke the convention of the large 6 to 10cm flat by reducing his figures to a constant 28mm, naturally sacrificing detail in so doing, but at the same time enabling complete armies to be assembled in a uniform size, which was what the German child wanted. Like any other innovator he had plenty of rivals, and flagrant piracy existed, sometimes two-way, so that only the expert can decide which particular model is by Allgeyer or Heinrichsen. Prices were naturally much lower than those of the makers of the conventional large models, and the firm virtually reigned supreme until the coming of the semi-flat. The founder of the firm began as an engraver, gaining a prize only three years' after beginning his own business, and he subsequently continued to engrave many of his figures, assisted by Alexander von Heidelof. In 1842 he exhibited models in 40, 50 and 70mm, and in 1848 he first introduced his 28mm scale, professedly for children, for whom he wrote a manual on *kriegsspiel*. It would be impossible to list the many sets issued, and all one can do is to record the most popular; medieval tournaments and battles, Greeks and Romans, the Seven Years' War, the Thirty Years' War, the Napoleonic Wars, the Franco-Prussian War and the Crimean War. Heinrichsens were probably the first to create the focal group of several characters moulded on one footstand — Hannibal and attendants, a knight under a tree defending himself against half-a-dozen assailants, two tilting knights with a dog running alongside, Poniatowski falling into the river at Leipzig, the death of Gustavus Adolphus at Lützen, Napoleon on the bridge at Arcole, Napoleon being urged by his staff to flee the field at Waterloo, Bismark surveying shell-torn ruins. Many of the sets were accompanied by printed booklets giving a history of the battle or war portrayed. A series of seafights consisting of ships and separately moulded waves were also issued, and, apart from military subjects there were numerous traditional country fairs and gatherings of townsfolk, farms with hedges, trees, flowers and buildings, and scenes from Grand Opera. The later Heinrichsens succumbed in most cases to the semi-flat and the interest died, probably the last models to be made being of First World War figures by Johannes.

Heiss, Wilhelm, Kulmbach. Listed in 1973 as a manufacturer of flats.

Heitz, Jean Henri, Strasbourg, (1779-1789). Was responsible, with Levrault, for the printing of five volumes of illustrations of military costume, engraved on wood after drawings by Pierre-François Isnard (1776--9) which had a profound influence both on the producers of paper sheets and on the early Strasbourgian makers of flats. He also issued large single woodcuts as recruiting posters.

Hellenic Miniatures. *See* Imrie/Risley Miniatures Ltd.

Heller, France. Manufacturers of polystyrene AFV and armament kits. In 1976 they began making figures in 54mm kits including an officer of the Sahara Company and a Bedouin with a camel.

Helmbrecht, Bernard, Munich. Listed at Kulmbach in 1973 as producer of copies of Haffner original museum pieces.

Helmet Products (Denis Knight), Betchworth, Surrey (1970-). A producer of 54mm kits in various plastic materials, mainly P.V.C. which needs a special adhesive and primer. The helmets, breast-plates, etc, are metal-plated, and wool and cloth fabrics are incorporated for helmet crests, etc. Foot soldiers were introduced in 1974. The figures are designed by David Pomeroy, the horses by Selwyn-Smith. The lively action is spoiled by the very thick stands.

Helwig, Brunswick (1780). Inventor of a form of *kriegsspiel*.

Hemphill, Michael, USA. A professional painter employed by Cowan.

Henderson, Patrick, Canada. A landscape artist employed on the D-Day diorama at the Canadian War Museum, Ottawa.

Henderson, R.E., Australia. One of the team that produced the dioramas at the Australian War Memorial, Canberra.

Hendl, W. *See* Holweg, J.

Henlo. *See* L & H Metal Miniatures.

Henniges, Ernst, Hanover. Publisher of flats, including 12 figures of the killing of King Philip of Swabia (issued in 1972).

Henning, K. Designer of flats for Von Droste.

Henry, J., England (c.1940). Carver of four wooden models, 90mm, depicting uniforms of the Border Regiment, exhibited in their museum at Carlisle.

Hentall, M.R.E. *See* 'Militia Models Worldwide'.

Hentschel, Dr Horst, Magdeburg, E. Germany. Publisher of flats.

Herald Miniatures Ltd, London (1953-). The most influential manufacturers of modern 54mm plastics, quite unsurpassed in their design and manufacture. In 1951 M. Zang and R. Selwyn-Smith, a designer of great merit, formed a small company issuing modern troops and traditional Westerners. In 1953 the now famous trademark 'Herald' was adopted, but some of the original figures still retained the name Zang on the underside of the base. By 1955 Zang and Selwyn-Smith became an associate company of William Britains and rapid expansion ensued. By 1958 Zang had retired, and Herald was formally incorporated into Britains. In the same year the famous 'Swoppets' range was introduced, breaking new ground. Since then they have remained the pre-eminent makers of English plastics, only the firms of Marx (on occasions), Starlux and Cavendish being in a class to be compared with them. The first models were of British infantry of the Second World War. Others that followed included the English Civil War, the American Civil War (including a fine gun team), Highlanders, Trojans, a Robin Hood set and a group of polar explorers with a miraculous sledge. 'Swoppets' featured Westerners and the American War of Independence, but the most famous and attractive set was the Wars of the Roses, incredible ingenuity being displayed in the minuteness of the weapons. Perhaps the most attractive of all are their non-military models, especially the farm and garden series, the show jumpers, the riding school, the ballet and national dancers, the Nativity set and the series of teenagers with motor-cycles and guitars. Latterly, the manufacture and painting is taking place in Hong Kong. Actually their sets, although separated in Britains' latest catalogues, are so intertwined with Britains' plastic products that they could well be classified as one. (*See also* Britains Ltd; Selwyn-Smith, R.; Zang, M.)

Herbu (Ruthard Bunzel), Hamburg. Publisher of 30mm flats, mainly of the Seven Years' War and civilians of the same period.

Hering, Werner, Bayreuth. Professional maker of dioramas. (*Kulmbach Almanac, 1977*)

Heritage (Dr Allan C. Scott), Austin, Texas (1971-). A Roman aquilifer and a Texas infantry sergeant (1839) were made in 54mm metal kits for Cowan. They had the alternative name 'American Classic.'

Heritage Miniatures (Victor Roming), New Canaan, Connecticut (1973-). Roming began making architectural models and scenic backgrounds some 45 years ago (dioramas of South Smith Street at the New York Museum and asphalt miners at the Smithsonian Institution). During the Second World War he made scale model ships for identification purposes for the Navy Department. (An aircraft carrier was made for the Roosevelt Collection at Hyde Park, New York.) Later he started making model artillery for various producers (e.g. Com-E-Tec) and in 1973 began to market his own models. These are in pewter, in 54, 70 and 90mm, mainly of the American Revolution, with good cannon of all periods, a series of Colonial craftsmen and women, and delightful animals and birds. He also makes facsimiles of buttons and historic coins. He dispenses with a plasticine model, working the master direct in the re-

quired pieces, which are then cast in kit form and assembled. Ill-health has caused a suspension of work.

Heritage Models Inc., Dallas, Texas (1975-). Makers of 25mm solids of the medieval period and mythical creatures, some inspired by Tolkien's *Lord of the Rings.* [*Anton*]

Heritage, New Zealand (1978-). Manufacturers of plastic semi-flat 45mm models: a set of six of New Zealand military figures from 1850 to the present date. [*Kearton*]

Hermua, Madrid. Publisher of paper sheets of the Spanish Civil War.

Hernando, Madrid (pre 1914-1936). Publisher of paper sheets of European armies. From 1914 to 1936 they were printed on inferior paper. [*Balil*]

Heroard, Dr John, France. Author of a delightful journal of great historical significance covering the years 1601-1628. An English translation occurs in Crump. The first ten years deal with the early life of Louis XIII, to whom he, as medical adviser to the household, appears to have been devoted. We learn that in 1604 the Dauphin 'played at soldiers with his little lords, dressed in a complete suit of armour, carrying a diminutive pike, and shouting "Come on, soldiers! March! On guard"'. He also possessed bows and arrows, arquebuses, swords, a black horse with a soldier on it, a mounted Turkish trumpeter, trumpets and drums in profusion, and a little silver cannon given him by Sully. In 1608 his indulgent mother, Marie de Medici, gave him a large army of silver soldiers, 300 in all, made by Nicolas Roger, and forgot to pay for them, which was a royal prerogative. Apparently he also attempted to make some models of his own, and in 1610 he 'cast some little lead soldiers' 7cm high, pegged to fit into a board, presumably to perform drill. He also made cannon soldered with 'Spanish iron, which fired without bursting', and made the year 1617 an alarming one for the good doctor, the nurses and governesses. Finally, he had other models of pottery, wood and cardboard in all shapes and sizes.

Heroics (R.B. & J.R. Styles), London (1972-). Manufacturers of 6mm solids: infantry, AFVs, and forts and castles in polystyrene, ready cut out, in the same scale; coloured prepressed cardboard landing craft, 1978.

Heron, Craig, Baltimore, Maryland (1973-). Maker of clothes-peg models, for sale, the legs from wire and tape, and with natural clothing, 65mm high.

Herrings Soldiers, Greenwich, Connecticut (1976-). Manufacturers of neo-Britain-style models in sets of four to eight pieces. Poor quality and production intermittently interupted.

Herzog, H., Hanover (c.1936). Publisher of flats.

Hetzer, Germany. Manufacturer of polystyrene AFVs.

Heuchler. *See* Pilz, C.F.

Hewitt, N., Australia. One of the team of dioramists employed at the Australian War Memorial.

Heyde, Dresden (c.1840-1944). The best known and the most prolific of the German manufacturers of solids and semi-solids, ranking alongside Britains of England and Mignot of France as the most important makers of toy soldiers. It is possible that the firm began operations at a much earlier date than that quoted in *Hannover's Gloria*, No. 84, which gives 'c.1870', although labels on boxes bearing mentions of prizes won are not known before 1872. The founder certainly made some tentative models c.1830 but the firm really became established

44 **Heyde.** *Examples of solid toys cast in soft metal (Wade).*

under Gustav Adolf Theodor (1855-) and was brought to fruition by Georg (1872-1939). As with Heinrichsen and his flats, success was assured by the enormous sets made and the quantity of output, together with the great variety of postures. Two main types of boxed sets were available, the 'Battle' and the 'Parade', both of which are self-explanatory. The general characteristic of a Heyde model is an overlarge body with short legs and overlong arms. The lead of which the earlier models were made was very pliable, enabling the manufacturer to bend arms and legs at will, thus achieving different postures at the expense of anatomy. The weapons were often of pure tin, easily bent; the heads were plugged in and riders carried a little peg which fixed them to their saddles. Sizes varied enormously from 40mm to over 110mm, and models were issued in various qualities, the larger models being on the whole the more accurate anatomically, and sometimes having the refinement of removable helmets, swords and bayonets. Horses in the largest sizes were hollow-cast. Overall, less accuracy was shown in details of uniform than by Britains, and the general impression is of a certain clumsiness. The collecting of Heyde models presents the same difficulties as those found by the Britains enthusiast – the wealth of different models, the sizes, and the qualities. Some of the later models, for example, display the influence of Britains, and are in hollow-cast, one of their catalogues, indeed, extolling their virtues as 'very light, especially suitable for exportation', and mentioning 'second quality' and sizes 'IB' and IC'. As well as the normal figures, they made groups of combatants, and armaments, wheeled transport, pontoons, camp-fires, trees, hedges and impedimenta likely to be found in a warlike situation. The horses in the smaller sizes were semi-solid, and rifles sometimes retained a coloured blob of fire inherited from Heinrichsen's flats. The whole range embraced history from ancient times to the First World War, and included such now famous sets as the

Greeks and Trojans, in which Hector is dragged along behind the chariot of the triumphant Achilles, and which incorporated weeping women and classical temples; the procession of Germanicus, complete with chariots and bound captives; gladiatorial fights; Hannibal's march on Rome, with magnificent elephants; incredibly romantic and impossible medieval warriors; a very fine and elegant British encampment during the American War of Independence; the Franco-Prussian War; North American Indians with tethered victims; an Arab camp; the Durbar of 1910, with foreign potentates, rajahs, elephants, Indian troops, and gilded Hyderabad artillery; the Negus Menelik receiving ambassadors; an incredible elephant gun-team; British Naval ratings; Boer War Royal Engineer balloon section, displaying remarkable ingenuity. (Other sets are mentioned on pages 155-157 and 194-195 of the author's *Model Soldiers for the Connoisseur.*) The sheer volume of production swamped England at the end of the 19th century, but Britains' hollow-casts gradually gained the upper hand, even though as late as 1940 Heyde sets were on sale in the larger stores. The factory at Dresden was obliterated during the bombing and thus died the work of a manufacturer who, although never achieving the elegance or precision of a Lucotte or a Haffner, holds an honoured place in the development of the miniature figure and still has countless admirers in many parts of the world. The influence exerted by the Heyde production is evident in the works of other contemporaries and later manufacturers, especially in Spain and Italy, and modern replicas are being made by Silvano (*q.v.*). Methods of recognition include the stepping-off on the right foot of a marching infantryman, weapons sloped on the right shoulder, and the comical belly-to-ground charging horses. Paint varies from eggshell to shiny. Mark on labels of boxes: ⇄

Heyde, Leipzig (early 20th century). Producer of a few flats.

Heydorn, Wolfgang, Hamburg (fl.1950-60). Manufacturer of flats, 30-50mm, many of peculiar anatomy. His range included Russia 15th-17th centuries, Poland 1792-94, Denmark 1849-50, China 19th century, German Wehrmacht 1939-45, and Mr Pickwick. In 50mm: North American Indians. The moulds were purchased by Kebbel in 1960.

Heyer, Vienna (c.1890). A little-known maker of 7-8cm solids, which were apparently of fine quality.

HH (Ole Høyer and J.W. Hansen), Copenhagen (1974-). These two artists joined together to produce a series of 54mm solids of Danish historical uniforms, the former as designer, the latter as caster. These are distinguished by their elegance and restraint, typical of Scandinavian makers. Like all the best designers, they know where to stop. A Høyer prototype is made of Isopon and balsawood. An equestrian Gustavus Adolphus is a fine, curvetting figure, awarded a medal at Milan in 1976. (*See also* 'Steadfast Lead Soldier'.)

Hibbert, R., London (1970-). Included as an example of eccentricity: he makes 20mm models out of clothes-pegs and matchsticks.

Hickmott, Allerton C., Hartford, Connecticut. In 1958 he donated a collection of models by Stadden, Métayer, Ballada, Courtenay, Greenwood and Ball, Berdou, Baldet and Victoire to Trinity College Library, Hartford. In his own words: 'I had reached a point when it seemed that my brigade of military miniatures crowded round me with a coldly possessive eye'. (*The Book Collector*, Summer, 1958)

Hicks, Peter, Seend, Wilts (1970-). Maker of 20cm solids in cold cast bronze, mainly for presentation to Regiments or commissioned by Regimental museums. In addition he paints a number solely for Zellis of Burlington Arcade. Other work includes jockeys in their owners' colours and non-military bronzes for such diverse firms as Avon Tyres and Unigate Foods.

Hierapolis, Syria. A semi-flat horseman with a conical hat dating from 5th century was found here.

Higgins, Leslie, Northampton (fl.1965-72). The tragic death of Leslie Higgins at the early age of 47 cut short a career which showed signs of such competence that greater things must surely have ensued. He began as a maker of tiny drivers for model cars for commercial toy firms, then turned to the production of 20mm solids which were of the same excellence as those of Niblett and, indeed, complemented them. The first were of the English Civil War, including a drumhead preacher and a standard bearer, Cromwell and Charles I, all on foot. At the same time he produced a Norseman, a Grenadier of 1745 and a Cameron Highlander. Later his range expanded to include a fine series of Marlburians in 25mm, which had the elegance of comparable flats of the same period. From these he turned to the slightly larger 30mm, making a fine but smaller series of the Civil War, including a serving wench, which was marketed under the name 'Jason'. These attractive models were superceded by others of the same period in 56mm (1965). Good though they were, they could not avoid a certain clumsiness and coarseness in the faces and hands, but his 'powder monkey' was an outstanding figure. A series of civilians including a suitably pompous Samuel Pepys and a refreshing set of Dickens's characters followed. A model of Hitler showed his antipathy to the man, and we wonder that he ever published it, but a range entitled 'Pagada' made for and marketed by 'Tradition', consisting of Elizabeth I, Henry VII, Henry VIII, Lady Jane Grey with executioner, a burgomaster, a Regency couple, Raleigh, and an officer, drummer, pikeman and musketeer of the 17th century (the name in cursive under the footstand) formed a fitting close to a distinguished career. After his death the moulds were taken over by B.L. Marlow, and a few castings are still available. (*See* Phoenix Model Developments.)

Higgs, David and **Richard.** *See* Miniature Figurines.

Hilditch, Graham. *See* Caberfeidh Miniatures.

Hill, John & Co. *See* Johillco.

Hillman, Frank, Leipzig, Publisher of flats. (*Katalog der Formen*, 1976)

Hilpert, Coburg/Nuremberg (1720-1822). The first and most important name in the history of the German flats, Andreas Hilpert, a tinsmith, was followed by his sons Johann Gottfried (1732-1801) and Johann Georg (1736-95), and Johannes Wolfgang, son of Johann Gottfried (1736-1800). The moulds were subsequently purchased, circa 1805, by J.H. Stahl (fl.1805-22), and later still by A. Haring. Marks: H;JH;JGH (sometimes dated, the earliest known being 1775); J.W. HILPERT FECIT. Tinsmithing had existed in Germany for centuries, the products being mainly of a religious nature, together with trinkets and furniture for dolls' houses. Military figures were made, but of an extremely clumsy nature, and anonymously. Gradually, however, a small but growing industry in martial figures emerged between 1750 and 1770, at Frankfurt in particular about the latter date. It is reasonable to suppose that Andreas Hilpert had some military models in his output, but nothing bearing his name appear to be known. Johann

45 **Hilpert.** *Frederick the Great, made and signed in 1777. Probably the most famous flat ever made.*

Gottfried learned the craft from his father between 1746 and 1750, and then left him to take up an apprenticeship in Nuremberg, where he received his Mastership and the freedom of the city. His son Johannes Wolfgang, although becoming a Master himself in 1787, remained with his father until his death. Johann Gottfried also trained J.C. Scheelhorn, who later left to form his own business. Johann Georg joined his elder brother after training with Andreas, and again stayed with Johann Gottfried until he died in 1795. Hilpert for a long time followed the traditional rococo style of civic worthies and tradesmen, hunters and gypsies, farm and pastoral scenes, public gardens and buildings, animals and birds, including a set of 19 monkeys with Latin inscriptions. Soon, however, the martial side of the Germanic character began to assert itself, and it may well have been the issue of the engraving by Chodowiecki of an equestrian Frederick the Great that fired Hilpert to create a series of military leaders. Certainly his own version of the portrait is a masterpiece. Issued in 1777, two versions are known, one signed 'H', the other 'J.H.1777'. The size was the traditional large one (15cm). Others followed of Voltaire (1778), the Prince de Ligne ('J.G. HILPERT, 1778') and others of a similar nature. In these figures the art of engraving has never been surpassed and they remain the earliest masterpieces of their craft. Frederick had to have troops and Hilpert proceeded to make them in great quantities and different sizes, as well as French, Russian and Turkish forces. An early Hilpert is quite unmistakable. In most instances he mastered the anatomy of the horse far more readily than his contemporaries (and many of his successors) and his figures have both animation and facial expression, even though conventions still prevail. The colouring, when full, is rich, but in many the painting was confined to the rider only, the horses being left blank. The later members of the family made use of inferior alloys so that much of the sharpness of the engraving was lost (e.g. the Napoleon), and when Stahl (probably a dealer) took over the stock, he began recasting from moulds that had almost worn themselves out; Haring, the last owner, did the same.

Hinchliffe, Frank and **Robert**, Meltham, Yorks (1967-). The Hinchliffes began with remarkably fine artillery pieces made by Frank, which were admirably suited for incorporation with the models of Gammage and Stadden. They had already (1966) exhibited 54 and 60mm military figures, but it was not until about 1973 that they added magnificent horses and men (by David Sparrow) to their artillery. In the meantime, due probably to their being joined by Peter Gilder, they had begun (1969) a series of 20 and 25mm wargame figures which many collectors cherish for their own sakes rather than for use (although the early specimens are thin and spindly products). The range is now extensive (at one time five masters a week were appearing) and features ancient times (including little-known tribes, auxiliaries and subdued races) and the Napoleonic period, besides 'personality' figures, the Middle Ages and the American War of Independence. In 1974 the riders of the 25mm range were cast separately for the first time. The following year science fiction and war elephants appeared. Again with the wargame in mind, they brought out a new venture in the form of a complete series of dioramic-scenic units, complete with 12mm

models by Gilder called System 12. David Sparrow began making 54mm models in 1973, beautifully sculpted, and comprising Napoleonics, Victorians, the American War of Independence and the Civil War. In 1974 an arrangement was made with the English agents of Historex whereby the English Ray Lamb was loaned, as it were, to Hinchliffe, who in effect did the casting and marketing of a series of 75mm models of the Napoleonic era designed by Lamb, which, although popular, were anatomically gauche. A 90mm Saburai kit, by the same man, however, is in a class of its own. These were followed by Prussians, a North American Indian in an unusual and attractive pose, and a mounted Assyrian archer and lancer. In the 90mm size again, 1974 saw the first of a series of Prussian and Cleve-Burg models by D. Roberts, which he might like to forget. The most outstanding contribution reverts back to 54mm, for, in 1975, Sanderson was commissioned to execute a splendid series of English soldiers and Zulus at Isandhlwana, used to great effect in various dioramas. Others to work for the firm are Benassi, in 78mm, his figures being of a rather grotesque and tasteless character, Stadden (1976, in 75mm, only one of a projected series being issued), Jarvis (90mm), and Paul Knight (1978), with an 80mm mounted knight with a variety of equipment. Reverting to smaller models, in 1976 Peter Gilder began a series in 25mm entitled 'Foremost', while in 1979 some 25mm sets were marketed under the name 'Calder Craft'.

Hingle, C.B.O. Associated with Stadden in the early days of the latter's career.

Hinote, Ronald. *See* Little Generals.

Hinsch, Bruno, Hamburg (1932–1957). Engraver of flats who began work in 1932 (*Ortmann*). His most important works are sets of Assyrians, Babylonians and Hebrews, slave markets and a 'drinking orgy'. These, together with his Wild West models, are now owned by Ochel. Before beginning flats, Hinsch had made tanks in the round.

Hinton Hunt Figures Marketing Ltd (Marcus Hinton) Taplow, Bucks, (1957-). Hinton began making models in collaboration with Simon Hunt, but the latter soon left to devote his energies to music. Hinton's interest in collecting actual military equipment has stood him in good stead for he has created a vast series of models of most periods in history. The Napoleonic era (including a chess set and separate portraits of the Marshals) is almost inevitably predominant, but he has also made Romans, Saxons, Greeks, Samurai, and more modern European armies, including the American War of Independence (again including a chess set), the Crimean War, the Risorgimento and the American Civil War. All these are in 56-58mm. He was one of the earliest makers of wargame figures, which are still in great demand, and of good quality when properly cast, but unfortunately many are issued that are so heavy with flash as to be unacceptable to the collector. His medieval range is impressive more by the number of subjects than in the quality of the models. Too often a basic torso with unfortunate knock-knees and inanimate arms create a row of models distinguishable only by the different periods of armour. One of the best is of the Black Prince, which has the leopards and lilies engraved on the jupon and the shield, and the herald is quite impressive. The range serves a useful purpose for the creation of heraldic

25 Far left: **Jackson.** *Large statuette made shortly before his death in a number of materials, some never used before (Private collection). 26* **Krauhs.** *Sultan Lamido of Rei Buba (Central Africa) with his ministers. Large composite figures (Krauhs).*

28 **Lelièpvre**. *Two 54mm solids. Left, Zimbalier gendarme Ecossair; right Louis XIV (Leliepvre).*

29 **Mignot**. *The staff of King Umberto I (Gennari).*

figures, but the 75mm models, begun in 1974, emphasize the inherent overall clumsiness of the conception. None of his horses is other than pedestrian, so to speak, but although it would be difficult to class his work in the top quality, he certainly deserves a place in history as filling a need at various times. Apart from military models, he also makes rifle stands, paved roads and the like, most useful for vignettes. His civilian figures should not be forgotten, including one of Mathew Brady with his camera. It should be noted that the Napoleonic and 58mm medieval ranges are also available unassembled under the name of Guard House. Hinton himself is one of the characters of the trade, and in this his whimseys are aided and abetted by his wife. He changed his trade name from Hinton Hunt Figures in 1974. His wargame figures have suffered more than many others from the indignity of piracy, especially in the United States, where even his name and the serial number remains on some of the castings.

Hinton, Peter, Chapel Hill, North Carolina (1976-). Freelance designer of Freehold Miniatures included in Monarch's range, including Thracians and hoplites, 17th-century troops and a set of the Four Musketeers. A Henry VIII is also included in Greenwood and Ball's (Pearce) list, and some of the medieval figures are modelled directly from actual armour in the Metropolitan Museum, New York, and in Vienna. In 1977 he issued 77mm models, to be followed in the same year by a 75mm winged Polish Lancer.

Hirn (or **Hoerner**), Strasbourg (1795). Publisher of paper sheets.

Historex S.A. Aeros (M. Gillet), Paris (1950-). Manufacturers of 54mm polystyrene kits of foot and cavalry of incredible intricacy and accuracy. The firm began in 1950 as makers of aircraft kits, but about 1964 turned their attention to the production of military models at the instigation of Eugene Lelièpvre, who has remained their chief designer and consultant. They have so far

concentrated on creating a vast number of models of French troops of the Napoleonic era, outstanding in their precision and delicacy. Each kit comprises many component parts, including straps and leathers, and such minute objects as buttons. The conversion angle is unlimited, and it might well be said that their sales are greater than those of any other maker in any material. Attempts at models in plastic in kit form had been made before, but the accuracy of the design and the skilful making of the parts singled them out as innovators of a new idea in model soldiers, wherein the amateur could create his own figure without any knowledge of anatomy, although strangely enough printed instructions as to assembly were not given with the kits. The French artillery team certainly stands as a masterpiece in its own right, and is of such intricacy that often it needs more than one pair of hands to complete. As with other innovations, it was a few years before the idea became firmly established, but it is certain that there can be no limit to their empire. In 1975 they introduced two ranges of accessories for an inn and a farmyard, to assist the makers of dioramas and, in 1977 a pair of nudes, ideal for imaginative clothing. Modern warfare is represented by their entrenching tools, water bottles, etc, supplied under the name of Armour Accessories. As was inevitable, other firms followed where they had led, but all except SEGOM, the originators of the idea in a somewhat different and more limited form, and Airfix, appear to have fallen by the wayside.

Historic. *See* Seamer Products Ltd.

'Historical Figures' series. *See* Ceramics.

Historical Miniature Figures. *See* Scruby, J.

Historical Model Figures, England (fl.1939). Makers of 40mm solids.

History and Adventures of Little Henry, The. S. and J. Fuller, Temple of Fancy, London (1810). A series of four coloured aquatint cards for cutting out and standing up, giving Henry a choice of costumes comprising those of a drummer, a midshipman, a naval captain, a schoolboy and a beggar. Probably the earliest English set of cut-out sheets. A pamphlet of 16 pages was issued to go with it. It was reprinted in 1976 by Scolar Press.

Hitcher, Gerald. *See* Saunders, N.

Hitchins, T.K., London (fl.1937). Maker of models in wood and in plywood, 6 inches in height.

Hitrovo, Michael V., Ambler, Pennsylvania. One of the outstanding collectors of modern times, not for the quality or quantity of his collection, but for his enthusiastic altruism. Now crippled by illness (which does not prevent his giving of his knowledge and assistance) he was formerly active in the making of his own solids, and a collection of his Russian troops is in the White Russian Museum at Lakewood, New Jersey. He was also an early inspiration to the then emergent school of native American model makers.

Hockley Shell Moulds, Laindon, Essex (1975-). Makers of replica Napoleonic 12-pounder gun and ammunition limber.

Hodapp, Wolfgang, Karlsruhe. Publisher of 30mm flats, mainly of the Napoleonic era (especially troops of Baden), designed and engraved by Sollner.

Hodge, M.D. *See* Parade Miniatures.

Hoene, K.P., Wurzburg. Producer of flats.

Hoffman, D., Nuremberg (c.1930). A gun carriage was listed in a Phillips auction sale in 1975.

46   **Hitrovo.** *A specialist American modeller (M.V. Hitrovo).*

47 **Hollow-casts** *from a wide variety of makers (Wade).*

Hoffman, E., Germany (fl.c.1965). A professional painter of flats.

Hoffman, Captain Fritz, Zurich (d.1965). A producer of 30mm flats, mainly of the modern Swiss Army. About 1930 he re-issued a number of Allgeyer's Swiss village scenes.

Hoffmann, Heinrich, Nuremberg (1870-?). Maker of flats, including an amusing *'Struwwelpeter'.*

Hohenstein & Lang, Berlin (c.1900). Publisher of 14 x 16 inch paper sheets.

Hohmann, Adolph, Kassel. Listed in the Kulmbach catalogue of 1973 as a manufacturer of flats.

Hohrath, Daniel, Esslingen (1979-). Publisher of flats.

Holden, Barry. Serving in the Royal Air Force, 1974. Professional painter for the Dover branch of Historex.

HOLLAND. A society was established in 1955, staging an important exhibition the following year, at which dioramas made from imported flats were the principal attraction. At the same time a number of collectors displayed their own original models, and it was thought that some commercial ventures might be started. However, this was not to be, and so far as can be ascertained one maker only, Schoppen, has emerged. A certain number of publishers of paper sheets exist, but the Dutch still rely on importations, even specimen figures in the Dutch Army Museum being by Stadden.

Holberg, J.G., the younger, Potsdam (c.1830). Employed as an engraver by Meyerheine.

Holloday, A.J. & Co. *See* Skybird.

HOLLOW-CAST. In 1893 William Britain placed on the market a revolutionary model formed by a shell of metal whose two sides had been soldered together under great heat. The moulds were similar to those used by the manufacturers of solids, but the leaden core was poured away through small vent-holes. The result was a much lighter figure which was also more fragile. The advantages were cheapness of production and a great increase in output, but the beginning was singularly inauspicious, and it was several years before the toy stores were convinced that this was to be a lasting form of toy soldier. However, once established, export soon followed, and practically every country in the world purchased them in ever-increasing quantities, sometimes to the detriment of their own aspiring native manufacturers, the one exception being the United States, where, we are reliably informed, the Grey Iron Casting Corporation more than held its own [*Zipple*]. At first Britains had a number of rivals (mostly short-lived) whose products were blatant piracies, but after the Second World War several firms were serious contenders in popularity. Of these John Hill (Johillco) made some solid-looking models of better design and more varied action than Britains, while at times Cherilea, Crescent and Charbens all produced satisfactory models. Those made by Timpo reached a high standard, especially their medieval and American G.I. ranges, but in many instances firms were content to produce models of small consequence, some being well below the standard 54mm in size. Even so, the hollow-cast provided the basis of the toy soldier trade, and, at the same time, and in the absence of something better, attracted the attention of serious collectors (albeit often for conversion). Many of the models, indeed, are now of historic interest, some occasionally being of surprisingly good quality, while others portrayed subjects not yet superseded by more sophisticated craftsmanship.

Hollow-casts differ from commercial solids in their weight and in the fact that riders are normally cast with the horse in a single piece (exceptions were Cherilea's 'Baronial' series, and Timpo's 'Ivanhoe' and 'King Arthur' sets). Up to the Second World War the models were packed in boxes containing on an average five to eight soldiers, each performing the same action, together with an officer. Larger boxes were made up of an amalgam of positions, with bands, and perhaps a sentry box or an extra officer as a bonus. Great ingenuity was displayed in the making of the musical instruments, and here the movable arm (not invented by Britains, but brought to perfection by them), was an obvious attraction. Boxes were attractively decorated and, being of a uniform size, could be easily and neatly stored. It was thus possible to build up large parades, and much use of the positions offered was made at the time of the Coronation of King George VI. The uniform size of the models was ideal for use in recruiting and military training and, although toys, they were extremely accurate as to uniforms and weapons, and re-issues were made from time to time as dress regulations changed.

After the Second World War much more freedom of position was expressed and, indeed, it is from this time that the emphasis on 'men of action' dates. The old tradition of the boxed set with its rows of stylized actions was no longer regarded as a requisite, and models began to appear in separate cardboard containers. Many anonymous firms were making the occasional model and identification of the odd model found in the junk shop is becoming increasingly difficult. Several Continental firms, including Heyde and Mignot, were influenced by what to them was an alien technique, but kept the process for their cheaper models. Vertunni, however, early recognized its potential in his superb portrait-models. Barclay and Manoil and a few other firms in the United States made their models in hollow-cast, but on the whole it remained a particularly British achievement. Nor must it be forgotten that the old German tradition of country scenes and farm life in flats was paralleled in Britain by the hollow-cast, and today these rural scenes, which were a commonplace in 1920-40, are eagerly sought for. Now that production has ceased, their collectability has increased, and the nostalgic element is being met by firms such as Nostalgia and Blenheim who, while not slavishly copying Britains, and, indeed, casting in solid, and with movable arms, are recreating the past. Many collectors, also, are re-casting from the original moulds, taking pains, it is to be hoped, that the models are marked as copies or facsimiles.

Holmes, W., England (d.1970). Modeller and designer for Deltorama.

Holst, Adolph, Copenhagen (c.1900-1940). Publishers of paper sheets of Danish Hussars and artillery, in two sizes and thicknesses.

Holt, John. *See* Dragon Miniatures.

Holtfort, Dr W., Germany (fl.c.1965). A professional painter of flats.

Holtz, J.A.A., Hamburg, (1820-30). Maker of flats. One in

10cm of Marshall Blücher, is illustrated in Kollbrunner.

Holweg, J. and **Hendl, Wilhelm,** Vienna (fl.1890-1914). Publishers of paper sheets of predominantly Austrian troops, but also featuring those of Germany, France, Camel Corps and Zulus.

HOME-CASTING. The provision of ready-made moulds from which the purchaser could cast his own models has been popular from early times, and it is possible that Hans Andersen's 'steadfast tin soldier', who lacked a leg because the metal (that of an old tin spoon) ran out, may have been made in this way. Normally the moulds were of execrable crudeness, as evinced by the numerous semi-flat examples found when digging the garden. In 1975 the author saw a collection of such, with flaking household paint, bandy and twisted legs, featureless in every way. However, on occasion manufacturers made their own moulds for distribution to the retail toy trade (e.g. Ace Toy Mold Company, Metal-Cast Products, Nathanson Brothers, Rapaport Brothers, and Schiercke), while a vastly superior set issued by Edman was designed by no less a person than Holger Eriksson. It is evident that some contemporary pewterers in the United States are using old American moulds of this type for the production of flats and semi-flats and since 1975 there has been a revival in Germany.

Home Founding Company, Chicago (fl.1933). Home-casting moulds.

'Home Pastimes'. *See* Griffin & Farran.

Hong Kong. A name of ill omen. Apparently native labour is so ill-paid there that Britains can afford to despatch vast quantities of their plastic moulds and pay for the return to England of the finished models and at the same time make a profit. Nowhere in the rest of the world is there such piracy of toys sold in the stores of the United States, Spain and Italy.

Honrath, G., Berlin. Publisher of pre-pressed cardboard trees. (*Ortmann*)

Hood, R.C., Tawa, Wellington, New Zealand (1970-). A commissioned maker of 54mm solids of British infantry. He uses a variety of materials to add to his own castings. He is represented at the Napier Museum, Wellington, and the Army Museum, Waiouru, New Zealand.

Hopf, Richard, Mengersgereuth-Hammern (c.1964-). Manufacturer of poor plaster-composition models of Westerners.

48   **Home-casting.** *From central Europe, except the large model which is from the United States (Author).*

Horlicks. *See* Ray, Don and Honey.

Horton, Sydney. *See* Chota Sahib.

Hourtoule, G. *See* D.F.H.

Howard, John. *See* Cody Models.

Howarth, J.R., Rochdale (1979–). Maker of a chess set in the medieval style in the form of flats.

Howell, E.V., Staines, Middlesex (c.1930). Maker of 9 - inch plywood figures, to be seen at the Border Regiment Museum, The Castle, Carlisle.

Hoy, Copenhagen (fl.1848-50). Apparently the only named maker of 7cm Danish flats. A handful of models only are known: a 15th-century knight, two different horseguards, and an equestrian Frederick VII. A limited edition of the latter has been recast by the Copenhagen Technical Museum.

Høyer, Ole. *See* H H.

Hoyles, D., Bridlington (1978–). Creator of a series entitled 'Folk Heroes' for 'On Parade'.

H.R. Products Ltd (Cy R. Broman), Morton Grove, Illinois (1968–). Originally producing solid models as a pastime, Broman began to market them around 1968, and has since built up a substantial volume, about half being of Americans in the Second World War. His earliest efforts of Indians were in kit form, and unusual in having scenic bases. By the alteration of equipment an Ojibwa hunter became a Hudson Bay trapper; other models included a Zulu, a Bulgarian officer and von Richtofen. Some of these early models were designed by Tom Sibbitt and Richard Kramer. Of his own designing is a self-portrait as a US Pilot when on duty in England. Today he concentrates more on armaments and extra weapons for 54mm models, of which he has made an extremely large and useful collection, and plastic battle-fields for 20mm models.

H.R. Products (H. Reynolds), London (fl.1955). A small manufacturer of 54mm hollow-casts, whose output included a set of thickset Vikings, a poor Roman centurion and a legionary, and a 'Treasure Island' set. All were issued with biscuit-coloured footstands.

HS-Zinnfiguren. *See* Deutsche Zinnfiguren-Werkstatte, Berlin.

Hubbard, William, USA. A professional painter employed by Cowan.

Huber, Baron Francis Xavier, London (d.1970). An eccentric collector who possessed a large number of the finest quality models.

Hubert, André (E. Baptiste). Paris (1968–). A maker of 54mm solids of fine quality in the traditional French method and limited in their edition.

Hubley Manufacturing Co., Lancaster, Pennsylvania. A firm making cast-iron toys such as carriages and miniature dolls' prams, said by McClintock to have been founded in 1894. In 1940 they were making metal tanks. Taken over by Gabriel Industries in 1965.

Hudson Pewter (Schmid Brothers Inc.), Barrington, Rhode Island (1975–). Publishers of a fine series of 60mm American War of Independence leaders, together with a group of four models on one stand entitled 'Spirit of '76' made for them by Lance Miniatures of New England. Other models were designed for them by Com-E-Tec, Baston and Sullivan.

Huelse, Dresden (mid-19th century). Carved wooden soldiers exhibited at the Paris Exposition of 1855.

Huen, V., Nancy, France (fl.1914). Designer of paper sheets published by *Imageries Réunies de Jarville Nancy.*

Hughes, General G.P., London. Responsible for one of the dioramas at Woolwich Arsenal.

Hugonnet, France (c.1970–). Manufacturers of 54mm plastics, including two 17th-century mounted musketeers, French Foreign Legion, 'Red Berets', United States troops and cowboys. Many are direct piracies from Lone Star, Herald, Timpo and Reamsa. [*Kearton*]

Hujos, Barcelona (19th-century). Publisher of paper sheets.

Hume, Ella L. *See* Moulded Miniatures.

Hummel House of Miniatures, London. One of the most elegant though restricted shops dealing with model soldiers. Formerly Morrell's, well-known to pre-war collectors of flats and specialist models, it was here, in the mid-thirties, that the author first saw an array of Courtenay's models, arranged as if on a battlefield, 'reduced to one guinea' each, which, although he had at the time never had a thought of collecting models, lingered in his memory as a blaze of colour. Mr R. Webb, the proprietor, has acted as agent for Ping, Courtenay (and the present Courtenay-Ping-Greenhill), Arthur, Greenwood, Stadden, Niblett, Patmore, Willetts, and occasionally Ségom and Alymer.

Hunt and Hoffman, Nuremberg (1867). Publishers of paper sheets. The Paris Exposition of 1867 contained an entry of stiff paper designs of farm animals, agricultural workers, haywains, farmhouses, etc.

Hunt, Simon, London (1957). Associated with Marcus Hinton in the commencement of Hinton Hunt Miniature Figures. He left to devote himself to music, but not before he had done a small amount of designing for The Sentry Box.

Hunter, David, Penshurst, Kent (1975). Creator of a diorama of the Battle of Hastings on exhibition at Battle Abbey, containing 1400 20-25mm metal and plastic models.

Huppertz, Gunther, Germany (1977–). Wooden accessories for Second World War dioramas.

Hurd, Beatrice and **Calvin,** USA (c.1968). Makers of 54mm solids. We know nothing further of them, nor can present-day collectors add to this.

Hurd, Major C. *See* Petit Soldat, Le.

Hure, Gilbert, Paris (fl.1938). A maker of 55mm solids; virtually unknown.

Huss, Herbert, Aldekerk, W. Germany (c.1960). Maker and professional painter of flats.

Hutchings, David. *See* Miniature Figurines.

HYDRASTONE. A cement-like plaster that yields a hard, water-resistant casting; used by L. Keenon.

I

ID, Hong Kong. 40mm plastic piracies seen in London in 1976.

Ideal Moulds, Germany. Home-casting moulds, semi-solid. [*Fischer*]

Ideal Plastics, New York (1958-). Manufacturers of 3-inch models in rubber-like plastic, mainly of G.Is, some with interchangeable equipment. Made and painted in Hong Kong for the juvenile market.

Ideal Toy Company (Lewis David Christie), Bridgeport, Connecticut (1920-1924). Manufacturers of 40 and 54mm hollow-casts of American forces and Indians, some with movable arms. Unusual for the period in that some were painted in matt colours. They were equivalent to poor-quality Britains. The moulds, made of bronze, were purchased from a Mr Hassellman, who obtained them in Germany. The figures carry no marks of identification. [*Anton*]

Ideal Toy Corporation, New York. According to McClintock the firm was founded in 1903, and made cast-iron wagons, horse-drawn carriages and the like. The first known military models made by them (in 1961) were 35-40mm plastic toys, of poor quality. It is possible that they are linked to Ideal Plastics (*see above*).

Iezzi, B. *See* Life Model.

Illuminated Games Co., London (1965). Makers of an electronically-controlled wargame battlefield seen at Hamley's in that year.

Ilse, E. Hanover (c.1840-55). A practically unknown engraver of flats. Mark: E. ILSE 1849.

Imagerie d'Épinal. *See* Olivier-Pinot.

Imagerie de Nancy, Nancy, (fl.1875). Publishers of paper sheets: may well have been an amalgamation of a number of publishers.

Imagerie Jarville Nancy, (fl.1865). Probably a predecessor of Imagerie de Nancy.

Imagerie Nationale, Paris/Grenoble (19th century). Publishers of paper sheets.

Imagerie Réunies de Jarville Nancy, Nancy/Paris (fl.1865-at least 1920). Probably successors to Imagerie Jarville Nancy.

Imageries de Pont à Mousson (M. Vagné et ses fils), Paris (fl.1900). Publishers of paper sheets.

Images Neurin, France (19th century). Publishers of paper sheets.

Imai, Japan. Manufacturers of AFV polystyrene kits.

IMP, Japan. Peter Greenhill owns a 54mm solid model of a Samurai, bearing the legend 'Made in Japan/IMP'. The date would be approximately 1970. A set of three 'Spirit of '76' models has also been heard of, but this is possibly a piracy.

Imperial, Hong Kong (1977-). Piracies in 54mm plastic of Airfix Australians masquerading as Americans. (*Kearton*)

Imperium Publishing Co., USA, (1979-). Publishers of scenic diorama card kits for use in 'fantasy' wargames, under the title 'Netherworld'.

Import D.E.N.T. *See* Oneto, A.

Imprenta Industrial SA, Bilbao, Spain (1972-). Publishers of stiff paper sheets.

Imprimerie Alsacienne. *See* Kieffer, F.

Imprimerie de Bouquet. *See* Support Breveté.

Imprimerie de Wissembourg, Alsace. Founded in 1833 by Ch.F.Wentzel. An establishment was opened in Paris in 1860, and a colossal number of paper sheets with titles in six languages, rivalling those of Pellerin, was issued. The business was run after 1880 by Ch. Burckardt, then from 1906 to 1920 by R. Ackermann. In 1960 it was revived by Ch. Euller who continues production.

Imrie/Risley Miniatures Ltd (William Imrie and Clyde Risley), Burnt Hills, New York (1954-). Imrie began in a tentative way making commissioned 54 and 60mm solid models for museums and private clients. This led to a certain small commercial outlet under the name of Imrie Custom Military Figures. Even in the early days the models were subjected to so much research that the purchaser could be assured of accuracy. In 1956 he was joined by his wife who had been trained as an artist, and they expanded their efforts with a series of models of the Napoleonic era in kit form, known as Hellenic Miniatures, these proving so popular that the original commissioned work had to be pared down. Joined by another artist, Clyde Risley, in 1962, the association grew in stature, mainly through Risley's knowledge of human and equine anatomy; indeed, Risley has designed horses for other makers. In the painting of exhibition models they can also call upon Risley's wife, another artist. They work basically to a 54-56mm solid torso, with separate heads and arms, and much animation goes into different models. In addition, spare parts are

49 **Imrie-Risley**. *German Infantry in winter dress (Imrie-Risley).*

available for collectors who wish to alter or add to their models. Where required the models are issued painted with their own particular make of colours. Their name is a household word in America and they hold a position similar to that of Stadden in England, although some harsh criticism has recently been levelled at them. A perusal of their catalogue discloses a preponderance of models of the American War of Independence, which is understandable, and, indeed, it would seem to many collectors that they are happiest in this period. Fifty-four different positions are available for the infantry and there are sixteen basic horses. These delightful, colourful models have formed the basis of many a diorama of Trenton or the Skirmish at Poundridge. One of the enduring masterpieces is the Trumpeter, First Troop, Philadelphia City Cavalry; and the heavy draught-horses, the six-pounder gun and the riders are an unforgettable achievement. The Napoleonic range is smaller and here the cavalry is the most important aspect, together with British and French field-guns. The broken-down parts are easily assembled, and the uniforms scrupulously accurate. The Civil War is adequately covered, again with cannon, but the horses in the main are those used for the earlier American war.

Apart from a few excursions into other periods, which will be considered later, their next most important contribution is in the Second World War where Germans and United States troops predominate, with a few British 'Desert Rats'. Camouflage is much in evidence, and a number of positions appear of a more violent nature than previously, dictated, no doubt, by the fact that violence in the Second World War seems, by its comparatively recent date, to be more pronounced than in earlier periods, paradoxical as this may seem, and a bayonet-charging British infantryman of 1775 has a dignity about him lacking in a grenade-throwing storm-trooper of 1941. The former is still a breathing human being, probably inwardly terrified, while his modern counterpart displays a ruthlessness which hardly commends itself to the traditional collector. This is no reflection on the ability of Imrie/Risley: it is merely symptomatic of the modern as against the traditional approach to the philosophy of the model soldier.

So far we have concerned ourselves with the mainstream of their models, but they have recently broken new ground with a series of 14th-century men at arms, archers and handgunners. The majority of these are based on the same torso and leg positions, but, although interesting, they do not achieve the spirit of the times. Nor is the mounted knight anything but ordinary. An Assyrian mounted archer, on the other hand, is a fine and colourful figure. More recent are a Roman centurion and a German tribesman, a Viking, a swashbuckling Landsknecht, a Musketeer of the time of Louis XIII, figures for the War of 1812, the Mexican and the Cuban Wars, First World War, Plains Indians, United States Cavalry and Prussians of 1910. A most interesting innovation is a series of carronades of the 18-19th centuries, with either an officer or a gunner. It is a pity that they have succumbed to the late '70s craze for nudes, as the slave-dealer and his captive group is far behind the creations of Gammage in a similar context. In 90mm two models are outstanding: an RAF and a German Air Force Pilot of the Second World War. These are cast in one piece. Another outlet is their French Renault tank (designed by Owen Gordon) in 54mm size.

Two things recently conspired to produce an impressive series of figures for the Franklin Mint: the bicentenary of 1776 and the growing popularity of pewter. The finely sculptured models of the American War of Independence are beautifully conceived, issued in limited numbers, and fit happily with the Colonial types already made by Chernak. In addition, a chess set of the same period was issued by The Soldier Shop, either in kit form, or a limited edition of 50 painted sets. In general, the models of the firm have a professional competence that is sturdy and unwavering among the mass of sometimes meretricious figures of contemporary makers, and at times a breathtaking example emerges. Certainly it would appear that, although one of the earliest exponents of the craft in the United States, they will remain the backbone of the American scene for years to come.

Incorporated Soldiers and Sailors Help Society, London (1914-18). The original name given to Lord Roberts' Workshop (*q.v.*) set up to provide occupation for wounded soldiers. Here they turned out 54mm hollow-casts, presumably of doubtful quality, and from moulds possibly made for them by Britains. Shamus Wade drew our attention to a label which was in his possession in 1972: 'Our Army and Navy. Models of His Majesty's Forces by Land and Sea. Seaforth Highlanders. Made in London by Disabled Soldiers and Sailors for the Incorporated Soldiers and Sailors Help Society, 122 Brompton Road, S.W. Correctness of detail in Uniform Equipment Guaranteed. To be obtained from all Toy and Athletic Dealers or from the Makers.'

Indestructible Speciality Co., New York (c.1910-30). Early American manufacturers of 54mm poor quality hollow-casts, mainly of the United States Army.

'In De Tinnen Wonderwereld'. *See* Spandauw, E.

Industria Argentina, Argentina (c.1935). Manufacturers of 54mm hollow-casts of native regiments. The mark appears on the footstand. (*Wade*)

Industria Nationale Giocattoli Automatici. *See* INGAPP.

INGAPP, Padua, Italy (1922-). Manufacturers of tin-plate vehicles.

Ingenia France, Paris. Publishers of stiff paper sheets of domestic and farm buildings.

Innovative Promotions Inc., Cherry Hill, New Jersey

(1973-   ). Manufacturers of 54mm plastic models. One set, in blue plastic, entitled 'Men of '76', is a blatant piracy of Britains' Swoppets, but crude in the extreme.

Instant Terrain. *See* Sinclair Toys Ltd.

International Silver Company, Meriden, Connecticut. In 1975 they issued a set of chessmen of the American War of Independence in pewter, in 500 numbered sets, and a series of 14 individual 3½-inch models, also in pewter, begun by Robert Sullivan and completed by Lloyd Lillie.

Ipey, J., Holland. Constructor (1950) of a model of a siege of a medieval castle for Leiden Museum.

'Iron Men'. *See* Grey Iron Casting Co.

ISA (Industria Soprammobili Artistici) (G. Pelli-Cini) Turin, Italy (1954-   ). One of the most prolific of Italian manufacturers of 54mm solids. A vast range covers most armies, with emphasis on those of Italy, marketed in boxes of 3, 4 or 6 pieces. Of the poorest quality (indeed, some are quite ludicrous), they have always been extremely popular in their native country. They are designed by Italo Cenni.

Isnard, Pierre-François, Strasbourg (1776-81). Designer

of five volumes of military uniforms, printed by Heitz and Levrault, containing wood engravings which were ideal for colouring, cutting out and mounting.

ISOPON. A chemical product of value in making prototypes or for conversion. When set it can be carved freely and cleanly. Only the resin and the filler is used, and it is cured by the addition of a hardener. The resin itself may be used for adhesion.

ISRAEL. The first Israeli production that can be traced dates from 1949, when there were large numbers of locally-made semi-flat 50mm troops, in all combat and marching positions, originally obviously representing British soldiers, but converted to Israelis by repainting. In 1950 they disappeared, not to be replaced until some seven years later, when two variants of 7cm lead military police were issued. These were so appallingly bad that they vanished overnight, to be supplanted by a plastic set of eight foot soldiers, which may, however, have been imported from England. In 1949 there appeared a sheet of a military aerodrome with planes, hangers, an A.A. battery and personnel. [*Roubicek*]

50   **Italy.** *Back row: Boggio (2); Pranzetti (in carved wood); middle row: Amati; front row: Parisini (2); Sideria (2) (Author).*

Italaeri, (Ital-Hobby), Bologna (1973–). Manufacturers of polystyrene AFV kits, and some 54mm plastic figures of fair quality, designed by Leonardo Bozzetti; German and Italian paratroops and artillery (1975).

Italia, Italy (c.1970–). Manufacturer of plastic composition models of the pre-war Elastolin style including Swiss and Scottish troops. [*Opie*]

ITALY. Flats appeared in Italy as early as 1770, a large collection being preserved at the Museo de Commune in Milan and at the Museo Civico in Turin. Research has failed to trace the names of the makers or the towns in which they operated. It may well be that the political refugees who later fled to Spain and began making models there learned their trade from these makers. There has been little attempt to continue the art, although the models of Mauke and Maraini are well known to modern collectors. The paper sheet, on the other hand, has always been most popular. Remondini, a firm which began about 1750 and lasted until 1859 (some of the sheets have been reprinted in modern times), may have been the first printers to realize the potential. A magnificent collection of over 2000 models of this period, cut out and mounted, was specially painted for the King of Naples by Emmanuele and Filippo Gin, and show great brilliance of movement and fine painting (illustrated in *Alberini*). It is certain that in 1878 the improvement in the art of lithography induced Lebrun and Boldetti to issue many sheets, to be followed by other printers such as Vedova Ventura, Mercenaro and Macchi, Giore, Castiglioni and others. Artistically the highest point was reached between 1895 and 1910, and commercially the First World War proved a profitable period. From 1930, however, a decline in standards set in. These are all now collectors' specimens (*Alberini*), but Morazzoni recalls that during the winter months working-class boys in Italy used paper sheets for a special game of their own devising. Boys between the ages of six and twelve cut out the figures and then placed them, five or six at a time, between the pages of a book, as a prize for a lottery. These 'working-class' sheets were printed in colour,

about 40 x 30cm, and purchasable from stationers.

Solid commercial models first appeared in 1927, when Francesco and Luciano Antonini began making their FIGIR series, based on the Heyde tradition of detachable riders. Still in existence, the models are as popular in Italy as Britains are in England, but they are of an incredibly naïve appearance, which is apparent also in the productions of L.A.R.G. (1934) and ISA (1954). However, this type of model is represented in bulk in the collections of several connoisseurs.

Specialist models are in the ascendant. The earliest maker we have been able to trace is Manfredini Otello (1958), who, however, we lost touch with until 1974, and it is good to know that after a lapse of several years he is beginning again. More recent makers are Bormioli and Parisini, while we have recently been privileged to see photographs of models by Boggio, Baschieri and Bragaglia which are quite breath-taking and equal to any. Amati and Sideria have also begun to make attractive models.

Italy has taken kindly to the composite figure, normally of wood clothed with actual materials, as exemplified in the work of Pranzetti, Chiappa and Battaglia. Wargame societies flourish, and collectors' clubs are in healthy existence. The one medium in which Italy seems indifferent to quality is that of the plastic or the plastic composition. We have seen numerous specimens from various makers and have been either unimpressed by their sameness or horrified or amused by their sheer inanity. On the other hand, it is said that the polystyrene A.F.V. kits that proliferate are acceptable.

Iturri, Father Carlos Garcia. *See* Assasition.

Ivanov, G., Stockholm. Maker of 30mm flats of the Russian Guard of 1913.

Iwaszko, Z.M., Ltd. *See* Miltra.

Izzard Century Toy Soldiers, London (1974–). 40mm semi-solids, 60mm semi-flats, cast from home moulds by Miles Izzard, on sale at Hummels. They are of parade troops and mounted Life Guards, sold in cylindrical chipwood boxes of antique style.

J

Jabey, M.J. *Call to Colors* magazine, vol 3 (c.1970) makes the assertion that M.J. Jabey, 'the noted figurine painter', together with Gunther von Wooster created the miniatures for the planning of the Coronation of Napoleon I! We cannot comment further!

Jac Models (J.A. & W.A. Collins), East Grinstead (1971-75). The first offerings were 30mm Napoleonic solids with cannon. In 1972 they began making 54mm solids, comprising some fifty-odd Napoleonics, together with British, Austrian, Bavarian, Spanish and Italian troops of the same period, British units of 1730-50 and 1878-1900, a mounted Cromwellian trooper and a Luftwaffe paratrooper. More important was their range of medieval figures, which reached considerable proportions. The footsoldiers would not satisfy the purists, being somewhat pigeon-chested (especially the archer) and many of the spearmen had very anaemic legs. Chain-mail, also, seemed to present some difficulty in portrayal. However, the knights (with various helms) were of better proportions than the men-at-arms, and the horses (riders cast separately) were really strong destriers. A quiescent knight, 'alone and palely loitering' as it were, with helm in hand and bent head, was a refreshing and unusual model, and one on a violently rearing horse could make a good centre-piece for a St. George and the dragon. They also made a few models in 75mm. The firm vanished as quickly as it appeared.

Jackboot (C. Robinson), Belfast (1970-). A trade name incorporating the work of Cliff Sanderson and John Barber. The solid models are of a true 54mm size, mainly of the Nazi army, but with breakaways in a First World War helmeted German, very stout, with beer stein in hand, and an unusual trumpeter of the Hillsborough Guard. The sculpture is rather shallow, with a tendency to an ovoid figure rather than a round one. Great confusion was caused at one time by Robinson's curious naming of his chief sculptor as 'Saunderson'. In 1975 Sanderson began a series of 90m models, the first being of Sepp Dietrich, an arrogant, posturing model, but indicative of the advance in technique he had made since his first efforts. Other, female, figures are in very bad taste.

Jacklex (E. Alexandre), Harrow (1972-). Delightful 20mm solid wargame figures, among the best on the market. His range covers British Colonial 1890-1910,

the regular Indian Army, the Zulu War, the North-west Frontier and the American Civil War.

Jackman, M. *See* Bofors Models.

Jackson, C. d'O. Pilkington, Edinburgh (1886-1973). A superb craftsman who is best remembered for his military statuettes in Edinburgh. These are of carved and polychromed wood, and most impressive in their reticence. He later turned to commissioned models, using a variety of materials, including polyester resin, non-ferrous metals, and gold and platinum leaf. These are mainly just over three feet high, and in his lifetime he complained to the author over his inclusion in the author's first book, as he could not reconcile the association of a 'statuette' with a 'model'. He was, however, mollified by the author's explanation that his statuettes were so well known that they could not possibly be omitted. A number (including one with a concealed turntable) have found homes in Calgary and in New York. His granite statue of The Bruce at Bannockburn (27 feet high) will be well-known, and has been copied in plastic by Niblett.

Jackson, Cecil. *See* Tru-Craft Models.

Jackson C. ('Jane Jackson'), Canada (1965-70). The first native Canadian maker of 54mm solids. During the short period in which he worked he produced an interesting series, including Fort Henry Guards, Butler's Rangers, Rogers' Rangers, Runchey's Negro Company, a Canadian Voltiguer, Major General Brock, gypsy girls, camp followers and a slave auction. He found marketing too difficult, and no English or American dealer was at the time sufficiently interested in stocking his models. The last time we saw him (1973) he informed us that the moulds had been destroyed. His was just another case where a model maker has been a generation too early. He used his wife's name Jane as his trade-name.

Jacobite Miniatures (W. Skinner and T. Park), Edinburgh (1978-). 15mm solid wargame models of the Napoleonic wars.

Jacobsen (Alfred) Forlag, Copenhagen (19th-20th centuries). Publishers of 'Danske Billeder', a series of paper sheets.

Jacques, Jeffrey, Rochdale, Lancs (1975-). Maker of 54mm solids, assembled, of 1854, 1914, 1916 and 1944 periods, of good quality.

51 **Jackson**. *Two 54mm solid examples by the first Canadian specialist (M.O'Brien).*

Jago, Esmond. *See* DEK

Jakobs, E.R., Grossenheim (fl.1900). Manufacturer of solids.

Janssen, J.P. *See* Black Watch, The.

JAPAN. A catalogue issued in America by Butler Bros, a wholesale toy dealer, lists in 1914 under the section 'Miscellaneous Japanese Toys' a set of 10 soldiers and sailors, 2¼ inches, made in papiermâché and painted to represent Japanese uniforms. Apart from this the only other reference to models actually made in Japan as against piracies is to a model made by IMP (*q.v.*), even though a few years ago Stephen Turnbull, an authority on Japanese armour, toured Japan in an effort to find specimens.

Jarville Nancy, Nancy (19th century). Publisher of about 40 paper sheets.

Jarvis, David, London, (1976-). Designer of 90mm Napoleonic models for Hinchliffe, and (1977) 100mm 'Dragoon Models' under his own name.

Jason. *See* Higgins, L.

Jay Line Manufacturing Co., USA (1943). Known to have made a cardboard camouflaged defence force, with aeroplane, soldiers, anti-tank unit and building, all prepressed for removal from the surround.

Jayman Manufacturing, USA (1939-44). Makers of cloth tents for miniature soldiers. [*Pielin*]

JC, Spain (c.1970). Manufacturers of 54mm plastics, probably piracies [*Opie*]. Possibly the same as Jecsan.

JEAN, Germany (c.1960-). Manufacturers of 52-54mm plastics. A number appear to be originals, but the bulk of their production consists of piracies of other makers. A siege tower (probably copied from Elastolin) is a remarkable achievement. Mark: W. GERMANY, the earlier models also bearing the name JEAN. [*Kearton*]

Jecsan (Javine Cuadrados Anton), Barcelona (fl.1965). Manufacturer of 54mm plastics.

Jenkinson, Jack, Kent (1970-). Has made master solids for several leading makers, e.g. Series 77 and, on occasion only, Gammage.

JER, France (c.1900-). Maker of a composition chess set representing France and Britain at war, with 20cm portrait models of George III, Queen Charlotte, Wellington, Nelson, Napoleon, Josephine, Talleyrand and Ney, and Britannia and La France (Marianne),

which was sold at Christie's, London, July 25, 1978 for £1,200.

Jervis, David, Lowestoft (1979-). Professional painter of solids.

JIM, Paris (1969-). Maker of good plastic 58mm models.

Jiminez, Angel, Barcelona (1920-36). Manufacturer of 45mm solids and a few semi-flats. The moulds of the former were later purchased by Castresana.

Job, Paris (c.1915). Designer of a series of volumes of figures for cutting out, published by Hachette. [*Schiller*]

Johansen, Stan. *See* Stan Johansen Miniatures.

Johanssen, I.H., Copenhagen (1968-). A private maker of 54mm solids, who some years ago joined with Anholm (*q.v.*) in the creation of some 65 models depicting uniforms at the time that Denmark was at war with Prussia and Austria. They were made for the Danish society.

Johillco (John Hill & Co.), London (c.1900-67). Manufacturers of 54mm hollow-casts, founded by a Mr Wood, formerly of Britains. A firm with a prolific output, little, if at all, inferior in quality to Britains. They were one of the first firms to make individual figures rather than boxed sets. They specialized in First World War khaki-clad troops, regimental series (some with movable arms), Arabs, Camel Corps, Romans (including a circus with gladiators), Crusaders and later medieval periods, the RAF, Civil Air Guard instructors and pupils, Westerners, Mounted Police, English police and policewomen, the Red Cross, United States Marines, West Point Cadets and Second World War combatants. Unusual models were those of a field-marshal with a baton, a steel helmeted infantryman with a small ring on the left arm to enable a change of weapon to be effected between an entrenching tool, a rifle or a Sten-gun, and a lifeboatman in various sizes. An exceptional model was a 16cm Knight of the Order of St John of Jerusalem, obviously made as a showpiece, as it was repeated in 54mm size. A coach originally designed for the coronation of George V, complete with outriders and attendants, was re-issued as required. Marks: JOHN HILL: J. HILLCO: JO HILL: JOHILLCO (some on the back of the figure, some on the underside of the footstand): ENGLAND on the bellies of some horses. Plastics, begun in 1956 (HILLCO/MADE IN ENGLAND) were undistinguished. The moulds were offered for sale in 1967 by Replicas of Liverpool, and it is probable that some at least (e.g., extra-terrestrials) were purchased by Cherilea. Some sets were issued as 'Britannia Brand'.

John Bull Miniatures (J. Stevenson), Vancouver. In 1974 an advertisement for three solid models in 54mm appeared in journals as being available in Canada and England, but no trace of them can be discovered.

John, Michael R. *See* Trophy.

Johnson, C.H., Wanannassan, New Jersey (1965-). Maker of polystyrene artillery of the period 1775-1783.

Johnson, Dennis. *See* Mitrecap Miniatures.

Johnson, D.M., New York (fl.1938). Assisted in the making of dioramas at the Museum of the City of New York.

Johnston, J.D. *See* Douglas Miniatures.

Johnstone, Peter. *See* Campaign.

Jones, J. Edward. *See* Moulded Miniatures.

Jones, M.E., Worcester, England (1973-). Maker of 10/12-inch-high wooden models, on foot and mounted.

Straps, etc, are made from lead. He prefers to make British or Colonial types. They have been on sale through Wade and have appeared in Phillips' auctions. He is represented by a series of figures of the Women's Army Services including colonials, at Staverton Skyfame Aviation Museum.

Jones, P. *See* British Bulldog.

Jones, Vernon, Australia. One of the artists employed on the dioramas at the Australian War Memorial.

Jonson, Ben, (1512-1637). English dramatist. His *The Devil is an Ass* (1616) mentions 'leaden men' representing 'Finsbury battles'.

José, Paris (fl.1880). Designer of an exceptional 8cm model for CBG. Unfortunately, it is a mere fragment, but enough remains to show that the rider, the saddle, and the horsecloth are removable. It is signed JOSÉ CBG PARIS.

Jouet Français, Paris (c.1940). Manufacturers of metal tanks of the smallest size.

Jouets la Moniquette, Hameau de Mery, France (fl.1958). Manufacturers of plastics of very poor quality.

Journal, The, USA, (1896). Battle of Bunker Hill as a paper sheet.

Journals. *See* Societies.

JOURNEYMAN. One who paints or animates for a maker. In the old days of the flat he would be known as an apprentice. A self-effacing and industrious person, often unhallowed and unsung, he gives life either to the casting of a master sculptor, or paints it for presentation to the public. A number of established makers in their own right began as animators (e.g. Robert Rowe). Journeymen compete for a trophy at the British Model Soldier Society's annual competition. To give them the credit they deserve, and for the purpose of this book, the author repeatedly advertised in military journals, asking for their co-operation, without result. One can only assume that they are bound by their employer to a vow of silence, and one maker went so far as to state that, as they were paid wages for their work, he had no intention of giving them any credit whatsoever.

Jowett, Trevor, Launceston, Tasmania. Converter of Britains' models for dioramas at the Queen Victoria Museum, Launceston, Tasmania.

J/R., Paris (c.1945-). The only models we have seen or heard of are a group of 4 French personalities 40mm in porcelain, one mounted. [*Greenhill*]

'Jubilee' series. *See* Sentry Box, The.

Juersch Boghandel (G.G. & E.C. Fillge), Copenhagen. Publisher of lithographed paper sheets.

Jugal, Buenos Aires (fl.1965). Manufacturer of 54mm and 10-inch plastics.

Julia (Vincente Julia Manuel), Madrid (1968-). Maker of 54mm solids of Spanish troops, well-designed and adequately painted. They include units of 1808-12, 1872-6 and 1936-9, with portrait models including José Antonia, General Franco, Valentin Gonzalez and General Mola. The sculptor very cleverly varies the faces according to the period they represent.

Julier, Keith, Leighton Buzzard. Advertises a professional painting service.

Jullemier, Paris. A professional painter of flats.

Junior Caster, USA (c.1930). A series of home-casting moulds.

Junker, Nuremberg (19th-20th centuries). Engraver of moulds for Spenküch.

Jupiter Models (B. Banbury), Ash, Surrey (1978-). Maker of cannon, in 16 pieces, the limbers in 22, with men in 7 (54mm, solid). He has produced a fine 80mm Nelson (commissioned by HMS *Victory*), an excellent mounted Oliver Cromwell and a standing Charles I, both in 75mm, to begin a Civil War series. He also works to commission. In mid-1979 he began a series of artillery, the first ones being a 38mm scale model of a 32-pounder naval cannon and a 68-pounder carronade, each with a set of five figures.

Jurdzinski, K., Hanover (1977-). Publisher of Napoleonic period flats. (*Klio*)

Just Models, London. The trade name for early models by Stadden, re-issued in a spread-eagle position ready for animation.

JVR Miniatures (John von Roepke), Woodbury, New Jersey (1976-). 'Toy' soldiers in 60mm, all in the same marching position, comprising the British Empire and Indian Army, French Army and Navy (1880-1914), and ancient peoples. The painting is kept to the minimum. [*Anton*]

K

Kaestlin, Major J.P., London. Constructor of one of the dioramas at Woolwich Arsenal.

Kahle, Conrad, Brunswick (c.1850). One of the more obscure makers of flats. A son, Wilhelm, is known to have sold some of the moulds in 1870 to a firm in Wolfenbuttel (Mark: KAHLE/WOLFENBUTTEL), while others appear to have been purchased by Rieche.

Kaiser, Hermann, Penig, E. Germany. Designer and engraver of flats. (*Katalog der Formen, 1976*).

Kannick, Preben, Denmark. A designer of flats for Tobinnus, also a well-known authority on all military matters, and a fine artist.

Kappel, Uwe, Bochum (1979-). Publisher of flats.

Karthage Figures (K. Arthur), London (1970-). Large figures of carved and painted wood, continuing the tradition set by his father.

Kaser, Gottlieb, Aarau (c.1830-60). Engraver of flats for Wehrli.

Kast A Toy (Ace Toy Mold Company), Toledo, Ohio (fl.1934). Manufacturers of moulds and equipment for home-casting.

Katie Kraft, Bourne End, Bucks (1975). Advertised a professional painting service.

Kaufmann, Martin L. *See* Cockade Miniatures.

Kavoteide (Øy Telgman A.B.), Finland (1940-50). Publishers of paper sheets.

Kayson, D. and **Phillipson, Trevor.** *See* DEK; Reider Design.

Kebbel, Harald, Weimar/Nuremberg (c.1950-). An intelligent maker of elegant flats, with a large output, embracing Burgundians, 1450, the Peasants' War, 1525 (drawn by Becker, produced by Starr), the Seven Years' War, the Napoleonic wars, First and Second World Wars. He also makes delightful civilians of various periods, including a sedan chair with weary bearers, and a chamber-music group. Mark: HK. He owns the moulds of Mauke and Heydorn. Some of the figures are designed by his wife, Renate, and engraved by Sollner and Staar.

Kec Kraft Designs, Waltham Cross, Herts. In 1973 they advertised a chess-set of medieval design.

Keenon's Design Establishment (L. Keenon) Pacific Palisades, California (1976-). Maker of 9in models in hydrastone with lead equipment, primarily for museums. [*Anton*]

Keester, George F., Annapolis, Maryland. A collector who displayed great enthusiasm for the hobby in the 1950s, and was of great assistance to enquiring minds.

Kehoe, E.J. *See* Wend-Al.

Keil, Günter, Advertised at Kulmbach in 1973 and 1977 as a maker of flats.

Kelle. *See* Wachsmuth & Kelle.

Keller, Ch-F., Paris (fl.1950-60). A private maker of flats of great importance in the development of the art in France. Several fine series stand to his credit: troops of Louis XV, Louis XVI, the Hundred Swiss, the Second Empire, the Swiss Army 1912-14 and 1935. (Mark: FK). He did a magnificent hunting scene engraved by Maier after tapestries by Oudry from paintings by Van Loon, produced with Brutsch; Third Swiss Grenadier Guards, with Brandt (Mark: KB); French Infantry 1786 (Mark: GB); representations of the Cantons at the Occupation of Basle 1792, designed by Rousselot and engraved by Sixtus Maier and Krunert (Mark: S).

Kellogg's Cornflakes, USA and Great Britain (1960-). Several sets of plastic models have from time to time been issued in their packets. The first we can remember is a set of Guards bandsmen, with plated instruments (made by Cherilea) in 1958. In 1969 a set of 16 45mm unpainted models ranging from Crusaders to Zulus (dare we think they were designed by Stadden?) was issued simultaneously by Peak Frean (*q.v.*) followed in 1971 by half-round kings and queens (40mm) in white Alkathene. The backs of their packets have often been used to display uniforms in colour, as in 1965, when a series of 20 figures in 54mm with front and rear views was issued. Another 12 in set followed, this time the front view only, and more recently still (1970) by four series: armour, British Cavalry, national costume, and Indians, in which parts could be cut out and fitted together, forming a three-dimensional figure. These were all issued with press-back stands.

Kellogg's Sugar Snacks, 1966. In the packets were to be found any one of a set of six 40mm plastic 'Thunderbird' figures.

Kemnow, G., Germany. Painter of flats for the R.U.S.I. dioramas.

Kemp, Alan, Whitley Bay, Northumberland (1970-). Maker of 54-60mm models in a variety of materials: wooden torso, faces of hardened plasticine, metal accoutrements, paper and other substances. He is adviser to the Regimental Museum of the 15th/19th King's Royal Hussars, Newcastle, who possess a number of his models.

Kemp, Stephen. *See* S.K. Models; Tanner Castings.

Kempin, Bernhard, Böblingen, W. Germany. Constructor of show cases. (*Kulmbach Almanac, 1977*).

Kemplay, Peter, Skipton, Yorkshire. A professional painter and dioramist and originally a collaborator with Lamming.

Kennedy, David, Baltimore, Maryland (1975-). Began by making some models in 54mm for Valiant, but later turned to 90mm size models in epoxy 'Sculptee'. [*Corning*]. (*See also* The Black Watch.)

Kennesaw Battlerama. *See* Pfab, Vincent.

Kenneth Speciality Company (Richard F. Brady) Baltimore, Maryland (fl.1950-60). A collector who made 90mm solids of American interest for United States museums.

Kentoys (Kenway Cycle Stores Ltd), London (fl.1958). A small range of 54mm plastics, heavily influenced by Herald, and issued as a side-line to their main business.

Kern, Werner, Feuchtwangen, W. Germany. Listed in the *Kulmbach Almanac, 1973* as a maker of flats.

Kerswell, A.W.G., London. Designer of a Western Front diorama exhibited at the Imperial War Museum in 1934-5.

Kessler, L., Bernburg am der Saale (c.1860). A producer of either flats or solids. (*Köllbrunner*)

Kews Ltd. *See* Ku-Zu Models.

Kidd, Glen E. *See* Ral Partha Enterprises.

Kiedorf, Germany. Designer and engraver of flats.

Kieffer, Fritz and **Fischbach, G.,** Strasbourg (1872-1914). Publishers of a great number of paper sheets. The imprint was 'Gustave Fischbach and Fritz Kieffer, l'Imprimerie Alsacienne'.

Kiker, Edward, Fort Belvoir, Virginia. A converter of Cameo, I/R, Historex and Almark models for United States Engineer Center. Up to 1976 he had made over 60, including portrait models of American Presidents and Generals, Sir Winston Churchill and Nazi officers. He specializes also in 4 x 5 in vignettes incorporating four or five models, and has made two dioramas in 1:72 scale. His present whereabouts are unknown.

Kiki. *See* Roma (Editorial).

Kilia. *See* Ochel, Aloys.

Kilmore Figures (Frederick Moore), Great Missenden, Bucks (1976-). A maker of aluminium-resin 90mm models of Romans and Second World War combatants, and kings and queens of England. In 1977 he converted them to bronze composition.

'King Arthur' set. *See* Timpo.

King White Figures, Hong Kong (1974-). 50mm metal models of Second World War figures indvidually boxed and inscribed 'Made for A.A. Hales in Hong Kong' (Hales is a dealer in models). They are unusual in that metal models rarely emanate from Hong Kong, and there is a possibility that they may be piracies of Mini-Models.

'Kings and Queens of England' series. *See* Franklin Mint; Saunders, Roger.

King's Art. *See* Moulded Miniatures.

'Kings Chess'. *See* Weikhmann, C.

Kintzel, Sonneberg, E. Germany (?-1840). An engraver of flats, as shown by thirteen Prussian Grenadiers signed 'Kintzel, Graviert' at Deutsches Spielzeugmuseum, Sonneberg.

Kirby, Alan, Rickmansworth, Herts (1974-). Maker of scale model cannon.

Kirk, W., Leicester (1970-75). Maker of 56-60mm solid models. An interesting range, with apparently no linking theme. The result is that there are such diverse subjects as 6th Dragoon Guards officers (1808-1810), 17th Lancers, Polish Lancer troopers and trumpeters, and The Black Prince (all mounted); and on foot Simon de Montfort, a Viking, Henry VIII, Oliver Cromwell, Bonnie Prince Charlie, Wellington, Napoleon, an able seaman, and a member of General Bolivar's bodyguard. The stiff wire-brush tail of the Black Prince's horse is unusual and not particularly effective. Kirk also made a small range of metal tanks.

KIT FORM. A model in which the component parts are cast or made separately, to be assembled by the purchaser. The first essays in this direction were in the form of large polystyrene figures, pioneered by Aurora in the United States, followed by Selcol and Airfix in England. An obscure firm, Rogard, of Wales, forestalled these efforts with at least one model consisting of two pieces only. In 54mm plastic Herald issued a fine range entitled 'Swoppet' in which much ingenuity was displayed; SEGOM was the first French representative, to be followed by Historex. These, being designed by a master and consisting of so many minute and intricate parts, were a great challenge to the purchaser, and naturally provoked rivals such as Prairial and L'Aiglon, who, however, did not last long, Airfix, in fact being the only comparable makers to Historex at the time of writing. In metal, Gammage must have been the first to issue models in this form (c.1956) and it is now the accepted presentation in most quarters, even with the large 90-120mm productions. There are, however, drawbacks to these unassembled figures. The maker is not always careful to ensure that arms fit into sockets, that necks plug accurately into the cavities prepared for them, or that the two sides of a horse align accurately. Much time often has to be spent in filing, cutting and plugging. Very often, also, the figure advertised as a 'kit' is merely an early effort withdrawn from the maker's list, either because of its imperfections or unacceptability, and offered at a cheaper price. Others masquerade under other names (e.g. Guard House for Hinton, Just Models and Standish for Stadden). Another drawback is that, coming as they do in separate parts in a plastic envelope, one cannot judge the quality of the model until it has been assembled. From the maker's viewpoint, however, it saves the expense of assembly or animation. The latest development is the kit in 120 and even 170mm, consisting of up to as many as 26 separate pieces. The thousands of AFV kits are of the greatest complexity.

K. & L. Company. *See* Thomas Industries.

Klaenschi, G.A., Strasbourg (1930-45). A manufacturer of paper sheets. He conceived the grand design of issuing a complete collection of every French uniform ever worn. He went into voluntary exile in 1939 and by 1945 he had completed 44 sheets. He also made decorative backgrounds for dioramas of paper soldiers in the Strasbourg Museum.

Klein, Dr Klaus G., Hamm, W. Germany. Listed in the *Kulmbach Almanac, 1973* as a maker of flats.

Klein, Ronald von. *See* Collector Enterprises.

Klement, R., Vienna (1965-?). Designer of flats.

Klenze, H.M. von, Germany. Maker of a diorama of the Battle of Leuthen, using 17,000 flats, in the museum at Ingolstadt.

K. Mart (S.S. Kresge Company), Troy, Michigan. Founded as a store in 1930 [*Anton*]. Importers of 54mm diecast models entitled 'Men of History' or 'Men of the West!' The range includes Vikings, pirates, Napoleonics, Wyatt Earp, Billy the Kid, Little Crow and Red Cloud. These all appear to be piracies (e.g. Little Crow is exactly the same model as the White Eagle of Gabriel Industries, except for the altered name, both models emanating from Lone Star). Marketers, also, of the Airfix 7½-inch polystyrene kits, but assembled, plated and boxed, and bearing Kresge's name (but made in Hong Kong) under the title 'Collector' series, and containing a printed leaflet headed Ward International Inc. Other models include facsimiles of Britains' 'Deetail' range of knights and Turks, with the difference that they are plated and the base is not of metal. Here again the inscription is 'Made in Hong Kong exclusively for Ward International' and with a curious trade mark: ⑤

Knie, Heinrich, Hellabrun. Maker of large wooden models.

Knight, Clive, London (1974-). Designer of 30 and 35mm First World War models for Tradition.

Knight, Denis. *See* Helmet Products.

Knight, Derek J., San Mateo, California (1975-). A maker of commissioned models of fine quality. In 1978 he was making plans for the formation of his own company under the title 'Knight Original Figures'. (*See also* Blenheim Military Models.)

Knight, Paul. *See* Hinchliffe, F. and M.

'Knights of Agincourt'. *See* Britains; Gottstein; Selwyn-Smith.

Knoeschen, Germany (1950-). Designer of flats for Blum, Gottstein and Ochel.

Knoll, Michael, Berlin. Publisher and engraver of flats for Sivhed and others, mainly of the Thirty Years' War, the Seven Years' War, 1813-1815, Nassau and East Prussian cavalry and infantry, and 1900-1913 Prussians. He is the possessor of Thiel's moulds.

Kober. *See* Wollner Figuren.

Koch, A.U., Bensberg, W. Germany. Publisher of flats of the 17th-18th century periods.

Koch, Gunther, Herford, W. Germany. Master-maker for Ara-Kunst.

Koch, Konrad, Fürth (fl.c.1920). A curious entry in Ortmann suggests that he was a maker of solids which were designed by Sixtus Maier.

Koch, L., Fürth (c.1870). A producer of flats.

Koch, Dr Ludwig, Germany (fl.c.1965). A designer of flats for Tobinnus and Vesely.

Koch, Paul F., Göttingen, W. Germany (1900-1914). A maker of 54mm solids.

Koekkoek, Holland (fl.c.1930). An artist who designed, painted and made his own incredibly active paper soldiers, which have found an honoured place arranged in diorama form in the Dutch Army Museum at Leiden.

Kok, O., Gebr, Amsterdam. Publishers of paper sheets of the 1812-1815 period.

Kolbitz, K.H., Berlin. Publisher of flats, designed by Mauke and engraved by Emmerling, of the Seven Years' War and civilians of 1770-1790.

Kollbrunner, Curt F., Zollikon, Switzerland. Owner of the Gottstein moulds, recast by Neckel in 1974.

Kollenz, Erich, Vienna (1975-). Designer of 30mm metal vehicles and guns, ancient siege artillery, cannon (c.1490), mortar (c.1672), field pieces (c.1675) and gabions (c.1700).

52 **'Kombination flat'** *by Gepner (Author)*

'*Kombination*' Figure. An ingeniously designed flat figure, invented by Schirmer, which may possess four arms, each holding a different weapon, and four to six legs in different positions, so that a collector may cut off the redundant limbs and thus vary the pose of the basic figure. Horses are similarly supplied with heads, legs and tails in varied postures. Excellent use of this device is displayed in many dioramas. Splendid examples are designed by Hafer, Scholtz and Geppner. The same principle was applied by Herald plastics, with their 'Swoppet' models, where the torso could be twisted at the waist, the heads were interchangeable and different weapons could be used. They were copied without taste or feeling by a number of firms. Segom did the same thing in a minor way in their 25mm polystyrene models.

Kometer, Baron de, Germany. Exhibitor of a diorama of the Battle of St Privat, exhibited at Berlin about 1930.

Kooken, Olive. *See* American Alloy; Barclay; Tommy Toy.

Korn, Gunther, W. Germany (1973-). Maker of 54mm solid models of the Blue King, in unlimited numbers for presentation only. To make solids today in Germany is an unusual achievement. Photographs indicate that they are of exceptionally fine quality.

Kostelnik, R., USA (1970-). He creates most delightful and colourful models from clothes-pegs clad in all types of material.

Kouchnir, Dr, Switzerland. Mentioned by Nicollier as a maker of many pieces of artillery.

Kovar, Ewald and **Peter.** *See* Wiener Zinnfiguren Ewald-Kovar.

Kowallik, Claus S., Germany. Designer for Ara-Kunst.

KPH, Argentina (1957-?). Manufacturers of 68mm

plastics.

Kramer, P. *See* K-S Miniatures.

Kramer, Richard, USA. Freelance designer of 54mm solids, including various models for H.R. Broman and Soldiers Unlimited.

Kramer, T. Robert and **Schwartz, A.** *See* Com-E-Tec.

Kratz, Edouard, Strasbourg (1814-60). Publisher of paper sheets.

Krauhs, Helmut, Salzburg (b.1912). A brilliant exponent of the larger model, he began making 32cm models professionally in 1945, using cotton over wire for bodies, limewood for heads, and natural materials and metals. His interest is mainly in historical Austrian uniforms from 1648 to 1848, especially in groups of eight to ten figures. He is represented at the National Army Museum in London, at West Point, Museo Navale (Venice), the Vatican Museum, the Danube Museum at Petronell near Vienna, the Haus der Natur at Salzburg, the Donaumuseum (Neider Osterreich), the Rainer Museum at Salzburg and the Stadtmuseum at Wels, among others. He is equally at home when illustrating the operas of Mozart. His carriages are wonderful examples of wood-carving and his mounted figures superb. Everything he makes carries the stamp of genius.

Krause, Theodore, Gotha (1853-1932). Producers of poor quality flats, solids, and hollow-casts. The founder (1853-80) used Schilling as an engraver. His son Carl (1849-1912) made mostly solids. His moulds are in the Heimatmuseum, Gotha, and the Stadtmuseum, Weimar. The final owner of the business was Rudolf Krause (c.1912).

Kredel, H.H., Germany. Designer of flats for Otte.

Kresge, S.S., Co. *See* K. Mart.

Krey, R. *See* Trentsensky; Verlagsbuchhandlung.

'KRIEGSSPIEL'. The German name for what has now developed into the wargame. Ortmann states that William I of Orange and his historian Everaed van Reyd used some sort of models to study projected reforms in the 16th century Dutch army, and undoubtedly many monarchs and commanders used models to plan their campaigns (*see* Evolutions). A game entitled 'King's Chess', based on sixty pieces comprising all ranks, was invented by Christopher Weikhmann in 1644, while in 1780 a scheme invented by Helwig used full-scale model armies, this being amplified in 1800 by Viturinus, who used some 2,500 pieces in his game. In 1811 von Reisswitz used a relief model with blocks rather than actual figures as military units, a scheme that remained in being until modified in 1824 by his son. About 1830 Major Kuntz wrote a pamphlet for the French Army explaining the use of wooden models. Other schemes were evolved by Generals Mieroslawski and Tschischwitz (1862), whilst Heinrichsen not only introduced the idea to children but issued printed slips on its use with a number of his sets of flats. The idea was used by most Continental countries during the Franco-Prussian War, and became firmly established as a method of working out actual strategic plans for real war, while in England Major W.R. Livermore in 1879 and Spenser Wilkinson in 1910 issued their own versons.(*See* Nash for an excellent evaluation of its subsequent use. *Stalin and his Generals*, edited by S. Bialer, 1970, throws light on *kriegsspiel* as used by the Russians. *See also* Wargame.)

Krischner, Professor Fritz. *See* Lübecker Spielfiguren.

Kroger, Henry, Hamburg (c.1880). Producer of flats.

Krolyn (G. Krohn Rasmussen), Copenhagen (fl.1945-74). Manufacturer of aluminium 75mm models of Vikings, knights, Ivanhoe, Robin Hood, the Danish Royal Guards, Westerners, etc. After 1946 they absorbed the firm of Rode Orm and retained the trade mark.

Kröner, Elisabeth, Austria (c.1973). Collaborator in Austrian dioramas.

Kröner-Grimm, Dr Erich, Vienna. A collector of international standing, and of great drive and initiative, responsible for many outstanding dioramas in Austria.

Kroschewski, Erika and **Georg.** *See* Ochel, A.

Kruger et Cie Editions, Paris. Publishers of large cardboard paper sheets of the Grande Armée, printed on stiff card, and in book form.

Krümpelbeck, Franze, Löhne, Oldburg, W. Germany (1977-). Producer of facsimiles of old semi-solids. (*Kulmbach Almanac, 1977*)

Krunert, Alfred, Vienna (c.1880-?1978). An engraver of flats for numerous editors, including Keller, Ochel, Scheibert and Vesely. Sets include Thirty Years' War, Hofer's Rising, the 1848 Revolution, First World War, Poland 1930-39, and the Conquest of Mexico. The moulds are now in the hands of Heinz Pohl.

Krupp, Frank. *See* All-Nu.

K/S Historical Prints. *See* Com-E-Tec.

K-S Miniatures (Donald K. Steiner and Peter Kramer), Alexandria, Virginia (1963-70). When we first saw the 40mm solids of these makers we envisaged a long life for them, owing not perhaps so much to any excess of ability, but to the unusual subjects they portrayed (e.g. the Mexican War, the Civil War Navy), little known fields at the time. However, the models were used for dioramas, to which the makers eventually turned their hands (e.g. Navy Museum, Washington).

K/S Pewter Miniatures. *See* Com-E-Tec.

Kuhn, E.G., Nuremberg (c.1770-?). In the early days of the flat the interest was by no means confined to military matters. Many manufacturers turned out delightful villages, farms, etc, and one in particular concentrated on garden scenes, with civilian figures, trees, flowers in pots and vases, statues of Venus and Cupid, refined *mannequins pis*, fountains and vines. The only clue we have to his name is a fountain signed 'Kuhn' and a vine signed 'K'. (*Hampe*)

Kuhn, Gustave, Brandenberg (1830-c.1900). One of the best publishers of paper sheets of the period. Later, when taken over by Oehmigke and Riemschneider, Kuhn's name was erased.

Kuhne, Walther, Berlin (c.1956). Maker of flats.

Kuhr, Heinz, Austria. Builder of dioramas for Plassenburg and Schloss Pottenbrun.

KULMBACH (Plassenburg Castle). A place of annual pilgrimage for all collectors interested in flats, as important to them as is nearby Bayreuth to devotees of Wagner. It was instituted before the Second World War by the publisher and collector Bonness, with assistance from Eric Wurzbacher. It was re-opened after the war, and, at the time of writing, contains about 375 dioramas, and, we understand, a Charge of the Light Brigade in 30mm solids by Surèn. Of late years publishers of flats and occasionally of the stray German and English solid have displayed their recent achievements.

'KUNSTSCHRANK'. In 1632 the town of Augsburg presented Gustavus Adolphus with a magnificent collection of bronze, silver and copper castings by their finest craftsmen. They are preserved at Uppsala, and include an equestrian 5cm chased and gilded bronze St George and the Dragon. There is no exact English equivalent for the word 'Kunstschrank'; it may be roughly translated as 'casket of works of art'.

Kunter, Dr Fritz, Berlin. Painter of flats exhibited at Kulmbach.

Kuntz, Major, Germany (c.1830). One of the early writers on *kriegsspiel*, based on carved wood models, and recommended to the French War Office.

Kurton Products Ltd, Colorado Springs, Colorado (1979–). Makers of diorama accessories and miniature buildings in plaster.

Kurz, G.L., Stuttgart (c.1760-1820). One of the early manufacturers of flats, including piracies of the large models by Hilpert and possibly Lorenz. Mark: GLK 1769.

Ku-Zu Models (Kews) Ltd, Brockley, London (1925-?58). A manufacturer of hollow-casts. In 1927 the name was changed to Brockley Forges. They turned out models of satisfactory quality of soldiers, sailors, cricketers, farms, gardens, village figures, hunting scenes, jungle animals, railway staff, nursery rhymes, RAF, Lifeguards, Highlanders, Grenadier Guards, Gurkhas, medievals, machine-gunners, gladiators and Zulus.

L

Laas, M., Paris. *See* Vasquez, F.

Labayen, Ramon, San Sebastian, Spain (1962-). One of the most outstanding of the present-day school of Spanish makers. When in London in 1961 he was tremendously impressed by the Staddens that he saw, and the influence of the latter is apparent. Beautifully sculptured, and in most cases excellently cast, the models he himself paints when requested are remarkable. His standards are such that if he is not satisfied with a figure he abandons it immediately. His range is confined to the Napoleonic army, with portraits of the Marshals. He informs us that at 'one time' his family was involved in the production of paper sheets as a sideline. In 1977 he began mounted troops and models in 30mm.

Lacina, Uwe and Gesa, Hamburg (1969-). Makers of what we are told are delightful 30mm solids to commission and, in 1977, models in 54mm. Unfortunately, their own reticence does not allow us to comment more fully.

Lacomblez, Gaston, Belgium. A leading Belgian figure painter and one of the first Belgian collectors and converters of solids.

Lacour, Nancy, France (c.1830). Publisher of paper sheets.

Laforet, Mayor. See V.

La Grande Illusion. *See* Roma, (Editorial).

La Guerra, Spain (c.1963-?). A small firm which turned out a modest range of 54mm plastics.

La Guerra (J. Capell), Barcelona (1896-1960). Founded by Baldomero Casanellas as a manufacturer of 45mm and a few 54mm solids.

Laing, Peter, Hereford (1973-). A maker of 15mm solids. His avowed intention was to cover, as completely as possible, the personnel and equipment of every period. He made a good beginning with the ancient world, the medieval period, the Marlborough wars and the American Revolution, together with camels and artillery and the total has now reached over 600 sets. The models are specifically designed for dioramas, but have undoubtedly been seized upon for wargaming. For the collector *per se* they serve no useful purpose, as the size allows for no individuality and painting becomes an intolerable burden. In 1977 he issued scale card buildings designed for him by John Mitchell.

Lamb, Ray, Northiam, Sussex (1969-). Known for some years as a skilful converter and painter of Historex kits for the Dover branch of that firm, in 1973 he began designing models in solid metal, starting with a group of Napoleonic troops in 75mm cast by Hinchliffe. Although they received lavish praise from practically every quarter, it was obvious to the more discerning collector that, although the idea of a slim, elegant figure had been discarded in favour of a more literal rendering, the anatomy left much to be desired, especially the heads, which were grotesquely large. No help, either, was afforded them by the incredibly tasteless overpainting which was prevalent at the time, and it seemed that it was a long time before Lamb realized the difficulties posed by original design and execution as compared with, bluntly, the sticking together of prepared pieces. Greatly to his credit his later models of a mounted Persian and two Plains Indians, one crouching by his horse, showed a vast improvement. To his credit also is a kit of 26 pieces which build up to a remarkable *saburai* which will remain as one of the modern masterpieces. In 1975 he began a series of 90mm models, the first two of Norman knights, under the name of Poste Militaire, which fell back into anatomical inexactitudes. A Saxon house-carl and a French cuirassier, however, proved fine pieces. In 1978 he began a series of medieval Japanese warriors to complement the *saburai*.

Lamb, Ray, USA (1974-). A free-lance designer of solids. He made a fine 54mm Napoleon for Bresica, an 'Empire' series in 80mm for Cameo, and for Superior in 90mm 'The Entertainers' (twelve models of famous film stars), nude female models and a series of figures to illustrate Tolkien's *The Lord of the Rings*.

Lambro Products Ltd. *See* Lamming, W.

Lamming, W., Hull, Yorkshire (1965-). Originally called Lambro Products. Solid 54mm Napoleonic troops were the first to be placed on the market. These were issued as spread-eagled torsos, the arms and equipment cast separately. Later he turned his talents to the making of 20 and 25mm solids, together with cannon and spare parts. Most of the figures are of the Napoleonic era, both foot and mounted, but there is an increasing range of ancient and medieval units. The horses, cast in two pieces, interlock accurately enough, but, with the exception of a standing one, are clumsy. However, with separately cast riders and good casting, they are ideal for the painting of heraldic devices. A variety of helms is available which screw into the neck socket. An Egyptian chariot is a good, clean piece of work, but some of the medieval models (especially the civilians) have deformed heads. A Waterloo chess set, the pieces in the form of busts, in 54mm, is available as a casting or in chrome and copper bronze, or gold and silver, or hand-painted. The features are well-sculpted, although one of the Queens has the type of masculine face reminiscent of the paintings of Fuseli.

Lance Historical Miniatures (Norman and Lisl Cooke) Chepachet, Rhode Island (1958-). Norman Cooke began as a collector and turned to making solid 54mm models in 1958, his wife painting them. Their first efforts were of the Austrian Army during the Seven Years' War, including many variations with little-known regiments, and the French on the side of the Americans during the Revolution. They extended this series to include British and Allied troops, and followed with Austro-Hungarians, 1798, Bavarians and Prussians, 1806-12, and the Napoleonic wars. Naturally enough, the American Civil War followed, together with a fine Polish winged lancer of 1683. Commissions, especially for portrait models, began to come in, and occupied most of their time. Free-lance work was also undertaken (e.g. American Revolution and Civil War models in antiqued pewter for Com-E-Tec) and for the same firm models of de Laudonnière and Floridian Indians and Spaniards (now transferred to The Barefoot Soldier). Meanwhile the great collector Lilly died and his son decided to extend his father's existing collection of models. He accordingly commissioned the Cookes to make a vast series of new models, some to be used in diorama form at Heritage Plantation. Dioramas were nothing new to the Cookes, as they had been experimenting with them for some years. For the last few years they have also been supplying models for a vast diorama of Waterloo commissioned by the City of Vancouver. In 1975 they returned to Com-E-Tec with a series of thirteen models of the American War of Independence in 85mm, and in 54mm new designs of the United States Army, 1851-86. In 1976 they made an exclusive series of fifteen 54mm models of the American West for The Marlin Firearms Company. A Cooke model lies outside the present tendency of the American model in that it is far more reserved in its action, and the painting makes allowance for imagination. However, their work cannot always be said to reach a high level, the height of some models being greater than their girth demands, giving a somewhat lifeless character.

Lance Miniatures of New England, Hudson, Massachusetts (1974-). Makers of 56-70mm pewter models of the American War of Independence. [*Anton*].

Lancer, USA. Mentioned in *The Soldier* in 1968 as a maker of 54mm solids, but nothing further is known.

Lancer Collectors Toys (D.J.Bracey), Farnham, Surrey (1977-). Maker of ancillary military vehicles to go with 'toy' soldiers. A converted mule stretcher-chair, c.1900, is at the R.C.T. Museum, Aldershot.

Landi (Valentino Ditta), Italy (1964). Manufacturer of plastic models.

Landl, Leo, Salzburg (1979-). Designer of flats.

Landmark, USA (1975-). Manufacturers of cardboard models of famous American buildings. (*Newman*)

Landmesser, Dr Michael, Neustad, W. Germany. Mentioned in the Kulmbach list of 1973 as a maker of flats.

Landsberg, Abbess Herrad of. The author of the 12th-century manuscript *Hortus Deliciarum* in which occurs a drawing of hand-manoeuvred fighting warriors. A facsimile reprint was made in Strasbourg in 1901.

Lange, J.W., Rellingen (1977-). Publisher of flats of folk-types of the early 19th century. (*Klio*)

Langham, Ulrich, Germany. Originator of a set of flats of Sikhs, published by Neckel in 1968.

Lanz, Hermann, Geneva (?1965). A maker of metal and wood artillery. (*Nicollier*)

L.A.R.G. (Laboratorio Romano Artisano Giocattoli) Rome (1934-47). Manufacturers of 42mm metal Heyde-type models of all ranges of Italian troops, including those used in the Abyssinian campaign, together with Askaris, and portraits of Badoglio and Mussolini. The mounted troops were very poor. During the Second World War manufacture ceased, but in 1945 a metal jeep with military police (American and British) appeared. The firm seems to have closed permanently in 1947.

Larson, John, USA. Constructor of dioramas at the US Army Military Research Collection, Carlisle Barracks, Pennsylvania.

Lasset (John Tassell), London (1970-). Tassell worked for some years as an animator and maker of dioramas for 'Tradition', and obviously gained much by the experience. His first appearance as a maker of original models was in 1970 when he and Pat Bird collaborated in the formation of Series 77. However, the partnership did not last long and in 1972 he joined the new Greenwood and Ball group. He immediately gained attention with a fine series of native tribesmen for the Omdurman Campaign (including troops mounted on horses and camels), and with Napoleonic, Hesse-Darmstadt and Second World War models. Following these came the American War of Independence, together with Indian scouts of that period. In 1973 he began a series of medieval warriors of various dates, admirable for the display of armour and heraldry. These, although beautifully clean in sculpture and casting, and admirably quiescent in posture, exhibited the all-too prevalent custom of a basic figure with only minor alteration to the positioning of the arms and the variety of the weapons. Hence a knight had the same face as a crossbowman (and all of them very like the facial expression of a Stadden!), so that a long series when grouped together appeared as the large progeny of the same parents. The mounted specimens were unambitious and the latest venture, dismounted knights in combat, does not come to life. Romans, however, are much more acceptable. Other miscellaneous models include a fine portrait model of Blücher, units of the British Army in the Peninsular War, a Persian camel trooper, a Scythian horse archer and a Celtic chariot (1975). In 1977 he began models in 75mm, as the start of a 'Jubilee' range for Greenwood and Ball (Pearce) and, with T. Reeves, founded Sovereign Miniatures.

Last Post, The. Dallas, Texas (1979-). 'Toy' soldiers in solid of British regiments, advertised as the 'largest selection in the world'.

'Last Soldier, The'. The Lichtenstein Army, comprising 80 men and one officer, was dissolved in 1868. The last survivor died in 1939 at the age of 95. A commemorative flat, 4 inches high, is alleged to have been made in 1969 at Vaduz [*Wiseman*] but extensive enquiries have not produced any concrete evidence of this.

LATEX COMPOSITION. *See* Composite Models.

La Tijera Ediciones, Barcelona (c.1936-). Publishers of paper sheets. These were colour-printed (from about 1940 on both sides) and of modern troops, up to 20 figures on a sheet, with tanks, guns, etc, in several sizes, both as separate sheets or in book form. In 1936 the Abyssinian War was commemorated, and there were sheets of Catalan Militia, mounted, or in groups, with artillery in action.

Laumonier, Dr, France. About 1900 he constructed a diorama of part of the Battle of Austerlitz, using thousands of flats. (*Nicollier*)

Laurent, J. A French collector and diorama maker. He was liberal in his gifts to Compiègne and he constructed a diorama of Waterloo containing 12,000 Heinrichsen flats.

Lauter, Rudolf, Nuremberg (fl.1900). Maker of flats. (*Scholtz*)

L.E., Nuremberg. Mentioned by Hampe and Kollbrunner as a maker of flats, but neither date nor place of origin is known.

LEAD DISEASE. A type of oxidization which has an adverse effect on metal, causing disintegration of the model. This may occur over a number of years. One of the causes is believed to be centrifugalizing the mould with the casting metal at too high a temperature, causing the metal to become porous. D.G. Glover and R.J. Marrion spent five years investigating causes and prevention. (See the *Bulletin* of the British Model Soldier Society, December, 1965 and April, 1966.) Both they and Stadden came to the conclusion that a casting should be coated with transparent varnish before undercoating is applied. Durethant or Resin varnish was recommended.

Leblich. Leipzig (c.1850). Producer of flats.

Lebrun & Boldetti. Milan (fl.1878). Publishers of paper sheets.

Lecke, Hans, Rehburg/Loccum (b.1920). A magnificent engraver of flats, and a worthy successor to Frank and Sixtus Maier. Since 1953 his work has been eagerly sought for by many agents and editors. He has engraved for Droste, Pahl, Wollrath, Grosche, Hafer, Schirmer, Vesely, Vorberg and others, and designed for many of them also. Since 1967 he has been his own publisher. Specially noteworthy are his 1756 English Foot Guards, his 14th-century series and his 1810-15 Prussian infantry and staff officers. He is interested in the traditional large flats, and has engraved for Scholtz and Manfred Walter in this size. Mark: HL.

Leclerc, J.P. Belfort (c.1850). Publisher of paper sheets.

Ledbetter, Humphrey. *See* Citadel Miniatures Ltd.

Lefèbvre, Pierre. *See* Pilef.

Legall, Paris (fl.1958). Manufacturer of 54mm plastics.

Le Gaulois France. *See* Ballada, M.

Le Gloahec, Alan, USA. Professional painter for Murray (before the birth of Old Guard) and at the moment for Cowan.

Lehmann, Artur-Andreas, Freiburg, W. Germany 1964-). Publisher of flats.

Lehmann, Horst, Allersberg, W. Germany (fl.1965). Maker of flats.

Lehmann, Hugo, Meissen, E. Germany (fl.1866). Noted by Hampe as becoming a master of flats in this year,

with a mechanized tournament with a mounted knight as a test piece.

Leipzig Exhibition, 1930. One of the first and most influential of exhibitions of dioramas. It was arranged and organized by *Klio* and was widespread in its implications.

'Leipzig' series. *See* Valiant Miniatures.

Lelièpvre, Eugène, Montrouge, Paris (b.1909). As official painter to the French Army, Lelièpvre has ample opportunities to display his knowledge of the anatomy of, and his profound feeling for, the horse. Nowhere is it more ably shown than in the models he designs for Historex. For some years he has been the most influential figure in France, both by virtue of his own example, and for his enthusiasm and his desire to hand on his knowledge to future generations; few of the modern French craftsmen have not at some time received instruction or advice from him. His research into the niceties of the uniforms of the French Army at all periods is on a level with that of Rousselot, and evident both in his own models and those that he designs for others. His influence on the diorama is also extensive, and his own writings on the subject display deep knowledge of the intricacies involved. He has collaborated on a number of occasions with Madame Métayer (e.g. 'Suffren à l'Ile de France', 'Bir Hacheim'). In his own work in this sphere he has studied profoundly the effect of distance on the rotundity of a figure, flattening and reducing in size his background models and gradually coming forward to the full roundness and larger size of those in the foreground. Nor does he restrict the nature of the substances used, and may well employ paper, cut, wrought, or shaped tin, wood or plasticine in addition to lead, as dictated by the subject. His 54mm solids are based on a lead torso, and built up in the traditional French style, but the larger (25-38cm) statuettes are normally of plaster or wax, built on an armature of steel wire, the hands of wood so carved that each finger is articulated for holding. The painting is of the highest order, while the figure is finished with a clothing of actual materials, tailored in the main by his wife. Moustaches and hair are of silk thread, bits and stirrups of metal, reins and slings of leather, and any other impedimenta made of the actual material. He was at one time connected with Mokarex and Café Storme, and began a short-lived venture with Rousselot and a collector, Mathiot, into plastic flats. With Rousselot he has created a series of porcelain models, with the addition of metal, and made primarily for van Gerdinge of Vaucluse. His latest ventures are solids for The Black Watch.

Lelong, G., Paris. A dealer and agent in France for Heinrichsen. In 1935 he made a few sets of flats himself, including trees and other accessories for dioramas.

Lemon, J., London (1876). Maker of a metal chess set, silvered and gilded, of medieval English and French monarchs, crusaders, and kneeling pikemen, varying in size from 4 inches to $2\frac{5}{8}$ inches, the maker's name stamped on the bases. Sold at Christie's, London, on 18 June, 1979.

Lemoyne, Paris (fl.1839-51). Manufacturer of what were probably solids.

Leonard, Michael, Massachusetts. Painter of figures for the dioramas 'They Nobly Dared'.

Leroux, M., Paris. Designer for Mokarex up to 1965.

Leroux, P.A., Paris (fl.1950-60). A designer of flats.

Leschhorn, Carl Gottlieb, Raudten, W. Germany (1806–78). One of an association known as 'Tinsmiths and Tin-figure Manufacturers'. Mark: C.G. LESCHHORN.

Le Seigne, Paris (fl.1743). 'The General of Engineers and later engineer in charge of constructions for the King' (*Baldet*). He was responsible for one of the first-known dioramas, that of Dettingen. The models were continuous strips of infantry, 6mm, and cavalry, 12mm. It can be seen in the Musée de l'Armée.

Le Sellier, Jacques, Brussels. A maker of 54mm solids to commission, conversions to order and 'toy' soldiers.

Lesney. *See* Matchbox.

'Le Soldat de Plomb Historique'. *See* FIGUR.

Le Sueur, Jean-Baptiste Denis, Paris (1748–1826). Publisher of magnificent paper sheets. (*See* Bibault de l'Isle collection at the Carnavalet Museum.)

'Les Petits Soldats de France'. *See* Métayer, F.

'Les Petits Soldats de Strasbourg'. A colloquial name given to the Strasbourg paper sheet industry, dealt with in a delightful book by Paul Martin of the same title.

'Les Tambours'. *See* Métayer, F.

Lethbridge, G.E.T., Tiverton, Devon. Converter (1975) of models for Tiverton Museum.

Leveille, Paris (fl.1830). A maker, supposedly, of solids.

Levi, Arturo, USA. A designer employed on the Authenticast figures (non-military section).

Leviathan Models (D.P. Bright) Malvern, Worcs. (1978–). Maker of 25mm science-fiction figures (e.g., swamp dragon, sky demon) sculpted by himself and Stewart Meikle.

Levine, Harry, USA. Sponsor, with Otto Gottstein, of the dioramas of Jewish history (models made by Greenwood and Ball) for the Jewish Theological Seminary, New York; now in Jerusalem.

Levrault, Strasbourg (c.1780). Collaborator with Heitz in the production of five volumes of engravings of military uniforms, many of which gave inspiration to the publishers of paper sheets.

Lewin, Peter. *See* Maritime Models.

Lewis Collection, Springfield, Massachusetts. A toy soldier collection at Springfield Armory Museum which is claimed to be the largest in any museum in the United States, but the curator is curiously reluctant to impart any further information.

Lewis, R.H. and **Howell, H.** *See* Pixyland.

Ley, Christian Friedrich. *See* Leyla.

Leyla, (Christian Frerich Ley), Roth (b.c.1936). Manufacturer of plastic composition 9–10cm models, mainly of popular subjects, and of poor quality. Mark: LEYLA/GERMANY.

Lezius. A review of the Ib Melchior collection, given in the British Model Soldier Society *Bulletin,* August, 1969, names him as an engraver, but verification is not forthcoming.

L & H Metal Miniatures, Freehold, New Jersey (1975–). Makers of 54mm solids of both World Wars, both leaders and combatants. The catalogue bears the cryptic name 'Henlo', which can be interpreted as being the name of the designer. To judge from the photographs the models are not of particularly good quality.

Libby's Milk, USA (?1935). A set of prehistoric figures were produced for them by Lincoln Logs.

Lido Toy Company, New York (1960–). Manufacturers of poor quality 54mm plastics.

Lief, Christopher. *See* Greenhill Medieval Miniatures.

Life Model (A.R. Repetto), Genoa (1978–). 90mm metal kits of ancient races, conceived by A. Daneri, C. Valente, B. Iezzi and A. Repetto, and sculpted by A. Mussini.

'Life Of A Soldier'. *See* Green, J.K.

Lillie, Lloyd, Meriden, Connecticut (1974–). Completed the set of figures begun by Sullivan for International Silver. [*Anton*]

'Lilliput' series, *See* Britains.

Lilly III, J.K. Sandwich, Massachusetts (1972–). Patron of the Heritage Plantation, Sandwich. His father was a noted collector of rare books, stamps and models, for whom Norman and Lisle Cooke made and painted some 2000 models between 1949 and 1951, all of United States troops up to 1900. Later they did perhaps another 200 miscellaneous models. J.K. Lilly III decided, on his father's death, to make a permanent exhibition and created the Heritage Plantation for this purpose. To the existing models the Cookes added several dioramas.

Linck, L., Brunswick (1870–1916). Producer of flats, who purchased the business of W. Denecke in 1870. It was subsequently left to two sons, of whom Albert, an engraver, died in 1916. The moulds were finally bought by Rieche.

Lincoln International, USA (1974). Plastic models, 5 inches high, of modern troops, probably imported from Hong Kong.

Lincoln Logs, Chicago. A firm with complicated origins. Milton Bradley, Playskool Manufacturing Company and J.L. Wright Inc. all appear to have been connected with the firm at various times. Founded about 1910, production of 54mm metal models began about 1929. The designers were W.H. Long and J.L. Wright, the mark LINCOLN LOGS/USA or NOVELTOYS, with a special American War of Independence range entitled 'Ticonderoga'. The majority of the figures depicted US troops, Westerners, West Point Cadets, and combatants of the First World War. The figures were crude and badly painted. Forts and log cabins and other structures were issued under the title 'Lincoln Lumber'. During the First World War they published a game entitled 'At The Front', the box containing 'soldiers which are to be taken out and fired at, for which purpose there are pistols enough for considerable execution. Each soldier stands until he is shot and then falls like a man and takes no further part in the game.' In 1936 they also produced moulds for home-casting. Although Playskool had been connected with them from 1928, it was not until 1946 that they began to make plastics under this name.

Lincoln Lumber. *See* Lincoln Logs.

Lindbeg, N.E. *See* Tenngjuteriet Mars.

Lindberg, USA (1966– ?). Manufacturers of polystyrene AVF kits.

Linden, Esaius zur, Augsberg (1609–32). Noted silversmith and maker of a silver parcel-gilt nef with soldiers and sailors (in the Rothschild Collection, British Museum).

Lindner, Doris, England (1947–). A ceramicist working for Royal Worcester. She has made outstanding equestrian models of the Queen as H.R.H. Princess Elizabeth, officers of the Life Guards and the Royal Horse Guards (1961) and a Royal North-West Mounted Police Con-

54 **Lineol.** *Examples of composition models (Hawkins).*

stable.

Lindu, Hong Kong. Manufacturers (probably piracies) of 54mm plastics of Westerners.

Line Mar, Japan (c.1950). Manufacturers of tin-plate military vehicles.

Lineol-A.G., Dresden/Brandenburg (before 1939- at least 1944). Manufacturers of plaster, glue, sawdust and linseed oil models, similar to those of Elastolin but with square footstands. Mark: LINEOL/GERMANY. At one time they rivalled Elastolin in popularity, generally overcoming more successfully than the latter the clumsiness inherent in the material used. Basically all troops have German equipment, and, whatever posture was used, variation in national costume was achieved by varying the headdresses and colours. They were exported in great quantity as a propaganda exercise, extolling the virtues of Nazi Germany. (It is recorded that a German alien living in Buffalo during the Second World War had his collection seized by the F.B.I.) Detail was superior to that of Elastolin, as shown by a series of Nazi leaders and their henchmen. Specially to be commended are their machine-gun crews, although the very thick footstands are an eyesore, as are the wheeled stands of the horses. Later, poorer models bore the inscription VEB LINEOL, with three walking ducklings as a trademark.

Linka (T. Salter) Ltd, Glenrothes, Scotland (1978-). Metal kits for making buildings.

Linus, Milan (c.1965-). Publishers of colour-printed paper sheets.

Linzer Zinnfiguren Arge, Linz (1974-). Manufacturer of flats of the period 1900-15; unusual in supplying spare heads for conversion.

Lion, Henri, Brookline, Massachusetts. Creator of the series, and painter of dioramas for, 'They Nobly Dared'. Possibly one of the finest professional painters of models in the United States.

Lipkin, London (1966). Manufacturer of plastic tanks. *(Opie)*

Lippett, Paul, & Co., Folkestone (1974-5). Makers of 90mm solids, marketed in kit form. Their first offerings were a series of medieval figures, the mounted ones in kit form or assembled, the horses ill-designed. One or two of the footmen were the same basic figure with different weapons, and had a somewhat gangling appearance, the faces in particular being unconvincing. Portrait models were included, and helmets and diorama impedimenta available. These were followed by equestrian models of the Earl of Cardigan, Alexander the Great, Cortez, Zapata and the Earl of Uxbridge. They had planned a series of the Seven Years' War and of the Napoleonic period but a disastrous fire in 1975 destroyed literally everything.

Lipton, (Thomas J.) Red Rose Tea, Canada (c.1965-73). A tea company which included plastic models in its packets. Two types were issued: a medieval series, sprayed gold, and a Canadian series, painted. The latter, of which several hundred appeared, included trappers, soldiers, Prime Ministers, Simcoe, Montcalm, Chouart de Groseilliers, Tecumseh and many others, all of quite good quality. Mark: MADE IN HONG KONG, enclosing a serial number. The name of the individual portrayed appears on the front of the footstand. [*Ray*]

Lito Lusitania (Ricardo Falcao), Lisbon. Publishers of paper sheets.

Little Generals (Ronald Hinote) USA, (1972-   ). Maker of solid 90mm lead models. At first the castings were rather crude and pitted, but redesigning of the moulds led to an immediate improvement. Hinote favours the miscellaneous approach, so that there is no set series. Early models include a British Pikeman (1660), a Dervish, a Scots Highlander (1880), a French Legionnaire (1904), a Bengal Lancer, a French Revolutionary figure, a British Cavalryman (1640), a Skinner's Horse, a Roman, a Cossack, a Moroccan halberdier, and a sprinkling of First and Second World War Germans. These early models were made in one piece with only the arms to be attached, but in 1975 he began issuing kits, and in the same year there appeared models of Josephine and a yawning Russian drummer. The portrait of Hitler appears to be the best extant, and the sculpting is becoming excellent. One may not like the 90mm size, but it is apparent that Little Generals is setting a high standard. In 1976 the size became even larger (140mm). Hinote has also worked for The Franklin Mint, adding 54 and 75mm models in pewter, besides working to commission in 90mm. It has been said that piracies have appeared in Hong Kong.

Little Wars. See Wells, H.G.

Livermore, Major W.R., USA. In 1879 he published rules for '*kriegsspiel*'. (*Nash*)

Lleonart, Joan, Barcelona (1870-90). Manufacturer of 40mm flats, especially a Corpus Christi procession of over 100 figures. He took over the moulds of Pirozzini.

Llopart, Juan. *See* REAMSA.

Llorens, Joan, Barcelona (1860-75). Publishers of paper sheets.

Llovera, Arturo, Barcelona. In 1927-30 he gave the bulk of his remarkable collection of Spanish models to the Castillo of Montjuich, Barcelona, and the remainder to the Museo Naval in Madrid.

Lloyd, S. Chichester. *See* Saint Louis Lead Soldier Company.

L.N. *See* Comet.

Loback, Tom. *See* Dragon Tooth.

Lobel, Jean-Pierre. *See* Art Miniature.

Lober, Edward. *See* Cavalier.

Löblich, Wilhelm, Leipzig (c.1850). One of the makers of flats who joined the Association of Tinsmiths and Tin-figure Manufacturers.

Lockwood, Charles, London. One of the earliest members of the British Model Soldier Society, instrumental in encouraging the hobby in England.

Lockwood, Walter, Chemnitz. A private collector of flats who also employed engravers such as Frank for the issue of his own series.

Lodin, Erik, Lovisa, Finland (1761-1801). He was apprenticed to a tinsmith, I. Burman, 1777-82, who, however, appears not to have made military figures. In 1786 he moved from Stockholm to Finland and made the first flats in that country. They exhibit all the tentative gropings of the rococo period. (*Gripenberg*)

Loebel Widman & Co., Hoboken, New Jersey (c.1917). Manufacturers of 54mm hollow-casts of poor quality, mainly of United States troops.

Loescher, Bert G., Burlinghame, California (c.1952-3). Maker of commissioned solids of American historical figures, including the Old French War, the American War of Independence, and portrait models.

Lohmann, Aimor R., Porvoo (Borgà), Finland. Listed at Kulmbach, 1973, as a maker of flats.

Lolo. *See* Roma (Editorial).

Lombardo, Frederick, County Club Hills, Illinois. A freelance maker of 54mm solids who has designed for Valiant and others.

London Toys, Canada (1939-45). Manufacturers of 7.5cm hollow-cast models of soldiers and airmen, all standing rigidly to attention, except in the case of an officer, who carries a swagger stick. Of the poorest quality, and obviously influenced by Manoil, they are important as an indication that Canada was trying to encourage its own native production when the usual imports were not available. [*Morrison*]

Lone Star Die-Casting Tools Ltd, London (c.1953-c.1970). Manufacturers first of hollow-casts and then of plastics, 54mm and 6cm size. Generally speaking their models were of toy-trade quality, though occasionally better ones occurred (e.g. their medieval siege weapons). The usual range was followed: Westerners, knights, battledress troops, Guardsmen, gauchos, Scottish regiments, Davy Crockett, tanks, guns and rocket warfare. After lying dormant for some years, they reappeared in a series pirated in the United States, dated 1974, called 'Metallions', and 'Made for Gabriel Industries by Lone Star'. These were unpainted, in plastic bubble con-

53 **Lodin.** *Officer of the Finnish Dragoons, 1789 (National Museum of Finland).*

tainers. Lone Star state that this was quite without their knowledge or consent. Mark: LONE STAR/HARVEY SERIES/MADE IN ENGLAND.

Long, William H. *See* American Metal Figures; Lincoln Logs.

Longhurst, Max, London. A professional painter for the Dover branch of Historex; in 1978 he began sculpting for 'Andy'.

Longley, Donovan, Meltham, Yorkshire. Master pattern-maker who prepares Hinchliffe's models for castings.

Lord Roberts' Workshop, London (1914–18). Model soldiers may have been made at this home for war casualties. Wooden toys were certainly made, though of a more peaceful nature. (*See also* Incorporated Soldiers and Sailors Help Society.)

Lorenz, Johannes Gottlieb, Fürth/Nuremberg (1800–c.1850). Maker of flats of various sizes to 8cm. His business was purchased by Gottlieb Schradin of Nuremberg in 1852, some of the moulds being owned in recent years by Artur Caspari of Hof. His most famous production was a set of large medieval knights of a highly 'gothic' flavour (illustrated in Garratt: *Model Soldiers: a Collector's Guide*). The mounted figure in this illustration figures also in Martin's *Le Monde Merveilleux des Soldats de Plomb*, where it is ascribed to a Stuttgart maker, c.1830. Correspondence with Martin revealed that the mark is K, indicating a piracy by Kurz (or the other way round). Very strange, almost Brueghelesque models, are illustrated in Ortmann. Marks: LORENZ: L [cursive].

Lotus Miniatures (W.E. Greer and R.G. Cade), Apalachicola/Eastpoint, Florida (1974–77). Makers of 54mm solids in kit form. The initial range included seven models of the American War of Independence, a Texas Cavalry trooper, a major-general and an infantry officer (1839) (all by Cade except four of the Revolution figures), courtesans, Romans, and Guardsmen. A splendid Nativity set was commissioned by New Hope Design, but advertised without attribution. The partnership dissolved in 1974.

Louis IX, Landgrave of Hesse-Darmstadt (1768–90). The owner of 600 wooden models which were destroyed during the French Revolution.

Louis XIII, XIV, Kings of France. *See* France; Heroard.

Loumar. *See* Marx Miniatures.

Loustalot-Forest, J., Sainte-Marie, France (c.1950–60).

Producer of 30mm flats of the 1812 and 1870 periods in France, designed by P.A. Leroux and engraved by R. Pepin.

Lowe (E.S.) Company Inc., New York (1974–). Producers of a rather clumsy Renaissance-period chess set. [*Anton*]

Lowe, Samuel, Co., USA (c.1942). Publishers of cut-out or pre-scored sheets, the figures 5 and 7 inches high.

Lowther Arcade, London. An Edwardian toy centre, where thousands of conjoint-tin models were sold.

Loxley, Peter. *See* Mitrecap Miniatures.

Loy, Hans, Munich (fl.1950–68). Publisher of 30mm flats of the 1760–80 American period, together with Canadian Indians, backwoodsmen, the British Army 1756–63, the Ancient World, Aztecs and Spaniards, and Burgundians of the Middle Ages. The moulds are now owned by Tilo Maier.

Loyart. *See* Moulded Miniatures.

LP, Paris (fl.1914–18). Manufacturers of 54mm solids. Shamus Wade has had models of Sir John French, a French general, British machine-gunners, and an officer with a movable arm.

L & R. An American collector, W. Meyer, wrote about this maker in the British Model Soldier Society *Bulletin* in December, 1965. One imagines that it is a misprint for I/R.

L & S Models, Holland (1960–). Folding cardboard sheets for the construction of farms and windmills.

Lübecker Spielfiguren Verlag, S.W. Wilner, Lübeck (c.1950). Publishers of paper sheets of the Ancient World, drawn by Professor Dr Fritz Krischner.

Lucas, Nicholas J.D., Leamington Spa, Warwickshire. Professional painter for The Old Guard (English branch).

Lucotte. *See* Mignot.

Lumbswitz, Dieter, Dortmund (1975–). Maker of flats including a 'Murder of Wallenstein' set, engraved by Lecke.

Lyman, Thomas, Massachusetts. Creator, painter and maker of dioramas of 'They Nobly Dared'.

Lynch, Guy, Canberra, Australia (b.1898). One of the artists employed on the dioramas at the Australian War Memorial.

Lyne, Captain J.H., Shilo, Manitoba. Creator of dioramas at the Royal Regiment of Canada Artillery Museum.

Lyon Ltd. *See* Battle Building Soldiers.

M

Mable, K.M. and **Mable-Gallacher,M.** *See* M & M Models.

McCalum, A. *See* Caledonian Castings.

McCandish, USA. Designer for Auburn Rubber Corpn.

McCarron, J.E. *See* Stone Mountain Miniatures.

Macchi, Elizeo, Fabbrica Nationale d'Immagini, Milan (c.1870–90). Publishers of paper sheets of Spanish huntsmen, French Lancers, Bersaglieri, Garibaldi's war. (*See also* Mercenaro.)

McClellan, Frank, USA. A woodcarver of model soldiers listed in a catalogue issued by The Barefoot Soldier in 1973.

McCubbin, Louis, Melbourne, Australia (1890–1932). Official War Artist to the Australian Government in the First World War. He was responsible for a number of dioramas at the Australian War Memorial.

McEnroe, USA. A group of three 'Spirit of '76' hand-carved wooden models on one base was advertised and illustrated by an American shop in 1976.

McEwan Miniatures (John McEwan), Salt Lake City, Utah (1965–   ). McEwan began with 'Medallion Miniatures' in 54mm solids. Few of these were published though included in them was the 'Miniature Americana' group [*Pielin*], and in 1974 he changed to 25mm models of Napoleonic artillery and troops, science fiction ('Starguard' series), and ancient and medieval periods under the present title. He claimed to be the first to supply separately cast weapons and shields for this size, but Lamming was before him.

McGerr, Joseph, USA. A free-lance designer and professional painter for Cavalier, Monarch, The Barefoot Soldier and others.

Machut, Gerhard, Berlin. Maker of flats. (*Katalog der Formen, 1976*)

McKenzie, B. *See* Castile Miniatures.

McKenzie, James, Edinburgh (fl.1925). The leader of the group of woodcarvers under C. d'O. Pilkington Jackson who created the 83 statuettes at the Scottish United Services Museum.

Mackenzie of London (1978–   ). Publishers of colour-printed sets of Guards regiments consisting of 10 figures each, including bandsmen, pre-pressed, with plastic foot stands.

McLoughlin Bros, New York/Brookline, Massachusetts (c.1852–1920?). One of the pioneers of American toy and toy-soldier making. The firm was founded by John McLoughlin as a publisher of childrens' books and games in 1828 (*McClintock*). In 1852 they were making 'toys of all kinds', including cast-iron carriages, wagons, and trains, and were early in the field as publishers of single cut-out and coloured cardboard military figures for children to shoot at with pop-guns or cannon. These figures were from 5 to 6 inches high, and mounted on wooden blocks. When iron was scarce during wartime they turned more and more to cardboard figures, one set in 1898 containing as many as 100 pieces (*Newman*). They continued to make these single figures up to about 1917, superseding them by the issue of paper sheets, $10\frac{1}{2}$ x $10\frac{1}{2}$ inches, with 10 infantry or six cavalry figures per sheet, for cutting out and mounting. Boxes of 60 of such were entitled 'De Luxe Soldier Review'. Metal soldiers were started about 1890, these being 56-60mm, hollow-cast, strongly influenced by either Heyde or Britains. Their output appears to have been prolific, and sets are illustrated in the catalogues of the large American stores over many years.

MacMurray, Dan, USA. Professional painter for Cowan.

McNeil, Gordon, Surrey, British Columbia (1972–   ). A maker of two sizes of solid models, 6 and 8 inches. The smaller size is entitled 'Austerlitz' and consists of some fifty models illustrating the Ancient World, the Seven Years' War (including Indians), Napoleonics and the Crimean War. They are made in kit form, soldered together, with weapons and slings cast separately. The designs cannot compare with similar productions by other makers; nor can the larger models ('Sculpted Marblex'), the hands in particular being singularly clumsy. These cover more or less the same range as the smaller models, but equipment is made of wood or leather. Perhaps the best figure is that of an aide-de-camp to Murat (based on an illustration by Preben Kannick).

McSweeney, C. *See* Wend-Al.

Madlener, Ludwig, Munich. One of the greatest designers of the renaissance of German flats, in demand by a host of publishers and engravers. Happiest, perhaps, with the Middle Ages, he created a whole range of magnificent figures, including the set of 'Knights of Agincourt' which were first produced in solid by Selwyn-Smith and then taken over by Britains for making in hollow-cast. Madlener died at a great age in 1977.

MAGAZINES. Society journals have always been the life-blood of the model soldier world, but they are of necessity limited to members, and within recent years magazines catering for collectors, model makers and converters have become readily obtainable by those not associated with a society or club. The greatest advantage of these magazines is that they bring to the notice of readers the latest productions of contemporary makers through the advertisements of the many dealers who now flourish. Every aspect of the modern scene is covered, but emphasis is mainly placed on polystyrene kits and their conversion, on the making of dioramas and on wargaming and armoured fighting vehicles. Painters, amateur and professional, and dioramists are commissioned by the publishers, sometimes with remarkable results. Information regarding uniforms also takes up a large part of each issue, displaying, to some readers, an unhealthy interest in the Third Reich. One is often amazed by the occasional total ignorance of some of the contributors and editorial staffs of the history of the model soldier, while reviewers of models and of books swing between sycophantic drooling over the latest flashy model and total insensitivity to anything of a more serious nature. Reports from toy fairs are also often misleading, some models being reviewed as 'new' or 'just issued' that have been on the market for years, dropped by the makers, and then revived. Probably the best of the magazines are *Campaigns* and *Tradition.*

Magdeburg. Provenance of a strip of lead tournament figures, c.1250, which have some affinity with the *minnesinger.*

Magg, Herman, Schwabach (1979-   ). Designer of flats.

MAGNESIUM. The only maker to use this material was Strömbecker.

Mahon, Japan. Manufacturers of polystyrene AFV kits.

Maier, Sixtus, Nuremberg (1875-1936). With Frank, one of the most significant engravers of 'specialist' flats, setting a tremendously high standard. He began as an engraver of solids for Konrad Koch, then in 1925, for Biebel; thereafter, in successive years, for Ochel, Armant, Diedrich, Mittman and Mauke. He signed his models in Roman letters. With his son Sixtus II (1907-1968) he worked under the trade name SIMA. It is difficult to distinguish individual models as he and his son worked closely together, but one notes Sixtus junior signed his footstands in Gothic script. Further complications occurred with the advent of grandson Tilo, who today carries on the tradition, engraving for a number of producers, including especially Scholtz. The moulds of Wimor and Loy are in his possession. Fine sets engraved by the Maier family include Austerlitz, a weapon smithy c.1450, a town fair comprising 50 figures, Pope Julius II with the Apollo Belvedere (10 figures), Napoleon at the pyramids, the *Thousand Nights and a Night,* robber barons, an 18th-century hunt, Tilly and Pappenheim (50mm) and Bavarian infantry 1870-1871.

Maier, Thomas, Cincinnati, Ohio. Sculptor for Ral Partha.

Mainly Military, Lichfield, Staffs (1976-   ). Publishers of 15 and 25mm wargame accessories for the medieval, 17th and 20th century periods, together with cottages and houses. Al Charles has sculpted semi-flats for them, 54mm in groups of three figures on one stand, and 75mm models euphemistically described as 'novelty girls'.

Maita Miniatures (A. Maita) Chicago (1956-?). Manufacturer of poor-quality 54 and 60mm solids and hollow-casts. Many of the solids were of the American War of Independence, sold unassembled. At one time he owned some of the Moulded Miniature moulds, and from them produced solids for collectors. An American Revolution infantryman signed AM in the possession of W.Y. Carman may be by Maita. He is still active, but as a dealer only.

Malcolm Miniatures (D. & S. van Ormer) Aliquippa, Pennsylvania, (1978-   ). Maker of solid 54mm neo-Britains, mainly conversions from the latter's Scottish officer, with a reduced sporran, with belts and scabbards removed, and with different heads, but still retaining the movable arms. The result is a series of Scottish clansmen of some charm.

Malleable Mouldings, Deal, Kent (1947-50). Established by Winkler, supported morally and artistically by Henry Harris, and representing the dying efforts of the Comet-Authenticast enterprise (*q.v.*). Many of the models were made from the original moulds or altered and cast in metal for collectors. Their importance is that they were probably the first English firm to make a type of plastic model in separate components which were then affixed to the torsos. They were issued in a basic red or blue, the horses (in two parts) being in black or white. Bases for infantry were round or square, for the horses oblong. The underside bore the simple inscription 'Made in England'. The most popular model proved to be an equestrian Princess Elizabeth. Unfortunately, they were a decade in advance of popular taste, and, despite their excellent quality, were nevertheless unable to make the business profitable. At least they had the distinction of being the only English models illustrated by Martin and Vaillant in *Le Monde Merveilleux des Soldats de Plomb,* where the caption reads *'l'Armée Britannique en 1890, figurines composée par un amateur à Londres'.*

Mallol Carreras, Vincente. *See* Miniaturas Militares.

Mambru (Carlos D. Avondoglio), Argentina (1955-62). Manufacturers of 54mm hollow-casts, similar in style to Timpo. Of good quality, they included Second World War Americans with interchangeable weapons, mortar crews and motorcyclists.

M.A. Model Accessories (John Piper), Kingston-upon-Thames (1977-80). Metal AFVs and diorama accessories. Taken over in 1980 by Miltra.

M & M Models (K.M. Mable and M. Mable Gallacher) Tuxford, Notts. (1976-   ). Makers of 25 and 54mm solids of the Napoleonic period and the English Civil War.

Mangold, G.A. *See* GAMA.

Manning, Peter. *See* Miniature Figurines.

Manoil, Jack and Maurice, Waverly, New York (1930-c.1955). Manufacturers of extremely crude 75-85mm hollow-casts for the juvenile trade. During the Second World War they changed from metal to composition. Similar in appearance to the models of Barclay, they have always been favoured in the United States, one of the reasons being the wide range of over 105 numbered models, some with unusual stances, and many with variations of production. They are distinguishable from Barclay by having a horizontal eyebrow over a dot to represent the eye. In 1976 the moulds were revived, and castings may by now have appeared on the market. Marks: MANOIL MADE IN USA (c.1938); later substituted by a single M.

Manufacture Historique de Soldats de Plomb (Jean Montagne) Paris (1975). A firm of jewellers who published a set of twelve 54mm foot and mounted Napoleonic-period figures, designed by Lelièpvre (the riders detachable), die-cast, silver-plated and lacquered, sold by subscription under the title 'Remanence'. In 1979 they were offered singly on a normal cash basis.

Manurba, Germany (1968-). Manufacturer of 54mm plastics of contemporary German troops.

Maraini, Nicolo, Rome (fl.1964). Publisher of 8cm flats, especially of the Italian troops at the time of Napoleon.

Marca Aquila, Italy (1910-30). Publishers of paper sheets.

Marca el Toro. *See* Toro.

Marca Stella Esercito Italiano Edizioni, Milan (c.1880–1914). Publishers of an immense range of paper sheets, comprising uniforms of all countries, with a natural preponderance of those of Italy. Of good quality, though not comparable with their French and German contemporaries. The oldest sheets bear the sign of a red star.

Marchand, Eugène, Strasbourg (1905). Chief producer of the last of the Strasbourg flats. His son, Florent, reproduced many of the historic figures for collectors.

Marchand, L. Paris (fl.1766). Manufacturer of paper sheets.

Marchant, Gardner H. Jr, Massachusetts. One of the creators and painters of the dioramas 'They Nobly Dared'.

Marchi, G., & Figli, Bagni di Lucca, Italy (c.1965-). Manufacturers of juvenile plastics, including United States Civil War combatants and Indians, both foot and mounted, the riders detachable, with a few swivelling at the waist. They are characterized by the crudity of design and child-like faces, are painted a basic black with coarse colour superimposed. Mark: ITALY.

Marchis, Carlo de. *See* Sideria Miniatures.

Marcino, Corunna, Spain (c.1930- ?). Publisher of paper sheets, especially of the Spanish Civil War.

Marcum, Donald E., Massachusetts. Designer and painter of dioramas for 'They Nobly Dared'.

Marine Model Co, Halesite, Long Island (1974-). Maker of a limber and ammunition carrier for the American Civil War (seen at Hamleys in London in 1974).

Maritime Models (Peter Lewin), Greenwich, London (1979-). An unusual series of naval personnel in 90mm kit form, with accessories such as binoculars, life jackets and fishing baskets, all sculpted by Peter Allen.

MARKETING. The popularity of the flat in certain European countries seems to imply that some system of advertising or visits from travelling salesmen must have operated; otherwise it is difficult to see how so many disparate places were served. The earliest known advertisement appeared in *The Royal Gazette* in New York, 1777: 'Christmas Presents for the Young Folks, cast in metal, in beautiful uniforms, 18s a dozen'. At this time the English occupied New York, and one must surmise that the flats in question were the traditional large German ones, shipped to America with the baggage of the Hessian and Brunswick troops serving in the British Army. The German toy firms of Catel and Bestermaier issued catalogues of their stock in 1790 and again between 1798 and 1809, while in 1805 Stahl in-

formed his clients that he had taken over the moulds of Hilpert. Various advertisements by French firms occur in *Le Bon Génie* and *Bazar Parisien* in 1825, while the Great Exhibition of 1851 featured toys of all kinds, and the catalogue contains a number of references, though no specific maker is named. This and exhibitions held in Paris and other Continental cities must have boosted the sales of toy soldiers. It was not, however, until the last years of the 19th century that large firms such as Heyde and Britain appear to have contemplated issuing catalogues of their own vast outputs. These were extremely detailed and, illustrated by many line drawings, had become an established feature by 1914 and proliferated thereafter. Advertisement by stores, however, were confined to the catalogues of such firms as Gamages in England and Marshal Field in America (sometimes without acknowledgement to the manufacturer) and how tempting they looked at the time; indeed, how tempting still in retrospect! In recent years some makers and manufacturers have issued elaborate catalogues, with many illustrations in colour, a practice followed by a number of hobby-stores. Those published by Alymer, Imrie, Merten, Gammage, Tradition, The Soldier Shop, Militaria and Historex set a very high standard, and it is a pleasure merely to contemplate the offerings. Some, notably Greenwood and Ball, add articles of military interest, but many still rely on printed or badly-duplicated and unillustrated lists, at times in so small a type as to be practically unreadable. Especially infuriating in this respect are many of the lists issued by publishers of flats, Scholtz being a notable exception.

Between the two World Wars and for some time after the Second, it was possible to find toy soldiers in every town. Mrs Doan's Post Office and General Store in John Moore's *Brensham* (really Evesham) is a typical example. Here, among the 'strange assortment of goods' were 'boxes of lead soldiers belonging to armies and regiments long disbanded—Montenegrin Infantry and Serbian Hussars'. The wares of certain larger makers would naturally predominate, but a strong regional bias was apparent, with the smaller Lancashire firms being strongly represented in the North of England and poorly in the South. The better class, or 'specialist', models were confined to a few enlightened shops such as Morrell's (later Hummel's) and the great toyshops such as Hamley's (now a shadow of its former self). Here, at what appeared even then to be exorbitant prices, one could see a Carman, a Greenwood, a Courtenay or a Niblett. Society journals occasionally featured a review of a new model, and the makers ventured a mild, self-effacing advertisement in the end pages. A photograph was a rarity. Flats, however, were better served, several of the German societies beginning a regular series of photographs printed effectively on black backgrounds, a practice which happily still continues.

With the gradual slowing-down in the 1960s and '70s of commercial manufacture, and the rise of the individual makers, came an influx of shops catering exclusively for model enthusiasts. These began in many cases primarily for the sale of aircraft kits, but they soon cast their nets wider to catch the emergent market in kits of armoured fighting vehicles, armaments and figures. Nor was this a phenomenon confined to Great Britain, but also covered Europe and the United States. The larger stores, surprisingly, remained conservative and if anything reduced their ranges, but the more enthusiastic shops stocked a particularly wide range. Here it was possible to purchase a casting, either in kit form or assembled and undercoated, or painted by a team of artists employed by the proprietor or the maker. Later the importation of foreign models began, so that it was possible to judge the products of Segom and Alymer, occasionally Starlux, Soldat and Brunoe, as well as increasing numbers from the United States. Later still, when the now obsolete hollow-casts began to be sold at auction, dealers were eager to stock second-hand models. An attempt was made to popularize flats, but with only moderate success, although inter-Continental activity is now much more evident, one shop in Denmark giving a home to the latest British and American productions, and the Americans importing large numbers of British ranges, and in some cases Spanish and French ones as well. Universally stocked are the Historex and Airfix kits, while the incredibly large wargame range of a number of makers is considered essential, one or two firms, indeed, setting up their own wargame tables.

Coincidental with the establishment of these shops came magazines for modellers. Here, for the first time, were long reviews of new models, often specially painted and photographed for the occasion, with ample space given over to the advertisements by maker and dealer alike, and, what is more, available to anybody who cared to purchase them from a newsagent. Catering, however, as they did and do, mainly for the converter, who came into his own with the advent of the polystyrene kit, they proved in their text to be incredibly naïve concerning the history of the model soldier, and pretty worthless in their assessment of models. The writers on the whole tended to be either extravagant in their praise or damning in their condemnation. On balance, however, their value as a medium for advertisement and as an introduction to new models has been proved, to the extent that they have largely taken the place of English society journals. Advertisers did not confine their propaganda solely to military magazines, however, but also made use of such publications as airline and model railway journals. One or two makers (Greenwood and Ball, The Barefoot Soldier) have gone further and issued a house magazine, in which they not only discuss their new models, but include articles on general military topics. One dealer, indeed, has added comments, often caustic, on the relative value of the works of other makers.

Military magazines should be read with a certain amount of caution, for, although most advertisers are the soul of honesty, there are others who seem extremely averse to supplying the models they advertise; in one instance cheques were taken from overseas clients for an item (not a model) that had never even existed.

Probably the most effective method of marketing used by makers is that of the society gathering where one finds a dozen or more stands set up for the display of the newest models. It may well be that a lowering of standards result from this hectic competition, making the meetings too commercial, but on the other hand it is certainly an advantage to be able to view the works of a number of makers brought together at the same time in the same place, and to form one's own unbiased judgment. (*See also* Magazines; Societies.)

Märklin, Göppingen, W. Germany (1865-?). Manufacturers of tin-plate mechanical military vehicles. Bethnal Green Museum possesses a gun carriage with horses and men of the early Elastolin-type period.

Mark-Time Figures (P.J. Cowan), Croydon (1976-). Makers of Britains-type 54mm figures, but solid, and filling the gaps in their range, e.g. Indian Army, Rifle Brigade, in boxes of four, including officer. The boxes bear Britains-style labels.

Marletti,F. & P. *See* Amati.

Marlin Firearms Co., USA (1976). Commissioned Lance Historical Miniatures to do a series of Westerners for them.

Marline. *See* Marx Miniatures.

Marlow, B.L. *See* Phoenix Model Developments.

Marrion, R.J., London (1968-74). He began as a private maker of 54mm solids, particularly of the South African War, expertly painted. On joining the Greenwood and Ball (Pearce) school, he issued more models under the title Olive, including British and Boers, a trooper of the Guards Camel Corps, a Zulu War lancer and infantryman, cavalry from the Egyptian and Second Afghan Wars, an off-duty infantryman, a United States cavalry trooper, an Indian scout and a French hussar in stable dress. All his models were dismounted and of high quality. His connection with Greenwood and Ball having ended, he turned his attention to book illustration.

Mars. *See* Tenngjuteriet Mars.

Marte (Julio Garcia Castresana) Madrid, (1945-65). Manufacturer of 45-55mm solids of Spanish troops of all periods. He made a large collection of models for Manuel Martin Gonzalez. Purchaser of the Jimenez moulds.

Martico Imports, New York (1976). A pseudonym for a short-lived group of seven metal British and Napoleonic figures imported from Hong Kong. An illustration suggests a piracy from Rose models. [*Pielin*]

Martin, Michael. *See* Cavendish Miniatures.

Martin, Paul. *See* Pastimes Metal Figures.

Martin, Dr Paul, Strasbourg. Formerly Curator of the Musée Historique de Strasbourg, Dr Martin is a respected collector devoted to the study of Strasbourg flats and *'les petits soldats de Strasbourg'*, about which he has written in a highly sensitive manner, as well as other books on collecting and military dress.

Martinez, Maure, Italy. Manufacturer of 54mm plastics.

Martin-Gonzalez, Manuel de, San Sebastian, Spain. A collector whose models, some designed by himself and made for him by Castresana, together with others by Britains, Almirall, Mignot and Ballada, were to be seen at his private museum at Castillo de la Mota until its partial destruction by fire in 1972. The owner died in 1975. The Castilla has been partly restored. The best of the models were kept at another of his establishments, and were sold in 1979.

Mar Toys. *See* Marx Miniatures.

Marvel, USA (c.1935). Makers of balsawood kits of armaments.

Marvel Comics Group Corp., New York (1967-). Manufacturers of huge rubber-like plastic models of such subjects as Batman, Captain America, Spider Man, Thor, etc. These are horrible confections in violent self-colours. Their trade mark is a direct copy of that of Marx Miniatures.

Marx, Dr, Germany. Designer of flats.

Marx Miniatures (Louis Marx & Co.) New York. At the end of the 19th century a large number of manufacturers of toys were turning out miniature items such as horse-drawn carriages, wagons, stage-coaches and artillery in either cast iron or sheet tin. One of these firms, that of Frederick Strauss, was founded in 1896. In 1921 a former employee, Louis Marx, purchased the business and the stock, remarking the toys with the names MARLINE or MAR TOYS. Lithographed, stamped-tin target models in boxed sets, named 'Soldiers of Fortune', and tinplate tanks with clockwork mechanism (including one which climbed an incline) were their main military products until about 1950, when they began making plastic figures. They began with a set of the United States Presidents and a scale replica of the White House. Thereafter they became the most prolific and outstanding manufacturers of 20, 54 and 70mm plastics in the United States. Their range covered practically every aspect of military history and also embraced many non-military subjects such as the English Royal family, Sir Winston Churchill, film stars, nursery rhyme characters, a Nativity, Roman slaves and ancient Mediterranean peoples. The majority were sold unpainted in plastic bags of around fifty to seventy models, but they also sold in boxed sets; for example: Frontier wars, American War of Independence, the Civil War, the Alamo, the Foreign Legion, Zorro, Robin Hood, a Roman circus, Ben Hur, each of which had a coloured-card building to be used as a background.

Pre-pressed paper sheets of forts were also made to accompany sets. At their best the 54mm range rivals the models of Herald, but the massive, violent action-figures of the Second World War (designed by Stadden) fall far behind them in quality. From 1967–70 a small number of models were marked MADE IN ENGLAND signifying the establishment of a factory or an agency in Swansea (Dunbee Combex Marx Group), but although models could frequently be found in England before 1970 they have now disappeared from English shops. Some sets were imported into England under the name 'Flexitoys'. Later, polystyrene sets were marked 'MADE IN WEST GERMANY' and included many of the designs previously made in Alkathene. Later still, another style, more rigid than Alkathene, and badly painted, was made in Hong Kong. The loss in quality may be seen by comparing one of these with the original of, say, figures for *The Robe*. From Hong Kong also emanated a polystyrene series, this time reasonably well painted, entitled 'Warriors of the World', some in boxed sets of four or five models. Anton says that occasionally all styles may be found together in American stores. Identification marks are numerous and are no guide to the date of issue. The earliest are found on the tin-plate models: MARLINE or MAR TOYS in a circle divided twice diagonally and with MARLINES underneath. The most usual mark on plastics is MARX in a circle surrounded by USA, heavily sunk into the footstand (in many cases a magnifier is needed to read it). Others are MAR on a cross within a circle, LOUMAR and MPC (Marx Plastics Company). Many models have been pirated in Japan, the most usual mark on these being LINE/MAR/TOYS.

'MASTER'. German tinsmiths employed apprentices who served the usual seven years as journeymen, doing necessary but prosaic work. At the end of this time they were expected to produce a model of their own conception for examination by the Guild. If it was passed, the journeyman became a 'master'.

Master Models, Bishop's Stortford (1979–). Makers of 15mm scale colour-printed card models in sheet form for assembly of houses, cottages and chapels.

Master Peace Models, Enfield, Middlesex. Professional painters of wargame models.

'Masterworks'. *See* Sea Gull Models.

Matai Industries, Greymouth, New Zealand. In 1973 they contracted to produce a number of 30, 54 and 90mm models designed by Gunson; at the time of writing the models do not appear to have yet been placed on the market.

Matarazzo, Argentina (fl.1950-60). Manufacturers of 54mm solids.

Matchbox (Lesney Products), London. Better known for their tiny models of civilian wheeled vehicles, they have also made a number of military ones, with tiny figures as drivers. In 1975 they issued tank kits, and are famous for a Coronation coach.

Matchlock. *See* Riviere, R. Briton; Willetts, H.

Matchsticks. Models in this unlikely object have been made in recent years by R. Hibbert.

Matheson Models, Penshurst, Kent (1975–). A group of four 54mm solids, under the title 'Chivalry Figures', was reviewed in *Military Modelling*, January, 1976, but was withdrawn before publication. The same may have happened with a further announced set of Arthurian knights.

Mathiot, M. France (d.1970). A collector for whom Lelièpvre made many models. He was also involved with the latter and with Rousselot in the abortive making of plastic flats.

Matson, Chriss, USA. A free-lance artist, who has designed for American makers, including Waterloo Galleries.

Mattel Toy Corp., USA. An American manufacturing firm with a confused history which is difficult to elucidate. At one time they appear to have issued Monogram Models, and are still making plastic figures under their own name. In 1974 they issued a series entitled 'Heroes in Action' (14 sets), one of which is a two-man 60mm plastic mortar team with movable torsos and arms, moulded base scenery, a recoiling mortar and a clicker to simulate rifle fire. Kits and figures were taken over from Revell in 1965.

Matthews, Neville, New Zealand (1977). Creator of an AFV diorama for the New Zealand Army Base.

Mattingly, Dieter. *See* Regent Miniatures.

Maty Models, Poland (1975–). Makers of cardboard buildings. *Newman.*

Mauke, G., Naples (1920–). A German-born enthusiast who was one of the strongest advocates of flats in Italy. In 1937 he organized an exhibition of dioramas at the Castel Sant'Angelo, Rome, which had a great success. His own flats of Neapolitan and Napoleonic troops (some engraved by Maier) are now in the possession of Donath and Neckel. He also designed for Kolbitz and Emmering (Seven Years' War), Lecke, Pahle and Schirmer.

MAX, USA. Manufacturers of polystyrene AFV kits.

Maxwell, Robert Jr, Massachusetts. Painter of figures

55   **Men O' War.** *'The Pensive Poilu' (Men O' War).*

for 'They Nobly Dared'.

May, John, Nova Scotia. Designed and executed the dioramas for his shop 'Sealladh Breagh', Margaree Harbour, Nova Scotia, and arranged the Poitiers diorama at Trinity College Library, Harvard, Connecticut.

Mayhew, E. A mysterious figure of the 1960s-70s, whose models—whether originals or conversions remains obscure—were advertised from time to time in the United States and in Denmark. He appears to have been in Leiston, Suffolk, in 1970, and to have produced 54mm solids.

'Maystetter' series. *See* Reider Design.

MAZ, USA. Manufacturers of polystyrene AFV kits. May be the same as MAX.

MCW, Denmark. Publishers of paper sheets.

MDM (René Daniel), Choisy-le-Roi, France (1956-). A maker of 40mm plastic models mainly devoted to the Napoleonic period. They are most attractive and seen frequently in foyers of the larger hotels in Paris and at Orly airport.

Meadows, Richard (1798). As a prisoner-of-war at Lille, he carved a model of an officer in the Coldstream Guards, now in the National Army Museum.

Meates, K.F. *See* Gunson, W.

Meccano. *See* Dinky; Sovereign Figures.

Medallion Miniatures. *See* McEwan Miniatures.

Meger, France (19th century). Publisher of paper sheets.

Meikle, Stewart. *See* Leviathan Models.

Meister, E. *See* Selcol Products Ltd.

Melco, USA (1936-?). Producers of cardboard forts.

Mellentin, Dr, Germany (1930). An arranger of several dioramas containing figures in plaster of Paris exhibited at the Leipzig exhibition, 1930.

Ménager, Raymond, St Geneviève-des-Bois, France (1965-). Maker of 54mm models in paper relief of military and peasant subjects.

'Men at Arms Autographed Collection'. *See* New Hope Design.

Mench, Henri. *See* Scharwalder Verlag.

'Men of History'. *See* K. Mart.

'Men of the West!'. *See* K. Mart.

Men O' War (Maurene Sandoe), Welling, Kent (1973-). Maurene Sandoe served an apprenticeship with Russell

Gammage and began sculpting 90mm models, which are issued in kit form or assembled. Being a wife and, in 1978, a mother, she has little time for model-making, so that her output is as yet small: a French Dutch Lancer (1812-1814), a British trumpeter and NCO in campaign dress (1810-1815), a Jacobean musketeer, Nazi officers and standard-bearers, Napoleonic Lancers and a French First World War infantry drummer. This model must surely be classed as one of the most sensitive ever made. He is depicted seated on the ground, gazing into space as he seeks inspiration for a letter to either his mother or 'the girl he left behind him'. There is resignation here, and pathos, and little evidence of *la gloire*. Apart from the aesthetic beauty, the competence of the model is evident, no detail being omitted, even the studs in the soles of the boots being depicted. All Sandoe's work is invigorating, but this model is worth a hundred others.

Menz, Fritz, Iserlöhn, W. Germany (b.1907). Publisher of fine 30mm flats, including Indian war elephants, Burgundian heavy horse, Landschnechts, winemakers, the building of Magdeburg, some being *'kombination'* figures. He also makes 50 and 90mm fictional models such as Don Quixote and Sancho Panza which do not have the quality of the smaller ones. All the engraving is done by himself. He also owns the Müller moulds.

Mercandino, Cesare, Milan (1973-). Publisher of flats of First World War.

Mercator, Great Britain (1975-). Manufacturers of tanks in metal.

Mercenaro & Macchi, Italy (19th century). Publishers of paper sheets.

Meredith, John. *See* Micro-Mold Plastics Ltd.

Merité Military Miniatures of Canada (c.1970). Makers of a small range of 54mm solids. Canadian collectors do not know of them, so perhaps the name as advertised is that given to Monogram-Merité in Canada.

Merleben. *See* Micro-Mold Plastics Ltd.

Merlin, Paris (1650). A goldsmith who made a silver army for Louis XIV.

Merten, Walter. *See* Berliner-Miniatur-Plastiken.

Messmer, Klaus, Germany. Designer of flats.

Metal-Art. *See* Moulded Miniatures.

Metal-Cast Products, New York (c.1915-30). Manufacturers of moulds for home-casting, available from retail toy shops.

Metallions. *See* Gabriel Industries.

Metal Miniatura, Italy (1972-1977). A small range of 54mm models appeared sporadically in shops in England. Die-cast piracies of early models by Minot. The boxes bear the initials FT on a shield.

Metal Miniatures Co. *See* Moulded Miniatures.

Metasol, London (?1950). Manufacturers of 54mm hollow-casts of which the only known models appear to be a set of the Coldstream Guards. [*Opie*]

Métayer, Fernande, Paris (1941-). She began by painting flats for the then newly-started series by Mignot, which led to her turning to existing solids. Eventually she decided to create her own 54mm solids. She worked on the basis of a seven-piece figure, soldered together, with equipment added. During her formative years she issued her models under the name of 'Les Petits Soldats de France', to immediately see them pirated in the United States as 'Les Tambours'. She had and still retains a preference for parade ground figures (some slightly pot-bellied), but has made many and

56 **Métayer**. *Napoleonic troops, 54mm (Trinity College, Harvard).*

varied poses for collectors. The diorama of Bir Hacheim, displays her adaptability and her ability to work with others, especially Lelièpvre (see their dioramas at the Musée de l'Armée, Paris, and others at Compiègne). Her corpus of work must be considered as part of the French contribution as a whole, and she makes no concessions to startling innovations or the latest fads in painting although she is a beautiful artist, and her models gain in stature and dignity accordingly.

Meteraux, Florimond (1961-6). Maker of dioramas at the museum of the Royal 22nd Regiment in Quebec.

Metralla, Argentine (fl.1970). War terrains for 54mm scale wargames or for diorama terrains. (The Argentina Club gives a date of 1953-4).

Mettoy Company Ltd, Northampton/Swansea (1934-   ). Founded by Phillip Ullmann, previously the owner of Tipp & Co. of Brun, Czechoslovakia, whose stock was taken over by Hausser in 1925. Ullmann was a political refugee, coming to England in 1926. In 1934 he began making stamped metal toys under the name of Mettoy, thus continuing the line of business that he had started in Brun in 1912. During the years 1941-1945 the making of toys was suspended. In 1948 plastics were commenced, and soon after that the famous Corgi range of cars was introduced. The Silver Jubilee saw the appearance of a delightful 1902 State Landau, with the Queen and the Duke of Edinburgh, and, of course, a Corgi dog. 'Stars of Soccer', 4 inches high, were made in 1974. They are agents for Big Spielwarenfabrik and make them at Swansea under licence.

Metzger, K., Nuremberg (19th-20th centuries). Manufacturers of flats and semi-solids.

MEXICO. There may have been, may still be, manufacturers or makers in Mexico, but if so they remain anonymous. They are certainly unknown to any institutions listed by the Mexican High Commissioner in London: the Instituto de Historia Militar, Mexico City (which does, however, have a model by Cassin-Scott) or the Museo Naçional de Historia, Castilla de Chapultepec.

Meyer, Gunther, Brandenstein, E. Germany. Designer of flats of Romans, engraved by Menz.

Meyer, Hermann, Brunswick/Hanover (fl.1890-1926). A collector and private maker of flats. In 1913 he made designs for Börnig for a diorama of Leipzig.

Meyer, Captain Leo, Washington, D.C. (fl.c.1958). Designer of a number of models for Bussler.

Meyerheine, Potsdam (c.1830-c.1920). A well-known family of makers of unusual flats in various sizes. J.K. was born 1793 and died 1843. The business was continued by his widow and son K.A., who died in 1901. In 1856 J.G. Hollberg was employed as engraver. The military range included Russians, Turks, Zouaves, the Coronation of Wilhelm I, Prince Friedrich Karl, Napoleon and King Wilhelm, Frederick the Great and his troops, the German Army in the Cameroons, and a medieval joust with movable figures. Fleets in 40mm were also made. Most original, however, and best-loved, were family groups and musicians. In 1891 Meyerheine's journal contains the interesting entry: 'Sales bad, competition. Lead soldiers appearing—not so fragile as the flat tin figures'. However, a grandson, Rudolf, continued the business until 1920. Many of the moulds were broken up, but a substantial number is preserved in the Heimatsmuseum at Potsdam. Marks: M.; A.M.; H.W. (ILDT); R.M.

Meyers Collection, Brussels. Includes a 6cm flat of a knight, moulded on one side only, c.1280.

Meyers Trenten, Holland (fl.1890). Publishers of paper sheets of the Dutch Army.

Meyniel, Jacques, Paris (fl.1965). Publisher of 20mm flats of the 1806 period, engraved by Heydorn or Sollner.

Mibike, (Hunters) Swansea (1978-   ). Producers of a 20-piece kit of Lawrence of Arabia as Aircraftsman Shaw on 'Boanerges'.

Michel, Ben, USA. *See* Campaign Miniatures.

Michel, France (1968-   ). Manufacturers of plastic models of the modern French Army and the Foreign Legion, which are piracies of Starlux figures. [*Kearton*]

Micro Armor. *See* GHQ.

Micromodelos Ibera, Argentina (1960). Manufacturers of ancient cannon.

Micromodels, Great Britain (fl.1950-55). Publishers of packets of cards, 3 inches x 5 inches, each containing an illustration of a tiny model to be cut out and assembled. Buildings issued include the Tower of London, the Globe Theatre, Westminster Abbey, Windsor Castle and the Houses of Parliament. (*Newman*).

Micromodels, Leicester (1972-   ). Manufacturers of metal AFVs and some tiny figures to go with them.

Micro-Mold Plastics (R.G. Scott), Goring, Sussex. Manufacturers of plastic buildings, war terrains, field works, diorama bases and 20mm models. The idea was begun by Merleben (John Meredith) of Bracknell about 1965, and taken over by Scott in 1969, who also incorporated Deltorama.

MIDDLE AGES. In medieval times model soldiers took on many forms, not necessarily all relevant to the subject of 'model' soldiers. However, the prototypes of the flat (as at Cluny) and the solid (as in the German jousting knights) cannot be disregarded. Domestic utensils such as the nef and the aqua-manile displayed opportunities for making military figures, and hand-manipulated puppet warriors of wood were popular. The normal occupation of the period was war, and many of the models were obviously intended to educate youngsters into the art of combat. In *Cry God for Harry*, Elizabeth Rofheart depicts Henry V of England as having been presented with the gift of a quantity of jewelled ivory models brought back from a Crusade to Palestine. He carries these about with him, and plans his tactics with them. Correspondence with the author reveals that although she had no concrete basis for the introduction of them into her novel, nevertheless her thorough reading of the period led her to the conclusion that such models undoubtedly existed, possibly as chessmen. The Nuremberg tin factories ensured a steady supply of religious tokens, leading to the development of military ones, while on the lowest level models of clay or wood were undoubtedly prolific.

Midgetoy, Great Britain (c.1955). Manufacturers of tinplate artillery.

Midleton Models (Major Alan Coppin, David Coppin), London/Kingsbridge, Devon (c.1955–). Major Coppin began making models after several years of converting Britains' hollow-casts. He was inspired by Patrick Synge-Hutchinson (now retired from the association) to design 12-15-inch-high models of plaster, wood and natural materials. Immense care is taken to ensure the accuracy of every detail. Commissioned models may be seen at the National Army Museum, the National Maritime Museum and the Canadian National Maritime Museum. His son is concerned mainly with the painting.

Midori, Japan. Manufacturers of polystyrene tank kits under the name RIKO. In 1975 they began making 54mm plastic figures of German Second World War occupants of tanks and carriers.

Mieroslawski, General, Poland (c.1830). A developer of *kriegsspiel*, using carved wooden figures.

Miersen, Annemarie, Gundelsby (Kappeln), W. Germany. Appears in the list of makers of flats issued at Kulmbach in 1973 and is the present owner of Rössner's moulds.

Mignalu, Paris (c.1930). A sub-division of Mignot, producing 54mm models in aluminium. A few of the 'kneeling-firing' models were provided with a hand mechanism which enabled a cap to be fired from the rifle. [*Wade*]

Mignot (CBG), Paris. The oldest firm of manufacturers of solid 54mm models still in existence. Time has passed them by and nothing new has been issued since about 1950. Their present business appears to be the re-issue

and re-issue again of sets of models produced from about 1890 to 1934, but only in the more popular ranges, and it is probable that no researcher will be able to discover all the types that they made. The general output is not to be compared with that of Heyde, but for years they and the latter held the monopoly of export, especially to the United States. Their range includes most of the European armies of the 19th-20th centuries, interspersed with excursions into the past, and many portrait models feature in their list. The Napolenoic period, naturally, is predominant. From time to time they have made a really good model, but on the whole they display the faults of the Germanic makers of solids in that the arms are too long for the bodies, and the medieval range is still and archaic. At the present time only the 54mm pieces are generally known, but there is evidence that they made models of a larger size, and, indeed, were commissioned by Royalty on special occasions. Occasionally they still attempt to invade the export market, but, generally speaking, their business methods are so haphazard and their prices so outrageous that they have achieved little success in Britain at least, where they are rarely seen.

Their origin is still veiled in mystery. Years ago an attempt was made to establish the true date of their foundation, but no help whatsoever was received from the firm (*See* France). The only concrete fact that can be established is that it, at some time or other, incorporated the firms of Cuperly, Blondel and Gerbeau, that Henri Mignot was in charge in 1921, and that the firm still continues to function in the Rue de Vieux Colombier. Besides their normal 54mm solids they experimented at times with hollow-casts and aluminium for cheaper ranges, and presented their sets in highly decorated boxes, often on two shelves with a dioramic background. One amusing set is a *plage*, or scene by the seaside, with a semi-dioramic surround. Some sets, such as the *pompiers*, are extremely rare. For many years they issued their own models and those of Lucotte concurrently. Of the types of models issued by the latter in the earliest days there seems to be no record, those which appear on the market or in private collections or museums appearing to date almost exclusively from 1860 onward. Certainly they have not appeared in

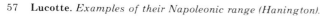

57 **Lucotte.** *Examples of their Napoleonic range (Hanington).*

Mignot catalogues for many years. The Lucotte models must have been outstanding in their day, anticipating commercially what was later achieved by the master-craftsmen: separate reins, saddles, saddle-cloths, weapons and riders. The five basic Mignot horses (all on stands) are more static, although one or two were undoubtedly based on those of Lucotte. Even so, the Lucottes are generally far superior to their German counterparts, although neither they nor Mignot used a pin protruding from the seats of the riders. Identification of mounted models may initially be found by the outstanding trademark of L and C on either side of an Imperial bee. Generally the horses are walking, with a raised foreleg, and the legs themselves are longer and thinner than those of Mignot, as are also the tails. The Mignot horses are rearing or trotting when mounted by personalities or colour bearers and, after 1918, galloping, and the saddles and reins are soldered on. The detachable riders sit a long way from the reins. In the case of infantry, the Lucottes stride forward purposely, nearly always on oblong stands, except for halted figures, whereas those of Mignot have a straight-legged walk, stepping off with the right foot from small square stands, painted either grey or dark brown, some embossed CBG, some with a paper label, some with no mark at all. The Lucotte packs are larger and longer, the bayonets shorter. With artillery, the Mignot guns and limbers are under scale, and the horses the same as those used for single figures. Gunners are dark blue, while those of Lucotte are grey. Painting in the older CBG models is of a dullish finish, in the more recent castings more shiny.

L.W. Richards wrote some valuable articles on the products of the firm which appeared in the *Bulletin* of the British Model Soldier Society, but he fought shy of investigations into dates, and one suspects that the members of the French Society might well be the only people who could conduct a proper enquiry into the problem. Whether they would obtain any assistance from the firm itself is a matter for conjecture. However, one aspect of their work is well documented. Apart from the Strasbourg industry, the flat in France had met with little response, but the spread of the 'connoisseur' flat as made in Germany by historically accurate and artistic craftsmen fired the imagination of a group of highly skilled French artists, and in 1936 plans were drawn up for a French product. Led by Pierre Armont (calling himself Petrocochino), the team comprised Rousselot, Hamel, Bombled and Martin as designers, Maier, Hahnemann and Frank as engravers, with Rousselot, Métayer, Sainte-Marie, Cosson, Martin and Hamel as the principal painters. They induced the firm of Mignot to publish the results and had an immediate success with the discerning collector. The sets they made were of outstanding quality, and the range fairly impressive: chariots of Assyria and Egypt, Numidian war elephants, Persians, Scythians, Greeks, Romans, the Field of the Cloth of Gold, Cortez and the Aztecs, the Valois, the Thirty Years' War, the Capets, the Franco-Prussian War, the war in Algeria and the 'war to end war'. Paramount was the Napoleonic set, far-reaching in its scope, and still by far the most popular, for here Rousselot was given full rein for his genius as a designer. The life of the Emperor is traced through all his campaigns, and a rich and outstanding set results.

On the other hand, and surprisingly, the Joan of Arc set is disappointing, with entirely lifeless figures. A full catalogue, with line drawings depicting the various positions, is kept on hand at their showroom, and one orders from the numbers. In keeping with Continental manufacturers, a series of 45 naval vessels, in small scale, was produced for some years, while some rare models were made in 60mm and 30mm semi-solid about 1910. John Lyle, writing in *Old Toy Soldier Newsletter*, June, 1978, describes the only known set, made about 1925, depicting *The War of the Worlds* by H.G. Wells.

Mike's Models (Michael Burton), Brighton, Sussex (1978-). Maker of vast quantities of wargame models in 15mm.

Milartex. *See* Sykes, John.

Militaria (Robert Cowan), Dallas, Texas. An enterprising dealer who has occasionally produced a beautiful catalogue fully illustrated in colour. He sets a worthy example for researchers by giving the names of converters where appropriate, and the names of the painters he employs. He also makes dioramas and figures of various kinds to commission, and combines with Dr Alan Scott in a small series called Heritage.

Military Buildings (Ken Chapman), Netherhampton, Salisbury (1971-4). Maker of cardboard models of Napoleonic War buildings.

Military Casts, Valley Stream, New York (fl.1960-65). Makers of 54mm solids.

'Military Commanders' series. *See* Ceramics.

'Military Figures' series. *See* Ceramics.

Military Miniature Reproductions, Hollywood, California (1968). Makers of metal cannon of the Napoleonic wars and the American Civil War.

Military Miniatures (John Scheid), New York (c.1948-55). A series of well-designed 54mm solids, designed by John Scheid and cast by Comet. They were issued unpainted, with the mark MIL MIN. The range comprised United States Dragoons, fifes and drums of 1779, a Drum Major of Infantry at the trail 1812, artillery of 1830, King's Rifle Regiment firing and British Guardsmen firing and marching.

Military Models, San Francisco (1958).Makers of 54mm solids of the United States Army 1865-85, Napoleonic units, the Indian Army (including groups of three figures), the Foreign Legion, the Royal Air Force, British Commandos and Indians, issued either plain or painted.

'Military Series'. *See* Airfix.

'Militia Models'. *See* Drumbeat.

'Militia Models Worldwide' (M.R.E. Hentall) Staunton-by-Coleford, Glos. (1979-). Manufacturers of neo-Britains, designed by K.V.T. Walter and Terry Witts. First marketed by Drumbeat under the name Militia Models.

Millat, Joan, Barcelona. A publisher of paper sheets who took over the business of Antoni Bosch in about 1875.

Miller, Anthony, London (1977-). Professional painting service offered.

Miller, D. *See* Tricorne Miniatures.

Miller, J.M., USA (c.1950-60). A manufacturer of 5-inch plaster models. Only a few are known, including a pair of stretcher-bearers. Signed on the top of the footstand **19◯50 J.M. MILLER** [*Anton*]

Milliken, E.K., (fl.1930-35). Founder-member and past President of the British Model Soldier Society, and one

30 Left: **Non-Military Models.** *'Homage to Watteau'. A superb group of 54mm solids by Rollo (Author).* Right: 32 **Painting.** *90mm solid of a Polish Lancer officer illustrating Sheperd Paine's impeccable painting (Sheperd Paine).* Below: **Non-Military.** *Two settings by P. van Tuycum, the models by Rose and Sanderson. (van Tuycum).*

Non-Military. *'Leonora' – a delightful evocation of the 18th century by Rollo. 54mm solid (Rollo).*

35 Above: **Palomeque**. *Spanish Orders of Knighthood, c.1925. Attractive metal figures by a Spanish commercial manufacturer (Allendesalazar). 36* Right: **Pranzetti**. *Italian hussar in polychrome wood (Pranzetti).*

of the first collectors in England to create dioramas and utilize model soldiers for educational purposes. In 1930 he showed at Croydon a series of models under the title 'A Page of History', consisting of Gulliver pegged down, the Sheriff of Nottingham and Robin Hood, Hiawatha's Encampment, the Pied Piper, Robinson Crusoe, Hansel and Gretel and the Jungle Book.

Mil Min. *See* Military Miniatures.

Miltra (Z.M. Iwaszko Ltd), Harrow (1977–). Makers of small plastic models of modern troops for use by the British Army, the United States Army and Marine Corps for tactical and recognition purposes. A small section is for sale to the public. They may be seen at various military establishments including the Parachute Museum, Aldershot, and the Ministry of Defence, Whitehall. In 1980 they took over the stock of M.A. Model Accessories.

MIM (Emmanuel Steinback), Belgium (c.1935-48). One of the best manufacturers of his time in 60mm solids. Each was numbered and certificated. Models included the French First Empire with musicians, Bonaparte with his family and his marshals, British and United States armies of the Second World War, the RAF, Military Police and the Ancient World. All models were specially painted and the cavalry had detachable riders. A lesser range of one-piece mouldings, sold at a cheaper price, with thick bases, were entitled NIMIM and comprised Napoleon and his staff mounted.

Mimic, London (c.1956). A manufacturer of non-military figures, with a few vehicles.

Miniaturas Militares (Vincente Mallol Carreras) Valencia, Spain (c.1972–). Maker of 54mm solids of all contestants of the First World War, including portrait models of Wilhelm II and Albert I. (*Allendesalazar*)

Miniature Americana, Mt Prospect, Illinois (1965-7). A small series of 60mm solids of a particularly crude appearance, designed by Sibbitt. They include the United States 7th Cavalry, a Mexican of 1519 and a Barbarian chief seated on what purports to be a throne. Each is a caricature, although possibly this is not intended. They were taken over by McEwan about 1967.

Miniature Figurines (Neville Dickinson), Southampton (1968–). Dickinson began making wargame figures in solid as a result of taking over a small range entitled Alberken, which was connected initially with Peter Gilder. The earliest models were ill-designed, with no uniformity of size, some horses being impossibly large, with horse and rider in one piece. On being joined by Neil Butcher, David and Richard Higgs, David Hutchings and H. Walters, scale became more uniform and tremendous output was achieved. It cannot be said that the quality improved overmuch, but the sheer volume was staggering. Almost every conceivable era has by now been produced, each in many dozens of models, so that complete armies may be achieved. All the usual periods have been well represented, together with war elephants, gun carriages and caissons. In 1974 they began a 'Middle Earth' (Tolkien) set that is still growing. One wishes they were in a larger size. In the same year they began 5 and 15mm figures, with fences and bridges added the following year, the smallest figures being in strips (an idea soon copied by United States makers). In 1976 they were joined by Peter Manning with new 15mm designs, followed by 25mm Waterloo personalities. At the time of writing they must be re-

58 **Miniature Figurines.** *Examples of 25mm solids.*

garded as the most famous wargame suppliers in the world, and are consequently pirated in the United States. It must in all honesty be said that few of the models have style or elegance, many are ill-proportioned, and many are armed with weapons of such size and thickness that they are out of all proportion to the bearer. Nor are they always historically accurate; their Alexander Nevsky knights were savagely attacked recently by an expert on Russian armour. Nevertheless, the Battle of Bosworth series issued in 1976 showed a great improvement, even though the choice of horses was restricted, and the latest Napoleonic personalities are in the 'collector' class. In justification it must be said that the models in mass provide just what is needed for wargaming, and on occasion they blend well with those of other makers.

Early on in his career Dickinson commissioned a number of solid 54mm models from Major Rowe, but difficulties ensued, they were soon withdrawn and are now scarce. Two unusual models in the same size, this time of early motorists, appeared in 1975, and it was mooted that Sykes had been approached for designs in this size, but nothing appears to have transpired. Unusual efforts are a 40mm chess set of the heads of Egyptian gods and goddesses and 18th-century artillery in 25mm. Tanks and polystyrene houses at the moment complete their output.

Miniaturen in Zinn (Manfred Walter), Porta Westfalica, W. Germany (1974–). A designer and publisher of $3\frac{1}{2}$ inch flats, engraved by Lecke. He has a keen interest in the Scottish regiments, and his first models included a piper in the Scots Guards. Other models are a Drum-Major of the 7th Middlesex (London Scottish) Rifle Volunteers (1893), a Sergeant of the Arab Legion with camel, a bass-drummer of the Kenya African Rifles (1970), an Indian in warpaint (after Bodmer), a mameluke and a winged Polish Lancer. His intention is to portray the most attractive uniforms of all countries. It is interesting to see a return to the *vitrinen* figure, as extolled in recent years by Rössner and Scholtz.

Minicraft Models Inc., Torrawell, California. Plastic piracies of Tamiya produced in Hong Kong.

Minifigure Co., Tucson, Arizona (fl.1950-65). Manufacturers of 54mm solids of American troops, Indians, Regimentals, painted or unpainted, issued seven to a box.

Mini-Mansion, USA (1975–). Publishers of historic American buildings. (*Newman*)

Minimarquet, Argentina (1956). Manufacturers of unbreakable model tanks. [*Basseterre*]

Minimen (J.B. Updyke). Chagrin Falls, Ohio (1975–). Maker of 35, 58 and 100mm solids. The first batch consisted of Pershing, Colour-Sergeant Bourne, Lieutenant Chard, an Isandhlawana Zulu, a Rorke's Drift Zulu and Captain Bligh. Later models included Lindbergh, Nelson, Geronimo and two versions of Robin Hood, one having shorter legs than the other. They are full of rugged action but the component parts do not always fit well together. Furthermore, the stands are decidedly lumpy in some instances. The varied facial expressions are good. In 1976 models in 35 and 100mm were begun with Wellington and Kitchener. For exhibition and advertisement purposes they are painted by Joe Berton.

Mini-Models, London (1967-?70). An offshoot of Triang, this military series consisted of 54mm plastic Japanese, Germans and Americans of the Second World War, designed by Stadden and issued between 1967 and 1968. In 1970 they took over a number of Almark designs which they issued as kits. In 1972 'Tradition' advertised them in metal. Their best effort was a set of chessmen depicting the Battle of Agincourt, designed by Stadden, and issued in 1970. These were beautifully (although in some cases not heraldically correctly) painted, and quite exciting to handle or contemplate.

Miniplast Miniatur-Plastiken (Ernst Schmidt), Berlin (c.1960-). Manufacturers of 60mm plaster composition juvenile models of knights and Westerners.

'Miniploms'. See Alymer.

Minitanks, USA (1975-). Manufacturers of the smallest size metal AFVs. Poor-quality plastic figures by Preiser of Churchill, Hitler, Goering, Mussolini, de Gaulle, Eisenhower, Stalin and Rommel appear in their latest catalogue.

Minnikin Figures, Japan (fl.1958). Manufacturers of solid 54mm piracies of Heyde, Britains, Pilkington Jackson, all with Oriental faces.

Minot, Barry, Elstree, Herts (1968-). Minot began with the Greenwood and Ball (Pearce) combine, designing for them dismounted 54mm solids of the Napoleonic period, naturally including the Emperor himself, and a British and Highland Infantryman and Fusilier of lesser quality. In 1973 he began making 30mm models of the Napoleonic Wars of the utmost grace and character, including a group of wounded and a 'Last Stand'. In 1974 he began work on his own account, issuing a Texas Ranger, a United States Dragoon of 1840, a fine Gaulish chieftain and a cavalryman of 1870 peeling potatoes. A splendid mounted British Light Dragoon, incorporating an imaginative balance for the rearing leg, and a Lieutenant Dieudonné after Géricault are outstanding models. The next year he received his first commission from Under Two Flags: an Indian gunner, mule and mountain battery, with a private of the East Lancashire Regiment, 1897. He started 90mm models in the same year, with Murat as Grand Duke of Berg. In 1977 he began 25mm Zulus under the name 'Genesis', mythological and fantasy models in 30mm, barbarians in 54mm, and in 1978 added a 100mm 'barbarian and fabulous female companion'.

'Mirror Signature'. In 1850 Allgeyer senior engraved his name the wrong way round on a mould, from which twenty castings were made, each of which, naturally, bore the signature in reverse. Only four specimens, all owned by Ib Melchior of the United States, are known.

Mitchell & Son, Glasgow (1930). Makers of a set of 30 stand-up cigarette cards, size 36 x 37mm.

Mitchell, John, Malvern (1977-). Designer of card build-

59 **Minot.** *Interpretation of painting by Géricault. 54mm solid painted by Bill Duinker (Author).*

ings in 15mm.

Mitrecap Miniatures (Dennis Johnson), Beighton, Sheffield (1979-). Maker of 54mm solids. From a modest start he hopes to develop two themes: the Life Guards and troops of the Second World War. He intends making a series of vignettes to comprise a British square at Waterloo, in the design and sculpture of which he will be assisted by Peter Loxley. At one time he designed and sculpted for Empire Military Miniatures, and four of the figures he did for them are now incorported in Mitrecap.

Mittmann, Franz, Schweidnitz (1901-59). He began making 20mm flats in 1930. Some were engraved by Ferner and S. Maier senior. They are still obtainable through his widow. Mark: FM.

Mivie, J., Argentina (fl.c.1960). Maker of carved and painted wood models, 10 inches high, clothed in natural materials.

M.J. Mode. See Douglas Miniatures.

Mleczko, Peter. See Saunders, N.

M.M.C., London (c.1930). Manufacturer of 54mm hollowcasts. The only traceable figures are of British soldiers in scarlet uniforms with pith helmets, on camels. (*Wade*)

Moberg, Major N.U., Stockholm. Creator of a diorama of 140 flats at the Army Museum, Stockholm.

MOD-AC Manufacturing Co., Los Angeles (c.1942). Manufacturers of wooden kits of army scout cars. (*Newman*)

Modakit, USA (1974). Manufacturers of polystyrene AFV kits, Nissen huts, etc.

Modelled Miniatures. See Dinky (Meccano) Ltd.

Model Mattel. See Monogram.

Model Toys Ltd. See Timpo.

Mohr, F. Karl. See Wimor.

Mokarex, Paris (1958-67). Manufacturers of hollow metallic plastic 54mm models, one being included in every tin of their coffee. These remarkable figures, designed originally by M. Leroux, and then from 1964 to 1967 by Lelièpvre, cover a tremendous range of French military and civil history, including portrait models and a chess-set. Many of the figures were copied from famous paintings. Issued unpainted, competitions were held for the best painted assembly, and an attractive catalogue issued. Certain sets (including the chess set) were revived as Figurines Historiques in 1976, and offered for sale by Historex. Polk says that he and the Brethiot family were responsible for this revival.

Molfort 'Sock Brand', Barcelona. Manufacturers of printed soldiers to be cut from the wrappers of packets of children's sweets.

Monarch, England (pre-1939). Manufacturers of 54mm hollow-casts of whom practically nothing is known.

'Monarch'. *See* Cherilea Products.

Monarch, (Dr August John Benkert) Long Island City, New York (1968-). Apparently a subsidiary of Research Collectors' Aids (one of the veiled peculiarities of the American sales-world of the time). Makers of 56-60mm solids, issued in kit form. A number of free-lance artists are employed, including Greer, McGerr, Olmstead, Fabre, Benkert himself, Raymond Crowe, Sanderson, Saunders and Sparrow. The range is prolific, including gladiators, Romans, the Middle Ages, Napoleonics, the Colonial Wars, both World Wars and United States forces of all periods. There are also portrait models of Gordon, Goering, Zapata, Rob Roy, Rommel, Frederick the Great, von Ziethen, Patton, Washington, Augustus, Julius Caesar, Nero and Caligula. Possibly the best model is that of a British naval Gatling gun crew, the gun itself being in minute and elaborate detail, frustrating to assemble and so like the Gardner gun made by Cavalier that it is possible that both were created by the same artist. In 1976 the Gatling gun crew was complemented by a British Naval Brigade supply wagon and working party. Of some models it is difficult to say much that is complimentary. Many exhibit the most glaring faults of anatomy, sculpture, casting and general presentation, even though designed by some of the best known of the free-lance artists. However, those issued in 1974, especially the medieval lady, the Black Prince and a series of 'The Spirit of '76' by Greer, together with some re-modelled figures issued earlier, are superior to the rest. In 1975 Chernak did a Second Virginia Regiment rifleman at Valley Forge for them, and in the same year they somehow acquired the mould from Old Guard of a mounted Emir. Hinton joined them in 1976, beginning with medieval figures.

Mond, Sir Alfred, London. In the 1930s he presented a fine collection of Lucotte models to the R.U.S.I. Museum. Their present whereabouts is unknown.

Monogram, USA. An example of the confused history of the ownership of models typical of the United States. Under the name Monogram, Model Mattel issued a series of plastic 54mm models (1956), comprising an 18-piece United States Infantry squad for use with tanks. Earlier models, issued from Chicago, were 40mm battle troops and AFV kits. The next stage was about 1965, when Monogram Models Inc., of Morton Grove, Illinois, issued a series of 54mm solids entitled Monogram Merité, which, again, were originally marketed by the Mattel Toy Corporation. These were discontinued in 1972, but revived with additions by Polk the following year under the name Aristo-Monogram Merité. With few exceptions they depict Second World War troops, and are issued in kit form, complete with adhesive and stand. Knowledgeable collectors consider the earlier

where the various techniques are discussed in detail. varying periods made for them in 1975 by Beverly Gordon are superior to any of the others.

Montagne, Jean. *See* Manufacture Historique.

Monta-Plex (Española de Juguetes-Garanta), Barcelona (1973-). Manufacturers of 20mm plastic modern battle-dress piracies of Airfix.

Monte Enterprises ASA. Publishers of cardboard models of famous American buildings.

Moore, Frederick. *See* Kilmore Figures.

Morawski, R., Warsaw (c.1960). Maker of 54mm solids. [*Ortmann*]

Morestone London Ltd (Morris & Stone) London (fl.1958). Manufacturers of 54mm plastic Davy Crockett characters.

Morica Stella Isercito Italiano, Rome. Publishers of paper sheets.

Morrell's. *See* Hummel.

Morris, Walter. *See* W.M.H. Models.

Morris, Wayne. *See* Hazelwood Miniatures.

Morris & Stone. *See* Morestone.

Morrison, J.F., Glasgow (c.1936). Maker of six models, 12 inches high, in barbola of units of the Royal Army Service Corps in the R.A.S.C. Museum, Aldershot.

Morrison, Thomas, Edmonds, Washington/Maine (1940-). A maker of models in various materials and sizes.Originally a collector, he turned to making models for himself and his friends. In 1940 he began original work in clay, porcelain, metal, wood, stone and aluminium paste, primarily for the toy and furniture trade, including over 100 chess sets of various designs. His first commission (1968) was a 50-piece set in 9-inch porcelain of the United States Army 1775-1880, limited to an edition of 100 figures of each type. Next came 100 pieces (3 inches) in aluminium paste for the Colorado Historical Society of uniforms of Colorado State Militia 1840-80. Other work includes models of 3 to 6 inches for the Alaska State Museum, of Alaskan natives and their body armour, decorative figures of the traditional costume of Europe (48 pieces, in porcelain), Indians of North America (100 pieces, porcelain) and natives of the North-West coast. He is at present working on ethnic costumes of 105 different countries, male and female, for issue in a limited edition, and a 6-inch porcelain version of the Alaska models. In addition, he has made some 700 military models on commission for collectors between 1947 and 1974. He was born on a cattle ranch near Los Angeles in 1924, and has been a professional soldier, engineer, business consultant and industrial designer. In 1976 he began a series of 200 units of local US Militia Companies 1800-80. He also indulges in 'whimsies' of turned wood and papiermâché in limited editions, one, of a 'Christmas Soldier', also being made in porcelain. One of his humorous series was made for the Wells Fargo Company, to be sold in towns on their original stage-coach runs.

Morsack. *See* Stockinger, L. von.

Moser, J. John, Magdeburg. *See* Neue Magdenburger Bilderbogen.

MOULD. The majority of models, even those made in the new materials such as fibre-resin and cataloy paste, need a mould for their production. So many and varied, however, are the materials employed, that it seems wiser to leave the reader to peruse such works as those written by Cassin-Scott, Dilley, Ortmann and Stearns, models to be the best, although a series of six models of Further information occurs from time to time in society journals and military magazines. At the same time it should not be forgotten that the process of moulding has changed vastly from the early days, and that versatility has been greatly increased by the more flexible materials now in use. One example may be quoted as typical of the 1930s. A certain maker wished to produce tiny railway figures and approached a professional sculptor. Plaster of Paris moulds were used, and the only way it was considered possible to produce a lead figure from them was to make a multipiece bronze master mould. Because of the rigidity of the metal, undercutting was not possible, so it was decided that each figure had to consist of the product of twelve plaster moulds, with eventual bronze castings. Therefore the 20mm models had to be assembled from twelve separate pieces! Lead was melted on a two-burner gas stove, and the hot twelve-piece mould had to be dismantled for each casting - a far cry from today's multiple production.

Moulded Miniatures (J. Edward Jones and Ella L. Hume) Chicago (c.1929-56). Makers of various sizes of hollowcast. Known under many names: Metal Miniatures Co to 1945 (sub-divided into Metal-Art, Universal, World Miniatures, King's Art, 1954), broken down again under the names Varifix and Loyart. Some of the moulds were sold to A. Maita, who cast them as solids. By 1954 they had produced 208 different designs, a number closely resembling those of Britains. Perhaps the first firm to represent the troops of the American War of Independence, and these of good quality. The catalogue of 1930 gives four sizes: Large (15cm) Medium (6.5cm), Small (54mm) and Midget (40mm). The medium size had horses to match. Footballers, farm animals and a model of Father Time were also made.

MPC. *See* Marx Miniatures.

MPC Model Products, Mount Clemens, Michigan (1973). Manufacturers of a Korean staff car in polystyrene.

MSR, Brighton, Sussex (1950-3). Three models only, a trooper of the Household Cavalry, on foot and mounted, and a Scottish infantryman, were made, in 58mm solid, as the offshoot of an insignificant and short-lived engineering firm.

M.S. Tank (Manuel Schmid), Higueras, Spain (1975-). Manufacturers of AVF kits in fibreglass-resin and white metal.

Mudie, David, London (fl.1902). A small manufacturer of 54mm hollow-casts prosecuted by Britains for piracy.

Muller & Freyer. *See* Elastolin.

Müller, Hans, Erfurt (1885-1967). Publisher of flats. He began by making fully round vehicles, but turned to the production of flats, some of which were engraved by Frank. These included Crusaders, Saracens, the storming of Acre (formerly at the R.U.S.I.), Crécy (also once at the R.U.S.I.), Greek athletes, the Battle of Tannenberg (1410), 16th-century Brandenburgers, Henry VIII and his wives, Holbein, Netherlands couples after Hals and Rembrandt. At one time he appears to have owned Biebel's portrait figures and troops of the Thirty Years' War. Marks: MR; (M).

Müller, Heinz, Halle a.d. Saale, E. Germany. Publisher of flats. (*Katalog der Formen, 1976*)

Multi-color, Spain (fl.1956). Maker of tiny plastic models.

Multiple Plastics Corp, New York (1965-). Manufacturers of poor-quality 54mm and 6-inch plastics of American infantry and African natives.

Multiple Toy Makers, USA (1975-). Manufacturers of a set of 35 models in 45mm, in blue plastic.

'Multipose'. *See* Airfix.

Mumoz, José Barinage, Spain. Publisher of paper sheets.

Munaña Miniatures (1974). A firm whose identity it was impossible to establish. A note sent to the author by an American collector stated that their models were available in the United States, but were of Spanish origin. Photographs published in *Military Modeller* in 1974 depict a German Admiral, a sailor and an Infantryman of the Second World War.

'Müncherier Bilderbogen'. *See* Braun & Schreider.

Munchow, Max, Schwerin, E. Germany (b.1896). A private maker of round artillery and flats. (*Ortmann*)

Munne, Lawrence, Augsburg (1973). Listed at Kulmbach as a maker of flats.

Murray, Patrick, Edinburgh. One-time curator of the Edinburgh Museum of Childhood. A keen collector, he has written a number of articles on early models, and has made researches into the folded-paper model.

Murray, William H. *See* Old Guard.

Musgrave, G. & Culpitt, P.S. *See* Gem-Models.

Musser, Edward, USA. One of the designers employed by the Grey Iron Casting Company.

Mussini, A. *See* Life Model.

Mutzbauer, Rainer, Nuremberg (1979-). Designer of flats.

M.W. (Albert Selley and Harry White), Tottenham, London (1972). A short-lived venture of 12-inch clay models, a few only and in limited editions, the models by Selley and the painting by White.

N

N.A. *See* Nessenius, J.A.

Nadebor, Gerald, Germany. Engraver of semi-solids.

Nadler, Axel, Landshut, W. Germany (1977-). Publisher of flats of a 16th-century wedding. (*Klio*)

Nahde, Munich (fl.1965). Publisher of Napoleonic and Bavarian flats.

Nalecz, Poland (1974-). Solids, 54mm, imported into Forest Hills, New Jersey. Polish troops, 1732-1939, some mounted, issued plain or painted. Probably piracies of Stadden.

Naon, Carlos Maria. *See* Figurines Karlis.

Napoleon III. He commissioned a set of himself and his marshals, in 13 large plaster models, which was exhibited in Paris in 1922.

Nardi, Italy (fl.1963-73). Manufacturers of 58mm plastics.

Nathan, Philip, Alfold, Crawley (1965-). Worker in silver and pewter. Joined the Franklin Mint as senior sculptor/designer, producing coins and medals. Became free-lance in 1973, producing sets of spoons with handles depicting *A Christmas Carol* (12) and *The Canterbury Tales* (24).

Nathanson Bros, Toledo, Ohio (c.1929). Makers of moulds for distribution to retail firms who cast the figures themselves and did their own marketing.

Natter, Karl, Stuttgart (1974). A designer of flats of Romans for the Württembergischen Landesmuseum.

NB, Belgium (before 1939-?). Manufacturers of poor-quality plaster composition models, similar to the pre-war Elastolin.

N.D.C., England (c.1910). Manufacturers of a breech-loading gun, $5\frac{1}{2}$ x $3\frac{1}{2}$ inches, which 'elevates and traverses with great accuracy'. The label says 'The Most Perfect Model Gun on the Market'. [*Opie, Wade*]

Neckel, F.C., Stuttgart/Hattenhofen, W. Germany (b.1906). One of the most important contributors to the history of flats, editing a large output, starting from about 1935. He covers a wide range of history: Numidians, Thessalonians, Greeks, Scythians, Carthaginians, Egyptians, Romans, Germanic tribes, tournament knights, Burgundians, Landschnechts, Prussians, Turks, Austrians, Brandenburgers, French, Russians and English, the Franco-Prussian War, the Indian Mutiny, South-west Africa, the Wild West, the American War of Independence and the Civil War. Also contained in his lists are Japanese (1900-18), Americans and other nations of the First and Second World Wars, including troops of the Third Reich. Many of them were engraved by Frank. In output he is second only to Ochel. In 1974 he was entrusted with the recasting of Gottstein's moulds.

Neckermann, Arthur. *See* Valiant.

Nedov, G., Tiraspol, USSR (c.1959) 'In Corrective Labour Colony No. 2 at Tiraspol, the sculptor G. Nedov, himself a prisoner, modelled the figure of a prisoner in his trusty's workshop, in plasticine to begin with. The disciplinary officer discovered it. "So you're making a prisoner, are you? Who gave you the right? This is *counter-revolution!*". He seized the figure by its legs, tore it apart, and hurled the halves on the floor (But he didn't go on to stamp on it, and Nedov hid the halves . . .). Only six months' later did Nedov dare retrieve the halves; he glued them together, made a Babbit metal cast, and sent the figure out of the camp with the help of a freeman' (Solzhenitsyn, *The Gulag Archipelago III*, 1976.) It was evidently preserved by someone, as a photograph of it appears in the book.

Neely, James, USA. Professional painter for Cowan.

NEF. A medieval utility table vessel, usually in the form of a ship on wheels, which could be coasted from one end of a table to the other. Obviously confined to the houses of the rich, numerous examples are preserved which exhibit the skill of the silver and goldsmiths in the making of little solid sailors and warriors manning the vessel, which are an indication of the style of the models prevailing at the period.

Nelli, Piero, Italy. A collector whose models are to be seen at Padua.

Nelson, Mrs Ann, Fairfax, Virginia (1975). Arranged a parade of commercial models on view at National Guard Association Museum.

Nesselberger, Hans, Austria (1975-). Designer of flats, some for Wagner and Scholtz.

Nessenius, Johann Arnold, Hanover (1760-1801). Engraver of flats. Marks: JAN; AN; JA. Ortmann found the initials AN on a 5cm flat of a Hanover Hussar, made about 1760. Kollbrunner goes further and identifies it as being the work of Nessenius.

'Netherworld'. *See* Imperium Publishing Co.

Neue Magdenburger Bildenbogen (J. John Moser) Magdeburg. Publisher of paper sheets.

Neumeister, Frank, Wallwitz Saalkries, E. Germany.

Publisher of flats. (*Katalog der Formen, 1976*)

Neumeister, Dr Horst, Marbitz/Halle (1960-). Publisher of flats, some designed by Madlener, others by himself, and engraved by Frank. Neumeister also engraves occasionally. He produces sets of the rococo period, Hanse port civilians, a Moorish ambassadorial suite and minnesingers. He has also designed for Ochel.

Neue Ruppin. *See* Kuhn, G.

'Neues Kriegsspiel'. See Viturinus.

Newberry, W/O II Reginald, Aldershot (1974-). A converter who makes models to order. He is represented at the Museum of Queen Alexandra's Royal Army Nursing Corps (with a converted Airfix model of Anne Boleyn), the R.A.M.C., Ash Vale, and the Welsh Depot Museum, Crickhowell (a small diorama).

New Hope Design (D. & Y. Winter) London/Rothbury, Northumberland (1974-). David and Yvonne Winter had been avid collectors while they were both serving in the R.A.F., and on their retirement they decided to go into business. They accordingly contacted Murray in America and proceeded to set up an agency in London for the importation into England of Old Guard models. Using the same name, they also began to employ freelance artists, whose models they exported to Murray in the United States. During this period they issued models of Indian Mutiny troops, a mounted Roman auxiliary of the second century AD by Malcolm Dawson (made in twelve pieces), Mary Queen of Scots, a Pipe Major of the Cameronians, and a series of railway figures in 20mm entitled Branchline Figures made by Malcolm Dawson, assisted by Roslyn Young. The connection with Old Guard terminated in 1976, and the firm moved to Northumberland under the new title of New Hope Design. Here some fine Landschnechts were made, accompanied by a pack donkey which was the first solo contribution by Roslyn Young, who at the time was only seventeen years of age. She has gone on to make Roman legionnaires and medieval figures. Dawson also did a medieval model for the Codrington family, originally as a special commission but later released in the ordinary way and now for sale to the public. This is a lifeless model, encumbered by an anachronistic shield. Confusion in the mind of the public had arisen as to which of the Old Guard models were English or American, and this was repeated when the Winters introduced Deauville Figures from the United States. It is known, however, that under this name they did a set representing the unhorsing of Blücher at Ligny, consisting of five models, the men by John Patterson, the horses by William Taylor. They also announced as 'New Hope Design' a nativity set which was actually made by Lotus. In 1976 they produced very poor models which purported to be ancient Greeks, but confidence was restored by quite brilliant work by Roger Saunders, with a long series of English troops of 1900, together with a most delightful 'officer's lady'. The following year a series of 54mm models was made by Malcolm Dawson, which were of much better quality than his earlier efforts. These were linked with illustrations in a series of books published by Osprey, and were given the title 'Men at Arms Autographed Collection'. They were followed by limited editions of 10 and 50 copies respectively of a Bavarian General and a Crusader by the same artist. In 1978 they enlisted the services of Cattle, who did a few medievals for them,

followed by a Murat and a Napoleon, while Dawson added a Nelson. More recent sculptors who have made models for New Hope include Peter Rogerson (gladiators, Dutch and Belgian troops 1804-15, Europeans of the 1900 period), 'George Ellison' (Burgundians, Austrians of the early 18th century), Keith Durham (White and Black Mercenaries 1965) and Ian Franklin (75mm Napoleonics). New Hope is an active concern, and, according to their catalogues, not only do they undertake special commissions, but use the facial features of Rothbury inhabitants in their models. The firm exhibited a fine chess set of 18th century troops at Kulmbach in 1979.

'New Machiavelli, The'. See Wells, H.G.

'New Metal' series. *See* Britain, William, Ltd.

Newson, Alan. *See* Starcast Miniatures.

Newton, Norman, Ltd. *See* Tradition.

New York Herald Magazine. (1 September, 1918). The stiffened back cover (17 x 12 inches) contained a complete US Aviation Corps for cutting-out.

New York Journal (1896). Cardboard cut-out figures for the Battle of Bunker Hill.

NEW ZEALAND. Geographic inaccessibility has been responsible for the collecting of model soldiers being of comparatively recent years. Those with leanings in this direction have had little opportunity to see old models, and even the ubiquitous Britains rarely reached the remote islands. By force of necessity enthusiasts began making their own models, J.K. Collins being represented at two museums in Australia and one in New Zealand, R. Allison making models to commision and founding a society in 1971, R.C. Hood (working in various media) exhibiting at two New Zealand museums, and Fritz Rietveld making Napoleonic styles to commission. Dinah Penman, also working to commission, in 1972 began carving 54mm models in wood, with slings, reins and weapons carved separately, with leather and metal attachments.

Two more imaginative ventures should also be mentioned. Billie Turton began in 1970 to market her 54mm models, each restricted to 50 castings, while William Gunson, starting in 1973, has been able to interest Matai Industries of Greymouth in the production of his 15, 30, 54 and 90mm figures. (It has also been reported that he has designed some in the last size for Scruby.) Wargamers flourish, and New Zealand appears to have taken its place on the model soldier map.

Niahon, Japan. Manufacturers of polystyrene AFV kits.

Niblett, John, Sidcup/Herne Bay (1948-). One of the first English makers to issue specially designed models, in this case, 54mm and 65mm medieval foot and mounted soldiers, the latter with detachable riders. From 1950 to 1963 he issued delightful 20mm figures of Romans and heraldic knights, bowmen and English Civil War foot and mounted soldiers (the riders again detachable),and a 95mm bowman on a black plinth (an enlarged version of the 20mm one), at the same time designing for Malleable Mouldings and The Sentry Box. From 1956 to 1974 he was immersed in the design of the now famous Airfix wargame figures, together with their other range of historical characters in 160mm polystyrene (with a skeleton used for instructional purposes for schools), and the first of their 54mm Napoleonic and modern models in polystyrene kit form. Meanwhile he designed and produced for the Ministry of Public Buildings and Works two fine models, one of Henry VIII, the other a mounted late Gothic knight modelled from a specimen in the Tower of London. In 1968 he produced a 90mm plastic gilded copy of the Pilkington Jackson statue of The Bruce at Bannockburn. In 1975 he opened a studio in Herne Bay for commissioned models and has designed and produced figures for Lesneys, Britains, etc. He decided in 1977 to reintroduce his 20mm metal models which had been discontinued in 1957 and created the first of a series of models in 170mm metal, in twenty-five parts. In the same year he began designing for Hall a series of 54mm Scottish troops.

Nichimo, Japan. Manufacturers of AFV kits in polystyrene.

Nicholson, Lieut-Colonel J.B.R., London (c.1965-). With Gammage made some of the Coronation set, and did other work for Graham Farish. In 1965 he designed for 'Tradition' a few separate sheets for cutting out, reviving the style of the early 19th century. He has had a long and intimate association with the trade.

Nicker, R., Strasbourg (1840). Publishers of paper sheets.

Nicolson, G.F., Canberra. Made the ammunition cases, ordnance and armoured vehicles for the 1914-18 dioramas at the Australian War Memorial.

Nicollet, Eugène, Strasbourg (fl.1817-30). Publisher of paper sheets.

Niederost, Switzerland (c.1810). As a youth he watched the Battle of the Muothatal Valley (1799) from the heights of Illgau. From memory he constructed a diorama of the battle, which took him two years to complete, using one-inch semi-flats. It is still to be seen at the Glacier Garden Museum, Lucerne. Later he became an artillery captain in the French Army. (*Nicollier*)

Niemojewski, M., Lvov, USSR (fl.1910). A publisher of paper sheets, based on drawings by Z. Rozwadowski. These were of cavalry and horse artillery, 1807-31.

NIMIM. *See* MIM.

Nitto, Japan (1970-). Manufacturers of polystyrene AFV kits.

Noble, London (c.1960). A small firm making 54mm hollow-casts with a small output. A European with an Arab guide, akin to Crescent, marked NOBLE diagonally on top of base, is known. [*Coutts/Juplin*]

Nolan, K. *See* Assegai Miniatures.

NON-MILITARY MODELS. It may come as a surprise to the reader of such a book at this to know that many collectors would not mind very much if model soldiers had never been made. Indeed, if human society were perfect, they never would have been, as they would never have existed in real life. It may further surprise many ardent AFV and wargame enthusiasts to know that there is a growing body of collectors who actually prefer the non-military figure. There is historical evidence that such 'civilians' were made in ancient times (e.g. at Tanagra) but little, if anything, survived the succeeding centuries, so our next landmark is the emergence of the tin-figure industry, where the concentration of the Guild of Pewterers (1578) was on religious figures. Successive generations (especially in Holland) produced little solid models, mainly in silver, of civilians going about their pastoral occupations. The great breakthrough came with the advent of the Hilpert family, and, anatomically correct as the latest models undoubtedly are, they cannot compare with the absolute rococo beauty of the 18th-century Watteau-like shepherds and shepher-

desses, country folk and country fairs. Curiosity engendered by the published accounts of voyages to faraway lands, and an awakening interest in natural history fostered by the works of such writers as Linnaeus and Peter Kalm, were rendered in flat figures by the Hilperts and the Fleegels. The former produced a series of 19 monkeys, each with the name of the species in German and Latin, and the latter at least 55 animals, birds and fishes, again scientifically labelled. Hilpert made not only country folk, but townspeople and musicians. All these models were large, a practice continued by Schweizer, whose 'Paradise' and other groups are perhaps the most delightful of all. With the advent of Heinrichsen and Allgeyer the models became smaller, but even with mass production there was no lack of charm. All the qualities of the previous decades were there, only in greater intensity; the country scenes became much more elaborate and were issued with fences, hedges and trees. Townscapes were introduced, including markets with booths and even houses and shops. Circuses were prominent, as also were menageries, with animals in cages. Technological progress was recorded, and the railway was an immediate success. Nor were the more solemn aspects of life forgotten: Hilpert is known to have made a Nativity, and a Flight into Egypt, and Corpus Christi processions by Heinrichsen undoubtedly influenced the early Spanish makers, who, indeed, appear to have begun their production with them.

As the military model acquired solidity of form, so also did the civilian model, and semi-flats, semi-solids and solids continued in the tradition of the flats. Söhlke, Heyde, Wollner and Mignot all made farms with hedges and trees, and town parks with workmen. Parallel with these were the wood figures carved throughout the 19th century in Germany, with the inevitable Noah's Ark as the prime factor. After 1918, in the light of public reaction to military affairs, Britains began the issue of farm animals and humans, together with all the necessary impedimenta. (A simple two-armed signpost cost one penny; it was recently catalogued at £3: a horse-drawn rake cost 5/- in 1928; today's price is £15.) Other makers followed, and the demand was such that thousands of toy farms appeared. The beauty of them was that they could be added to indefinitely by the purchase of single pieces, unlike the military models which had perforce to be bought in boxes. Nor was the demand any less when plastics took over. Indeed, Herald set a standard with their ballet dancers and national dances never previously achieved and still supreme.

The growth of the model train industry inspired by Bassett-Lowke provided another outlet for the manufacturers, who peopled their railway stations with travellers, porters and ticket-collectors, as well as luggage and slot machines. Models of the police, the fire-service, the Salvation Army, boy scouts, football teams and mounted jockeys in their owners' colours all followed and when the Second World War broke out A.R.P. Wardens and decontamination squads were quickly on the scene. Crescent added variety by a series of shops: a fishmonger, a barber, a butcher and a milk bar, each with customers.

The specialist makers of flats were as venturesome as their predecessors and, by employing historical experts as their draughtsmen, were able to translate their efforts into authentic miniatures. Delightful sets resulted, such as the series of Kings and Queens of England and the Court of Henry VIII by Gottstein, Chinese mandarins by Müller, French *incroyables* by Rössner, Holbein by Müller, Pope Julius and the Apollo Belvedere by Maier. Marvellous peasants, burghers and noblemen have been created by Rössner, Scholtz, Hafer and Wimor, including several hawking and hunting sets, while Blum, Ochel and others have produced captured men and women to add to the drama of their battle scenes. Exploration into ancient times has resulted in notable achievements by Hafer, with a host of mythological and Old Testament studies, and by Neckel with his 'Judgment of Paris' and Caesar and Cleopatra. In several instances complete sets of furniture have been made to go with the figures, so that small dioramas may be made. Scholtz has made a complete history of costume, a delightful street photographer group and a delicious rococo garden.

The first of the modern craftsmen in solids to break away from the military aspect were Vertunni with a whole host of monarchs and historical characters, both male and female, Carman with Dickensian and Shakespearian characters, and Courtenay with Nefertiti and Akhnaton, Nell Gwynne, 'Garter' ladies and King George V and Queen Mary. The coronation of Queen Elizabeth II gave makers the opportunity to satisfy a ready market (e.g. Chiswell, The Sentry Box, Willetts, Eriksson, and Gammage). Stadden began a long series of female models to go with his military characters. The non-military figure gradually spread into the lists of many of the more recent makers. Fowler had made a few Dickensian characters, and Higgins, during his brief career, left his own inimitable series of varied content entitled Pagada. Ping was early in the field with Scottish clansmen, and his subsequent men and women of all periods have left an indelible mark. Gammage went back to Egyptian, Minoan and Babylonian times, and in his remarkable style achieved a new standard of craftmanship and historic research. Nobody could object to his female nudes, nor to those of Sanderson's 'Slave Market', but a certain salaciousness occurs in the camp-followers created by Surén and in the 'Barrack Bawds' of Murray. Sanderson's later figures can be put in the same category; indeed his 'Stripper' and the nudes by the American Ray Lamb are unnecessary and unworthy models. Sanderson's 'Pirates of Tortuga' series is outrageous, while a completely erotic 'Rufus' series, said to be by the same maker, leeringly advertised and purchasable only 'under the counter', was quite rightly rapidly withdrawn.

Fermor and The Sentry Box have made a number of non-military types as has Jackson of Canada; those of Brunoe are outstanding in quality and feeling for period. Surén has made some delightful 30mm character studies, while Sanderson's series of 17th-century tavern roisterers and 19th-century press-gangers have given makers of dioramas ample scope to display their art.

Perhaps the most interesting and attractive series has been that by Phoenix of Regency dandies and their ladies. The group is complemented by the diorama settings which Phoenix also make, and is a sheer delight in all aspects. A sedan chair with occupant and bearers by The Sentry Box is also an outstanding achievement in

60 **Non-military models.** *Back row: Higgins, Courtenay, Fontanini, Sanderson; middle row: The Sentry Box (2), Café Storme (2); Ara Kunst; front row: Café Storme, Caiffa, Courtenay (3) (Author).*

this field. In the larger size the composite models by Krauhs of Mozart and his operatic characters are unforgettable, and Cassin-Scott has made a series of male and female civilians in various walks of life. The civilian models of Marx, the Airfix kits, and the 40mm Merten medievals and modern bathers are most attractive, as are Elastolin's 14th-century ladies. A longer range is afforded by the two coffee firms, Café Storme and Mokarex, each offering a number of non-military models.

Reverting to Herald, notable contributions are a riding school, show jumpers, figures in a suburban garden, and a brilliant series of motorcyclists. Arctic exploration has attracted a few makers (Söhlke, Mignot, Herald, Comet) and Heinrichsen did a delightful mountaineering party. Painting and painters have featured in Müller's Holbein and his mounted couples after Hals and Rembrandt. Rössner's has gained inspiration from Bosch, Pisanello, Memling, Rubens and Hollar, whilst a delightful set of Rembrandt together with Banning Cocq and von Ruytenburgh of *The Night Watch* fame was engraved for the Dutch Society in 1956. Hafer has published a Leda after Michaelangelo; sets by Braune depict Leonardo da Vinci displaying his *Mona Lisa*, Goya with his models and Riemenschneider carving an altarpiece. Café Storme's Rubens is sitting at an easel, their Van Dyck standing. Heinrichsen made a whole series of models depicting Wagner's operas; William Tell has been made by Stemmerman, Heinrichsen, Gottstein, Ochel and Series 77; Faust by Unger and Wimor; Don Giovanni by Gottstein and Krauhs; while the theatre is represented by Carman (Hamlet and Ophelia),Fowler (Hamlet and Othello), and by Rieche (*Die Hermannschlacht*).

One of the first to make musicians was Hilpert; others have been made by Meyerheine, Neckel, Kebbel, Duffy and Phoenix, and we have seen a solid group of 45mm

American Negro jazz players by an unknown manufacturer. Figures from literature include the Dickens series by Fowler and Higgins and Carman's David Copperfield, Söhlke's Gulliver and Robinson Crusoe (also made by Maier), Black Beauty by Britains, Cooper's 'Red Stocking' novels, the *Thousand Nights and a Night* (both by Wimor), Karl May's novels (Elastolin) and science fiction by a number of makers, either in metal or plastic. Dickinson, with his long range of characters from *The Lord of the Rings*, set the precedent for a number of other makers, some piracies, others of a fevered imagination and clumsy workmanship. Sherlock Holmes and Dr Watson have been created by Old Guard, while nursery rhyme characters have been featured by Söhlke (Hop o' My Thumb, Puss in Boots), by Britains (Cinderella, Red Riding Hood), by Pixyland, Kews and Marx, and in flats by Rossner and Menz. 'Whimsies'. in the form of the 'Cocoa Club' were made by Britains and Teddy Tail by Pixyland.

Films and television inspired Timpo's *Quentin Durward* and *Ivanhoe*, Elastolin's *Prince Valiant*, Reynolds and Marx's *Treasure Island*, Sacul's *Andy Pandy*, Timpo's *Hopalong Cassidy*, Trojan's *Roy Rogers*, and a set of twelve film stars by Superior. Dances were a feature of the early makers of flats, either the rustic ones of Schweizer or the more refined waltzes by Heinrichsen. Herald and Cherilea made ballet dancers, and Herald dancers of Russia and Spain. In the Argentine numerous manufacturers commemorated their own national dances.

Legendary heroes have naturally attracted attention, Robin Hood in particular being represented by Niblett, Greenwood, Erik, Benbros, Marx, Courtenay, Doran, Airfix, and Minimen, Gunfighters such as Belle Star, Billy the Kid, Ned Kelly, Pat Garrett and Bat Masterman have been depicted by Lone Star, Marx, Wooten and others, while there is a whole gallery of Westerners and Indians. The Americans have of recent years become much more aware of their pioneering history and groups and portraits of Whites and Redskins feature prominently.

Athletic pursuits have been portrayed by numerous makers; skating (Hilpert, Heinrichsen), racing (Britains), baseball (Marx), football (Britains), bicyclists (SEGOM) and the Tour de France (Cofalu, Starlux), bullfighting (a number of Spanish makers, including portrait models by Reamsa), Minoan bull-jumpers (Hafer, Gammage), Greek athletics (Scholtz, Neckel), bathing (Merten, Grey Iron Casting Co., Mignot), motoring (Dickinson); and here one might perhaps include gladiators (Heinrichsen, Heyde, Sanderson, Garrison, and, rather woodenly, Murray). In 1975 Britains issued a pair of Kung Fu exponents.

During the past few years a weird offspring has grown up. A number of makers have inundated the market with unbelievable witches, warlocks, werewolves, 'undead', 'living dead' and other strange hallucinations. Thankfully the majority are in wargame size, and can therefore be ignored by the serious collector. However, it is disturbing to some collectors to find that such firms as Phoenix, Squadron/Rubin and Minot have begun to make 54-70mm models, beautifully sculpted, of so-called 'lost civilizations', consisting of bestial, jock-strapped males and erotically nude or near-nude females, some of whom are the unclothed parallel of Hitler's women prison guards. It is sad to see talents so abased.

It is obviously impossible to mention here more than a very small fraction of the non-military models that have been and are being made, but even so slight a reference to the output of the makers, whether commercial or 'specialist', should convince any reader that the civilian model can more than hold its own with the military one.

Nonsuch. *See* Series 77.

Norden, Copenhagen (after 1940). Publisher of paper sheets of modern troops.

Norey, Harry. *See* Warrior Miniatures.

Norman Miniatures (K.A. Norman), Brighton (1976). Maker of 54mm solids of vehicles (with figures) and 19th-century cannon.

Norman, Victor. *See* The Barefoot Soldier.

North Park Toys, London (c.1958). Manufacturers of copies of Charben's 54mm Westerners and Indians, but in solid, not hollow-cast. [Opie] It is possible that the name is that of a toyshop rather than a manufacturer.

North, René, England (d.1971). Around the 1940s-50s he produced a series of plywood models, mainly about six inches high, with some smaller ones, which he designed and painted himself. He also drew and published line drawings in postcard size of uniforms (still being produced), and 30mm cut-outs of the Napoleonic Wars. A Past-President of the British Society, and author of a number of authoritative works on uniform.

Nostalgia (Shamus O.D. Wade), London (1974-). A collector of many years' standing, he then became a dealer in rare and unusual models. In 1974 he conceived the idea of reviving the traditional 'toy soldier' of the Britains variety, with the theme of the uniforms of exotic and little-known British forces and native auxiliaries overseas at the time of the height of the British Empire. He contacted Frank and Janet Scroby, who agreed to sculpt, cast and paint the models from his designs. Coming as they did when collectors were being subjected to models of German, Russian and Japanese troops of the Second World War, they appealed greatly to those who welcomed the colour of the past. Issued in sets of seven or eight figures, each with an officer, they filled the gap left by Britains by presenting colourful examples of hitherto unproduced uniforms. Detailed research by Wade ensured accuracy. A large number of sets have been published all in limited editions, and already 'Old Nostalgia' sets, even single figures, are obtaining more at auction than the price of the original sets.

Nouvelle Imagerie D'Épinal. *See* Pellerin & Cie.

Novell, Domenc, Barcelona (c.1820). Publisher of paper sheets.

Noveltoys. *See* Lincoln Logs.

Noyce, D.J. *See* Hampshire Figures.

Nuffield, Lord, England (1935). Financed Treforest Mouldings.

Nuremberg Scale. First put into operation about 1848 by Heinrichsen as a standard 28mm for flats.

Nuovi Soldatini di Carta, Italy (1977). Publishers of paper sheets in book form.

O

Oat Crunchies, London. Publishers of figures for cutting out, printed on the back of their packets.

Ochel, Aloys, Kiel (c.1925-). The most prolific contemporary publisher of flats, issued in two styles: (1) 'Kilia', the finest quality metal: (2) 'Oki', castings in an inferior metal. In either case they are issued plain or painted, but normally the collector would remove the paint, which is only an approximation. Ochel was formerly employed by Hähnemann, and prior to 1939 was an agent for Heinrichsen. Practically every period of history is covered in his output, and there can hardly be a collection of flats or a diorama that does not contain some of his productions. The 'Joan of Arc' set is based on paintings by Boutet de Monvel, and he has a long range of individual portrait models from Hannibal to Generals Lee and Grant. Siege weapons, war elephants, chariots and a 1943 Soviet tank are included in his productions. Boxes are labelled 'Kilier Zinnfiguren'. Maier, Geppner, Sambeth and Sollner engraved for him at various times, and he purchased the moulds of Meyniel, Bretegnier, Hinsch and Vollrath. On his retirement the products passed to Erika and Georg Kroschewski. Collectors will remain in Ochel's debt for his kindness and patience, and his willingness to teach a few selected pupils to learn the art of casting flats. Mark: ᴋ.

Oddy, David. *See* Cody Models.

Odhams Press, London (1953). Publishers of a coloured model of the Royal State Coach, with horses, outriders, grooms, Yeomen of the Guard, Household Cavalry, Buckingham Palace and Westminster Abbey. The figures were pre-pressed, and the Palace, the Abbey and the coach were in layers to form three-dimensional models.

Odiot, J.B. Claude, France (early 19th-century). A goldsmith who designed a set of wargame pieces for the King of Rome. Their romantic history is told by Harris (*Model Soldiers*) and Nicollier.

Oehlslagel, Germany. A designer of flats for Dietrich and Otte.

Oehmigke & Riemschneider, Neue Ruppin (19th-century). Successors to Gustave Kuhn as publishers of paper sheets.

Oesterreich, R.G., Switzerland (fl.1960). Publisher of flats.

'Official Western Sculpture Collection'. *See* Chang, W.

OH & Co Unity Toys, London (? 1940). Producer of a 3¼ x 3-inch grenade-thrower in metal, with mechanism adjusted to hurl up to five missiles, together with a sheet of instructions. [*Wade*]

O.K., Japan (pre-1939). Flagrant piracies of 54mm hollow-casts of existing models. Mark: ᴏ.ᴋ. ᴊᴀᴘᴀɴ.

Okakura Mfg Co., Japan. Piracies in plastic of models by Lone Star.

'Oki'. *See* Ochel, Aloys.

Oklahoma, Argentina (1975-). Manufacturers of 54mm plastic Westerners and vehicles. [*Basseterre*]

Olbia. The site on the Black Sea of a find of semi-flat lead 40mm models dating from the 5th-4th century ʙᴄ.

Old Campaign Figures (C. Stobart), Northampton (1978-). Maker of 127mm metal kits, designed by Stobart, sculpted by Stephen Farmer, beginning with an officer of the King's German Legion, 1815.

Old English. *See* Pearce, W.F.

Old Guard (William H. Murray), Plainfield, New Jersey/ Rothbury, England (1958-). Murray began making models for his own pleasure to add to his collection. He was then commissioned by Polk to make a range of medieval models, with poor results. However, he made his name with a group of sturdy Romans, with detachable cloaks and weapons, of which a marching Legionary with wine flask and looted chicken bears comparison with anything made since. Urged by Henry Becker, he made Civil War contestants to go with Becker's cannon. He was helped considerably by Custer and Greer, who together furthered his interests. He also obtained great assistance from the painting skill of Alan le Gloahec. His next interest was the Russian army, 1805-1815, of which he made a considerable number of good models, the details excellent, but rather dumpy in the legs and with a certain sameness of facial expression. In about 1971 he appears to have abandoned his own designs, to have employed free-lance artists (e.g. Stackhouse, Cade and Gordon Owen for artillery) and to have introduced the title 'Old Guard'. Other ranges of variable quality appeared, leading in 1973 to a splendid Nicholas II of Russia by Chernak. The following year he set up an agency with David Winter (later New Hope Design) and his models became more widely known in England. As Winter produced models designed by English artists and marketed them under the name Old Guard, collectors were confused as to which were by Murray's artists and which by Winter's. Before this Murray produced some poor gladiators, together with Second World War German paratroopers and assault troops, Spanish-American War contestants, Local Defence Volunteers and specimens of United States troops, 1878-1902. After this his models (some of which were advertised but never appeared) became inextricably mixed with those of Winter until, in 1976, the connection ended. Murray then began to design 25mm 'fantastics', such as 'The Empire of the Petal Throne'.

Olive. *See* Marrion, R.J.; Greenwood and Ball (Pearce).

Olivier & Delhaaert, France (19th-century). Publishers of paper sheets.

Olivier-Pinot, Épinal, France (19th-20th century). Publisher of paper sheets, under the imprint of Olivier-Pinot and Imagerie d'Épinal. (*See also* Pinot, Ch.)

Ollesschau, Germany (c.1920). Cigarette cards bearing pressed-out uniforms of the German Army.

Olmes, Jurgen, Krefeld, W. Germany. Designer of military costume plates, and a skilful painter of flats.

Olmsted, A.G., Las Vegas, Nevada. A free-lance designer whose drawings for Second World War figures have been used by Monarch and Valiant. An abortive partnership with Columbo dissolved in 1973.

Oneto, Andrea, Genoa. Maker of 54mm solids to commission, using his agent 'Import D.E.N.T.'

Onken, Germany (fl.1965). Professional painter of flats.

On Parade (G.A. Philip), Bridlington (1978-). Agent for a series of neo-Britains by M.J. Mode of 1937 Coronation pieces, and of 'Folk Heroes' by D. Hoyles (Robin Hood and his men, the Battle of Hastings, the Battle of Trafalgar).

Oracle Miniatures, Edinburgh (1978-). Makers of 15mm fantasy wargames models.

Ordnance Miniatures. *See* Black Watch, The.

Ordonneau, Paris/New York (fl.1960). Maker of flats for the Battle of Austerlitz.

Ormer, D. & S. van. *See* Malcolm Miniatures.

Ortelli, Jean Girault Carlos, Barcelona (c.1828-1847). Manufacturer of 4.5cm flats. An Italian refugee from Lake Como, he settled in Spain and in 1830 employed Salvatore Bacciarini as his engraver. He was succeeded by Juan Pera (1841-47). No marks are to be found on the flats. Some 900-odd moulds of military subjects, religious images, dancers, animals, ships and vehicles are to be seen at the Museo de Industrias y Artes Populares del Pueblo Español in Barcelona. Descendants of the original founder will, if pressed, supply models from their private stock, and they are occasionally obtainable at the museum.

Ortmann, Erwin, Weimar (fl.1960-). Maker of flats of the Thirty Years' War for private publication and a designer of same. The author of one of the best modern books on flats.

Oscar, USA. Manufacturer of very crude home-cast wargame figures.

Otaki, Japan. Manufacturers of polystyrene AFV kits.

Otani, T., London. Maker of 45mm models for a diorama at the Airborne Forces Museum, Aldershot.

Otello, Manfredini, Rome (1956-). A maker of fine solid 8cm models of the Napoleonic era. For a number of years he made nothing, but began again in 1975.

Otte, Werner, Barnten/Münster/Delitzch, W. Germany (1950-). Maker of flats. In 1955 he assisted in a diorama of Waterloo at Hanover. He was responsible for a small series of Charles V, Napoleon and Murat, the French Revolution, and the periods of 1848 and 1864-69, some designed by Kredel. He was still advertising in 1977.

'Over There' series. *See* D.J.'s Miniatures.

Owen, Brian. *See* Valda.

OXYDIZATION. *See* Lead disease.

P

PACKAGING. Flats in the early 19th century were packed between shavings in oval-shaped, extremely thin chipwood boxes, each bearing the label of the maker. Surprisingly, little transport damage appears to have ensued. Later, towards the end of the Heinrichsen period, small cardboard boxes were substituted for wooden ones, each model being placed between layers of the thinnest paper with the footstand in alignment with the edge of the box. The maker's label now bore a handwritten inscription stating the contents. Solids and semi-solids were much more elaborately packed in large cardboard boxes, or if the quality warranted it, of polished wood. The ones in cardboard bore the maker's label, often decorated in gold with facsimiles of medals awarded at exhibitions, the wooden ones had the decoration and descriptive lettering in gold directly on to the box. Cuperley, Blondel and Gerbeau issued large boxes in red and gold, the label bearing the gold medals; Trousset & Laumonier advertised models encased in wood and glass, whilst Mignot used oval wood boxes well into the present century. Hollow-casts began by being packed so many to a box in a single line, each model being held securely in place by an ingenious method of threading thin twine through holes and round the models to a thin piece of card. This card was then inserted in a substantial card box, in the case of Britains of a unique dark shiny red, and the makers' label, in this case a long one, covering the entire length of the box, affixed to the lid. Often this was of a pictorial nature, many being designed by Fred Whisstock for Britains. The designation of the regiment was also given, and larger assemblies packed in several lines. The advantage of the uniform size for storage purposes will be apparent. Some of Mignot's boxes up to 1914 were designed in tiers with scenic backgrounds. In 1913 Britains issued a set of Zulu warriors with papiermâché kraals, the whole boxed in a diorama-like form, but it was not until much later that departure from standardization became commonplace. The same firm broke tradition in 1957, when they began the issue of special models in single, transparent-fronted boxes, a practice soon followed by Timpo and other firms (although in this case the boxes were of cardboard). With the advent of new plastic packaging materials such as polystyrene, Britains and others lined their boxes with these instead of cardboard, each model being placed in a shallow depression of approximately the same dimensions as the model itself. Mignot now began to display single figures in individual plastic boxes, with the model mounted on a stand, a practice followed by Alymer with great distinction. Cheaper plastics were sold in polythene bags, and, beginning about 1970, 'blister' packets began to be made by certain manufacturers of die-cast and metal models. In 1974 a return to the old German tradition was made when Miles Izzard's recasts of old moulds started using late-19th century-style boxes.

The 'specialist' makers adopted a variety of methods for the enclosure of their models, including plastic envelopes, the component parts of the model being placed in loose, together with a diagrammatic drawing or a colouring guide. In the United States this was often accompanied by a full-scale photograph or drawing, often in colour. Transit through the post was a hazardous business, for when the envelope was prepared and packed into a box little attention was paid to the alignment of weapons, so that a lance could easily arrive bent, or even broken. (Five mounted models by Alymer were sent from the United States. Although stuffed with foam rubber and enclosed in their plastic boxes, the feet of all the horses were broken.) Norman Cooke was much more careful and despatched his models in small wooden boxes, the figure itself securely screwed to a small block of wood. Assembled models were normally wrapped with swathes of tissue or plastic paper, again with little thought for the bending of weapons, or placed between layers of flexible foam rubber. Perhaps the most impressive and effective of the more recent ideas is that invented by Bressica. Here we have a square or oblong box of finest transparent tough plastic, lined with foam rubber, completely insulating the model from damage, a card describing the figure cut to the correct size and laid face upwards in the base, and the whole sealed by a built-in snap-closure.

Paestum. Italy. Excavations made in 1954 at Tempa del Prete revealed a rich store of archaic figurines.

Pagada. *See* Higgins, L.; 'Tradition'.

'Page of History, A'. *See* Milliken, E.K.

Pahle, Heinrich, Quedlinburg/Magdeburg (fl.1968). Producer of flats of the Thirty Years' War, engraved by Emmerling and Lecke.

Paine, Sheperd. A free-lance designer for US makers, and a skilled professional painter who conducts his own classes in the art.

PAINTING. Commercial solids and hollow-casts were issued painted, the work being done in the main by teams of housewives or relations of employees who worked at home on batches collected and delivered at stated times. The painting was accurate and sufficient for the purpose. The colours were applied flat, without shading, and in enamels. Gold was used sparingly. Faces were conventionalized, with a slightly deeper dab of pink on the cheeks and a dot for an eye. Bases were nearly always a uniform dark green or sandy colour. Plastics were factory-painted in the same way, except that no 'blushes' or eyes were indicated. A much brighter range of colour was used, with a preponderance of very light blue and orange, making the result much gayer. The paint of the hollow-casts tended to rub off after considerable use, while that of the plastics soon began to flake. Much of the recent work has been done in Hong Kong owing to the cost of labour in England and the United States. The early flats were only partially painted, the horses usually being left blank. When, in the Heinrichsen era, full paint was applied, this again was done by families. In Fürth, for example, in 1898, 151 schoolchildren between the ages of 6 and 13 were employed, using enamels. Here again the colours were put on flat, with a mere blob for the eye. (It is interesting in this connection to note that in April, 1977, the *Daily Telegraph*, reporting on 'sweated labour', disclosed that women were being paid £3.50 per thousand for painting models in three colours. They did not say whether these models were 25mm or 54mm 'Britains revivals'.) The advent of the less commercial maker saw the more careful application of paint by the maker himself, the more limited number of castings enabling him or perhaps a few friends to cope. Courtenay was scrupulous in the use of his colours, often adding gold to his heraldry, while the skilful brush of Miss Ball earned the firm of Greenwood and Ball much praise. The early Staddens and Gammages were similarly treated, but the former went further, and began the style of painting that is prevalent today, that of the 'naturalistic' as against the conventional. Here there was greater emphasis on folds and highlights, and features were given more prominence. At the same time this was done with reticence, and there are many collectors today who feel that a return to this ideal is overdue. It was really the issuing of models in kit form that began the 'paint it yourself' era. The maker no longer did his own painting, but had a sufficient number of samples painted by studios to supply dealers with examples, and left it at that. A few, such as Ping, Labayen, des Fontaines, Brunoe and Berdou still felt justified in doing their own finishing, but they are now the exceptions. The result was that not only the collector but also professional artists working free-lance were able to exercise their skills. Some of the results are good, some lamentable. In a final analysis it is not the technique that counts but the taste of the artist. Present-day flats by the large groups of makers may be purchased as castings or painted, in which case the painting will only be an approximation, and a moderately gifted collector can always do better. Professional painters of flats, however, are in a class of their own, and one has seen some wonderful examples of how these tiny flat objects can assume three dimensions.

Modern methods of painting have been influenced by the greater variety of types of paint available. Oils are still, in the opinion of many, unbeatable, but water- or cassein-based colours have a wide following, and they have the advantage of drying much more quickly; acrylic colours undoubtedly have their uses in certain circumstances.

Painting, like so many other pursuits, is dependent upon a good eye and a steady hand. Whether the brush used is an 00 or a number 4 is immaterial, although, as in watercolour painting, there is often a tendency to use a brush with too fine a point.

The one subject in the collecting of model soldiers which is likely to cause the most controversy is the way to paint a model. One can be taught how to play the piano as far as the manipulation of the notes is concerned; but the interpretation of the music depends on the player. He may turn out a note-perfect and soulless performance, or he may err occasionally in the technical sense (as did Paderewski, Rubinstein and the rest) but give a memorable rendering because of his innate feeling for the music. So with painting. The collector is bombarded on all sides with instructions on how to paint his models, and the subject has become too scientific. Suffice it to say that he should evolve his own technique which will come to him through blood, toil, tears and sweat. It is not the amount of detail that makes a successful model but the knowledge of where to stop, and, above all, the realization that a model is after all an approximation in greatly reduced facsimile of a human being. If the collector is no hand with the brush, he will ask a friend to do it for him, or purchase it already painted from the maker, or employ an artist from one of the many professional studios. If he does this he must be prepared to pay accordingly. A well-sculpted model should supply the necessary creases and folds and crinkles, and it is refreshing to turn to a Høyer or a Brunoe or a Schreiber to see how imagination is allowed to function. (As for castings, there is sheer joy in painting the models of Major Rowe, and sheer misery or desperation with those of many another maker.) Nationally the painters of Scandinavia, France and Italy are the most reticent, while those of the United States and certain sections in Great Britain go out of their way to emphasize every crease, fold and wrinkle. Flagrant examples of overpainting appear in many a magazine and journal, and what better (or worse) example than the step-by-step photographs (and on an anatomically incorrect model at that) shown in all good faith by Philip Stearns in his *How to Make Model Soldiers*. A more reticent, but still highly complex, technique is demonstrated in Lion and Bean's *My Way*. The painting of wargame figures is another subject on which opinions differ widely, and it might be better for the reader to refer to the many publications on that pastime, so that he may judge for himself the extent of work he is prepared to put into a 20mm model.

P.A.L., Greece (1978-). Manufacturers of 60mm plastics of Evzones. [*Kearton*]

Palmer Historic Cannon (Tottenham Models), London (1971-). Manufacturers of scale models of cannon.

Palmer Plastics, USA (c.1960–?). Manufacturers of polystyrene models in kit form of Romans and

Spaniards.

Palomeque, M., Madrid (1922-36). A prolific manufacturer of fair quality 54mm solids, including Romans, crossbowmen, Spanish troops (1718-1928), and Columbus at the Court of Spain. Some enormities, however, occurred. Special collections in sizes ranging from 19 to 59mm were made on commission. Several thousands of the moulds were destroyed during the Spanish Civil War.

Paluzié, Barcelona (c.1900-1914). Publishers of paper sheets of the Spanish Army, coloured or plain.

Palx, Alexandre, Paris (fl.1950-65). Palx was a renowned painter of flats and solids, at the same time creating his own 50mm models of French non-military types of the period of Louis XIII, somewhat clumsy in appearance, but with a fascination of their own. For some years it was not recognized that 'Palx' and 'Alexandre' were one and the same person, so for the benefit of collectors a cross-reference to Alexandre is included.

Panache, Hawarden (1979-   ). Manufacturers of perspex display cases.

Panache Figures. *See* Roberts, Derek.

Panda (distributed in New Zealand). Hong Kong piracies of plastic Airfix 30mm British Second World War troops.

P & Co., Lisbon (c.1920). Publishers of paper sheets, possibly the same as PC & Co.

'Papal Figures' series. *See* French, Neal.

PAPER, FOLDED. Pinched or folded paper had a vogue around 1800. The figures, bearing only the slightest resemblance to soldiers, were about 5-6cm high. They are preserved in several Continental museums and illustrated in Hampe, Gröber and D'Allemagne. 'We were so enamoured of these little triangular figures that seemed to us so much more natural than those flat metal heads which look as if they had escaped from an herbarium' (*Freeman*). Patrick Murray is of the opinion that they all emanate from a single artist named Senff and that the military types were based on French and German schoolboys' *cocottes* (chickens) and *krähen* (crows). Today one imagines that they might be made by *origami*.

Papermade Models (Seeley Service & Cooper Ltd) London (1975). These publishers projected a series of booklets in which the parts necessary to build up a three-dimensional thin cardboard figure were presented as colour-printed press-outs. In their own way they were as intricate as a Historex kit. The complete proof models as seen at the publisher's office stood approximately 6 inches high and were most attractive. The project was not proceeded with and a few proof copies of the booklets and the made-up prototypes are all that exist.

PAPER SHEETS. Woodcut blocks pre-dated engraving, and continued throughout the centuries, not only as book illustrations, but as a 'visual aid' for the illiterate. Probably the oldest example, apart from the 'block book' is the playing card, and there seems evidence to suggest that the latter influenced the production of later single cuts of a military nature, especially in Spain. During the early 17th century books on the military art and on uniforms, illustrated by engravings, were extremely popular, and it is not impossible that these were from time to time coloured by juvenile hands, mounted on card, cut out and stuck to small blocks, thus creating a home-made army. We know that the Dauphins of

France possessed a number. In fact in 1670 Henri de Gissey, engraver, and Pierre Couturier, painter, were paid '6,000 milles francs' [*sic*] for the creation of a special army of '*XX escadrons de cavalerie et X bataillons de l'infanterie*'. Early examples exist in numerous Continental museums, but the evidence suggests that individual engravings were used, and it is probable that the first example of sheets of paper containing a number of figures was issued by Seyfried at Strasbourg in 1744. The first sheets expressly designed for cutting out followed when the same engraver produced a series depicting mounted troops of the Regiment Orléans-Cavalerie, to be followed by others by Isnard, printed by Heitz and Levrault between 1776 and 1779, and copper engravings by Striedbeck, who in 1780 set up a regular factory. These were accurately printed, and proved of immense popularity. Thus began *Les Petits Soldats de Strasbourg*, so lovingly depicted by Paul Martin in his book of that name. Interesting examples of how the paper sheet influenced other forms of art is provided by two disparate items which were on show at the '1776' Exhibition held in 1976 at the National Maritime Museum, London. One (from the Brown Military Collection at Providence) was a sheet of original watercolour drawings (c.1775) of American Light Cavalry and Dragoons, each figure being identical with the others (*Exhibition catalogue, illustration at p.194*). The other (from the Museum of Fine Arts at Boston) was one of the earliest surviving pieces of Irish linen, illustrating the military life of 1782. In this five separate lines of designs of soldiers, guns, tents, trees, etc., are repeated in a regular series. (*Exhibition catalogue, illustration at p.99.*) Other producers early in the field were Bader, Gerhardt and Benjamin Zix, and while some of the sheets were issued plain, others were painted most elaborately in gouache, and printed on both sides, thus giving front and rear views of the same figure. The invention of lithography helped to reduce printing costs, and such printers as Pflüger, Havard, Nicker and Boehm took full advantage of it. Further progress was made when Silbermann (1801–76) invented in 1845 a form of colour printing, enabling him in one year alone to issue 130,000 sheets. Others to follow suit were Berger-Levrault, Pellerin, Gangel & Didion, and Wentzel. The geographical bounds having been broken, countries such as Italy (probably Boldetti in 1878) and Spain (Simo, 1790, Sola, 1794, Gran, 1821, Bosch, 1823, and others) established an enduring industry that is still flourishing. In general the best work was done before the Second World War, and many crude and clumsy juvenile products are still available in most countries, even those of Eastern Europe.

The scope of the paper sheet is immense: every conceivable uniform from every country being represented; but whereas the earlier printers were content to represent serried rows of parade troops, later ones incorporated artillery and more vigorous action, so that in many present-day sheets each figure is different. Again, many of the earliest efforts have an anachronistic charm (especially in the 'Gothic' sheets) which echo the flat models of the time, while those of the latter part of the 19th century have the more solid and mundane bearing of the comparable Heydes and Mignots. Present-day sheets combine the violent action of grenade throwing with massacre by machine gun and tank destroyer, and

IMAGERIE DE NANCY

ARMÉE RUSSE. Artillerie.   771

61   **Armée Russe.** *Artillerie. Small portion of a coloured paper sheet consisting of seven rows of figures, published by Imagerie de Nancy, c.1875.*

whereas there are a few individual firms who maintain tradition and quality of printing, they are outweighed by a load of crudities hardly worthy of attention. (A parallel could be drawn between them and recent plastics.) Literally hundreds of printers have been involved since those early Strasbourg days, and the number of amalgamations, transferences of businesses, changes of name, incorporation of other family members, etc, would take a lifetime of study to disentangle. Large and varied collections of sheets have been preserved by the owners and passed on for safe-keeping to various museums, and to cut out and mount them is now a heresy. However, occasionally they have been used in dioramas, as at Strasbourg and at Leiden. As the original sheets get rarer and rarer they are sometimes being replaced by facsimile reprints, as in Spain and in America by the Paper Soldier, while Norman Newton (Tradition) and Robinson-Sager in Canada have issued fresh interpretations in recent times. Variations on an original theme are sheets printed on thicker paper, or cardboard, and those which will eventually make a three-dimensional model. Reference to the relevant sections should be made.

Paper Soldier, The (Barbara and Jonathan Newman) Clifton Park, New York (1970-). Essentially dealers in all forms of paper and card sheets and cut-outs, military and non-military, they from time to time make facsimile reprints of sheets by Silbermann and others.

PAPER, THREE-DIMENSIONAL. Most models in this category are non-military; windmills, houses, castles, bridges, railway stations and trains and carriages have been produced in large numbers. On the military side cannons and aircraft predominate, and it is only occasionally that one comes across a model soldier in this medium. The putting-together of card usually creates great difficulty with the planes, and Kellogg's did a series of well-known faces which were disastrous in their results. About 1930 a box was issued entitled 'Prince Albert's Own Eleventh Hussars', containing a large number of colour-printed pieces which, when assembled, resulted in a remarkable three-dimensional model standing 2 ft 6 inches high. Facially it bore a caricature-likeness to Lord Cardigan. The box itself had a plan of Sevastopol, drawn by Gower. No publisher's name appeared on the box, but it is understood that it was purchased at the London store of Heal's.

PAPIERMÂCHÉ. Paper soaked and then moulded in layers. It was popular in France, where it is known as *carton-comprimé*, for commercial use between 1870 and 1900, and used, at times, even before then. (We hear, for example, of the artist Ridinger of Ulm making himself a complete army in 1675.) Fleischmann of Sonneberg showed a model in this material at the Great Exhibition of 1851, while Ken Schwartz is today quite famous in his own field for his original conceptions.

Papillon, Jean-Michel, Nuremberg (1698-1776). A designer of fine-quality engravings on wood, issued between 1730 and 1740, which influenced the style of the makers of flats.

Parade Miniatures (M.D. Hodge) London (1979-). Publishers of 80mm metal kits, designed by Stephen Attwood. The first three were of a French Line Dragoon, 1815, an officer of the Royal Horse Guards, 1815, and a Grenadier, 1690.

'Parade Soldiers'. See Britain, William, Ltd.

Parade Square (R.G. Garfield and Alan C. Beckman) Sheridan, Chicago/Highland Park, Illinois (1973-76). Makers of four-piece sets of 54mm solids, boxed, with old-style labels. They were originally made in pewter, then turned to lead alloy, and painted in enamels. The production includes Gordon Highlanders, Zurcos, Zouaves (all 1910); British Infantry (1815); Foreign Legion; US Infantry (1898); German Infantry (1910, 1914, 1918 and 1939). Inspired, admittedly, by Britains, they are so similar as to raise doubts as to their absolute originality. Suspended in 1976 for lack of painters.

Paramount Plastic Products Ltd, London (fl.1968). Manufacturers of poor quality plastics for juveniles.

Parcella, James, USA. A painter of figures for the diorama sequence 'They Nobly Dared'.

Parisini, G.R. *See* Rifle Miniatures.

Park, Thomas. *See* Advance Guard; Authentic Miniatures; Jacobite Miniatures; Scottish Soldiers.

Parker Bros. *See* American Soldier Co.

Parker, R.A., Carmel, New York (c. 1961). A fantastic eulogy appeared in *Dawk*, (the journal of the American Model Soldier Society of California) in 1961, in which Parker was called 'the finest maker ever', who apparently only executed commissions for friends. No American collector has been able to verify this statement.

Parsen, Vienna (fl.1960s). Publisher of 30mm flats.

Parsons-Gorham, C.P.D. *See* Christopher's Model Outfitters.

Pascoe, Henry, USA (1979-). Sculptor of 90mm solids for Series 77.

Pastimes Metal Figures (Paul Martin), Kenilworth, Johannesburg (1977-). Maker of 54mm solid models of fine quality of Dutch troops (1700), Zulus, Frontier Police, Maritzburg Rifles, Cape Mounted Rifles, etc.

Patmore, Clive, Ilford, Essex (fl.1962-65). A maker of 12-inch plaster composition models, all in limited editions. They included a Guards Officer, Royal Horse Artillery, 7th Queen's Own Hussars (1807), the 42nd (The Royal Highland) Regiment of Foot (1808), and the 1st Battalion 73rd (Highland) Regiment of Foot (1778). For a few years they were very popular and could be purchased from Hummel. Patmore ceased production owing to the competition from Willetts and The Sentry Box.

Pattegay, Mulhouse (1850). Publisher of paper sheets.

Patterson, John. *See* New Hope Design.

Patti, Graf Ferdinand. Owner of a private collection of dioramas at Schloss Loosdorf, near Vienna.

Patzsch, Paul, Dresden (1908-24). A maker of flats, and also of vehicles and guns in the round.

Pauer, Vienna (fl.1830). Producer of 6cm flats. He was awarded a copper medal for a group of Austrian cavalry.

Payette, James, Kansas City, Missouri (1976-). Freelance sculptor. He worked for Bivouac and also (1978) The Black Watch.

PC & Co. May be the same as P & Co. (*q.v.*).

Peacock, Charles, USA. A professional painter employed by Cowan.

Peak Frean, England. Manufacturers of biscuits. With their 'Pom Pom' biscuits in 1969 they issued a set of 50mm plastics of sixteen figures in all. These were the same as those enclosed in packets of Kellogg's cornflakes.

Pearce, S.A., London. A 17-inch lead, mounted kettle-drummer of the 11th Hussars, Crimean War period, by him, was sold at Phillips' sale rooms on 11 December, 1969.

Pearce, W.F., London (1966-1975). Pearce, a lifelong friend of Greenwood, took over the original Greenwood and Ball figures until his own retirement, when he handed them to John Braithwaite. As a sideline of his own he made a 54mm hollow-cast highwayman which sold under the name 'Old English'. This was the precursor of a still-born venture intended for the souvenir market. One other model (that of a cook) was seen by a Canadian collector during a visit to Pearce. (*D. Frost; Pielin*) (*See also* Greenwood and Ball (Pearce))

Pearlytoys Mfg Co. (C. Rosenberg Inc.), New York (fl.1928-36). Manufacturers of hollow-cast 54mm models of poor quality, including Westerners, United States infantry of the First World War, and baseballers. They were on thick bases, mostly oblong, the metal tapering up curiously between the lower half of the legs. In 1930 they were known as Soljertoys, and in 1936 they used the moulds of Metal-Cast Products.

Pech Hermanos, Barcelona (c.1950-1960). Manufacturers of a wide range of slightly rubber-like 55-65mm plastics, of fair quality, including the American Civil War, Moorish Guards, pirates, Westerners, and animals, both wild and domestic. Riders were detachable. They also copied the models of Sanquez.

Peipp, Helmut, Germany. Designer and engraver of semi-solids.

Pellerin & Cie, Épinal, France (1703-c.1935). One of the most important family firms of publishers of paper sheets, both of military and non-military subjects. Nicholas was born in 1703, dying in 1773, but most of the inspiration and drive was provided by his son Jean-Charles (1756-1836). Sheets were issued in extensive series, for example the French Army (37 sheets), German, British, Italian and Japanese troops (a total of 52 sheets), Imperial Russian, Bulgarians and Napoleonic troops (a total of 63 sheets). Immediately upon the outbreak of a war in any part of the world, sheets of the participants were issued. An exhibition held at Pollock's Museum in London in 1965 displayed their immense and varied range, from the simplest single figure to the most elaborate working model. Later sheets were printed from zinc plates, and coloured by stencil. The firm was later renamed Nouvelle Imagerie d'Épinal, probably another family amalgamation.

Pelli-Cinni family. *See* I.S.A.

Peltro, Italy (1976-). Manufacturers of a series of six pewter 4-inch models of a Roman, a hoplite, a Saracen, two medieval warriors and a 16th-century halberdier. The same models are repeated in 30mm.

Pembroke, Earl of. The inheritor of a vast collection of 19th-century German semi-solids, now arranged in diorama form at Wilton House.

Pendragon, EMI Film Studios, London (1978-). Makers of 20mm 'fantasy' figures.

Penman, Mrs Dinah, Dunedin, New Zealand (1972-). Using two small gouges and a penknife, Mrs Penman has created a range of 60mm models in wood, all to private commission, including mounted cavalry of New Zealand, Commonwealth and British troops (1750-1910), particularly of the Crimean War. She has made models of other countries, including Cossacks, but no German, Chinese or Japanese. Leather is used for bridles and saddlery, metal for bits, buckles and swords, wood for stirrups. Some of the men have movable arms. The horses are painted in oils on gesso, the men in Humbrol. Personal examination of a model shows a decided sympathy for horses, but the men have a somewhat stolid expression.

Penney Packets. *See* Clarke, H.G. & Co.

Penny Srl., Turin (1975-). Makers of a set of six silver 54mm models of Italian troops of 1705-1788, in a limited edition entitled 'Valorosi', designed and sculpted by T. Schudin.

Pepin, R., Paris (fl. 1950-70). Designer and engraver of flats: for Boverat, charging horses, (1806): for Bittard

37 Left: **Revell**. *54mm plastic. Artillery and crew (Custer).*

38 Left: **Ping**. *Richard III and his associates. 52mm solid (Miss Taverner and Miss Elins).*
39 Below: **Palomeque**. *Spanish artillery, 1910 (Allendesalazar).*

43 **Rollo**. *Beautifully made and painted 54m solids: 'Arretez, Madame (Dubarry): l'ordre Dauphin.' The maker also made the gates pilasters.*

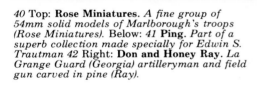

40 Top: **Rose Miniatures**. *A fine group of 54mm solid models of Marlborough's troops (Rose Miniatures).* Below: 41 **Ping**. *Part of a superb collection made specially for Edwin S. Trautman* 42 Right: **Don and Honey Ray**. *La Grange Guard (Georgia) artilleryman and field gun carved in pine (Ray).*

and for Bretegnier.

Pera, Francisco and **Juan,** Barcelona (1841-47). Engravers of flats for Ortelli.

Percy, Henry, Earl of Northumberland (1564-1632). Possessor of an army of 4,000 'leaden soldyers'. (*Rukeyser*)

Peres, René, New York (1974-). A Brazilian maker of solids of various sizes, of female figures only, mainly for Monarch.

Perez Arias, Jésus, Barcelona, Spain. Contemporary wargame solids in 30mm designed by Casadevall. (*Allendesalazar*)

Period Setting. *See* Cawkwell, L.W.

Perlasca, Strasbourg (fl.1800-10). An obscure producer of paper sheets.

Perry, Alan and **Michael.** *See* Citadel Miniatures Ltd.

Pesaro, Italy. Archaic models of gods and goddesses and one of Julius Caesar were unearthed here.

Peter III (Czar). He is known to have possessed models in brotteig, Nuremberg flats and polychrome wooden cutouts. His collection was formerly at the Hermitage Museum, Leningrad.

Petermann, Helmut, Germany (fl.1965-70). A collector and professional painter of flats. In Nicollier's book he is illustrated extensively and listed (one feels wrongly) as a manufacturer.

Peter Pan Playthings. *See* Timpo.

Peterson, John, jr., Massachusetts, USA. One of the painters employed in the making of the dioramas 'They Nobly Dared'.

Petit Soldat, Le (Major C. Hurd) USA (1963-?). A dealer who named his shop thus, giving the name 'Black Eagle' to such items as mounted models by Stadden.

Petrich, Max, Hanover (fl.1960). Manufacturer of aluminium 54mm models.

Petrocochino *See* Armont, Pierre; Mignot.

PEWTER. A composition of zinc, antimony, tin and alloys, which in the middle of the 19th century also contained lead. Many of the earlier tinsmiths produced their models in a material more akin to pewter than to lead, German manufacturers of semi-solids advertising them as being in this material. During the past decade it has come back to favour, primarily for models intended to remain unpainted. Imrie/Risley have done a number of models for themselves and for The Franklin Mint, as has Chernak. Ewer of Colonial Craftsmen reproduced a number of solids and flats from old moulds in pewter. Stadden has also used the material extensively during the last few years, especially for his 80mm models.

Pfab, Vincent, Petersburg, Virginia (1960-). Vincent and his wife began by making 54mm solids entitled Realistic Miniatures. They then abandoned these in order to create an incredible 'Battlerama' of the battles of Kennesaw Mountain and Atlanta, which comprised many thousands of models of their own making. These are somewhat crude and painted in flat unadorned colour. Some of the arms are fitted with a ball and socket joint. The 'Battlerama' was put into cold storage in 1965. The Pfabs have now revived their Realistic Miniatures, creating Colonial frontiersmen, the American War of Independence and Indians, and are beginning peoples of the Bible. Meanwhile, the American Civil War range has increased to about 5000 models. Mrs Pfab has for some years been working on a series of twelve very large Colonial figures in ceramic,

62   **Phoenix.** *54mm solids made by T. Richards (Phoenix Model Developments).*

and hopes to add to these in due course. The sizes range from four to ten inches. A number of dioramas (many in museums) and commissioned models fill in their spare time.

Pfeiffer. Vienna (1898-1904). The first Continental firm to use the Elastolin-type composition for vehicles, which they also made in tin-plate. They were taken over in 1904 by Hausser.

Pfitzner, H., Kulmbach (fl.1955-69). Producer of flats and maker of dioramas. Many of the latter are in the museum of that town.

Pfluger, J.G., Strasbourg (c.1835). Publisher of paper sheets.

PGD Co., USA (c.1968). Manufacturer of 11-inch juvenile plastics.

Philadelphia Tin Toy Manufactory (Francis, Field & Francis), Philadelphia, Pennsylvania (1847-50). An advertisement of a mounted trooper with guidon, the horse on a wheeled board, appeared in the catalogue of an American toy wholesaler.

Philip, G.A. *See* On Parade.

Phillipot, Maître, Paris. Patron for many years of the French society, he has had a tremendous personal influence on the development of taste and style in collecting.

Phillips of England. *See* Quorn Collection.

Phillipson, Geoffrey. *See* Elite Figures.

Phillipson, Trevor. *See* Reider Design.

Phobel, Liège (19th century). Publisher of paper sheets.

Phoenix, London (fl.1961-2). Manufacturers of 54mm plastic models, utilizing the moulds of Johillco.

Phoenix Model Developments (B. Marlow) Earls Barton, Northants. On the death of Leslie Higgins (q.v.) the moulds were taken over by Marlow and a new outlet established. In successive years Marlow extended the range and scope, and, while still preserving the essential Higgins characteristics, designed fresh models himself and employed the services of Tim Richards and John Hanscomb in the production of 20, 25, 30 and 54mm ranges, the latter mainly in kit form, although the 30mm bandsmen were also issued in this form. A number of the original 20mm Higgins models of the Civil War were added to by Marlow, as were the Marlborough war models by Richards, who also designed the horses (used in both this and the 25mm Indian Wars series, the Infantry for the latter being by Marlow) and the original Higgins Napoleonics. Richards also made the 30mm British Line Bandsmen, and the 25mm 'Command

Group'. Higgins' small line of 30mm Greeks was paralleled by a 25mm range with a couple of anonymous figures added. Of the larger models, the Civil War infantryman made by Higgins, together with his 16th-century French arquebusier, were expanded by Marlow, and Richards has added a couple of mounted figures: a Cromwellian officer (far too small for his horse), and a magnificently arrogant Cavalier. Other models by Richards are a galloping French Cuirassier, 'Young Winston', a British Colonial Lancer (the horses very similar), a mounted Imperial Guard Lancer, two subalterns of the Coldstream Guards, 1815, a Captain of the Royal Navy, 1800–1812, a *Chef de Bataillon*, French Imperial Guard, a seated cavalry officer in a nonchalant pose, Hitler in a greatcoat, and (1975) an appalling Zhukov, looking more like an oversized dwarf. The original and very bad Hitler by Higgins has been thankfully withdrawn, and Marlow has added an RAF officer.

The greatest impact that Phoenix has had, however, is through a most delightful series of Regency and Directoire non-military models produced first in 1974. These are the last word in elegance and grace, and give special pleasure to the author, as he sees his years of advocacy of civilian models, issued commercially, bearing fruit. These models, by Richards, are of splendid quality and, to display them to perfection, he and Marlow combined in the making of furniture of the period. The whole scene can then be assembled in the specially designed interior, made of white polystyrene, which can be painted to taste. Other periods are also available. In the same year the firm began a delightful series of vehicles of the past, including a brougham, a milk float, a knife-grinder's barrow, a stage coach and a barrel organ. In 1975 finely made figures to accompany these were begun. 20 and 25mm guns and vehicles were begun by Handscomb in 1973 in a range which the firm calls Renown. It seems certain that Richards is a sculptor of the highest class, and all collectors must look forward to a long series of fine figures. 'Under Two Flags' set a good example in 1975, when they commissioned him to make an equestrian model of the Duke of Wellington from a portrait at Apsley House, to be marketed by that firm only and in a limited edition. In 1976 he began making models in 75mm. Another addition to the group is Roger Saunders, who is making 54 and 30mm models. Other recent models include a 75mm Chesty Puller (a famous US Marine Second World War hero). Richards has made a not very attractive pair of figures on one stand depicting a Viking killing a monk, entitled 'Lindisfarne 793', and has succumbed to the latest science-fiction craze by producing a set (which is being added to from time to time) of 'Atlantis' male and female nudes and semi-nudes of a sadistic nature. A special and unusual commission was the making of several 45mm models of the 1st Queen's Dragoon Guards, 1973, to decorate the wedding cake made for the wedding of Princess Anne and Captain Mark Phillips in 1974.

PHOTOGRAPHY. The first advocate of 'table top' photography of model soldiers was a Brighton collector, J.P.B. Veale, who published about 1930 *Table Top Photography of Model Soldiers*. This was a crude attempt, and aroused little interest. A new standard, however, was set by Edwin Smith, with his photographs for *The Saturday Book No. 20* (1960), but this was an isolated exercise by a photographer better known for

landscape and architecture, and it was not until the advent of Philip A. Stearns that photography of groups in outdoor and indoor setting reached a level that has persisted through the last decade. Since then one of the military magazines has regularly offered prizes for the best amateur pictures of the month, and surprisingly good results have been forthcoming. There are, however, dangers inherent in 'artistic' photography. One is the glamorizing of an inherently vulgar model, and the other the startling emphasis of disproportionate detail (such as the eyes of a 75mm model perpetrated by Stearns of all people in his close-ups of the painting by stages of a face on a Hinchliffe-Lamb model in his book *Making Model Soldiers*). The same falsity was apparent in certain colour illustrations in *Model Soldiers for the Connoisseur*, where over-enlargement occurred. Stearns' usual treatment of single figures and dioramas is superb, especially when he is cooperating with Surén.

P.I., Brunswick. An engraver known only by his signature. (*Hampe*)

Picco, Louis. *See* American Alloy.

Pickles, Timothy, Knaresborough (1977–). Painting and diorama service offered.

Piecha, W., Germany (1974–). Designer of flats for Scholtz.

Pierce, Leslie. *See* Thomas Industries.

Piferren, Francesco, Barcelona, 1822. A publisher of paper sheets who later joined Bosch.

Piggott, K., Hanwell (1973–). Maker of 80mm Scottish troops to commission.

Pilef (Pierre Lefèbvre), La Baule (1962–). A converter of plastic kits, mainly those of Historex, and all of the Napoleonic period, to which he adds actual cloth, feathers, hair, etc. What distinguishes him from thousands of others of the same ilk is that he issues a catalogue, in which illustrations are given of about a dozen basic positions (including portrait models) which he has established as being most likely to attract buyers.

Pilgrims' Tokens. Medieval articles of religious significance, usually about 6cm high, moulded in flat lead. Some of semi-military types may, if the feet are damaged, be mistaken for early military flats.

Pilz, Carl Friedrich, Freiburg (c.1755–1823). One of the earliest makers of 9cm flats ('Master Craftsman' in 1778). He produced cavalry with movable arms (engraved by Heuchler), knights, miners, hunting scenes and markets.

Ping, Frederick, Slough/Kingston-upon-Thames/Salisbury/Wylye (1930-77). To any collector of sensitivity, the models of Frederick Ping evoke respect and affection. A maker of world renown, who confined himself to commissioned 50mm solids, and then only the type in which he was himself interested. He began making models early in the 1930s, when a chance meeting with Courtenay led to a long and fruitful friendship. Ping made a number of designs which Courtenay turned into models, and he also assisted Carman in his initial efforts. His first commercial venture was a set of Scottish clansmen, each a unique figure, which proved immensely popular when placed with Hummel. He devised a prototype male torso of a malleable consistency, and a number of horses in different postures, and was thus able to ring the changes on every model by the amount of extra soldering and building up in the French

Ping. Models commissioned by the author: Louis IX and standard-bearer; five models of Chaucer's Canterbury Pilgrims; Henry V.

style that appeared to be necessary. The result was a model that was unique, or in the horrible current jargon, a 'one-off'. By some wizardry peculiar to himself, however, every face had its own particular characteristic, hence his employment by Peter Cushing for making portrait models for his working model theatre. It would be difficult to say exactly how many models by Ping there are throughout the world. His range was from ancient times to the present day, but although his 18th-century figures have a charm of their own, it is obvious that his great passion was for the Middle Ages. Here he was supremely himself, and his figures breathe the very essence of those enigmatic times. His chief delight was the portrayal of non-military costume (his females are particularly lovely), of armour and heraldry and the warrior in his leisure pursuits. No model is ever bombastic, indeed, each is a personal portrait, and usually in an attitude of quiet. His painting is imaginative and meticulous, but the heroics of the current style of shading and lining and high-lighting in detail were not for him. He managed in a few subtle blendings of colour to convey all that was necessary. That is why so many collectors commissioned him to convert and paint their Britains' 'Agincourt' models when they were issued. Upon Courtenay's death his son, together with Webb of Hummels, entrusted Ping with the moulds, hence the reissue of many of the favourite or rare models, including the six-inch Black Prince. At the same time he was given licence to alter the originals, and a new and greatly varied Courtenay/Ping emerged. The original horses carried new riders; figures slashed at each other in different ways; helms acquired new crests; standards were carried by different bearers; a mace replaced a sword, a lance a warhammer. The painting was not in Courtenay's glowing, slumberous hues, but an entirely new conception, translucent and alive. It might be said that Ping *was* a latter-day Courtenay, so linked in spirit with his great friend was he that whatever model he turned out has a trace of both artists, and, even in the civilians, a Courtenay horse, much altered, may well appear. Although he has his admirers all over the world in little dedicated groups, he offers little for the younger collector, reared as he is on kits and military magazines, on Nazis and Samurai and Plains Indians, while Ping's models gain stature by their isolation from the hurly-burly. Ping himself did not seek publicity, and his clients did not provide him with designs and instructions – they left it to him, in the knowledge that he knew his craft to the finger-tips. After his death the Courtenay moulds passed to Peter Greenhill.

Pinot, Ch., Épinal (19th century). Paper sheets.
Pinot-Sagaire. Probably part of the Pinot group.
Pinpoint Series, USA. (1973–). Manufacturers of terrains for military dioramas or wargames.
Piper, John. *See* M.A. Model Accessories.
PIRACY. The darker side of human nature crops up from time to time in the model soldier world. Certain unscrupulous individuals, knowing that they were without the necessary ability to create original models, would take an existing one and from it cast others which they would proceed to market as their own product.

Heinrichsen and Allgeyer stole frequently from each other, as did Kurz and Lorenz, and many of the early German makers in semi-solid did a thriving business in this way. The first-known firm to actually take rivals to court were Britains, and it is interesting to note that they were successful in their prosecutions. It would appear that an ancient Act of 1814 stated that a manufacturer of any kind of article had to stamp his wares with his name and a date, but this no longer appears to have any relevance, as it is often impossible to identify certain models. Canadians are reproducing Britains in solid lead, and an American is doing the same with old Heydes. However one may applaud the idea of wishing to perpetuate one's favourite models, the act is tantamount to forgery if these models are offered for sale unless the copier marks them on the base or elsewhere as facsimiles. One flagrant example, that of an English collector issuing plastic copies of Eriksson's tiny models, has now ceased, and he is now making genuine originals. However, one firm that advertises itself so prominently in the United States that it has created its own eponymous magazine has the effrontery to illustrate it with its own dubious 'original' models. Knowledgeable collectors in the States are all agreed that these are clever adaptations of existing examples, two firms in England being the chief sufferers. Nor, it would seem, is this an isolated example, as it was recorded in 1973 that in California many recasts of Stadden and Gammage, and, what is more surprising, the contemporary models of Cameo, Valiant and Superior were all being offered and sold at much lower prices.

Makers of wargaming figures also fare badly in America, in Japan and in Hong Kong, in one case Hinton's name and serial number remaining on the base and being offered as an original, and in another Surèn's horses being dissected and put together again by another firm. One also has one's suspicions of the appearance overseas of Dickinson's 'Middle Earth'

64 **Piracies.** *Examples collected by the author deriving from Hong Kong, U.S.A. and Spain and companies such as Gabriel, Kresge, Reamsa and Birmania.*

characters so soon after their appearance in England. Birmania of the Argentine issued box after box of forgeries of Britains' models, with perhaps some extra item such as a trophy of swords in an attempt to disguise them. Piracy has always reigned supreme in the world of the plastic and the die-cast, with Hong Kong being the main home of the offenders. Hardly a firm has not been treated in this way, and the piracies of Airfix 20mm models are legion. Britains' 'Swoppets' have had their fair share of copying too, including their American Revolution models. An Italian maker of plastics (Fontanini), only to be identified by the trademark of a crab, has had 8-inch and 54mm models blatantly pirated in Hong Kong, even down to the special screw-on base. A collection of plastic models emanating from America in 1975, enclosed in plastic-covered boxes, were liberally sprinkled with the name of the firm in the United States for whom the models were 'specially made in Hong Kong'. It took no time to establish that they were blatant forgeries of Britains' Turks and a mounted knight from their 'Deetail' series, the only variation being that the bases were plastic and not metal, and the figures were plated and not painted. What interested Britains when they were sent a sample was that although their Herald models had for some time been produced by themselves in Hong Kong, not so their Deetail range. Another curiosity is a collection of die-cast models from S.S. Kresge and Gabriel Industries. One model, that of a running Indian entitled 'White Eagle' was stated on one box to have been made by Lone Star for Gabriel Industries: on another the same figure, now with 'White Eagle' erased from the base and 'Little Crow' substituted, was marked 'MADE IN HONG KONG FOR S.S. KRESGE CO'. The figure of Billy the Kid was identical in both. Lone Star's comment, when these figures were brought to their attention was, 'The items were in fact copied from our models, and as is common in that part of the world produced in an inferior style at a very much lower price.' These piracies are designed to bring in a quick return over a cheap expenditure and one supposes that they will continue. It is, however, sad to know that at least one firm is doing the same thing with 'specialist' models, and blatantly at that. What is more distasteful is that the piratical firm has no need to en-

gage in such activities. It is itself thriving and employs free-lance artists for its own original models. It transpires that the firm in question bought up the remaining stock of Sanderson's nudes and semi-nudes from an American dealer, erased the name Sanderson from the rim of the base, and then promptly advertised them as 'Buccaneer Models, made in the United States' (and, of course, at a cheaper price than those imported from Sanderson). To the uninitiated the Buccaneer is an original. Furthermore, the proprietor of the firm spoke of one of his artists 'altering' the larger Sanderson nudes. One would hope that this dubious practice will cease forthwith, as, with the passing of time, memory will fade, and who will distinguish the true Sanderson from the false?

In the middle of the 19th century a nest of forgers was uncovered in Paris. The little figures they made were castings from rare originals of the 16th century, and they marketed them by depositing them in the mud of the River Seine and then guiding avid antiquaries to them. Similar forgeries of pilgrims' tokens occurred in London at about the same time, the mudbanks of the Thames being the market place. Unconscious piracy, however, is inevitable. Two free-lance artists in the United States, for example, each recently made a design of Lawrence of Arabia, and offered them to two different firms. Both firms accepted them, and the resultant models appeared on the market at the same time. Both models were in a similar stance, and it might well be thought that one was a copy of the other. But with a subject of this kind there is little latitude for treatment, and the artists, in this case both completely blameless, each seized upon the same posture at the same time. On the other hand there is on occasion the tendency to use parts of any existing model as a basis for another which, while not coming directly under the heading of piracy, may be classified as a quasi-piracy.

Pirozzini, Barcelona (c.1830). Manufacturer of flats, later taken over by Lleonart. His moulds are in the Puebla España.

Pither, R. *See* RA Cannons.

Pitman, Theodore B., USA (d.c.1970). Creator of dioramas for US museums, using beeswax for his figures, which were graded in size.

Pixyland Toy and Manufacturing Co. (R.H. Lewis and H. Howell) London (c.1920-33). A small firm of manufacturers of 54mm hollow-casts. Beginning with a few military models they proceeded in 1925 to make farm and zoo animals, station staff, nursery rhyme characters and a box of ten models of 'Teddy Tail'. A large bust of Madame Tussaud was an unusual model. The activities of the firm were recorded in *Industrial World* in July, 1930. The author met Mr Lewis about the year 1957, but all that he could show was the set of 'Teddy Tail' characters.

PLAGIARISM. *See* Piracy.

Plagwitz, Wolfram von, (1914-1918). Maker of portrait models in flat. (*Hampe*)

Plank, James, Grand Rapids, Michigan. Models by him are on view at the Grand Rapids Public Museum.

Plasençia, Angel Comes. *See* Alymer.

PLASTER. *See* Composition.

PLASTER (METALLIZED). *See* Composition.

PLASTICS. Material akin to hard, compressed rubber. The models made by Herald are in I.C.I. Alkathene (a proprietary name) and the majority of other makers use a similar material. Granules are liquefied under intense heat and poured along channels into prepared moulds. Equal, if not greater, detail can be obtained by the use of plastic rather than metal, but the main drawback is the lack of stability, resulting in the bending of weapons, especially annoying if the model itself is a good one (as in the set of chessmen designed by Stadden for Triang). On the other hand it is ideal for toy-making. A few firms were experimenting as early as 1935, but the first serious attempt to achieve a good model was not made until 1947, when Malleable Mouldings made models of a plastic composition similar to Alkathene, in which several pieces were moulded separately and then affixed to a torso. Of excellent design, they still failed to attract a wide enough public to be viable, and many of the moulds were subsequently used for the making of metal models for collectors. About the same time a Pole, M. Zang, who had lived in England since 1908, began making British battledress troops in plastic as we now know it. They were slightly more successful, and, having been joined in 1951 by Roy Selwyn-Smith, sales began to soar. Smith brought expert craftsmanship to the production, and in 1955 Britains, possibly foreseeing the end of their hollow-cast empire, took control, Smith being retained as chief designer. Under the name of Herald these models continued to be made, and it is no exaggeration to say that only once have they produced anything other than a first-class model, and that a cheaper version of the 'Wars of the Roses' set. The standard of excellence which they achieved was not equalled by any of their rivals, many of whom (Timpo, Cherilea, Charbens, Lone Star) were simply using their old metal moulds rather than re-designing. In fact, the only link that Herald had with the Britains' tradition was concerned with their 'Eyes Right' series of British Regimental bands. Their importance is that they filled the gap between the dying hollow-cast and the specialist

model, and at the same time created a model well worthy of preservation. An ingenious attempt at a convertible model was made for some years in their 'Swoppet' series, in which the upper part of the body was plugged at the hips, enabling it to be either completely removed or twisted; and arms, legs and heads were detachable, as were weapons, sword belts, scabbards, and the like. Riders, horse trappings and saddles were also removable. The idea was quickly pirated by other firms, but the very clumsiness of their efforts brought the whole thing into disrepute, and Herald decided to discontinue their own 'Swoppets'. Herald made beautiful civilian ranges, the Polar sledge with huskies and removable storage boxes showing great ingenuity. In their painting Herald anticipated later trends, the colours being matt, no doubt being forced on them by the type of material. Unfortunately the binding quality of the paint has not proved stable and many a model has been ruined by peeling of the paint in later years. The only English models that approached Herald in quality were the products of a very minor firm called Cavendish Miniatures who, about 1959, placed on the market a box of assorted London tourist-attraction figures, a group of four 18th-century Grenadiers and a box of Henry VIII and his wives, all of which were designed by Stadden. Generally speaking, although certain individual models by other makers showed imagination, the standard was depressingly ordinary both in range and execution. The flow has slackened during the last few years, although Timpo is still active in re-issuing its old models, though now unpainted, while Britains, in their Deetail models (plastic with metal bases) show a falling-off in the standard of design, and use a highly incongruous support for the horses. The only French firm to hold a candle to Herald is Starlux. They created a whole range in 60mm of magnificent medieval and Roman troops, and a not-so-good Napoleonic set, while in the United States the firm of Marx became a latter-day Heyde in the size and

65 **Plastics (English).** *Back row: Cherilea, Niblett, Kellogg's, Niblett, Walt Disney; middle row: Timpo, Crescent, Cherilea, Crescent, Cherilea, Charbens, Crescent, Cherilea, Crescent, Timpo; front row: Lone Star, Kellogg's (4), Timpo (Author).*

scope of their unpainted, often extremely well-designed models. On the other hand, some grotesque monstrosities appeared (and still do) in the United States, where makers appeared to vie with each other in the production of giant-size figures. Nor were the products of Spain very much better, although George Erik enabled the long-established firm, Reamsa, to improve their models in some directions; while in Italy manufacturers were, and still are, content to make the worst possible use of the material. Manufacturers of plastics have suffered much with piracy, the chief offenders being the Japanese and the people who inhabit Hong Kong. One curious aspect is the use made by respectable firms of the services of moulders and painters in that outpost of Empire.

The greatest impact made by the plastic model was the creation by Airfix in 1960 of armies of 20mm figures, sold uncoloured and attached to the sprues in boxes of 48 for a very modest price. Many a wargaming enthusiast was created by the possession of these boxes, long before many of the present-day makers of tiny metal models realized their potential. That the use of plastic can reach greater heights is shown by Niblett's models of the Bruce at Bannockburn and the Tower of London models. The great difficulty that a historian encounters is the anonymity of so many models. Small firms rose and vanished quickly, unable to compete with their larger competitors. In most cases their models are marked merely with the country of origin, and there must be many still unrecorded.

PLASTIC COMPOSITION. A non-metallic substance taking various forms and used mainly by European manufacturers. The main characteristic is rigidity and a brittleness not associated with the more general plastic (or Alkathene). Its use appears to have begun after the Second World War with the re-appearance of Elastolin models after their factory had been rebuilt. The firm turned out a whole range of sets – Roman, Huns, quasi-Normans, Turks and Landschnechts, all in colourful array and violent postures. The most effective were the quiescent civilian models. Riders and weapons were moulded separately, the painting appeared to be fused into the model, and two sizes were available. Cannon and siege weapons were also obtainable. Another firm, Berliner-Miniatur-Plastiken, produced models in a similar substance, mainly in 40mm, again with the riders and weapons detachable, but apparently painted in the traditional manner. A variety of the same material was used by Minimodels (1967) in a series of 50mm models designed by Stadden, and by the makers of a series of models of armour from the Real Armoria. Another variation was achieved by two firms of coffee-importers, one Belgian, one French, using in this instance a hollow-cast version, unpainted, one model being enclosed in each tin of coffee. The first, Café Storme, starting about 1963, had by 1969 issued several hundreds of figures illustrating the history of Belgium, including many civilians. Riders were detachable, and conversions could be undertaken. A regular magazine illustrating conversions and the making of dioramas was mailed to all subscribers. The second, Mokarex, first issued models about 1958, and later ones (1965–67) were designed by Lelièpvre. Competitions were held to determine the best set of painted figures.

PLASTIC FLATS. Attempts have been made from time to time to produce a flat figure in plastic. The most distinguished effort was made by Lelièpvre and Mathiot (c.1968), but it never matured, and apparently only two sample figures exist. Marx is said to have produced a few in 1966, and one or two Polish, Czech and U.S.S.R. manufacturers have had them in their lists.

PLASTICINE. More normally used for preliminary studies, it is occasionally used for finished models. Around 1954 W.A. Thorburn created a series of 6-inch equestrian models moulded on a wire armature. Horses were made of wood, the plasticine being worked upon it as a base, and saddles and equipment added. The figure was then varnished and japlacked and painted in matt colours. In 1970 John Ciuffo began making plasticine models in 54mm for museums, and later for sale. They differ from those of Thorburn in that the only painting involved is that of the face, various shades of the natural material being cleverly used. Their disadvantage appears to be in that they cannot be handled, but must be kept in sealed transparent boxes. In 1975 David Roberts announced that he intended making a series in the same material and the same size, but apparently he turned his attention to the metal model instead. T. Anderson coats his models with enamels.

Plasticum-Spielwaren (F. Plawner), Nuremberg. Mentioned in *Dawk*, 1975, as a manufacturer of plastic models. No further information could be obtained.

Plastoform Ltd, La Paz, Bolivia. A manufacturer of plastics. The name appeared in the Bolivian Board of Trade list in 1975, but no further information could be obtained.

Plastone. An extremely fragile form of plaster. Models made in it will certainly not arrive intact if sent by post. To our knowledge the only exponent of it is D. Evans (*q.v.*).

Plastray Corporation, Mt Clemens, Michigan (c.1968–). Manufacturers of a 22-inch vinyl plastic kit of a United States Civil War cannon. Advertised in *The Soldier*, 1968.

Platignum Pen Co., London (1973). Publishers of a set of coloured pens on cardboard with military cut-outs for colouring.

Plato Painting Service, Chelmsford, Essex (1972–). Advertisers in military magazines.

Plawner, F. *See* Plasticum Spielwaren.

Playbook of Columbus. See Harpers.

Playskool Manufacturing Co., USA (1928). Employed John Lloyd Wright to design its Lincoln Logs productions.

Playtime Products, New Zealand (fl.1966). Manufacturers of juvenile plastics.

PLYWOOD. A hybrid, achieving neither the three dimensions of the solid nor the delicacy of the flat. It might in fact be called the poor relation of the wood-carved figure. Two distinct categories emerge: first, the printed figure, simply mounted on thin wood and then cut with a fret-saw. Numerous examples of these may be seen in toy museums, and between the wars they were sold as targets for toy cannon. (Some were made in the United States in 1919, size $12\frac{1}{4}$ inch, on a stout base.) The second is the original design from an authentic source of reference, and carefully drawn on to the wood, painted and shaded, and cut equally carefully. In this form they represent a serious form of expression. E.V. Howell was one of the first specialists, working around 1930, and a number of his 9½ inch cut-outs may be seen at the Border Regiment Museum at Carlisle; there may well be more scattered through Great Britain which are not recognized as by him. T.H. Hitchins worked in the same style in London about 1937, and René North some years later. The models of both the latter were on an average 6 inches high.

POACHING. *See* Piracy.

Pock, Professor A., Germany (fl.1960s). Designer of flats for Vesely.

Pohl, Heinz, Vienna. Publisher of several series of flats, including Huns, medievals, Austro-Hungary 1837-48. He collaborated with Kröner-Grimm in the construction of the dioramas at Schloss Pottenbrunn, and is owner of Kruner's moulds. He is named in the Kulmbach list of 1977 as still working.

POLAND. Great difficulty was experienced as far back as 1957 in trying to get any information regarding model soldiers in this country, and actively hostile opposition was encountered. It is known, however, that in 1921 30mm flats were made in Lodz, with a label inscribed 'Wojsko Metalowe' (metal army). There were also large boxes of Polish naval artillery in action (the guns flat, and belching fire and smoke) and smaller boxes of the Napoleonic period, the 1830 Revolt, and modern troops, with barbed wire entanglements. Paper sheets were popular, the best being by Nimojewski of Lvov, one series depicting cavalry and horse artillery of 1807-31. Stiffer sheets of Polish Winged Hussars in violent action were in the author's possession in 1958. S. Gepner, former Curator of the Army Museum in Warsaw, made a number of designs for flats for the French society and for Ochel; in 1939 he started his own production, beginning with Prince Poniatowski, and including '*kombination*' figures. Pestana describes some modern models (1970). They were, he says, all plastic, some being semi-flat, others fully round, ranging in size from 40 to 54mm, the majority unpainted. Several firms featured Winged Hussars, others the Napoleonic period, and there were also Kościuszko's soldiers, medieval Teutonic and Lithuanian knights, and both World Wars. Those which were painted were quite adequately done. The makers one has been able to trace rejoice under the names of CZZPP, WYROB, WZUP and PZG. In 1972 54mm solids in small quantities were obtainable in New York.

'Polar Exploration' set. *See* Herald; Timpo.

Polistil, Italy (1974-). Manufacturers of polystyrene AFV kits and a few figures in plastic; in 1975 three soldiers in metal appeared.

Polk's Hobby Store, Jersey City, New Jersey. A big name among dealers, stocking many of the better known native makers and more adventurous than most in their importation of foreign models. They now control the Aristo-Merité range and have an interest in the recreation of Mokarex. Nathan Polk himself has an enviable collection of the models of des Fontaines.

Polland, Donald, USA (1965-). A maker who began with military miniatures in 54mm, but later made models in pewter for Lance Corporation and large action groups in bronze.

Pollock, Benjamin, London. A Victorian firm specializing in toy theatre sheets, complete with libretti. He took over the firm of Redington and Skelton who issued similar items. The only set of interest to collectors of paper sheets is the typical 'Battle of Waterloo', and that solely because of the title. Pollock was the originator of the term 'penny plain, twopence coloured'. The firm still exists and does reprints of the original sheets and theatres.

Pollock, Ivor. *See* Crown Personalities.

POLYSTYRENE. A hard, tough composition, used mainly in the construction of separate parts for kits. The first exponent was probably Segom, about 1950, but their models differed from those of later makers in that each part of the body was solid, and five or six parts only were necessary to complete a figure. Horses were in several sections. Early designs were clumsy, but they improved over the years. In 1957 the first large (12-inch) kit was made by Aurora Plastics of Long Island. This was the 'Blue Knight of Augsburg', followed shortly afterwards by six others, all beautifully designed, metallized to the appropriate colour of the armour, and quite a joy to assemble. The *tour de force* was the 'Gold Knight of Nice', complete with armoured horse. They were certainly pieces for adults, but later models from the same firm were intended more for the juvenile market. Selcol (1962) made two kits of excellent quality, designed by E. Meister, one of Queen Elizabeth I containing a mass of intricate detail, the other, Richard I, being a fine sturdy figure. A show-jumper was also contemplated, but never issued. The idea was quickly taken over by Airfix, who issued smaller and less elaborate kits at much cheaper prices, forcing Selcol off the market. The Airfix models, although not in the same class as those of Aurora or Selcol, achieved a mammoth sale, some adults even converting them, one in particular, Enno Spandauw, opening his own museum of conversions. A chariot issued in 54mm by Revell opened up possibilities for collectors of the traditional size models, which were seized on in 1964 by Historex, who were soon competing with metal models for popularity. Each kit consisted of innumerable separate pieces, including such minute items as bits and buttons, reins, scabbard-slings and the like. Each model was designed by Lelièpvre; the whole range of the First Empire was contemplated and is now well on its way to achievement. At first the models when assembled had little success, but the potential for assembly and painting was realized by certain enthusiastic collectors, and the name of Historex became a household word. They were imitated by several competitors, all of whom fell by the wayside except Airfix. The latter, naturally enough, concentrated on British troops during the Napoleonic wars and, the kits being far less complex than those of Historex, their impact was more immediate. The whole idea derived originally from the aeroplane kit and spread to the production of kits of artillery and AFVs.

Pomeroy, David. *See* Helmet Products.

Poplar Playthings Ltd, Bridgend, Wales (1958-65). Manufacturers of large-size Romans with chariots, spacemen and Westerners for the juvenile trade.

Popular Plastics. *See* Timpo.

Porcelain. *See* Ceramics.

Porcelain Enamel & MFG Co. Ltd, USA (c.1950). Publishers of a cardboard cut-out West Point cadet, 6 inches high. [*Newman*]

Porter, D. & J. *See* D.J.'s Miniatures.

Portoli, Spain (c.1830). Manufacturer of flats.

PORTUGAL. The earliest models known are flats engraved by Symon Roualle, or Roullé, a Dutchman, around 1762 at the express command of Dom José, Prince of Brazil. They seem to have made no impact, the later industry proving to be of solids or semi-solids made mainly by Almeida (1870, and still producing from the original moulds), and Cutileiro (naval painter, sculptor and engraver for the Museo de Marinha, where some of his woodcarvings may be seen).

Posas, Joan, Barcelona (fl.c.1855). Manufacturer of flats.

Possnecker, E., Austria (d.1960). A publisher of flats of Romans, war-elephants, Prince Eugen, French troops (1793-98), Bavarians (1809-13) and Tyroleans (1809). His moulds, purchased by Pohl, are now with the Austrian society. He also at one time was the possesor of the Wollner semi-solid moulds, now owned by Kober.

Poste Militaire. *See* Lamb, Ray (England).

Potsdam Zinnfiguren (Colonel Joseph Shimek) US Army in Germany (1976-). Replicas of Heyde in 45mm.

Pouilhac Collection, Paris. Contains a model of a 16th-century armoured knight, without the horse, 14cm high, with detachable and jointed armour, bearing serial numbers; undoubtedly a model tilting figure.

Powell, R., Moorabin, Victoria, Australia (c.1970-?). A maker of a small range of 54mm models: no further information could be obtained.

Prairial System, Paris (fl.1970). Manufacturers of polystyrene kits 54mm high, including a Duke of Wellington in four poses, the horses sold separately, and four models of the 42nd Highlanders. The firm could not compete with Historex.

Prandell, Germany (1977). Homecasting kits for flats.

Pranzetti, Augusto, Sassari, Sardinia (1948-). A skilled woodcarver who imbues his subjects with character. The equipment is made of natural materials, and the models are normally 15cm for mounted troops and 54-60mm for infantry. His range is wide, and he particularly favours British regiments, although for the Municipality of Sassari he did a series in 1951 of 54 Italian types from the 18th century to the present day. It was stated in 1972 that Figir was negotiating with him for the design of his models to be translated into lead. (*Alberini*)

Pratt, Judson, Massachusetts. One of the designers of the dioramas and a painter of some of the actual models for 'They Nobly Dared'.

Preiser Plastiken Figuren, Rothenburg, W. Germany (1965-). Manufacturers of plaster composition, and later plastic, models of military subjects and wild and domestic animals and civilians, the sizes of which vary enormously from 20mm to go with Minitanks to 20cm horrors. They also issue cardboard sheets of buildings for dioramas.

Prell, Emil, Nuremberg. Mentioned in the Kulmbach list of 1973 as a manufacturer of flats.

Premiere, Japan (1966). Pirates of Britains' guns and vehicles.

Presentation Associates, USA. Makers of dioramas for the National Guard Heritage Gallery.

Pressman, J. & Co., New York (c.1910-45). Manufacturers of hollow-cast 54mm models, mainly of US troops for the juvenile trade. A list issued in 1929 contained 1040 items. A 'Soldier Set' comprising five card figures prepressed for cutting out and mounting, together with a supply of marbles, was marketed in 1940.

Pride of Europe (J. Dew), Hoyle, Cornwall (1977-). Manufacturers of Britains-style toy soldiers in solid, designed by A. Rose.

Prins August. *See* Edman, Ab. Jan.

Priors Forlag, Copenhagen. Publishers of paper sheets.

Pritchard, William, USA. A painter of figures and designer of houses for the diorama series 'They Nobly Dared'.

'Proclaim Freedom', (c.1945). A series of dioramas of Jewish history now in Jerusalem made by Stokes and Greenwood and Ball at the instigation of Gottstein and Levine.

'Pro Patria'. *See* Bouquet, H.

Prudenziali, Fabrizio. *See* Grifo.

PSEUDONYMS. Many makers use a trade-name (e.g. Rose, Brigadier, Helmet, Lasset) which makes a direct impact on the public. The majority of them do their own designing, but larger groups (e.g. Cavalier, Monarch, Greenwood and Ball/Pearce) employ a number of free-lance designers. This makes it difficult to discover the name of the artist and confusion is worse when the same artist may work for several firms, or when, as in the United States, parent firms issue their models under several different guises. Another type of pseudonym occurs when a maker, usually known under his own name, has his models issued by various agents under other trademarks. Tradition, Standish, Just and Buckingham are all Stadden figures; Pagada is Higgins, and Guard House is Marcus Hinton, while Murray suddenly becomes Old Guard, which again is confounded by his former English agent, New Hope Design, employing English artists, and at the same time embracing Deauville (an American firm), but again with English designers.

PVC. *See* Helmet Products.

PYROGRAVURE. An indispensable aid to the converter of polystyrene kits, being the equivalent of the soldering iron to the expert in metal. It is capable of fusing and moulding the material upon which it is used.

Pyro Plastics, New York (c.1968-). Manufacturers of polystyrene kits of Westerners and Indians.

PZG, Warsaw (fl.1970). Manufacturers of 50-54mm plastic models of Napoleonics and Teutonic and Lithuanian knights, all mounted and well painted. [*Pestana*]

Q

'Q' Models. *See* Rose Miniatures Ltd.

Quadri-Animata (Maria Grazia), Italy (1975-). Publishers mainly of toy-theatre sheets, but one is of the Coliseum at Rome, with modern soldiers, tanks and trucks. (*Newman*)

Quality Model Soldiers (M. Haley) Bradford, Yorks. Designer in solid in the Britains' tradition, with Continental regiments, and in two styles - 'marching' and 'action' - boxed in traditional fashion. Mark: QMS.

Quarré-les-Tombes, France. White clay mounted soldiers of the 15th century were found here.

Queen's Dolls' House, The. Windsor Castle, Berks. The most lavish model of its kind in the world. It contains tiny boxed replicas of the Royal Horse Guards and the Life Guards, complete with label, being the smallest models ever made by Britains.

'Queen Victoria's Fighting Men' series. *See* Rowe, R.

Quinn, R. Watford, Herts (c.1939–45). A minor maker of 36mm solids of the United States army, each with a removable helmet.

Quinnell, C.R., MM, ex-Royal Fusiliers, Royal Hospital, Chelsea (b.1885). Chelsea Pensioner Quinnell learned, with help from Chelsea College, to make moulds, and in 1978 began making 9-inch polychrome plaster models of Chelsea Pensioners. These are reinforced with armatures. They are obtainable in the Great Hall of the Hospital.

Quiralu (Hubert des Granges) Luxeuil-les-Bains (c.1935–60). Makers of aluminium models, 60mm, for the toy trade. Dies of a selected range were also sent to Wend-Al for production in England. They appear to have used the alternative name Quirinal indiscriminately [*Information from E.J. Kehoe of Wend-Al*]. A number are identical with Frenchal [*Brett*] and it is further suggested that they were taken over by Starlux and the name changed to Quiralux. [*Opie*]

Quirinal. *See* Quiralu.

Quorn Collection (P.A. Taylor), Nottingham (1978-). Agent for silver models, 55mm of military and civilian subjects, published by Phillips of England.

Q.T. Models, Bridlington, Yorks (1978-). Diorama accessories.

R

Raab, Johann, Nuremberg (19th century). Publisher of paper sheets.

Rabe, Dr Willi, Karlsrühe (1979-). Producer of flats.

RA Cannons (R. Pither, A.J. Clarke) Tilehurst/Reading/Frimley (1977-). Makers of hand-made scale cannon.

Rachmaninov, Jacob, & Co., Wokingham, Berks (1978-). Makers of metal cannon.

Racine, Stephen, Ottawa, Canada. Landscape artist employed on the 'D-Day' diorama at the Canadian War Museum.

Rae, J. *See* Castile Miniatures.

Railroads, USA (1970-). Manufacturers of 20mm plastic civilians.

Ral Partha Enterprises (Glenn E. Kidd) Cincinnati, Ohio (1975-). Makers of 15, 58, 65 and 75mm solids, sculpted by Tom Maier. A series of small figures to illustrate *The Lord of the Rings*, with reasonably well-made models of Gandalph, the Riders of Rohan, Sauron and Saramun, a Balrog and a Ringwraith, was followed by a degeneration into American 'pulp magazine' monstrosities. As a complete change, there is an excellent 58mm windswept American sentry at Valley Forge. In 1977 Kidd reverted to the 'fantastic' with a 65mm 'Angel of Death'.

Ralston, USA, (c.1945). Manufacturers of metal tanks.

Ramin, Wolf-Dietrich von, Spaden-über-Bremerhaven, W. Germany. Appears in the 1973 Kulmbach list as a publisher of flats.

Ramm, Luneberg, Germany (1830-1904). Makers of non-military flats, begun by Johann Christoph (d. 1870), succeeded by Johann Heinrich Friedrich (d.1904). Marks: R; RAMM.

Rammelt, Hans-Jorg, Dessai-Ziebigk, E. Germany. Designer of flats for Hartmann.

Rap-a-Jap. *See* Woodburn Mfg Co.

Rapaport Bros, Chicago, Illinois. Advertisers of home-casting moulds, which, although not mentioned as such, are those designed by Eriksson for Edman.

Rapaport, David. *See* Woodburn Mfg Co.

Rapi, Germany. Publishers of paper sheets of Westerners, Indians and United States Cavalry.

Raretanks, USA. Manufacturers of polystyrene AFV kits.

Rasmussen, G. Krohn. *See* Krolyn.

Rathgeber, Josef, (1812-75) Diessen-Ammersee. Producer of flats. He began in 1812 as a journeyman to Schweizer, becoming a partner in 1816, and later starting his own business. Mark: JR.

Ray, Don and **Honey,** England/Calgary, Alberta (1933-). The Rays began by converting Britains' models with barbola, and made many such for Charles Lockwood and also sold them through Hamleys. Honey painted many flats for Gottstein, some of which were used in the RUSI dioramas. They were then commissioned by Lord Greenway to make ten models of every regiment in the Indian Army, and were working on them in their Conduit Street studio when war broke out. In the meantime they had also produced solids for Horlicks. Their studio was completely demolished by enemy action in 1940, with the loss of all their equipment. Before their involvement with model soldiers they had worked as circus performers, being known as the 'Del Rios', their act including the throwing of knives by Don around the outline of Honey, one mis-throw through the hand being reported. After the war they re-commenced their act, but on the birth of a son they decided to resume their modelling interests. Settling in Calgary, they started wood carving, and their models (now made only to commission) are to be seen in a number of Canadian collections. They also made 54mm moulds of infantry of both World Wars from which they cast when requested. Their collection of Britains and other hollow-casts (inherited from Don's father) now form the nucleus of a permanent display of dioramas, 'Fields of Glory', begun in 1968, intended as a kind of history through the ages, which is housed at the Empress Hotel, Victoria, B.C. To these models others such as those of Elastolin and Herald have been added. Civilian subjects such as what the Rays claim as the world's largest doll's house, and Old London Bridge, are incorporated in the display. The large wooden figures are carved by Don, with Honey painting them in oils. Buttons are applied, swords are removable from scabbards, while belts, slings, knapsacks and the like are of leather, and metal parts are added where necessary. Honey also produces most beautiful carvings of birds. Boundless in energy and enthusiasm, at the end of 1975 they began making one thousand 'folk art' wooden models, each 12 inches tall, entitled 'Ray's

Armies', ten models to each troop, with artillery, baggage wagons, cavalry, line regiments and skirmishers. As a happy and generous thought, they are calling each troop by the name of a friend, e.g. 'Garratt's Rangers'. At the same time they have been making very small, carved wooden figures and accessories for 12 x 14-inch dioramas of New Testament history. Thirty of these have been exhibited at St Mary's Roman Catholic Cathedral and (1977) at the Hudson Bay Company Stores, Edmonton.

'Ray's Armies'. *See* Ray, Don and Honey.

RD. Shamus Wade possesses a costermonger in hollow-cast so marked.

Ready-Brek, London (1975). A cereal company which produced a series of 3-inch pre-pressed cards (similar to cigarette-cards) of pirates and civilians.

Real Armoria, Madrid. This enterprising museum has had made a series of 54mm models in a metallic composite plastic of replicas of historic pieces of armour, some mounted, in the museum.

Realistic Miniatures. *See* Pfab, V.

Real Models. *See* Sea Gull Models.

REAMSA (Resinas Artificiales Moldeadas, S.A.) (Juan Llopart), Barcelona, (1955-). Manufacturers of 54-60mm plastic models of considerable variety, generally deriving from the designs of Elastolin. As far as the medieval range is concerned, the armour is entirely anachronistic, and the same set serves equally for 'The Knights of King Arthur' and 'Richard the Lion-Heart'. Many are also direct piracies from those of Starlux. However, from 1964 to 1970 they employed G. Erik of Wimbledon, who designed for them some good models of French and Spanish soldiers of the Napoleonic period, a set of portrait-figures of famous bull-fighters, and an excellent 'El Cid', based on the film starring Charlton Heston. The foot models and the removable riders are quite in keeping with the period, but unfortunately the horses are as illogical as those of the earlier sets already mentioned. Further models were of authentic Apache Indians, North-West Mounted Police and trappers, and a train hold-up. Some of the later models are issued unpainted in packets with colours and brushes, under the name 'Decofigur'.

Recordez Bruguera, Malaga, Spain. Publishers of paper sheets.

Red Box. *See* Blue Box/Red Box.

Redington, J. and **Skelton, M.**, London (fl.1850). Publishers of paper sheets for the juvenile theatre. The only military ones were a short uncoloured series, very Victorian in feeling, entitled 'Redington's New Foot Soldiers'.

Redlin, Richard, Potsdam (1932–41). An engraver of flats, who began in 1932 by engraving his own designs, together with some by Hans Fritsch.

Red-Y-Cut, USA (c.1935). Makers of balsawood kits of armaments.

Reed (W.S.) Toy Co., Leominster, Massachusetts (fl.1875-90). Maker of wooden soldiers. It may safely be assumed that these would be of the skittle type.

Reeves, Ronald, London (1974-). Maker for Warrior of 14-inch models of synthetic resin with metal, cloth and leather, including a member of the Kaiser's Private Bodyguard, 1900, each priced at £200. In 1975 models in 90mm were begun.

Reeves, T. *See* Sovereign Miniatures.

Regalia. *See* Superior Models Inc.

Regent Miniatures Inc. (Dieter Mattingly) Elk Grove Village, Illinois (1977-). Publishers of 54 and 100mm solids by Hans Reuters and Gregg Volke.

Regimental. *See* Cassin-Scott, Jack.

Regimental Enterprises (R. Banks), Warwick (1974-). Constructors of dioramas for military museums (e.g. Welch Regimental Museum) using commercial models where possible, originals being made as required. Banks has also done extensive repairs to some of the RUSI dioramas, and is an agent for Bisgood.

Regiments from Canada's Colourful History. *See* Robinson-Sager, A.

Reh, D, Munich, (b.1920). Maker of flats of the French Revolution and Napoleonic periods, and civilians. A tendency to caricature is evident in all his models.

Reh, Heinz, Penig, E. Germany. Publisher of flats.

Reiber, Paul, Strasbourg (fl.1830). Publisher of paper sheets, a large collection of which may be seen at the Museum at Strasbourg.

Reich, Johann Christian, Fürth (18th-19th century). A manufacturer of tin medallions, who may also have made flats of a military nature.

Reid Brothers. *See* Charbens & Co. Ltd.

Reid, Peter, New Zealand. A maker of 12-inch models in balsawood to commission.

Reider Design (D.G. Kayson, Trevor Phillipson) Leicester, (1979-). Makers of 80mm solids, sculpted by Kayson (who had previously made one or two models for DEK). A range of models of the 17th century is subtitled 'Maystetter'.

Reimann, Franzi, Nittenau, W. Germany (1973-). Publisher of flats.

Reisberg, Eward, Aschersleben, E. Germany. Maker of flats. (*Katalog der Formen, 1976*).

Reisler (Kai) Samleserier, Copenhagen (1950-). Manufacturer of 55mm plastics of the modern Danish army and mounted troops of the Middle East, in which the design is obviously based on that of Timpo. (*See also* Fischer Thermoplastics.)

Reka Ltd (C.W. Baker) London (c.1910-33). Manufacturer of hollow-casts. Marks: REKA COPYRIGHT; REKA/COPYRIGHT/C.W. BAKER/MADE IN ENGLAND. Many models were not marked, but some were dated. The quality ran from good to very bad. Their range was similar to that of Britains, and some details derive from the latter. However, some unusual and original models were produced such as a Bersaglieri with detachable entrenching tools, and Australian Mounted Lancers where the rider is cast separately from the horse. The moulds may have been purchased by Cherilea, and certainly some were used by the St Louis Lead Soldier Company.

Reliable Toys, Canada (1939-45). One of the earliest native producers of Canada, and important as such, even though their 54mm plastics were very crude.

Remanence France. *See* M.H.S.P.; Lelièpvre, E.

Remondini, Giuseppi, and family, Bassano, Italy (c.1750-1850). Prolific publishers of paper sheets. Reprints by Zillio were made about 1970.

Rendall, Martin, Brighton, Sussex (1960-). A creator of carved polychrome wood models in varying sizes, from 77mm to 14 inches, mainly to commission, some in violent action. Some were made for Surén, and others (caricatures) for 'Tradition'. In 1973 he made a series of 12- to 14-inch models of the troops of the United States from 1775 for the Maritime Museum, Boston, together with dioramas using 10-inch figures.

Renfeld, Henning. *See* Comet.

Renner, G.-N., Nuremberg (19th century). Publisher of paper sheets.

Renown. *See* Phoenix Model Developments.

Renvoize, James, London (c.1900-1914). Manufacturers of 54mm hollow-casts. Mark: J. RENVOIZE (date) COPYRIGHT on the bellies of the horses. His large range was so similar to that of Britains that he was sued for piracy by the latter.

Renwall Blueprint Models, Mineola, New York (fl.1950-60). Manufacturers of polystyrene kits of armaments with a few figures in plastic to go with them.

Repetto, A. *See* Life Model.

Replicas, Liverpool. Advertised Johillco's moulds for sale in 1967.

Research Collectors' Aids, USA. Forms either part of the Monarch establishment, or is controlled by Monarch.

Resinas Artificiales Moldeadas Sa. *See* REAMSA.

Retter, Alfred, Stuttgart (b.1906-   ). Publisher of flats, many to his own designs, including the Siege of Troy, Diogenes and Alexander, ancient India (with a tiger hunt), German medieval folk-tales, Wurtemburgers (1900-1914), Prussians (1914), and Afrika Korps. One outstanding set is the arrest, trial and crucifixion of Christ (40 figures), and another a 62-figure 'Snow White'. A zeppelin set includes the longest casting ever made, that of the zeppelin itself, which is over two feet in length. Mark: RE. [*Bean*]

Reuters, Hans, Hartland, Wisconsin (1977-   ). Creator of a 100mm French dragoon, off duty, sitting on a chest, for Regent Miniatures. Has also designed for Valiant, and works to commission.

Revell Inc., Venice, California (c.1951-   ). Manufacturer of plastic and polystyrene figures and A.F.Vs. Some of the figures achieved a remarkable competence, especially in the grouping of mortar teams. They also made one of the earliest and best of the 54mm kits, of a Roman chariot, inspired no doubt by the film *Ben Hur*. Some figures appear to have been taken over by Monogram in 1965.

Rey, Jules, Monaco (1910-20). Publisher of paper sheets. A large collection may be seen at Strasbourg Museum.

Reycels, Corunna (fl.1926-35). Publisher of paper sheets.

Reyco (Carlos J. Reynal & Co.) Argentina (1952-55). Manufacturer of copies in solid 54mm of Britains' hollow-casts, including sailors and guns. [*Basseterre*]

Reynal, Carlos J. & Co. *See* Reyco.

Reynard (John Carrington), London (1973-   ). Maker of 75mm solids of the Napoleonic period for 'Tradition'. Facially they show a strong Stadden influence.

Reynolds, H. *See* HR Products.

Reynolds, Lloyd. *See* Tru-Craft.

Rhoederer, Achille. A collector who left his collection of paper sheets to Strasbourg Museum.

Ribes, Manuel. *See* GAMA.

Rich, Major M.E., Shiloh, Manitoba. The creator of dioramas at the Royal Regiment of Canada Artillery Museum.

Richards, L.W., London. An ardent and learned advocate of hollow-cast and solid commercial models. His researches into the complexities of the productions of Britains, Heyde and Mignot were pioneer efforts that have never been surpassed, and his altruistic comments

or advice were typical of the ideal of the true collector.

Richards, T. *See* Phoenix.

Richards, T.C., (c.1930-50). A manufacturer of hollow-casts of small consequence.

Richardson, Sir Albert E. (d.1964). The former owner of a magnificent Agincourt chess set made for Louis XV and illustrated in the author's *Model Soldiers: A Collector's Guide* (pl. 71).

Richter, Adolf Christian and **Johann Gottlieb,** Celle (1814-30). The business was carried on by Adam Gottlieb Christian Richter (1830-1849) and was then purchased in 1852 by H. Heine (d.1940). Marks: J.G.; J.G. RICHTER IN CELLE.

Rich Toys, Clinton, Ohio (c.1955). Manufacturers of a pressed wood and metal fort with two 54mm guardsmen.

Ridinger the Elder, Ulm (c.1675). An artist who made himself an army in papiermâché.

Rieche Gebr., Hanover (1866-1929). Manufacturers of flats, for whom Franz was the engraver and Ernst the painter. They were the first to break away from the Heinrichsen tradition, and the wide range included portrait models of Napoleon, Wellington, Blücher and Gneisenau, as well as medievals. In 1916 they purchased Link's moulds, and, says Ortmann, those of Ammon, Kahle and Haselbach.

Riedder, Paris. A collector who presented a series of dioramas to the Musée de l'Armée in Paris in the early part of the present century.

Riedmatter, Roger de, Vienna. A member of the prominent contemporary Austrian school of makers of dioramas.

Rieger, K.W., Kiel, W. Germany (1977-   ). Publisher of flats and maker of solids, 17th-18th century. (*Klio*)

Ries, USA. Advertised in *The Soldier*, October, 1968, as a maker of solid 54mm models, but no collector in the United States appears ever to have heard of him.

Rietveld, Fritz, Tawa, New Zealand (1972-   ). Maker of mainly Napoleonic 54mm solids to commission.

Riffet, Marcel, France (1969-   ). Maker of 7-inch solid models with cloth uniforms. These appear to be known only in France and in the United States, where he has an agent.

Rifle Miniatures (Gian Roberto Parisini), Genoa (1970-   ). Parisini began making models in card and in wax before turning to metal. His 54mm solids are divided into two categories: (1) a single-mould casting ('Standard') and (2) a 'Super' model, hand-cast, built-up and added to, and limited to fifteen numbered copies. Those issued coloured are painted by the maker. The models are beautifully made and refreshingly original, and cover Continental and British troops from 1713 to 1775 and Italian uniforms from 1861 to the present day. They were first seen in England in 1974 when Jock Coutts of Under Two Flags began to import the 'Standard' range.

Rigaud, Paris (fl.1850). Manufacturers of '*cavaliers sur resorts, et militaire de toutes armes*'. (*Almanach Bottin*)

Riko Tanks. *See* Midori.

Ringel, Pierre, Paris (fl.1850). Manufacturer of models mounted on springs.

Rivière, Captain (fl.1860). Inventor of evolution models. (*See* Evolutions.)

Riviere, R. Briton, London (fl.1948). On the dissolution of the Carbago venture some of the models were marketed under the name Argosy. Riviere then took over the rights, added to the historical figures, and also produced a series of military ones in hard plaster. The historical models were then marketed as Faber, the military ones as Matchlock, which caused a clash with Willetts, whose models already bore that name. He then linked up with The Sentry Box, for whom he and Simon Hunt designed some 18 to 33cm plaster models, which were then metallized, as were subsequently a small number of the Matchlock figures.

'Rivollet'. *See* Berne, Maurice.

Roberts, Derek, Yorkshire (1974–). A series of models in metal announced as Panache Figures in *Military Modelling* failed to appear, but in 1974 he joined Hinchliffe with 90mm models. One of these was so ill-constructed that the separately cast arm was impossible to attach to the shoulder, and the whole model was extremely clumsy.

Robinson, Cameron, Belfast (1970–). Known principally as a dealer who was responsible for launching Barber and Sanderson in the Jackboot series and, later, Sanderson alone as Acorn; also agent for Fermor and Saunders. At the same time he is a keen collector and himself makes the occasional model or diorama.

Robinson, H. Russell, London (c.1945-77). A free-lance artist on the staff of the Armouries of the Tower of London who collaborated with Carman and a number of later makers. Author of *Medieval Knights for Colouring and Cutting Out* (Colchester, 1977), a revival of the paper cut-out, in book form, the figures 11 inches high, with separate equipment.

Robinson-Sager, Allan, Toronto. A private collector who in 1972 published in book-form a set of paper sheets entitled *Regiments from Canada's Colourful History*, in which seventy-four figures were illustrated, in an edition limited to 500 copies. This was followed in 1976 by sheets depicting the Heights of Abraham.

Robrach & Co., Magdeburg. Publishers of paper sheets.

Rocchiero, Italy (1976–). Conversions of Historex and Rose. The Italian journal *Warrior* describes them as 'a true pirating' [*sic*].

Rocco Plastics Ltd, Preston (1956-?). A small manufacturer of plastic 30mm guards, knights and Westerners with detachable riders for the juvenile trade.

Roche. *See* Austrandia.

Roche-Kelly, Major E., London. Maker of six conversions, 54mm, depicting uniforms of the Border Regiment, at their Museum, Carlisle.

Rochelle, USA. Classified in a Polk catalogue about 1970 as on a par with Berdou, but Polk himself cannot even remember him.

Rockwell, Annette, USA. Assisted in the creation of the diorama of Bunker Hill at the First National Bank, Boston.

Roco, Vienna (1965–). Manufacturers of metal tanks of tiny size, with figures to complete.

Roco Minitanks, New York. In 1974 they issued a group of 54mm plastic models of Axis and Allied Second World War models. Also known for their polystyrene A.F.Vs.

Rodden, Brian, Rollinsford, New Hampshire, (1970–). A maker of polychromed pewter models, 8½-10 inches high. His work includes the American Revolution and the Middle Ages; future projects embrace characters from Shakespeare and Israeli history, and Western pioneers. He issues his models in ordinary and in limited

editions, these mainly of 150 castings. As a comparison, the ordinary 'Hotspur' is priced at $600 and the limited one $3,500. A set of representatives of the original thirteen colonies are all the same basic casting. His portrait of the 'infamous' Banastre Tarleton after the painting by Reynolds is magnificent.

Roddy, Kenneth, USA. Professional painter for Cowan.

Rode Orm, Copenhagen (c.1910-46). Manufacturers of aluminium 76mm models of Vikings, knights, Robin Hood, Ivanhoe, Danish Royal Guards and Westerners. Mark: RODE ORM. The firm was taken over in 1946 by Krolyn, but many of the models still retained the trade name.

Roder, Anton, Mengersgereuth-Hammern (1965). Manufacturer of plaster composition figures of Westerners of very poor quality.

Roders, Jasper, Soltau, (1800-1840). Producer of flats. His son Georg Andreas (1840-70) engraved for Du Bois, Engels and Ramm.

Rodriguez, Teodor. *See* Teo.

Roederer, Achille, France (1816-26). Publisher of paper sheets.

Roepke, John von. *See* JVR Miniatures.

Roer, Dr Hans, Mainz. Named in the Kulmbach list of 1973 as a publisher of flats.

Rogard Ltd, Penmaenmawr (c.1935). An obscure maker of one of the first of the polystyrene kits, consisting of a 6-inch Lifeguard, only two pieces and a base being required.

Rogean Advertising Associates. *See* Rowe, R.

Roger, London (c.1940). A model of a frog in the possession of Shamus Wade is all that can be discovered.

Roger, Nicolas, Paris (fl.1608). A silversmith who made 300 silver models, commissioned by Marie de Medici for the Dauphin.

Rogers, Frank. *See* Comet Metal Products Inc.

Rogerson, Peter. *See* Caledonian Castings; New Hope.

Rohm, Germany. In 1908 designed a medieval battle set for Schweizer.

Rollo (Søren Brunoe) Copenhagen (1948–). The official artist to the Danish Navy. He started making 54mm and 22cm solid models in 1948, solely for himself. About 1965 he began tentative marketing, and found an

66   **Rowe, Major Robert.** *A small group of his 'Ensign Miniatures' (Author).*

immediate response among a limited number of collectors in his own country. Since then he has gradually established himself as one of the leading model makers of the world, even though his time is limited. He models his prototypes in wax, plasticine or Isopon, in separate parts which are then cast in metal and soldered together and equipment added. His larger models are confessedly influenced by 18th-century porcelain figurines, as, indeed, one feels his smaller models are also. It seems natural therefore that the 18th century is his special interest, and he has made some most evocative models, especially of Danish and Swedish troops of this period, and has extended it to include a fine 'Clive at Plassey'. He is, however, equally at home with a Roman Forum scene. He bases small groups on contemporary paintings. A Victoria Cross winner at Dargai is an unusual model for him. He is also intensely interested in the portrayal of the female sex, clothed or partially nude, but never is he anything but tasteful in this sphere. Indeed, elegance may be said to sum up all his achievements. His 'Homage to Watteau' group is probably the most perfect ever made. He mixes his own colours, and paints with taste and restraint. Of recent years he has been concentrating on the creation of dioramas, including seascapes such as the sinking of the *Titanic*. His work may be seen at the Swedish Army Museum and the Warsa Museum, Stockholm. In 1975 he was commissioned by Ewing of Houston, Texas, to make six masters for the American Revolution.

Roma (Editorial), Barcelona (before 1950-). A prolific publisher of paper sheets and precut sheets in booklet form. Productions include the Spanish armed forces from 1920 to the present day. British of 1918, Second World War US troops, menageries, circuses, the Wild West, guns, tanks and a castle. The sheets, containing the same illustrations, are issued in different sizes (30, 50 and 70mm) under the names Construcciones Pepi, La Grande Illusion, Kiki and Lolo. [*Balil*]

Romanelli, Carl, Encino, California. Designer and modeller for the original Tru-Craft.

Romanoff's Military Miniature Casting Moulds, Ann Arbor, Michigan. Agents for the Eriksson home-casting moulds which he designed for Edman, which go under different names according to the country or even the State in which they are issued.

Romero de Cidou, Spain. Publishers of paper sheets.

Roming, Victor and **Gael**. *See* Heritage Miniatures.

Romund, Karl, Hanover (b.1903). He began making flats in 1956, which he designed and engraved himself. He has made many sets of Romans, Huns, cavemen and prehistoric animals, the Seven Years' War and the American Civil War, including artillery teams. His chief contribution has been an outstanding series illustrating North American Indians, including Apaches, Little Big Horn and plains wagons and oxen.

Roscini, Count Maurice, Italy (1977-). Noted for his busts in bronze of famous people, he made two full-length models, 43cm, in bronze, each signed and numbered, and limited to 12 copies, under the title 'The Roscini Collection', which were published by Geoffrey George Warner of Kingston-on-Thames, who advised him on the details of the uniforms.

Rose, Andrew, London (1976-). Designer of modern 'toy' soldiers for M.J. Mode, Pride of Europe, Under Two Flags, and for his own Steadfast Soldiers.

67   **Rose Miniatures.** *One of the finest of Gammage's models, painted by Le Gloahec (Custer).*

Rose Miniatures (Russell Gammage) London. (1954-). One of the few makers of 54mm solids of whom it may be said that over the years the excellency of his creations has remained unvaried. His first commission was for a series of Coronation figures for Graham Farish, in which he was assisted to a limited extent by Nicholson. The pleasure which these models gave led to other commissions, and finally to the setting-up of his own business. For some time he experimented in methods of production: a spread-eagled 'Cabalt' figure for individual animation, bodies with separate legs, and 'Q' models with sets of arms. The spread-eagle casting, though no longer made in Cabalt, is still done for basic male and female bodies, which are extensively used for diorama work. But for the last twenty years models have been either single-piece castings, which help the beginner as yet unskilled in assembly, or bodies with separate heads, arms, bases, equipment etc. He was at the same time one of the first in the field for the production of 25mm wargame models, and has since extended into the 30mm field for these collectors. In 1974 he introduced a new series entitled 'Elite Models', the initial offering being of Musketeers of 1608 taken from engravings by Jacob de Gheyn. His range is extensive, and he has the habit of breaking off a series to introduce a new line and then continue with the original. In some instances this has led to the withdrawal of a model with which he was dissatisfied and its replacement by another version. He has made basic nudes for the collector who wishes to experiment with adornment, Achaean troops (with the figure-of-eight shield) and stricken Greek warriors from antique sculptures, Romans (including musicians), Egyptian soldiers, Normans*, English bowmen (of whom only one is now available), men at arms, the English Civil War*, the Seven Years' War (including French and the troops of Frederick the Great), the American War of Independence (increasing in number, and including British troops), English and French of 1795-1815, the Royal Navy of the present day and earlier times, Germans 1880-1914, the Indian Army, British County Regiments, Lowland* and Highland Regiments, Russians of 1880-1914, First and Second World War combatants, Gurkha and Pakistani Pipe Bands* and portrait models of Napoleon, Wellington, Montgomery, Wavell* and Rommel, and a swaggering Tambour Major.* (Those marked * have now been withdrawn). During the last ten years, while adding fresh models to those already mentioned, he has broken new ground with Gauls, Celts and Germanic tribes, Persian Immortals, Assyrians, Landsknechts, Aztecs and Conquistadores, the American Civil War, the Honourable Artillery Company 1900, the Royal Marines, and the Afghan Wars. A mortar team is now included, and gunners of Waterloo and later periods to serve Hinchliffe artillery. There is now a mounted Napoleon and a swaggering Murat to go with his Napoleonic cavalry, together with mounted British and Germans and the Indian Army, and a marvellous Officer of the 4th Light Dragoons, 1822. Occasionally he is assisted by research from collectors such as Schriltz (Zouaves, Turcos, and the Imperial Russian Army), and designers such as Turnbull (12th-century Japanese Yama-Bushi and Samurai). He was the first to break away from the military model, and, beginning with Cro-Magnon Man, create the finest of series of non-combatants. It is possible, by means of these models, to create vignettes of prehistoric men and women. Grecian and Minoan women and a Minoan bull-jumping set complement a whole series of wonderfully colourful Egyptian gods, goddesses, Pharaohs and their consorts, concubines, slaves, fanbearers and tumblers, and captives at a Roman slave market. The crowning glory is a magnificent chariot, a *tour-de-force* of craftsmanship and elegance. Amazons are not quite so successful, and many may well regret the portrayal of the flogging of Boadicea. A number of collectors have successfully combined Gammage's females with Sanderson's males in dioramas. The latest of the 25mm models include the English Civil War and the Zulu War, and the 30mm figures gladiators, Napoleonic troops and a slave market. In 1979 Gammage began the production of 90mm models in hollow-cast with a portrayal of a Hussar of Von Belling's Regiment, c.1758. In announcing this Gammage said 'We have several more in progress, both in 90 and 150mm. . . We have experienced great difficulty in casting the master models hollow, due mainly to the shrinking number of companies supplying metals. . . The figure is in two halves, front and back, and these are hollow'. In all his work Gammage is exceptionally consistent, and he has always offered not only quality of execution but dignity and integrity, and is certainly the most reliable of contemporary makers. One is not always particularly enamoured of his horses, apart from those for the chariot and a few others, but by and large they are as good as any others. While it is known that Sandoe and Turner worked for him at one time or another, and Jenkins gave occasional free-lance assistance, the whole accent of Gammage's workshop is a steady and thorough training of his assistants into the niceties of the art, thus lending homogeneity to the finished *corpus* of his work. Well could one reviewer remark that he had not yet seen a newly announced group, but that he would have no hesitation in giving it the praise that he was sure it deserved. Of few contemporary makers can this be said.

Rosegg, Carinthia. Miniature horsemen of tin and lead c.1000 BC were unearthed here.

Rosenberg (C.) Toy Manufacturers Inc. *See* Pearlytoys Manufacturing Co.

Roskopf-Miniaturmodelle, Berlin (1925-?). Manufacturers of metal tanks and armoured vehicles. A small number of solid modern troops in 20mm were made, one foot of each figure fitting into a tiny circular base.

Rossetti, Roberto, Benevento, Italy (?1972–). A maker of 54mm solids to commission only, mainly of the Neapolitan Army of 1700–1860. Unfortunately, he appears to be somewhat of a recluse and averse to giving more information about himself. [*Gennari*]

Rössner, Professor Georg Walter, Schleswig-Holstein/Stockholm, (d.1973). One of the most original of the modern school of engravers of flats, he began work in 1925, and has encompassed the sizes of 30, 45mm and 7cm. He greatly appreciated the potential scope for detailed engraving offered by the 18th-century large flat, and in this size made a delightful Persian fairy tale set (from the *Poems of Nizami* manuscript), an equestrian George Washington, and *Les Incroyables*. Normal-size figures include Swedish troops of the Seven Years' War in many actions, and most accomplished medieval crossbowmen and non-combatants. He also designed and engraved for Scholtz, Ochel and Waibel and did a set of the American Revolution which were designed by Captain James S. Tily. Marks: WR; W. ROSSNER (cursive), occasionally with the addition of SW (Sven Wentzels, his former agent). His moulds are now in the possession of Annemarie Mierson.

Rothe, H., Kulmbach. Publisher of flats of the Napoleonic period and of Hanseatic Landwehr.

Roualle, or Roulé, Symon, Portugal (fl.1768). A Dutch emigré, employed by Don José, Prince of Brazil, as an engraver of flats for the first time in Portugal. A few moulds are still in the possession of the Portuguese society. It was rumoured in 1968 that an attempt was being made to reproduce them in plastic, but this cannot be confirmed.

Roundhouse, Hawthorne, California (1974). Manufacturers of plastic building kits.

Rousselot, Lucien, (c.1930–). Paris. Maker of large, mannequin-like models, utilizing all types of materials. As one of the instigators of the Mignot flats, he brought his profound knowledge of the Napoleonic army (as displayed in his magnificent series of designs on uniform sheets) to bear, and his influence on other makers has been profound.

Rowe, Major Robert O., Southampton/Woburn (1970–). Rowe served an apprenticeship as an animator with 'Tradition', which stood him in good stead when asked to convert some 400 Staddens for the Woburn Abbey collection. At the same time he learned much about sculpting and casting, and had a series of twenty models of unusual military subjects accepted by Dickinson. They are, however, no longer obtainable. He then designed a few models for The Barefoot Soldier, but really found himself when he began his Vallance series for Rogean, the rights being purchased in 1977 by Cavalier. These models, cast in a single piece apart from the weapons, although in style as old as the hobby, were something new to the American market, with its cost-saving emphasis on models in kit form. The quality of the sculpture and the finish were far superior to any others in the 54mm size. They were also refreshing in their relaxed positions. In making them he was later joined by his son, Robert, and his son-in-law, John Goddin. In 1974 he began another series, Ensign

Miniatures, inspired by visions of the British Army of the 1900s. This took the form of a number of soldiers in off-duty poses, together with accessories such as benches, chairs, tables, beer tankards, books and separate head-dresses. These again were single-piece castings, with an incredible exactitude of balance, so that no footstand was required. The proof of the quality of any casting is the smoothness of the surface to be painted, and in this aspect the models were of the highest. They were linked into a homogeneous whole, so that small tableaux could be formed. A series of French Napoleonic figures followed, with pairs of soldiers chatting by a stile, or, freezing in an icy wind, gazing hopefully at a signpost half obscured by snow. To an ultra-critical mind it is possible that the French models are not quite so distinguished as their English counterparts. More recently Rowe has been concentrating on a neglected subject, the British Navy in all its aspects. Added to these are 'Queen Victoria's Fighting Men', the Indian Mutiny, and the American Revolution, without repeating those already made under the name Vallance. His first model in 100mm appeared in 1978.

Rowe, Sergeant Robert, Woburn. Son of Major Robert Rowe. Active in assisting his father and designer of a French Revolution group originally intended for The Barefoot Soldier, but eventually published by Cavalier.

Roxtantius. A white clay equestrian Gallic toy c.AD600 found at Cologne bears this name.

Roy. *See* Thomas et Roy.

Royal Doulton Tableware Ltd, Stoke-on-Trent. Makers of a magnificent set of models in porcelain of the American Revolution, begun in 1969, and introduced by the first four figures in 1975, for the United States only. Designed, sculpted, and supervised by Eric Griffiths, they represent the finest and most accurate in porcelain models of this epoch in history. Immense care was taken to ensure accuracy, advice being obtained from the Corporation of Colonial Williamsburg. Rifles and other equipment were made separately. In due course there will be a total of thirteen pieces, the last being an equestrian one. The whole edition will be limited. A series of Colonial people, made in 1960 by the same designer, for Colonial Williamsburg only, should also be noted. The set comprises a hostess, a lady and a gentleman (both seated), a boy and a girl, the Royal Governor's cook, a blacksmith, a silversmith and a wig maker. The average height is 14 inches.

Royal United Service Institution Museum. From 1937 to 1967 this was the home of the remarkable collection of dioramas conceived by Otto Gottstein, Denny R. Stokes, W.Y. Carman and other members of the British Model Soldier Society. Originally planned to be constructed on the Continent, using flats by Continental makers, they were eventually made in England, with Stokes as the chief designer of the overall layout and of the scenic effects, the flats being imported from Germany until that became impossible. The series was completed by the use of Greenwood and Ball 20mm figures. Siborne's first model of Waterloo was also exhibited there for years, as was the Mond collection of Lucottes, and exhibitions by members of the British Society were held, culminating in one concentrating on the Battle of Waterloo. It was the Mecca of visitors from overseas, and it was nothing short of lunacy to split up the dioramas and dispose of them to different places. They are now to found as follows: Flers, D-Day: Imperial War Museum; Ulundi: Staffordshire Regiment, Lichfield; Plassey: Museum of the Dorsetshire Regiment, Dorchester; Quebec: Royal Sussex Regiment Museum, Chichester; Marston Moor: Castle Museum, York; Acre: Royal Artillery Museum, Woolwich; Hastings: Hastings Museum; Balaclava, Waterloo, Blenheim and Crécy: Glenbow Institution, Calgary, Alberta (where they have been disgracefully neglected); Tilbury: Thurrock Museum; The Field of the Cloth of Gold: Kneller Hall.

Royal Worcester Porcelain. *See* Ceramics; French, N.; Gertner, F.; Lindner, D.; Winskill, B.

Roydon, London, (c.1960). A manufacturer of hollow-casts, mainly of non-military figures.

Rozniecki, Lieut-General, Poland (fl.1812). Commander of the Light Cavalry Division in the *Grande Armée,* and later Inspector of Polish Cavalry. He used models to demonstrate tactics and evolutions.

Rozwadowski, Z. *See* Niemojewski, M.

Rubin, Raymond. *See* Squadron/Rubin.

Rucker Gebr, Hanover (1960-). Professional painters of flats and publishers of a long set of Germans of 1939-45, German South-West Africa, wild animals, birds and trees.

Ruckert, Würtemberg (1785-c.1875). A family of makers of 6-23cm flats, somewhat crude in production. The founder, Philip, an engraver, employed his sons J.S., Martin and Anton. Marks: M.R.; A.M.; A.F. RUCKERT; F. RUCKERT. Martin (b.1785) was apprenticed to Stephen Heber, succeeding his father in 1821.

Ruddle, John, Hampton-on-Thames. The possessor of a private out- and indoor layout, complete with a vast contingent of Britains, and home-made streets and buildings, which he opens to public view at certain times of the year.

Rudiger, Hildesheim (1814-1920). A family firm of manufacturers of flats. Founded by August (1814-69), succeeded by his son (1869-1920).

Rudolph II, Emperor (1576-1612). Owner of a clock, now in the British Museum, made by Hans Schlott in 1580. Of silvergilt, it is in the form of a ship, with the Emperor and his court on the poop. On the striking of the hours the figures revolve.

'Rufus' Figures. *See* Sanderson, C.

Rupp, Fritz, Nuremburg (c.1965). Manufacturer of plaster composition 6cm knights, civilians, etc, for children.

Russell Mfg Co. Ltd London, (1914-18). Manufacturers of poor-quality hollow-casts in 54mm size.

Russell, Stephen, Littleport, Cambs. In 1977 he announced a professional painting service.

'Russian Warriors' series. *See* U.S.S.R.

Russo, Michael. *See* Collector Enterprises.

S

Saalfield Publications, USA (1963-). Publishers of cardboard pre-pressed figures in book form, such as *The Lieutenant*.

Sablock, Peter, Massachusetts. Assisted in the creation of, and made models for, the dioramas 'They Nobly Dared'.

Sachs Soldier Manufacturing Company (S. Sachs) New York (c.1899-?1946). Maker of home-casting moulds, apparently the first such to appear in the United States (*Old Toy News Letter*). In 1933 he introduced hollow-casts, changing the name to Metal Cast Products Company. In the catalogue issued in the same year it is stated that the firm had been 'thirty-four years in business'.

Sacul Playthings Ltd, London (post-1945-55). Manufacturer of 54mm and 6cm hollow-casts, all of poor quality, but surprisingly expensive for their time. They were mainly of knights, with movable visor and silver-plated, Crusaders, Highlanders, Guards, Household Cavalry, children's television characters and dogs. The large models included Peter Pan, Captain Hook, Rob Roy and a Redcoat.

S.A.E. Sculptured Figures (Swedish African Engineers, F. Winkler and C. Wennberg) Cape Town (c.1955-70). Manufacturers of 30 and 54mm solids. Their 30mm solids, sold in boxes, of three to five models, made quite a sensation on their appearance. They were designed by Eriksson and bore his unmistakable stamp of quality, but their poor casting and painting were a disgrace to this great master. A large series was issued, embracing many periods and countries, including civilian subjects such as Papal choirboys. The 54mm models were reminiscent of Authenticast, and were later sold un-assembled and unpainted in the United States. The firm was founded by Winkler and Wennberg after the failure of the Irish headquarters of Authenticast. After about 1970 Wennberg intimated that reproduction in Madeira of Heyde models was contemplated. The 30mm models were imported into Canada as EMI and pirated in Hong Kong as AHI.

Saez-Alcocer, Lucio, Barcelona (c.1965-). An accomplished maker of solids, in 30, 45 and 54mm. An extremely wide range is available, especially of the Napoleonic wars, and he himself estimates that he lists over 5000 models. Artillery also features large in his output. The larger models are well designed, and in particular a modern-style Scottish clansman with fishing rod rather than claymore is a welcome change. Those in 54 and 45mm are sold painted, the 30mm as castings.

Saint George Miniatures, Genoa (1976). *Warrior*, 26 July, 1976, advertised Italians of the First World War, 'the best made in Italy', to start in October of that year.

Saint Louis Lead Soldier Company (S. Chichester Lloyd), Detroit, Michigan (1925-?). An oddity in model soldier history, who produced 54mm solids, 'giants' (horses 18cm in length) and semi-flats of various sizes, painted and unpainted. An ancient catalogue shows a conglomeration of the poorest quality castings from moulds purchased from Metal-Cast Products, Schiercke, Schneider, Reka, and probably Heyde and Haffner, together with piracies of Britains and other hollow-cast makers.

Saint-Marie, Mlle, Paris (c.1950). Painter of flats for Mignot.

Sala, George Augustus. A percipient Victorian journalist and author, one of whose interests was toy soldiers. He had some pertinent remarks to make regarding the preponderance of German 'aggression' in playthings: 'The number of military toys in the German courts is truly remarkable. There are whole *corps d'armée* in tin, lead and zinc, with encampments on the vastest scale of which miniature is susceptible, squadrons of cavalry, parks of artillery, and gabions, fascines and pontoon bridges without number. It is significant that the smaller German states contribute the largest number of these bellicose playthings . . . To the martial display of Bavaria, Hesse and Wurtemberg there is no end.' (*Notes and Sketches of the Paris Exhibition*, 1868). His remarks give a fair indication of the prominence of the German toy industry of the period.

Salas, Delfin, Madrid (1977-). Publisher of paper sheets. Assisted in the formation of a large collection in the museum at Santo Domingo.

Salter, Thomas, Ltd. *See* Linka.

Salvatalia Editorial (A. Miguel), Barcelona. Publisher of paper sheets of historical figures.

Sambeth, Kiel (fl.1950-60). Designer and engraver of flats for Ochel, Bolling, Schirmer, Tobinnus and Waibel.

Samtgemeinde, Schoppenst, W. Germany (1977-). Producer of flats illustrating *Til Eulenspiegel.* (*Klio*)

Sanderson, Clifford, Sutton-in-Ashfield, Notts (1967-). Sanderson will, in the years to come, be regarded as one of the most enigmatic of makers of model soldiers, capable of making the most technically perfect figures and yet indulging at times in incomprehensible coarseness of subject. His first professional assignment was the creation (with John Barber) of a series for C. Robinson entitled Jackboot, and owing to Robinson's persistence in naming him 'Saunderson' it was some time before it was realized that the two men were one. These early efforts were inauspicious, being more oval than round. They dealt mainly with the German Army of the Second World War, and included an officer with a map, and a private with a guard dog. The First World War was represented by a portly beer-swilling *pickelhaube*-helmeted infantryman. A Cameronian at Aden brought history nearer, but the most unusual model, never previously presented, was a trumpeter of the Hillsborough Guard, a most colourful model. Sanderson then began a series of male and female models depicting a Roman slave market for Greenwood and Ball/Pearce. These were well received, as the only comparable ones at the time were those made by Gammage. The faces and togas were crisply sculpted, although the figures in themselves were still slightly oval in shape. The nudes in the group were followed by a series of what were euphemistically called 'novelty girls' or 'fun figures', that is girls nude other than for a helmet or a pair of boots. Surén had made similar figures in somewhat larger size, as had Murray, who was honest enough to call them 'Barrack Bawds'. It was the slight eroticism of these figures, far removed from those made by Gammage, that led him to perpetrate a series of frankly erotic models, in pairs, entitled 'Rufus' figures, which even his agent was compelled to sell under the counter. Two more semi-naked females, one entitled 'The Stripper' in 80mm, followed in the Acorn range for C. Robinson, culminating in a vicious and violent series of buccaneers engaged in rape and torture for Monarch, and a series of two- and three-piece 'fantastics' in the same vein. A further series (announced in 1979 as being contemplated), illustrating the classic Arabian *Thousand Nights and One Night* (for Greenwood and Ball/Pearce) may be assumed to contain the same erotic element.

Turning away from these salacious figures, the real Sanderson emerges in his tavern gallants and wenches, his gladiators, and his press gang set. Many of these are in pairs, ideally suited for making into dioramas. Equally effective is a group of Normans harrying Saxon villagers, an 80mm Sepp Dietrich and a 75mm Gustavus Adolphus (both for Acorn), and a series of Swedish monarchs for Sebastian Tamm. However, the models which have made the greatest impact are those in 54mm done for Hinchliffe in 1975, comprising a large number of figures to illustrate the Battle of Isandhlwana, each being made of a number of interchangeable parts so that conversion can be effected, a fact that has resulted in a number of dioramas being made. A series of Spanish infantry (1811-15), also for Hinchliffe, confirms the verdict that Sanderson is one of the most notable of contemporary sculptors.

Sandoe, Maurene. *See* Men O' War.

Sandor, W., Germany (fl.1965). Minor publisher of flats.

Sandow, D., Berlin (d.c.1970). A maker of flats, specializing in the Boer War and South-West Africa. He also engraved for Schirmer and Tobinnus. His moulds are now owned by Scholtz. Mark: DSW.

Sandré, Charles, Paris (fl.1920). Expert maker of 38cm mannequins clothed in natural materials.

Sandré, Charles. While a prisoner-of-war on Dartmoor during the Napoleonic wars, he carved a remarkable series of 14-inch-high wooden models, clothed in actual material, with metal accoutrements. The collection was illustrated in *The Illustrated London News*, 25 June, 1932.

Sandy, John. *See* Britannia Ltd.

Sangster, Lynn, Dover, Kent. A professional painter and converter of Historex kits. He acts as English agent for that firm.

Sanquez, Madrid (c.1940-50). A manufacturer of extremely attenuated 50mm solids, and a reasonably good range of 30mm flats.

Santessonska Tenngjuteriet, Stockholm (1843-1930). A prolific manufacturer of 35mm flats, 40mm semi-solids, and 50mm and 8cm solids. The firm was founded by Nils Abraham in 1839, but no military subjects were made until 1884. Abraham himself died in 1886. The flats, mainly of Swedish history, were of sound quality, but most probably engraved in Germany. The semi-solids (definitely from German moulds) included figures for Lützen, Breitenfeld, Narva and Poltava. The solids, of equestrian Swedish monarchs, were made in three pieces.

Sanz, José-Maria, Las Avenas, Vizcaya, Spain (1973-). Publisher of a series of cut-out cardboard figures (14 x 8cm) of the Spanish Army of 1910.

SARDINE-TIN MODELS. *See* Stamped Tin.

Saunders, E. W., Taunton, Somerset (fl.1960-70). A maker of commissioned models, he used 54mm solids for the American Civil War, the Seven Years' War and the Napoleonic period. He then began to investigate the possibilities of the 6- to 9-inch figure, making the torsos from plastic wood turned out from plaster moulds, the heads of plaster from Silicone rubber moulds, and the whole figure then clothed in natural materials.

68 **Sanderson.** '*Isandhlwana*', *models assembled and painted by Norman Abbey (Greenwood and Ball).*

Saunders, N., Metal Products Ltd, London. Producers of Stadden's Buckingham Pewter models, his chess sets, ballet dancers by Gerald Hitcher and Victorian characters by Peter Mleczko. (*See also* Sovereign Figures.)

Saunders, Roger, London (1974-   ). One of the most consistently excellent makers of 54mm solids. He has designed for Monarch (Landschnechts and 20 First World War figures), for New Hope (24 in all, ending in 1976), C. Robinson, Cavalier, Phoenix (4 models in 1977), and The Franklin Mint (a series of 43 English monarchs in 60mm, issued by subscription, under the aegis of the Society of Portrait Sculptors). He also works in 77mm and does much work to commission.

'Saunderson'. *See* Sanderson, C.

Scad, Germany (1977-   ). Home-casting kits of semi-flats of Napoleonics and the Franco-Prussian War.

Scale Specialities Miniatures (B. Gordon) USA (1972-   ). A firm founded by Beverly Gordon which has made 54mm solids of German paratroopers, the French Foreign Legion, and a Flying Column officer of the Free French Forces, 1940, in tropical dress with a desert turban.

Schalk Bros. *See* Schiercke, H.C.

Schaper, C., Hanover (fl.1846). Engraver of flats 5cm tall for the widow of Demong (e.g. at Braunsweig Museum).

Scharlowsky, Günter, Delmenhorst, W. Germany. Engraver and publisher of flats, especially of the Second World War, some figures having separate attachments. He has also designed for Heydorn, Sandow, Schirmer and Sollner.

Scharwalder Verlag (Editions Henri Mench, Paris), Freudenstadt, W. Germany. Publishers of historical buildings in paper, forming dioramas.

Scheibert, Teuber & Edward, Vienna (1882-1930). Publishers of flats and semi-flats, specializing in the Thirty Years' War and Austrians and French of the early 19th century, many of which were engraved by Krunert. The business was carried on later by a female member of the family until 1960.

Scheid Miniatures (John Scheid) Easton, Pennsylvania (c.1948-60). A maker of fine quality 54mm solids of American historical figures and uniforms and European troops of 1900-1918. The models were sold unpainted, and only to selected clients. He also made commissioned models, and did some masters for Military Miniatures.

Scheidel, H., Rottweil, W. Germany. Producer of large-size flats. (*Klio*)

Scheinemann, David, London (1974-   ). A maker of 30mm American Civil War solids for 'Tradition' who also assisted Caton in making 54mm models.

Scheller, Carl, Kassel (c.1840-1924). One of the manufacturers of flats who joined the 'Association of Tinsmiths and Tinfigure Manufacturers'. Before 1893 he used the services of Frank as an engraver. The last of the family, a great-grandson, died in 1924.

Schellhorn, Johann Christoph, Nuremberg (c.1800). A manufacturer of flats who learned the art from Hilpert. Mark: J.S.

Schepp, Carl Gottfried and **Robert Julius,** Breslau (c.1840). Manufacturers of flats, and members of the 'Association of Tinsmiths and Tinfigure Manufacturers'.

Schiercke, Henry C., Germany/Ghent, New York. A distributor of home-casting moulds between the two World Wars. These were of flats and semi-flats and in-

cluded a remarkable pressure cannon. The moulds were later purchased by Schalk Brothers.

Schildknecht, Conrad & Son, Fürth (1840-c.1900). A manufacturer of flats, semi-solids and solids (the latter made about 1870). He bought Besold's business in about 1890. Marks: K. SCHILDNECHT; C.S.; C.SCH.

Schildkrot, Mannheim (1977-   ). Manufacturer of home-casting moulds.

Schiller, Ulla, Vienna (1973-   ). Publisher of flats, designed by Winter, engraved by Kovar, of the Thirty Years' War, and Austrians of 1780 and 1914.

Schilling Gotha (1860-80). Engraver of flats for Krause.

Schirmer, Friedrich, Hanover (1899-1973). A maker and publisher of 20 and 30mm flats. He began making his own moulds (using Frank as an engraver) in 1937, turning later to the smaller figures. He was especially interested in the Seven Years' War, particularly the uniforms of the Hanoverian regiments, and also made diorama accessories. Other excursions were made into the 1670-1700 and the Napoleonic periods. He was intensely interested in all activities of the world of flats, and for many years edited *Die Zinnfigur*, abandoning this to start the production of *Alte und Neue Zinnfigur*. He is accredited with the introduction of the 'kombination' figure.

Schlott, Hans, Germany (fl.1580). A silversmith who created the Rudolph II clock in the British Museum.

Schmid Bros Inc. *See* Hudson Pewter.

Schmid, Manuel. *See* M.S. Tank.

Schmidt, Ernst. *See* Miniplast Miniatur-Plastiken.

Schmidt, F. His collection of paper sheets was auctioned at Strasbourg in 1972.

Schmidt, Hans, Wuppertal (1960-   ). A publisher and designer of flats, mainly of the Napoleonic era, including Brunswickers, Dutch KGL and British.

Schmidt, Samuel S., USA. Designer for Grey Iron Casting Corp.

Schneider Gebr Gieffssformen Fabrik, Leipzig (c.1913-c.1928). Manufacturers of very crude 45-60mm semi-flats for juveniles. Some of the moulds were purchased by the St Louis Lead Soldier Co.; others are now being re-issued by Greiner.

Schneider, J., Strasbourg (c.1930). Publisher of paper sheets.

Schnug, L. Strasbourg (1908-20). Publishers of paper sheets.

Scholtz, Hans Günther. *See* Berliner Zinnfiguren Werner Scholtz.

Scholtz, R. Überlingen, W. Germany (1968-   ). Publisher of flats of the Thirty Years' War.

Scholtz, Werner. *See* Berliner Zinnfiguren Werner Scholtz.

Scholz, Joseph, Mainz (1860-1940; possibly also after 1945). Publishers of paper sheets of all countries (14 sheets alone of the Reichswehr), average size 13 x 16 inches, together with cardboard village cut-outs.

Schoppen, W.C.J., The Hague (1974-   ). Maker of 54mm solids. He is also experimenting with 200 and 300mm figures in polyester, with cloth and metal.

Schotts, William C. *See* Scrimshander, The.

Schrader, Hanover (19th-20th century). Manufacturer of flats.

Schradin, Gottlieb. *See* Lorenz, J.G.

Schreiber, Carl, Fürth (19th-20th century). Manufacturer of flats and possibly semi-solids.

69 **Schreiber.** *Delightful examples of peasant costume (Tennfigurmuseum, Leksand).*

Schreiber, J.F., Esslingen (c.1844-   ). Publishers of paper and cardboard sheets of houses and castles; one of the oldest surviving firms specializing in this medium. Sheets of a military nature appear to have been issued only around 1910.

Schreiber, Magnus, Lidingö, Sweden (c.1968-   ). A maker of 54mm solids to commission and for his friends. An ex-naval officer, he began making models about 1968. He starts with a prototype in kit form, made in Isopon, and any models not commissioned are issued in a limited edition of ten copies each. His interest is largely confined to the 1790-1813 period of Swedish history. The sculpting is crisp and elegant, his horses delightful, and his painting follows the restrained Scandinavian type. For the Army Museum, Stockholm, he has made a complete squadron of the Royal Pomeranian Mounted Legion ('The Green Squadron'). This unit was formed in 1813 in Stralsund, Swedish Pomerania, and consisted of 60 volunteers under Major Ernst von Quistorp. It was disbanded in 1814. For the Tennfigurmuseum at Leksand he has made or converted 70 delightful models of Swedish national costume.

Schreiber, O., Waldheim (fl.1867). A firm which exhibited children's toys in tin and wood at the Paris Exposition in 1867.

Schreiners Söhne (Anton Schreiner), Nabburg, W. Germany (1973-   ). Publishers of flats.

Schreuder & Olsson Leksakfabrick, Stockholm (1896-1920). Manufacturers of naive 40mm semi-solids. The moulds were of German origin, and the range included troops of the South African War and European armies between the two World Wars.

Schroetter, J.N., Strasbourg (1791). Publisher of paper sheets.

Schubert, Dieter, Grenzach-Wyhlen, W. Germany (1977-

). Publisher of flats of country folk from the 14th to the 19th century. (*Klio*).

Schuco, (c.1930-?) Germany. A firm noted for mechanized tin-plate vehicles. About 1960 they produced some poor quality plaster composition models.

Schudin, T. *See* Penny Srl.

Schultz, Friedrich J., Stuttgart/Mainz (19th century). Publisher of paper sheets.

Schulz, Dieter, Berlin (1976-   ). Producer of 30mm flats.

Schundler, J., Leipzig (c.1850). One of the members of the 'Association of Tinsmiths and Tinfigure Manufacturers', later joining Bunau in the production of semi-flats.

Schutz, Matthias, Bavaria (fl.1674). A woodcarver who was commissioned to make model troops for the Prince Elector of Bavaria.

Schwartz, A. *See* Com-E-Tec.

Schwartz, K., Pittsburgh, Pennsylvania. A maker, to commission, of 10-inch models in papiermâché.

Schwarz, Dieter, Hannstetter (fl.1960). A maker of flats which he himself engraved.

Schwarz, F.A.O., Illinois. Agent to whom Britains supplied specially assembled specimen boxes.

Schwarz. *See* Spenküch.

Schweigger, Nuremberg (1763-1886). One of the earliest German firms to make flats: founded by Christian G. (1763-1829), succeeded by Ludwig F. (d.1886). Besold served an apprenticeship with the firm.

Schweizer, Diessen-Ammersee (1796-   ). The oldest firm of makers of flats still in existence. Founded in 1796 by Adam (d.1848), succeeded by Anton (d.1896), his widow Babette and her son Adam (1896-1914), Anton's widow Wilhelmine and their two children Wilhelm and Anny, and finally the present Babette. The most romantic and at the same time the most naive of the rococo period, their 'Paradise' set will serve as an excellent example. The sizes vary from 20 to 40mm up to 15cm, and one only has to glance through their catalogue to see how individual in style are their products, and how free from other influences they have remained. Apart from the Adam and Eve group, they made a beautifully child-like series of sets of the Nativity and Corpus Christi processions, fairy tales and country dances. They were, however, not above piracy, copying exactly Hilpert's Frederick the Great. Another unusual feature is a range of filigree metal hedges and doll's furniture, still being issued. In 1908 a medieval battle-scene was designed for them by Hans Rohm, but generally speaking military subjects in their earlier period are not prominent, their *ritters* and trumpeters being particularly ungainly. In

70 **Schweizer.** *'Paradise'. Late 18th-century flats (from Ortmann).*

view of their charming earlier pieces, it is quite a shock to see a particularly crude series of 40mm semi-flats of the Franco-Prussian War, which are not illustrated in their catalogue, but are featured in books by Alberini and Mackenzie (in both instances from recent re-casts). The ascription was so puzzling that confirmation was obtained from the firm that they were indeed the makers. The true Schweizer's are to be seen in excellent examples in Ortmann (plates 76-84).

Schwetter, J.N., Strasbourg (1791). Publisher of paper sheets.

Scimitar Miniatures, Canada (1974-). What purported to be a new firm, beginning operations with 54mm solids of a Zaporozhian Cossack Hetman (1901), H.H. Maharaja Sir Pratap Singh Bahadur (1900), and an Indian Army cavalry officer (1900), was advertised by a Canadian dealer and an English agency in 1974, but repeated enquiries proved fruitless.

Scott, Dr Allan C. *See* Heritage.

Scott, R.G. *See* Micro-Mold Plastics Ltd.

Scottish Soldiers (Thomas Park), Glasgow (1977-). Maker of 75mm metal kits, starting with an equestrian Queen Elizabeth II and Scottish infantry and officers, continuing soon afterwards with models in 90mm.

Screiber, J.G., Germany (1870-1920). Publisher of sheets for the juvenile theatre. During the 1880s they employed Th. Guggenberger, who raised the standard of design with several fine sheets of medieval costume and a military camp. (*Newman*)

Scrimshander, The (William C. Schotts) USA (1971-c.1974). Maker of a small series of solids, issued in kit form, under the title American Heritage, and signed on the base in varying forms. The sizes and subjects were disparate, and included a Texas Ranger, Jim Bridger, a Plains Indian chief, a Mountain Man, and a Vaquero, all in 60mm, and a crouching Indian brave reaching over his shoulder for an arrow from his quiver (54mm), which is the best of an undistinguished collection.

Scrine, T. One-time director of Britains and designer of a few labels for them.

Scroby, Janet and **Frank.** *See* Blenheim Military Models; Nostalgia.

Scruby, Jack, Visalia/Cambria, California (1953-). One of the earliest of the post-war makers of solids, 20, 30, 40, 54 and 90mm models. A prolific producer, in 1953 he and Frank Conley formed Historical Miniature Figures, with 54mm models of no particular quality. The partnership dissolved in 1958 and Scruby began producing wargame models. He had already been making these for his own collection, and has since issued vast numbers of Napoleonic and American Civil War figures. The 9mm models, begun in 1970, are sold in groups of three, attached to a solid metal base, making them difficult to remove. Gunson says that he supplied Scruby with designs for models in 90mm, but this cannot be verified. Somewhere about 1965 he called himself Armbrite Industries, but later resorted back to his own name. As a writer, he began *The War Game Digest* in 1957, which lasted until 1962, when it was superceded by *Table Top Talk*. In 1978 he began selling in limited numbers specimens (painted by himself) of Britains-type 'toy' soldiers.

SCULPTURE COPYRIGHT ACT. The protection against plagiarism given by this Act of 1814 was conditional on the proprietor 'having caused his or their name to be put on every sculpture before the same shall be put forth or published'. It was also necessary for the models (in the context of the date of the Act not necessarily applying to toy soldiers) to be anatomically and technically correct, and that they displayed artistic skill and merit. Although the Act was archaic, Britains successfully invoked it against several firms who were pirating their products.

Sea Gull Models (A.M. Campbell), London. A firm of dealers who have actively, and sometimes confusingly, acted either as agents for, or commissioned models from, various English makers. In the early 1970s they were the sole agents for Ciuffo and for Valda. In 1975 they announced a 'splendid' King Kenneth II of Scotland in 160mm, with winged helmet, in metal with cloth additions, whose authorship is still unknown. In the event the casting of the 37 different parts proved so difficult that production was deferred indefinitely. A series entitled Real Models in 90mm was started for them in 1976 by William Hearne, subsequently being enlarged in size to 120 and 140mm, and added to in the following year by Richard Almond. The designing, casting and assembly of these were long situated in different places, causing the firm to set up a special base in 1979 in Earitch, Cambridgeshire, adding at the same time a sub-range entitled 'Masterworks', the first three models (1980) in 130, 100 and 90mm being by David Grieve and Colin Bramwell. In the same year they released models of the Chinese T'Sung dynasty in 54mm by George Haines and Imperial German cavalry by Martin Feldwick, followed later by a 'Personality' range in 80mm, the first model being of Alexander the Great, dismounted, with horse, by James Staines. In 1978 a 'New Series Classics' group appeared, this time in 100mm, in a limited edition of 250 castings. Other makers may well be represented in their production, but it was not always possible to discover the authorship of individual models. They also publish a series of card models including a fine and elaborate one of York Minster.

Seamer Products Ltd, Hull (1979-). The firm has long made latex and plastic moulds and toys and games. In 1979 they issued a 'Historic' range of 54, 75 and 90mm metal models in kit form, made for them by a firm whose name they would not disclose. Future models were to be made for them by Graham Cattle.

Sebastian Miniatures. *See* Baston, Prescott.

Seeley Service & Cooper Ltd. *See* Papermade Models.

Segal, Philip, Christchurch, Hants (1938-50). A minor manufacturer of 54mm hollow-casts of Westerners, Cossacks, Guards, RAF, Highlanders, modern troops, Marines, Nigerian Rifles, Canadian North-West Mounted Police, and Australian infantry. A set of footballers is very rare. Also produced a semi-flat 1¼-inch series of wild animals, farm animals and people, one box of which is entitled 'Dorset Box No. 16 Farmyard Series'.

SEGOM (Sociétié d'Édition Générale d'Objets Moulés) Paris (c.1950-). One of the first manufacturers of polystyrene 54mm models in semi-kit form. Where they differ from later manufacturers is that their kits consist of a solid torso, solid buttocks, thighs and legs in one piece, and separate arms, legs and equipment, rather than a multitude of tiny thin pieces. Where broad-skirted figures are required (as for the 17th-18th century), these are moulded to the torso, and the

71   SEGOM. *Later-style plastic kits (Author)*.

buttocks and legs fitted beneath them. The horses are in two or four pieces, and the whole is produced in a pleasant cream-coloured material. Occasionally hats are trimmed with simulated lace, weapons are separate, as are flags and standards in stiff parchment-like paper. Early models were extremely clumsy, with pouter-pigeon chests, but with the advent of Peter Biéville a greatly improved model appeared. Wargame figures in 25mm (foot and mounted, the riders detachable) are clumsy, with white or dismal chocolate-coloured horses. At their best, the 54mm models are most attractive when painted, and there is a range of spare parts from Elizabethan times to 1945. Mark: MADE IN FRANCE.

Seibt, Vienna, (1977–). Publisher of flats. (*Klio*)

Seidel, Ernst, Germany. Designer and engraver of flats.

Seix y Barral, Barcelona. Publishers of paper sheets whose original foundation date is unknown, but who are still in business. [*Balil*]

Selchow & Richter Co., New York (1910–30). Manufacturers of 54mm hollow-casts of the modern American army for the juvenile trade.

Selcol Products Ltd, London (1955–60). Manufacturers of 54mm plastic models and 12-inch polystyrene kits. The smaller models were oval in shape, and included a small range of medieval figures for which the horses were in polystyrene. The larger kits, of Richard I, Elizabeth I and Henry VIII, were designed by E. Meister, and are the finest of their kind.

Seldenslagh, Brussels (fl.1950–60). An eccentric collector who owned a clothier's shop, and invited favoured patrons to an inner room in which his collection was kept. It is possible that some of these were made by himself.

Selley, Albert. *See* M.W.

Selwyn Miniatures. *See* Selwyn-Smith, R.

Selwyn-Smith, Roy, London (1951–). One of the most intelligent, capable and versatile makers of the models of the present century. In 1951 he made a small range of medieval knights, now extremely rare, designed by Madlener and sponsored by Gottstein, for export to the United States only, under the name Selwyn Miniatures. They were not a financial success and were perhaps ahead of their time, but Britains stepped in and purchased the moulds, subsequently issuing them as 'Knights of Agincourt', when they had an immediate success. One or two of the originals so impressed

Courtenay that he purchased castings and painted them himself [*Greenhill*]. Selwyn-Smith then joined Zang, a Polish refugee who had started a small plastics business. The models they jointly produced began to achieve such popularity that once more Britains became interested and acquired both the designs and the designer, for some time retaining the trade mark of Zang under the footstand. Eventually they were re-named Herald. Smith has made a valuable contribution to the art of the plastic figure, especially in his non-military designs, a set of Polar explorers being a masterpiece. Apart from published works, he made a number of models for his own pleasure, including one in 40mm which was included in the 'Waterloo' exhibition staged by the British Model Soldier Society. Gradually his eyesight failed, and he is now a director of Britains, leaving the designing of figures to other craftsmen. (*See also* Britains; Zang, M.*)

Senff. *See* Paper, folded.

Sentinel Series. *See* Almark.

Sentry Box, London (c.1965). Manufacturers of tiny metal tanks.

Sentry Box, The (J. Lovell Barnes, Yvonne Edmonds, Mrs P.T. Edmonds), London/Wisborough Green, Sussex (1952–). Soon after the Second World War several makers began large plaster models, and in 1952 Barnes went into partnership with Nancy Wynne-Jones in a range of 12cm figures representing the British Army. Owing, however, to the fragility of the substance used, they decided to 'cupronize' them with metal to ensure strength. A number were designed by Barnes and others by Riviere and Hunt, and all were somewhat lacking in detail. At the same time they inherited a small miscellaneous line of 54mm models from the Carbago venture. When Miss Wynne-Jones retired in 1965 her place was taken by Yvonne Edmonds, who had been a kind of 'Girl Friday' since 1954. Having in the course of her duties picked up a knowledge of production processes, she began an all-out effort at re-creation and it is from about this date that the present system of newly-designed, all-metal foot and mounted models in kit form appeared. Constant changes were made to existing models, some being ruthlessly re-designed. The resultant figures are infinitely better than the original ones and form a worthy tribute to the glory of British regimental uniforms. In 1975 a numbered 'Jubilee' range of limited editions appeared, including models of a Royal Scots Dragoon Guards drum horse, and, strangely enough, George Washington. They were originally intended to be sold as fully assembled units, but later in the year were made available as kits. In the 54mm range the historic personalities are unimpressive, but of late an attractive series of civilians has emerged, even though the facial detail leaves much to be desired. These include gentlemen of 1700 and 1740, and ladies of 1650, 1750 and 1906, the latter being a basic casting with alternative head-dresses but each with an open parasol. One or two of the models are designed to sit on chairs made by Phoenix. A special commission was a set of models for the Duke of Beaufort.

Series 77 (Pat Bird) Gravesend/Canoga Park, California (1970–). In 1970 the first of what was to prove a very long and interesting range of solid models in what was then a new size (77mm) was issued by Pat Bird and John Tassell. Both had previously worked as animators and dioramists for 'Tradition' and the first batch of models was obviously derivative. Although announced as being in 77mm, the size was nearer 75mm. The models were at times awkward in anatomy although the sculpture was excellent; they were over-painted, with the emphasis on large oval-shaped eyes and very emphatic creases around the noses. Happily this was rectified as a result of criticism by collectors. Napoleonic types predominated, but, after Tassell left to go free-lancing, Bird began a complete reconstruction of the existing series of some thirty or so models, redesigning them in a true 77mm size. They were issued in groups, usually of six figures entitled 'Stages'. To an historian the task of recording which models formed the original and which the later 'Stage' is impossible, owing to a number of the earlier models having either been completely withdrawn or so completely altered as to be unrecognizable. Eventually the tally of 'Stages' was 15 (actually 14, as 'Stage 13' for some unknown reason was never made). They were: 1. French infantry 1804-1815; 2. French Hussars 1794-1815; 3. French Lancers 1807-1815; 4. British Cavalry 1790-1815; 5. British infantry 1815; 6. Pilots 1939-45; 7. Landschnechts; 8. Canadian Militia; 9. Greeks, 500-300 BC; 10. English Civil War; 11. Camel Troopers (French and Turkish) 1453-1793; 12. Warriors in history, including an Assyrian archer, a gladiator, a samurai, Henry VIII (no warrior this!), a Prussian Fusilier 1776, George Washington, and a French Foreign Legionnaire 1905; 14. Prussian Heavy Cavalry 1900; 15. Romans AD 100. They were normally on foot, with an occasional mounted figure. At times there was too much facial likeness, in the Greeks almost amounting to vacuity, but the chariot was most impressive, and a fascinating pair was of a Greek warrior carrying his son on his shoulder. A number of the Greeks were completely nude and were subjected by agents to the crudest painting. An attractive feature was a double-tier circular footstand which lent an air of distinction to the figure. The idea of 'Stages' appears to have come to an end about 1974, when models in 54mm (some designed by Jenkinson) were announced, and the following

year a project was underway in which Embleton was to design figures in pairs. However, Bird had for some time contemplated moving to the United States, and it was not until 1976 that the Jenkinson models were issued under the name of Nonsuch and the Embleton pairs began to appear. Since then Bird has been concentrating on single, disparate models, many in 54mm, but also including a multi-kit Landschnecht and a peg-legged pirate, both in 154mm, and both anatomically suspect. In 1978 Bird announced that he was re-issuing the original 'Series 77', and the same year saw the appearance of a Gatling gun team, with two horses and two men.

Serig, F.A., Leipzig (1815-29). Producer of flats.

Seton, G.R. *See* Warrior Miniatures.

Seyboth, A., Strasbourg (1744). Publisher of paper sheets.

Seyfried, Strasbourg (1744). Publisher of paper sheets.

SFJB, Paris (c.1910). Manufacturer of composite models. A box, sold at Phillips' auction on 11 December, 1969, and purchased by Wade, contained French Infantry, the rifles detached, and the figures held in place by small metal clamps, the outside of the box marked '*soldats colouriers inoffensives depose*'.

Sforza Castle, Milan. The *Club Italiano Modellismo Militare* has for several years running held here an international exhibition of fine models, at which craftsmen of all nations are invited to show their products.

Shackman, USA (1978-). Publishers of a cardboard fort with eight tiny plastic models made in Hong Kong. (*Newman*).

Shakespeare, J.D., Blackpool (1973-). A maker of 13-inch commissioned foot figures, with mounted ones in proportion, of cataloy paste resin, with occasionally barbola, lead and wood added.

Sharna Ware Mfg Co. Ltd. *See* Cherilea.

Sharp's Toffee, London (c.1935). Producers of a hollow-cast 'Mr Sharp'. [*Wade*]

Sheet Tin. Thin tin, cut out and affixed to a base. In the late 19th and early 20th centuries the design was usually printed in colours, but some modern exponents (e.g. Weiss and Debler, and, says Nicollier, Varloud) do their own painting.

Shideler, Mrs Linda J., Visalia, California (1972-). A free-lance artist who works both for her own pleasure and to commission. She has two styles of procedure - either to design from scratch in 54mm using plastic or metal on a nude torso, or by direct conversion. She tackles all periods, but is especially fond of American troops prior to the Second World War. An imaginative Merlin might equally serve as a portrait for Tolkien's Gandalph. Her models are to be seen at the Los Angeles County Museum.

Shimek, Colonel Joseph. *See* Potsdam Zinnfiguren.

Shingle, Paul. *See* Eagle Miniatures.

SHIPS. The range of constructed or individually made ship models is outside the scope of this book, but it should be mentioned that many model-soldier makers, old and contemporary, made and are making scale-model vessels as an ancillary to their normal range. Flats of rigged ships, for example, were made in the 18th century and Heinrichsen produced a notable series of warships and trading vessels, as also did Krause and Heyde (semi-solid), examples being illustrated in Ortmann's book. Haffner made a 'Grand Review at

72
Series 77. *An early issue in 77mm solid showing the influence of Stadden (Pat Bird).*

Spithead', comprising eight battleships together with their jolly-boats, all in semi-flat, while Meyerheine departed from his usual civilians to make ships in 40mm. Mignot included a long range of modern warships, and Segom four ships of the line from the time of Louis XIV to the Second Empire. Viking longships were made by Elastolin, and pirated by an anonymous Spanish firm. Amati make larger vessels, and are the only firm that can be traced who make 22mm figures of mariners to go with them. There are, of course, a number of firms whose sole output consists of waterline models.

Shipton, W. *See* Trojan.

Sibbitt, Thomas, Schaumberg, Illinois. A free-lance designer who did all the original H/R models and those of Miniature Americana. He has also worked for Valiant.

Siborne, Captain William, London/Dublin (1797-1849). Assistant Military Secretary to successive Commanders of the Forces in Ireland (1826-43); Secretary of the Military Asylum, Chelsea (1844-49). Author of an account of the Battle of Waterloo, at which he was present. He was commissioned by the Commander-in-Chief to supervise the making of a model of the terrain on which the battle was fought. For this he received a first payment of £350 (of a promised £1,400), the rest of which was apparently repudiated by a change of Government, forcing him to place the model on exhibition so that he could recoup part at least of what was owing to him. This, the first of two models, including 190,000 half-inch pin-like figures in the round, occupying an area of 18ft x 7ft 10 inches (scale 9ft to 1 mile), was shown at the Egyptian Hall in 1838, was for years at the RUSI, and then at the National Army Museum for repairs before its transference in the future to Stratfield Saye. The second model, one of a number intended to embrace various moments in the battle, but never realized, was made between 1840 and 1844, of approximately the same size, but this time on a scale of 15ft to 1 mile. It portrays the charge of the Heavy Cavalry round La Haye Sainte. This time the models are individually identifiable, with movable arms and removable headgear and breastplates, each being about 1½ inches in height. This model is now at Dover Castle. A few models were left over, and W.Y. Carman owns one or two. A fully detailed history of the models and Siborne's financial difficulties are given in Garratt, *Model Soldiers: a Collector's Guide* (pp.65-68). The author had been under the impression that Siborne himself had made the models, as no mention of payment to anybody is contained in Siborne's voluminous correspondence, but it now seems more likely that they were made in Germany. Contemporary appreciation of the two models is shown by extracts from papers of the time, which include *The Morning Post, The Globe, United Service Gazette, Court Journal, Courier, Naval and Military Gazette, John Bull, The Times* and *The Atlas:-*

'The model is on the scale of about nine feet to the mile, and gives a complete and most vivid representation of the scene of action. every village, every house and farmyard, every knot of trees, every undulation of surface, every field, nay, every crop of wheat which the field bore at the time . . . is given with the closest accuracy. . . The position of all the various troops engaged at the moment selected for representation is marked out with the utmost exactness, and in the most graphic manner.

The models of all the buildings and natural objects, the figures of the soldiers and the horses are, in every instance, elaborately executed.' 'The ensemble is very striking. . . the smoke is formed by cotton of the finest texture, attenuated to an almost impalpable substance.' 'The battlefield and the details are most exquisitely modelled . . . every individual figure is a perfect study-every group is full of life, the figures are large enough to allow the recognition of the persons most distinguished during the action.' 'The mechanical part of the model is very well managed, the little figures carefully constructed and painted . . . they seem to start to life and to carry the spectator's imagination into the very heat of the action. In point of execution, the model is perfect, but it possesses even a higher attraction than its artistic excellence. It is a national momento of one of England's most glorious triumphs.'

Sichart, Joseph, Vienna (1825-). A colourful circus in semi-flats by this maker is illustrated in Ortmann (plate 128).

Sideria Miniatures (Carlo de Marchis), Rome (1974-). Maker of attractive 54 and 94mm solids in kit form, with oval bases, of Italian forces 1650-1870. The earliest models were of Romans and the Papal Guard, which the maker himself deprecates. Certainly the larger models do not compare with those in 54mm size.

Siege Weapons (medieval). *See* Artillery.

Siemens, K. *See* Simmy.

Sigaard Figures, Denmark. Listed in a Danish dealer's catalogue in 1970 as producing 54mm solids of Robinson Crusoe, William Tell and Hamlet. The dealer was not listed in the provision of any further information.

Signature series. *See* Black Watch, The.

Silbermann, H.R.G., Strasbourg (1800-1876). The most prolific of the Strasbourg school of paper sheet producers, at one time turning out some 130,000 sheets per year. In 1845 he perfected his own method of printing in oils, and heightened many sheets with gold and silver. A curious offshoot was the discovery in 1900 of a remainder, which was put to use by a shoe company who printed their advertisement on the verso (*Newman*). The original company was taken over by Fischbach and Kieffer until 1914 under the name '*L'Imprimerie Alsacienne*'. Modern reprints are made by The Paper Soldier.

Silhol, A. Maker of a diorama of the parade of the French army before the Czar and the Czarina and President Loubet at Betheny, near Rheims, in 1901. The maker was present at the parade, and took 32 years on the construction of the diorama, utilizing some 12,000 semi-solids. (*Compiègne Museum*)

Silk, Allan. *See* Cavalier.

Silvercross (A. Graham), London (1970-74). A minor maker of 20mm wargame figures of Napoleonic and British First World War figures. An ancient British chariot is pleasing.

Sima. *See* Maier, Sixtus.

Simbas Arts Ltd. Hoddesdon, Herts (1979-). Makers of military plaques in relief, in frames with velvet backgrounds.

Simmy (K. Siemens), Lüdenscheid, W. Germany (1958-?). A minor manufacturer of poor-quality 8cm plaster composition figures of Westerners and animals.

Simo, Pere & Josep, Barcelona (1790-1840). Publishers of paper sheets.

Simon, Pierre, Paris. Collaborated in the Mignot flats.

Sinclair Toys Ltd, Romford, Essex (1975-). Manufacturers of materials (i.e. moulds and plaster of Paris) for the construction of medieval castles. These can be quite attractive when completed, and numerous permutations may be made, including the incorporation of buttresses and ecclesiastical pillars for chapels. They are marketed under the name of Castlemaster. Another range of artificial stones and bricks for battle scenes carries the name Instant Terrain.

Singleton, A.M., USA (1940). Publishers of pre-cut, press-out card figures, 1 inch high, with stands, of the American War of Independence, the War of 1812 and the Civil War.

Sisley, Jenny, London (1978-). Designer of a three-sheet cut-out of the Tower of London.

Sivhed, Thorold, Trelleborg, Sweden (b.1915-). The foremost modern publisher of flats in Sweden, concentrating mainly on the Thirty Years' War (including several examples of multiple figures on one stand) with an excursion into Grecian times. He employs as designers Martin Block, Roland Backman, William Ericsson and Mano Winter, and as engravers Franke, Knoll, Peter Kovar and Hans Walz.

Sjosward, Holm, Sweden. Designed 40mm solids of Vikings and the 15th-century Battle of Brunkeberg for Tenngjuteriet Mars.

Skelton M. *See* Redington.

Skinner, Denzil, Hartley Wintney, Hants (fl.1965). Manufacturer of tiny metal tanks.

Skinner, William, *See* Jacobite Miniatures.

S.K. Models (S. Kemp), Morden, Surrey (1977-). Began with scenic bases for the display of models by Kemp himself. These were soon followed by the actual models. In 1978 he issued a weird eleven-piece dragon and an equally curious 65mm draped skeleton with a scythe. The following year a 1st Bombay Lancer officer (1897) appeared in 130mm, being the first of a 'Connoisseur Figure' range in cold-cast aluminium.

Skybird, (A.J. Holloday & Co.) London (1939-51). Manufacturers of a wide range of 30mm solids of the British army (1939-51), also some unusual ones of the Royal Flying Corps, with accessories. They were revived in 1970 by Douglas Miniatures.

Skytrex, England. Manufacturers of metal tanks and 25mm models under the name Conquest. In 1978 they made a German 800mm railway gun in 21 pieces.

Slonim, A., J. and S. *See* Comet.

S.M.C., Czechoslovakia. (1960-). Manufacturers of 60mm plaster composition models of the modern Czech Army. [*Kearton*]

Smit, J., Holland. Restored a model of the Dutch Light Brigade at Leiden Museum in 1973.

Smith, A, New Orleans, Louisiana (c.1970-). Maker of 54mm solids including the Brigade of Guards, US Marine Corps and German troops 1939-45.

Smith, C.E. and Mrs Margaret E., Canada. Assisted in making the diorama of the Battle of Waterloo at the Canadian Forces Base, Chilliwack.

Smith, George H. *See* Ye Olde Soldier.

Smith, William, Essex, Connecticut (1975-). A freelance designer, especially for Superior Miniatures.

Smyth, Lieut-Colonel M., England. Assisted in the construction of the dioramas of Arroyo dos Molinos and the Landing Zone at Arnhem at the Border Regiment

Museum, Carlisle.

Snyder, Willard P., USA (c.1945). Probably one of the first Americans to take an interest in flats, he designed American Civil War figures for Ochel to make and export to America. (*See* Ochel, *Sorten Liste E,* numbers P.703, 757-9, 763-5, S705-6.)

Société d'Édition Générale d'Objets Moulés. See SEGOM.

SOCIETIES. When kindred spirits decide to gather together at periodic intervals for the mutual airing of views and opinions the usual result is the eventual formation of a society. Small bands of enthusiasts undoubtedly met one with the other informally during the early part of the present century, and it was from these gatherings that the present societies evolved. The first of these was the *Société des Amateurs de Jouets et Jeux Anciens* (1905), which did not confine itself strictly to the model or toy soldier and soon went out of existence. The first strictly military one was the German 'Klio' (also founded in 1905), followed after a long interval by the French (1931) and British (1935) Societies. They all exercised a profound effect on the collectors of their respective countries. Others quickly followed and today they are to be found in most parts of the civilized world. If conducted by officers with tact and courtesy they can be extremely beneficial to the collecting world. A newcomer, however, or one who for geographical or domestic reasons is only able to make a rare appearance, may well form the impression that it is a 'closed shop' and diffident collectors are apt to resign. One of the troubles of the fast-growing interest in the hobby is that large societies become even larger, and it is up to the President to ensure that the occasional visitor is welcomed and not left to drift around. This difficulty overcome, much mutual benefit may be derived. The sight of other collectors' models is stimulating, often leading to conversation regarding the origin or the painting. Exhibitions (usually accompanied by a prize-giving ceremony) are frequent; indeed, fierce competition is apparent among the contestants for the cup or spoon or whatever it is. Generally it is the most spectacular model that receives the greatest acclamation, which is a pity, as many a quietly-conceived and restrained model is overlooked. Perhaps this accounts for the growing extravagance in many of the styles and sizes of the models currently being made. The most profitable for the hobby in general are those exhibitions which are planned to commemorate an historic event such as the Battle of Waterloo, where the set theme is represented by members, without the competitive spirit being present. The result is a well-balanced survey of the best available talent.

Most societies issue some kind of journal or bulletin for circulation to their members. These vary greatly from an elaborate magazine, with coloured illustrations, and articles written by leading authorities, to duplicated sheets with atrocious drawings and ill-digested and ill-informed contributions by self-styled experts. However, even the worst has something to offer in the way of advertisements of new models; and makers are beginning to realize that many of their orders accrue from these advertisements. Journals in general can be beneficial, providing the collector uses caution and is not carried away by the sometimes fulsome description of some new comet. Many of the articles, indeed, are worthy of a permanent place in the literature of the model soldier (e.g., Richards on Britains, Heyde and Mignot; Greenhill on Courtenay; Bean on flats). Too many, however, say little about the model *per se* and concentrate on military history, a subject treated more efficiently by magazines of a purely historical nature.

At the meetings of a number of societies the makers or their agents are present in strength, each having a stand displaying their latest products, and it is not unusual for much business to be done. To the older members this is objectionable, but others would argue that the result is beneficial, provided the meeting does not turn into a buying session. The best-run society allots a time for discussion and a time for buying, just as a Parochial Church Council should divide its agenda between spiritual and temporal matters.

The average society begins with a haphazard gathering of enthusiasts representing not only varied facets of a mutual interest but of the social stratum. It is sometimes a case of 'where two or three are gathered together', as often occurs in a boarding or grammar school, or in the remote regions of Canada and Australia, where distance is a formidable barrier to frequent meetings. But they can take heart from the fact that the British Model Soldier Society had quite a humble beginning. Contact with the French and the Germans (through Gottstein) led to a gathering in 1935 of fifteen ardent collectors, at which E.K. Milliken was elected President; they called themselves the British Society of Collectors of Model Soldiers. After the war the energy and drive to regather the scattered members was provided by Charles Lockwood.

Just before the beginning of the War an attempt had been made to create a permanent exhibition, with the British troops at Waterloo as a centre-piece. Although this idea failed, a permanent home for exhibitions was established at the RUSI but disbanded when the dioramas were dispersed.

Membership of most societies expanded rapidly after the war, especially in the United States, and while many of them have remained faithful to the original concept, others have succumbed to the prevailing mood of the times, and embrace conversions, Armoured Fighting Vehicles and wargames within their scope. Smaller, regional groups, owing allegiance to the mother society, proliferate, some occasionally breaking away and becoming independent. There are now probably more societies devoted to the wargame and the AFV and the conversion of plastics than there are of the original collectors' gatherings. Even the collecting of model soldiers has its pathos, or bathos, according to one's interpretation. A certain society, which shall be nameless, claims to have been founded in 1971 with the express object of restricting membership to collectors of solids and flats with no commercial interests. For some years afterwards it regularly advertised itself as having international off-shoots, but locked itself in a mystery more profound than that of a Secret Society, and the only conclusion one can draw is that it was as insubstantial and mythical as King Arthur's Round Table. No tangible proof could be offered by its organizer of the existence of any member other than himself. If such evidence is forthcoming, the author will willingly make suitable amends in public.

Society To Advance the Retarded. *See* S.T.A.R.

73   **Soldat.** *60mm solids (Soldat).*

'Sock Brand'. *See* Molfort.

Söhlke, F. Hanover/Regensburg/Augsburg (1810–20). Maker of flats.

Söhlke, G., Berlin (1819–72). A manufacturer of a wide range of flats, semi-solids (40–50mm) and solids (10–12cm). The flats included a set of Queen Victoria and her officers at a review at Windsor (exhibited at the Great Exhibition, 1851), infantry, cavalry and artillery of many nations, the Battle of the Alma, stag-hunting, railways, literary scenes and fairy-tale characters. The semi-solids and solids were unremarkable, and exported in great quantities to an uncritical Britain. 'Metal Soldiers' were exhibited at the Paris Exposition of 1867, and a catalogue was issued in the following year. The moulds were sold in 1872 to Haselbach, Scheller, Heinrichsen and Haffner. Söhlke's son continued the business until 1881, but probably only to dispose of remaining stock, and passed it on to Paul Wetzel in 1896.

Solá, Francesco, Barcelona (1794). One of the first Spanish firms to issue paper sheets. A Josep Solá, also of Barcelona, known to be a publisher in 1821, was probably a son.

Soldalu, Paris (c.1940). A manufacturer of aluminium figures. W.Y. Carman considers that these were imported by Wend-Al and re-christened.

Soldat (José Alarçon), Madrid (1970–). A maker of 54mm solids designed by Ramon Casadevall, and so far consisting entirely of Germans of the Second World War. They are reasonably well-made, but the cost of the painted model when imported into England is prohibitive. Originally called Franco.

SOLDER. A fusible metal for uniting joints, normally used for putting metal kits together, but also used with great effect in the creation of tiny pieces of equipment such as buttons and badges. (For its actual use in creative modelling *see* Clarke, Frederick.)

SOLDERING IRON. An instrument used in the soldering of models, and still superior to all the impact and other adhesives on the market.

'Soldier Set'. *See* Pressman, J. & Co.

Soldier Shop, The. *See* Blum, Peter.

'Soldiers of Fortune' series. *See* Marx Miniatures.

'Soldiers of the British Empire'. *See* Trophy.

Soldiers' Soldiers (J. Tunstill and A. Rose), London (1976-
). Solid 54mm revivals of Britains-style models. To
date over 200 different series (eight to a set) have been
issued. They are obtainable in boxes or individually, as
castings or painted.

'Soldiers to Shoot'. *See* Britain, William, Ltd.

Soldiers Unlimited (Michael Ferguson), Wyndmoor,
Pennsylvania (1970-). A minor producer of a small
range of 54mm solids in kit form, some designed by
Kramer, including Assyrians and Persians, a Royal
Marine Light Infantry Officer and a Royal Engineer
Gunner (both 1900), a British Hussar of 1880, and a set
of three native gunners with a British N.C.O. of the
Madras Foot Artillery, 1845. Ferguson plans an issue of
Indian Army infantry from 1757 to the Mutiny. He has
also designed one or two models for Superior.

Solido-Belge, Belgium (1977-). Manufacturers of 54mm
plastics of the Belgian Army in ceremonial dress.
[*Kearton*]

Solido, France (1960-). Manufacturers of metal tanks
and artillery.

SOLIDS (Commercial). As the name implies, a solid
model is made of a heavy material, usually of lead or
pewter or an amalgam of metals. Consequently it is not
only resistant to damage, but is in many cases malleable
to a greater or lesser extent, thus lending itself to
animation. Both these characteristics endeared themselves to collectors and led to the solid model's pre-
eminence over other materials such as plastic or plaster.
A solid model occurs when the pouring of molten metal
into a mould and the consequent cooling and removal
from the mould results in a 'casting'. This may be either
in the form of a complete figure or in various parts to be
subsequently assembled. This holds good whether the
model is a mass-produced article for the toy trade or a
better-quality production aimed at a more sophisticated
audience. In the case of the commercial solid, an
infantryman is usually cast in one piece, weapons being
soldered on, while cavalry consist of two pieces – horse

74 **Solids** *by Minot in 30mm (Author)*.

and rider, the latter in the smaller models having a tiny
spike in his seat and a corresponding hole in the saddle.
In the better-quality models (e.g. Lucotte, Haffner)
saddles, stirrups and reins are also cast separately. A
few solid models have been handed down from antiquity
and there is evidence that they were made in France in
the 16th and 17th centuries. (Forgeries were produced in
Paris at the end of the nineteenth century and seized
upon eagerly by antiquaries.) The first commercial
venture appears to be that of Lucotte right at the end of
the 18th century. Obviously there were other makers, as
is shown by Paul Martin's 1815 Officer of the Mounted
Artillery of the Garde Royale (*Le Monde Merveilleux*,
p.55). Cuperly, Blondel and Gerbeau flourished in the
middle of the 19th century and, when that firm later became Mignot, produced a vast quantity of models, many
being exported to Britain and the United States. Apart
from these commercial products Mignot executed commissions such as the seventy-five different units of the
French Army of the Second Empire, designed by
Fremiet for the Prince Imperial. In Nuremberg in the
mid-18th century a small industry of tiny solids with
wooden accessories had no influence, and the flat remained paramount until, by the 1860s, the Germans developed a much more solid and heavy model. The
pioneers were Heyde and Haffner, the former eventually
sweeping all competitors before him and continuing in
production until 1939, although increasingly
diminishing in numbers owing to the competition of
British hollow-casts. Haffner models were undoubtedly
superior in quality and worthy museum pieces, while
those of Heinrich were almost as good. Heyde's great
success was due to the massive number of miscellaneous
figures and accessories that went with each set,
together with the various sizes and qualities that were
available. They are pre-eminently the 'toy soldier' and
as such will always have a nostalgic attraction, even
though still frowned upon by German collectors, the
majority of whom are still wedded to the idea of the flat.
Their defects are their lack of anatomy and their
malleability, especially in the weapons, but they display
more vigour than the contemporary Mignot, and in certain quarters are being recast for collectors.

Other countries soon followed suit in the early days of
the 20th century, making their own models rather than
relying on German and French solids or on English
hollow-casts. Prominent among them was Emmanuel
Steinback (MIM) of Belgium, whose models were of excellent quality, Banner-Model and Brigader-Statuette in
Denmark (still surviving), Francesco and ISA in Italy in
their own peculiar manner, Casanellas and Palomeque in
Spain, Santessonska and Mars in Sweden, and the
American Soldier Company and the Warren Company in
the United States. Even in Latin America native solids
were to be found, while at the beginning of the Second
World War Canada made its own contribution with a
few models which are best forgotten. Vast numbers
were churned out year after year, first leading the
hollow-cast and then competing with and finally
succumbing to it. Indeed, many collections consist entirely of the commercial solids of the nineteenth and
20th centuries. There are many manufacturers whose
models are unidentifiable for lack of trade-marks,
specimens seen from time to time appearing to have no
known provenance, and much more research is still

needed into styles and types of figure. There has of recent years been such a resurgence of interest in these 'toys of the past', which is reflected in the prices paid at auction, that a full-scale book dealing solely with these products is becoming increasingly necessary. (McKenzie's *Collecting Old Toy Soldiers* merely skims the surface.) The main way in which these models differ from later productions is in the limited range of position. An excellent example is illustrated in the catalogue of Gammage's stores for 1913, which shows boxes of Heyde and Mignot models: six Romans marching, three cavalrymen trotting, five riflemen firing, and the like. Variety there was of course, especially with Heyde, but on the whole commercial solids were sold in stylized positions.

SOLIDS (Semi-). A form of model probably dictated by economy and the advent of '*kriegsspiel*'. The large heavy German models must have been expensive to produce and the size of the figures too large for organized play. The manufacturers therefore produced a hybrid, often as small as an inch or so, where the cavalryman was solid, and could be fixed on to the saddle by a tiny peg. The horse, however, was in the nature of an emphasized flat, the feet being in alignment. Haffner, Ammon, Allgeyer and Spenküch produced vast quantities of these curious models, which appear to have had a ready sale in England. The 40mm size was most popular, and all the impedimenta of war were made, including vehicles in the round, although still drawn by semi-flat horses, the latter often linked together by footstands. Later still (c.1880) such firms as Wollner made their models in an oval rather than a round shape. Eventually, and possibly due to the spread of Britains' hollow-casts, the idea died a natural death, and nobody mourned its passing, although many unusual groups of models were produced. An echo remained in the form of the home-casting mould, and has persisted in some Eastern European countries.

SOLIDS (Specialist). A distinction must be made between the models made specifically for the toy trade ('commercial') and those for a more discriminating market. The 'toy' soldier is a mass-produced item, normally sold in boxed sets and, though research is necessary to provide the model with some veracity as to uniform, anatomy is of secondary importance, and facial expression is the same in every model. The model has to be produced at a price commensurate with the market it is intended to reach, and costs accordingly have to be kept to the minimum, and no single figure can be given special treatment. Thus mass-production in a certain limited range of positions is essential if the product is to be viable. These 'commercial' figures have been the backbone of the model-soldier trade, and their simplicity, allied to their mass-painting in basic colours, has proved acceptable to many who have collected them as a reflection of the times in which they were made, ignoring the fact that in actuality they have always been at best merely an approximate attempt to portray a military figure. However, there has always existed a number of collectors who would prefer to have a single figure of a better quality than a whole collection of 'toys'. It is evident, for example, that in the early days of flats Hilpert made specially fine figures for distinguished patrons, as did later both Mignot and Heinrichsen. For years serious collectors made their own improvements to existing toys, especially those of the hollow-cast variety, which proved suitable for conversion, but around the 1930s there occurred in several countries (notably France, Germany and Great Britain) a desire for a 'specialist' model hitherto unobtainable either in flats, solids, hollow-casts or by home-conversion. This, by a process of artistic evolution, led to the emergence of a number of artists who spent much time on research, casting and painting, in order to produce single models rather than massed assemblies. In Great Britain W.Y. Carman produced a number of models which were available at 7/6d each, as compared with a box of Britains' infantry at 1/6d. It cannot be said that they were much better than those of the commercial houses. Richard Courtenay, having made commercial figures in alliance with Doran, branched out on his own and began the production of an astonishing series of medieval warriors in varied poses, some mounted, and made in solid metal, only a handful of early models being in hollow-cast. He charged two guineas and more for each of his models, all brilliantly painted and with impeccably researched heraldry. His friend Ping soon followed his example, together with Niblett and Greenwood. Gradually more 'makers' – rather than 'manufacturers' – followed suit, especially after the end of the Second World War, the most notable being Stadden, Gammage and Hinton, each in his own way adding an ever-spreading range of models specially designed for collectors. Whatever the difference in their subject matter, each followed the same method of production. A particular example of military history having been decided upon (sometimes at the suggestion of a collector), the artist proceeded to research his subject to an extent that the resultant model would represent a facsimile in every detail. This often entailed hours of searching through reference books, manuscript material, regimental histories and visits to military museums. Detailed drawings would then be made of every visual aspect. These would then be transferred to actual production by the making of a prototype, usually in plasticine or some other malleable material. When the maker was satisfied with all aspects of the model, it would, by a process of making plaster of Paris moulds, pouring in molten metal (usually a mixture of antimony and lead), removal of the 'master' model from the mould, filing or trimming of extraneous material or 'flash', and possibly small adjustments by file or chisel, be considered ready for production. Final casting being completed, more filing and corrections would be made, the figure cleaned, primed, and painted as carefully as possible. The whole process being slow, production was limited, but with later improved methods of casting, production was speeded up. There were two methods of producing a solid model open to the maker: making a single-mould figure, in which clothing, headgear and the like formed an integral part, or the production of a torso, with separately-cast heads, limbs, accoutrements, etc, which would then be soldered together.

These early makers often worked from their own homes, with simple equipment, and painted their own models before placing them on the market, so that each figure they made was their own from start to finish. It must not be forgotten that although the collector was potentially there, marketing was not easy. The higher price asked by the maker deterred many a shop from

75 **Large solids.** *Back row: Almirall (90mm), Superior (80mm), Imrie-Risley (75mm), Poste Militaire (95mm), Almirall; front row: Niblett (170mm prototype), Stadden (80mm), McNeil (140mm), Acorn (80mm), McNeil: Series 77 (72mm), Niblett (Author and Niblett).*

adding his products to their more easily saleable lines, and it was a hard and long struggle for Courtenay and Stadden to become established. Gradually, however, one or two dealers with vision such as Morrell's in Burlington Arcade (later Hummel House of Miniatures) and Hamley's of Regent Street, began to feature their models, at times making special displays of them. Thus the continued success of the specialist solid in Great Britain was assured. As the makers became established, so their business expanded, and in the majority of cases the home-workshop was abandoned for the small factory and the consequent employment of workshop personnel for casting and painting. (Courtenay, however, preferred to continue personally to produce his work from start to finish.) In some instances this popularity proved a mixed blessing, as standards of production and of painting decreased in quality; 'animation' took place and makers began to vie one with another in an ever-increasing search for a new or novel figure. (Gammage, however, although employing labour, never relinquished his overall control and maintained a consistently high standard.) The 'specialist' figure increased in momentum, more and more artists entering the field from 1960 onwards. Higgins and Surén were among the most successful, followed by a revived Greenwood and Ball combine and the emergence of Hinchliffe, both of the latter employing numerous artists to work for them. Methods of presentation changed, the models now being mainly marketed in 'kit' form, that is, in separate parts to be assembled by the purchaser. While enabling the collector to animate the figure, this could be a drawback in that the separate parts did not always match, and frustrating filing or filling-in of gaps resulted. This method of production is now the normal practice, although a few makers, such as Gammage, Rowe and Tassell, prefer to issue their models assembled.

In the United States the specialist model was pioneered by Bussler and Scruby, followed by Murray and Imrie, who, on being joined by Risley, became the most prolific of makers. In their early days the single-mould model prevailed, but as times changed the makers with few exceptions adopted the 'kit' form. They also formed combines similar to those of Greenwood and Ball and Hinchliffe, employing free-lance artists of varying degrees of ability. Within the last few years there has been a steady increase in transatlantic trade, so that many models from the United States may be seen in Great Britain and many English models find their way to America.

Of all nations in Europe, France has always been more interested in the specialist model than in the 'toy', and the models of Berdou, des Fontaines and Lelièpvre are probably the most elegant and accomplished ever made. The first of the French specialist makers were Baldet, Bittard and Métayer, each contributing a quality peculiarly French. The French, moreover, used a different method of production to that of the English makers. They began with a basic torso, to which was added the head and limbs. The clothing or uniform was then built up by successive layers of the thinnest sheet lead, and such items as headgear, saddles, reins, stirrups, sabretaches, swords, bits, and buttons were sculpted separately and then soldered on. Thus each model differed slightly from another. The majority of their work was to commission, and it is known that Berdou kept an immaculate record of every detail of every model that he made, so that no two models would be identical. Never have any of the French masters attempted to compete with the number of models produced by the English or the Americans, the sole exception perhaps being that of Fouillé, and then only to a minor degree.

In Scandinavia the first to produce the specialist model was Eriksson, bringing with him a Nordic freshness and directness of approach, while those of Brunoe and Schreiber combined both strength and elegance. Spain and Italy has produced a number of fine makers, working either to commission or for the collector in general, while Canada, Australia and New Zealand have all made their own contributions.

So far the models discussed have been of 54 to 60mm size, but from about 1972 onwards makers gradually increased the size of their models, and it is now commonplace to find them in anything up to 150 or 180mm. Although their continued popularity seems assured, they do not fit easily with the models of the more traditional size; any anatomical clumsiness is naturally exaggerated and painting may well become overdetailed. The smaller model has also increased in popularity since Niblett produced a delightful series in 22mm in 1954, to be echoed some time later equally expertly by Higgins. The most popular of the smaller sizes is 30mm, splendidly made by Surén, Gammage, Stadden, Eriksson and Lacina. An intermediate size of 25mm was begun by makers of wargame models, resulting in many new makers who produced some good and some distinctly shoddy work.

The immense variety of the specialist solid may be shown by the fact that although there would appear to be hardly a period or an era not already covered, new models continued to pour from the moulds. With this tremendous output came the danger of issuing work that was poor in quality, and there are indeed many models that reflect no credit on their designers. This is most apparent in the work of many of the younger present-day artists, especially in the United States, where swagger and bravado was used to cover up technical and artistic shortcomings. It was here that the greatest unevenness occurred, especially in the models issued by large combines employing free-lance designers, where in any batch of, say, twenty models from the same firm perhaps only four or five would be of desirable quality. The reasons appear to be three-fold: first, pressure to issue a certain number of new models each month: second, the employment of free-lance modellers, irrespective of their abilities or otherwise; and, third, poor and hasty production due to haste in getting on the market in advance of competitors. These strictures, of course, do not apply to the specialists who work to commission, or the long-established craftsmen who endeavour to sustain their hard-earned reputations; but many a maker is tempted to use the same basic model for any number of figures, the only alteration being perhaps a different head or weapon, a practice known in the United States as 'spin-off'.

The latest feature is the 'group set', consisting of two or three models engaged in some occupation. Thus, one maker has a scene of Normans at a Saxon village forge, one kicking a recalcitrant native, while a blacksmith is forced to shoe the horses of the Normans. Another maker portrays a set of press-gang officers in a quayside tavern, or a group of Royalists carousing, or a bevy of brawny Romans lashing a pinioned Boadicea. Each of these sets lends itself admirably to the creation of a vignette-diorama.

The variety in the whole vast range of specialist solids cannot be described in detail. Three aspects, however, are obvious. The first is that although a number of makers, such as Gammage, Rowe and Stadden, keep several themes running at the same time, adding gradually to each, others, particularly the American combines, jump from subject to subject without any obvious reason, due, one must assume, to the employment of free-lance artists with their own particular interests. The second is that there is a great disparity in the quality of models, ranging from the exquisite productions of Berdou, des Fontaines, Lelièpvre, Rowe, Gammage, Saunders, Sandoe, Barrientos, Parisini, Eriksson, Surén, Courtenay and Brunoe to the vague gropings of many a lesser light.

The final feature that emerges is that of 'playing the market', or the production of models to meet a supposed demand, or even the attempt to create a demand. The obvious example is the two- or three-year period when the model soldier collector was bombarded from all sides by a barrage of Germans and Japanese of the Second World War (a trend still continuing in the form of plastic kits of AFVs). This was followed by the cult of the Japanese medieval warrior, of which the most memorable is the 120mm multiple-piece kit by the English Ray Lamb.

Finally, there are two subjects hardly linked to the model soldier, but in many cases made by established makers, the first being the 'fantasy' figure. It is possible that Tolkien's *The Lord of the Rings* was the unconscious instigator; at any rate a host of weird and repulsive witches, warlocks, werewolves and other monstrosities culled from neurotic American pulp and science fiction magazines have appeared, and a whole literature of wargame rules for them has been published. Even more curious to the collector is the eruption of nude or near-nude male and female figures under such titles as 'Atlantis', the sculptor taking advantage of what is commonly called the 'permissive age' to go as near the erotic as is possible. These figures, although in many cases most admirable in execution, are far removed from the nudes and near-nudes of Gammage, and many are an affront to human dignity. The sociologist may be interested in the fact that they are peculiar to Great Britain and America.

Soljertoys. *See* Pearlytoys.

Sollner, Gerhard, Karlsruhe/Aachen (1950-   ). Producer, designer and engraver of flats, including the Thirty Years' War, a Prussian artillery train of 1813, Napoleonic troops, the Franco-Prussian War and the Second World War. He has designed and engraved for Hodapp, Kebbel, Scholtz (in 12cm.), Tobinnus, Kreddel, Meyniel and Otte.

Sommer, Carlos, Buenos Aires, Argentina (1947-66). A German expatriate, Sommer made a number of good-quality 35mm semi-solids of soldiers, sailors, Westerners, Arabs, circuses and safaris. [*Basseterre*]

Sorgente, La, Italy (c.1966). Publisher of a number of small booklets with figures for cutting out, of modern and historic Italian uniforms.

SOUTH AFRICA. Although there are a few collectors, models in general do not appear to attract much attention, and, apart from the ephemeral appearance of Swedish African Engineers, the only native makers we can trace are Nolan (who gave up the struggle early) and

Pastimes Metal Figures.

SOUTH AMERICA. Apart from Argentina little has emerged from the South American states, except for one or two isolated instances of makers in Bolivia and Colombia.

SOUVENIR FLATS. From time to time flats of a commorative nature have been specially made. The best known are those issued annually for presentation to visitors to the Kulmbach meetings, the best designers, engravers and casters being employed. The Dutch society has also issued a number to illustrate its country's history. Of a more permanent nature are the figures of Anton-Gunther von Oldenburg (c.1680) made recently for the Oldenburg Tourist Board, a set of *minnesingers* at Eisenach Museum, and peasant scenes at Leuchtenburg bei Kahla.

Sovereign Figures (N.T. Boland) London (1974-). A series of 70mm pewter models of Yeomen of the Guard, Guardsmen, etc, clumsy and uninspired, designed and produced for Meccano by N. Saunders Metal Products Ltd. They are marked on the footstand 'Association of British Pewter Craftsmen',

Sovereign Miniatures (J. Tassell and T. Reeves) Chatham, Kent (1977-). A series of 60 and 75mm solids of Romans, Russo-Japanese War, etc. A splendid medieval knight is marred by the skimpy reins and head harness of his horse. In 1979 they issued a set of white metal parts to add to a Britains' elephant comprising a mahout, two warriors, a fighting castle and trappings.

76   **Sowden.** *A 10-in. stone ware model entitled 'Gas' (T.B. Sowden).*

Sowden, T.B., Ilford, Essex (1968-). A maker of commissioned models in clay, fibreglass, metal or stoneware. Normally they are about 12 inches in height, but he has also made a small range of 30mm models. He encompasses many periods from the English Civil War to the First World War. He is one of the few artists who approach his subject with a view to personality and stark reality, no concessions being made to pedantic accuracy. The result is a vivid reconstruction of action, in which the material used is strained to the utmost. On the lighter side, he has made a caricature of Surèn.

SPAIN. The making of flats began in 1828 in Barcelona by Carlos Ortelli Dotti, an Italian emigré from Lake Como, who employed as an engraver Salvatore Bacciarini, another Italian, and later two Spanish brothers Francisco and Juan Pera [*Allendesalazar*]. Many were of the Corpus Christi processions, changing only gradually to military subjects. The original moulds still exist in Spanish museums. He was soon followed by Pirozzini, and the craft was carried on by Lleonart (1870-90). Solids and semi-solids by Capell and Gonzalez made their appearance in the 1890s. These continued to be made by both firms until about 1945, being joined in the meantime by Palomeque and Sanquez. These commercial figures were stopped by the '*Código Alimentoso*', which prohibited the making of metal figures for children in view of the supposed danger of lead poisoning. This led to the introduction of plastics by Reamsa, Pech Hermanos and Dia-D-Hora. Soon the 'specialist' model began to be made, notably by Saez-Alcocer and Almirall, who quickly attracted attention outside their own country, while Alymer, although beginning production in 1928, did not become universally recognized until he added models in 55mm to his earlier ones in 20mm. Others, such as Julia, Soldat, Barrientos, Rodriguez, Mallol, Gutierrez, Echeverria, and Labayen have been instrumental in creating a now well-established Spanish school.

An aspect which continues to flourish is the paper sheet. These were started early in the 19th century, and reached their apogee around 1850-70 — especially those issued by Abadal, Llorens and Paluzié — having as their inspiration those imported from France, Germany and Italy. They began as single or double figures of Corpus Christi processions, triumphal arrivals of monarchs, zoos and circuses. They were put to various uses, including the zoëtrope, childrens' tableaux and greetings cards [*Balil*]. They reflect practically every aspect of life in Spain and portray, somewhat naïvely, the mood of the times. The military sheets were mainly of the wars with the French or the Moors, and later, of course, the Spanish Civil War. Other countries, however, including the French in Algeria and the British and the allies in the Crimean War can still be seen in the collections of J. Amades, J.M. Colominas and P.Vila held by the *Instituto Municipal de Historia de la Ciudad* at Barcelona. Later sheets, especially contemporary ones, vary considerably in quality, many being obviously designed for the juvenile market, but reprints are being made of some of the early sheets.

Spandauw, Enno, Groningen, Netherlands (1965-). A collector of large polystyrene kits who converts them, and has so far made more than fifty dioramas for his shop and museum 'In de Tinnen Wonderwereld'.

Sparrow, David. *See* Hinchliffe; Monarch.

Speedwell Manufacturing Co. London (1958–68). A manufacturer of a very small range of plastic 54mm models, obviously based on Herald's modern British troops.

Speich, R., Strasbourg (1930–50). Publisher of paper sheets.

Spencer, Major H.A.V., York. A maker of 15-inch carved wooden models rather naïve in appearance, with equipment of leather and metal. Twenty-one models, depicting uniforms of the Prince of Wales's Own (West Yorkshire Regiment) from 1685 to 1866 were commissioned by the Regiment for their museum at Imphal Barracks, York.

Spencer-Smith Miniatures (Ronald W. Spencer-Smith) Frimley Green, Surrey (1965–). A small manufacturer of 30mm plastic wargame models of the American War of Independence, the Seven Years' War, the Napoleonic period, the American Civil War and modern (Field Dress) troops, together with naval and army artillery. Before 1973 these were re-pressed from existing models as a spare-time activity, but in that year he began designing his original 'Connoisseur Range' in nylon plastic.

Spenküch, Georg, Nuremberg (1870–1924). A prolific manufacturer of undistinguished flats, semi-solids and solids, of varying sizes. Besides the military ranges, unusual sets included the Nuremberg-Fürth railway, houses, gardens and townsfolk, and bullfights (engraved by Frank). Some of the flats were engraved by Junker. The last owner was a Herr Schwarz, who, it is stated, sold the moulds to Sweden. Mark on labels: an exploding bomb with G.S. below and 'EXTRAFEINE MASSIVE ZINNFIGUREN-FIGURES D'ÉTAIN SUPERFINES-SUPERFINE SOLID PEWTER FIGURES'.

Spicer, Ronald, Llanerch, Pennsylvania. A free-lance designer of solid models, especially for Superior, and an expert at modelling artillery.

Spilz, Charles, Strasbourg (1930–50). Minor publisher of paper sheets.

'SPIN-OFF'. An Americanism used to describe models from the same mould masquerading as different ones. Thus, the same stance does duty for perhaps half-a-dozen allegedly varying figures, where apart from trifling details of uniform added later, or a head turned another way, or a different painting, the unsuspecting customer ordering by post receives not six distinct models but six almost identical ones. This, of course, was a characteristic of the commercial solid or hollow-cast, being brought about by economic necessity, which naturally is as relevant today as yesterday; but the maker could at least state that all the models are in the same pose.

'Spirit of '76' set. _See_ Hudson Pewter.

SP Manufacturing Co., Walthamstow (1917). Producers of a tin-plate anti-aircraft gun. (_Model Soldier_, October, 1978)

Springwood Models (A.C. Collett) Oxford (1972). A short-lived venture into the manufacture of a set of 48 figures in 25mm in white polystyrene, comprising twelve each of British, French, Prussians, and Russians, on the sprues, with a sheet of colours.

SPRUE. The residue on a plastic figure formed by the pouring channels, especially when in kit form. This usually takes the form of a slender stem from which the figure or part of the figure has to be removed. Intelligent enthusiasts preserve this for melting down when

engaged in the conversion of a kit.

Squadron/Rubin (Raymond Rubin) USA (1972–). Rubin began by making 54mm solids for Cavalier, then transferred his allegiance to The Squadron Shop. As with so many other present-day American makers, no cohesive theme appears to be followed, so that all types of models appear in the lists of his productions. The earliest of his works were dull and anatomically incorrect. This applies especially to the model of a pilot, where the head is too large, and many of the figures were, like the early ones of Sanderson, oval rather than round. Later models, however, have rectified this impression, and are crisply sculpted. The fact that they are cast in one piece with only a weapon to add makes them a change from most contemporary models. Although he linked up with Chernak in 1974, making 25mm models under the name of Grenadier, up to the time of writing models have also continued to appear under the original Squadron name, although the quality of the latest ones is extremely variable, due perhaps to haste in production, over two hundred models having appeared since 1976. In 1977 he succumbed to the 'fantasy' figure, one in particular, 'The Death Rider', bearing a remarkable resemblance to one in 30mm issued in 1975 by Ral Partha. This is probably co-incidental, both makers probably basing their figures on a painting issued in an American 'pulp' magazine.

Squadron Shop (J. Campbell) Detroit. A publisher of models under various names: Squadron/Rubin, Squadron/Combat, Squadron/Signature and Squadron/Waterloo. Many of the figures are made by Rubin and Chernak, and doubtless there are other designers whose names may emerge in due course. (The Squadron/Waterloo models proved on examination to be actually Historex infantry kits in polystyrene). In 1975 he acquired a number of nudes or semi-nudes which had been made by Sanderson, and re-issued them under the name of Buccaneer, expressly advertising them as having been made in USA. Examination showed that Sanderson's name had been removed from the side of each footstand.

S.R. [**Ivollet**], France. a two-horse limber and gun team with three outriders produced by Maurice Berne was sold at Phillips in London on 19 December, 1974.

Staar, Germany (19th century). A minor publisher of paper sheets.

Staar, Friedbert, Jena. An engraver of flats of fine quality, who has worked with Emmerling and Kebbel; especially noted for a set of Louis XIV.

Stack, Commander. _See_ Tenngjuteriet-Mars.

Stackhouse, Kurt, New York. A free-lance designer of solids, especially for Cavalier and Old Guard, and a professional figure-painter.

Staden, C.L. van, Amsterdam (fl.1830). Publisher of paper sheets.

Stadden, Charles C., Rustington, Sussex (1950–). The most prolific of makers of modern specialized solids. In the 29 years since his tentative entry into the professional world he has made literally thousands of models and has achieved a fame far beyond parochial boundaries. Whereas English dealers of the period were loath to import models by foreign makers, the United States was early to recognize Stadden's figures and they still form the basis of countless dioramas and collections. They have also proved extremely popular in

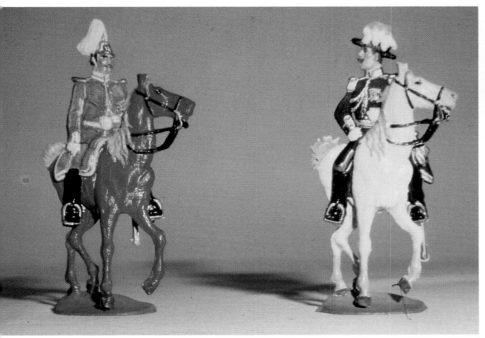

44 Left: **Santessonska**. *Prince Karl and King Gustav V of Sweden. Solid 54mm (Allendesalazar).* Above: 45 **Rose Miniatures**. *A selection of Greek warriors and females. Solid 54mm (Rose Miniatures).* 46 Below: **Solids** *(Commercial). Typical specimens of Germanic solids. The Foot Grenadiers are by Heyde; the mounted staff officers by Haffner (Gennari).*

47 Above: **Semi-solids**. *Although a hybrid, German models of the late 19th – early 20th centuries are often interesting in the variety of subjects which they portray (Gennari).* 48 Right: **Saez-Alcocer**. *Spanish infantry, 1910. A colourful group (Allendsalazar).* 49 Below: **Superior**. *A fine 90mm solid of Cortez by Ron Spicer painted by A. Etchells (Eugene and Wilma Custer).* 50 Below right: **The Sentry Box**. *Three 17cm metal models (The Sentry Box).*

77 **Stadden.** *A typical group displaying insensitive painting ('Tradition').*

Australia, New Zealand, Scandinavia and even in Germany, where solids were, and still are, generally regarded as a lower grade of art. There were perhaps three reasons for this early popularity: the sheer industry of the man; the quality of those early models and the making of a large number of period-linked models. Thus, one could start a collection of American Revolutionary troops or the Napoleonic Wars in the knowledge that additional models would soon be forthcoming, and would not merely be 'spin-offs', as so many present-day figures are. Indeed, the early models, made before about 1965, were of a splendid character, with an original mind expressing itself with conviction and freshness of approach, together with impeccable painting, so that they have become treasured pieces (see those at Blenheim Palace, for example). In justice to Stadden, it should be clearly pointed out that once the master-figure left his hands, and was taken over by Belmont-Maitland's team for 'animation', the resultant model often bore no relation to the original. Hence the fact that the vast majority of Staddens are pedestrian. (He has made no models for 'Tradition' since 1973). However, it is safe to say that his place in the history of the model soldier will remain firmly entrenched as the most influential and internationally known figure of the last two decades. The early models have always been those which he himself prefers, certainly those of the British troops of the 18th century, but the most popular have always been his Napoleonics, especially those of the great man himself and his staff of colourful marshals. Here the physiognomy of each individual is admirably caught, even though there is a certain dumpiness of the legs. The greatest disservice from which he has suffered of recent years has been from the team of painters who produce specimen models for exhibition and shop sale, as shown in the colour plates of Nicholson's *Model Soldiers*, where any disaffinity is emphasized by the appalling coarseness of the facial lining and shading. To appreciate Stadden to the full one should therefore buy an unpainted casting. He has never been able to make a convincing female, except on the rarest occasions. On the credit side is the all-embracing sweep of his talents, and some delightful out-of-series individuals. Beginning commercially in 54mm, the models increased to 56 or 58mm, and probably suffered in consequence. To his credit also is the vast range he has created: his British troops; his Romans; his Marlburians and his troops of Frederick the Great. His later excursions into the Franco-Prussian War, the Crimean War and the World Wars are adequate though not particularly distinguished, and his medieval models, although beautifully painted and with much better horses, are still somewhat top-heavy, even allowing for the tortoise-like immobility of a dismounted heavily armoured knight in combat. To many a collector the extremes of size of those in 30mm and those in 80–90mm show Stadden at his best, although his real masterpieces are those he has specially created to commission. The smaller models are little gems, and the larger ones in pewter display a dignity worthy of any collector's cabinet.

Stadden began carving models in wood, but, these not proving successful commercially, he joined an old friend, C.B.O. Hingle, and in 1950 began working in metal in the $1/1\frac{1}{2}$-inch size, changing a year later to 54mm. In 1953 Belmont-Maitland began to market his models, and in the course of a few years Stadden was able to devote himself to the making of masters, leaving the rest to a professional team. When Hingle left in 1957 he was replaced by Alex Griffiths.

One thing that emerges from a study of Stadden's models is his profound knowledge of uniform, in which department he led the field for many years. Not all his figures are designed by himself, of course, and although he has been assisted over the years by Lawrence Archer, Embleton, Nicholson and Belmont-Maitland, the actual sculpting has been done by him. Nor has he confined his talents exclusively to the production of models for 'Tradition'. This most versatile man has been withdrawing, redesigning and reissuing his models for many years, and has made a large number of armies in 20 and 25mm, some designed by other makers, which, while not competing with his splendid models in 30mm, have been of great assistance to those wishing to build up wargame armies. At the other extreme 80 and 90mm models in pewter appeared from 1973 onwards (*See* Stadden, Chas. C. Studios). Normally his 54 to 60mm models are found as complete entities, though they have also been issued in kit form under the names of Standish, Just and Tradition. However, the quality of the casting in these cheaper issues is such that much work has to be done on them. He has designed for Hinchliffe, Old Guard and Almark in 54mm and for Marx in 6 inches. A fine medieval chess set was made in 1973 for Triang, and, outside the military range, he has worked for Bowaters, Waddingtons, Meccano and Subbuteo. Born in 1919, he is capable of producing many more models.

Stadden, Chas. C., Studios Ltd (N. Saunders Metal Products Ltd), Twickenham, (1975-). Feeling dissatisfaction with the treatment that his models had for years undergone, Stadden joined Saunders in a venture whereby every stage of the making is controlled and supervised by himself. He uses two types of metal – a mixture of tin and lead for 'The Stadden Edition' and hand-sculpted pewter for 'Buckingham Pewter', where the 80mm models each have a sloped base engraved with a regimental badge. The latter are sold either plain or, with Harrod's as the only London agent, hand-painted under Stadden's supervision. Apart from individual figures, he and Saunders have made three admirable chess sets. The first, that of the Battle of Waterloo, was thus described in an advertisement in *The Sunday Express* (20 September, 1975): 'The importance of this edition may be measured by the fact that Charles Stadden, determined to ensure that the quality of finished painting matched the exactness of the original sculpture, spent eight months in recruiting a team of artists to complete the individual pieces. So painstaking is the work that it takes as long as five days to complete the painting of just one major figure in all its lavish detail'. A set featuring the American Revolution followed in 1976, and a most unusual one depicting major personalities in history who were connected with the Tower of London completes the trio.

Stadtler, Albrecht, Fürth/Nuremberg (c.1893). A publisher of flats who was originally an engraver for Heinrichsen. He purchased Haffner's business in 1893, and was joined by Frank in the same year.

Stahl, Johann Ludwig, Nuremberg (fl.1805-22). Mainly a dealer, he purchased Hilpert's moulds, as mentioned in a catalogue dated 1805. The more clumsy Hilpert castings may well have emanated from Stahl around 1822.

Staines, James. *See* Sea Gull model.

Stamped Tin. One of the cheapest forms of models, they were paramount in the late 19th and early 20th centuries and sold in the penny bazaars, but were advertised in Paris as early as 1840. A jig having been made, the forms were stamped out from flat sheet tin in their thousands, painted by a mechanical process, and then fitted with a flange for the feet. M.D. Griffiths (*The Toy Armies of the World,* 1898) describes what he saw when he visited a factory: 'The artisans [there] make common soldiers out of old sardine tins. . . Into a sort of witch's cauldron are flung these old boxes, smelling of oil and grease. When sufficiently heated they become unsoldered, and, when cool, are hammered, straightened, flattened, and sorted to their primitive state and then converted into common tin soldiers. . . The enamelled soldiers – a recent invention – are cut by means of a knife, from sheets of metal, and afterwards have to pass through the painting rooms, in which two hundred women are employed'. Still come across in some of the more backward or remote parts of the world, and made in thousands by Marx for target practice.

'Stamford Bridge' series. See Greenwood and Ball (Pearce).

Standish. A trade-name given between 1970 and 1972 to early Staddens in kit form by a dealer, Standish-Hardie, of Harrogate.

Stange (Edition), Berlin, (19th Century). Publisher of paper sheets.

Stan Johansen Miniatures (Stan Johansen) Naugatuck, Connecticut (1973-). A maker of 30mm solids of Napoleonic and medieval Japanese subjects. Comparison of models seems to point to the fact that Johansen not only copied many of those of Surèn, but actually cut them up and fitted them together in different positions. Formerly traded under the name of Victory Miniatures. In 1977 he abandoned his Napoleonic range to concentrate on 'fantastics' and figures from science fiction.

S.T.A.R. (Society To Advance the Retarded), Norwalk, Connecticut (1977-). Victor Roming began making 'toy' soldiers for use in therapy, but production was suspended owing to a prolonged illness.

Starcast Miniatures, Erith, Kent (1973-). A company which manufactures tiny metal A.F.Vs. In 1977 they began an 80mm solid range by George Haynes, and the following year mythical figures in 25mm by Newson and 80mm models by Feldwick.

'Starguard' series. *See* McEwan Miniatures.

Starlux (Beffara et Cie), Chamiers-Perigueux, France (1900-). Manufacturers of 25, 35 and 60mm plastics. The firm was founded in 1900 by Elie Tarroux, the models being made in a composition called *blanc de Meudon.* In 1936 the firm was taken over by Beffara, and in 1945 the modern style of plastic was used. These excellent models are beautifully painted, and second only to those of Herald in quality. The spirit of the Middle Ages lives in their knights, men-at-arms, squires and ladies, who are especially attractive. The mounted models are less accurate in detail, with a leaning towards the modern style of Elastolin. The Romans are no more than interesting, as is the Napoleonic range. Other models include Chasseurs Alpins, Marines, parachutists, legionnaires, Arabs, Westerners and Indians, Mexicans and corsairs. Many of these are also available in 35mm, while in 1971 plastic 25mm wargame models of Napoleonic troops were issued, the riders detachable. Opie considers that they may have taken over the firm of Clairet about 1968.

STATUTORY REGULATION. A British Act of 1967 prohibited the manufacture of any toy soldier having a coating of paint containing lead. Britains were forced to acknowledge that there was a 'very real danger in lead if it falls into a child's hand'. Although the prohibition apparently did not cover the importation of foreign models, and one can see no recorded evidence of a sudden plague of infantile deaths from the early days of Mignot and Heyde and Britains, the fact remains that the threat of prosecution evidently loomed large in the minds of all makers of hollow-casts, and was one of the reasons that led to their turning to plastic. Britains' recent zinc models are apparently within the law, as are also those of Nostalgia and Trophy and the other neo-Britains makers. (*Compare* the '*Código Alimentoso*' in Spain.)

Staudt, Hans von, Dusseldorf (1933). Publisher of flats.

Stauffler, P., USA. Professional painter for Cowan.

Steadfast (Lee N. Daniels) Las Cruces, New Mexico (1977-). Re-casts of original Heyde models.

'Steadfast Lead Soldier'. The Scandinavians Anholm, Brunoe, Høyer and Hansen mark some of their models thus.

Steadfast Soldiers. *See* A. Rose.

Stearns, Philip O., USA/London. The first occasion one had to see the work of this photographer was probably the little book he did in collaboration with Peter Blum. One was immediately struck with the quality of his colour compositions. While living in London he did more than anyone else to record by photography the works of contemporary makers. Allied to this he has a keen appreciation of quality, has an enviable collection of models, and has added his own contribution to the literature of the model soldier. His latest venture is his co-operation with Dilley in *Model Soldiers in Colour.* (*See also* Photography.)

Steinback, Emmanuel. *See* MIM.

Steiner, Donald K. *See* K & S.

Steinmann, Helmuth, Great Britain. A maker of three-dimensional paper figures. An example of his work is given in the *Bulletin* of the British Model Soldier Society, October, 1973.

Stemmerman, Wolfgang, Freiburg/Berlin (fl.1950). Known mainly for the war machines he made for the R.U.S.I. dioramas. Is known also to have done a hunting scene and a William Tell, presumably in flats.

Stern, R., Germany (fl.1950). Connected with the construction of the R.U.S.I. dioramas.

Steudner, J.Ph., Augsburg (17th century). His wood-engraved, hand-coloured illustrations were the precursor of the paper sheets.

Stevens Foundry, Cromwell, Connecticut (c.1960). Manufacturers mainly of cast-iron home-banks, but may possibly have also made some flats.

Stevenson, R.L. and **Osbourne, Lloyd.** Stevenson's only interest in models was as an aid to his and Osbourne's particular brand of harmless and juvenile games. He was a child at heart, as is shown by his mention of toy soldiers in his poems, and it would be fatuous to link him with H.G. Wells as a serious advocate of the wargame.

Stewart, D.S., Los Angeles (1969-). Maker of a series of 54mm solids for Waterloo Galleries. These consisted of a range of American Revolution and Napoleonic troops, cast in a metal so malleable that the arms and the legs were easily animated (and the bayonets easily broken). They were not particularly noteworthy, except for a certain ruggedness, which was refreshing, but a mounted knight was so badly designed that the fitting together of the two parts of the horse was impossible, and the making of the figure a sheer waste of time.

Stirling Castle. A series of paper cut-outs of Scottish troops on packets of Danish tobacco.

Stirnemann, J., Aarau (1830-60). Engraver of flats for Wehrli.

Stobart, Colin. *See* Old Campaign Figures.

Stock, J. Duke, USA (fl.1950-65). One of the earlier of the United States makers of solids, with a small output of 48 to 50mm models of the Ancient World, Romans and Aztecs.

Stocken, Nevile. *See* Archive Miniatures.

Stockinger, A.F., Linz (1977-). Publisher of flats of the First World War. (*Klio*, 1977).

Stockinger, L. von and **Morsack,** Vienna (fl.1850-70). Publishers of paper sheets of the Austro-Hungarian army.

Stoddart Ltd, London (fl.1950-55). Manufacturer of a small range of 54mm hollow-casts, including a polar exploration set with Eskimos and igloos.

Stokes, Denny C., London/Deal/Harpenden (d.1975). A pioneer in the making of dioramas in Great Britain, setting the pattern for many later conceptions. He was a prime mover in those at the R.U.S.I. and collaborated on many occasions with Greenwood and Ball. An exhibition of his work in London in 1958 revealed an intelligent mind, so elastic as to be able to create a perfect reconstruction of Egyptian times by placing, within a designed framework, a single figure, that of Courtenay's figure of Nefertiti, or to be equally at home with a vast panorama in flats. He also created many dioramas of social life and work for industry, and his models are to be seen in many institutions.

Stoll, Hans Jorg, Konstanz, W. Germany. A publisher of flats of the Seven Years' War, some engraved by Lecke or by Trips.

Stone Mountain Miniatures (J.E. McCarron), Denver, Colorado (1977-). Maker of 25mm wargame solids of the American Revolution and the Civil War, together with Civil War cannon, including a parrot gun. Riders are removable, separate heads are available, and colour-printed flags are a useful addition. McCarron also produces 54mm models to commission.

Stonesypher, John R. *See* Deauville Models.

Strettweg Idol Cart. One of the finest known specimens from antiquity, found near Judenberg, and including 13cm high horsemen with helmets, shields and spears, dating from about 1000 BC. There is a copy in the Ashmolean Museum, Oxford.

Striedbeck, Jean Frederic, Strasbourg (fl.1780-90). One of the early publishers of paper sheets.

Stringer, South America (pre-1939). Manufacturer of 54mm solids.

Strola, Italy (c.1935). Manufacturers of Elastolin-type composition models.

Strombecker Corporation, Chicago, Illinois (c.1936-). A firm of toy makers. In the 1940s they produced balsa-wood kits of armaments. Between 1968 and 1972 they made several sets of badly cast 54mm solids in magnesium, each consisting of up to five figures, including one of American combat troops of the Second World War in the Pacific Islands, and one of Germans of the same war. The amount of flash left on some of the models was quite remarkable.

Structo, USA (fl.c.1930) Manufacturers of tin-plate army vehicles and tanks. [*R. O'Brien*]

Stuttgarter Bilderböger, Stuttgart (1860-90). Publishers of lithographed uncoloured paper sheets of world-famous events.

Styles, R.B. and **J.R.** *See* Heroics.

Success, Hong Kong. Contemporary piracies of Herald models. [*Opie*]

SUGAR. *See* Edible Models.

Sullivan, Barry, Monkstown, Dublin. A maker of 12.5cm semi-flats, engraved on one side only, designed for Irish Regimental messes and for the Naval HQ at Haulbowline, and including a set of Regimental uniforms of 1930 to 1940.

Sullivan, Robert, USA (1935-74). Maker of pewter models for Hudson Pewter, and a chess set of the American War of Independence for International Silver Company.

Sun Rubber, USA (c.1935-1960). Makers of poor-quality rubber models.

Supercast (Calex International), Torrance, California (1970-). Makers of solid 54mm Second World War action troops, ten figures in all. Photographs suggest that they are derivative.

Supercast Ltd, Hull (1974-). Manufacturers of home-casting kits consisting of eight 54mm rubber moulds of Napoleonic troops.

Superior Models Inc., (Lionel Forrest) Claremont, Delaware (1967-). One of the most important makers of solids in the United States. Beginning with 90mm models, they have also issued specimens in 54 and 88mm. Forrest had been known for some years as a skilled professional painter, and he himself set the standard for Superior by designing a number of the first models, especially those in 90mm which were entitled Regalia. Others employed by the firm are William Smith, Don Spicer and M. Ferguson. Probably the most impressive productions are the assembly of men and artillery making up an Austrian First World War Skoda mortar team. The kit is infinitely detailed, and must be one of the artillery masterpieces of all times. Others in the same vein are an 88mm anti-aircraft gun, a 7.5mm German Second World War howitzer, and a Rennaissance cannon, also with crew. Other fine models are a mounted Cortez, a series of medieval armour copied from actual specimens in the Metropolitan Museum (these can also be obtained plated as paper-weights), a pair of tilting knights, and an officer of the Bengal Lancers. An American War of Independence group includes Burgoyne, Kościuszko and a very poorly made George Washington. They have also produced a French artilleryman, Napoleon, Murat and Ney, a German Panzer Grenadier and the Kaiser, while a Robert E. Lee and a Jebb Stuart represent the Civil War. In 1976 they issued their first 150mm model and a series of twelve famous film stars, 'The Entertainers', by Ray Lamb. In the following year they joined the 'fantasy figure' fetish.

Superquick, USA. Publishers of pre-pressed cardboard models of domestic buildings.

Support Breveté SGDC Imprimerie de Bouquet, Paris. Publishers of pre-pressed cardboard sheets, one series consisting of 112 figures of infantrymen.

Surén, E. *See* Willie.

Sutton, Lieut-Colonel Thomas, Lewes/Eastbourne (d.1970). A connoisseur and collector of chess sets (one of which he bequeathed to the National Army Museum). Turning later to model soldiers, he commissioned the diorama of the Battle of Lewes (at the East Sussex Schools Museum Service, Lewes), and left part of his collection of flats and Britains' models to the Sussex Archaeological Society.

Sutty, Michael, Knockholt, Kent (1968-). A sculptor in bone china who has established an international reputation. His very large military models, sometimes consisting of several figures grouped together (e.g. the Capture of the Eagle at Waterloo), are unique in that detail is of secondary importance, and the whole fluidity of his material expresses itself in exciting movement. His Henry V appears to be creating an impossible situation for himself in the manner in which his lance and the reins of the horse are being handled, and his Richard I is far from the usual image, yet such is the balance achieved that the models appear to be impelled by some irresistible force. The only comparison one can make as far as this urgency is concerned is with that of the creations of Angenot. Sutty's Black Prince is surely unique in this context, but, ironically, the Hussar that was commissioned by Fortnum and Mason and which really started his career is a woeful effort. Not all his models, however, are in such violent action. The 'American Heritage' series is of a calmer nature, as are his collection of Lancers at pistol shooting and his Dragoon Regiments, and, naturally, a series of evocations from medieval statues and brasses, while his Robert the Bruce is expressed with nobility. In 1976 he began a series of fourteen models, 'The Glory that was India', which may be added to over the years. To mark the Silver Jubilee Sutty created an equestrian group of the Queen and the Duke of Edinburgh in an edition of fifty at the price of £3,000. Other models marking the occasion were a Sowar of the Bengal Lancers, a Grenadier Guards pioneer, a Gordon Highlanders drummer and a few other similar subjects, all in editions varying between 25 and 50 copies, and a mounted British officer of the Bengal Lancers. Sutty also makes delightful nursery-rhyme characters, animals, birds and a heraldic zoo.

Swartz, Germany. It has been alleged that he purchased

78 **Sutty.** *'The Black Prince'. English redstone; decorated in enamels and lustres; reins and sword in hall-marked silver.*

Spenküch's moulds and sold them to Sweden.

SWEDEN. There is no evidence of model-making in Sweden prior to 1843, when the firm of Santessonska Tenngjuteriet was founded. They produced 40mm semi-solids, probably from moulds imported from Germany, mostly of Swedish subjects, together with special 50mm solids of Swedish sovereigns, semi-solid 4cm and 12cm models, and poor 35mm flats. Production ceased about 1930. Schreuder and Olsson Leksfabrick (1896) made 40mm semi-solids of naïve quality, but not after 1920. The most popular firm was that of Tenngjuteriet Mars, founded in 1913 by a banker named Aschberg, together with Commander Stack and N.E. Lindbeg. They appear to have had a ready sale for their 30mm flats and 40mm solids both in Denmark and in Russia, a market that of course was brought to a halt in 1917. After 1945 Swedish interest in military affairs dwindled and, about 1947, Lindbeg sold about a thousand sets of moulds to Curt Wennberg, only to buy back again the Romans, Teutonic Knights, Westerners and Lapps. Wennberg continued to cast from the remaining moulds, of which some were in turn sold to Neckel. Wennberg also bought about half of Schreuder's moulds (it is said for a 'song') and what he could of the moulds formerly made for Santessonska, who, however, refused to sell those of the Thirty Years' War, Charles XII and the Finnish War of 1808.

The most outstanding figure is Holger Eriksson. Early in the 1930s he began carving large equestrian models in wood, but soon turned his hand to the production of lead models in 54, 40 and 30mm. Each of these displays an economy of effort, a beautiful sense of proportion and a severe rectitude. Wennberg was instrumental in introducing him to Comet, for whom he designed the majority of the Authenticast figures, which made him famous in a larger sphere, and later his association with S.A.E., badly cast though the models were, ensured him lasting fame. While still marketing a certain number of castings, he has of late retired even further into his self-imposed shell and is happiest working to commission. Magnus Schreiber, a comparative newcomer, concentrates on Swedish history and limits his models to a few castings, normally for presentation. He, too, displays a Nordic austerity. Flats are championed by Sivhed, employing the services of several designers and engravers, and depicting principally the wars of Gustavus Adolphus. These contain many examples of groups and '*kombination*' figures. The hobby stores in Sweden stock many British and American models. There is a flourishing school of Historex converters, and a well-established society.

Swedish-African Engineers (1955–58). *See* S.A.E.

'Swoppets'. A type of plastic model invented by Herald Miniatures in 1965, which caused a minor sensation when first issued. Basically the idea was that of a model made in several interlocking pieces, so that the torso could be swivelled at the waist, the head could be turned sideways and alternative weapons and headgear be removed at will. The 'Wars of the Roses' set had everything – a fine basic design obviously derived from Britains' Agincourt series, different shields and swords, battleaxes, maces, lances, pennons, alternative movable visors and a whole series of different crests. Even the misericords were made separately and the swords were removable from the scabbards. Horses had two styles of trappings, which were removable, as were the riders, the bridles and the saddles. The only blemish was an anachronistic red or white rose on shield or banner. They were followed by an equally good set of Westerners and Indians, and a slightly less impressive American Revolution set. Other firms followed suit without having the slightest idea of the proportion of the equipment, and some quite laughable examples were produced. The idea died as the polystyrene kit took over.

Sykes, John, Mosman, New South Wales (1965–   ). A maker of 54mm solids. He began with a series entitled Australian Military Miniatures, comprising a small range of mainly Australian forces of 1900. These, being marketed by Eric Wiseman, an Australian dealer, were thought for some years to be his work, as Wiseman made no mention of Sykes' name in advertisements. They are to be recognized by the trade-mark on the underside of the base – a castellated barbican. Although featured in the *Bulletin* of the British Model Soldier Society in 1971, they had no more fortune than those of Wooten. Sykes then came to England to improve his technique. On returning to Australia in 1972 he began producing further models of the Napoleonic era in 15 and 25mm, the Crimean War, the Seven Years' War, the Napoleonic Wars and the United States Civil War in 30mm, and a 'Collectors' Series' in 54mm of Australian troops 1860–1900, the Black Watch, Lord Uxbridge, and the 17th Lancers 1879, in kit form. He now has his own shop, The Anatomy of Glory, in Sydney, where all his models, under the name Milartex, are to be found. It was rumoured that in 1974 he had been commissioned by Miniature Figurines to design 54mm models for them.

Synge-Hutchinson, Patrick. *See* Midleton Models.

Synthetic Resin. *See* Composite Models.

'System 12'. *See* Hinchliffe F. and R.

T

T. & B. *See* Taylor & Barrett.

Taffy Toys, Hong Kong (1966). Manufacturers of plastic horrors.

Tag, England (c.1970). Manufacturers of plastic composition 70mm models of Second World War (British Infantry), Paratroopers, WAAFS, ATS, RAF Regiment, United States Infantry and Cossacks. [*Opie*]

Talim, Argentina (1955). Manufacturer of 54mm metal guns. [*Basseterre*]

Tallon, Germany (1964).Manufacturer of plastic models of modern troops.

Tamiya, Japan (1970-   ). Manufacturers principally of polystyrene AFVs and armaments in kit form, in about 1974 they began producing troops to go with them. These consisted of 25mm models, which were then pantographed to 54mm size and cast in metal, together with 75mm solids of Germans of the Second World War. In 1975 they issued a Wehrmacht mounted infantryman, the horse and figure in a 48-part kit, and, in 1976, medieval Japanese, 'The Forty-seven Ronin', and a USA command group.

Tamm, Sebastian, Sweden. In 1977 he projected a series of Swedish models by Sanderson to be issued in a limited edition, silver-plated, on presentation stands.

Tanner Castings, London (1978-   ). Their first offering was an anatomically inexact Chevaux-Légers Lancer, 1814, in 100mm, by S. Kemp.

Tapavica, Michael, Mission Viejo, California (1968-   ). Maker of commissioned 150mm solids, his first commercial venture being a series for The Black Watch.

Tassell, John. *See* Lasset; Series 77; Sovereign Miniatures.

Tauber, Austria. A producer of flats of the Austrian Landwehr, 1809, and Military Academy figures, 1780.

Tavener, Ray, Farnham, Surrey (1970-   ). Served for some years as a caster for Trussler of Tooting, London, who made moulds for many toy firms. On settling in Farnham he began making 90mm models to commission.

Taylor & Barrett, London (c.1930-?). Manufacturers of 50 and 55mm hollow-casts of khaki-clad troops (1914-18), naval ratings and a good sled and dog team with Eskimos. The partnership dissolved, one becoming F.G. Taylor & Sons Cast Metals, turning later to plastics, and the other Barrett & Sons. Mark: T&B/ COPYRIGHT/ENGLAND.

Taylor, P.A. *See* Quorn Collection.

Taylor, R. *See* Tricorne Miniatures.

Taylor, William, Newcastle. In 1966 he was featured in the *Bulletin* of the British Model Soldier Society as a carver of 12-inch models in yellow pine. In 1975 he reappeared as a designer of horses for the Blücher group produced by Deauville.

T.B.S., Italy (fl.1965). Manufacturer of composition figures similar to the pre-war Elastolins.

TBS. *See* The Barefoot Soldier.

Teague, Dennis, Plymouth, Devon (1968-75). A dealer who, until serious illness procluded such activity, was also occupied making commissioned dioramas. As these were for agencies, the eventual locations were usually unknown to the artist, but he has been seen some in television films such as *The Battle of the Atlantic* (B.B.C., 1974) and *Blue Peter*. In the main they consisted of converted kits of aircraft and naval vessels, but he himself cast a number of the latter, and made occasional original military models which fitted in with the commissioned conversions. A collection of 25mm models, mainly converted, but painted by him, was commissioned by the Leicester Education Board. He also wrote a small but useful book on the making of dioramas.

Telgman, Øy A.B. *See* Kavoteide.

Tellos, Madrid (1925-45). A carver of 60mm infantry in wood, which are rarely seen outside Spanish museums.

Tempa del Prete, Paestum, Italy. A rich hoard of archaic military figurines was found here in 1954.

Tenngjuteriet Mars (Aschberg, Commander Stack and N.E. Lindbeg), Stockholm (1913-47). Manufacturers of flats and 40mm solids. The moulds for modern troops were made in Germany, and issued in sets of 18 infantry or cavalry. Models of Vikings and the Battle of Brunkeberg were designed by Holm Sjosward, those of Lapps and reindeer by Ossian Elgstrom. The flats were particularly lively and attractive. The moulds of these were purchased by the dealer Wentzels.

Tenngjuteriet Schreuder. *See* Schreuder & Ohlsson.

Teo (Teodor Rodriguez) Barcelona (1928-31). A maker of excellent solids mainly of Spanish cavalry, the swords, helmets and cuirasses of steel. They proved too expensive for the times and are now rare and eagerly sought after. (*Allendesalazar*)

Terana, Christian, Paris. Professional painter of flats.

Teremy, David J., Mindenerheide (1979-   ). Producer of flats.

Ternisien, Alfred. A French collector who donated 30,000 flats and solids to Compiègne in 1927.

Terry (Carlos Rodriguez Zambori), Argentina (1953-57). A producer of hollow-casts based largely on Britains' originals. [*Basseterre*]

Tessière, Paris (fl.1839-51). Mentioned in the *Almanach Bottin* between 1838 and 1951 as a manufacturer of 'soldats'.

Testi, Commendatore, Italy (d.1972). His vast collection of mainly Italian commercial solids is at Ponte di Brenta.

Tetra, Italy. Manufacturer of polystyrene AFV kits.

Tetzel, Heinz, Magdeburg. Publisher of a few flats, engraved by Frauendorf, including the Swiss Guard and an equestrian hunting scene of the 18th century.

Teuber-Weckersdorff, Colonel Willy, Vienna/Bad Gastein (c.1880-1974). In 1909 he made a diorama of the Battle of Aspern, using 30,000 flats. Another of Prinz Eugen crossing the Danube (1717), with about the same number of Heinrichsen's models, was shown in Vienna about 1915.

Teubner, B.G., Leipzig. Manufacturer of cardboard models of houses. *Ortmann*)

The Barefoot Soldier (R. Victor Norman) Bloomsbury, New Jersey. An agent who had a pungent way of writing in his house magazine. Under the name TBS he issued a series of five models of early Americana (purchased from K/S Historical Prints), and designed by Greer, Cooke, Scruby and McGerr. Although of no great quality, their subject matter was interesting. In 1972 he published a four-piece set by the Rowes, only to sell them in 1977 to Cavalier. The firm closed down in 1978.

'The British Army' series. *See* Caton, A.

'They Nobly Dared'. A series of dioramas of the American War of Independence, made by members of the Military Collectors of New England, headed by Henri Lion. Work began in 1973, and the models used were mainly those of Rose and Imrie/Risley, with additional ones made by Cooke and Greer. In one instance 9mm Scruby figures were incorporated. The dioramas were exhibited at the offices of The American Mutual Insurance Company at Wakefield, Massachusetts, in 1975, and later at the Boston Museum of Fine Arts.

Thiel, H.H., Ruhla, E. Germany (1900-70). A maker of flats, known mainly for his French Napoleonics. The moulds were purchased by Knoll. Mark: T.

Thiemiel, Otto, Germany (fl.1960s). Maker of 30mm flats of the United States Civil Wars.

Thien, Erwin, Ratingen (1979-   ). Producer of flats.

Thies, M., Germany. Designer of flats.

Thirot, Paris (fl.1817). A carver of 20mm wooden figures for a diorama of the bridges of Paris.

Thomas & Skinner, Indianapolis (c.1950). Manufacturers of a wood and steel coastal defence gun.

Thomas et Roy, Metz (19th century). Publishers of paper sheets.

Thomas, G.B., London (fl.1960). Manufacturer of plastic piracies.

Thomas Industries (W.A. Thomas), Shawnee, Oklahoma (1950-   ). One of the earliest and still one of the best makers of 20mm solids, mainly of the American Civil War. He was allowed by Arquette to pantograph his large wooden models and to issue them as 54mm solids. About the year 1970 the firm was taken over by Leslie Pierce, the name being altered to K. & L. Company.

Thompson, Glenn, Dublin. Designer of 5-inch semi-flats for Cork Museum.

Thompson, Jeffery, U.S.A. Professional painter for Cowan.

Thompson, Peter, Cincinnati, Ohio. A publisher of paper sheets, 13 men and one officer, 3 inches high, with wooden blocks.

Thompson, Robert, Stockton-on-Tees. Converted 15 Stadden models into uniforms of the Durham Light Infantry 1750-1915, at the request of the Regiment in 1968, for their museum at Aykley Heads. A similar collection was commissioned by the Durham County Hotel, Durham, and others were done for the Queen's Dragoon Guards, 9th/12th Lancers and 4th/7th Dragoon Guards.

Thorburn, W.A., Edinburgh (1954-   ). A maker of models in plasticine, 1 inch to 1 foot, built up on a wire armature, varnished, japlacked and painted, with wood or metal accessories, the horses of wood. These are of Scottish troops, and are at the Scottish United Services Museum.

Thorne, E.A. & Son, London (fl.1957). Listed in an official journal that year as makers of hollow-casts, but repeated inquiries elicited no reply.

Thornton, London (1975-   ). Manufacturers of polystyrene battlefield scenery, pre-flocked in green, for wargamers.

Thorp Modelmakers, London. Makers of dioramas to commission. Three were shown at the '1776' exhibition at the National Maritime Museum (1976), two of which incorporated specially made models by Series 77, the third a kind of Siborne layout involving half-inch butterfly pins, the heads appropriately painted. They have renovated the models in the London Museum, and have added others to the recently formed Museum of London.

'Those Valiant Upstarts'. A series of 15 of the 'They Nobly Dared' dioramas, with three others, exhibited at the Boston Museum of Fine Arts in 1975.

Thurman Publishing, Great Britain (1975). Publishers of elaborate cardboard cutouts in book form of Salisbury Cathedral and Culzean Castle.

Tibidabo Toys, Italy (fl.1965-   ). Manufacturers of 56mm plastic models of modern Italian troops and carabinieri in ceremonial dress.

Tichband Brothers, London (fl.1965-70). Free-lance artists who, besides animating models for 'Tradition', also did a fine diorama of the Battle of Alexandria, which was for years on loan to the Gloucestershire Regiment at Bishop Hooper's House, Gloucester.

'Ticonderoga' series. *See* Lincoln Logs.

Tiddle-Toddle, Austria (c.1960). Manufacturers of papiermâché 7cm models of Westerners, knights and contemporary troops. Even worse than the name would lead one to imagine.

Tihm, Nuremberg (fl.1935). Maker of flats.

Tilo. *See* Maier, S.

Tily, Captain James C., USA. Designer of an American Revolution set which Rössner made in flats.

Tim-Mee Figures (F. Baumgartner), Karlsruhe (fl.1958). Manufacturers of 8cm plastic composition figures of Westerners, knights and contemporary troops.

Tim-Mee Toy Co., Aurora, Illinois (fl.1965). Manufacturers of 6cm unpainted plastic monstrosities of modern troops.

Timms, Richard, London (d.1975). One of the original designers for Valda.

Timper, Gertraude, Linsengericht, W. Germany (1979-). Producer of flats.

Timpo, London/Shotts, Lanarkshire (1943-79). Manufacturers of hollow-casts and plastics, 56-60mm. In 1953 they changed their name to Model Toys Ltd, only to revert later to the original. Marks: (Hollow-cast) TIMPO/TOYS—ENGLAND across shoulders or base of stand; (Plastics) TIMPO; TIMPO TOYS/MADE IN ENGLAND under stand, or simply MADE IN ENGLAND on top of stand. Although not so prolific in their range as Britains, shunning the traditional style of presentation in rows of models undergoing the same actions, Timpo achieved a solidarity of style and a variation in posture that the older manufacturer never possessed. Remove the sentiment attached to Britains and Timpo emerges as probably the most consistently good of the later manufacturers in this medium. The slightly increased size and greater bulk of the models was to their advantage, and the more adventurous positions added greatly to their reputation. Especially noteworthy were their American combat troops of the Second World War, and their excursions into past history. While their Romans were not particularly distinguished, they opened up a new era for painters with a bent for heraldry with the introduction in 1955 of their 'Ivanhoe' series, the riders being cast separately and the lances detachable. Even with the simple painting in which they were issued they were impressive, and, indeed, the first models the author ever bought were these. The horses were solid enough to carry the weight of armour, but were all in one position. The lance was originally of metal, but it had a tendency to break where it slid into the hand, and, regretfully, a poor one in plastic replaced it. A set of King Arthur and his knights, in the Malory tradition of armour, soon followed, admirably stocky fellows, all in different action poses, with adjustable visors and tufted helms. The set of 'Quentin Durward' opened up a new interest for many collectors, that of the Landschnecht, some of whom had separate crossbows or handguns. The models in all these sets were issued in separate cardboard boxes, each with its own name, and were better than the British battle-dress troops, Westerners and farm animals, although a now rare big game set with bearers, elephants and white hunters set a good standard. The hollow-casts were replaced in 1956 by plastics, mainly based on existing models (except for the knights) with the addition of the French Foreign Legion, Romans, Robin Hood, West Point cadets, Guardsmen, etc. The horses were the same for all sets. The quality was not to be compared with the hollow-casts, but a 'Waterloo' proved successful, though more research could have made them memorable. These models were all orginally sold painted, but for the last few years have been obtainable only in their natural state. They now produce their models under the various names of Action Pack, Famous Fighters and Tiptops, the latter for the artillery. Opie considers that a number of sets of cowboys and Indians in unpainted plastic, under the name of Peter Pan Playthings, and a similar range with the addition of a covered wagon and combat infantry called Popular Plastics, may also be products of Timpo. About

1949 they made an abortive effort to produce models in plaster.

Tin Plate. *See* Conjoint Tin.

Tinsmiths and Tinfigure Manufacturers, Association of. A group of small manufacturers of flats who pooled their resources in the mid-19th century. They were: Scheller (Kassel), Schindler, Bunau and Loblich (Leipzig), Vaterlein (Freiburg), Schepp (Breslau) and Leschhorn (Randten).

Tipp & Co. *See* Mettoy.

Tipple-Topple. *See* Elastolin.

Tiptops. *See* Timpo.

Titan Manufacturing Co. Ltd., Southall, Middlesex (1973-). Manufacturers of dust-covers for large models.

Tobinnus, Gerhard, Hanover. A prolific publisher of flats. It is difficult to establish which ranges Tobinnus produces himself and which he markets for others. He acts as agent for Sollner, Meyniel, Beck and Schirmer.

Todd, William, USA. Professional painter for Cowan and others.

Tomker Accessories, Antwerp (1978-). Makers of metal accessories such as tankards, candlesticks, etc., in 75, 80 and 90mm scale.

Tommy Toy (Dr Albert Greene, Charles E. Weldon, John Zeman) New York (c.1935-1938). A minor firm making hollow-casts. A total of twelve military figures, one nurse and ten nursery-rhyme characters, the latter by Kooken and Margaret Cloninger. Some bases were marked Tommy Toy, others unmarked, which have been confused with those of American Alloy. A few vehicles were also made. [*R.O'Brien; Pielin*]

Toms, Paul. *See* Hazelwood Miniatures.

Tootsietoys. (Dowst Manufacturing Co.) Chicago (1928-41). Manufacturers of 35mm semi-solid figures for use with their tin-plate military trucks and cannon.

Topper Toys, USA (fl.1965). Manufacturers of 8-inch plastic models.

Toray (Ediciónes Recontables). Barcelona/Buenos Aires (1962-65). Publishers of paper sheets, usually numbered four to eight, in covers, of Vikings, Bedouins, Napoleonics and the Second World War.

Torn, Edmond M., Munich (1979-). Producer of flats.

Toro, Marca el, Spain. Publishers of paper sheets, especially of the Spanish Civil War.

Tottenham Models. *See* Palmer Historic Cannon.

'Tower of London' chess set. Commissioned by the Constable of the Tower to commemorate 900 years of history. Sculpted in pewter by Stadden, and painted under the control of N. Saunders Ltd. The figures are: William I, Anne Boleyn, Elizabeth I, Duke of Monmouth, William de Mandeville, Archbishop Laud, Duke of Exeter, Archbishop Cranmer, Sir Thomas More, Bishop Gundulf, Sir Walter Raleigh, Saint Thomas à Beckett, with pawns in the form of an archer of the time of Edward III and a Yeoman Warder and castles as the Bloody Tower. Issued in a strictly limited edition.

Tower of London, The. A small wooden model, 3 x 1½-inches, circa 1485, and possibly of the Bloody Tower, was unearthed in London in 1964.

Townley, USA. One of the earliest pirates of Stadden, who departed unwept, unhonoured and unsung.

Toy Creations. *See* American Alloy.

Toydell Ltd, (P.B. Ducker), London (? -1954). Manufacturer of plaster composition 60mm models of the Household Cavalry dismounted, Highlanders, Foot Guards, Chelsea Pensioners, Westerners. These were well painted, and highly glazed. Mark: J.W.D.

'TOYS'. The name given to bulk-manufactured figures intended primarily for the juvenile trade. Apart from the specially commissioned or superfine models made as either single items or in limited quantities, the term embraces practically the whole of the pre-1939 output of flats, semi-flats, solids, semi-solids, hollow-casts, composition figures and, later, plastics. Indeed, a number lingered on in diminishing quantities in hollow-cast and other materials until the middle of the 1960s. As has been said elsewhere, the influence of the collector led to the rise of the individual maker of a more highly sophisticated model, and the mass-produced item, apart from those in plastic and composition, became things of the past. However, their place in the history of the model soldier is indestructible, embracing as it does the products of the early makers of flats, (the Heinrichsens and the Allgeyers in particular), the semi-solids of Ammon, Spenküch and Wollner, the home-casting moulds, the early American efforts of Barclay, Manoil and McLoughlin, the solids of Heyde and Mignot, the hollow-casts of Britains and their rivals and competitors, the naïve productions of I.S.A. and Antonini, the Scandinavian Mars and Brigader, the plastics of Cherilea, Timpo, Reamsa and Marx, and the everpresent Elastolin and Lineol. Originally made to be expendable, they are now treasured by a number of collectors as reminders of the past. It must in all fairness be said that, while many are of extremely poor quality, both in design and execution, there are also countless models which are unique in their action or historic witness. Production was enormous in quantity and scope, and the collector is constantly finding a figure of whose existence he was ignorant. Even if one is fortunate enough to possess a manufacturer's complete catalogue, it is today highly unlikely that one could collect every single item contained therein: indeed the works of Britains, Barclay, Heyde and Mignot were so subject to alteration or modification that a lifetime devoted to one manufacturer is needed. One is constantly reminded of the 'fringe' items that they made, such as farm scenes and miniature gardens, walls and hedges and telegraph poles, railway staff and army equipment of the most amazing variety. Nor can it be denied that the sight of thousands of enamel-clad figures of a folk naïvety is impressive, and a reminder that the 'steadfast toy soldier' has its honourable and in some quarters honoured place in history. The powerful fascination that it now exerts is evident from the number of enthusiasts who are re-creating the idea in solid at what are by no means negligible prices, and the sums to which devotees are prepared to go at auction for the acquisition of these 'toys', scorning the productions of present-day master craftsmen in favour of the past.

TRADE-MARKS. These are most useful for accurate identification, but unfortunately many makers do not stamp their figures. There are in consequence many unidentifiable models whose parentage can be surmized only on style and general character, particularly Germanic solids and toy-trade plastics. The former normally carry no legend whatsoever, the latter often merely the country of origin. Ideally the underside of the base of the model is the best place for a trademark, but if the model is glued to a stand it is impossible to see. With the older models identification may be achieved if they are preserved in the original box, but in early days no thought of later interest could have been in the minds of the makers. Modern makers of flats, however, are scrupulous in giving the initials of the designer, the engraver, the publisher and the number of the series. These are usually found on the upper surface of the footstand and even when painted over they can often still be seen. Wargame models are particularly irritating in their lack of identity, with the exception of Garrison, on the foot of whose figures is a deeply engraved trade-mark.

'Tradition' (Norman Newton, incorporating Charles C. Stadden Ltd., R. Belmont-Maitland) London (1962-). One of the most renowned of dealers, this magnificent shop in Mayfair is the culmination of years of enterprising planning by Roy Belmont-Maitland. (q.v.). The name Norman Newton has over the years become synonymous with the models of Stadden, so that on the Continent they are thus falsely called. The range of models that they stock and produce is dominated by those of Stadden, but they have always encouraged Arthur (father and son) Rendall from time to time, and more recently Cameron. Under the name 'Tradition' will be found Stadden's models of various periods, early, withdrawn, remade, in kit form, etc, together with incorporations such as the Pagada range made by Higgins, 54mm, 80 and 90mm models, either single castings of infantry, or elaborate mounted specimens, with metal attachments, issued in limited editions, by Alan Caton, and 75mm Napoleonics by Carrington and 80mm Napoleonics by Jeff Willis (1976). A series of wargame figures by Stadden has been added to by Surèn, Hinton, Clive Knight and David Scheinemann. 'Tradition' also has its own staff of animators, painters and dioramists, and a number of artists who have served what might be called an apprenticeship with the firm have gone on to join the ranks of makers in their own right. The firm has also issued paper sheet revivals by Nicholson, and deals in older types of historic models.

Tradition. A book of illustrations in colour, devoted entirely to Stadden models and published by 'Tradition' in 1967.

Tradition. The official journal of the International Society of Military Collectors, published by 'Tradition'.

Trafalgar Models, Walsall (1978-). Manufacturers of Britains-style 'toy' soldiers, under the name of Victoria Toys.

Tranquil, Jonny. *See* Grifo.

Trautner, J., Nuremberg (18th century). Publisher of paper sheets.

Trauttmansdorff, Count Johannes. Owner of the Pottenbrun Castle, the tower of which collapsed and, when rebuilt, was designed so that it could house fifty dioramas, including those of Mohacs, Nagy Kamzca, Lützen, Belgrade, Vienna, Sacile, Leipzig and Custozza, under the name of *Zinnfigurenmuseum.*

Treacy, William P. Jr. *See* Warwick Miniatures.

Treforest Mouldings Ltd. *See* Winkler, F.

Trellis Tongs. *See* Automata; Evolutions.

Trentsensky, Vienna (fl.1850). Publisher of paper sheets. Over 40, in line, with captions in three languages and a colour guide, were reissued by Verlagsbuchhandlung (R. Krey) in 1975 as a 125th anniversary issue.

Triang, England. Manufacturers mainly of toy motor-cars, they have also produced castles and forts. (*See also* Minimodels.)

Triangle, South Carolina (1977-). Pirates of Miniature Figurines models.

Trico, Japan (c.1930). Pirates of Elastolin models.

Tricorne Miniatures, England (R. Taylor and D. Miller) Kenilworth, Warwicks (1977-). The *Kulmbach Almanac* for 1977 announced a series of solids under this title, comprising 70mm 'Deutsche Landsknechte (Pludertract)' 1550-80; 54mm Der Grosse Deutsche Bauernkrieg ('Das Blutgericht' 16 models), and Prussian infantry 1740-86 in the same size. It was discovered that the modeller, D. Miller, had had considerable difficulties with production, but that the models were scheduled to appear 'at some time in the future' under the aegis of Zens Zinnmodelle.

Trips, Johannes, Empfingen. A publisher, designer and engraver of flats, including 20mm Carthaginians with heavy artillery, the Ancient World in general, Hittites designed by Blumentritt, a K.G.L. battalion and Danish, French and Prussian troops of 1805-15.

Trojan (W. Shipton) Ltd, London (fl.1958-63). Manufacturers of plastic 54mm models of modern troops, Westerners, a mortar set, ambulances, sandbags, and a Roy Rogers - quite reasonable on the whole. A series of 8cm mounted Westerners in polystyrene were quite ridiculous.

Trophy (Michael R. John) Penarth, Glamorgan (1971-). As Harlech Models he began with 58mm kits of solids of a mounted knight (with three detachable and alternative helms), an English bowman and a mounted Samurai with its own base scenery. The knight, although well-proportioned, had a horse with a very uneasy balance, but the Samurai made quite an impressive figure. A Murat and two Napoleonic infantrymen (all ill-conceived and ill-made) followed, together with an undistinguished George Washington. In 1975, however, better models followed in the shape of a mounted Robert Devereux, Earl of Essex, and a mounted Sioux. In the same year, John began a series of 'Soldiers of the British Empire', foot and cavalry, in Britains' style.

Trousset et Laumonier, Paris (fl.1876). A catalogue of French manufacturers issued in 1876 advertises 'boxes of wood and glass containing artillery, infantry and cavalry'. No further evidence is available as to whether they were solids or composition. The models would not have been imported, as the firm were evidently not dealers.

Tru-Craft Models (Cecil Jackson), Santa Monica, California (1939-62): (Donald Felton and Lloyd Reynolds), Encino, California (1974-). Jackson was one of the pioneers of the better-class commercial solid in the United States. A missionary in China, he returned to America and started with tiny models of railroad crews and passengers. When America became involved in the Second World War he obtained the services of Carl Romanelli, and began a series of G.Is, Marines and Japanese that proved extremely popular. To these he gradually added forces of the United States Civil War, the French in Mexico, the Foreign Legion and the Second Empire. A Civil War 13-inch mortar was an achievement, as was a horse cast in one piece. All the models were painted by home labour and attractively boxed. Eventually he found that he and his wife were being swamped by business and like a wise man retired from the field. In 1974 Donald Felton and Lloyd Reynolds took over the moulds, and now market the figures discreetly. The mortar has been remodelled, and in 1975 a 75mm Samurai appeared.

Trussler, Tooting, London. Makers of moulds for commercial firms including Britains.

Tschischwitz. The author of a treatise on *kriegsspiel*, 1862.

Tubbs, Christopher. *See* Edman, Ab. Jan.

Tuck, Raphael & Co., London. A firm of well-known British publishers. About 1910 they issued a series of highly coloured pre-cut and embossed military scraps, with stands.

Tudor Rose, England (c.1966). Manufacturers of plastic models, chiefly of King Arthur and spacemen.

Tunison, Ron, USA. A maker to commission of large, 10-inch clay models. Usually featured in the catalogues of The Soldier Shop.

Tunnicliffe Leisure Craft Models (R. Tunnicliffe) Thornaby, Cleveland (1979-). Maker of a scale-model, 9 inches in length, 6 inches in height, in wood and brass, of a 15th-century breech-loading peterara (or cannon), modelled from an original at the Tower of London.

Tunstill, John, London. Proprietor of Soldiers, a retail store selling a wide variety of models. Instigator with A. Rose in 1976 of Britains' type 'toys', entitled Soldiers' Soldiers. He has also made for Bethnal Green Museum a series of the Bethnal Green Volunteer Regiment, after the drawings by Rowlandson.

Turnbull, Charles Edward, & Co., London (fl.1914). A manufacturer of poor-quality hollow-casts of which only a few specimens are known.

Turnbull, Stephen, Northants. An authority on early Japanese armour, Turnbull regularly produced his own originals or conversions at club exhibitions, and took part, incidentally, in the B.B.C. television programme *Mastermind*, where Magnus Magnusson was at sea with his pronunciations! In 1975 he designed one or two medieval Japanese warriors for Rose Miniatures.

Turner, Alex., Perth (1966- ?). Mentioned in the *Bulletin* of the British Model Soldier Society, February, 1966, as a maker of 54mm commissioned solids. No further information has been forthcoming.

Turner, Pierre, Bridport, Dorset (1968-). A maker to commission of 77 and 230mm models in fibreglass resin, with wire armatures, the arms and headgear made separately and adhered. He served for a few years with Gammage. His models are most elegant in style, perhaps, in one or two instances, almost effeminate.

Turton, Byllee. *See* Frances Turton Figures.

Twist, Peter. *See* Coronet Miniatures.

Tyler, Lieut-Colonel E.S., Fort Devens, Massachusetts. A commissioned converter of 18-inch models in composition and actual cloth. His models may be seen at West Point, Fort Sill and Fort Leavenworth.

Tylinski, Horst, Berlin (1976-). A publisher of flats depicting Austrians and Russians.

U

Ubl, Hans-Jorg, Kutzendorf (1977–). A publisher of flats of ancient Germanic people. (*Klio*).

Uhlmann, Walter, Chemnitz (c.1930). Maker of accessories for dioramas.

Ullmann, Martin, USA. Designer of packages for Auburn Rubber Corpn.

Ullmann, P. *See* Mettoy Company Ltd.

U.N.A., London (c.1970). Manufacturers of plastic piracies of Timpo, Johillco and Herald's 'Swoppets'. [*Juplin*]

Un-Art Co, Norwell, Massachusetts (1964–). A firm that took over Hamblen's moulds.

'Uncle Sam's Defenders' series. *See* Grey Iron Casting Co.

Under Two Flags (J. & C. Coutts) London. Enterprising dealers who in 1975 began commissioning models from Minot and Phoenix and at the same time are skilled professional painters. They are to be commended for encouraging designers with limited finances by taking them under their wing (e.g. Ducal, Union Jack) and are ardent in their promotion of neo-Britains models.

Unger, Ing Wolfgang, Leipzig. A publisher of unusual flats, such as sets of a witches' kitchen from *Faust*, Leipzig Fair crowds (1825), and reproductions in miniature of Meissen porcelain vases.

UNIDENTIFIABLE MODELS. Throughout the years many manufacturers have refrained from placing any mark on their models. (Conversely, some have spoiled a model by placing their name across the buttocks, for example.) The German makers of solids were particularly perverse, and it is only in recent years that research has established that many of those formerly ascribed to Heyde may well be by either Heinrichs or Haffner. In the case of semi-solids it is only when they have been preserved in the original box and it can be proved that the contents are original that Ammon or his contemporaries can be named with certainty. Many of the hollow-casts remain anonymous, as the makers in many instances copied Britains slavishly, and were reluctant to give their name for fear of prosecution. Similarly, there is a vast concourse of plastics, the identity of which may well never be discovered, and once a collection of wargame models becomes mixed one is rarely able to identify the maker's name. In this context, the Garrison trademark is to be applauded. The Italian plastic and the Elastolin-type figure is the most frustrating, normally being marked 'Made in Italy (*déposé*)' and sometimes bearing a symbol only. The researcher works practically blind in a case like this, no matter how many correspondents he has in any country. Nor are enquiries from Consulates, Trade Agencies, Chambers of Commerce and the like often fruitful. As an example, the Greek Consulate General in London supplied the author with a list of 22 native makers of plastics. A letter was sent to each, explaining the nature of the enquiry. After six months replies had been received from three, two soliciting bulk shipments of dolls at a cut price, the other sending a catalogue of mechanical ducks and mice. Paper sheets in a number of instances bear neither the name of the printer nor the publisher; the collector Testi actually had a number of figures printed for him, and subsequently coloured by pencil, varnished and cut for standing, but no indication is given anywhere of this fact. Even Cornelius Frazer, who has thousands of sheets, can supply no clue to the publisher of many of them. It is probably safe to say that there are almost as many unidentified models in collections all over the world as identified ones. Modern makers have the advantage of photographic records of the majority of their work, even if it is not signed, but for pre- 1939 models the task is sometimes hopeless.

Union Jack, London (1976–). Britains-style revivals in solids, under the patronage of Under Two Flags.

Unione Nazionale Collezionisti d'Italia, Rome (c.1860). A little-known publisher of paper sheets.

Unique Art, Newark, New Jersey (c.1950). Manufacturers of tin-plate caricature-like military toys.

Unique Miniatures (Ronald White) Chelmsford, Essex (1974–). Maker of commissioned solids, mainly of Plains Indians and Westerners, 120mm to 150mm, in a resin-bound compound, with natural cloth and accessories. The horses are particularly well-made.

United Crafts, Mitcham, Surrey (1976–). Manufacturers of a 54mm Napoleonic chess-set, painted with a simulated pewter finish.

UNITED STATES OF AMERICA. The first record of model soldiers in North America occurs in an advertisement in *The Royal Gazette* of December, 1777: 'Christmas Presents for the Young Folks'. New York at this time was occupied by the British and their German

79 **United States** - *solids. Back row: About Face, Aristo-Merité (B. Gordon 2), Bressica, Brundick, Bugle & Guidon (2); middle row: Cameo (Boutet 2), Cavalier (2), Cockade (2), Aztecs (2); front row: Cockade (2), Greer (3), H-R (2), HAM (2) (Author).*

allies, and the models would undoubtedly be large flats imported from Germany, transported in British ships along with the Hessian troops, and intended for the children of both the British, the Germans and the Americans loyal to the crown. As to flats actually made in the United States, Ortmann illustrates three models, an animal up a tree, a large parrot and a lady sitting in a chair, which he states are of American origin and dating from the beginning of the 19th century. However, such is their affinity with the Schweizer type of model of that period that it appears more likely that they were importations from Germany, as were certainly the tin Prussians given by George Washington to his stepson John Parke Custis in the 1750s. There is, of course, the possibility that they are the work of an emigré, but much more evidence would have to be produced to establish that flats were made in any quantity (if indeed at all) in America at this time. Michael V. Hitrovo has a small number of semi-flats, engraved on one side only, of impeccable pedigree, depicting Civil War cavalry which would certainly appear to have been made in the United States. (Carman states that modern copies emanating from Japan are known.) Referring again to Ortmann, it will be seen that he illustrates (*plates* 139, 141) what purport to be United States flats of the middle 19th century. A curious one of a balloon is labelled 'Spencer N. York'. It could conceivably not be a native product at all, but imported for a special occasion, possibly to commemorate the observation balloons used during the Civil War. Of the naïve OMIBUS (*sic*) Michael Hitrovo says that this name was never used in America, nor is the type of vehicle an American one. Similarly a flat of a railway engine is of a type that might emanate from anywhere other than the United States. Importation of toys began early, as is shown by the advertisement in

the *Philadelphia Public Ledger* of 1850 of Louis C. Bauersach, Importer, stating that he had just received '100 cases of Penny Toys, including soldiers and seamen' (*McClintock*), and the flats illustrated by Ortmann might easily have been imported. McClintock also states that from about 1840 to before 1900 there were several hundred toy-makers in the United States, all engaged in the production of iron and tin-plate wheeled carriages, dolls' house furniture and the like. The manufacture of tin-plate began in the United States as early as 1740, so that it was a well-established industry before it turned to the production of toys. Conjoint tin was used from 1870 to 1914, cut-out tin from 1919 to 1930, both for the production of cheap models of soldiers, while from 1889 iron and coppered-iron toys including soldiers and artillery teams were advertised in toy catalogues, mainly by Parker Bros and Butler Bros, both importers.

Models in wood were made from the 1880s, some in the form of trellis tongs, one firm advertising in 1894: 'Buffalo Bill . . . A new departure in wooden toys . . . it illustrates how Buffalo Bill and his scouts overcame a party of ambushcading Indians', and would appear to have been of a panoramic nature. Many firms also issued plywood cut-outs, some mounted on metal bases, complete with toy pistols with which to shoot the soldiers down, one in particular in 1894 consisting of 'one large army gorgeously arrayed', while another of the same date, 'The Royal Guards', consisting of 33 men $7\frac{1}{2}$ inches high, with band, two cannon and flags, 'all on wheels', which could be made to 'march company, front, or right and left oblique', may well have been of wood mounted on metal, with mechanism so that they could perform their drill. Just as popular were great quantities of cardboard cut-out figures, again provided with toy pistols, many being made by the firm of Parker Bros, who, indeed, issued many wargame board games (one advertised in 1892 as 'The Battle Game'), varying the uniforms of the troops as successive wars occurred in which the United States was involved. The first solid lead models to appear were imported Heydes and Mignots (President Lincoln's son Tad certainly had some), and they are shown in line drawings in *The Tin Army of the Potomac*, published about 1880.

The first American makers of metal models appear to have been Beiser in 1900 and McLoughlin Bros, who, although founded in 1828, did not add soldiers to their cast-iron and cardboard toys until 1902. Their models were closely based on those of Heyde and Britain. They were followed by the American Soldier Company, owned by Parker Bros, and a few small firms, a number of whose models still cannot be identified. From 1914 the field was held by the Warren Company, Barclay, Manoil, the Ideal Toy Company and Comet. Models in cast-iron came from the Grey Iron Casting Corporation, as popular in America as the imported Britains. Comet, after starting with their own rather clumsy Brigadier models and ship recognition vessels for the US Government, were persuaded to employ Holger Eriksson for the design of an entirely new range, Authenticast.

Up to the era of the 'specialist' figure many other firms emerged, some good, some indifferent, some negligible, such as Lincoln Logs, Military Miniatures, Metal-Art (later Moulded Miniatures), St Louis Lead Soldier Company (an eccentric firm if ever there was one), Tru-Craft, and Colección Mexico. Many of the firms ceased production when the making of plastics started. Beton Toys had experimented in 1938 with models in various materials, but the chief exponent was Marx, whose excellent specimens were destined to be exported to many European countries. As for polystyrene kits, America was early in the market, and manufacturers continue to proliferate.

Around the 1930s the need manifested itself for a better model, and here, as in other countries, the impetus was provided by collectors who began making their own models, such as Brady, Hitrovo, West and the Harles. After 1945 the pace accelerated. Murray and Imrie began operating, the latter was joined by Risley and their models immediately commanded comparison with the recently imported Staddens; in fact, Imrie/Risley may be compared with Gammage in that they avoid the extravagancies and eccentricities of many of their contemporaries. They were soon followed by Kaufmann (now retired), Norman Cooke (now engaged mainly on diorama work), Ahrens, Broman (now specializing in accessories and artillery), and K-S, now defunct. In the last few years the pattern has changed. New firms have sprung up like mushrooms, and a school of free-lancers has emerged, creating difficulties in identification, especially when any one firm may engage the services of as many as a dozen designers. One advantage, however, accrues from this practice – a vast expansion in the range of subjects. Whereas Imrie/Risley have pursued traditional lines such as Napoleonics, American War of Independence and Civil War figures, other firms such as Monarch, Valiant, Cavalier and Little Generals work to no set plan, and are as likely to follow the issue of a Lawrence of Arabia by that of a Hun or a Brunswicker at Leipzig. At times there has been a preponder-

ance of Second World War troops, some poor excursions into Roman times, and equally dull figures purporting to represent the Middle Ages, and above all a feverish attempt by the less experienced maker to produce something novel, usually resulting in a figure of exquisite ineptitude. On the other hand there are some good efforts by Greer, the later models of Beverly Gordon and the vigorous Updyke, as well as splendid models by Chernak and Boutet.

American museums have always favoured the large model for their dioramas, and oversize figures are now dominating the market in the work of Superior, Little Generals, Lamb, Caldwell and Rodden. On the other hand there are few makers of wargame figures, apart from Scruby, Bussler, Wall and Pierce, but a number of makers are turning out great numbers of very poor 20 and 25mm creatures of a fevered imagination. The paper sheet has never been very popular with American publishers, but they have made valuable contributions in the form of beautifully printed books of pre-pressed figures.

Societies abound and English models are extremely popular, while imports of Spanish and French models, fostered by Polk and The Soldier Shop, appear at regular intervals. There is also a small but healthy appreciation of the flat. Some of the younger collectors have yet to appreciate the artistry of some of the more reticent classics of both old and recent times, their time

80 **United States** – *solids. Back row: Covington, B. Gordon; second row: Squadron/Rubin (4), Stewart (2); Third row: The Barefoot Soldier (3), Thomas (after Arquette), Valiant (3); front row: Valiant, Imrie (Author).*

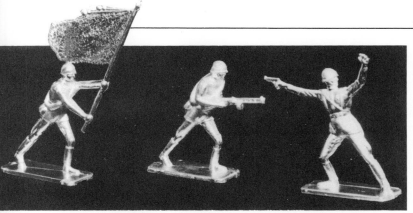

81   U.S.S.R. *Modern hard plastic, 40mm (C. Robinson).*

being occupied mainly in assembling Historex kits and making at times quite incredibly beautiful conversions. The models of most makers can be found in the shops of dealers in most areas of the United States, where blatant piracies may also be seen. Tremendous interest is shown by countless exhibitions; indeed interest in the hobby has never been higher. Above all, there is a healthy interchange of ideas between American and British collectors.

United Toy Factories. *See* Haffner, Johann.

Universal. *See* Moulded Miniatures.

Uno-A-Ekke, Germany(?). A solid silver 54mm Maximillian-period knight with plumed close-helmet and two-handled sword, Assay Office mark 925, seen in London in 1977.

Unwin & Wrigglesworth, London. Toy dealers. In 1760 George Washington ordered from them, among other toys for his stepson, a 'Prussian Dragoon' costing 1s 3d.

U.P.C. (Universal Powermaster Corporation) New York (before 1974–). Manufacturers of models exclusively for dioramas.

Updyke, J.B. *See* Minimen.

Urich, Heidrun, Munich (1979–). Designer and publisher of flats.

U.S.S.R. As is inevitable in any country abounding in forests, the Russian peasants were adept at carving wooden soldiers, some of which were mounted on trellis tongs. Paper sheets were also popular up to the Revolution, some being of the Russo-Japanese and First World Wars. The latter were pre-pressed and coloured, and sold in boxes of about 100 figures, ready for attaching to tiny circular metal flanged stands. The collection of Peter III, formerly at the Hermitage, but now at the Artillery Museum in the suburbs of Leningrad, contains a large number of flats and solids imported from Germany, together with flat wooden painted figures representative of eighteenth-century troops. Here also, are dioramas with flats and pre-Revolution Imperial Guards units, made of plaster with metal equipment [*C. Robinson*].From 1900 to 1917 a few firms produced crude 40mm flats and semi-flats, while one firm, making flats in 25mm, pirating the designs of Heinrichsen, went so far as to imitate the actual boxes. Allendesalazar illustrates (p. 47) solids of 1925 where mere round blobs without eyes or eyebrows, noses or mouths represent the faces. Miniature tin and wooden soldiers were shown to satellite countries at the Leipzig Trade Fair in 1957. At another trade fair, this time in Britain, the author was unable to obtain any information regarding the making of models, the blank wall of a representative at the stand having a chilling effect on the inquirer. Again in modern times paper sheets of Budenny's troops, dated 1945, have been seen in Turin, while in 1969 the great store GOUM carried stocks of troops made by co-operatives. These were all flat or semi-solid, 54mm, all of Russian troops, including bandsmen and Guards, with painted plastic flats. Other sets included Russian uniforms of all periods, entitled 'Glory to the Russian Weapon', a medieval series 'Russian Warriors' (actually supposed to portray Alexander Nevsky and his troops), in 60mm unpainted plastic, and 'Chapayev's Soldiers', mounted, with horse-drawn machine guns and weapons. Hitrovo and Pestana, who both saw them, summed them up as atrocious. In 1977 C. Robinson saw hard plastic sets, some in neutral plastic colour, others sprayed to simulate metal, size 40, 45, 54 and 60mm, some semi-solid, which may be the ones already mentioned.

Utexiqual, Moorestown, New Jersey (1973–). 54mm plaster composition models, rather doll-like in appearance, but well painted in what appears to be watercolour, including 16th Bengal Cavalry (1801) Cavalry and Lancer officers (1850, 1860, 1881 and 1910). [*A. Robinson*]

V

V (Mayor Laforet) Barcelona (1945-55). Manufacturer of 50mm solids, sold in boxes of 8 to 10 figures.

Vagné, M. *See* Imagerie de Pont-à-Mousson.

Valda Military Miniatures (R. Timms, B. Owen) Coventry (1969-c.1974). This partnership began with a small series of handcast 54mm solids of female army types, in limited editions, marketed by Sea Gull Model, from whom the names of the designers were unobtainable. However, their identity was disclosed when they set up an establishment at Coventry, and advertised an extension of their range to include Bombay, Madras and Bengal Native Infantry (c.1850) and the 24th Regiment of Foot (1879) in kit form with alternative heads and, in some cases, arms. Timms died in 1975, and the production of models ceased. The original conception was imaginative and some good models resulted.

Valente, C. *See* Life Model.

Valentino (Ditta Landi). *See* Landi, Ditta.

Valhalla Wargames Ltd, (R.A. Buxton *et alia*) Bathampton, Bath (1972-). Diorama specialists, formed from the nucleus of the only professional wargame team in existence, under the auspices of the Department of Trade & Industry and the Ministry of Defence, while being serving members of H.M. Forces. Exhaustive research with authorities is done before any commissioned diorama is begun. Models (usually 20mm) are all multi-conversions. Specimens of the firm's work can be seen at Towneley Hall Museum, Barnsley; Lancashire Fusiliers' Museum, Bury; HQ 13th/18th Royal Hussars, Cannon Hall Museum, Barnsley; Fleet Air Arm Museum, Yeovilton. They have their own personal dioramas of Waterloo, each using about 18,000 models, as (1) a portable wargame-type layout, (2) as a static model (exhibited at Woburn Abbey, 1973-74). An exhibition hall at Bathampton was commenced in 1974.

Valiant Miniatures (Arthur Neckermann & Shepard Paine) Chicago (1969-). A firm that has turned out one of the most prolific series of 54mm solid models in kit form, in that some are of the finest quality and others sink to the lowest depths of inanity. This is explained in part by the practice of having no set theme, and by employing free-lance artists of variable ability. Among these are Anderson, Paine, Boutet, Cade, Berton, Bihari, Greer, Lombardo, Fabre, Sibbitt, Olmstead, Kennedy, Reuters, Voeke and others who, the firm say, wish to remain anonymous. The series of models depicting participants at the Battle of Leipzig are full of character and élan, as are those of Second World War Americans, although peculiarly similar to those of Imrie/Risley. The Germans of the same war are pedestrian. An Irish Republican Army soldier (1921) captures the spirit of the times. The 'Barbarian' range (a Nordic warrior, a Teutonic chieftain, a Vandal, a Visigoth and a Berserker), followed chronologically by El Cid and a Crusader, on the other hand, are all best forgotten. The same has to be said of Hans Brinker, a Conquistador, Myles Standish and Winston Churchhill, while Don Quixote, Micawber, and a cruel caricature of President Nixon could well sink into oblivion. A mounted Mameluke is an unusual model which is, however, excellent. Recent additions are a US Navy Pilot (Second World War) a North-West Mounted Policeman, a Dutch Horse Artilleryman (1815), a First World War Poilu, a Wild Bill Hicock, Plains Cavalry, a combat pair of Germans and Americans at the Battle of the Bulge and a 90mm Rommel. Valiant will undoubtedly continue to be one of the most prolific of modern United States producers, and many more models will have been issued by the time this appears in print. One hopes that they will be more critical of their future efforts, as the best are undoubtedly of excellent quality.

Vallance (Rogean Advertising Associates). *See* Rowe, Robert.

'Valorosi' series. *See* Penny Srl.

Valverde, Captain Carlos Martinez, Barcelona (fl. 1955-). A converter of large collections of 45mm solids for the Museum at Pontevedra, the Naval Museum at Madrid, the Military Naval School, the school-boat of Marine Guards *Juan Sebastian de Elcano*, the Submarine Arms School at Sollér and the Marine Infantry Application School.

Van Gerdinge, J.-J., Vaucluse, France. Maker of fine porcelain chess sets, especially notable being one of Crusaders and one of the Field of the Cloth of Gold, issued in limited editions. Producer also of the fine porcelain and metal statuettes designed by Lelièpvre and Rousselot.

Vanguard Miniatures, USA (c.1974-76.) A short-lived venture of 54mm solid Napoleonic and Franco-Prussian War troops, possibly pirates. [*D. Frost; Pielin*]

Vanot, Bernard, Paris (1956-   ). A maker of commissioned 54mm solids in the traditional French style. A protégé of Lelièpvre, his work is to be found in diverse places. He apparently made models during periods when he was not actively engaged in acting. Collectors with a knowledge of his work say that his technique is on a par with that of des Fontaines and Lelièpvre, whether working in metal or plastic. He converts models for SEGOM, but again only when commissioned.

Van Tubergen, George. *See* Command Post.

Varifix. *See* Moulded Miniatures.

Varloud, France (c.1960). A modeller in sheet-tin. *(Nicollier)*

Vasco Americana, Bilbao. Publishers of a long series of books of cardboard cut-out figures, with different sets on each sheet, under the title 'Soldados'.

Vasquez, Paris (c.1919). Linked with Mignot in one of their catalogues. It is possible that he was responsible for a box of conjoint tin, once in the posession of Wade. These were 54mm, each marching infantryman having the front foot directly in front of the other. Cavalry were semi-flat. They represented British Infantry of the Line, with spiked helmets, and equipment added. The box was signed FV, with the name M. Laas, (probably a shopkeeper).

Vaterlein J. & G., Freiburg, (fl.1866-80). Producers of flats. The stepson of Carl Gottfried Daniel Bruck and the inheritor of his business. One of the Association of Tinsmiths and Tinfigure Manufacturers.

VDP (Vendita a Diretta Prezioso), Valenza, Italy (1975-   ). Makers of a set of 24 silver models, 12-15cm, in a limited edition, of troops of the Napoleonic period. [*Vergnano*]

Veale, J.P.B., Brighton, (fl.1930-58). A solicitor by profession, he was one of the first to advocate table-top photography and wrote a small brochure on the subject.

VEB Espewe, USA. Manufacturers of polystyrene AFV kits.

VEB Lineol. *See* Lineol -A.G.

Vedova Ventura, Italy, (c.1895-1910). Publishers of paper sheets.

Vendita a Diretta Prezioso. *See* VDP.

Verdener Heimatbund, Verden, W. Germany (1977-   ). Publisher of flats. *(Klio)*

Verkehrsverein Mulheim Ruhr, Mulheim (1977-   ). Producers of civilian flats of the Middle Ages and the 18th to 19th centuries.

Verlagsbuchhandlung R. Krey. *See* Trentsensky.

Verlinden, François, Lier, Belgium (1978-   ). Originally known as a brilliant converter of AFVs placed in life-like diorama settings, he entered the professional world with his own Diorama Construction Sets in brick and stone material for use with 54mm models.

Verol, Lisbon (c.1900). Publishers of paper sheets.

Verronais, Metz (fl.1870-90). Publishers of paper sheets.

Vertunni, Gustave and Madame, Italy/Paris/USA (c.1900-c.1955). Certainly the earliest of the specialist makers, their models, of which upwards of five hundred are known, were made in solid, and occasionally in hollow-cast, in sizes ranging from 54 to 58mm. They embraced not only military types such as Napoleon, his marshals and his troops, but included portraits of wide-ranging diversity from the early Middle Ages to the early 19th century. Gustave was originally a carver in wood. Although Italian, he worked in France and later

82   **Vanot.** *54mm solid, (Vanot).*

emigrated to the United States. Especially able are his portraits of Frenchmen and women of the 13th to the 15th centuries. Each of his models is an excellent achievement, and a Vertunni is now eagerly sought for, and, if found, given an honoured placed in any collection. He would never entrust the painting to anyone other than his wife.

Vesely, Julius, Vienna (fl.1960s). A maker of 30mm flats of the Austrian Army before 1914.

Victoire. A name that crops up occasionally when a collection is talked or written about. All that can be established is that he was a Frenchman who worked on 54mm solids on commission from about 1925 to 1930.

Victoria Toys. *See* Trafalgar Models.

Victors, Johannesburg (1975). Manufacturers of scenic accessories for wargames.

Victory Miniatures. *See* Stan Johansen Miniatures.

Viking, USA. Manufacturers of polystyrene AFV kits.

Vila, P. An avid collector of Catalan paper sheets who bequeathed them to the nation.

Vincents Kunstforlag (Alex Vincent), Copenhagen (c.1910). Publisher of paper sheets of Hussars and Dragoons.

Viruta (Enrique Wernicke), Argentina (1947-52). A manufacturer of 54mm solids in the Mignot style, including Argentine troops, Gauchos, Conquistadores and South American patriots. [*Basseterre*]

Viturinus (1800). Inventor of *Neues Kriegsspiel.* *(Nash)*

Achaean Greek. 1300. BC. Old kingdom. Inf. 1st. Cent. AD. German.

-52 Right: **Wilcox.** *Two composite models -*
ove Ancient Tribesmen; below Alexander the
eat (Military Modelling; photos by R.A.
e). 53 Below: **Shakespeare.** *Corporal, 40th*
giment of Foot, 1815. 10in. high, resin paste
hakespeare).

54 **Willie**. *Diorama with 30mm solids. 'Friedland', after the painting by Meissonier (Forbes Foundation).*

55 **Wood**. *A model in polychrome wood with metal additions by Martin Rendall (Rendall).*

56 **Valiant**. *US Navy pilot, World War II. Solid by Valiant painted by Sheperd Paine (Sheperd Paine).*

57 **Valiant**. *Rommel. 90mm solid. Painted Sheperd Paine (Sheperd Paine).*

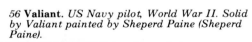

Vliet, Jerre van, Weare, New Hampshire (1974-   ). Carver of 4- and 9-inch basswood figures.

Volke, Gregg, New Berlin, Wisconsin (1975-   ). Free-lance artist of 54mm solids for Valiant, Regent Miniatures and to commission.

Volker, G., Leipzig. Producer of flats of the Napoleonic period including a portrait of Nelson, and Napoleon's postilion at Leipzig.

Vollrath, Wolfgang, Duisberg (d.1968). A publisher of flats notable for his models of ancient times, the Incas, medieval German monarchs, slaves moving an Egyptian sphinx, the Coronation of Maximilian, the Court of Justinian, sleigh ride of Sobieski, the Battle of Rocroy, and a masked ball. The moulds are now owned by Ochel.

Volumetrics, Editions. *See* Editions Volumetrics.

Von Droste, F. See Droste, F. von.

Von Ramin, Wolf-Dietrich. *See* Ramin, Wolf-Dietrich von.

Von Reisswitz, Prussia (1811). Inventor of a *kriegsspiel* using blocks on a relief model. His methods were revised in 1824 by his son. (*Nash*)

Von Roepke, John. *See* JVR Miniatures.

Von Schriltz, Lieut-Colonel Dick, Garrison, New York. Possessor of one of the largest collections in the world. He has for years planned to portray every unit of all the American Wars and all the British Empire troops, employing, even while in the Far East, a host of workmen to convert and paint Rose and Stadden models. He has worked out an ideal exhibition hall and hopes that the collection will be purchased *in toto* by an Institution which will conform to his plan. Included in the collection are a number of dioramas loaned by, and extra to, the Lilly Collection, the bulk of which is at the Heritage Plantation, Sandwich, Mass. At the time of writing von Schriltz's collection is housed in three places - his own home, Dick's Castle (Garrison, New York) and Fort Leavenworth. His industry and planning ability must be unique in the annals of collecting.

Von Staudt, Hans. *See* Staudt, Hans von.

Von Wooster, August Paul, Clyve and **Earl,** California. A magazine entitled *Call to Colors* (c.1972) devoted almost exclusively to a firm of this name probably emanated from the firm itself. Some curious points emerged from the first few issues. The first was occasioned by a series of colour plates of mini-dioramas, mainly of models of Prussians, which seemed extremely similar to some English products of long standing. The second was a series of photographs purporting to be moulds of flats of such an early date (starting in 1636) as to necessitate a complete re-appraisal of the history of the *zinnfigur*. These were said to emanate from the 'von Wooster' workshop, and extended into the early 19th century. The photographs themselves were so bad that few details could be established. The third point was the statement (complete with a colour plate by Job) that the models for Napoleon's coronation were made by the von Woosters. The fourth was the publication of a series of photographs of eight castings of medieval monarchs 'just released'. The Editor was asked to forward a letter to the von Woosters; a letter was written to them at their shop in California, asking for certain details and for their sources of information, and again to a certain collector mentioned in the magazine as the owner of the various models displayed. A second letter to all these persons received no reply.

Von Wooster, Gunther. *See* Jabey, M.J.

Vorberg, H.R., Bonn. A publisher of flats, of Romans and the Seven Years' War, engraved by Lecke and signed VR.

V.P., London (c.1970). Manufacturers of 54mm plastic copies of Herald, Timpo and unpainted Speedwells. [*Juplin*]

Vulcan Miniatures (Dale A. Bilsland), Glasgow (1977-   ). Makers of 25mm solids of 'fantasy', Norman, medieval, Renaissance and Hun models. The designs are by a large team of directors and associates.

W

Wachsmuth & Kelle, Neustadt bei Coburg. Described in *Dawk* in 1975 as a manufacturer of (presumably plastic) models. No reply to correspondence was received.

W.& C., London (fl.1914). A minor manufacturer of 54mm hollow-casts.

Waddington, John, Ltd, Great Britain. Publishers in 1966 of a board game entitled 'White Knights' containing, not counters as usual, but 9 25mm plastic models, 3 white, 6 red, of medieval warriors.

Waddington's House of Games Ltd, Leeds (1966). Manufacturers of a set of chessmen of Norman type in polystyrene. Their advertisement stated that they were created by a 'young Welsh designer', but they would not disclose his identity.

Waddy Productions, London (c.1935). A publisher of paper sheets, in four parts, in book form, comprising the Grenadier, Welsh and Irish Guards and the Black Watch, the figures printed on the left and right sides of a castle background.

Wade, Shamus O.D., Dublin/London. As a collector he made a number of commissoned 54mm models in solid. Later he became a dealer, and was instrumental in the creation, the design and the fostering of Nostalgia.

Wagner, Siegbert, Hanover. A publisher of flats of the War of the Spanish Succession, 17th-century Prussian Infantry, French Infantry 1701-14 (designed by Nesselbeyer, engraved by Lecke), the Seven Years' War (designed and engraved by Grunewald), troops of 1810-15 to complement those issued by Grunewald himself, rococo civilians, and a set of the Blue King of which the moulds are owned by Neckel.

Wagstaff, Bristol. Offered a professional painting service in 1974.

Wahnschaffe, A., Nuremberg (1907). A boxed set of solids, practically indistinguishable from those of Heyde, of the Battle of Sedan, with bomb bursts, trees and ruined houses, bears the initials A.W.N. on the box. Possibly a marketer rather than a manufacturer. (*Macoir*)

Waibel, Dr Helmut and Frau, Austria. Publishers of sets of flats of Spanish Artillery 1808 (designed and engraved by Rössner). Turks (engraved by Sambeth and Frau Waibel), Belgian artillery (engraved by Sambeth), Frederic VI of Denmark 1813-15, the Napoleonic Wars, Brandenburger Grenadiers 1700, and, unusually, medical personnel of various countries and periods.

Walker, R.T., Australia. One of the sculptors who assisted in the dioramas at the Australian War Memorial.

Wall Figurines (Ronald Lloyd Wall), St Louis, Missouri (1975-). Maker of 25mm solids, especially of the American War of Independence, also of personalities, notably a mounted Washington, and of the Napoleonic wars. In 1977 he made a Continental Marine and a modern Master Sergeant, which is anatomically incorrect, for the United States Marine Corps in 54mm, each commissioned in 15,000 copies, and began a full-scale Battle of Tarawa, with 2,500 models. Of his figures he says, 'More for historians, collectors and artists than for wargamers'. Mark: WALL on top of footstand.

Walsh, Thomas G., Massachusetts. A painter of models for the dioramas 'They Nobly Dared'.

Walt Disney Productions, London (1965). Manufacturers of a 60mm plastic, mounted Zorro.

Walter, K.V.T. *See* Drumbeat; 'Militia Models Worldwide'.

Walter, Manfred. *See* Miniaturen in Zinn.

Walters, Hugh. *See* Miniature Figurines.

Walthers Historical Miniatures (William K. Walthers Inc.) Milwaukee, Wisconsin. *The Scabbard* advertised in 1973 the production of models of the First World War: American officer, doughboy, two poilus and two Germans, which, it was discovered, were the first efforts of Chenak, made about 1970. The models had not appeared by 1975, and a request for further information was ignored.

Walz, Hans, Altensteig-Walddorf, W. Germany. A publisher of flats of the Thirty Years' War, a group of Cortez and Pizarro, and a town guard of 1840. Also engraves for Sivhed. (*Klio*)

Walz, Karl, Germany. Engraver of flats.

Wanderer, Friedrich, Germany (fl.1880). Engraver of flats for Heinrichsen. (*Scholtz*)

Ward International. *See* K. Mart.

Ward, J., New Orleans, Louisiana (1974). A designer and sculptor of 54mm solids which were intended to be marketed by a firm in New Orleans. However, this never materialized. [*Wohl*]

Ward Lock & Co., London (c.1910). Publishers of highly coloured, embossed 3/5-inch military scraps, pre-cut,

83 **Wargame models** *by Wall (on stand at rear), Garrison (5), McEwan (2), Hinchliffe (2), Miniature Figurines (2) (Author).*

with movable parts and tabs to form a two-dimensional picture.

WARGAME (ACTUAL). *See Kriegsspiel.*

WARGAME MODELS. In the early days of the 20th century a group of eminent French collectors used to meet and indulge in imaginary battles with model soldiers, but the first general idea of the game was given in a little book for children *The Tin Army of the Potomac*, by W.H. Downes, published in Boston about 1880. Written to give American boys a knowledge of the history of the Civil War, it introduced the idea of using toy soldiers, with hints on the use of building blocks for bridges and breastworks. The line illustrations, endorsing the statement in the text that the only models available were those imported from Germany, are obviously based on Heyde, even to the uneasy seats of the obviously detachable riders. The same idea re-occurred after a long interval, when in 1908 Britains issued the anonymous *The Great War Game*, now known to have been written by H.G. Wells, who, with his brother and Jerome K. Jerome, played a type of wargame with hollow-casts and blocks, described in two books: *Floor Games* (1911) and *Little Wars* (1913). Very popular at the time, the second work has been reprinted several times. Both, however, were merely extensions of the book by Downes. Britains continued to foster the idea with a box specifically marked 'War Games for Boys and Girls Played with Metal Soldiers' (1913). The modern pioneer book on the subject was Morschauser's *War Games* (New York, 1961), and the present-day application dates from around that time, though Grove and Benoy had made 30mm hollow-casts fitting into slots in about 1945, possibly with the wargame in mind.

The game itself suddenly blossomed in the late 1960s and societies sprang up overnight. This was now no light-hearted pastime, but a relentless battle; young and not so young were stricken as by a plague, and wives and families either drawn into the maelstrom or cast aside. Sets of rules for battle, from antiquity to the modern holocausts, were drawn up feverishly by military experts, and published in printed form in ever-

increasing numbers. Battles were fought on elaborate mock terrains or on no terrain at all. They were waged by telephone or post, and bitter altercations, denunciations and counter-charges reverberated in society journals. Battles were fought in private and in public, and conventions held as frequently as possible. The provision of terrains now became a matter for serious thought. Logically, there appears to be no need for either terrain or models: colour-printed battlegrounds and symbols were easily obtainable. The simplest solution was an approximation of the battleground achieved by pieces of wood cut to shapes simulating contours, but the wargamer derived greater satisfaction by building as complete a facsimile as was possible with flock grass, wooded hills, standing corn, hedges and ditches, escarpments, trenches, shell-craters and so on; while models of houses, castles, forts, churches, indeed complete villages and towns became readily available from manufacturers. On this base the commanders-in-chief of both armies could deploy their dozens or thousands of troops and artillery.

The technique of wargame play has its own literature, but it is relevant to survey the actual models with which the game is played, even though they are usually regarded as means to an end rather than a theme for collecting. The sudden surge of popularity of the game necessitated a greater range of figures than were then available, leading to the creation of the Airfix 20mm plastics, the price of which was such that whole armies could be amassed for a nominal outlay. Even so, they did not cover all the periods required by the wargamers, so conversions became commonplace. However, they held the field until Dickinson began a steady stream of metal models. Within a few years the range reached considerable proportions, and no longer was there any need for conversion. The scope of Dickinson's production can best be seen from his numerous lists and catalogues, ranging over many eras and including characters from Tolkien's *The Lord of the Rings*. The earliest of his models were poor specimens, the heads of the infantry being too large, the riders either too large or too small for the horses, and weapons such as pikes impossibly cumbersome. But a gradual improvement took place, and there are now a number of good sets to his credit. Hinchcliffe, who had already been making artillery models of the finest quality, was joined by Gilder, who began a series of 30mm models, followed soon after by models in 20 and 25mm, of which the Napoleonic period was the best, the models of ancient and medieval times being far too reminiscent of the semi-flat. Next in volume of production came Garrison, the work of John Braithwaite of the Greenwood and Ball (Pearce) combine, the majority of which surpassed in quality the figures made by their competitors. The work of all these makers, together with that of Stadden, Gammage, Hinton, Scruby, Thomas and Bussler, constituted the bulk of the wargame figures. Other smaller makers, however, began to fill the gaps (e.g. Silvercross, Douglas, Jacklex, Lamming, Phoenix, Minot, Surén and Warrior). Of these many were worthy of removing from their wargame context and preserving as miniature works of art. Plastics were made by Segom, Almark (designed by Stadden) and Spencer-Smith, who, having begun by making copies of Eriksson's delightful models, in 1973 created an entirely original range. In the United States new makers appeared: C. & C., GHQ, McEwan, Ral Partha and Wall, in some cases blatantly copying English models. The Italian firm Atlantic turned out as prolific a range as Airfix, with some especially delightful Egyptians and Romans, but generally speaking the wargame has had little impact on the Continent.

One would have imagined that models in 20 and 25mm were small enough, but in 1974 the size was reduced to 15mm by Peter Laing, who has by now made over three hundred sets. It would be idle to suggest that any artistic definition is possible in this size, but a number of makers went even further and produced ranges in 5, 6, 9 and 10mm. Wargame armies on the whole consist of figures made for the re-enactment of historic and documented battles, the players being guided by a flood of printed historical notes, but new aspects have gradually emerged, such as the 'space-age' game, originating in science ficton, 'inter-galactic' wars and a form of what can only be called 'mythical' or 'fantasy' play, wherein witches and warlocks, dwarves and creatures of evil act out strange fantasies. It will be interesting to see how long these ghoulish creations last. One thing at least is certain, that the models themselves are contemptible.

WARGAME TERRAINS.
The wargame purist explores the possibility of the use of every conceivable object that may enable him to create a facsimile terrain and takes advantage of the numerous products that are commercially made in polystyrene or in cardboard and which may equally be used for the making of dioramas. Forts, castles and miscellaneous buildings have already been mentioned, and to these may be added the ones in polystyrene by Airfix and other makers, while Heroics have similar items for use with 6mm models. A number of makers have provided dugouts, entrenchments and the like, mostly scaled to the 20 and 25mm model. Hinchcliffe in 1975 went further with their System 12, which incorporated 12mm figures and guns, adding refinements in the Calder Craft series. Natural objects, such as trees, bushes, hedges and simulated ponds are available from a number of makers, so that the present-day wargamer has practically everything to hand.

84 **Warrior**. *A 14-in. composite model by Reeves (Warrior).*

Wargames Publishers (Scotland) Ltd, Glasgow (1978-). Producers of 25mm fantasy wargames, designed by New Hope, and issued as 'Warriors of the Lost Continent'.

Warneford Bros, London (1975-). Marketers in England of anonymous Italian-made 30cm moulded plastic specimens of French Grenadiers of fine quality. It has been established that they are actually made by Fontanini.

Warner, G.G. *See* Roscini, Count Maurice.

Warren Co., USA (c.1914-40). Manufacturers of 57mm solids. A small range only was made: United States troops of 1914 to 1930, with movable arms and the heads plugged in, excellent artillery, the horses full of action, the riders removable, the reins and harness cast separately. The moulds were purchased by Comet.

Warren Paper Products, Layfayette, Indiana (c.1930- ?). Producers of cardboard 'Built-Rite' forts.

Warrior Miniatures (G.R. Seton, H. Norey), Stony Stratford, Bucks. (1972-). A series of 30mm wargame models was produced in 1972. They were hurriedly withdrawn, as being incompetent, but in 1974 a fresh start was made with better designs, and to date Warrior is one of the most prolific producers. In 1975 they commissioned Ronald Reeves to design 14-inch models of synthetic resin with metal additions and cloth uniforms, issued in a limited edition at £200 each. These are entirely lacking in the competence of their Continental counterparts. In the same year models in 9-inch size were announced, but do not appear to have ever been issued. The following year they issued one or two 75mm models by Benassi: and in 1978 a 'Crécy' chess set in 54mm and a kit in 240mm of a World War I infantryman by S. Williams.

'Warriors of the Lost Continent' series. *See* Wargames Publishers.

'Warriors of the World' series. *See* Marx.

'Wars of the Roses' set. *See* Herald; Swoppets.

Warwick Miniatures Ltd, (William P. Treacy Jr.) Portsmouth, New Hampshire (1979-). Maker of Britains-style models, designed by himself, sold individually painted or as castings, and in boxes of five or six figures. Of variable quality: in one cavalryman seen the man is far too large for the horse. [*Anton*]

Washington, US Quartermasters' General Office, Washington, D.C. (1970-). Makers of dioramas for museums.

Wasit, Iraq. A toyshop containing 400 terracotta figurines, c.1400 AD, was unearthed here in 1942.

'Waterloo' chess set. *See* Lamming, W.; Stadden, Chas.

Waterloo Galleries (William Connolly), Irving, California (1968-). An agent who has promoted the work of D.S. Stewart, Beverly Gordon and van Tubergen, as well as that of free-lance artist Chris Matson, and has done some original work himself. In 1977 the firm was in the hands of Arthur T. Emerson, Jr., of Coronado, California, who converted the original Stewart and van Tubergen models into 'toy' soldiers, besides adding a few of his own design.

Waterloo Toy Company, Waterloo, Liverpool (fl.1906-1914). Manufacturers of hollow-cast 54mm models of British infantry in khaki and Highland troops. Mark: WTC. [*Opie; Wade*]

Wathen, Captain Augustus, England. In 1832 he interested the War Office in a device whereby cavalry drill could be demonstrated by the use of small model rocking horses on springs. (*United Services Gazette*)

WB & Co., New Zealand. A set of Maoris in 54mm was made probably about 1970.

'WD' series. *See* Almark.

Webb, C., London. Proprietor for many years of Hummel House of Miniatures, and responsible for the initial marketing of models by Niblett, Greenwood and Ball and Courtenay.

Webb, Terry Lea, USA. Professional painter for Cowan.

Webster, Gerald. *See* W.M.H. Models.

Wee Warriors, USA (1977-). Manufacturers of wargame models.

Weglewski, Hans-Heinz, Munich. Producer of flats.

Wegmann, Brunswick (1820-95). Manufacturers of 30mm-10cm flats. Begun by Carl (1820-25), carried on by Theodore (1825-95). Many of Denecke's moulds were used (purchased in 1820), with the substitution of the mark CW. The business was subsequently purchased by B. Bornig. J.E. du Bois served his apprenticeship with Wegmann. The models are noted for their naïve and large portrayal of the troops of Napoleon, and Prussian and French Infantry of 1866. A medieval tournament, with stands and trophies of war, was a remarkable achievement.

Wehrli, Rudolf, Aarau/Nuremberg (1801-1887). A remarkably prolific and early manufacturer of flats, Rudolf was orginally apprenticed to Gottschalk. He was succeeded by his son Friedrich. The large number of 1963 moulds is preserved at the Landesmuseum, Zurich. They consist of military models, zoos, circuses, gymnasts and hunters. He called his productions 'zinnkompositionsfiguren'!

Weikhmann, Christopher, 1644. Inventor of a '*kriegsspiel*' entitled 'King's Chess'.

Weineck, Horst, Böhl-Iggelheim (1979-). Publisher of flats.

Weiss, Wolfgang, Brunswick. (b.1941). A maker of 6cm flats in sheet tin, he is rapidly establishing himself as one of the finest of painters.

Weisskünig, Der. A monumental volume, published c.1516, of Hans Burgkmair's wood-engravings glorifying the achievements of the Emperor Maximilian I. It is notable for containing an illustration of hand-manipulated tilting-knights.

Welch, Robert, Quincy, Massachusetts. A painter of models for 'They Nobly Dared', and maker of a diorama of Major James Ferguson at Brandywine at Heritage Plantation.

Weldon, Charles E. *See* Tommy Toy.

Wells Fargo, Argentina, (1975-). Manufacturers of 54mm plastic models of Westerners.

Wells, H.G. (1866-1946). In a novel published in 1911 entitled *The New Machiavelli*, the hero, Dick Remington (obviously Wells himself), played 'games upon the floor that must have spread over several years', and with his friend Britten (a name perhaps suggested by William Britains?) developed a wargame of his own devising using nearly 200 models including 'a detestable lot of cavalrymen, undersized and gilt all over' as well as spring cannons. In his *Autobiography* (1934) Wells says that up to 1914 he found a lively interest in playing a wargame with toy soldiers and guns, which obviously correlates with his *The Great War Game* (published anonymously in 1908) his *Floor Games*, which, although primarily of a peaceful nature, does contain an element of warfare, and with his *Little Wars* (1913). Although hardly the kind of occupation in use today, involving as it did the damage of models by projectiles, his name will long be remembered as one who wrote openly of adults playing children's games, and as an advocate of tape measure control of tactical moves.

Wells, John. *See* Evolutions.

Wend-Al (Wendan Manufacturing Company Ltd), Blandford/Byfleet/Liphook (1947-). The original partners were E. Davies-Sparke, W. Hebden, Clive McSweeney and E.J. Kehoe, the last being still active. At Blandford in 1947 they imported dies from Quiralu (known also as Quirinal) and produced toys in aluminium. For a time they were assisted in the operation by Frenchmen for the casting and French girls for the painting. These girls, says Mr. Kehoe, were so skilled that they could handle five brushes loaded with different colours at the same time. When they left, their skill could not be matched. Great quantities of what appears to have been a comparatively small range were turned out, and even exported to the United States. Few of the models were marked. The venture lasted until 1953. The aluminium models were succeeded by plastic models of wild animals from moulds supplied by a London firm, flock material being added to the animals, and sold mainly to zoological gardens, although they were also obtainable at Selfridges in London (but still unmarked). One of the curiosities of this production is that for some years the models were produced by inmates of Lewes gaol. Another surprise is that a limited range of the original Wend-Al models is still available at Liphook. (The continued existence of the firm was brought to light by Brett, and further research was then conducted.)

Wennberg, Curt, Sweden/USA/Eire (1939-1970?). As Swedish Ambassador to the United States, he arranged with Comet for the production of models now familiarly known as 'knees-bend', which were designed and moulded by him. They had thick oval stands with rectangular projections at the ends. Later he persuaded Eriksson to work with Comet on the production of Authenticast. On the failure of the Irish venture, he launched S.A.E. with Winkler in South Africa, again with Eriksson's designs, but this time in 30mm. Manufacture of these ceased when he moved to Madeira. In 1970 he himself stated that he had been able to secure a large number of original Heydes previously in the possession of Kaiser Wilhelm II, and intended to reproduce both these and copies of old flats of 1790 to 1843 at King William's Town in South Africa, using native labour. No more has been heard of this venture. (*See also* Winkler, F.)

Wentzel, Ch. F. *See* Imprimerie de Wissembourg.

Wentzels, Sven, Stockholm (fl.1960). Purchaser of the flats of Tenngjuteriet Mars and agent of Rössner and Eriksson.

Wernicke, Enrique. *See* Viruta.

West, Mr., London (1797). An inventor of instructional drill blocks. A set was exhibited at the Antiquarian Book Fair in London in 1975. (*See also Evolutions*).

West, Mrs. Helen S., Baltimore, Maryland. A collector who exercised a profound influence on the taste and critical intuition of the American quest for the specialist model. Early in life she made her own models, dealing mainly with early times and the Middle Ages. According to Hitrovo they are highly prized.

Western Dioramas. *See* Anderson, Raymond.

Western Front, Panorama City, California. (1977–). Manufacturers of simulated barbed wire.

Westfalische Zinnfiguren, Nuremberg (1975–). Manufacturers of home-casting outfits for the making of semi-flats.

Westgate Models, Westgate-on-Sea, Kent (1977–). Manufacturers of perspex wall display cabinets.

Wetzel, Paul, Berlin. Purchased G. Söhlke's business in 1896.

Weygang, Göttingen (c.1810–1919). A father-and-son production team of a vast number of flats in 40mm to 10cm: Carl (1810–72), Carl Friedrich Victor (1863–1919). Military types of many nations were made, very much in the style of the times, some being frank caricatures.

Ships in conjoint tin are also known. The moulds are preserved at the Staatisches Museum at Göttingen, and some reprints were made by August Weygang in 1932. Marks: C.W.G.:C.W.:W:FW, and occasionally in full.

WHEELED TRANSPORT (non-military). As a corollary to military vehicles, makers of all ages have been interested in the creation of transport of other types. Everyone is familiar with the models of trains, buses and motorcars that have delighted children and adults alike, but less prolific are representations of coaches and the like. The most popular materials for these in the days before polystyrene were wood and lead, and a 9cm coach, made about 1780, and incorporating clockwork, is at the Nuremberg Museum, and two others, unmotivated, at Munich and Augsburg. Conjoint tin was cheap, and coaches, wagons, fire-engines and similar objects were made for the toy market, especially in the United States, but the early makers of flats produced many fine models, often gaily painted. An extraordinary open landau, 4ft 6 inches long, containing figures of Queen Victoria and the Prince Consort, was exhibited at the Great Exhibition; Mignot's Coronation coach of Napoleon is still available, while state coaches were made by Heyde and Birkman. Coronations have proved a good opportunity for modern makers to exhibit their skill, and Britains, Timpo, Johillco and Dinky took advantage of those of George V and Queen Mary and of Queen Elizabeth II. Phoenix have recently started a remarkable series of carriages, broughams, milk-floats (also made by Britains and other past hollow-cast makers) a knife-grinder's cart and a barrel organ. The best of all is the unique coach of Charles VI of Spain made by Helmut Krauhs. Death conquers all, and funeral hearses have been made by Ballada ('The Return of the Ashes of Napoleon' at Compiègne) and of the funeral of Gustavus Adolphus in flat by Wimor. Sedan chairs in flat by Keller and in solid by Phoenix and The Sentry Box, and medieval litters designed as a Kulmbach souvenir, are delightful additions to any collection, but a rickshaw by Atlantic is a pedestrian effort.

Whisstock, Frank. For many years designer of labels for Britain's boxed sets.

White, Harry. *See* M.W.

85 **Weygang.** *Caricature flats, 8-10cm (Gottinger Museum).*

'**White Knights**' (Boardgame). *See* Waddington, J., Ltd.

White, Ronald. *See* Unique Miniatures.

Whitehead, P. *See* Glassorama.

Whitelaw, R. & William R., Massachusetts. Assisted in the building of the 'They Nobly Dared' dioramas.

Whitman Publishers Inc., USA (1964). Publishers of cardboard models in book form with such titles as *The Big Invasion, Battle* and *Action Soldiers.*

Wieger, Strasbourg (c.1900). Publisher of printed sheets.

Wiener Metallfigurinen, Vienna (1974-). Maker of a small number of 54mm solids of the Austrian army, 1900-1914. No further information could be obtained from the firm.

Wiener Zinnfiguren Ewald-Kovar (Peter Kovar), Vienna (1965-). Ewald is known as an engraver of flats, including sets of Rudolf von Habsburg (1291) and Friedrich von Hohenzollern (1415). Whether Kovar retired or died is not certain, but his son Peter now owns the business and is also an engraver.

Wilcox, Peter, London (c.1966-). A maker of commissioned 54mm models in various materials, including plaster, wood, metal, nylon and paper on a lead torso. He is also not averse to incorporating spare parts from other makers. He concentrates on ancient times and the Middle Ages, and his creations have great flair and distinction, commanding a high price when sold at auction.

Wildner, Herbert, Vienna (1977-). Publisher of flats of the Great War (*Klio*, 1977).

Wildt, H., Berlin (fl.1848-1890). An engraver of flats for Haselbach and a designer for Buliker.

Wilke, C.F., Grossenhain (fl.1870). Engraver of flats. Marks: F.W.; F. WILKE; WILKE.

Wilke, Florian, Germany. Designer and engraver of flats.

Wilke, Horst, Fürstenwalde, W. Germany. Designer, engraver and publisher of flats.

Wilke, K. Alexander, Vienna. A towering figure in the world of Austrian flats, encouraging collectors and holding regular classes for diorama building and figure painting. He was responsible for the Marston Moor diorama originally at the R.U.S.I.

Wilken, Alexando, Gerhagen. Publisher of a set of French Revolution flats after paintings by Job.

Wilkinson, Spenser, England (c.1910). An advocate of '*kriegsspiel*' for the use of the British army. (*Nash*).

Willetts, Howard Francis, St. Ives, Huntingdon (1950-1974). A maker of high-quality models of plaster in statuette-size, and one of the first of the moderns to produce models in this size. Willetts did all the research, the drawings and the sculpture, the casts and moulds being made by Joseph Grassi, and T. Allen, beginning in 1954, doing the painting. The plaster was strengthened by a wire armature, and finishing details were sculpted directly from the completed casting. Swords and other weapons were made of the appropriate material, and each model limited to seventy copies, each bearing a certificated number and signature, and the name 'Matchlock'. Comprising the British army from 1900, they were often confused with the early efforts of The Sentry Box.

William I, of Orange. *See Kriegsspiel.*

Williams, Stanley, Leighton Buzzard, Beds (1978-). Maker of a British World War I infantryman in 240mm for Warrior.

Willie (Edward Surén), London (1964-). A maker of 30,

86 **Willie.** *Part of a diorama with his 30mm models (Marquis of Cholmondeley).*

40, 54 and 60mm solids, whose productions are among the finest in their field. An immense talent is allied to a profound knowledge and intelligence. His integrity is akin to that of Berdou, Eriksson, Ping, Schreiber, Barrientos and Brunoe. He is traditional in style, so that his series of 60mm nudes or semi-nudes must be regarded as a *jeu d'esprit*, divorced from the rest of his work. Few would take exception to them, as they are devoid of the salacious undertones of similar models made by other makers. His main output, in 30mm, covers a wide range, with many portrait models included. Many are mounted, the riders detachable, as are also such items as pistol holders. There are a few disappointments, such as the Norman footmen and the disproportionate size of the horses of their Saxon adversaries, and a mounted 40mm knight in Maximilian armour, but these are more than compensated for by the remainder of his production. The most difficult model to obtain is a pair of medieval mounted knights in combat, only cast rarely, and sold painted only at an exorbitant price. Two other sets, also only issued painted, and in limited editions, are an 18th-century stag hunt, comprising eight mounted figures, with six couple of hounds and a stag, and a pig-sticking group: four mounted figures and a pig. Single figures of Polish Winged Lancers and Turkish cavalry are others only available painted. A range entitled 'Harlequinade' is made up of such diverse figures as pirates, monks, harem beauties, Lady Godiva and inhabitants of the Barbary Coast. Surén's horses are beautifully done, and he has suffered much from piracy. In 1977 he started issuing his 30mm models in kit form owing to the rising cost of metal. Three chess sets are outstanding, one of the Battle of Pavia, another of the Battle of the Pyramids, and the third of the American War of Independence, each in figures ranging from 30 to 54mm, and each limited to 25 sets either painted or in gold and silver. He has constructed many dioramas with his models which have found homes in museums and institutions, and he owes much to Philip Stearns, who has taken many fine photographs of his work.

Willis, Jeff, London (1976-). He has made a large number of rather clumsy 80mm solids of the Napoleonic era for 'Tradition', together with a vulgar series in 90mm of nude females slaves and their masters.

Willis, J.B. and **F.A.**, Petersfield, Hants. Responsible for the display in five showcases of some of the models at Wilton House.

Wilner Verlag S.W. *See* Lübecker Spielfiguren.

Wimor (K.H. Winkelmüller & F.K. Mohr), Leipzig. Karl Mohr (1896-1969) of Wiederitzsch started by making silhouette-style flats in tinplate. In about 1950 he combined with Winkelmüller in the production of some outstanding sets of flats of the normal kind, such as Napoleon in Egypt, the funeral procession of Gustavus Adolphus, a Burgundian wedding, an exotic and erotic *Thousand Nights and One Night*, robber barons, an 18th-century hunt, 1848 street barricades, Goethe's *Faust*, and a sadistic set of central European gypsies. Mohr was also a professional painter of flats, and a designer and engraver for Bittner. Mark: MOHR.

Winar, Don. *See* Armtec.

Winkelmüller, K.H. *See* Wimor.

Winkler, F., Germany/England/Sweden/South Africa. (d.1959). Assisted by Curt Wennberg, he escaped to England from the emergent Nazi Germany, and, helped financially by Lord Nuffield, established Treforest Mouldings in 1935, for the production of scale ship models. In 1939 he began the manufacture of 45mm military models, some designed by Henry Harris, others based on Heyde. Having been interned during World War II, he helped, with Harris, to found Malleable Mouldings. Prior to this he had ordered several hundreds of castings of the Authenticast models from Wennberg at Cladagh, but these were so badly cast or broken on arrival that they were virtually useless. However, a few of the better specimens were re-cast in solid for collectors. Winkler and Wennberg then set up SAE in South Africa. Production of these ceased when Winkler moved to Madeira.

Winskill, Bernard, England (1969-). Employed by the Royal Worcester Porcelain factory in the production of the first two of their 'Military Commanders' series: Napoleon on a rearing horse, 1969, and, 1974, the Duke of Wellington. They are about 16½ x 14½ inches.

Winter, David & Yvonne. *See* New Hope Design; Old Guard.

Winter, Mano, Vienna (b.1900-). Designer of flats for a number of makers, including Vollrath, Ochel, Lecke and Sivhed.

Wippler, Keith, New York. A professional painter of flats for Old Guard, Cowan and others, and maker of commissioned 54mm solids.

Wirkner, M., Germany. Designer of flats.

Wirths (husband and wife), USA. Pioneers in the American effort to create specialist figures. Their own conversions are in several American museums.

Wise, Terence, London (1972-). Manufacturer of cardboard domestic buidings; designer of war terrains for Micro-mold Plastics.

Wiseman, Eric, Sydney, N.S.W. A dealer who endeavoured without success to introduce the work of Wooten and of Sykes to the world market.

Withers, Captain R.W., New Zealand. Maker of 6-inch models of the R.N.Z.I. Regiment and Special Air Services for the Army Museum, Waiouru, New Zealand.

Witts, Terry. *See* Drumbeat: Militia Models Worldwide.

W.M.H. Models, Hanwell, Middlesex (1978-). Makers of 90 and 130mm solids in kit form, the range varying from a Greek hoplite to a Skinner's Horse, a number being

mounted. The designers, Michael Hearn, Walter Morris and Gerald Webster, can be identified by the intial H, M, or W before the number of any specific figure mentioned in their catalogue.

Wmon, Poland (fl.1963). Publishers of paper models of armoured vehicles. (*Newman*)

Wohlmann, Wolfgang, Berlin (1979-). Publisher of flats.

Wolavska, Franz, Murztal, Austria (1914-). Unique in that he has made an assembly of First World War battle and trench scenes which he exhibits at his own private museum, constantly adding to them since he began in 1914. A torso of wood, with added limbs, is dipped into a molten hard-wax substance of his own composition. After cooling, detail is worked onto the wax, which is still pliable. Helmets, weapons and equipment are made of lead. The wax cools to a dull colour and is finally shaded with copper-bronze. The self-imposed task would appear to some to be masochistic, as there is great evidence of barbed wire, dying horses, and other horrors which Wolavska must himself have witnessed.

Wolfram, Plagwitz/Leipzig (c.1900). Maker of flats. (*Hampe*)

Wolfram, Ernest, Leipzig (fl.1895). Maker of wooden vehicles, guns, booths and houses.

Wollner Figuren, Vienna (c.1868-1914). Manufacturers of solid and semi-solid 38 and 55mm models, foot and mounted, mainly of the Franz Josef period. These naïvely crude models are greatly favoured by Austrian collectors. Apart from the military figures and campsites, they made carriages, civilians and park scenes, as may be seen in the illustrations in Alberini. The moulds, once in the possession of Possnecker, have for some time been the property of Kober, and they are still being cast, although in decreasing quantity.

Wolrab, Jacob, Nuremberg. A silversmith who flourished around 1672. *See* France.

'Women at War'. *See* Dorset.

WOOD. Carved wood models of a military nature date back to the beginning of history. The earliest known are those found in Egyptian tombs, and there are many specimens of the Middle Ages in the form of military saints in museums all over the world. The peasant

87   **Wood.** *Late 18th-century 'trellis tongs' figures 2 in. high. The headgear is detachable. (Strangers' Hall, Norwich).*

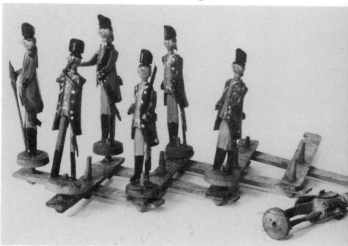

population of the Bavarian forests eked out a precarious existence by a cottage industry: the material was to hand, and folk art has its legitimate place in any history of the model soldier. Stylized they undoubtedly are, but the sheer simplicity and honesty of purpose of these toys is not to be despised in relation to those of our own sophisticated age. Especially charming were the tiny carts and horses and people which were still available in the author's childhood. The lathe-turned skittle-like soldiers, standing stiffly to attention, destined to be knocked down by the projectile of the spring-gun, will be known to many collectors, and indeed were noted by Charlotte Brontë in 1829. Much more elaborate examples were made commercially in Germany and France, as noted under 'Automata' and 'Evolutions'. The King of Rome had a mounted mameluke, and a carved wood equestrian model of Napoleon could be regarded as the inspiration of the lead model made by Mignot. These wooden models are amply documented in contemporary paintings and satirical engravings from the time of Gillray onwards, and that they were the staple diet of children is self-evident. An outstanding example of skilful carving is evinced in the remarkable series of units of the Napoleonic Army which were carved by Charles Sandré, while a prisoner of war in England. The greatest modern achievement was the creation of a team led by Pilkington Jackson of a group of 83 polychrome oak statuettes for the Scottish United Services Museum at Edinburgh. Having laid down the main guide-lines, he employed James McKenzie as overseer to this outstanding series.

H.J. Arthur began (c.1950) a series of large carved models of the American Revolution, the American Army from 1830 to 1865, and many others, including British troops from 1650 to the present day. On his death his son continued in a similar vein, marketing them as Karthage Figures (1970). All are extremely attenuated and caricature-like. Other makers with whimsical fancies are Cliff Arquette and on occasion Rendall, who, however, has turned out much more serious work. Large wood models have been made by Españocraft (1972), J. Henry (for the Border Regiment), M.E. Jones (including the Women's Army Services), Heinrich Knie, Frank McClellan, Mivie of Buenos Aires, Don and Honey Ray (Honey also makes beautiful bird studies) and Major H.A.V. Spencer (for the Prince of Wales' Own Regiment of Yorkshire). Far removed from these in style are the remarkable conceptions of General Angenot, who concentrates on movement and artistic thought in his bass-wood equestrians. Tiny models (28mm) were made by Samuel and Dr Ernest Augustus Dancaster (before 1900 to 1914) in the island of Jersey. They were unique in that even in this small size the rifle slings were made separately. (Wade had a large number for sale in 1970.) In 1963 Joseph Gryiewicz began a large series of 8-inch pine models of Police of all periods and nations for the US Military Police School, and the art is being perpetuated by Pranzetti (54mm) and in remote New Zealand, where Dinah Penman started in 1972 a series of 54 to 60mm carved polychrome examples, mainly of cavalry, some with movable arms and with

separate, attached swords, slings, sabretaches and harness, Peter Reid does a series of 12-inch balsawood models, and Captain R.W. Withers has a series of 6-inch models in the Army Museum, Waiouru.

Wood, G.W., London (fl.1912). An ex-employee of Britains and maker of an extremely small range of hollow-casts. Richards, indeed, was only able to trace one item, that of a Lifeguardsman with a fixed arm, but Shamus Wade has been able to identify one or two others which bear Wood's signature.

Woodburn Manufacturing Co., USA (c.1943). Publishers of cardboard sheets of press-out soldiers, together with aeroplanes, $9\frac{1}{2}$ x $8\frac{1}{2}$ inches, boxed, designed by D. Rapaport, and entitled Rap-a-Jap.

Woodland Scenes, USA (1976–). Manufacturers of 20mm plastic trees.

Woolbro, Hong Kong (1970). Piracies of plastics by various makers.

Woolford, Arthur, Marlow, Bucks. A designer of 54mm fibreglass models. Although strictly a private maker, a number of his models, especially those of women, have influenced the productions of certain professionals.

Wooten, Peter, Sydney, N.S.W. (1963–4). Wooten started with a British Grenadier of 1792, but, as a mere half-dozen models were made before the mould fractured, the figures are now rare. Assisted by the Rev. Sir Dickon Durand in casting new models, he produced a short series of 54mm solids, comprising a New South Wales Lancer, 1905, a First World War Guardsman, an S.S. Guard Officer, a Victorian Scot, a Ballarat Ranger, an Australian Light Horseman, an Afrika Korps infantryman, and a Roman General. Separate caps or helmets, blunderbuses and flintlock muskets were also made. All the models were limited in number. They were placed in the hands of a dealer named Wiseman, and Durand tried hard to raise interest in England with no success, which is to be regretted, as the models were of good quality. It has been suggested that 7–9 inch models were also made, but it appears more likely that they were never issued, as Wooten made a regretably early retirement. [*Durand; Wiseman*]

World Miniatures. *See* Moulded Miniatures.

Worster, Terry, USA (1975–). Maker of 90mm solids, including several for The Black Watch.

W.R.G., USA. Manufacturers of plastic armament kits.

Wright, J. Lloyd. *See* Lincoln Logs.

Wrightsville Hardware Company. *See* Grey Iron Casting.

Wünsch, Richard, Germany. Designer of flats.

Wurzbacher, Erich, Germany. Assisted Bonness in the foundation of the Plassenburg Museum.

Wynne-Jones, Nancy. *See* The Sentry Box.

Wyrob, Warsaw (fl.1970). Manufacturers of 54mm plastics. A Winged Polish Lancer is described as having the armour painted gold, a red cape and grey wings, and mounted on a standing white horse with gold saddle, blanket and harness, with a lance of sharpened aluminium wire. [*Pestana*]

Wzup, Warsaw (fl.1970). Manufacturers of 54mm plastic Polish troops of the Napoleonic era, Second World War and the present day. Equivalent in style and execution to Britain's models. [*Pestana*]

XYZ

Xiloplast, Italy (c.1950-). Manufacturers first of Elastolin-type composition figures, then of rubber-like plastics of particularly uncouth appearance, painted over a black foundation colour which shows through. The range consists of modern Italians, the Risorgimento, Romans and the Middle Ages.

X.R., Paris (c.1935). Manufacturers of 60mm solids, 56 and 58mm hollow-casts similar to Mignot. The badly designed horses have no bases, the trademark appearing only on the footstand of the infantry. [*Roche-Kelly*]

Yelmo-Batalla. *See* Girardo, Ernesto.

Ye Olde Soldier (George H. Smith) Torrance, California (1979-). Britains-style figures cast in solid.

Young, Roslyn, Newcastle-upon-Tyne (1975-). Aptly surnamed, at the age of sixteen she produced a Landschnecht's donkey for New Hope Design, and also did some of the same firm's 'Branchline' models. (*See also* New Hope.)

Yule, Jimmy, Perth. A professional painter for the English branch of Historex.

Zambori, Carlos Rodriguez. *See* Terry.

Zang, M., London. He came to England from Poland in 1908, and made toys of many kinds. In 1951 he was joined by Selwyn-Smith and they began plastic 54mm models marked 'A Zang Product. British Made Catalogue number'. In 1953 the mark was changed to the figure of a herald with the substitution 'MADE IN ENGLAND'. Although soon taken over by Britains (1955), and the numbering made to conform with that of Britains' register, some models bore the original mark as late as 1957 (*See also* Britain, William, Ltd.; Herald; Selwyn-Smith, R.)

Zellis. *See* Hicks, P.

Zeman, John. *See* Tommy Toy.

Zens Zinnmodelle Gmbh., Nuremberg. Producer of three-dimensional vehicles and artillery of the 16th-20th century, in 30mm (*Kulmbach Almanac, 1977. See also* Tricorne Miniatures).

Zerwick Gebruder, Vienna (c. 1806-70). Manufacturers of 45mm semi-solids, sold in boxes with trade initial ℨ on upper cover. The labels bear gold medallions and are marked 'MADE IN GERMANY'. A number of the models are two-on-a-stand, with arms animated, and on Heinrichsen-like flat bases. (*See* Rattelmuller, p.127; additional information from Speyer and Wade.)

Zeumer, Richard, Dresden. A publisher of cardboard models of fortifications, houses and countryside scenes. (*Ortmann*)

Zeuner, K. Dresden (?1930-1939). Maker of flats and 20-30mm solids. Known chiefly as a maker of diorama accessories, in 1930 his advertisement read: 'Tin figures and soldiers of all times and nearly all in great choice and style - exceptional kinds of special exhibitions'.

Zinsler, George, Austria. Producer of dioramas for Pottenbrun, and also a painter of many of the figures.

Zix, Benjamin, Strasbourg (1796-1805). One of the first and best of the publishers of '*Les Petits Soldats de Strasbourg*'. Born in 1772, he may have worked for Striedbeck. In 1798 he produced sheets for the Swiss campaign, followed by his '*États Major Autrichien en Campagne de l'An IX*', consisting of fifty horse, 15cm high, painted in gouache, with every possible detail, each figure having its own individuality.

Zorn, Dr Hans Gunter, Camberg, (1973). Publisher of flats. They are now marketed by Frau Henny Zorn.

Zuber, J., France (c.1960). A maker of 54mm solids of whom no further information has so far been forthcoming.

Zurich Central Library. (1978-). Publishers of a set of five black and white plates of Swiss soldiers, reprinted from early sheets. (*Newman*)

PERMANENT EXHIBITIONS OF MODELS

AUSTRALIA

BALLARAT, Eureka Stockade (Cassin-Scott).

CANBERRA, Australian War Memorial (dioramas, 1914-18, 1939-45, models varying from 3 to 30 in, First World War in lead, Second World War in plaster, artists; *Anderson, Bowles, Bridges, Browning, Evans, Ewers, Feltham, Gilbert, Jones, Lynch, McCubbin, Nicolson).

SYDNEY, Rocks Historical Gallery (diorama by A.J. Collins).

TASMANIA, Queen Victoria Museum, Launceston (150-200 Britains representing Tasmanian military history 1803-70, Imperial troops and Local units from 1860-1930, converted by Trevor Jowett).

AUSTRIA

ALTENBURG, Afrikamuseum Deutsch (Krauhs).

DONAU, Museum (Krauhs).

HEZOGENBURG, Schloss Heiligenkreuz (Krauhs).

KLAGENFURT, Landesmuseum für Kärnten (archaic).

LINZ, Schlossmuseum (Krauhs; dioramas).

MELK, Museum.

MISTELBACH, Schloss Loosdorf (private collection of Ferdinand Graf Patti, thirty dioramas).

MURTZAL, Wolavka Privat Kriegsmuseum (dioramas of 1914-18 by Franz Wolavka).

PETRONELL, Danube Museum (diorama by Gärtner, Riedmatter, Kröner-Grimm).

ST FLORIAN, Jagdmuseum (Krauhs; dioramas).

ST POLTEN, Schloss Pottenbrun Zinnfigurenmuseum (50 dioramas, mainly by Kröner-Grimm and colleagues).

SALZBURG, Haus der Natur (Krauhs).

Rainer Museum (Krauhs).

Schloss Mirabell (Krauhs).

VIENNA, Heeresgeschichtlichemuseum (dioramas by Kröner-Grimm and colleagues).

Kunsthistorischesmuseum (medieval; flats).

Museum der Ersten Österreichischen, Ischen-Spar-Casse (Krauhs).

Wiener Neustad, Military Academy (Krauhs; dioramas of Wagram and Sacile, each approx. 5000 Heinrichsens).

WAGRAM, Deutsch-Wagram Heimatsmuseum (dioramas).

WELS, Schloss Wels (Krauhs).

BELGIUM

BRUGES, Musée Grandhuse (late 18th century flats).

BRUSSELS, Royale de l'Armée (flats).

CANADA

National Historic Sites Service, (planning to distribute Lelièpvre statuettes to various forts).

ALBERTA, Provincial Museum.

Calgary Museum (Cassin-Scott).

Edmonton (pre-Second World War Elastolin, Lineol).

Glenbow Institution (four dioramas, ex-R.U.S.I., in neglected condition), Calgary.

BRITISH COLUMBIA, Empress Hotel, Victoria, ('Fields of Glory': the Ray collection of dioramas).

Forces School of Canadian Military Engineers Museum, Canadian Forces Base, Chilliwack, Vedder Crossing (diorama, 'Part of the Afternoon, Waterloo', diorama, using 1,500 Britains, a few plastics, and Napoleon's coach, designed, constructed and painted by C/WO C.E. Smith, Mrs. M.E. Smith, Lieut. Dennis Amesbury).

Fort George Military Museum.

MANITOBA, Museum of Man and Nature, Winnipeg (dioramas by Series 77).

NOVA SCOTIA, Canadian National Museum, The Citadel, Halifax (Midleton).

Sealladh Breagh ('Beautiful View') on the Cabot Trail at Mouth of Margaree River (dioramas: Waterloo, in three phases; Bunker Hill; the Civil War; medieval castle - all by John May, using 20-54mm commercial models).

Shilo, Royal Regiment of Canadian Artillery Museum (two dioramas: 9-pounder detachment by Series 77 and Cut Knife Creek, 1885, converted models by Major E. Rich and Captain J.H. Lyne: diorama of Batoche).

ONTARIO, Fenelon Falls Museum (Ray diorama of Pickett's Last Charge).

Minden Museum of Dioramas (dioramas).

Ottawa, Canadian War Museum (very large dioramas of Paardeburg, 1900, and D-Day Normandy Beachhead, viewed through a simulated concrete bunker opening, plastic-kit vehicles, plastic wargame men, converted where necessary, supervised by Rear-Admiral C.J. Dillon, the diorama (24 x 8 ft) made by the staff, including Stephen Racine and Patrick Henderson as scenic artists, and Florence Galipeau as part-time painter of models, aircraft models made by the Ottawa Chapter of the International Plastic Modellers' Society; simulated sounds and smells).

Toronto: Casa Loma (Britains).

Dalziel Barn, Black Creek Pioneer Village (Britains; Percy Band Collection).

Metropolitan Central Library (Cassin-Scott).

Royal Canadian Military Institution (periodic displays).
Upper Canada Village, Morrisburg (a few Staddens).
QUEBEC, Montreal: Lake St Louis Historical Society (Baldet; dioramas).
Montreal Military Museum.
Quebec City. Musée du Citadel (dioramas in 30-40mm paper in semi-relief).
Musée de Fort (dioramas).
Regimental Museum of the Royal 22nd Regiment (small collection of solids).

CYPRUS
NICOSIA, Museum (archaic).

DENMARK
COPENHAGEN, Bymuseum (wood).
Dansk Folkemuseum (flats; old moulds).
Orlogsmuseet (Anholm, Brunoe, Høyer).
Teknisk Museum (moulds of flats 1760–1791; moulds by Høy).

EGYPT
CAIRO, Museum (archaic wood).

EIRE
CORK, Public Museum (eight models, 5-in flat, engraved one side, by G. Thompson and M. Casey, painted by I. Green).
CURRAGH, THE, Military Museum, County Kildare (miscellaneous, founded by Henry Harris).
DUBLIN, Hawlbowline Naval Headquarters (models by O'Sullivan).
Kinsale Folk Museum (plywood; dioramas in conversions).
Order of Malta HQ, Ballsbridge (Harris dioramas).

FINLAND
HELSINKI, Finlands Nationalmuseum (flats; solids).
Kriegsmuseum (flats).
PORVOO, Museum (flats).
TURKU, Stadhistoriska Museum (flats).

FRANCE
ARROMANCHES (D-Day diorama).
BALLEROY, Musée des Ballons, Château de Calvados (dioramas by Lelièpvre).
CHABOLTENE, Vendée, Musée Militaire (flats).
COMPIEGNE, Musée (magnificent collection of all types).
EPINAL, Musée (paper sheets).
GRAVELOTTE, Musée (Franco-Prussian War dioramas).
JANESSY, Musée (dioramas).
MARS-LA-TOUR, Musée (dioramas).
PARIS: Arc de Triomphe.
Musée Carnavalet (paper sheets by le Sueur; 17th-century solids; dioramas)
Musée de la Marine (Fouillé; dioramas).
Musée de l'Armée (flats; Collection Rieder, paper sheets; dioramas; Britains; Heyde; one of the largest collections in existence).
Musée de Cluny (medieval flat; 16th-17th century solids)
Musée des Arts Decoratifs (Hilpert chess set).
PAYLOUBIER, Musée de Legion Etrangers (Bir Hacheim diorama).
PERIGUEUX, Musée (paper sheets).
PHALSBOURG, Musée (paper sheets).
ST SULPICE LE VERDON, Vendée, Musée d'Histoire Militaire, La Chabottèrie (part of the Boersch collection of paper sheets).
SALON-DE-PROVENCE, Musée de l'Empèrie, Château de l'Empèrie (Collections Raoul et Jean Brunon).
SAUMUR, Musée.
SENLIS, Musée.

STRASBOURG, Musée Historique (very large collection of paper sheets, some as dioramas; Strasbourg and other flats; medieval).
TARBES, Musée International des Hussards (over 700 models).

GERMANY
Those places marked with an asterisk are in the G.D.R.
AALEN, Limesmuseum (flats)
AUGSBURG, Museum (medieval: flats).
BAMBERG, Museum (flats).
BERLIN, Museum für Deutsche Geschichte (flats).
Schlossmuseum (gum-tragacanth).
BIBERACH, Museum (gum-tragacanth).
*BISCHOFSWERDA, Heimatsmuseum (flats).
BRUNSWICK, Stadtischesmuseum (flats; workshop of Bornig).
CELLE, Bomann Museum (flats; solids).
DINKELSBURG, Museum (flats).
*DRESDEN, Heimatschutz (peasant wood-carvings).
Oscar Seyffertmuseum (peasant wood-carvings).
Staatliches Kunstsammlungen ('The Grand Mogul's Birthday Party').
Staatliches Museum fur Volkunst (flats).
*EAST MECKLENBERG, Museum (flats).
*EISENACH, Thüringer Museum, Wartburg Castle (flats).
EOBOE (Private collection of dioramas by E. Schmidt).
*ERFURT, Historisches Museum (dioramas; history of horticulture in flats).
GOTHA, Heimatmuseum (flats; Krause moulds)
GOTTINGEN, Staatliches Museum (flats; Weygang moulds).
HALLE, Heimatsmuseum (flats).
HAMBURG, Museum für Hamburgische Geschichte (flats).
HANOVER, Museum (flats; Waterloo diorama).
INGOLSTADT, Bayerisches Armeemuseum (flats).
KREFELD, Stadtische Museum (flats).
Kaiser-Wilhelm-Museum (flats).
KULMBACH, Schloss Plassenburg (extensive collection of dioramas in flats; diorama by Surén; annual meeting place for collectors).
*LEIPZIG, Stadtgeschichtliches Museum (flats; dioramas of Leipzig).
Torhaus Dolitz (dioramas; single models).
LEUCHTENBURG, Heimatsmuseum auf der Kahla (commemorative flats).
*MAGDEBURG, Technical High School (large flat of Otto von Guericke).
MUNICH, Bayerisches Museum (medieval; flats; solids, including Haffner).
Hersbruck, Museum (dioramas).
OBERAMMERGAU, Langsches Museum (dioramas made for Napoleon using 50mm models).
*OLDENBURG, Tourist Board (large commemorative flat).
PEGAU, Heimatsmuseum (flats).
PLAUEN, Vogtlandisches Kreismuseum (flats).
*POTSDAM, Heimatsmuseum (flats, especially by Meyerheine).
ROSTADT, Historische Museum (flats).
*ROSTOCK, Museum (flats).
*SCHWERIN, Staatliches (flats).
*SONDERSHAUSEN, Kreis-, Heimat-ind Schlossmuseum (flats).
*SONNEBERG, Deutsches Spielzugmuseum (flats; gum-tragacanth).
STUTTGART, Würrtembergerischen Landesmuseum (flats).
WEIMAR, Stadmuseum (flats, moulds by Krause).
WURZBURG, Burggaststatte Festung Marienberg (flats).
*ZEULENRODA, Museum (flats).
*ZITTAU, Stadtmuseum (flats).

*ZWICKAU, Stadtischesmuseum (flats).

GREAT BRITAIN

ALDERSHOT, Airborne Forces Museum, Browning Barracks (diorama of Merville by Greenwood-Stokes; diorama of Raid on Tragino Aqueduct, Apulia, 45mm models made by T. Otani).
Queen Alexandra Royal Army Nursing Museum, Royal Pavilion (conversion by Newberry).
Royal Army Service Corps Museum, Buller Barracks (barbola models by J.H. Morrison).
Royal Corps of Transport Museum (conversion by Lancer).

ANGLESEY, The Museum of Childhood, Menai Bridge (old toys).

ARBORFIELD, REME Depot (diorama of Light Aid Detachment in action in Western Desert, October, 1942, by Valhalla).

ARMAGH, Royal Fusiliers Regimental Museum (three conversions by Rose; ten carved wood models, 140-165mm, made anonymously in 1945).

ASH VALE, Royal Army Medical Corps Museum (conversion by Newberry).

BAGSHOT, RAChD Museum (dioramas by Rev. J. Bell).

BARNSLEY, H.Q. 13th/18th Royal Hussars, Cannon Hall Museum (diorama of the Charge of the Light Brigade, number of participants, 673 British, 580 Russians, at the point of contact 20mm conversions made in 1973 by Valhalla).

BATH, C.A. Bell-Knight Collection of British Bygones, Freshford (50 dioramas of Agincourt, Culloden, American Wars, Waterloo, etc., all conversions, loaned for exhibition purposes; selection of models, all periods. By appointment only).

BATTLE ABBEY, (Battle of Hastings diorama by David Hunter, 1400 converted 20 and 25mm Stadden, Warrior, Miniature Figurines and Airfix figures).
Museum (diorama of the Battle of Hastings).

BEVERLEY, East Yorkshire Regiment, Victoria Barracks (dioramas by Greenwood-Stokes: Normandy Assault, 1944, Heights of Abraham).

BIRMINGHAM, City Museum (flats).

BISHOP'S STORTFORD, Rhodes Museum (dioramas of South African history, military and civil, by Stokes).

BOSWORTH, Ambion Farm (diorama of the Battle of Bosworth, 54 and 60mm models, by Kirk, Herald, Airfix, designed, supervised and many of the models painted by George Farnham).

BRECON, Regimental Museum of the South Wales Borderers and the Monmouthsire Regiment, The Barracks (diorama: Defence of Rorke's Drift, by A. Grimes, 20mm Airfix; 50mm clay models by H. Griffiths, d.1972).

BRIDGWATER, Blake's House Museum (diorama by Greenwood-Stokes).

BURNLEY, Towneley Hall Museum (diorama of the Charge of the Heavy Brigade, 20mm, by Valhalla, made 1973).

CAMBERLEY, Sandhurst Infantry School (Cassin-Scott).

CAMBRIDGE, Folk Museum (wood).

CANTERBURY, Museum (medieval).

CARDIFF, Awgeddfa Wercymon, St Fagan's Castle (wood; flats; three dioramas of fishing villages by Greenwood-Stokes).
Welch Regimental Museum, The Castle (Cassin-Scott, solids; dioramas by Regimental; separate models).

CARLISLE, Border Regiment and King's Own Border Regiment, The Castle (six 54mm lead conversions by Roche-Kelly; four carved wood 90mm models by J. Henry, pre-Second World War; dioramas: Battle of Arroyo dos Molinos, 1811, commercial 5 and 54mm solids by Lieut-Colonel M. Smyth and F. Gibson; Landing Zone at Arnhem, 1944, gliders, etc. by the same team; plywood cut-outs, 9½ in, by E.V. Howell, c.1930).

CASTLETON, Isle of Man, Government Museum (eight dioramas of interiors by Greenwood-Stokes).

CHELMSFORD, Chelmsford and Essex Museum incorporating the Essex Regiment Museum (Elastolin and Lineol pre-Second World War Germans; trellis-tongs).

CHESTER, The Museum of the 22nd Cheshire Regiment, The Castle (dioramas: the Battle of Meeanee; the Death of Wolfe, both by Greenwood-Stokes).
King Charles' Tower (diorama of the Civil War).
Water Tower (model: Chester in the Middle Ages).

CHICHESTER, The District Museum, incorporating the Royal Sussex Regiment Museum (diorama, Quebec, ex-R.U.S.I.).

CULLODEN, National Trust for Scotland's Battlefields Museum, Old Leanach Cottage (six models by members of the N.E. Branch of the Scottish Military Collectors' Society, 1972).

DERBY, Sudbury Hall (English turned wood; Heinrichsen flats; 'The Castle of the Commander in Chief', c.1840).

DORCHESTER, Dorsetshire Regiment Museum, The Keep (diorama: Plassey, ex-R.U.S.I.).

DORKING, Museum (automata).

DOVER, The Castle (the second Siborne model of Waterloo, on loan from the Tower of London).

DURHAM, Light Infantry Museum, Aykley Heads (conversions of Stadden by R. Thompson, 1968: Elastolin Nazi leaders).
Durham School Services, on tour, headquarters Bowes Museum (Roman and Norman forts with converted 20 and 54mm plastic models by Airfix and Britains by Michael H. Brown).
Royal County Hotel (converted Staddens, 1758-1915, by E. Thompson).

EDINBURGH, Museum of Childhood (solids; flats; wood).
Regimental Museums of the Royal Scots, the King's Own Scottish Borderers, the Highland Light Infantry, the Cameronians, the Black Watch, the Gordons, the Seaforth Highlanders (plaster replicas of the Pilkington Jackson wooden statuettes).
Scottish United Services Museum, The Castle (Pilkington Jackson wood-carved statuettes; dioramas).

GATESHEAD, Saltwell Park Museum (Timpo Coronation coach of Queen Elizabeth II).

GLASGOW, Royal Highland Fusiliers H.Q. (diorama: 21st Foot at Dettingen, 173 models, 1 in high).

GLOSSOP, Centurian Public House, Gamesley (life-size centurion commissioned by Hyde Breweries from Michael Brown).

GUILDFORD, WRAC Barracks, Queen Elizabeth Park (plywood cut-outs).

HALIFAX, Duke of Wellington's Regiment (33rd Foot), Regimental Museum (18 conversions with added equipment by Rear-Admiral C.M. Blackman, D.S.O.).

HAMPTON-ON-THAMES (private collection, indoor and out, of John Ruddle, open to view).

HASTINGS, Municipal Museum (diorama: Battle of Hastings).
Triodome (diorama: Battle of Hastings by Featherstone and Bath, using flats by Müller).

HENDON, The Royal Air Force Museum (one or two small dioramas produced by personnel, using mainly converted 20mm models, but including those of U.P.C.).

HOVE, The Museum (Britains' Coronation Coach of Queen Elizabeth II).

KINGSTON-UPON-THAMES, Queen's Regiment (Queen's Surreys) H.Q. (dioramas by R.W. Hayward: Defence of Hill 60, Ypres, 20mm Airfix; Football Attack, East Surrey Regiment at Montauban Ridge, first Battle of the Somme, 30mm Staddens; 42 plywood models by R. North).

LEEDS, Abbey House Museum (a few Britains, some in boxes; Elastolin; Hong Kong plastics).

LEICESTER, Newarke House Museum (Britains, Elastolin;

Dinky).

LEWES, Anne of Cleves' House (Collection of Britains commenced by Thomas Sutton).

East Sussex Schools Museums (diorama with flats: Battle of Lewes, by Garratt).

LICHFIELD, The Staffordshire Regiment (The Prince of Wales'), Whittington Barracks (nine wooden models, 300mm, acquired 1956; 130 plastics; dioramas; Battle of Ulundi, ex-R.U.S.I.; Nicosia, 44mm models).

LIVERPOOL, Merseyside County Museum, King's Liverpool Regiment (diorama: a World War battle, 25mm plastics, by Alan Gosling; Britains, not on display);

TAVR Association for the North of England and the Isle of Man (Cassin-Scott; models on tour for recruiting purposes).

LONDON, Bethnal Green Museum (Allgeyer, Heinrichsen, Elastolin, Märklin, Fry, Stadden, semi-permanent collection of Britains, Soldiers' Soldiers; German carved wood; diorama with semi-solids dated 1834).

British Insurance Association, Aldermary House (Stokes' diorama of Parade of Pikemen and Musketeers of the Honourable Artillery Company).

British Museum (medieval nef; 16th-century clock; archaic).

Commonwealth Institute (miscellaneous).

Guards Museum (Greenwood-Stokes dioramas).

Gunnersbury Park, Museum (field hospital by Britains).

Honourable Artillery Company, Armoury House (diorama: Edgehill, by Surén).

Imperial War Museum (Elastolin, Lineol, Mignot; plaster, 300mm models in cloth uniforms; dioramas: Flers, D-Day, both ex-R.U.S.I.; Landing at V Beach, Gallipoli; several by Cawood, in plaster, wood and metal, of First World War; Royal Marine Commandos scaling cliffs, Second World War, 20mm).

Kneller Hall, Royal Army School of Music (diorama, Field of the Cloth of Gold, ex-R.U.S.I.).

London Museum, Kensington Palace (flats; hollow-casts; solids; conjoint tin; civil dioramas; 'Edward VII' clock: much reconstruction on dioramas done by Thorp Modelmakers, and many transferred to Museum of London).

Museum of London (dioramas, some from the London Museum, some new ones by Thorp Modelmakers: museum opened 1976).

National Army Museum (extensive collection of flats by Ochel; semi-solids by Allgeyer; Heyde, 40 and 90mm; Britains, Stadden, Carman, Greenwood and Ball, Métayer, Lucotte, Midleton Models; dioramas: Rorke's Drift, by Surén; Siborne's first Waterloo model due to be transferred to Stratfield Saye; part of collection still stored at Camberley).

National Maritime Museum (Midleton Models; Quebec assault barge in cork).

Pollock's Toy Museum (hollow-casts; paper sheets).

Regimental Museum of the London Scottish, 59 Buckingham Gate (diorama; Messines Ridge, by Greenwood-Stokes).

St James's Palace (instructional blocks).

Tower of London, Royal Fusiliers Museum (four dioramas by Greenwood-Stokes; Cassin-Scott).

Victoria and Albert Museum (medieval nef).

Wellcome Medical Museum (semi-permanent display by Mr. John Hanington).

Woolwich, Royal Artillery Museum (dioramas: Mountain battery, by General G.P. Hughes, using Scruby and Cox models; Peninsular War, Stadden models, by Major J.P. Kaestlin; Maiwand, by Colonel Brown; Neri and Minden, both by S. Brookes).

LUTON, Museum (semi-solids; flats; wood).

NEWCASTLE-UPON-TYNE, H.Q. 15th/19th The King's Royal Hussars

(Heyde, four models by Alan Kemp).

NORWICH, Stranger's Hall (hollow-casts; solids; trellis-tongs; wood-carving by Fichtel).

NOTTINGHAM, The Castle.

OXFORD, The Ashmolean (copy of the Strettweg idol-cart).

PENICUIK, The Scottish Infantry Depot, Glencorse Barracks (15 models by Gammage).

PERTH, The Black Watch Museum, Balhousie Castle (commercial models; diorama of Quatre Bras, by Surén).

Killiecrankie, Information Centre (diorama of Killiecrankie by Surén).

ROTTINGDEAN, The National Toy Museum, The Grange (Britains; Heyde; Ochell; trellis-tongs; carved wood; papiermâché).

ST ALBANS, Verulamium Museum (figures to go with models of Roman Britain).

SALISBURY, Museum (diorama).

SANDWICH, Kent, Precinct Toy Collection (small collection of hollow-casts; Elastolin Indians; Söhlke flats in original box).

SHEFFIELD, The Museum, Weston Park (tiny collection of flats and solids).

SHEPTON MALLET, Oakhill Manor (dioramas).

SHREWSBURY, KDG Museum, Clive House (military band by Blenheim).

SOUTHAMPTON, The Royal Marines Museum, Eastney Barracks (35 converted models with hand-made equipment by Rear-Admiral Blackman).

STAVERTON, Skyfame Aircraft Museum (wooden models by M.E. Jones).

STIRLING, Museum of the Argyll and Sutherland Highlanders (diorama of 'The Thin Red Line', by Greenwood-Stokes).

STOCKPORT, Torkington Lodge (permanent display by the northern section of the British Model Soldier Society).

TIVERTON, Museum (conversions by Lethbridge).

TUNBRIDGE WELLS, Museum (Lucotte, Allgeyer semi-solids).

WALMER, Castle.

WARWICK, Queen's Own Hussars Museum (diorama: Rahman Ridge, El Alamein, by Greenwood-Stokes; models by Bisgood).

WESTERHAM, Quebec House (Wolfe-period landing craft, figures in metal, by H.R. Allen).

WILTON HOUSE, Earl of Pembroke's collection (German 19th century semi-solids in dioramas, the best by Gammage, the remainder by John Copinger, Mr, Mrs and Miss Wills).

WINDSOR, The Castle ('The Queen's Dolls' House' containing tiny models by Britains).

WOBURN ABBEY (Rowe collection of converted Staddens; complete set of Ensign and Vallance models).

WOODSTOCK, Blenheim Place (large collection of Lucotte, small collection of Stadden).

WORCESTER, Worcestershire Regiment and Worcester Yeomanry Museum (Carman, Britains' 'Eyes Right'; diorama of Albuhera, 1811, the models in plasticine).

WORTHING, Museum (miscellaneous).

YEOVILTON, Fleet Air Arm Museum (dioramas, including aircraft: Airstrike at Taranto, by Stokes; Operation Tungsten — attack on the *Tirpitz*, scale of models diminishing from 54mm, by Valhalla; Swordfish attack on *Prinz Eugen*, *Scharnhorst* and *Gneisenau*, by Valhalla).

YORK, Castle Museum (wood; paper sheets; flats; hollow-casts; dioramas of Balaclava and Marston Moor, both ex-R.U.S.I.).

The Prince of Wales' Own Regiment of Yorkshire, Imphal Barracks wood, 15 in tall, by Major H.A.V. Spencer.

GREECE

ATHENS, Museum (archaic).

ISRAEL
JERUSALEM, Religious Centre ('Proclaim Freedom' dioramas by Greenwood-Stokes).

ITALY
FLORENCE, Bargello (aqua-manile).

MILAN, Museo del Commune (flats).

Sforza Castle (paper sheets).

NAPLES, San Martino Museo (2,260 paper figures, 70mm, painted by Emanuele Gin, b.1817, and Filippo Emilio, b.1845, made for Ferdinand II of Naples, acquired 1923).

PADUA, Ponte di Brento (Testi coll. of Italian commercial solids).

PINEROLO, Museo Nazionale dell'Arma di Cavalleria.

ROME, Torre di Conti (small museum of the *Unione Collezionisti d'Italia*).

The Vatican (Krauhs).

SASSARI, Sardinia, Municipality Museum (Pranzetti).

TURIN, Museo Civilo (flats).

Pietro Millo Museo (composite models).

Risorgimento Museo (composite models).

VENICE, Museo Navale.

MEXICO
MEXICO CITY, Instituto de Historia (Cassin-Scott).

MOROCCO
TANGIER, Forbes Museum of Military Miniatures, Palais Mendoub, (dioramas by Surén, Ciuffo: hollow-casts, flats, Heyde, Mignot Spanish manufacturers, modern makers, conversions by Harris).

NETHERLANDS
GRONINGEN, (Spandauw collection of converted kits).

LEIDEN, Koninklijk Netherlands Leger Museum (undergoing rebuilding, stock stored in the Armoury, Delft, and in storehouses in Leiden and The Hague (dioramas by Koekkoek of cut-out paper; a display 20 x 5 ft. of Spanish army detachment during Spanish-Netherlands war, made 1900; Airbase, R.A.F., Second World War; crude flats; model by Stadden).

NEW ZEALAND
WAIOURU, New Zealand Army Base (figures by Hood and Withers; diorama by Matthews).

WELLINGTON, Napier Museum (models by Hood).

NORWAY
OSLO, Norsk Folkmuseum (wood carvings).

STAVANGER, Ledaal Museum (flats; solids).

POLAND
CRACOW, Museum (selection of models by the Polish society of Collectors of Historical Figurines, 1966).

PORTUGAL
LISBON, Centro de Coleccionadores (flats; semi-solids).

Museo de Marinha (Cutileiro).

SPAIN
BARCELONA, Museum de las Reales Altarazanas (Valverde conversions).

Museo del Castillo de Monjuich (Llovera Collection solids).

Museo de Industrias y Artes Populares del Pueblo Espanol (moulds by Ortelli; flats).

Museo Instituto Municipal de Historia de la Cuidad (paper sheet collections of J.M. Columinas and P. Villa; flats by Lleonart).

CADIZ, Escuela de Guerra Naval (Valverde conversions). San Fernando. Pantéon de Marinos Illustres (Valverde conversions).

MADRID, Museo del Ejército (carved wood by Tello; Nuremberg flats; Ortelli; Julia).

Museo Naval (Capell; Valverde conversions; part Llovera coll.)

MAJORCA, Submarine School (Valverde conversions).

PONTEVEDRA, Museo (Valverde conversions).

SAN SEBASTIAN, Museo del Monte Urgall, Castillo de la Mota (Gonzalez collection of miscellaneous solids).

SWEDEN
ENSKEDE, Tennfigurmusei Vanner (flats).

GOTEBORG, Historical Museum (flats).

LEKSAND, Tennfigurmuseum, Hjortnas (old flats; dioramas by Dählback and Berglund; 54mm solids; military models and folkcostume by Schreiber, Eriksson).

LUND, Cultural Museum.

STOCKHOLM, Kungl. Armemuseum (flats; solids; plastics; dioramas by Moberg and Ewart)

Nordiska Museet (small collection).

Statens Sjöhistoriske, incorporating Warsa Museum (Brunoe).

UPPSALA, Universitets Konsthistoriska Institution ('*Kunstschrank*' of Gustavus Adolphus).

SWITZERLAND
AARAU, Museum Schlossli (flats).

ALTDORF, Musée (diorama of Waterloo with tiny, clumsy figures of dried dough on wire).

BASLE, Musée (flats).

BERNE, Musée (flats).

CANTON AARGAU, Museum Zofingen (pilgrims' tokens).

COPPET CASTLE, Musée des Suisses au Service Etrangers (Baldet).

GRANDSON CASTLE, (solids; dioramas).

LAKE GENEVA, Vieux-Morges Musée (Réné Morax collection).

LAUSANNE, Cantonal and University Library (flats).

LUCERNE, Alte-Rathaus Museum (flats from Keller collection).

Glacier Garden Musée (diorama by Niederost).

MORGES, Waadtlandisches Arméemuseum (flats).

SCHAFFHAUSEN, Musée (flats).

SION, Valiere Musée, Valais (flats).

ZURICH, Schweizerisches Landesmuseum (collection of flats).

UNITED STATES OF AMERICA
NATIONAL PARKS: Fort Sumter; Vicksburg; Yorktown (K/S pewter).

WELLS FARGO STAGING POSTS (Morrison caricatures).

ALASKA, State Museum, Juneau (Thomas Morrison models).

CALIFORNIA, Los Angeles, County Museum of Natural History (B. Gordon).

Los Angeles, Museum of Science and Industry (semi-permanent collection of Gordon, Shideler; loan exhibition of the Model Soldier Collectors of California).

San Francisco, Presidio Military Museum (dioramas: the Presidio in 1806; aftermath of the earthquake of 1906; semi-permanent loan exhibition by the American Model Soldier Society of California).

Santa Anna, Charles Bowers Memorial Museum.

COLORADO, State Historical Society of Colorado, Denver (Morrison, Cassin-Scott).

CONNECTICUT, Danbury, Scott Fanton Museum.

Hartford, Trinity College Library (Hickmott collection of solids, including dioramas of Poitiers with models by Courtenay, arranged by John May; Waterloo, 30mm Staddens by May and Peter Kemplay).

DAKOTA, Custer Museum, Little Big Horn.

DISTRICT OF COLUMBIA, WASHINGTON, Museum of the

Cincinnati, Anderson House (Baldet groups).

National Guard Memorial (dioramas; wood by Vliet).

Navy Department, Smithsonian Institution (history of the United States Marine Corps by Bussler; models by the Harles, the Wirths; diorama by Roming).

U.S. Government Defence Mapping Agency (8 dioramas by the National Capital Military Collectors).

GEORGIA, Atlanta, Coca-Cola Bottling Company, Troop Hunt House (diorama by Pfab).

Dobbins Air Force Base (five models).

Museum, (diorama, Capture of General Sherman).

Six Banks (diorama, Peach Tree Creek, by Pfab).

Fort Benning, National Infantry Center (4 dioramas: Gatling gun and crew, Monongahela, First World War, Ludendorff Bridge, all by James H. Copestick).

Fort Gordon, Naval Air Station (permanent exhibition by the Atlanta Soldier Society).

U.S. Military Police School (collection of 8 in carved polychrome wood models by Grykiewicz, moving to Fort McClellan, Alabama in near future).

ILLINOIS, Metamore Court House, State Memorial Museum, Lincoln Room (B. Gordon).

INDIANA, Indianapolis, Locke, Reynolds, Boyd & Weisell, Attorneys-at-Law (diorama, Bautzen, by Surén).

KANSAS, Fort Leavenworth (exceptionally large collection of 54mm solids in conversion on loan basis from von Schritz; 18 in conversions by Tyler).

Fort Riley, U.S. Cavalry Museum (Confederate Cavalry column, Lieut. Godfrey, K. Troop, 7th Cavalry at Little Big Horn, by Bugle & Guidon).

Fort Scaranworth, Museum.

KENTUCKY, Belmont-Columbus State Park (diorama of Belmont-Columbus by Pfab).

Blue Lick State Park (diorama of Boone and the Indians, by Pfab).

Fort Knox, Patton Museum of Cavalry and Armor (dioramas: Civil War; Germans in Russia; U.S. Tanks breaching the Siegfried Line; U.S. and German troops in combat; Renault tanks attacking at San Mihiel; U.S. tanks and troops in Korea).

MARYLAND, Aberdeen Proving Ground Ordnance Museum, U.S. Ordnance Center and School (3 dioramas, portraying ordnance, 1918 and 1962, using plastic vehicles, guns and figures, constructed by Museum staff).

Annapolis, Military and Naval Academy (dioramas; Paul Jones, by Dwight Franklin, 7 in models; Gettysburg, 4-8 in models, in beeswax).

MASSACHUSETTS, Boston, Bunker Hill Museum (Battle of Bunker Hill by Pitman; the same, by members of the Military Collectors of New England).

Maritime Museum (single figures, 12-14 in from 1775 onwards and dioramas, 10 inch, all in wood by Martin Rendall).

Charlestown, Balto County Library Branches, Fort Tabor and Fort Rodman Museums (an appeal was made in 1975 for models to start a collection to illustrate American history from the War of Independence).

Sandwich, Heritage Plantation (Lilly collection of models by Cooke, with dioramas by the same artist, with one by Welch).

Springfield, Armory Museum (Lewis toy soldier collection, claimed to be 'the largest in the United States - some are several hundred years old - others were purchased in dimestores during the thirties'; flats; semi-flats; solids up to 10 in. Receives active support from the Connecticut Valley Miniature Figure Collectors).

Swansea, Museum (dioramas from King Phillips' War to the War of Independence, by Cooke).

Wakefield, Mutual Insurance Co. (dioramas by members of the Military Collectors of New England, 1975).

MICHIGAN, Detroit Children's Museum.

Grand Rapids Public Museum (permanent collection of the Michigan Company of Military Historians and Collectors, including models by W. Alexander, R. Barecki, R. Gryga, J. Plank).

NEW JERSEY, Lakewood, 'Rodina' (White Russian) Museum, (Hitrovo bequest).

Princeton, Battlefields Preservation Society (every unit of the American War of Independence by Scruby).

Trenton, Old Barracks (dioramas by Greer, Imrie).

NEW YORK STATE, Albany, Museum (dioramas: Yorktown; Clinton's Southern Expedition; Discovery of Hudson's Bay; Champlain).

Fort Ticonderoga (dioramas by Stadden, Imrie).

Fort William Henry.

Garrison, Dick's Castle (part of the von Schriltz collection).

Gettysburg, Cliff Arquette Museum (carved wood).

New York, City Museum (9 in models; wood; paper sheets; 19th century German solids; early Britains; diorama by Roming).

Forbes Foundation (diorama of Friedland by Surén).

Roosevelt Collection, Hyde Park (aircraft carrier by Roming).

Vail's Gate, Newburgh Museum (dioramas by Imrie, Buckley).

West Point, United States Military Academy (dioramas: Cynocephalae; Adrianople; Crécy by Greenwood-Stokes; Breitenfels, by the same; Saratoga, 54mm, by Scheid; Gettysburg, wax and card, 35-110mm, by staff; Parade, by Phoenix, 35mm, scenery by Christophers; models by Métayer, Mignot, Cassin-Scott, Tyler, 21 in plaster by U.S. Quartermaster General's Office).

OKLAHOMA, Fort Sill.

PENNSYLVANIA, Carlisle Barracks, U.S. Military History Research Collection, Hessian Powder Magazine Museum (models and dioramas by, Imrie, P.A. Buckley and J. Larson).

Pittsburgh, Historical Society of Western Pennsylvania (permanent exhibition by the Assembly of Historical Collectors).

Quantico, U.S. Marine Corps Memorial Museum (dioramas; 2 models in 54mm by R.L. Wall).

RHODE ISLAND, Providence, Mrs. J.M. Brown Museum (solids).

SOUTH CAROLINA, Ulmers, Museum (Civil War dioramas by Pfab).

VERMONT, Shelburne Museum (carved wood model, 18th c.)

VIRGINIA, Colonial Williamsburg (Royal Doulton porcelain).

Fort Belvoir, U.S. Army Engineer Center (over 60 conversions, dioramas and vignettes by E. Kiker).

Newport Mews, War Memorial Museum (Landing of Rochambeau, by Baldet; early Britains; contemporary makers; permanent exhibition by the Pennsylvania Military Historical Society).

Yorktown (dioramas: Surrender of Cornwallis; Washington's Battery).

WASHINGTON, Seattle Art Museum (models by T. Morrison).

WEST VIRGINIA, Harper's Ferry Privately Owned Park and Museum (dioramas: Antietam; Fredericksburg; Fort Stevens; Gettysburg; Harper's Ferry, all by Pfab).

WYOMING, University of History Department (models painted by J. Christensen).

USSR

LENINGRAD, Artillery Museum (dioramas with flats; composite).

Museum of the Revolution (dioramas).

MOSCOW, Museum of the Revolution (dioramas).

Red Army Museum.

Russian Artillery Museum.

BIBLIOGRAPHY

'Aaurauer Zinnkompositions-Figuren in Landesmuseum', *Neuew Zurcher Zeitung*, 1 September, 1935

Achilles, Walter. *Zinnfiguren als kulturhistorische Quelle*, Brunswick, 1968

'1000 bunte Zinnfiguren', *Zeitschrift des Museums zu Hildesheim*, Heft 25, 1974

'Die altesten niedersachsischen Zinnfiguren des Meisters AN', Brunswick, 1976

Adhemer, J. *Imagerie Populaire Française*, Paris, 1968

Airfix Magazine Annual. 1973- (mainly concerned with conversions)

Alberini, Massimo. 'Le Armate in Vetrine', *La Vie d'Italia*, 10 October, 1965

Allendesalazar, J.M. *Coleccionismo de Soldados*, Madrid, 1978 (Spanish models)

Almanach Bottin, Paris, v.y.

Alte und Neue Zinnfiguren, Germany, 1970-

Althoff, Shirley. 'Military Miniatures', *Globe-Democrat Sunday Magazine*, U.S.A., 18 January, 1976 (models made by Wall)

Amades, J., Columinas, J., and Vila, P. *Els Soldats*, Barcelona, 1936. 2 vols. (exhaustive treatment of Catalan paper sheets)

Andress, Michael. *Scale Model Buildings*, 1973

Armies and Weapons, 1973- (an occasional illustration of a model)

'Armies Made to Order', *Everybody's*, 23 August, 1958

Armont, Paul. *Soldats d'Hier et Aujourd'hui*, Paris, 1929

Arque, L. *Les Faiseur de Jouets en Franconia*, Paris, 1908 (incidental references to models)

Ashley, J. 'Toy Soldiers and Military Miniatures', *Out and About* (International Police Federation, 1973) (conversions by Dilley)

Aslin, E. *Toys*, 1967 (incidental references)

'At Ease', *True*, U.S.A., March, 1954

Athletic Sports, Toys and Games, Journal of, 1895

Axel-Nilsson, Goran. *om tennsoldater och tennfigurer*, Fataburen, 1971

Bachman, M. and Langner, R. *Berchtesgardener Volkskunst*, Leipzig, 1957

Baecker, C., and Haas, D. *Die Anderen Nurnberger Techniches Spielzaug*, Frankfurt, 1973-4 (incidental references)

Baecker, C., Haas, D., and Jeanmaire. *Jouets techniques au Fil du temps.-Mäerklin*. 2 vols. Frankfurt, 1975-76 (the firm of Mäerklin)

Baier, Ursula. 'Das Thema fur den Sammler Zinnfiguren', *Die Kunst*, September, 1971

Bainbridge, H.C. 'Fabergé Figures in Russian Coloured Stones', *The Connoisseur*, April, 1938

Bakshian, A., Jr. 'Model Soldiers on the March'. *Reader's Digest*, December, 1976.

Baldet, Marcel. *Figurines et Soldats de Plomb*, Paris, 1961

'Les Troupes Françaises aux XVII et XVIII siècles', *Armi Antiche* (*Bolletino dell'Academia di S. Marciano*) Turin, 1970 (models by Lelièpvre)

Bangs, J.K. *In Camp with a Toy Soldier*, New York 1892

Bard, R. *Making and Collecting Military Miniatures*, New York, 1957

Baring, E. *Rules for the Conduct of the War Game*, 1872

Bast, J. 'Kleine grosse welt in zinn', *Neu Stafelte; die moderne Bildungszeitschrift für junge Menschen*, Berlin, July 1964

Baterschon, H. *Life of a Mogul Princess*, 1931 (incidental references)

Battle, 1975 (incorporated in *Military Modelling* 1977)

Battles for Freedom: a New Charter Exhibition of Battle-Dioramas and Model Soldiers (1974) (Stokes-Greenwood dioramas)

'Battles for Freedom from Magna-Carta to D-Day', *The Illustrated London News*, November, 1947 (Stokes-Greenwood dioramas)

Bayonet, The (Journal of the Horse and Musket Society), Margate, 1968

Beard, Charles R. 'Miniature Armours', *The Connoisseur*, December, 1928

Beaumont, C.W. *The Strange Adventures of a Toy Soldier*, 1926

Beauplan, R. de. 'Jouets d'Armistice: la Vitrine disarmée', *L'Illustration*, Paris, 28 December, 1940

Beavan, G. Phillips, (Editor). *British Manufacturing Industries: Toys Section* by George C.T. Bartley. 1877

Bedford, Paul. 'Toy Soldiers Never Die', *Courier*, U.S.A., December, 1948

Belsky, M. & F. 'Sculpture to be Eaten', *The Studio*, October, 1949

Benson, A.C. and Weaver, Sir Laurence. *The Book of the Queen's Doll's House*, 2 vols, 1924 (Britains' tiniest models)

Berling, Karl. *Altes Zinn*, Leipzig, 1919

Bernard, Jean. *Le Jouet Français*, Paris, 1956

Bertarelli, A. *L'Imagerie Populaire Italienne*, Italy, 1929

Bertram, Fritz and Zimmermann, Helmut. *Begegrunden mit Zinn*, Prague, 1967

Birnback, R.J. 'Name Your Weapons', *Nation's Business*, New York, March, 1952

Blake, M. *Making Model Soldiers*, 1976

Blum, Peter. *Military Miniatures*, New York, 1964
The Model Soldier Manual, New York 1970

Boersch. (Auction Sale-preface by Paul Martin) Angers, March, 1971

Boesch, Hans. *Kinderleben in der deutschen Vergangenheir*, Leipzig, 1900- Jena, 1924 (incidental references)

Bolletino, Accademia di S. Marciano, Turin, 1963 (A few illustrations of models in each issue)

Bonnes, Aug. *Die Zinngiesserfamilie Meyerheine*, Potsdam, 1937

Bory, Jean-René. *Les Suisses au Service Etranger et leur Musée*, Nyon, 1965

'Boston Tells the War Story in Table-top Battles', *Art & Antiques*, New York, June 21, 1975 (on the dioramas 'They Nobly Dared')

Bottiger, J. *Philip Hainhofer und der Kunstschrank Gustave Adolf in Uppsala*, 4 vols, Stockholm, 1909-10

Bourson, P. 'Les Petits Soldats de Strasbourg et leurs Peintres', *La Vie en Alsace*, Strasbourg, 1931

Bréviaire du Collectionneur des Figurines Historiques, Tom. 1, Paris, 1958

'Britains' Private Army on Parade Round the World', British Industries Fair Press Office, 1955

British Empire, The, Part VI, B.B.C., London, 1970 (diorama of Plassey)

'British-Made Toys', *Industrial World*, July, 1930

British Toy Fair Catalogue. Various Issues.

Brown, J.A. *Das Zinngeisserhandwerk der Schweiz*, Solothurn, 1930

Bruckner, A. and B. *Schweizer Fahrenbuch*, St Gaul, 1942

Bruckner, W. *Imagerie Populaire Allemande*, Paris, 1969

Bucquoy, E.-L. *Petits Soldats d'Alsace*, Valognes, 1913

Burgkmaier, Hans. *See* Treitzsaurwein, M.

Burial, Jan. *Arbeitsbeding-ungen und Klassenkampfin romischen wissenschaft*, Berlin (1957)

Cadbury, Betty *Playthings Past*. 1976 (incidental references)

Calgary Herald, 16 November, 1974 (the Pottenbrun Zinnfiguren Museum)

Call to Colors Magazine, Culver City, 1970-

Calmettes, Pierre. *Excursions à travers les Métiers*, Paris, c. 1904 (chapter on flats)

Campaigns, Los Angeles, 1975-

Carlet, C.H.C. 'Petits Soldats Strasbourgeois', *Album Historique de l'Armée et de la Marine*, No. 7, Paris, 1905

Carlos, A. 'Coleccionismo vuelven los recortables', *Los Domingo de ABC*, Madrid, November, 1979

Carman, W.Y. *Model Soldiers*, 1973

Carson, Jane. *Colonial Williamsburg at Play*, Colonial Williamsburg, 1965

Cassin-Scott, Jack. *Historical Military Models of the World*, 1973
Models in the Making, 1973

'C. Frazer Bezit 2000 Miniaturen', *De Noord Amsterdammer*, 22 November, 1974 (article on Cornelius Frazer's collection)

'Charlie Weaver', *Look*, New York, 26 May, 1959 (on Cliff Arquette)

Childrens' Paradise. A Christmas Exhibition of Toys through the Ages, 1957-8

Christmas Exhibition of Model Soldiers. (British Model Soldier Society) 12 December - 10 January, 1959

Churchill, Sir Winston S. *My Early Life*, 1930

Clarétie, L. *Les Jouets Historiques: Fabrication*, Paris, 1894
'Childhood through the Ages', *Cosmopolitan*, New York, January, 1904

Jouets de France, Paris, 1920

Compiègne Museum, *Origine du Musée de la Figurine*, Paris, c. 1950

Consolidated Encylopaedia. Vol. 10: Toys, New York, 1938

Consumer's Union, USA, 1936- (American toys)

'Couple re-create Biblical scenes', *Calgary Herald* (Ray biblical dioramas)

Craig, G. *A Book of Penny Toys*, 1899

Crump, L. *Nursery Life Three-Hundred Years' Ago*, 1929

Cruse, A.J. 'Parade of the "Tin Soldiers"', *Collins' Magazine Annual*, Vol. 5, 1952

Culff, Robert. *The World of Toys*, New York, 1956

Cummings, R. *Make your own Forts and Castles*. New York, 1976

Czolowski, Ted and Richards,Babynn. *Victoria Calling*, Victoria, B.C. 1973 (note on the Ray dioramas)

Dahlback, Ake. *Fran Tennsoldat till Tennfigur* (n.p., n.d.) (catalogue of the Leksand Tinfigure Museum)

Daiken,. L. *Children's Toys through the Ages*, 1953
The World of Toys, 1963

D'Allemagne, H.R. *Histoire du Jouets*, Paris, 1903
'Les Soldats de Plomb', *Jouets et Jeux Anciens*, Paris, June 1, 1905

David, H. *Jeux de Plombs*, Paris, 1949

Dawk. San Carlos. Various Issues

De Forest, K. 'Playthings of Kings', *Harper's*, New York, April, 1900

'De Maarschalk van Amsterdam', *Nieuwe Revu*, Amsterdam, November 15, 1974 (on the Frazer collection)

'Der Erbhuldigungzug für Maria Theresia', Museum der Ersten Osterreichishen Spar-Casse, Vienna, c. 1970 (models by Krauhs)

Deronville, Dr Jean. *Les Cahiers de Marottes & Violons d'Ingtes*, No. 2, Paris, 1949 (incidental references)

Der Stern, Hamburg, 1956

'Der Zinnsoldat', *Neue Mannheimer Zeitung*, Mannheim, 1 December, 1935

Descalves, L. *L'Imagerie Epinal*, Paris, 1918

Deutsches Spielwaren-Fachmesse, Nuremberg, v.y.

Diedrich, J. 'Geschichte in Zinn', *Die neue Molkerbastei*, Heft II, 1978

'Die Kunst der Zinnsoldaten', *Velhagen & Klasings Monatshefte*, Bielefeld, December, 1930

Dilley Captain R. *Scale-Model Soldiers*, 1972 *Beginner's Guide to Military Modelling*, 1974 and Fosten (B.) *Painting and Detailing Military Miniatures*, 1977 and Stearns (P.O.) *Model Soldies in Colour*, 1979

'Don't Say "Toy Soldier"', *Time*, U.S.A., 19 January, 1953

Dowdall, H., and Gleason, J. *Sham Battle*, New York, 1929

Downes, W.H. *The Tin Army of the Potomac*, Boston 1880, (line drawings of models)

Duchartre, P-L., and Saulnier, R. *L'Imagérie Populaire*, Paris, 1925

Dumont, J.M. *La Vie et l'Oeuvre de Jean-Charles Péllerin*, Epinal, 1956

Duplessie. 'Les Soldats de Plomb', *La Révue Britannique*, Paris, 1889 (article on flats)

Eipper, P. 'Zinnfiguren; ein vergessebes Spielzeug', *Westermann's Monatshefte*, Berlin, December, 1926

Elderkin, K.M. 'Jointed Dolls in Antiquity', *American Journal of Archaeology*, Vol. 34. Washington, D.C., 1930

Elgström, O. *Wir Man mit Soldaten Krieg Fuhrt*, Leipzig, 1916

Engström, Jarl. *Historia i tenn*, Sweden, c.1954

'En lille Kanoner til "Wasa"', *Berlingske Tidente*, Copenhagen, March, 1970 (article on Rollo)

'Etudes en Allemand: 1960-1970', *Atlantis*, Paris, 1971 (including paper sheets)

Ewing, J.H. *A Soldier's Children*, (illustration showing German automata)

Exhibition of Armour of Kings and Captains from the National Collections of Austria, Tower of London, London, 1949 (including model tilting knights)

'Exposition International des Arts Decoratifs et Industries Modernes', *Rapport Génèral*, Tom. VIII: Jouets, Paris, 1925

Featherstone, Donald F. *Tackle Model Soldiers this Way*, 1964
Handbook for Model Soldier Collectors, 1969
Military Modelling, 1970
Better Military Modelling. 1977

Ffoulkes, Sir Charles. *Arms and the Tower*, 1939

'Fields of Glory', *Toys International*, Vancouver, B.C. May-June, 1969 (the Ray dioramas)

Flick, Pauline. *Discovering Toys and Toy Museums*, 1971

Floericke, K. *Strategie und Taktik des Spiels mit Bleisoldaten*, Dresden, 1924

Foley, J. *Toys through the Ages*, Radnor, Pennsylvania, 1962

Forgeais, A. *Notice sur les Plombs historique trouvés dans la Seine*, Paris, 1858

Forrer, R. *Les Etains de la Collection Alfred Ritleng à Strasbourg*, Strasbourg, 1905
'Mousquetaire en plomb du 17e siècle trouvés dans la Seine,' *Jouets et Jeux Anciens*, Paris, August-September, 1905

Fosbrooke, T.D. *Encyclopaedia of Antiquities*, 2 vols. 1825

Fowler, R. *Making Military Models in Rubber Moulds*, Tipton, California, 1957

France, Anatole. 'Childrens' Playthings', *On Life and Letters. Second Series*, translated A.W. Evans, 1914

Franchey, J. 'Gettysburg in Miniature', *Popular Mechanics*, New York, September, 1956

Fraser, Lady Antonia. *A History of Toys*, 1966

Frauendorf, Johannes. *Die Zinnfigur und ihre Entwicklung in Natur und Heimat*, Berlin, 1955

Fredericks, P.G. 'Miniature Militias', *New York Times Magazine*, New York, 2 October, 23 October, 1955

Freeman, R. & L. *Cavalcade of Toys*, New York, 1952

French Toys, Paris, 1915

Friends (Citroen Co.) U.S.A., February, 1956

Fritzch, K.E., and Bachmann, M. *An Illustrated History of Toys*, New York, 1966 (incidental references)

Führer dürch die I. Internationale Zinnfiguren-Austellung des Deutschen-Zinnfiguren-Sammlerbundes Klio, Leipzig, 1930

Galter, J.S. *El Arte Popular en España*, Barcelona, 1948

Games and Toys, New York, *v.y.*

Garratt, John G. 'Model Soldiers', *Connoisseur Year Book*, 1957
'Model Solders', *Concise Encyclopaedia of Antiques*, Vol. 3, 1957
Model Soldiers: a Collector's Guide, 1959
'Little Armies', *The Saturday Book*, No. 20, 1960
Model Soldiers for the Connoisseur, 1972
Collecting Model Soldiers, 1975

Gay, Victor. *Glossaire Archaeologique du Moyen Age et de la Renaissance*, Paris, 1887

Gayle, M. 'Lead Soldier Parade', *Nation's Business*. U.S.A., January, 1951

Gazzetta Antiquaria, Italy, October, 1975 (article on Strozzi Palace exhibition)

Gebert, Carl Friedrich. 'Die Zinngiesser Hilpert', *Nurnberg Mitteilungen aus dem Germanischen National Museum Nurnberg*, Nuremberg 1914-15

Geist-Mahlan. *Spiegzeugfibel*, Leipzig, 1930

G.E. News, Nela Park, U.S.A., June, 1972 (Updyke's 'Rorke's Drift')

German Toy Industry, The, British Intelligence Objectives Sub-Committee Final Report, No. 1371. H.M.S.O., London, 1947

Geyman, R. 'Little Wars Can be Fun', *Sports Illustrated*, New York, January, 1965

Gilly, Wilhelm. 'Zinnfiguren-Sammler Karl Keim', *Oldenbourg Museumsführer*. Isenss, 1973-1974

'Glorious Past in Porcelain'. *Daily Telegraph*, 3 February, 1977 (models by Sutty)

Goethe, Wolfgang von. *Dichtung und Wahrheit*, 1811, (revised edition, translated by John Oxenford, 1891)

Goldkuhle, Fritz. *Rhenishe Geschichte in Zinn*, Dusseldorf, 1965

Goodenough, Simon. *Military Miniatures*, 1977 (the art of Charles Stadden)

Gordon, L. *Peepshow into Paradise*, 1953

Gosforth, J.C. 'Transmutation. The Art of Changing the Characters of Tin Soldiers and Leaden Models', *News Chronicle 'I Spy' Annual*, No. 2, 1955

Grant, Charles. *The War Game*, 1972

Great Exhibition, The, Official Catalogue, 1851

Great War Game, The by H.G. Wells Britains Ltd, 1908

Greenhill, Peter. 'Greenhill Miniatures – heirs to the Courtenay Tradition', *Master Craftsmen*, Winter, 1979

Griffiths, M.D. 'The Toy Armies of the World', *Pearson's Magazine*, 1898

Grimaldi, Emilio. 'Un Secolo di Uniformi per i Dragoni di Piemente', *Armi Antiche, Bolletino dell' Accademia di S. Marciano Turin*, Turin (models by Chiappa)

Gripenberg, Øle. *Tenngjutaren Erik Lodin och hans Soldatfigurer*, Osma, 1962
Tennsoldater. Som Leksaker Samlarfigurer och Undervisningsmaterial, Helsinki, 1973

Gröber, C. *Childrens' Toys of Bygone Days*, (translated by P. Herford) 1932

Guide to Captain Siborne's New Waterloo Model, 1844

Hahnemann, Max. *Führer durch die Kulturhistorische Kieler Zinnfigurenanstellung*, Kiel, 1929

Hammond, Alex. *The Book of Chessmen*, 1950

Hampe, T. *Der Zinnsoldat*, Berlin, 1924

Hannover's Gloria, Althannoversche und Andere Historische Zinnfiguren, Bomann Museum, Celle, 1956

Harris, Major H.E.D. *Model Soldiers*, 1962
How to go Collecting Model Soldiers, 1969

Hauscher, Hans. *Wirtschaftgeschichte der Neuzeit vom Ende des 14. bis 17. jahrhunderts*, Weimar, 1954

'Hearth Rug Rearmament', *Picture Post*, 11 March, 1939

Hellwig, Gerhard. *Vierzig jahre Berliner Zinnfiguren Werner Scholtz, 1934-74*, Berlin, 1974 (history of Scholtz's achievement)

Helm, R. *Nurnberger Zinnfiguren, Anzeiger des Germanisches National-Museum*. Nuremberg, 1935

Helmbrecht, B. and Reischl, J. *Geschichte der Firma Haffner*, Munich, P.P., 1973

Hercik, E. *Folktoys*, Prague, 1957

Herrad von Landsberg, Abbess. *Hortus deliciarum* (Twelfth century manuscript). Facsimile reprint by A. Straub and G. Keller, Strasbourg, 1901

Hert, L.H. *Handbook of Old American Toys*, New York, 1947 (incidental references).
The Toy Collector, New York, 1969

Hillier, Mary. *Automata & Mechanical Toys*, 1976

Hinchliffe (the firm of) *Handbook for Wargamers and Collectors*. Meltham, 1976

Hintze, Erwin. *Die deutschen Zinngieser und ihre Marken*, Leipzig, 1921

Nurnberger Zinn, Leipzig, 1921

His, H.P. *Jouets anciens de Basle*, Basle, 1973 (incidental references)

'Historic Battles in Miniature', *Civil & Military Gazette*, Lahore, 1937

Hiutorie in Tin, Amsterdam, 1956 (catalogue of noteworthy exhibition by the Dutch Society)

Hitrovo, Michael V. 'History on a Tabletop', *Aerotex Industries Review*, New York, Summer, 1964

Hobbies, various issues, 1940-64

Hofmann, K.B. *Das Blei beiden Volkern des Altertums*, Berlin, 1885

Holladay, Sergeant J. *War Games for Boy Scouts Played with Model Soldiers*, 1909

Holme, C.G. (editor) *Children's Toys of Yesterday*, 1932

Homes and Gardens, November, 1955

Horrath, Lt. G. von. 'The War Game', *Scientific American*, New York, March–June, 1916

'How and Where Toys are Made', *The Graphic*, 16 December, 1871

'How to Build your own Army', *Eagle*, 1 October, 1962

Hugo, T. 'Notes on a Collection of Pilgrims' Signs', *Archaeologia*, vol. 38, 1859

Huntley, T.D. *Painting and Lining Scale Models*. 1976

'Hvem kender tinsoldatens hemmelige kodesprog', *Berlingske Tidende*, Copenhagen, May, 1970 (article on Brunoe)

Illustrated London News, The, Various issues

Industrial Arts and Vocational Education, Various issues, 1931-56

'International Exposition', *The Graphic*, 15 July, 1871

Introduction to the Exhibition Commemorative of the Battle of Lewes, Lewes, 1964 (note on the Garratt diorama)

International Vorstilling af Tinnsoldater og Modelfiguren (Chakoten), Copenhagen, 1963 (exhibition by the Danish Society)

Jackson, Mrs. Neville. *Toys of other Days*, 1908 (chapters on flats)

Jackson, R. Toy 'Soldiers are on Draft', *Illustrated*, 8 January, 1947

Jacquermin, A. *Le Musée International de l'Imagerie à Epinal*, Épinal, 1958

Jean-Bernard, F. 'L'Enfant et la Figurine', *Le Jouet Francais*, Paris, April, 1956

Johnson, Curt. *Battles of the American Revolution*, 1975 (illustrations of wargame models)

Jones, J. Edward. *Looking for a Good Hobby — Miniatures Provide the Answer*, Chicago, 1948 (on Metal Miniatures)

Kant, Hubert. *Alt-Wiener Spielzeugschachtel*, Vienna, 1961

Katalog der Formen Kulturgeschtlicher Zinnfiguren in der Deutsches Demokratischen Republik. East Germany, 1976 (important list of makers of flats)

Kayser, E. *Die Zinnfigur in Gartenlaube*, Leipzig, 1929

Kebbel, Harald and Renate, *Bruckmann's Handbuch der Zinnfiguren*, Munich, 1978

Keller, Charles-Felix. *Eloge des Soldats Fins*, Paris, 1928

'K. Ewer, Pewterer', *Tuesday, The Star Ledger*, New Jersey, 3 April, 1973

King, Constance Eileen. *The Encyclopaedia of Toys*, 1978 (one chapter on models)

King's Armies through the Ages in Dioramas, The, Royal United Service Institution, 1935; revised edition, 1952

'*Kleine, grosse Welt'. Eine Figuren - Austellung*, Hamburg, 1954

'Kleines Rokokotheater. Mozartfigurinen aus Wien', *Westermann's Monatshefte*, Heft 2. Brunswick, 1957 (Krauhs' Mozart models)

Klio, Germany various issues (information on flats)

Kollbrunner, Curt F. *Zinnfiguren-Zinnsoldaten-Zinngeschichte*, Munich, 1979 (authoritative work on flats)

Krischen, Fritz & Hahnemann, Max. *Führerdurch die Weibnachtsamstellung*, Berlin, 1914

Kulmbach Almanac. Germany. Various issues (information on flats)

'Kulmbach Standiger Korgessort', *Bayerische Bundschad*, 26 August, 1957

Kulturhistorische Austellung Torhaus Dolitz, Leipzig, 1976

La Nature, Paris 1896

Lange, Hellmuth. 'Berliner Zinnfiguren von Werner Scholtz', *Schmalfilm*, Berlin, December, 1973

Lectures pour Tous, Paris, February, 1967

Leipzig Trade Fair. Various issues

Lenox, B. 'Parade of the Christmas Soldiers', *American Home*, New York, December, 1958

'Les Figurines Historiques' *L'Estampille*, Paris, January, 1975

'Les Figurines Militaires de Léon Hames', *Le Courier de Verviers*, 16 November, 1967

Les Images Populaires, Catalogue of an exhibition held at Pollock's Toy Theatre Museum, 1960

Lewis, G.H. 'Tin gee-gee', *Vogue*, New York, 5 October, 1955

Lill, Georg. 'Nurnberger Zinnfiguren der Familie Hilpert', *Kunst und Handwerk*, Munich, 1920

L'Illustration, Paris. Various issues

Lion, H., and Bean, V. *My Way*. Boston, 1977 (on painting models)

Loewenstein, Prince John of. 'Tin Soldiers', *Everybody's*, April 14, 1945

Look and Learn. Various issues, London 1962-66

McClintock, Inez and Marshall. *Toys in America*, Washington, 1961

McFadden, G.H. 'Eleven Hundred Years of the Worship of Apollo'; *The Illustrated London News*, 5 April 1952

McKenzie, Ian. *Collecting Old Toy Soldiers*, 1975

Mackett-Beeson, A.E.J. *Chessmen*, 1967

Macoir, Jean-Leo & Ch. *Jouets, Jeux, Livres d'Enfants*, Brussels, 1974 (a bibliography, containing a section on models)

Mais, Adolf, *Die Zinngiesser Wien, Jahrbuch der Vereine für Geschichte der Stadt Wein, Band 14*, Vienna, 1958

Makinson, J.T. *Toy Manufacture*, 1929

Marlin Sporting Firearms. North Haven, Conn. 1977 (on Lance models)

Martin, Dr. Paul. 'Les Collections de Soldats Peints ou Imprimés du Musée Historique de Strasbourg'; *Le Passepoil*, No. 3. Paris, 1938

Les Petits Soldats de Strasbourg, Strasbourg, 1950

Der Standhafte Zinnsoldat, Stuttgart, 1962

L'Imagerie Wentzel de Wissembourg, Paris, 1967

'Art Populaire de la France de l'Est', Strasbourg, 1969 (article on paper sheets).

and Vaillant, Marcel. *Le Monde Merveilleux des Soldats de Plomb*, Paris, 1959

'Medic Commands 117-Men Police Force', *Military Police Journal*, Augusta, December, 1968 (article on the Military Police models of J. Grykiewicz)

Men of Waterloo, Catalogue of British Model Soldier Society Exhibition, 1960

Meyer-Zschokke, L. 'Die Schweizer Zinnfiguren-Industrie', *Wegleitungen des Kunstgewerbemuseums der Stad Zurich*, Zurich, March-April, 1916

Michel, Colonel Albert. *Les Petits Soldats de Carton au Musée Historique, Strasbourg*, 1935

'Military Miniatures', *Gun and Cartridge Record*, USA., May, 1952

'Military Miniatures', *Trinity College Bulletin*, Hartford, Conn. February, 1959 (article on the Hickmott collection)

Military Modeller, New York. Various issues

Military Modelling, Hemel Hempstead, 1971-

Military Modelling Annual, No. 1-, Hemel Hempstead, 1974-

Military Modelling Clubs Directory, Hemel Hempstead, 1975

Milliken, E.K., *A Pageant of History and Romance in Miniature*, Croydon, Alder's Stores, October, 1935 (a pioneer exhibition). 'The Teaching of History by Means of Models', *History*, Vol. XXII, No. 86, September, 1937

Mills, G. *Painting, Detailing and Converting Napoleonic Figures.* 1978

'Miniature Pewter', *Acquire*, New Jersey, July, 1974 (article on C.K. Ewer)

Miniature Warfare and Model Soldiers, 1967-

Miniature-World, Pictorial Souvenir Guide Book, Fields of Glory, Victoria, Vancouver Island, 1973 (the Ray Collection of dioramas)

'Model Call-up for the Toy Generals. Armies in Miniature', *Eastern Daily Press*, Norwich, 8 April, 1975 (Series: 'The Collectors', refers to Garratt's first book.)

Model Maker, London, 1972-3 (mainly for converters)

Model Maker, New York. Various issues, 1963-5

Model Soldier, Ilford, 1978-

Model World, Learning with the B.B.C., 1975

Modell-Fan, Germany. 1974- (mainly plastic aircraft).

Modelling Military Figures, edited Bruce Quarrie, Cambridge, 1975

Modellini Militari. Italy, 1976- . Various issues

Modellismo Militaire, Florence, 1973-

Model Soldier Exhibition, Catalogue of exhibition held at the Charter Club, London, 1950

Model Soldier Manual, edited by C. Ellis, 1976

Model Soldiers, Armies in Miniature, introduction by A. Massimo, Novaro 1972

Modelworld Magazine, 1972-4 (conversions)

Modrijan, W. *Die figurale Bleiplastik von Frögg*, Germany, 1950

'More Discoveries at Cologne', *The Illustrated London News*, 22 November, 1930

Morgan, Mike. 'Old Soldiers Never Die in Mini-Wars', *Living; Fort Lauderdale News*, 17 September, 1973 (Fort Lauderdale Military Collectors)

Morris, E. 'Their Little Hobby Means a Lot', *US Lady Magazine*, New York, March, 1958

Morris, F. 'Toy-Making among the Germans', *Harper's Weekly*, New York, 14 December, 1901

Morris, Michael. 'Wild Man from Mount Idy', *Coronet Magazine*, New York, August, 1956 (on Cliff Arquette)

Morschauser, D. *War Games*, New York, 1961

Motson, Anna. 'Profiteering in the Ranks', *Daily Telegraph Magazine*, 6 June 1975 (conversions by members of the British Society)

Mr Punch's Picture Book (edited E.V. Lucas, 1900)

Murray, Patrick. *Toys*, 1968 (incidental references)

'Napoleon's Men in Tinycraft — Models made by a Prisoner-of-War', *The Illustrated London News*, 25 June, 1932 (carved wood models by Sandré)

Nasemann, Theodor. *Nostalgie in Zinn*, Munich, 1979 (brief introduction to flats)

Nash, David. *Wargames*, 1974 (excellent, informative introduction on the wargame as used by various European powers)

Neudorfer, Johannes. *Nachrichten von Nurnberger Kunstlern und Werkleuten aus dem Jahr 1547* (edited G.W.K. Lochner) Vienna, 1875

Newman, Barbara and Jonathan. *The Paper Soldier*, Elmora, New York 1972- (periodic catalogues of paper sheets for sale)

New York Journal. 19 April, 1896

Nicholson, Lieut-Colonel J.B.R. *Model Soldiers*, 1969 (catalogue of models made by Stadden for Tradition)

Nickel, E. 'Ein Mittelalterlicher Zinnfiguren-Streisser aus Magdeburg', *Ausgrabungen und Freunde*, Band I, Heft 5. Berlin, 1956

Nicollier, Jean. *Collecting Toy Soldiers*, (translated R. North) Fribourg, 1967

Notizia dell'Accademia di San Marciano, Italy, December, 1967 (models by Pranzetti and Ménager)

'Nuragic Art shown in Rome', *The Illustrated London News*, 21 May, 1932

Nurnberger Post, Nuremberg, December 1962; July, 1964

O'Brien, Richard. *Collecting Toys*, Montclair, New Jersey, 1979

O'Brine (—). 'Miniature Battlefields saves Lives in Invasion', *Popular Science*, New York, January, 1941

'Old Silver Nefs from Germany', *The Illustrated London News*, 28 January, 1933

'One Man's Hands make History Live', *Sentinel*, U.S.A., April 13, 1973 (article on Ray Anderson)

O'Neill, W.J. History in Miniature, *Philadelphia Enquirer Magazine*, 21 November, 1954

Onken, Walter. *Zinnfiguren*, Munich, 1976

Ortmann, Erwin. *Zinnfiguren Einst und Jetzt*, Leipzig, 1972 (excellent treatise on flats, complementing Hampe)

Osbourne, Lloyd. 'Stevenson at Play', *Scribner's Magazine*, December, 1898 (reprinted in the 'Tusitala' edition of Stevenson's *Collected Works*)

Panorama, No. 435 Milan, 1974 (article on Italian collectors)

Panyella y Juan Elias y Garriga. 'Los Soldatitos de Plomo', *Monografias de Arte Roca*, Barcelona, 1976

'Paris Exposition, The', *The Illustrated London News*, 1867

Parker, G. *The Army of Flanders and the Spanish Road.* 1969

Parsons, L.C. 'Toy Soldier', *Educational Review*, New York, June, 1915

Pember, C. 'The Lost Villa of the Younger Pliny', *The Illustrated London News*, 23 August, 1947 (on dioramas)

Percout, R. *Les Images d'Epinal*, Paris, 1912

Perry, F.E. *A First Book of Wargaming*, 1977 (using 54mm models)

A Second Book of Wargaming, 1978

Petermann, H. 'Das Hobby fur kleine und grosse Leute, Zinnfiguren-Sammler', *Durch die weite Welt*, vol. 45. Stuttgart, 1971

Petrikowits, H. von and Hubatsch, Walter. *Rheinische Geschichte in Zinn*, Dusseldorf, 1965

Pielin, D., Hillman, R., and Parker, E. *The American Dime Store Soldiers.* USA (1977)

Pierrelé, S. 'Les Soldats de Plomb', *Revue Illustré*, Paris, 1899

Playthings of Yesterday, Toronto, 1963 (on the Percy Band Collection)

Pleticha, Heinrich. *Weltgeschichte in Zinn*, Berlin, 1976

Polaine, R. *The War Toys I*, 1979 (on Elastolin)

Popular Science, New York. Various issues, 1936-50

'President Lincoln and his Problem Son', *McCall's*, New York, January, 1956

Pressland, D. *The Art of the Tin Toy* 1976 (tin-plate models)

Prima Mostra Internazionale di Antiche Soldatini da Collezione (Catalogue) Spoleto, 1977

Proclaim Freedom, A Pageant of Jewish History, An Exhibition of Thirty-five Dioramas, Jewish Museum, New York, c.1959

(Stokes-Greenwood dioramas)

'Progress in Education', *Christian Science Monitor*, New York, December 31, 1934

Pylkkanen, Ritta. *Dockor och tennsoldater*, Helsinki, 1961

Rabecq-Maillard, M.M. *Histoire du Jouet*, Paris, 1962 (incidental references)

Radius, E. 'La Grande Armata dei Soldatini di Piombo', *Le Lettura*, Italy, January, 1943

Ramsay-Kerr, Jane. 'Gallant Tin Soldiers of Fairyland', *The Illustrated London News*, 25 November, 1929

Rattelmuller, P.E. *Die grosse Welt in Kinderstuben. Zinnfiguren aus dem 19 Jahrhundert*, Munich, 1970

Reallexicon Vorgeschichte, Vols. XI, XII, Germany

'Rearmament in the Playroom', *Exchange and Mart*, 30 March, 1939

'Reduction of the World's Armies', *The Sun*, Baltimore, 20 May, 1954

Remise, J. and Fondin, J. *L'Age d'or des Jouets*, Lausanne, 1967 (chapter on models)

Reppert, R. 'Soldiers down the Ages', *Sunday Sun Magazine*, Baltimore, 13 March, 1955

Reveille, 22 November, 1956

Richards, L.W. *Old British Model Soldiers, 1893-1918*, 1969

Riff, A. *Les Etains Strasbourgeois du XVe au XIXe Siècle*, Strasbourg, 1925

Ringelnatz, Joachim. *Gedichte, Gedichte, Zinnfiguren*, Berlin, 1936

Ripley, Damon. 'Small Businesses and Crafts', *Yankee*, New Canaan, April, 1975 (article on Victor Roming)

Risley, C.A., and Imrie, W.F. *The Model Soldier Guide*, New York 1967

Ritter, Joachim. 'Der Standhafte Zinnsoldat', *Monatszeitschrift*, No. 4, Leipzig, October, 1934

Roh, Juliane. '*Altes Spilzeuge. Kleine Welt in Zinn*', Munich, 1958

Rosenhaupt, Karl. 'Die Nurnberg fürer Metallspielwaren-industrie', *Munchener Volkswirtschaftliche Studien*, No. 82. Stuttgart, 1907

Rossi, G. 'Une Collection de Soldats de Plomb', *L'Illustration*, Paris, December 29, 1928

Rowlands, Phyllis. 'The Porcelain Manufactury'; *Tableware International*, London, January, 1975 (illustrated article on Sutty)

Royal Gazette, The, New York, December, 1777 (the earliest record of flats in America)

Rukeyser, Muriel. *The Traces of Thomas Hariot*, 1970. (contains reference to the earliest military models made in England)

Saez-Alcocer, Lucio. *El Libro Miniaturismo Militar*, Barcelona, 1978 (Spanish models)

Sala, G.A. *Notes and Sketches of the Paris Exhibition: Dolls and Toys*, 1868

Sanders, H. 'Pre-Roman Bronze Votive Offerings from Despanaperros in the Sierra Morena', *Archaeologia*, Vol. 60, Pt. 1, 1906

Sanpére, Agustin Duran. '*Grabados Populares Espanoles*' , Barcelona, 1971 (paper sheets: based on the book by Amades)

Santesson, B.O. *Gammalt Tenn*, Uppsala, 1962

Scabbard, The, U.S.A. Various issues

Scale Modeller, 1970- (mainly conversions: a few metal figures)

Scale Modellers, New York, December, 1965

Schindler, Regina. *Das Steckenpferd. Kinderspiele aus Alter Zeit*, Freiburg, 1965

Schirmer, Friedrich. *Vom umfang mit Zinnfiguren*, Burgsdorf-Hanover, 1967

Schlisse, Otto. *Apfel Nuss und Mandelkern*, Stuttgart, 1953

Schlosser, J. *Festschrift für . . . Herausgegeben von Arpad Weixlgartnes und Leo Planiseig*, Vienna, 1927

Scholtz, Werner. *Bemalungsaulteitung für Zinnfiguren*, Berlin, 1971, 1974

Schweizer, Bruno. *Die Geschichte der Kleinzinngiesserei*, Diessen Ammersee, 1930

Schwindrazheim, Hilmarie. *Altes Spielungans, Schleswig-Holstein*, Heide, 1957

Scientific American, New York, various issues, 1893-8

'Scottish Military Statuettes', *The Studio*, December, 1933 (the Pilkington Jackson wood-carvings)

Scottish Military Statuettes at the R.B.A. Galleries, Catalogue of an Exhibition of the Works of C. d'O. Pilkington Jackson, Introduction by Stanley Casson, 1933

Scrine, J. *A Short History of Britains Ltd*, 1955

SEGOM. *How to Animate Models*, Paris, 1970

'Seine Majestat-Der Kamerad Zinnsoldat', *Haupstadt Mannheim Hatentreuzbanner*, 15 December, 1935

'*1776*'. *The British Story of the American Revolution. Catalogue of an Exhibition at the National Maritime Museum*. 1976 (dioramas)

Seyboth, Adolph. *Strasbourg Historique et Pittoresque*, Strasbourg, 1894 (article on Striedbeck and Silbermann)

Shreve, Crump and Low Co. (*Advertisement*) Boston, 1973 (on Brian Rodden)

Siborne, Captain W.M. Unpublished MS Correspondence, 6 vols. (at the British Library) *The Original Large Model of the Battle of Waterloo (and) the New Model . . . at the Egyptian Hall*, 1845 (broadsheet)

Slovak Folk Art, Prague, 1954

Snehsdorf, A. 'Cigarette-size Kings', *Argosy*, U.S.A., June 1953

Society of Antiquaries, Proceedings of The, New Series, Vol. 1, 1860

Soldier. Various issues, London, 1965-

Soldier, U.S.A. 1968-9 (incidental references and photographs)

'Soldier Review-Tin Reflections of Glories Passed', *Los Angeles Examiner*, 26 October, 1957

Souto, Gabriel de Rocha. 'Coleccoes de Armas, e Equipamentos, Modelose Miniaturas Militares', *Arqueologia e Historia*, IV, Associacao dos Arqueologos Portugueses, Lisbon, 1972

Spanner, Adolf. *Deutsche Volkunst*, Sachsen-Weimar, 1954

Speaight, M. *Toys in the London Museum*, H.M.S.O., London, 1969 (two illustrations of Britains and Heyde)

Specovius, R. *Die Zinngiesserei Weygang in Göttingens*, Göttinger Blatter, Heft 2, 1936

Spielberg, H. von. 'Der Stadhafte Zinnsoldat', *Velhagen & Klasing's Monatsheften*, Bild I., Bielefeld, 1898-9

Stahl, Johann Ludwig. *Verzeichnisuber vershiedens fein und ordinaire gemehlte Zinnfiguren. . .Hilperts seel*, Nuremberg, 1805

Stearns, Philip O. *How to Make Model Soldiers*, 1974

Stokes, Denny C. *Exhibition of Dioramas* (Catalogue), 1958
   The Miniature Diorama (Catalogues), 1959, 1967-1969

Stokes, I.N. Phelps. *New York Past and Present*. New York, 1939 (dioramas)
   Sword and Lance. Darlington, various issues, 1974-

Tarr, Laszlo. *Karren, Kutsche, Karosse. Eine Geschichte des Wagens*, Berlin, 1970

Tavard, Christian. 'Model Soldiers', *Model Maker*. November-December, 1955

Taylor, Arthur. *Discovering Model Soldiers*, 1970

Teague, Dennis. *Discovering Modelling for Wargamers*, 1973

Tennfigur Museum-en varld i miniatyr. Tennfigurmuseum, Hjortnas. Leksand, c. 1970

'The Collector's Dream for a Living Museum', *Western Daily*

Press, 3 April, 1973 (the Bell-Knight Collection)

'Three Centuries of Scottish Soldiers', *The Illustrated London News*, 1 April, 15, 1936

Thrienal, S. *Miniature World in Tin*, G.D.R.5.E. Berlin, 1964

Time-Life Magazine. No. 8. New York, 1970 (Plassey diorama)

'Tin Soldiers and Noah's Arks Six Hundred Years Ago', *The Illustrated London News*. 25 July. 1942

'Tin Soldiers in Excelsis: Models with Correct Accoutrements', *The Illustrated London News*. 25 December, 1948 (models by French masters)

Tinge-linge-later, tinsoldater, Copenhagen, 1966 (on Danish models)

Todd, Colonel F. *Notes sur les dioramas du West Point*, Paris, 1961

'Touching Playthings from Childrens' Tombs of 2,300 Years Ago', *The Illustrated London News*, 10 July, 1921

'Toy Battle of Pound Ridge, The', *Look and Learn*, No. 199, 1965, (Imrie/Risley models, photographed by Stearns)

'Toy Territorials: where the lead Soldiers are Made'. *The Boy's Own Paper*, 20 August, 1910 (Britains' models)

Toy Trader and Exporter. Various issues

'Toys', *Oxford Junior Encyclopaedia*, Vol. IX, 1953

Toys and Games, Coburg

Toys and Novelties. USA, 1936- (American toys)

'Toys with which Queen Mary Played', *The Illustrated London News*, 10 October, 1936

Tradition (Norman Newton Ltd), 1963-

Treitzsaurwein, M. *Der Weisskünig*, Vienna, 1775 (woodcuts by Burgkmaier, c.1515)

Tschleschnitz, T. von. *Anleitungzum Kriegspiel*, Neisse, 1862

T.V. Mirror, July, 1957

Two Centuries of Military Mapping. Defence Mapping Agency, Washington, D.C. 1976 (dioramas)

Uhlfelder, Wilhelm. Die 'Zinnmalerinnen in Nürnberg und Fürth', *Schriften des Vereins für Sozialpolitik*, Vol. 84. Leipzig, 1899

'Uitbeelding van Stad en Ommelund', *De Groninger Gezinsbod*, July 22, 1974 (article on Spandauw)

Ullrich, F. 'Mit Pauker und Trumpeter', *Neu Stafette dei Moderne Bildungs-Zeitschrift für Junge Menschen*. Berlin, 1964

United Services Gazette, 1832

United Services Journal, Pt. 2, 1833

Valverde, Carlos Martinez. *Serie de Modelos de Plomo del Museo de Pontevedra*, 1951 (conversions by Valverde)

'Van boerenoorlog tot slag de Ardennen', *Aspekt*, Amsterdam, 27 November, 1974 (article on Frazer)

Vaultier, R. 'Prestige des Figurines Historiques', *Le Jouet Francais*, No. 27, 30. Paris, January, April, 1956

Vauson, General. 'Petits Soldats d'Alsace', *Carnet de la Sabretache*, Paris, 1896

Veale, J.P.B. *Table-top Photography with Model Soldiers*,

Brighton, 1930

Verster, A.S.G. *Das Buch vom Zinn*, Hanover, 1963

Villefosse, H. de. 'Jouets à la Cour de France', *Connaissance des Arts*. Paris, January, 1959

Von Böehn, Max. *Dolls and Puppets* (translated by Josephine Nicoll) 1932 (incidental references)

Vos, Olof. 'Frän Viking till tamburmajor. En lekfull tennsoldatskavalkad genom Svenska historia', *Julstamning*. Stockholm, 1957 (article with coloured plates on the Tennfigur-museum, Leksand)

Wace, A.J.B. 'Fifty Years of British Archaeology in Greece', *The Illustrated London News*, 17 October, 1936

Wade, Shamus O.D. *A Short History of Nostalgia Models*, 1976

Walston, Sir C. *Alcamenes and the Establishment of the Classical Type in Greek Art*, Cambridge, 1926

War-Game Digest Quarterly, edited J. Scruby and J. Conley, Tipton. Various issues

'War in Lilliput', *Illustrated*, 25 September, 1943

Warrior: La Rivista del Modellismo Militaire. Genoa, 1975-

'War's a Game', *She*, December, 1965

Washington, George, *The Writings of*, edited John C. Fitzpatrick, New York, 1931

Waterloo-Austellung, Heimatsmuseum der Kreistaat Burgdorf, Hanover, 1955

Weiglin, Paul. 'Der standhafter Zinnsoldat', *Velhagen & Klasings Monatshefte*, Bielefeld, December, 1914

Wells, H.G. *The Great War Game* (anonymous) 1908
'Citizens of Toyland', *Everybody's*, December, 1911
Floor Games, 1911
Little Wars, 1913
Experiment in Autobiography, 2 vols, 1934

'Weltgeschichte in Miniature'. *Ausstellung Kultur-historischen Zinn-und Bleifiguren*. Vienna, 1959-60

White, Gwen, *A Book of Toys*, 1946
Antique Toys. 1971

Wiegand, Virginia. 'One Renaissance Man works for Bicentenniel', *Patent Trader*, Mount Kisco, N.Y., 17 April, 1975 (article on Roming)

Wilsdorf, Helmut. 'Bergleute und Hittenmanner', *Altertum bis Zinn Ausgang der Romischen Republic*, Berlin, 1952

Windrow, M., and Embleton, G. *Model Soldiers*. Airfix Magazine Guide No.19, Cambridge, 1977 (conversions)

Wittichen, J. *Celle Zinngiesser*, Celle, 1974

Wonderful World of Toys, Games & Dolls, 1860–1930, edited J.J. Schroeder, Jr. U.S.A., 1971 (facsimile pages from toy-dealers' catalogues)

Young. Brigadier Peter. *Charge!*, 1975 (The Wargame).

Zinnfiguren, Einst und Jetzt. Ein Führer dürch die Grosse Sonderschau im April 1956. Weimar, 1956

'Zinnfiguren-Museum', *Frankische Presse*, Germany, 22 August, 1958 (article on Kulmbach)

THEMATIC INDEX

Holland:
De Gruyter
Hong Kong:
Blue/Red Box
CK
Clifford
CMV
Grace
Imperial
ID
Lindu
Panda
Success
Taffy Toys
Woolbro
Italy:
Atlantic
Baranella
Bozzetti
Confalonieri
Dulcop
Dullap
Fontanini
Italaeri
Landi
Martinez
Nardi
Polistil
Tibidabo
Xiloplast
Japan:
AHI
Arpax
Fujimimokai
Minnikin
Okakura
Mexico:
Copada
New Zealand:
Heritage
Playtime
Norway:
Fischer Thermo
Poland:
Centrum
CZZP
PZG
Wyrob
WZUP
Portugal:
Almeida
Spain:
Aries
Aster
Dia-D-Hora
Exin
Gama
JC
Jecsan
La Guerra
Monta-plex
Multi-color
Pech
Reamsa
UnitedStates:
AMT
Andy Gard
Auburn
Aurora
Beton
Breyer
Disney

Elite Toys
Giant
Gibbs
Gilbert
Ideal Plastics
Ideal Toy Corp
Innovative
Lido
Lincoln Internat
Lincoln Logs
Marvel Comics
Marx
Mattel
Monogram
Multiple Plastics
Multiple Toy
Palmer Plastics
PGD
Playskool
Railroads
Renwall
Revell
Roco Miniatures
Tim Mee Toy
Topper

POLYSTYRENE
France:
Aiglon
Heller
Historex
Lelièpvre
Leroux (M.)
Prairial
Segom
Germany:
Big
Great Britain:
Airfix
Rogard
Selcol
Springwood
Trojan
Waddington's House
Hong Kong:
Einco
Fairylite
Italy:
Bozzetti
ESCI
Japan:
Aoishima
Fujimokei
Spain:
Exin
United States:
Anderson (R.)
Aurora
Mark
Palmer Plastics
Pyro
(See *also* Armoured
  Fighting Vehicles)

SOLIDS (Commercial,
and semi-solids):
Argentina:
Alaiss
Astesiano
Austrandia

Birmania
Casa Pardo
Falucho
Girardo
Grafil
Matarazzo
Reyco
Sommer
Stringer
Viruta
Belgium:
Le Sellier
MIM
Canada:
Reliable
Denmark:
Banner-Model
Brigader
Sigaard (?)
Eire:
Authenticast
Wennberg
France:
Berne (M.)
Blondel
Cuperly
Delacroix (?)
Emmanueli
Figur
Gerbeau
José
Lemoyne
Leveille (?)
LP
Lucotte
Mignot
Tessiere (?)
XR
Germany:
Allgeyer
Ammon
Baselsoder
Berliner
Bischoff (J.)
Diezemann
Dorfler
Fraas
Greiner
Haffner
Heinrich
Helmbrecht
Heyde
Jakobs
Kessler (?)
Koch (K.?) : (P.)
Kopien
Krause
Krumpelbeck
Metzger
Nadebor
Peipp
Potsdam
Roco
Roskopf
Schildnecht
Screiber (C.?)
Söhlke (G.)
Spenküch
Wahnshaffe (?)
Wiener Met
Zerwick
Great Britain:

Almark
BG of GB
Blenheim
British Bulldog
Bull (?)
Caberfeidh
Campaign
Copy-Cat
Crown
Dorset
Douglas Hall
Drumbeat
Ducal
Gould (R.)
Greening
Historical Model
Izzard
Malleable
Mark-Time
Militia
Militia Models Worldwide
MJMode
MSR
North Park
Nostalgia
On parade
Pride of Europe
Quality
Quinn
Rose (A.)
Skybird
Soldier's Soldiers
Sovereign
Steadfast
Trafalgar
Treforest
Trophy
Union Jack
Winkler
Hong Kong:
King White
Italy:
Figir
ISA
LARG
Metal Miniatura
Peltro
Polistil
Japan:
IMP
Minikin
Tamiya
Mexico:
Coleccion Mexico
Portugal:
Almeida
Campos
South Africa:
SAE
Wennberg
Winkler
Spain:
Barrieira
EKO
Gonzalez
Jiminez
La Guerra
Palomeque
Sanquez
Sweden:
Elgstrom
Santessonska

Schreuder
Sjosward
Tenng Mars
Wennberg
United States:
American International
American Metal
Autopiano
Best
Britannia
Colonial
Comet
Cromwell
DJ's
Eureka
FHQ
Fife & Drum
Fleischman
Gabriel
Hamblen
Herrings
JVR
Last Post
Levi
Lincoln Logs
McLoughlin
Maita
Malcolm
Military Casts
Minifigure
Parade Square
Realistic
Romanelli
Saint Louis
Scruby
S.T.A.R.
Steadfast
Strombecker
Supercast
Thomas (W.A.)
Tootsietoys
Tru-Craft
UN-Art
Vanguard
Warren
Warwick
Waterloo Galleries
Wennberg
Ye Olde Soldier

SOLIDS (Specialist
makers and commissioned
artists)
Argentina:
Balaguer
Figurines Karlis
Roche
Australia:
DP
Powell
Sykes
Turner (A.)
Wooten
Belgium:
Le Sellier
Seldenslagh (?)
Canada:
Betts
Coronet
Harling
Jackson ('Jane')

Ries (?)
Rochelle (?)
Rodden
Scale
Scheid
Scrimshander
Scruby
Series 77
Shideler
Sibbitt
Smith (A.) : (W.)
Soldiers Unlimited
Spicer
Squadron/Rubin
Stackhouse
Stan Johansen
Stewart
Stock
Sullivan (R.)
Superior
Tapavica
Townley
Valiant
Vallance
Wall
Walthers (?)
Waterloo Galleries
West (Mrs.)
Wippler
Wirth
Worcester

TIN (Conjoint, sheet or stamped)
Argentina:
Anteojito
Czechoslovakia:
Tipp
France:
Bouquet (H.)
Varlaud
Vasquez
Germany:
Bing
Debler
DRPA
Elastolin
Gama (G.A. Mangold)
Lineol
Mäerklin
Schuco
Tipple Topple
Weiss
Great Britain:
Mettoy
Midgetoy
SP
Italy:
INGAP
Japan:
Line Mar
United States:
Barclay
Chein
Marx
Philadelphia
Structo
Tootsietoys
Unique Art

WARGAME (Models, buildings, terrains, accessories)
Argentina:
Metralla
Belgium:
Verlinden
France:
Armour Access
Segom
Starlux
Germany:
Roskopf
Uhlmann
Great Britain:
Advance Guard
AirFix
Alberken
Almark
Alpha
Andy
Asgard
Castile
Cedarwood
Citadel
Dixon
Dorset
Dragon
Frei Korps
Garrison
Gilder
Greening
Greenwood and Ball
Hampshire
Heroics
Higgins
Hinchliffe
Hinton
Illuminated
Jacklex
Jacobite
Laing
Lamming
Leviathan
Mainly Military
MA Model
Micro-mold
Mike's
Military Buildings
Miniature Figurines
Oracle
Pendragon
Silvercross
Sinclair
SK
Skybird
Spencer-Smith
Springwood
Stadden
Starcast
Thornton
Tradition
Valhalla
Vulcan
Warrior
Willie
Italy:
Atlantic
ESCI
South Africa:

Victors
Spain:
Arm-model
Monta-plex
Perez
United States:
Archive
Bresica
Bugle & Guidon
Bussler
C & C
C.S & D
Custom
Dragon Tooth
GHQ
Grenadier
Heritage Models
McEwan
Modakit
Pin Point
Ral Partha
Roundhouse
Scruby
Stan Johansen
Stone Mountain
Thomas (W.A.)
Triangle
UPC
Wall
Washington
Wee Warriors

WOOD
Argentina:
Mivie
Canada:
Ray
Colombia:
Acuña
France:
Angenot
Clemence
Durinage
Fichtel
Foulley
Sandré
Thirot
Germany:
Huelsa
Knie
Krauhs
Schreiber (O.)
Schutz
Great Britain:
Arthur (H.J.) : (K.)
Bryant & May
Chad Valley
Dancaster
Henry
Hibbert
Hitchings
Howell
Jackson (C.d'O.)
Jones (M.E.)
Lord Roberts
McKenzie (J.)
Meadows
North
Rendall

Spencer
Taylor (W.)
Italy:
Cantelli
Pranzetti
New Zealand:
Penman
Reid
Spain:
Españocraft
Tello
United States:
Ace Model
Arquette
Austincraft
Brückner
Columbia
Grykiewicx
Heron
Kostelnik
Marvel
McClellan
McEnroe
Morrison (T.)
Rey-Y-Cut
Reed
Strombecker
Vliet